Political and Administrative Development

The Committee on Commonwealth Studies of Duke University

Political and Administrative Development

Ralph Braibanti, Carl J. Friedrich,
Giovanni Sartori, Henry S. Kariel,
Joseph LaPalombara, Fred W. Riggs,
Martin Landau, Harold D. Lasswell,
Allan R. Holmberg, Lucian W. Pye,
John D. Montgomery, Warren F. Ilchman,
R. Taylor Cole, José V. Abueva,
Joseph J. Spengler

Edited by Ralph Braibanti

Number 36 in a series published for the
Duke University Commonwealth-Studies Center
Duke University Press, Durham, N.C.
1969

Library of Congress Catalogue Card Number 75–79965
S.B.N. 8223–0022–2

Printed in the United States of America
by Kingsport Press, Inc., Kingsport, Tenn.

To

L. K. B.

Preface

This volume results from an international conference convened at the Rockefeller Foundation's Villa Serbelloni, Bellagio, Lake Como, Italy, July 16–22, 1967, to explore the theoretical issues implicit in transnational efforts to improve the administrative capability of developing political systems. Much attention in recent years has been given to the problem of the relationship of administrative reform to political development. This has been generated to a considerable extent by the extensive operations of the Agency for International Development designed to induce administrative reform in developing states, and by comparable programs of the United Nations technical assistance program and the Ford Foundation. The implications for theory as well as the operational pertinence of the subject are suggested by the fact that several conferences on closely allied problems were held prior to the 1967 Bellagio meeting and several more have been held since. The Brookings Institution sponsored a conference at Williamsburg, Virginia, in November, 1965, on the topic, "Research Needs Regarding the Development of Administrative Capabilities in Emerging Countries." In the fall of 1966 the Brookings Institution sponsored another conference at Airlie House in Virginia on the topic, "The Theory and Practice of Political Development." Subsequently, the development administration seminar of the Southeast Asia Development Advisory Group, organized by the Agency for International Development, devoted several sessions to the general problem of administrative reform. The introduction of Title IX in the Foreign Assistance Act of 1966 and its re-enactment in the 1967 act have also generated interest in the relationship between political and administrative development. To explore this problem the Massachusetts Institute of Technology convened a five-week conference at Endicott House in the summer of 1968 sponsored by the Agency for International Development. The Institute of Development Studies at the University of Sussex, England, convened a conference from June 28 to July 1, 1968, on political modernization with particular attention being given to the evolution of British thought on the problem. In September of 1968 a Round Table of the International Political Science Association meeting in Salzburg, Austria, was devoted to the problem of political modernization with particular reference to European and Communist theory as well as American theory on the subject. Many of the contributors to this volume participated in or were convenors of these closely related activities. The extent of this interlocking involvement is indicated in the biographical statements which are part of this volume.

The activities held prior to the international conference at Bellagio, from which this volume results, and the operations of AID provoked a series of perplexing theoretical questions which had not then been systematically analyzed. The present volume, like the conference from which it is derived, conjoins the insights of established scholars who have given much attention to political theory and who have had extensive experience in political and administrative reform in developing states. The conference brought together the multinational experience in administrative reform of the United States, the United Kingdom, India, France, Pakistan, the Philippines, and the West Indies.

The conference was sponsored by the Center for Commonwealth Studies of Duke University, assisted by the Comparative Administration Group of the American Society for Public Administration and the Committee on Comparative Politics of the Social Science Research Council. The conference was planned by a committee representing these organizations and consisting of Ralph Braibanti, chairman, Fred W. Riggs, and Joseph LaPalombara. The honorary chairman of the conference and its presiding officer at all the sessions was A. R. Cornelius, then chief justice of the Supreme Court of Pakistan. The superb facilities of the Villa

Serbelloni at Lake Como, Bellagio, Italy, operated by the Rockefeller Foundation, were made available for the conference.

Except in the three instances noted below, all of the papers included in this volume were presented at the Bellagio conference and were subsequently revised. The exceptions are the chapters by Henry S. Kariel and Martin Landau, which were commissioned after the conference, and the chapter by Harold D. Lasswell and Allan R. Holmberg incorporated in the series after the conference. Professor Lasswell was originally scheduled to participate in the conference and to write a paper for it but was obliged to withdraw from participation. He had, with the assistance of the late Professor Allan R. Holmberg of Cornell University, earlier written a paper for the Foundation for Research on Human Behavior under contract with the Agency for International Development. The topic of that paper was almost identical to the one which Professor Lasswell was to have prepared for the Bellagio conference. Since the paper, appearing in an electrotyped publication released by the Foundation for Research on Human Behavior, was not widely distributed, both the foundation and Professor Lasswell were pleased to have it included, with revisions, in the present volume. The decision to include Professor Landau's chapter came about in a different way. Professor Fred Riggs, as chairman of the Comparative Administration Group, suggested that a proseminar of that group held in conjunction with the annual meeting of the American Society for Public Administration in April, 1968, be devoted to a discussion of the results of the Bellagio conference. Accordingly, the proseminar was held at the Harvard Faculty Club on March 27, 1968. Professor Riggs had invited Martin Landau to prepare a critique of several of the Bellagio papers, and I invited Professor Riggs to discuss his own paper. As plans for the proseminar proceeded, Professor Landau was invited to prepare his paper for publication in the volume.

Each of the papers presented at the conference was criticized by an appointed discussant. Not all of the critiques took the form of essays; and some of the more detailed critiques were eventually incorporated in the revisions made by the writers of the paper. For these reasons, only two of the critical essays are included in the present volume. In addition to Professors Cole and Sartori, whose comments are included in this volume, the following persons served as discussants at the Bellagio conference: Michel Crozier, Professor of Sociology, Centre de Sociologie Européene, Paris, who discussed Professor LaPalombara's paper; Brian Chapman, Professor of Government, University of Manchester, was the critic of Professor Abueva's paper; A. W. Singham, Reader in Government at the University of the West Indies, was discussant for the present writer's paper. The paper by Professor Spengler was discussed by W. J. M. Mackenzie, Professor of Government at the University of Glasgow. Fred W. Riggs's paper was the subject of a critique by Samuel E. Finer, Professor of Government at the University of Manchester. Dwight Waldo, Albert Schweitzer Professor of the Humanities at Syracuse University, was discussant of Professor Montgomery's paper; and G. S. Sharma, Director of the Indian Law Institute at New Delhi, was discussant of Professor Pye's paper. W. H. Morris-Jones, Professor of Commonwealth Affairs, Institute of Commonwealth Studies, University of London, and Richard A. Preston, William K. Boyd Professor of History at Duke University, served as discussants-at-large. The success of the conference was due in no small measure to the vigorous intellectual exchange which resulted from the carefully prepared comments of these discussants. The final published versions of the papers which appear in this volume as chapters are the result of revisions which benefited from those comments. The author of each paper joins with the present writer in recording indebtedness to the discussants.

No effort was made to standardize the terminology used in the various chapters integrated in this volume. Such standardization might seem to have great advantage, but it is not possible at this stage in the development of the highly dynamic interdisciplinary study of political development in the new states. Nor was an effort made to make the length of the chapters uniform. Such standardization of length may have advantages for elementary textbook purposes, but it cannot constructively serve the purpose of an analytical discussion for which a totally different purpose is contemplated.

The financial assistance of Duke University, the American Society for Public Administration, the Social Science Research Council, and the Rockefeller Foundation, all of which made this conference possible, is gratefully acknowledged. In addition, individual authors have expressed indebtedness to other organizations and persons for assistance in the original research which made these papers possible, or in subsequent revisions of them. Such individual acknowledgment is made, where appropriate, in a footnote on the first page of the chapter. The thanks of all the participants in the Bellagio conference go especially to Mr. and Mrs. John Marshall, who direct the activities of the Villa Serbelloni and whose sensitive understanding of the subtleties involved in creating a context for productive research and speculation cannot be excelled. The editor is especially grateful to Mr. and Mrs. Marshall for a valuable two weeks spent at the villa with Mrs. Braibanti following the conference. There, as one of a congenial band of "scholars-in-residence," he revised and prepared part of the manuscript for publication.

None of the institutions which supported the Bellagio conference or this volume is in any way responsible for the contents of this volume. Such responsibility rests exclusively with each individual author.

RALPH BRAIBANTI

Durham, North Carolina
November, 1968

Contributors

José Veloso Abueva was born in the Visayas, the Philippines, in 1928. He was educated at the University of the Philippines and subsequently received the degrees Master of Public Administration and Ph.D. in political science from the University of Michigan. He has served in advisory positions for the government of the Philippines and was organization analyst and staff assistant to the chairman of the Government Survey and Reorganization Commission from 1954 to 1955. He served as secretary-general of the first Asian regional conference on public administration held in Manila in 1958. He drafted the chapters on public administration and administrative reform in the five-year integrated socio-economic program released by the government of the Philippines in 1962. He has been guest lecturer at the Ateneo de Manila University, the Local Autonomy College of Japan, the University of Hawaii, the University of Oregon, the University of Michigan, Cornell University, and Duke University, and in 1965–66 was senior specialist at the East-West Center in Honolulu. He joined the faculty of the University of the Philippines in 1951 and is professor and assistant dean of the College of Public Administration of that university. In 1966–67 he was visiting professor of political science at Brooklyn College of the City University of New York. He is the author of *Focus on the Barrio* (1959) and is co-editor (with Raul P. de Guzman) of *Handbook of Philippine Public Administration* (1967) and *Foundations and Dynamics of Filipino Government and Politics* (1968). He is a contributor to Edwin O. Stene (ed.), *Public Administration in the Philippines* (1955); Raul P. de Guzman (ed.), *Patterns in Decision-Making: Case Studies in Philippine Public Administration* (1963); Socorro C. Espiritu and Chester L. Hunt (eds.), *Social Foundations of Community Development: Readings on the Philippines* (1964); Robert O. Tilman (ed.), *Man, State and Society in Contemporary Southeast Asia* (1968); Richard Butwell and Felix Gagliano (eds.), *Politics in Southeast Asia* (1968); and Edward W. Weidner (ed.), *Development Administration in Asia* (1968). He has contributed to various learned journals and has served as editor-in-chief and chairman of the editorial board of the *Philippine Journal of Public Administration*. He has completed a political biography of Ramon Magsaysay resulting from research conducted under a grant from the Rockefeller Foundation.

Ralph Braibanti, born in Danbury, Connecticut, in 1920, received his doctorate in political science from Syracuse University. His service in World War II included two years as a military government officer in Japan for which he was decorated for meritorious achievement. On the faculty of Kenyon College from 1949 to 1953, he was on leave in 1950–51 as assistant director of the American Political Science Association. In the summer of 1952 he was in Okinawa as political adviser to the Civil Administrator for the Ryukyu Islands. He held Ford Foundation and Social Science Research Council fellowships for research in Pakistan in 1957, and in India and Pakistan in 1958 and 1959. A frequent consultant for the Agency for International Development, from 1960–62 he was chief adviser to the Civil Service Academy in Lahore and was also political consultant to AID on planning in Pakistan. In the summer of 1967 he was in Pakistan and Turkey as consultant to AID on aspects of the Foreign Assistance Act of 1966. In the summer of 1968 he participated in a six-week planning conference at the Massachusetts Institute of Technology on political development. A member of the executive committee of the Comparative Administration Group, he is also on the editorial board of the *Journal of Politics, Comparative Political Studies,* and *Comparative Politics,* and formerly was on the editorial board of the *Journal of Asian Studies.* He is also vice-chairman of the development administration seminar of the Southeast Asia Development Advisory Group. He is the author of *Research on the Bureaucracy of Pakistan* (1966) and is editor and co-author of *Asian Bureaucratic Systems Emergent from the British Imperial Tradition* (1966), and of various studies in learned journals. He is co-author (with P. H. Taylor) of *Administration of Occupied Japan: A Study Guide* (1950); co-editor (with J. J. Spengler) and a contributor to *Tradition, Values and Socio-Economic Development* (1961) and *Administration and Economic Development in India* (1963); and is a contributing author to such volumes as Joseph LaPalombara (ed.), *Bureaucracy and Political Development* (1963); John D. Montgomery and William J. Siffin (eds.), *Approaches to Development: Politics, Administration and Change* (1966); W. B. Hamilton, Kenneth Robinson, and C. D. W. Goodwin (eds.), *A Decade of the Commonwealth: 1955–1964* (1966); and Myron Weiner (ed.), *Modernization* (1966); R. R. Wilson (ed.), *International and Comparative Law of the Commonwealth 1907–1967* (1968); and Fred W. Riggs (ed.), *Frontiers in Development Administration* (1969). He is James B. Duke Professor of Political Science at Duke University, where he has been a member of the faculty since 1953. Since 1966 he has been chairman of the Committee on Commonwealth Studies.

R. Taylor Cole was born in Bald Prairie, Texas, in 1905. He received his doctor's degree in political science at Harvard University and subsequently held Guggenheim and Fulbright fellowships. He taught at Louisiana State University and at Harvard University and joined the faculty of Duke University in 1935. During World War II he served as a special assistant in the War Department, as special assistant to the United States Minister in Sweden, and during the summers of 1948 and 1949 as a consultant to the Office of Military Government of the United States in Germany. He was awarded the Medal of Freedom by the United States. He was editor of the *Journal of Politics* from 1946 to 1949 and editor of the *American Political Science Review* from 1950 to 1953. He has done extensive research in Germany, Italy, Commonwealth countries, and in Africa, and has served also in advisory capacities to the United States Agency for International Development on problems of education administration relating to African states and to the Ford Foundation on problems of international education in Europe. A member of the American Academy of Arts and Sciences, he has served also as a member of the Social Science Research Council, and is a member of that organization's Committee on Comparative Politics. He has also been a member of the Fulbright Committee on International Exchange of Persons. He is a member and was first chairman (1955–60) of the Commonwealth-Studies Committee of Duke University, president of the Southern Political Science Association in 1951–52, and president of the American Political Science Association in 1958–59. In 1965 he was at Harvard University as Ford Foundation Research Professor of Government. He is co-author (with Carl J. Friedrich) of *Responsible Bureaucracy* (1932); author of *The Canadian Bureaucracy* (1949), and is the editor and co-author of *European Political Systems* (1953). He is also co-editor (with Robert O. Tilman) of *The Nigerian Political Scene* (1962); and co-editor (with Don C. Piper) of *Post Primary Education and Political and Economic Development* (1964). A frequent contributor to European and American learned journals, he has also contributed to symposium volumes, including Volume XIV of *Public Policy* (1965) and W. B. Hamilton, Kenneth Robinson, and C. D. W. Goodwin (eds.), *A Decade of the Commonwealth 1955–1964* (1966). Since 1953 he has been James B. Duke Professor of Political Science at Duke University and from 1960 to 1969 was Provost of the University.

Carl J. Friedrich was born in Leipzig, Germany, in 1901. He received the Ph.D. from the University of Heidelberg and subsequently has been awarded honorary degrees by several institutions, among them the Juris utriusque Doctor from the University of Heidelberg, the Dr. rer. pol. from the universities of Padua and Cologne, the LL.D. degree from Duke University, and the L.H.D. from Columbia University. He taught at the University of Minnesota and has been on the faculty of Harvard University since 1926. During World War II he served as director of the School for Overseas Administration and the Civil Affairs Training School at Harvard University, as a consultant to the Select Committee for AID of the United States Congress, and was constitutional and governmental affairs advisor to the United States Military Governor in Germany from 1946–49. His experience as governmental consultant includes also his service as advisor to the Preparatory Commission of the Constitutional Assembly of Puerto Rico, to the Ad Hoc Assembly for a European Political Community, and to the Constitutional Convention of the Virgin Islands. He is co-founder of the American Society of Political and Legal Philosophy and edited its yearbook, *Nomos*, from its inception in 1958 until 1965. He has been editor of *Public Policy*, the yearbook of the Harvard University Graduate School of Public Administration until 1963. He has been president of the American Society of Political and Legal Philosophy and the American Political Science Association, and is president of the International Political Science Association and president-elect of the Institut International de la Philosophie Politique. He has been awarded the Knight Commander's Cross of the German Order of Merit and is a member of the American Academy of Arts and Sciences. His books include: (with Taylor Cole) *Responsible Bureaucracy* (1932); *Constitutional Government and Democracy* (1937; 4th rev. ed. 1968); (with associates) *American Experience in Military Government in World War II* (1948); *Inevitable Peace* (1947); *The New Image of the Common Man* (1950); *The Age of the Baroque* (1952); (with Z. K. Brzezinski) *Totalitarian Dictatorship and Autocracy* (1956; rev. ed. 1965); *Constitutional Reason of State* (1958); *Puerto Rico: Middle Road to Freedom* (1959); *Man and His Government* (1963); *Transcendent Justice* (1964). His latest work is *The Impact of American Constitutionalism Abroad* (1967). Since 1955 he has been Eaton Professor of the Science of Government at Harvard University and since 1956 has had the concurrent appointment of professor of political science at the University of Heidelberg.

The late **Allan R. Holmberg,** who collaborated with Harold D. Lasswell in Chapter 8, was professor of anthropology at Cornell University.

Warren F. Ilchman was born in Denver, Colorado, in 1934, and received the doctor of philosophy degree at the University of Cambridge where he was a Marshall Scholar. He has taught at Magdalene College, Williams College, the Center for Development Economics, and is presently associate professor of political science at the University of California at Berkeley. He has been a visiting lecturer at the International Center for Advanced Management Education at Stanford University and at training programs of the Peace Corps and the Agency for International Development. A member of the executive committee of the Comparative Administration Group, Professor Ilchman is also a consultant on technical personnel for the United Nations. In 1962 and 1963 he did field research under the auspices of the Rockefeller Foundation in India and the Middle East on political problems of social and economic change. He is the author of *Professional Diplomacy in the United States* (1961), a monograph on time in development administration and one on planners, and articles in various learned journals. Two books are scheduled for publication in 1968: *The Political Economy of Change* (with Norman T. Uphoff) and *The Foreign Policy of a New Nation: The Case of India.* Professor Ilchman is also collaborating on a text on *Comparative Public Bureaucracies.*

Henry S. Kariel, born in Plauen, Germany, in 1924, received his doctor's degree in political science from the University of California at Berkeley in 1954. During World War II he served in an engineer combat battalion, as *Stars and Stripes* correspondent, and as war crimes investigator. He has taught at Harvard University, Bennington College, the University of Georgia, and the University of California at Santa Cruz. His publications include *The Decline of American Pluralism* (1961); *In Search of Authority* (1964); and *The Promise of Politics* (1966), in addition to journal articles and chapters of books edited by others. He has edited *Sources in Twentieth-Century Political Thought* (1964); *Frontier of Democratic Theory* (1968); and (with Michael Haas) *Approaches to the Study of Political Science* (forthcoming). A series of lectures given at Loyola University will shortly be published under the title of *Open Systems: A Reaction to Closure.* He has been the recipient of grants from the Rockefeller, Volker, and Huber Foundations. He has been professor of political science at the University of Hawaii since 1965.

Martin Landau was born in New York City in 1921 and received his doctorate from New York University in 1952. He served in the United States Army Signal Corps from 1942 to 1946, completing his tour of duty as control chief, United States Ninth Army Multi-Channel Radio Link. He is presently professor of political science at City University of New York, Brooklyn, where he was awarded the Distinguished Teaching Medal in 1963. He has been visiting professor at the

University of Michigan, the Graduate Faculty–New School, and the Graduate School of Public Administration, New York University. He has been a Fellow of the United States Air Force Office of Scientific Research (Behavioral Sciences Division) and was a senior specialist at the Institute of Advanced Projects, East-West Center, in 1965–66. He has served as a consultant to various organizations, including the New York State Constitutional Convention Commission and the New York City Charter Revision Commission and has lectured often at the United States Civil Service Commission Executive Seminar Center, the New York City Executive Development Program, the United States Naval Applied Science Laboratories and the Institute for Mental Health Research. He is also chairman of the Committee on Organization Theory of the Comparative Administration Group. He is a contributor to Norman Washburn (ed.), *Decisions, Values and Groups* (1962); S. M. Mailick and E. Van Ness (eds.), *Concepts and Issues in Administrative Behavior* (1962); Glendon Schubert (ed.), *Reapportionment* (1964); edited (with Hans Jecht, Glenn D. Paige, and Dwight Waldo) and contributed to *The Study of Organizational Behavior* (1966); is both editor and co-author of *Management Information Technology* (1965). Professor Landau is presently completing *Political Science and Political Theory* and is writing *Decision Theory and the Process of Development.*

Joseph LaPalombara, born in Chicago, Illinois, in 1925, received his doctor's degree in political science from Princeton University in 1954. He studied at the University of Rome in 1952–53 and later was a visiting professor at the University of Florence, the University of California at Berkeley, and Columbia University. He has held a Social Science Research Council fellowship and a research award, as well as Fulbright appointments in 1952 and 1957, and research awards from the Rockefeller Foundation. In 1961–62 he was a Fellow at the Center for Advanced Study in the Behavioral Sciences. He taught at Oregon State College and at Princeton University and from 1953 to 1958 was at Michigan State University where he was professor and chairman of the department of political science. He has been a consultant to the Federal Civil Defense Administration, the Agency for International Development, the Carnegie Corporation, the Twentieth Century Fund and the Ford Foundation, and a member of the board of editors of the *Midwest Journal of Political Science.* He has studied administrative development and reform in such countries as Italy, Vietnam, India, and Pakistan. He is currently a member of the Committee on Comparative Politics of the Social Science Research Council, as well as liaison officer for the SSRC Committee on Italian Social Science. His publications include contributions to various learned journals and *Ini-*

tiative and Referendum in Oregon (1950); *Guide to Michigan Politics* (1956, 1960); *The Italian Labor Movement, Problems and Prospects* (1957); *Interest Groups in Italian Politics* (1963; published in 1967 in an Italian edition); *Italy: The Politics of Planning* (1966). He edited and was a contributing author to the volume *Bureaucracy and Political Development* (1963); co-edited (with Myron Weiner) and contributed to *Political Parties and Political Development* (1966); and was one of several authors of *Crises of Political Development* (1967). He has also contributed to such symposium volumes as Don Piper and Taylor Cole (eds.), *Post Primary Education and Political and Economic Development* (1964); Myron Weiner (ed.), *Modernization* (1966); Lucian Pye and Sidney Verba (eds.), *Political Culture and Political Development* (1967); Charles Press and Alan Arian (eds.), *Empathy and Ideology* (1967); Robert T. Holt and John Turner (eds.), *The Methodology of Comparative Research* (1969); and Fred W. Riggs (ed.), *Frontiers in Development Administration* (1970). Since 1963 he has been professor of political science at Yale University.

Harold D. Lasswell was born in Donnellson, Illinois, in 1902. He studied at the universities of Chicago, London, Geneva, Paris, and Berlin and received the doctor of philosophy degree in political science from the University of Chicago in 1926. A fellow of the Social Science Research Council in 1928–29 and later of the Center for Advanced Studies in Behavioral Sciences in 1954, he taught at the University of Chicago from 1922 to 1938. He has been on the faculty of Yale University since 1938 where he was formerly Edward J. Phelps Professor of Law and Political Science and is now Ford Foundation Professor of Law and the Social Sciences. Cited by the American Council of Learned Societies in 1960 as "a master of all social sciences and a pioneer in each," his methodology itself has been the subject of extensive research in political science. He has served as a consultant at various times to the Department of Agriculture, the Department of Justice, and the Department of State of the United States government, and has served on the Research Advisory Board of the Committee on Economic Development and also as Director of War Communications Research in the Library of Congress. In 1956 he was president of the American Political Science Association. Professor Lasswell is the author of a number of works, among which are *Psychopathology and Politics* (1930; rev. ed. 1960); *World Politics and Personal Insecurity* (1935; republished as *A Study of Power* in 1955); *Politics: Who Gets What, When, How* (1935; rev. ed. 1950); *Power and Personality* (1948); *Analysis of Political Behavior: An Empirical Approach* (1949); *The Future of Political Science* (1963). He is co-editor and co-author (with

Nathan Leites and others) of *Language of Politics* (1945); (with Daniel Lerner) *The Policy Sciences* (1951); (with Daniel Lerner and Ithiel de Sola Pool) *The Comparative Study of Symbols* (1952); (with Daniel Lerner and C. Easton Rothwell) *The Comparative Study of Elites* (1952). He is also co-author (with Myres S. McDougal and I. A. Vlastic) of *The Public Order of Space* (1963); (with Richard Arens) *In Defense of Public Order: The Emerging Field of Sanction Law* (1961); (with Abraham Kaplan) *Power and Society* (1950); (with Robert Rubenstein) *Power Sharing in a Psychiatric Hospital* (1966); (with Myres S. McDougal and James Miller) *The Interpretation of International Agreements* (1967). He was also associated with Bruce Russett, Hayward Alker, and Karl Deutsch in preparation of the volume *World Handbook of Political and Social Indicators* (1964) and contributed to Richard L. Merritt and Stein Rokkan (eds.), *Comparing Nations* (1966).

John D. Montgomery, born in Evanston, Illinois, in 1920, received the Ph.D. in political science from Harvard University in 1951. In 1962 he was awarded the honorary doctor of laws degree from Kalamazoo College. During World War II he served as a military government officer in the occupation of Japan. He was chairman of the Department of Government and Law at Babson Institute for a decade starting in 1947 and during part of that time was dean of the faculty. He has served as consultant to various organizations, including the Operations Research Office of Johns Hopkins University, the Ford Foundation, the Agency for International Development, and the Department of Health, Education, and Welfare. In 1957 he was in Saigon for two years with the Michigan State University Vietnam project as head of the academic instruction section. He was research fellow in the Council on Foreign Relations from 1959 to 1960 and was director of the Center for Development Research and Training, the African Studies and Research Program at Boston University from 1960 to 1963. He has studied administrative reform in a number of countries in Africa and Asia, and in the summer of 1965 was in Malaysia with Milton J. Esman under Ford Foundation auspices to survey that country's needs in administrative reform. In the summer of 1967 he was in Vietnam studying land reform and political development in that country. He is a member of the executive committee of the Comparative Administration Group and is chairman of the Development Administration seminar of the Southeast Asia Development Advisory Group and of the Committee on International Development Research of the Society for International Development. He is on the editorial board of *Comparative Politics*. In the summer of 1968 he participated in a six-week planning conference at the Massachusetts Institute of Technology on political development. His publications include: *The Purge in Occupied Japan* (1954); *The State versus Socrates* (1954); and *Forced to be Free* (1957). He is editor and co-author of *Cases in Vietnamese Administration* (1959). He has contributed to various symposium volumes including Ralph Braibanti and J. J. Spengler (eds.), *Tradition, Values and Socio-Economic Development* (1961). His most recent books are *The Politics of Foreign Aid* (1962) and *Foreign Aid in International Politics* (1966). He is co-editor (with William J. Siffin) and a contributor to *Approaches to Development: Politics, Administration and Change* (1966). He succeeded Carl J. Friedrich as editor of *Public Policy* in 1963. Since 1963 he has been professor of public administration and secretary of the John F. Kennedy School of Government at Harvard University.

Lucian W. Pye was born in China in 1921 and received his doctor's degree in political science at Yale University in 1951. During World War II he served in the United States Marine Corps. He has done extensive field research in Asia and was a Fellow of the Center for Advanced Study in the Behavioral Sciences in 1963–64. He was on the faculty of Washington University from 1949 to 1952 and subsequently was a research associate in international relations at Yale University and later at Princeton University. Since 1956 he has been at the Massachusetts Institute of Technology, where since 1960 he has been professor of political science and for several years was chairman of the department. He has been on the editorial board of the *Journal of Asian Studies* and on the Board of Directors of the Association for Asian Studies, the executive committee of the New England Political Science Association, the Council of the American Political Science Association, and has been a member and is presently chairman of the Committee on Comparative Politics of the Social Science Research Council. He is on the editorial board of *Comparative Political Studies* and *Comparative Politics*. He organized, with Max Millikan, a six-week planning conference at the Massachusetts Institute of Technology in the summer of 1968 on the strategies of political development. He is the author of *Guerrilla Communism in Malaya* (1956); *Politics, Personality and Nation Building* (1963); *Aspects of Political Development* (1966); editor and contributing author of *Communications and Political Development* (1963); and co-editor (with Sidney Verba) of *Political Culture and Political Development* (1965). He has contributed to various learned journals and to such symposium volumes as Gabriel Almond and James S. Coleman (eds.), *The Politics of the Developing Areas* (1960); Max F. Millikan and Donald L. M. Blackmer (eds.), *The Emerging Nations* (1961); John J. Johnson (ed.), *The Role of the Military in Developing Countries* (1962); Irving Swerdlow (ed.), *Development Administration: Concepts and Problems* (1963); Harry

Eckstein (ed.), *Internal War* (1964); Myron Weiner and Joseph LaPalombara (eds.), *Political Parties and Political Development* (1966).

Fred W. Riggs, born in Kuling, China, in 1917, received his doctorate in political science from Columbia University in 1948. He served as a research associate of the Foreign Policy Association from 1948 to 1951, as assistant to the director of the Public Administration Clearing House in New York from 1951 to 1955, and as a member of the Department of Government at Indiana University, where he held the Arthur F. Bentley chair, from 1956 through 1967. Since 1967 he has been professor of political science at the University of Hawaii and a member of its Social Science Research Institute. During 1957–58 he held a fellowship from the Committee on Comparative Politics of the Social Science Research Council for research in Thailand. He has been a visiting professor or lecturer at Yale University during 1955–56; at the National Officials Training Institute in Korea in 1956; at the University of the Philippines in 1958–59; and at the Massachusetts Institute of Technology, 1965–66. He has also been a senior specialist at the East-West Center, University of Hawaii, 1962–63, and a Fellow of the Center for Advanced Study in the Behavioral Sciences, Stanford, 1966–67. Professor Riggs has been chairman of the Comparative Administration Group of the American Society for Public Administration since 1960 and is a member of the Southeast Asia Development Advisory Group. He is on the editorial board of *Comparative Political Studies* and *Comparative Politics.* He is the author of *Pressures on Congress* (1950); *Formosa Under Chinese Nationalist Rule* (1952); *The Ecology of Public Administration* (1962); *Administration in Developing Countries* (1964); *Thailand, the Modernization of a Bureaucratic Polity* (1966); and is co-author and editor of *Frontiers in Development Administration* (1970). He is also the author of many articles on international relations and comparative administration, including essays in William J. Siffin (ed.), *Toward the Comparative Study of Public Administration* (1957); Klaus Knorr and Sidney Verba (eds.), *The International System: Theoretical Essays* (1961); Joseph LaPalombara (ed.), *Bureaucracy and Political Development* (1963); John Montgomery and William J. Siffin (eds.), *Approaches to Development: Politics, Administration and Change* (1966); James C. Charlesworth (ed.), *Contemporary Political Analysis* (1967); and William J. Crotty (ed.), *Approaches to the Study of Party Organization* (1967).

Giovanni Sartori was born in Florence, Italy, in 1924. He received the Italian Ph.D. (*libera docenza*) both in history of modern philosophy and in theory of the state. In 1949 he did research in the United States under auspices of the Viking Fund and from 1950 to 1956 he taught history of modern philosophy at the University of Florence. Since 1956 he has been associate professor and subsequently professor of political science at the University of Florence. For three years he has also held a chair in sociology. During the fall term 1964–65 he served as visiting professor of government at Harvard University, and during the year 1966–67 he was a Fellow of the Concilium on International Studies and visiting professor of political science at Yale University. His publications include *Democrazia e Definizioni* (1957); *A Teoria de Representacao no Estado Representativo Moderno* (1962); *Democratic Theory* (1962, 1965). He is editor and co-author of *Il Parlamento Italiano 1946–1963* (1963). He has also written *Stato e Politica nel Pensiero di B. Croce* (1966); *Parties and Party Systems—A Theoretical Framework* (1967). He has also contributed to a number of symposia, such as Joseph LaPalombara and Myron Weiner (eds.), *Political Parties and Political Development* (1966), and is the author of the articles "Democracy" and "Representational Systems" in the forthcoming *International Encyclopedia of the Social Sciences.* He is presently professor and director of the Institute of Political Science at the University of Florence.

Joseph J. Spengler, born in Piqua, Ohio, in 1902, received the Ph.D. in economics from Ohio State University, which also awarded him the degree of Doctor of Humane Letters in 1965. He taught at Ohio State University and the University of Arizona before joining the Department of Economics at Duke University in 1934. During World War II he served as Southeastern Regional Price Executive for the Office of Price Administration. He has been frequently a consultant to government, foundations, and business, and has lectured in such countries as Israel, Ethiopia, Japan, and Pakistan. He has held fellowships from the Ford Foundation, the Brookings Institution, and the John Simon Guggenheim Foundation. He is a Fellow of the American Philosophical Society, the American Academy of Arts and Sciences, the American Association for the Advancement of Science, the American Statistical Association, and the Mount Pellerin Society. He is a former president of the Population Association of America, the Southern Economic Association, and the American Economic Association, and former vice-president of the Economic History Association and of the Association for the Advancement of Science. His major works include: *France Faces Depopulation* (1938) *and French Predecessors of Malthus* (1942). He is editor and contributing author of *Natural Resources and Economic Growth* (1961), and co-editor (with O. D. Duncan) and contributing author of *Demographic Analysis* (1956), *Population Theory and Policy* (1956), and (with W. R. Allen) *Essays in Economic Thought* (1960). He is co-editor (with Ralph Braibanti) and a contributing author to *Tradition, Values and Socio-Economic Development* (1961) and *Administration and Economic Development in India* (1963). He has contributed to such symposium volumes as N. Mansergh (ed.), *Commonwealth Perspectives* (1958); B. F. Hoselitz (ed.), *Theories of Economic Growth* (1960); Robert O. Tilman and Taylor Cole (eds.), *The Nigerian Political Scene* (1962); Joseph LaPalombara (ed.), *Bureaucracy and Political Development* (1963); A. P. Sindler (ed.), *Change in the Contemporary South* (1963); Juanita Kreps (ed.), *Employment, Income and Retirement Problems of the Aged* (1963); E. A. G. Robinson (ed.), *Economic Development for Africa South of the Sahara* (1964); Stuart Mudd (ed.), *The Population Crisis and the Use of World Resources* (1964); Ronald Freedman (ed.), *Population: The Vital Revolution* (1964); B. R. Barringer, G. L. Blanksten, and R. W. Mack (eds.), *Social Change in Developing Areas* (1965); J. C. McKinney and E. T. Thompson (eds.), *The South in Continuity and Change* (1965); W. B. Hamilton, Kenneth Robinson, and C. D. W. Goodwin (eds.), *A Decade of the Commonwealth 1955–1964* (1966); J. C. McKinney and F. T. de Vyver (eds.), *Aging and Social Policy* (1966); Myron Weiner (ed.), *Modernization* (1966). Dr. Spengler is presently James B. Duke Professor of Economics, a member of the Commonwealth-Studies Committee and director of the Population Studies Center at Duke University.

Contents

1. External Inducement of Political-Administrative Development: An Institutional Strategy

Ralph Braibanti

3

2. Political Development and the Objectives of Modern Government

Carl J. Friedrich

107

3. Comment on "Political Development and the Objectives of Modern Government"

Giovanni Sartori

136

4. Goals for Administrative Reform in Developing States: An Open-Ended Design

Henry S. Kariel

143

5. Values and Ideologies in the Administrative Evolution of Western Constitutional Systems

Joseph LaPalombara

166

6. The Structures of Government and Administrative Reform

Fred W. Riggs

220

7. Political and Administrative Development: General Commentary

Martin Landau

325

8. Toward A General Theory of Directed Value Accumulation and Institutional Development

Harold D. Lasswell and Allan R. Holmberg

354

9. Bureaucratic Development and the Psychology of Institutionalization

Lucian W. Pye

400

10. Sources of Bureaucratic Reform: A Typology of Purpose and Politics

John D. Montgomery

427

11. Productivity, Administrative Reform and Antipolitics: Dilemmas for Developing States

Warren F. Ilchman

472

12. Comment on "Productivity, Administrative Reform and Antipolitics: Dilemmas for Developing States"

R. Taylor Cole

527

13. Administrative Doctrines Diffused in Emerging States: The Filipino Response

José V. Abueva

536

14. Allocation and Development, Economic and Political

Joseph J. Spengler

588

15. Conspectus

Ralph Braibanti

638

Index

668

Tables

The Structures of Government and Administrative Reform

1. Types of Complex Bureaucracy, Classified Structurally by Echelon-Staffing 257
2. Degrees of Bureaucratic Politization and Partisanship 260
3. Hypothesized Functions of Complex Bureaucracies for Their Polities 267
4. Types of Tonic Polities 301
5. Classificatory Equivalents—Riggs, Shils, Apter 314

Toward a General Theory of Directed Value Accumulation and Institutional Development

Figure. The Value-institution Model 385

Sources of Bureaucratic Reform: A Typology of Purpose and Politics

1. Increase in Commoners among Chinese Officials 434
2. Political Forms and Administrative Reform 458
3. Localization of the Public Service in Ghana, 1952–58 460
4. Localization of the Public Service in Malaya, 1956–58 460

Comment on "Productivity, Administrative Reform and Antipolitics: Dilemmas for Developing States"

1. Country of Origin of United Nations Public Administration Experts, 1950–1966 543
2. Contemporary Concepts and Practice: United Nations Handbook of Public Administration, 1961 544
3. Aid-Assisted Public Administration Projects in the Philippines 559
4. Classifications of Political Systems in Southeast Asia 565

Political and Administrative Development

• 1 •

External Inducement of Political-Administrative Development: An Institutional Strategy

Ralph Braibanti

In this chapter we seek to relate certain aspects of bureaucratic improvement in developing states to four selected conditions of political growth. Our assumption is that the strengthening of administration must proceed irrespective of the rate of maturation of the political process. Nevertheless, in recognition of the stress involved in rapid bureaucratic development occurring simultaneously with expanded mass participation in political life, we seek here to explore means of increasing the capability of other institutions not only to stimulate bureaucratic innovation but also to moderate administrative discretion, to enhance the symmetry of political growth, and to improve the quality of participation. It is assumed that a symbiotic relationship exists between administration and the political, indeed the total, social order and that in a mature system bureaucracy is articulated to more or less evenly developed attitudinal and structural components of that order. In new systems the levels of institutionalization and the consequent strains are uneven partly as a consequence of structural weaknesses often neglected both by internal reformers and by externally induced instruments of change. We shall first review new developments in foreign assistance in the United States which may signal efforts to induce institutional changes in total political systems externally. We shall then examine certain aspects of political development in an effort to relate administrative growth to the larger context. Finally, we shall suggest certain institutional and structural changes which might contribute to a constructive symbiosis of administration and the total political system.

We shall draw on experience in Pakistan, India, and, to a lesser extent, in Turkey and Japan as being suggestive of propositions. The design for strategy is tentative and the propositions scattered throughout require testing.

In this chapter the relationship of the party process to administration will be passed over since this is explored in this volume by Riggs[1] and, insofar as electoral mechanism is concerned, elsewhere by Sartori.[2] Further, we shall ignore the social-psychological context created by and contributing to the symbiosis between bureaucratic systems and personality development, aspects of which are explored in this volume by Kariel and Pye.[3] These omissions do not suggest the unimportance of the approaches or phenomena. On the contrary, it is this writer's view that the impact of institutions on human behavior and the value-content of institutions are problems at the frontier of political science which require increasing exploration. Their omission in this chapter is dictated by economies of time and space and by the distribution of emphases among other chapters.

I. New Challenge of the Foreign Assistance Act of 1967

Doctrinal antecedents and supports of Title IX

The relationship of induced administrative change to the development of political systems has been given fresh cogency in United States foreign aid doctrine by certain amendments to the Foreign Assistance Act first made in 1966 and strengthened in

1. See the chapter by Fred W. Riggs in this volume.
2. Giovanni Sartori, "Political Development and Political Engineering," in John D. Montgomery and Albert O. Hirschman (eds.), *Public Policy*, XVII (1968), 261–298. See also his "Constitutionalism: A Preliminary Discussion," *American Political Science Review*, LVI (1962), 853–865, and the subsequent exchange between W. H. Morris-Jones and Sartori, "Constitutionalism," *ibid.*, LIX (1965), 439–444.
3. See the chapters by Henry S. Kariel and Lucian W. Pye in this volume.

1967.[4] One effect of these provisions and particularly of Title IX is to sharpen our awareness that virtually no coherent systematized doctrine of political development existed in the foreign assistance policy of the United States prior to the elaboration of Title IX in the 1966 Foreign Assistance Act. This is not to say that American policy had been totally devoid of general predispositions relating to political development as such development affects the absorption of economic aid. Three categories of such predispositions antedating Title IX can be identified: (1) hortatory injunctions embedded in the statute, usually in the preamble on policy, (2) administrative statements in programs and reports of the Agency for International Development (AID), as well as implicit assumptions and attitudes of AID administrators, and (3) particularistic emphases written into the statute and relating to a part of the development process. In the first category we find generalized statements of an ideal polity included as a preamble in the basic Foreign Assistance Act of 1961 and its subsequent amended revisions of 1966 and 1967. In the 1967 act there is a resolve to help people of less developed countries "in their efforts to acquire the knowledge and resources essential for development and to build the economic, political and social institutions which meet their aspirations for a better life, with freedom, and in peace."[5] The same section of the act pledges Congress's support of "freedom of the press, information and religion" in such friendly nations and declares that our help to less developed countries is "not only expressive of our sense of freedom, justice and compassion, but also important to our national security." An effort by the executive branch to insert a policy statement was rebuffed by the Senate, which at the same time proposed the repeal of the 1966 policy statement as well.[6] The House Committee on Foreign

4. Foreign Assistance Act of 1966, Public Law 89–583 (80 Stat. 795). Foreign Assistance Act of 1967, Public Law 90–137 (81 Stat. 445).

5. Foreign Assistance Act of 1967, Part I, chap. 1, Sec. 102.

6. A year before, however, the Senate Foreign Relations Committee, in a less truculent mood, approved the policy statement as part of the 1966 act (United States Senate, *Foreign Economic Assistance Report of the Committee on Foreign Relations on* S. *3584*, 89th Congress, 2nd Session, *Senate Report No. 1359* [Washington, 1966], pp. 39–42). In considering a similar policy statement in 1967, the Senate committee thought that such statements were "so broad . . . as to be meaningless" and "too often become the tools of special bureaucratic

Affairs restored a statement of policy, longer than the 1966 statement and somewhat different from the 1967 version proposed by the executive branch. The House statement, part of which is quoted above, was accepted by the Senate in conference committee and is now part of the Foreign Assistance Act of 1967.[7] This statement is the principal source of the hortatory injunctions mentioned above as the first category of prevailing doctrine. These generalized ideals of the 1961 and 1967 acts were shaped more definitely in the 1967 act by the addition of seven basic principles, some new and some stating in clearer form assumptions scattered in other parts of earlier versions of the act. The first principle picks up the "self-help" theme strongly emphasized by President Johnson in his 1967 message to the Congress on foreign aid.[8] In the act as finally approved this theme appears in a somewhat weaker form than the President's earlier proposal for establishing a national advisory committee on self-help. Though the Senate committee approved the Johnson proposal,[9] it was rejected by the House committee. The resulting compromise was affirmation of the concept but not the structure of "self-help" as the first of seven basic principles. That principle declares development to be "primarily the responsibility of the people of the less developed countries themselves" and that United States assistance "shall be used in support of rather than substitution for . . . self-help efforts and shall be concentrated in those countries that take positive steps to help themselves." This first "self-help" principle also embraces the doctrine of "involvement of the people in the development process." This latter provision is almost identical to Title IX as it appears in the 1967 act. Its repetition as

interests." Moreover, the Senate resented the executive's drafting policy statements which it felt should be initiated by Congress: "the trend toward submission of packaged policy statements to the Congress by the executive branch illustrates how the principle of separation of powers has been deeply eroded in recent years" (United States Senate, *Foreign Assistance Act of 1967, Report of the Committee on Foreign Relations on S. 1872*, 90th Congress, 1st Session, *Senate Report No. 499* [Washington, 1967], p. 16).

7. Foreign Assistance Act of 1967, Part I, chap. 1, Sec. 102.

8. Agency for International Development, *Proposed Foreign Aid Program FY 1968 Summary Presentation to the Congress* (Washington, 1967), pp. 13–22, 272–283.

9. Text of this proposal as accepted by the Senate committee and included in its version of the bill can be found in Senate Calendar No. 484, *S. 1872*, Report No. 499, Sec. 209.

a policy at the beginning of the act accentuates the importance of the Title IX doctrine and expands its applicability to all programs authorized by the act. The second and third principles suggest that other "prosperous" nations be encouraged to share in the development responsibilities of the new states. Regional co-operation by emerging nations is also encouraged; improvement in food production and voluntary family planning are stated as principles. Finally, three administrative policies are enunciated: use of United States commodities and services to improve its balance of payments position, maximum efficiency and economy of operation of the aid program, and co-ordination of disposal of agricultural surplus and payments to international lending institutions with other programs of foreign assistance. In this first category of policy, we thus find repeated in the act from 1961 on a set of transcendent objectives not unlike the fourfold classification of Friedrich—security, external peace, prosperity, and internal peace—and his triad of subobjectives—justice, freedom, and equality.[10] Nor are these objectives much dissimilar from the "political goods" of security, liberty, welfare, and justice elsewhere espoused by Pennock[11] or from the elegant formulary of the papal encyclical, *Populorum Progessio*.[12]

The second category of sources of doctrine are sets of implicit assumptions and attitudes in AID administration of foreign assistance. Among these is the view that economic and administrative reform cannot be pursued in isolation from total political reform. This seems to have been a propensity not only in AID's operating disposition but in United Nations technical assistance doctrine and in academic thought as well. The need for dealing forthrightly with issues of political development received attention by a few political scientists before it was widely acknowledged as a conceptual problem by the discipline. This early recognition came within the ambit of foreign policy analysis. As has been mentioned elsewhere in this chapter, Friedrich consistently rec-

10. See Carl J. Friedrich's chapter in this volume, pp. 115–123.

11. J. Roland Pennock, "Political Development, Political Systems and Political Goods," *World Politics*, XVIII (1966), 418.

12. See below, n. 88.

ognized the problem.[13] Montgomery, surveying the occupations of Japan and Germany which he regarded as "artificial revolutions," asserted that "these considerations justify a retrospective analysis of the German and Japanese occupations as an innovation in American statesmanship and the forerunner of a new political consciousness in our foreign policy."[14] He regarded the occupation aims as the elimination of despotic elites, the support of new leadership, and "constitutional, legal, and institutional assurances of a new order."[15] A similar view was expressed by Cleveland: "The essence of overseasmanship is the building of political and social institutions."[16] More recently this view finds renewed expression in various studies.[17] The first major codification of administrative reform doctrine by the United Nations cautioned that "profound changes are required in political and social attitudes in governmental structure, institutions, behavior and skill."[18] This view was espoused even more strongly by academics and officials alike in relation to American aid by the Brookings Study Group convened for AID (then ICA) in 1960.[19] With respect to the view of AID on this question, as early as 1961 AID public administration advisors were told in official briefings that their work was closely related to the development of "political democracy."[20] Packenham culled from a variety of sources such as reports of AID officials, program reports, and interviews with AID personnel sets of assumptions and attitudes relating to political development.[21] He found that explicit attention to politi-

13. See below, nn. 62, 63, 85, 87, 108.

14. John D. Montgomery, *Forced to be Free: The Artificial Revolution in Germany and Japan* (Chicago, 1957), p. 3. See also his "'Gilded Missiles': Reflections on the Politics of Foreign Aid," *Far Eastern Survey*, XXVIII (1959), 81–89.

15. Montgomery, *Forced to be Free*, pp. 4–5.

16. Harlan Cleveland and Gerard J. Mangone (eds.), *The Art of Overseasmanship* (Syracuse, N.Y., 1957), p. 3.

17. See, for example, Robert M. Macy, "The Need for Guidelines to Political Development," in William Y. Elliott (ed.), *Education and Training in the Developing Countries: The Role of U.S. Foreign Aid* (New York, 1966), pp. 197–205.

18. United Nations, Department of Economic and Social Affairs, *A Handbook of Public Administration: Current Concepts and Practice with Special Reference to Developing Countries* (New York, 1961), p. 6.

19. See official report of this meeting by Mary E. Robinson, *Education for Social Change* (Washington, 1961), esp. pp. 12–13.

20. See José V. Abueva's chapter in this volume, p. 549.

21. Robert A. Packenham, "Political Development Doctrines in the American Foreign Aid Program," *World Politics*, XVIII (1966), 194–235, esp. 209–235.

cal development (as of 1962–63) was slight, that there was a gap between declared purpose and policy, and that there was uncertainty in AID about the relationship between economic aid and political development. Yet there was awareness particularly at higher levels of the importance of political development.

A third category of development doctrine can be found in particularistic provisions such as the Humphrey amendment of 1961 and the Zablocki amendment of 1962. Both emphasized popular participation in development, and in that respect they were direct ideological forerunners of Title IX. The first amendment, introduced by the then Senator Hubert Humphrey of Minnesota, declared that the policy of the United States was, *inter alia,* "to encourage the development and use of cooperatives, credit unions, and savings and loan associations."[22] In the Senate debate, Humphrey made clear that his amendment did not force co-operatives upon aid-receiving nations but that it would require AID to encourage these institutions in a more systematic and positive way.[23] Senator John Sherman Cooper of Kentucky, defending the amendment, declared that "these institutions are good in themselves. They have been good in this country. I think they would be good in other countries."[24] Cooper specifically related co-operatives to the participative emphases of the then unborn Title IX. He referred to a conversation he had with Arnold Toynbee about countries whose masses of people had no experience in democratic practices. Toynbee had mentioned co-operatives as an institution providing such necessary experience "from the bottom." The Humphrey amendment, which remains intact in the 1967 act, stirred some activity in AID in 1961 and 1962[25] but has now been eclipsed by the newer, more comprehensive doctrines of participation in Title IX of the 1966 and 1967 acts. A second particularistic provision conceptually related to Title IX is the amendment on community development intro-

22. Foreign Assistance Act of 1961, Public Law 87–195 (75 Stat. 424), Part III, chap. 1, Sec. 601.
23. *Congressional Record—Senate,* 87th Congress, 1st Session, August 18, 1961, pp. 16392–16394.
24. *Ibid.,* p. 16392.
25. For a description of this activity, see United States Senate, *Implementation of the Humphrey Amendment to the Foreign Assistance Act of 1961,* 87th Congress, 2nd Session, *Senate Document No. 112* (Washington, 1962).

duced by Representative Clement J. Zablocki of Wisconsin. This provides that in recipient countries with agrarian economies, "emphasis shall be placed also upon programs of community development which will promote stable and responsible governmental institutions at the local level."[26]

The foregoing brief analysis of three categories of doctrine antedating Title IX of 1966 suggests that there has been some semblance of doctrine reflecting in a sincere but perhaps platitudinous way American political experience. An inchoate body of policy with increasingly stronger emphasis on popular participation can now be discerned. Judging from these provisions, particularly the Humphrey and Zablocki amendments, it would be easy to conclude that the emphasis in foreign assistance had been on the participatory elements and to fear that this probable escalation of expectations might have strained the capacity of the apparatus of government to convert rising demands into policy or action. But such a conclusion is not warranted, even though it may be suggested by the statutory evidence. Analysis of country programs reveals a significant level of AID activity in building and strengthening the institutions of government. In such activities as administration, planning, agriculture, public health, and education, for example, even though they may not have been singled out for the same statutory attention as co-operatives and community development, such institutional strengthening has occurred.

It is clear that the foreign assistance program included allusions at least to rather generalized political doctrine, but it is probable that the vagueness of the doctrine somewhat reduced if not nullified their significance. The elasticity of interpretation of the statutory injunctions analyzed above is suggested by the diversity in political systems to which we gave 87 per cent of our foreign assistance in 1967. The sixteen major countries in this group include Brazil, Thailand, Vietnam, Nigeria, Pakistan, Tuni-

26. Foreign Assistance Act of 1962, Public Law 87–565 (76 Stat. 255), Part I, chap. 6, Sec. 461. For the committee's justification of this amendment, see United States House of Representatives, *Foreign Assistance Act of 1962*, 87th Congress, 2nd Session, *House Report No. 1788* (Washington, 1962), p. 26.

sia, Turkey, Laos, and India.[27] To determine whether each of these systems is committed to and is seriously implementing the directive principles set forth in the statute's preamble is to suggest both the vagueness of those principles and the almost total absence of a formula for political development which might be used effectively as a measure of a nation's political condition.

Title IX and related provisions

Provisions added to or reinforced in the foreign assistance acts of 1966 and 1967 bring us closer to the formulation of political development policy than we have ever been in the history of the United States foreign assistance program. Ambiguities remain and certainly we are far from a formulation which has immediate instrumental value; nevertheless the 1967 act is richer in political development implications than any of its earlier versions. These implications may, for expository convenience, be arranged in four groups. The first of these are declamations of the preamble reinforced in the 1967 act by the seven principles alluded to earlier,[28] the first of which relates to self-help and includes almost verbatim some of the Title IX doctrine as well. The second, relating to loans made from the Development Loan Fund, to technical cooperation and development grants, and to the Alliance for Progress, specifies as a criterion for aid "the degree to which the recipient country is making progress toward respect for the rule of law, freedom of expression and of the press, and recognition of the importance of individual freedom, initiative and private enterprise."[29] It is not without significance that this rule of law formulary appears three times in the act and covers virtually all aspects of foreign aid. Enmeshed in this doctrine is the familiar dilemma of reconciling institutional growth, which we here assume to be the principal means of achieving rule of law, with

27. *Proposed Foreign Aid Program FY 1968*, pp. 3, 4.
28. See above, pp. 6–7.
29. Foreign Assistance Act of 1966, chap. 2, Sec. 20 (b)(7), Sec. 211 (a)(7), Sec. 251 (b)(7). These provisions appear also in the 1967 act. This criterion had been included in the Senate foreign assistance bill of 1965 as a "principle to be taken into account in shaping a new aid program" but did not appear in the act. Its inclusion in the Foreign Assistance Act of 1966 was due to Senate insistence. See *Senate Report No. 1359*, pp. 7–8.

canons of mobilization implicit in the remainder of the provision. The ambiguity of the requirement and the difficulties of discriminating between ideological aspirations and effective implementation of a rule of law formulation may nullify its latent effervescence. As a consequence it is doubtful that the dilemma will be resolved by United States operations abroad. Nevertheless, the rule of law doctrine, with its implicit assumptions of building viable institutions and its foundations in personal liberty, might well have led to the same objective of political development for which Title IX was designed. This would have been the inevitable consequence of the relationship between popular sovereignty and participation necessarily stabilized within a framework of law. In the context of renewed concern for law as a positive instrument of social change rather than as a bulwark of impedance, this possibility might have been enhanced by active programs under the rule of law rubric. It is not an unexpected curiosity that this provision has been not only unexploited but totally ignored. The strategy of political development now being evolved is rising primarily from a base of popular participation rather than of legal institutions.[30]

The second relevant amendment,[31] reflecting admiration for the Joint Commission on Rural Reconstruction in China as "one of the most successful ventures of the United States in aiding under-developed countries," authorizes agreements for establishment of bilateral joint commissions on rural development in less developed countries. This provision first appeared in 1966 and was reincorporated in the 1967 act. The Senate Committee on Foreign Relations cites the JCRR (new versions of which are to be called joint commissions on rural development—JCRD) approach as enabling American aid to be made "available directly to the people of a recipient country without being channeled through bureaucracies."[32] The new institution (JCRD) on which

30. For further analysis, see Ralph Braibanti, "The Role of Law in Political Development," in Robert R. Wilson (ed.), *International and Comparative Law of the Commonwealth, 1906–1967* (Durham, N.C., 1968), pp. 3–26. See also n. 93 below.

31. Foreign Assistance Act of 1967, chap. 7, Sec. 471.

32. *Senate Report No. 1359*, p. 18.

reliance is placed combines in one entity elements of rural uplift and scientific agriculture with regulated participation in economic and agricultural affairs. Here the potential conflict between participative needs and infrastructural viability appears to be resolved, at least theoretically, by recasting dispositions, skills, and substantive concerns into a new mosaic.[33] The JCRD pattern also permits a bilateral collegiality based on parity of esteem in which there can occur an ecological adjustment of ideas and techniques introduced by the aid-giving nation. However enthusiastic the Congress, and especially the Senate, may have been about the possibility of establishing JCRD's, none had been established a year later when the 1967 Foreign Assistance Act was discussed in committee in June and July, 1967. AID Administrator William S. Gaud informed the Senate committee then that efforts were made in several countries but that "it takes two to waltz in this particular situation which entails setting up an independent organization . . . composed partly of Americans and partly of citizens of [the recipient country]."[34]

The most important element of doctrine in United States foreign assistance policy is Title IX—first introduced in the 1966 act and re-enacted with strengthening amendments in 1967 and 1968. Title IX was added to the act in 1966 at the initiative of and as a result of a motion by Representative Donald M. Fraser of Minnesota. Representative Clement G. Zablocki was co-sponsor.

33. For an account of the genesis of the JCRR by its principal initiator, former Congressman Walter H. Judd, see his testimony in United States House of Representatives, Committee on Foreign Affairs, Hearings Before the Subcommittee on Asian and Pacific Affairs, 90th Congress, 1st Session, *Rural Development in Asia* (Washington, 1967), Part II, pp. 223–262. Judd assumes the transferability of the JCRR concept and attributes its failure to spread to AID opposition and to the inability of Americans abroad "to work with other people or under one of them as chairman" (*ibid.*, p. 239). This appears to the present writer to be an oversimplification. The domestic and international contexts in which the JCRR was first organized in 1948 are markedly different from those now prevailing in developing states. For a suggestion that the JCRR model has little applicability to other situations see Max F. Millikan and David Hapgood, *No Easy Harvest: The Dilemma of Agriculture in Underdeveloped Countries* (Boston, 1967), pp. 116–118. For an analysis of preconditions and for a note of caution about its applicability, see also John D. Montgomery, Rufus B. Hughes, and Raymond H. Davis, *Rural Improvement and Political Development: The JCRR Model*, Papers in Comparative Public Administration, Special Series, No. 7 (Washington, 1966).

34. United States Senate, Committee on Foreign Relations, *Hearings on the Foreign Assistance Act of 1967* (S. 1872), 90th Congress, 1st Session (Washington, 1967), p. 173.

On the Republican side, passage of Title IX received considerable help from Representative F. Bradford Morse of Massachusetts. It reflected also the viewpoint of twenty-five Republican members of the House who, on the initiative of Representative Morse, had written a statement which included as its third recommendation a provision virtually identical to Title IX.[35] Title IX was not the natural outgrowth of extensive academic analysis specifically aimed at the problem of participation in political development;[36] nor was it an equally favorite project of both houses of Congress.[37] It emerged almost entirely from the initiative of Representative Fraser as a crystallization and refinement of earlier congressional sentiments on co-operative and community development.[38] It was supported with considerable enthusiasm by other members of the House Committee on Foreign Affairs, especially Zablocki and Morse.

35. Text of the Republican provision is accessible in *Congressional Record—House,* July 13, 1966, p. 14674. Statements vigorously supporting Title IX can be found in *ibid.,* pp. 14716, 14755–14757, 14764–14767, 14773–14776.

36. The issue of popular participation in local institutions of government does not appear, for example, in the report, *Some Important Issues in Foreign Aid,* prepared by the Legislative Reference Service for the Senate Committee on Foreign Relations, 89th Congress, 2nd Session (Washington, 1966). This report lists five problems in the political realm, but participation is not one of them (pp. 13–14).

37. That the Senate committee did not suggest Title IX is indicated by its silence on the issue in committee hearings and reports. See *Senate Report No. 1359* for the 1966 act and *Senate Report No. 499* for the 1967 act. Nor was Title IX proposed by the executive branch, which was officially silent on the matter in its proposals for the 1966 act. See Agency for International Development, *Proposed Foreign Aid Program FY 1967* (Washington, 1966). In its proposal for the 1967 act, after Title IX had already been included in the 1966 act, the executive branch continued its official silence. It may be that the President's espousal of "self-help" criteria was designed to lead to the same ends as those envisaged in Title IX. See *Proposed Foreign Aid Program FY 1968,* esp. pp. 13–23. Yet the specific provision for popular participation [Sec. 208 (c)] which ultimately appeared in the 1967 act in four places was inserted by the House committee; it had not appeared in the President's analysis of "self-help" criteria.

38. The role of Congressman Fraser as initiator of Title IX is generally accepted both in Congress and in AID, and there are frequent references to it in reports and hearings. See, for example, United States Senate, Committee on Foreign Relations, *Survey of the Alliance for Progress—The Political Aspects,* 90th Congress, 1st Session, Committee Print (Washington, 1967), p. 22. Statements of Fraser's views on political development can be found in *Congressional Record—House,* July 13, 1966, pp. 14755–14767, and United States House of Representatives, *Report of the Committee on Foreign Affairs . . . on H. R. 12048 . . . ,* Foreign Assistance Act of 1967, 90th Congress, 1st Session, *House Report No. 551* (Washington, 1967), pp. 117–221. See an earlier expression of his views and the reactions of Secretary of State Rusk in *House Report No. 1224* (complete citation in n. 66 below), pp. 117–121.

The text of Title IX as it appeared in the 1966 act consisted of a single sentence: "In carrying out programs authorized in this chapter, emphasis shall be placed on assuring maximum participation in the task of economic development on the part of the people of the developing countries, through the encouragement of democratic, private and local government institutions."[39] Programs authorized by Chapter 2 cover nearly the full ambit of foreign assistance activities. Included are development assistance, programs financed by the Development Loan Fund and those involving technical co-operation, development grants, the Alliance for Progress, and multilateral and regional programs in Southeast Asia. The skeletal generality of Title IX was given welcome fleshing-out by the report of the House Committee on Foreign Affairs.[40] Justifying the insertion of Title IX, the committee observed that "there is a close relationship between popular participation in the process of development and the effectiveness of that process." The aim of the committee was to tap the human resources of developing countries by associating people with various developmental organizations. Specific mention was made of co-operatives, labor unions, savings and loan-type institutions, voluntary organizations, community development and local government. The committee contemplated increased reliance on non-governmental organizations capable of mobilizing public efforts. The committee also made clear that it planned to check on the manner in which the intent of Title IX was carried out; AID was enjoined to develop criteria for judging the results of this effort.[41]

The assignment thus given AID in November, 1966, was virtually impossible to fulfil. The Title IX mandate was premised upon ascertaining the complex relationship between popular participation and building viable institutions. This relationship presented

39. Foreign Assistance Act of 1966, chap. 2, Title IX, Sec. 281.

40. United States House of Representatives, *Report of the Committee on Foreign Affairs, Foreign Assistance Act of 1966*, 89th Congress, 2nd Session, *House Report No. 1651* (Washington, 1966), pp. 27–28.

41. For AID responses to committee inquiry into implementation of Title IX, see United States House of Representatives, Committee on Foreign Affairs, *Hearings before the Committee . . . on H. R. 7099 and H. R. 12048, Foreign Assistance Act of 1967*, 90th Congress, 1st Session (Washington, 1967), Part II, pp. 448 ff.

the risk of precipitating a demand-conversion crisis, the result of too much participation in a system with weak institutions. This condition can presumably lead to mounting frustration over unfulfilled demands and thence to political disintegration. By May, 1967, AID had taken initial steps to respond to Congress's mandate. A Title IX division was established in the office of program and policy co-ordination and an intra-agency committee of fourteen senior officials was formed. Twenty-two field missions were asked as early as November, 1966, when the Foreign Assistance Act of 1966 was passed, to analyze their programs in the light of Title IX; academic consultants were engaged in the summer of 1967 to make preliminary surveys. Meantime the Title IX division formulated the broad outlines of an AID strategy.[42] The strategy was based on three themes: (1) recognition of differing conditions in each country, (2) co-operation between the mission and the host country, and (3) the interrelatedness of social, economic, and political factors. The challenge presented by the very appearance of Title IX stimulated further collaboration between academic research and AID. A panel on Title IX was organized by the present writer at the annual meeting in Washington of the American Political Science Association in September, 1968. Panel membership included Congressman Donald M. Fraser, author of Title IX, and John R. Schott, chief of AID's Title IX division. In the summer of 1968 a six-week "brainstorming" work session organized by Max Millikan and Lucian Pye was held under auspices of the Massachusetts Institute of Technology at Endicott House. The conference, financed by AID, included twelve academic political scientists (including David Bayley, Marcus Franda, John D. Montgomery, Pye, John Plank, Myron Weiner, and the present writer) as well as some twenty State Department and AID officials from overseas missions and from Washington headquarters. Its purpose was to summarize and evaluate the condition of analysis of political development as it has evolved in academic and government thought and to formulate strategies

42. Agency for International Development, "Report to the Congress on the Implementation of Title IX" (Washington, May 10, 1967, mimeographed).

for political and social development within the terms of the Foreign Assistance Act.

During the months between enactment of Title IX in 1966 and hearings on the 1967 Foreign Assistance Act, the new provision was favorably commented on by academic and other interested groups. The risks and delicacies enmeshed in the implicitly manipulative aspects of Title IX were mentioned only once and then inferentially.[43] Testimony given at hearings of the Subcommittee on Asian and Pacific Affairs not only applauded Title IX but suggested enlarging the scope of direct leverage of political development by the United States. Kenneth T. Young, president of the Asia Society and chairman of the Southeast Asia Development Advisory Group, referred to two memoranda he had written in 1957 (both of which the subcommittee inserted in the record) in which specific proposals were made for "getting increased political impact out of U.S. overseas programs."[44] With reference to Title IX, he suggested negotiating "modernization agreements" with countries receiving foreign assistance. Such agreements were to provide for "concrete kinds of advisory political assistance with escape clauses for nonperformance."[45] Samuel P. Huntington, pursuing a theme advanced earlier in an article,[46] urged the committee to amend Title IX "by adding the words 'and democratic political parties' to the existing language."[47] He also argued that assistance should be given to political parties, that we embark on the training of political leaders, and that an office for political development be created within AID. The vice-president of the National Farmers Union praised Title IX as a reiteration and expansion of the 1961 Humphrey amendment on co-operatives.[48] The vice-president of the Cooperative League of the

43. *Rural Development in Asia,* Part I, p. 114.
44. *Ibid.,* pp. 48–75.
45. *Ibid.,* p. 75.
46. Samuel P. Huntington, "Political Development and Political Decay," *World Politics,* XVII (1965), 386–430.
47. *Rural Development in Asia,* Part I, p. 121.
48. House of Representatives, Committee on Foreign Affairs, *Hearings before the Committee . . . on H. R. 7099 and H. R. 12048 . . . ,* Part IV, pp. 706–707.

U.S.A. voiced similar sentiments.[49] Communications specialists hailed Title IX, seeing its success contingent upon improved communication technology.[50] This relationship was supported by the House Subcommittee on International Organizations and Movements in its report on communications and foreign policy.[51]

The reincorporation and strengthening of the concept of Title IX in the 1967 Foreign Assistance Act appeared, as is suggested by the foregoing analysis, to be a not unnatural outgrowth of congressional and articulate academic and interest group sentiment. In the interim between passage of the 1966 and 1967 acts, the House Committee on Foreign Affairs considered its views on participation corroborated by findings of other subcommittees.[52] Although in the 1966 Foreign Assistance Act the formulary for popular participation appeared only once—in Title IX itself—it appears four times in almost identical language in the 1967 act. It is accorded more universal applicability by being included (with the self-help concept discussed above) as the first of seven principles in the statement of policy: "Maximum effort shall be made . . . to stimulate the involvement of the people in the development process through the encouragement of democratic participation in private and local governmental activities and institution-building appropriate to the requirements of the recipient nations."[53]

It appears a second time in the context of a statement of the purposes of development assistance. The executive is enjoined to place appropriate emphasis in furnishing such assistance on "assuring maximum participation in the task of economic development by the people of less developed countries through the

49. *Ibid.*, p. 882.

50. United States House of Representatives, Committee on Foreign Affairs, Hearings before the Subcommittee on International Organizations and Movements, *Modern Communications and Foreign Policy, Part X Winning the Cold War: The U.S. Ideological Offensive,* 90th Congress, 1st Session (Washington, 1967), pp. 87, 121, 153.

51. United States House of Representatives, Committee on Foreign Affairs, Report No. 5, *Modern Communications and Foreign Policy,* 90th Congress, 1st Session, *House Report No. 362* (Washington, 1967), p. 13R.

52. *House Report No. 551,* p. 30. The committee referred specifically to *Rural Development in Asia, Modern Communications and Foreign Policy,* and *Behavioral Sciences and National Security.* These reports are cited above in nn. 33, 50, 51 and below in n. 66.

53. Foreign Assistance Act of 1967, Part I, chap. 1, Sec. 102.

encouragement of strong economic, political, and social institutions needed for a progressive democratic society."[54]

Its third appearance is as the third of seven "self-help" criteria: "the extent to which the government of the country is increasing the role of the people in the developmental process."[55]

The fourth and principal appearance of the doctrine is the expansion of the text of Title IX proper, which now reads:

> *Title IX—Utilization of Democratic Institutions in Development*
>
> Sec. 281. (*a*) In carrying out programs authorized in this chapter, emphasis shall be placed on assuring maximum participation in the task of economic development on the part of the people of the developing countries, through the encouragement of democratic private and local governmental institutions.
>
> (*b*) In order to carry out the purposes of this title, programs under this chapter shall—
>
> (1) recognize the differing needs, desires, and capacities of the people of the respective developing countries and areas;
>
> (2) use the intellectual resources of such countries and areas in conjunction with assistance provided under this Act so as to encourage the development of indigenous institutions that meet their particular requirements for sustained economic and social progress; and
>
> (3) support civic education and training in skills required for effective participation in governmental and political processes essential to self-government.
>
> (*c*) In the allocation of funds for research under this chapter, emphasis shall be given to research designed to examine the political, social, and related obstacles to development in countries receiving assistance under Part I of this Act. In particular, emphasis should be given to research designed to increase understanding of the ways in which development assistance can support democratic social and political trends in recipient countries.
>
> (*d*) Emphasis shall also be given to the evaluation of relevant past and current programs under Part I of this Act and to applying this experience so as to strengthen their effectiveness in implementing the objectives of this title.

54. *Ibid.*, chap. 2, Sec. 207(a).
55. *Ibid.*, chap. 2, Sec. 208(c).

(*e*) In order to carry out the purposes of this title, the agency primarily responsible for administering Part I of this Act shall develop systematic programs of inservice training to familiarize its personnel with the objectives of this title and to increase their knowledge of the political and social aspects of development. In addition to other funds available for such purposes, not to exceed 1 per centum of the funds authorized to be appropriated for grant assistance under this chapter may be used for carrying out the objectives of this subsection.

The elaboration of paragraphs (*b*), (*c*) (except the last sentence), and (*d*) was added in 1967 and was due mainly to the initiative of Representative John Culver of Iowa. The last sentence of paragraph (*c*) and (*e*) were added in 1968 on the initiative of Congressman Fraser. The brief one-sentence principle in the original 1966 Title IX remains intact in the 1967 version but is fortified by the new provisions, the first of which recognizes the contextual relativity of the problem of assessing and implementing popular participation. Yet while the act acknowledges the "differing needs, desires, and capacities of the people"[56] of developing states, the House committee does not construe this as an excuse for not implementing Title IX; on the contrary, it enjoins AID to find new and imaginative ways of involving the people in development.[57] The new provisions also seek to link the intellectual resources of the recipient countries with foreign assistance so as to encourage evolution of indigenous institutions.[58] This rather vague provision is defined further by the House committee as the channeling of the "vast creative energies of the people" in the development of "an infrastructure of self-sustaining, viable institutions on the local, provincial, and national levels."[59] Specific reference is made to "public and private entities, including credit unions, cooperatives, labor unions and other voluntary associations." The third provision calls for support of civic education and training in skills required for effective self-government. This paragraph was supplied to Congressman Culver by Congressman Fraser. The House committee suggests

56. *Ibid.*, chap. 2, Sec. 281.
57. *House Report No. 551*, p. 29.
58. Foreign Assistance Act of 1967, Title IX, Sec. 281(b)(2).
59. *House Report No. 551*, p. 30.

that in this area the role of AID should be supportive and that the initiative should come primarily from the recipient countries. These three new provisions are buttressed by two subsections directing that research be undertaken to examine "political, social, and related obstacles to development" and to evaluate AID programs both past and present to determine what is effective in promoting "democratic development."

Title IX as well as the JCRD and rule of law formularies mark a crystallization if not a shift in United States foreign assistance policy. A "larger measure of popular participation in government"[60] through the medium of explicitly listed social and political institutions is now a criterion for determining the allocation of foreign assistance. We now have a statutory compilation of heretofore loosely defined, disconnected, and unarticulated assumptions, policies, and practices which have undergirded much foreign assistance activity. Though this may not be a new departure, the formulation signals what can become, although with considerable difficulty, a new era in induced political change. Only the future will reveal if international politics and national sensitivities will prevent the emergence of anything more than a passing nod to the new Title IX. One approach can be that of building into existing programs participatory structures, e.g., citizen advisory councils. A more ambitious and far more difficult approach would be the design of a comprehensive strategy for total political development. The latter hardly appears feasible now and its prospects appear to this writer to be diminishing. The former can probably be implemented. Nevertheless, the principal value of Title IX appears to be as a powerful generator of political development thought rather than as a means of actually implementing a political development strategy.

Academic research and foreign assistance operations

The idiom. Under conditions of the best possible rapport between academic theorizing and AID field experience, the gradual codification of such doctrine might be the new gristmill into which the now elusive, unsystematized speculations and experi-

60. *House Report No. 1651*, p. 27.

ences relating to political development might be fed.[61] The consequence might be, in a decade or so, the articulation of strategies of administrative reform to those of political growth, and of experience in transnationally induced change to academic theory construction. The statutory prescriptions for political development blend leverage of participative entities with the strengthening of political institutions. The most delicate of these participative entities—political parties—are not specifically mentioned in that policy. This blend may serve as a paradigm for the evolution of doctrine tested by practice. This possibility appears at a time of increasing awareness that unplanned sequential timing of participation and institutional viability, while perhaps irreversible, suggests the need for rapid strengthening of institutions.

The absence of a codified doctrine to which we can turn for immediate instrumental use may appear strange in view of extensive American experience in the Philippines, Cuba, and Puerto Rico and subsequently in the civil affairs administration of Korea and the military occupation of Japan, Okinawa, and Germany. These experiences were largely pragmatically evolved, although substantial intellectual effort was made to relate them to the classic doctrines of constitutional evolution.[62] The linkages between these separate national experiences with explanatory potential have been almost totally lacking,[63] and there is virtually complete discontinuity between those early insulated episodes and post-1947 analysis of political development phenomena. The rise of new states following the Second World War has been accomplished almost completely without (except for a constitution) a scheme of priorities, with little consideration of the interaction of economic and political development, and with little careful, rational articulation of externally induced and internally felt needs. There has been no design, no codification of past

61. For a general analysis of the phenomenon of disconnected research activities (not, however, specifically directed to political development problems) see Gordon Tullock, *The Organization of Inquiry* (Durham, N.C., 1966).

62. The outstanding of these efforts was Carl J. Friedrich and Associates, *American Military Government Experience in World War II* (New York, 1948).

63. Two exceptions are Montgomery's *Forced to be Free,* which compares denazification in Germany with the political purge in Japan, and Friedrich's *American Military Government Experience in World War II,* which includes chapters on Okinawa, Korea, and Japan as well as Germany. These are cited above in notes 14 and 62 respectively.

experience which might have served as a guide. There have been five-year plans, often including useful analyses of administrative needs and local government institutions. But, significantly, such plans have not included equally elaborate schemes for long-range political development articulated to the economic sequences of the plans. There has been some attention also to the mechanism of elections,[64] the most recent concern being the "freedom" of the 1967 election in South Vietnam. But these are particularistic, segmental interests focusing on only limited aspects of the political process. Theorizing on development in political science, little of which has yet attained international utility, emerged more than a decade after the establishment of the new states. Its usefulness in 1968 can be suggested by the imaginary creation of a new state patterning its development after the advice extracted from American political development writing. Recent efforts to search in the development of European states for patterns of significance to new states,[65] while highly important in the evolution of a theory of development, have minimal immediate utility because of differences in concentration of crises, in time-span, in internal cultural setting, and in pressures endemic in the maelstrom of international politics.

In the absence of a doctrine of political reform, the gradually revealed intelligence activities of the United States seemed to suggest reliance on manipulation of internal political forces as a means of moving political systems in particular directions.[66] At best this is a crude and naive shifting of power from often

64. An example of this concern can be found in Theodore Paul Wright, *American Support of Free Elections Abroad* (Washington, 1964).

65. See, for example, C. E. Black, *The Dynamics of Modernization: A Study in Comparative History* (New York, 1966); J. H. Plumb, *The Origins of Political Stability—England 1675–1725* (New York, 1967); Seymour M. Lipset, *The First New Nation: The United States in Historical and Comparative Perspective* (New York, 1963); and Samuel P. Huntington, "Political Modernization: America vs. Europe," *World Politics*, XVIII (1966), 378–415, and "The Political Modernization of Traditional Monarchies," *Daedalus*, XCV (1966), 763–788.

66. For an indication of the magnitude of these operations see United States House of Representatives, Committee on Foreign Affairs, Subcommittee on International Organization and Movements, *Behavioral Sciences and the National Security*, Report No. 4, together with Part IX of the *Hearings on Winning the Cold War: The U.S. Ideological Offensive*, 89th Congress, 1st Session, *House Report No. 1224* (Washington, December 6, 1965). See also Irving Louis Horowitz, *The Rise and Fall of Project Camelot* (Cambridge, Mass., 1965), and Robert A. Nisbet, "Project Camelot: An Autopsy," *Public Interest*, No. 5 (Fall, 1966), pp. 45–70.

evanescent coalitions which appear to be either "more democratic" or more friendly to American interests. The vacuum created by the absence of a positive doctrine of political development may have been filled by covert manipulation of participative mechanisms as a means of directing political change. It would perhaps be too extreme to suggest that covert manipulation was the direct consequence of the absence of an official, publicly revealed doctrine of political development. It is more likely that what appears to be the diminution, perhaps even abandonment, of covert manipulation as a consequence of the Bay of Pigs, Vietnam, and Camelot revelations and the emergence of the rudiments of political development doctrine is a fortuitous congruence.

The new awareness of the need for systematizing political development in foreign assistance conjoins in point of time with an inclination in some new states to solicit help in constructing more capable political institutions, despite simultaneous distrust of American designs. To a very limited degree the air has been cleared by Camelot and by percolation into foreign assistance activities of a new commitment to bilateral relations characterized by collegiality, parity of esteem, and equality of responsibility. American foreign operations practice is now harvesting the yield from sustained training efforts of nearly two decades based on the professional counterpart arrangement. In consequence, trained professional staff are more available in strategic places and a tutorial is giving way to a consultative relationship. On the other hand, these trends are countered and perhaps overpowered by increased sensitivity to foreign "intervention" in domestic affairs, and by a self-assertiveness not at all conducive to the reception of engineering of political systems. This attitude is especially significant in Pakistan, where it has been dramatically canonized by President Ayub Khan's autobiography, the theme of which is that "people in developing countries seek assistance, but on the basis of mutual respect: they want to have friends not masters."[67] Granted, in Pakistan there are special circumstances

67. Mohammad Ayub Khan, *Friends Not Masters: A Political Autobiography* (Karachi, 1966), title page. For an example of the mood of rather exaggerated independence, see the editorial in the *Pakistan Times,* August 23, 1967, p. 6, which asserts that Pakistan "is no longer faced with a crippling shortage of trained

conditioning this sense of independence, namely, disenchantment with the United States because of its military aid to India and the consequent desire to broaden its base of support. Nevertheless, there are more universal factors which operate in other countries to increase the resentment toward too penetrating an American involvement. Foremost among these is the increased technical competence which creates overconfidence and which acts as a barrier to advice which becomes regarded as "interference." The restructuring of world power because of the emergence of China and France as units detached from the Soviet Union and the United States and new opportunities for assistance from new regional (such as the Regional Cooperative Development scheme and the Asian Development Bank) and new multi- and unilateral sources have encouraged postures of independence and often xenophobia. Animosities created by such conflicts as the Israeli-Egyptian war of 1967 and the conflict between Turkey and Greece over Cyprus also condition attitudes toward the United States.

It is difficult, if not impossible, to assess these conflicting trends in the "Third World" of the developing nations; certainly any meaningful analysis would have to be made separately for each country. On the one hand, the awareness that institutions need strengthening and the increased technical efficiency of the infrastructure would appear to enhance the possibility of evolving a pattern for political development. On the other, these advantages seem to be neutralized by the diminishing prestige and hence effectiveness of the United States. This is coupled, on the part of the "Third World," with renewed insistence that development must be indigenized or ecologically adapted. It may be that the concept of political participation implicit in Title IX may be incongruent with new national sentiments in the "Third World" and that the idea which seemed attractive when conceived in 1965 from impressions of the early sixties will be even more incongruent with reality in 1968 when presumably it must be implemented. A final reason for a less than optimistic view is the growing disenchantment with foreign aid at the very time when

manpower" and that the 6,500 trained Pakistani serving abroad "should be happy to return if offered attractive assignments."

the coherence of economic doctrine and the organization of AID are better than ever before.[68] This "American retreat from foreign aid" resulting in reduced appropriations, combined with the mandate to use loans rather than grants and to use multilateral entities, may shrink the scope of political operations, thus reducing the probability of effectively implementing Title IX.

The institutional linkage. The potential for more productive interplay of academic theorizing and official government operations in foreign assistance is enhanced by Title IX. An obvious benefit is the statutory mandate for research in the realm of political development. Since there is no retrievable institutional experience in this activity, reliance must be placed on theory and speculation, and thus far this has been done almost exclusively in academic political science. An important statutory provision making possible a stronger link between relevant academic research and official experience is the allocation of funds to research and educational institutions in the United States to strengthen their capacity to carry out programs related to developing countries.[69] Included for the first time in the 1966 act with a recommended allocation of ten million dollars, the amount was raised to twenty million in the 1967 proposal[70] but reduced to five million in the appropriation. One link between academic research and AID is the research advisory committee within AID but composed of both AID officials and academic scholars. That committee was consulted on Title IX implementation soon after the amendment appeared. Another potentially effective link between the academic community and the Agency for International Development is the Southeast Asia Development Advisory Group (SEADAG), established by David E. Bell, administrator of AID in June, 1965.[71] The need for a more productive and more meaningful relationship between foreign assistance operations and academic

68. This point of view is forcefully presented by John D. Montgomery, "The Political Decay of Foreign Aid," *Yale Review*, LVII (1967), 1–15.

69. Foreign Assistance Act of 1967, chap. 2, Sec. 211 (d).

70. For examples of research undertaken under this provision see *House Report No. 551*, p. 14.

71. An official account of the operations of SEADAG can be found in Department of State, unclassified aerogram, "Southeast Asia Development Advisory Group: Its Initiation and First Year," July 26, 1966.

research was a major theme of the Gardner report of 1964[72] and was a concern of Bell as administrator of AID in 1965. Bell deplored the absence of effective research and evaluation programs in AID and suggested that "the whole process of foreign aid might be seen as a research process."[73] One institutional response to this clearly felt need was the creation of SEADAG, a multidisciplinary group of about 150 social scientists and development program executives from some thirty-four universities, fifteen private foundations and research institutions, and several government agencies, principally AID. Members of SEADAG are appointed as individuals whose interest and research are deemed relevant to AID operations. There is no formal representation based on institutional affiliation or academic discipline. The organization is loosely structured. There is no stated term of service; it is assumed that membership may not necessarily be fixed and that there will be movement in and out of the group reflecting changing research interests of the academic community. This flexibility has many advantages over a more rigid organization especially since development as a field of interest is highly dynamic and rapidly changing. Political science is more heavily represented in SEADAG than other disciplines, as is indicated by membership distribution by academic discipline:[74]

Agricultural economics	10
Anthropology	16
Development administration	18
Economics	22
Education	15
Geography	11
History, international relations, and area studies	19
Law	6
Natural sciences	6
Political science	39
Sociology	9
Urban-regional planning	12
Total (including about 30 double entries)	183

72. John W. Gardner, *AID and the Universities* (New York, 1964).
73. David Bell, "The Quality of Aid," *Foreign Affairs,* XLIV (1966), 601–608, at 606.
74. The source of these data is Asia Society, *SEADAG—Directory 1966–67* (New York, April 1, 1967).

The membership analysis given above is suggestive only of gross composition. There are several multiple entries in the tabulation (the total actual membership is about 150 rather than 183), and since most of those tabulated more than once are political scientists who are listed also in such groups as development administration and urban-regional planning, the actual proportion of political scientists is greater than the tabulation above suggests. SEADAG is administered for AID under contract by the Asia Society. Its chairman is the president of the Asia Society, the former United States ambassador to Thailand, Kenneth T. Young.[75] SEADAG is divided into seminars, each under the chairmanship of an academic member. SEADAG meets in plenary session twice a year and the seminars meet from three to five times a year.[76] The seminars are development administration, education and manpower, Indonesia, Mekong development, political development, regional development, rural development, urban development, and Vietnam: the problems of development under conditions of insurgency. SEADAG has three functions: advisory discussion, identification and promotion of research, and serving as a clearinghouse for information relating to development. An important principle governing SEADAG's operation as well as all of AID's research activities is that of collaboration with nationals of countries receiving United States foreign assistance. AID research projects must have the support of responsible institutions and individuals in the recipient country, even though the projects may be directed by American scholars. SEADAG similarly reflects the principle of collaboration of American and other scholars on the basis of parity of esteem and responsibility. For example, the SEADAG seminar on development administration held at Carmel, California, in November, 1967, included one Indian and four Pakistani scholars. In the case of the development administration seminar, an additional co-ordinative link is provided by drawing membership from the Asia Committee and from the executive committee of the Comparative Administration

75. See above, p. 17.
76. For an official description of SEADAG functions by William S. Gaud, AID administrator, see *Rural Development in Asia,* Part I, p. 202. Cf. *ibid.,* pp. 126–128, 148–149.

Group (CAG) of the American Society for Public Administration.[77] Although, as Administrator Gaud testified, SEADAG "is no longer an experiment,"[78] it is certainly too early to evaluate its effectiveness. Thus far the SEADAG structure is too loosely put together to permit much discussion or research of direct, operational significance. On the government side, the shifting demands of Congress, rapid turnover of leadership and crucial subordinate personnel in AID both in Washington and in the field, the short institutional memory of AID, and the absence of a permanent institution linking academic research with operations are weaknesses difficult to surmount.[79] On the academic side a serious obstacle is the escalation of theorizing divorced from government operations in the field. It is generally not noted that what little academic theorizing is based on field work is more often than not based on field *observation* of political development divorced from contact with official foreign operations. There is often an antipathy, if not disdain, on the part of the American researcher at least, for the official operation in the country whose development is being studied. Yet the dependence of the political scientist on AID missions abroad is likely to increase rather than diminish. This condition will be the consequence of the congruence of two events: the possible expansion of AID activity into the realm of political development through Title IX and the steadily shrinking corpus of research data available to the private researcher in many developing states. This latter condition is the consequence of either suspicion, deterioration in diplomatic rela-

77. For a survey of the important work of the Comparative Administration Group, see Milton J. Esman, "The CAG and the Study of Public Administration," in Fred W. Riggs (ed.), *Frontiers of Development Administration* (Durham, N.C., forthcoming). Several contributors to the present volume, namely, Riggs, John D. Montgomery, Warren Ilchman, and Ralph Braibanti, are active in both CAG and SEADAG. Riggs is chairman of CAG; Montgomery and Braibanti are chairman and vice-chairman, respectively, of the Asia Committee of CAG and the administrative development seminar of SEADAG.

78. *Rural Development in Asia,* Part 1, p. 202.

79. These weaknesses which have characterized United States foreign aid operations almost from the beginning flow primarily from the "temporary," improvising quality of planning and fiscal support for what in reality has become a permanent aspect of American foreign affairs. These weaknesses are felt not only in public administration and political development affairs but in other aspects of AID's operations as well. See, for example, a similar catalogue of deficiences in educational assistance in Philip H. Coombs and Karl W. Bigelow, *Education and Foreign Aid* (Cambridge, Mass., 1965), esp. pp. 27–40.

tions with the United States, or sheer inability to meet the increasing demands of the American research appetite, which appears to be unreasonable, imprudent, and insatiable.

Relevance of other national experiences. A different approach to academic-government relations in foreign assistance has emerged in the United Kingdom. There a justifiable preoccupation with immediate problems of transfer of power delayed the systematic conversion of long experience in imperial administration into a doctrine and practice of induced development within the context of a relationship between a former imperial power and newly sovereign states. Establishment of the Ministry of Overseas Development in 1965, a counterpart of the Agency for International Development, now consolidates British foreign aid into a separate, specialized entity.[80] The linking of academic research and government operations has been accomplished in a much more formal institutional manner than the SEADAG-AID arrangement in the United States. This has been done by the creation in 1966 of the Institute of Development Studies located at the University of Sussex. The institute is an incorporated, limited company whose six subscribers are from the Ministry of Overseas Development, the University of Sussex, other agencies of British government, and the Commonwealth Secretariat.[81] The institute organizes courses of study for the training of senior

80. The relevant statutes under which the ministry operates are Overseas Development and Service Act 1965 (1965 chap. 38) and Overseas Aid Act 1966 (1966 chap. 21). See also *Overseas Development: The Work of the New Ministry* (Cmnd. 2736, August, 1965) and the subsequent white paper, *Overseas Development: The Work in Hand* (Cmnd. 3180, 1967). For a review of British activity in foreign assistance before the consolidation of effort in the Ministry of Overseas Development, see the white papers, *Assistance from the United Kingdom for Overseas Development* (Cmnd. 974, 1960); *Technical Assistance from the United Kingdom for Overseas Development* (Cmnd. 1308, 1961); *Technical Co-operation: A Progress Report by the New Department* (Cmnd. 1698, 1962); and *Aid to Developing Countries* (Cmnd. 2147, 1963).

81. *Memorandum and Articles of Association of the Institute of Development Studies* No. 877338 under the Companies Act, 1948 (incorporated April 20, 1966, London). While the Institute of Development Studies is concerned with the whole spectrum of overseas development, it has had a particular interest in administrative training. Organization of the institute was first suggested in 1962 in the (Bridges) *Report of Departmental Committee on Training in Public Administration for Overseas Countries* (London, 1963). See also the related white paper, *Policy on the Recommendations of the* [*Bridges*] *Committee* (Cmnd. 2099, 1963).

administrators from overseas countries, British graduates who want to specialize in overseas development, and British government officials concerned with problems of development. The concentration of training and research in one center is characteristic of the British pattern not found in the United States where AID contracts for such training are made with a wide variety of institutions in the United States. A constructive relationship between government and academic research is expected to result from the physical location of the institute at the University of Sussex where there is considerable innovation in curriculum and university organization. This relationship is already manifested by certain joint appointments to the university faculty and the institute, by sharing of library facilities, and by participation of both advanced degree students and senior government officials in seminars.

While these developments in attitude and institutional links between theory and operations in both the United States and the United Kingdom appear to be significant, our projection for a paradigm in which theory can enrich the practice of political development may be too sanguine. It is possible to develop an effective reciprocity between AID operations and academic research (and such a link has already been forged in SEADAG), but meaningful exchange of ideas is much more difficult and has not yet been achieved.

Some degree of liaison between developments in the United Kingdom and those in the United States is likely to be mutually advantageous. The beginning of such liaison was the participation of B. B. Schaffer of the Institute of Development Studies at the Carmel meeting of the development administration seminar of SEADAG in November, 1967. A second connecting link was a conference at Sussex in June, 1968, on the politics of development at which British thought on development was presented. There were two American participants at this predominantly British affair sponsored by the University of Sussex. One advantage of such collaboration is that the barometric variations in acceptability of American official and private research and foreign assistance are likely to be evened out by different patterns of British and American influence in different groups of states. The consequence could be the conjoining of the richness of British imperial experience and the pragmatism of Britain's current overseas operations linked historically to the past with the massiveness of the American operation and its limited historical imperial links. Further, the extremely empirical and systemic bias of American political science scholarship might be tempered by the more historical, law-oriented, and pragmatic disposition of British scholarship. To this must ultimately be added Soviet practice and French theory and practice with respect to foreign assistance and political development in former French colonies.[82] But this must necessarily come later; the stage is now set by Title IX for analysis of American practice, and this is an auspicious beginning.

II. Characteristics of Political Development Especially Relevant to Administrative Development

It is pertinent to the subsequent argument of this chapter to set forth certain attributes of political development, not necessarily identical, however, to those which have been singled out by other students of development. Such is the primitive nature of the study of development that identical concepts are often expressed in different terminology and different attributes are given varying emphases. Summarizing and analyzing the works of some thirty writers—and reaching back to such students as Woodrow Wilson, John W. Burgess, and Max Weber—Packenham conveniently identifies five conditions commonly stressed: a constitution, an

82. For an example of the potential insights which such comparative research on foreign assistance and political development research can yield, see Robert B. Charlick, "U.S. and French Foreign Aid Rationales," in John D. Montgomery and Arthur Smithies (eds.), *Public Policy,* XIV (1965), 116–140. On French foreign assistance, see *French Aid: The Jeanneney Report, an abridged translation of La Politique de Cooperation avec les Pays en Voie de Developpement* (London, 1964), and Teresa Hayter, *French Aid* (London, 1966). Both of these are publications of the Overseas Development Institute, an important private research organization in London. See also Elizabeth Kridl Valkenier, "Recent Trends on Soviet Research on the Developing Countries," *World Politics,* XX (1968), 644–660.

economic base, administrative capacity, a social system, and a political culture.[83] Huntington has succinctly analyzed varying lists of criteria as used by Ward and Rustow, Emerson, Pye, and Eisenstadt.[84] He identifies four sets of categories which recur continuously: rationalization, national integration, democratization, participation. Noting that the last-mentioned characteristic is given greatest emphasis,[85] he deplores the failure of most definitions to emphasize or even to mention political institutions essential for converting demands produced by accelerated participation. Reviewing the first three volumes of the Social Science Research Council's Committee on Comparative Politics series, Lasswell folds them into the context of his own six-part model: self-sustaining power accumulation, power-sharing, national independence, a responsible role in world politics, an internal decision-making process conducing to wider participation in all values, and timing of elements in the sequence of development.[86] Friedrich rather cautiously projects a "model political order for an emergent world." He deems this to be merely a minimal statement of a "good political order"—good for the present, but not necessarily the best for all times and places. He suggests six features.[87] The first is the capacity to act effectively to cope with technological requirements of survival. Second, enforcible restraints on government. Third, operative popular participation in rule-making. Fourth, existence of general rules reflecting shared values and beliefs of the community. Fifth, a judiciary to interpret these rules and define terms of settlement. Sixth, voluntary associations, such as parties, which provide alternatives to exist-

83. Robert A. Packenham, "Approaches to the Study of Political Development," *World Politics*, XVII (1965), 108–121.

84. Huntington, "Political Development and Political Decay," 386–430.

85. See also Friedrich's observation on this point in his chapter in this volume, p. 114.

86. Harold D. Lasswell, "The Policy Sciences of Development," *World Politics*, XVII (1965), 286–310.

87. Carl J. Friedrich, *Man and His Government: An Empirical Theory of Politics* (New York, 1963), pp. 657–675. See also his "Power, Authority and Legitimacy: Political Theory and the Problems of Developing Countries," in Brookings Institution, *Political Theory and the Problems of Developing Countries* (Washington, 1968). In the Brookings paper, Friedrich includes a seventh feature, namely, "decentralization to the greatest possible extent compatible with effective government." In *Man and His Government* (p. 666) he had mentioned this as being presupposed by popular participation but had not listed it separately.

ing government, implement participation, and continually re-examine existing rules.

The universe of empirical referents is too vast and too disordered to allow for any rigorously constructed meaningful relationship between experience and definitions of development. Probably the best to be expected is the combining of intuitive theoretical insights in proportions varying with the definer with empirical analysis of some new political systems and with some historical perspective or older (e.g., European) systems. In such conditions there are as many sets of criteria as there are definers, each set suiting some immediate expository purpose. Certain attributes, four in number, which seem to have an important relevance to administrative reform are selected and discussed in the following pages.

For the moment in informal terms (coming later to a classification of more technical characteristics) it might be said that political development is in quintessence the ordering of the affairs of men into a polity more or less commonly agreed upon, clearly known, capable of rational adjustment, the whole being infused with qualities of freedom ennobling the puny lives of those who have formed the state. In terms of the Platonic Socrates and of Aristotle, "political society exists for the sake of noble actions, and not of mere companionship." Political development can be viewed as a series of ultimate progressions (with periodic regressions and even oscillations) from ascription to personal achievement, from ambiguity to certainty in the use of public power, from alienation and withdrawal to enlightened participation in collective social life, from coarseness and coercion to refinement and sensitivity in public action, from contraction to expansion of free choice. In the encyclical of Paul VI, *Populorum Progressio* of March, 1967, it was put with simple elegance that the basic aspiration of man is "to do more, know more and have more in order to be more,"[88] and that it is this aspiration which the state

88. *Encyclical Letter of His Holiness, Paul VI, Pope. On the Development of Peoples Populorum Progressio,* March 26, 1967 (official translation into English distributed by the United States Catholic Conference, Washington, D.C.), Part I, par. 6, p. 9. There is some controversy over the accuracy of the meaning conveyed in various translations of this encyclical. See New York *Times,* March 29, 1967, p.

through its political system must seek to fulfil. The last words of this portion of the encyclical, *ut ideo pluris valeant,* allude to the quality of physical and spiritual life to be attained by individual man—a dimension overlooked in virtually all political development literature, except Friedrich's chapter in this volume and the analyses by Pennock,[89] Steere, Sibley, and Goulet,[90] and Lasswell in this volume and elsewhere. Lasswell has been consistently and explicitly concerned with the capabilities of institutions and processes of decision for projecting societal values. "The social process can be characterized as *man* striving to optimize *values* (preferred outcomes) through *institutions* using *resources.*"[91] He clarifies the apparent ambivalence of the content of *values* regarded as preferred outcomes by other extensive analysis. The eight values to which he repeatedly returns in a variety of contexts are

---

1, and *National Observer,* April 3, 1967, p. 5. Apparently, there can be little argument that the English version has correctly transferred the meaning of this particular section. In the official Latin version issued by the Vatican, this expression appears as "hoc est, ut magis operentur, discant, possideant, ut ideo pluris valeant" (*Sanctissimi Domini Nostri Pauli Divina Providentia Papae VI, Litterae Encyclicae . . . De Populorum Progressione Promovenda* [Typis Polyglottis Vaticanis, 1967], Part I, par. 6, p. 7). In the official Italian version, the expression appears as "in una parola, fare, conoscere, e avere di piu, per esser di piu:" (*Populorum progressio, Lettera Enciclica di S. S. Paolo VI sulla sviluppo dei popoli* published in a special issue of *Quaderni di Ekklesia,* I [1967], 127–172, at 131). *Populorum Progressio* has been quoted with admiration and indorsed by other religious groups including Reform Judaism, the National Council of Churches, and the Church of the Brethren. See statements of these groups in United States Senate, Committee on Foreign Relations, *Hearings on S1872 . . . Foreign Assistance Act of 1967,* pp. 109–115, and House of Representatives, Committee on Foreign Affairs, *Hearings . . . on H. R. 7099 and H. R. 12048 . . . Foreign Assistance Act of 1967,* Part IV, p. 893.

89. "Political Development, Political Systems and Political Goods."

90. Douglas V. Steere, "Development: For What?" in John H. Hallowell (ed.), *Development: For What?* (Durham, N.C., 1964), pp. 213–235. Steere suggests that the effect of the process of foreign assistance in reciprocal, that is, it may not only enhance the human dignity of recipients but may also deepen a sense of worth and responsibility in those who are agents of the aid-giving country (pp. 222–224). See also Mulford Q. Sibley, "Development for What? Civilization Technology and Democracy," in Charles Press and Alan Arian (eds.), *Empathy and Ideology: Aspects of Administrative Innovation* (Chicago, 1966), pp. 226–253, and Denis A. Goulet, "Development for What?" *Comparative Political Studies,* I (1968), 295–312.

91. Harold D. Lasswell, "Conflict and Leadership: The Process of Decision and the Nature of Authority," in A. V. S. de Reuck and Julie Knight (eds.), *Ciba Foundation Symposium on Conflict in Society* (London, 1966), p. 211. For an exploration of the antecedents of Lasswell's philosophical assumptions, see Heinz Eulau, "The Maddening Methods of Harold D. Lasswell: Some Philosophical Underpinnings," *Journal of Politics,* XXX (1968), 3–24. Eulau relates the premises of Lasswell to the philosophy of A. N. Whitehead.

power (P), enlightenment (E), wealth (W), well-being (B), skill (S), affection (A), respect (R), and rectitude (D). For the sake of expository convenience, he has devised the acroynm PEWBSARD to stand for these values. He has examined the outcomes of these values in terms of leadership,[92] legal institutions,[93] conflict resolution,[94] the transnational world order,[95] and the development of new political systems.[96] In his chapter in this volume he suggests a provisional method for evaluating institutions in terms of these eight values.

It is probable that this qualitative and spiritual objective is implicit in all economic and political development analyses and that it has been detheologized by being couched in secular terms suggestive of material improvement and psychological well-being from which ennoblement is assumed to flow inevitably. Perhaps to a certain extent this is true. But it appears equally true that much economic and political development analysis, by failing to make explicit the purpose (*ut ideo pluris valeant*) fails also to place in proper perspective the many features of political order which are assumed to conduce to this end. Thus, too much emphasis may be placed on bureaucracy, or parties, or participation as ends in themselves. In reality they are means which human experience prompts us to believe under certain conditions lead to these ends. But these conditions and human dispositions vary in time and place. The precise nature of these features, their preferential order, and the intensity of their development lead us to a position of flexibility and relativity regarding their utility. In sum, an explicitness with respect to the condition of man as the aim of development may force upon us a deeper sense of contextuality in approaching the myriad prescriptions which accost us.

92. *Ibid.*, pp. 210–228.

93. Harold D. Lasswell, "Toward Continuing Appraisal of the Impact of Law on Society," *Rutgers Law Review*, XXI (1967), 645–677, esp. 650–653.

94. Harold D. Lasswell and Richard Arens, "The Role of Sanction in Conflict Resolution," *Journal of Conflict Resolution*, XI (1967), 27–39, esp. 29.

95. Myres S. McDougal, Harold D. Lasswell, and W. Michael Reisman, "The World Constitutive Process of Authoritative Decision," *Journal of Legal Education*, XIX (1967), 253–300, 403–437.

96. Harold D. Lasswell, "The Policy Sciences of Development." See also Lasswell's "The Uses of Content Analysis Data in Studying Social Change," *Social Science Information*, VII (1968), 57–70.

Architectonics

The first attribute of political development here selected is the requirement of common agreement on a fundamental polity of the state—an overarching purpose which gives form, cohesion, and direction to all public action within a sensed community. Older and once eminently useful terms which have been and continue to be used to express roughly the whole or parts of the same attribute are advisedly rejected. In several drafts of this chapter and in earlier published formulations the term "polity" was used with its meaning changed and narrowed from its original Aristotelian usage. But this appears now to be somewhat of an impertinence as well as perplexing, since "polity," so ancient a term and with little change in connotation, fulfils an important expository and conceptual need, and is comfortably seated in the literature. "Constitutionalism" appears inadequate because it is merely a first step and is now a relatively easy accomplishment in the attainment of political order. "National integration" connotes the submersion, deflection, conversion, or elimination of differential ethnicities within a given system, and, as we shall argue shortly, this is precisely what is not occurring in new systems. "Community" again suggests too much emphasis on common sharing of values and in this respect is related too closely to utopian, monastic, and other ideologically motivated communal organizations. "Legitimacy" focuses excessively on the capacity of the state to maintain its identity. This capacity is the first and elementary requirement of a political order and must be subsumed in any catalogue of attributes of political development. The useful term "political order," the continued use of which in contemporary political thought has characterized the influential work of Friedrich,[97] also seemed attractive especially because of its freedom from connotative encumberment and its plenitudinous embrace. The latter characteristic reduces its utility for our immediate purpose; political order, like polity, really includes the four attributes here being discussed rather than only the first.

97. The final chapter of his *Man and His Government* is entitled "A Model Political Order and the Emergent World."

It is with some hesitation and not with complete satisfaction that use is made of a venerable term, "architectonics," to designate this aspect of development.[98] Architectonics embraces values held dear in a society which penetrate the social fabric and generate positive action. It is a "consensus of sentiment." Ortega has dealt with this admirably in his analysis of Cicero's *Concordia et Libertas.*[99] Strata of discord are necessary, but they cannot reach the deeper layers of "concord," the "dogmas about life and the universe, moral norms, legal principles, rules regulating the very form of the struggle." "Concord," Ortega continues, "in its pure and radical form implies a firm and common belief regarding the exercise of supreme [political] power." The term "architectonics" approximates the definition of ideology set forth by LaPalombara which he asserts to be suggested by Garstin. LaPalombara regards ideology as involving "a philosophy of history, a view of man's present place in it, some estimate of probable lines of future development, and a set of prescriptions regarding how to hasten, retard, and/or modify that developmental direction . . . a set of values that are more or less coherent . . . [and the linking of] given patterns of action to the achievement or maintenance of a future, or existing, state of affairs."[100] We have not used the term "ideology" here because of its pejorative connotation and because it does not adequately direct attention to the rather special condition of values in a developing state as against a mature political system. That condition is the highly dynamic transformation of values as they settle in an amalgam in which tradition is reconstructed in terms of new ideas and structures. It is the search for roots, the identification of strands of indigenous thought which may have the capacity to sustain new technology,

98. In so doing we take shelter in (and courage from) the comment of Lasswell and Kaplan on uniformity and harmony of vocabulary: "Such expectations are of course, doomed to disappointment: uniformity of usage cannot be brought about by either fiat or exhortation. Nor is this uniformity of any transcending importance. What does matter is self-consistency, and clarity sufficient to make translation and empirical reference always possible. Our concern, moreover, is not with words but with concepts" (Harold D. Lasswell and Abraham Kaplan, *Power and Society* [New York, 1960], pp. x, xi).

99. José Ortega y Gasset, *Concord and Liberty* (New York, 1946), pp. 15–21. The Norton Library edition of 1963 is used here.

100. Joseph LaPalombara, "Decline of Ideology: A Dissent and an Interpretation," *American Political Science Review,* LX (1966), 5–18, at 7.

which is distinctive. The use of history for analytical effect is important in the process,[101] but it carries with it risks in interpretation.[102] Typically the constitution is the legitimating source of architectonics. Its very existence, the deference it commands, and its capacity to suffuse its norms through the whole system are a means of binding the state together. Its symbolic value can scarcely be overestimated; the more sacral its position the more effective its symbolism. But there may be some values which are not expressed in the constitution. There may be a kind of ethos (spirit, overtones, feeling) which has powerful force in holding the political system together yet is outside the legal writ of a constitution. Thus in such countries as Pakistan, Israel, or Turkey where there has been a profoundly emotional common experience based on religion and on real or imagined discrimination certain reactions internally and to religious affairs throughout the world can be expected. Historic animosities which bind the state together—for example, the enmity of India in Pakistan and of Israel in Egypt—are also part of the national spirit which generate particular policy or action.[103] What is here suggested is that the constitution, even when it includes (as in India and Pakistan) segments of architectonics such as the non-justiciable but ideologically significant directive principles of state policy, is but one of several sources of values held dear. In Pakistan, for example, so important an ideological component as basic democracies is not included in the constitution, although in India the analogous village panchayats are included as Article 40 of the directive principles of state policy. It would appear that the presence of values outside the formal constitution is especially important

101. This point has been developed in John D. Montgomery, "Pride and Progress: A Dilemma of Nation-Building," in Elliott (ed.) *Education and Training in the Developing Countries.* Here he discusses the dual deficiencies of legitimate nationalism, which he deems to be ignorance of national culture and interdependence of human culture (p. 191). See also his "Public Interest and Ideologies of National Development," in C. J. Friedrich (ed.), *Public Interest,* Vol. V in the Nomos series (New York, 1962), pp. 218–236, and "The Challenge of Change," *International Development Review,* IX (1967), 2–9.

102. On the role of history in this process of transformation, see Ralph Braibanti, "The Role of Political Science in the Study of Underdeveloped Areas," in Braibanti and J. J. Spengler (eds.), *Tradition, Values and Socio-Economic Development* (Durham, N.C., 1961), pp. 148–149.

103. For a general treatment of this phenomenon, see David J. Finlay, Ole R. Holsti, and Richard R. Fagen. *Enemies in Politics* (Chicago, 1967).

when the social order is torn into many pieces by linguistic and cultural cleavages or when the values of the constitution and the ruling elite are divorced—even in language as in the case of Pakistan—from the mainstream of the social order. Obviously this is not a new problem; it is essentially that of adjusting custom and a rationalized legal order. But it is a problem made much more difficult by the possibility that the rationalized legal order may lose its effervescence and may be overwhelmed by the surrounding tissue of custom. Further, the sharpness of the divisions usually gives rise to mediational processes which one way or another establish linkages between the strata.

In the context of administrative reform, Asoka Mehta, India's minister for planning, and long an important intellectual figure in India, alludes to this problem: "The dichotomy," he said, "between the traditional order and rational organization bears a certain relevance [to India]. In the developed countries, modern writing on administration has moved away from this dichotomy. . . . [L]eaders of administration in developing countries must learn to operate at two distinct levels—the levels of sophistication and of somewhat primitive preoccupation." Mehta relates this problem to what we have here called architectonics: "specialization is necessary but it is even more necessary that all specializations are related to each other. The need for an integrated approach demands that all specializations must be subordinated to a larger whole. There has got to be an administrative *gestalt* which inspires each segment of specialization. . . . In the quest for new tools and techniques it is necessary that you balance them by some kind of overriding purpose and understanding."[104]

The problem of linguistic, cultural, and other cleavages is aggravated by new significance of the old problem of polycommunality, a term aptly used by Montgomery in his chapter in this volume. The complexity of this problem confronts us, as it did in the instance of architectonics, with difficulties in terminology. The old terms "racial" and "multiracial," the newer term "communalism," the more restricted term "tribalism," and the expres-

104. Asoka Mehta, "Administrative Leadership," *Indian Journal of Public Administration*, XI (1965), 674–675.

sion currently in vogue, "ethnicity," are not of sufficient explanatory power or precision. Each of these terms embraces only a part of the total problem. Race and ethnicity do not always permit delineation of religious and linguistic differences. "Communalism," a term in use from the middle of the nineteenth century on, became identified with India and referred to the granting of local autonomy to identifiable communities, usually based on religion. Since we need a term to describe this phenomenon in all systems, it is essential to avoid an expression identified principally with India, even though it may be a useful one for that system. Moreover, the term "communalism" used without a prefix does not adequately convey the external or intergroup dimensions of the problem. For these reasons the term "polycommunality" is more suitable. It allows for the varying mixtures and interlacings of ethnic, caste, tribal, religious, and linguistic differences which are found in varying patterns in different systems. It thus has the qualities of range and precision. The prefix "poly-" directs attention to the inter- rather than the intragroup nature of the problem.

We witness in most states, both developing and mature, a resurgence in pride of culture, religion, language, and ethnic origin.[105] The concept of the "melting-pot" or absorption of some communalities into a dominant group no longer has great force. A simple yet rather dramatic manifestation of this in Britain is a rising pride in Cockney accent as a cultural expression of validity equal to that of Oxbridge;[106] comparable developments such as the Black Power movement with its emphasis on African culture and even on African sartorial and tonsorial modes are evident in

105. The complex changes occurring in ethnic awareness in the United States are suggested in Michael Parenti, "Ethnic Politics and the Persistence of Ethnic Identification," *American Political Science Review*, LXI (1967), 717–727. The literature on communal problems in developing states is immense. Especially pertinent dimensions of the problem may be found analyzed in Philip Mason (ed.), *India and Ceylon, Unity and Diversity* (London, 1967); Gerald D. Berreman, "Stratification, Pluralism and Interaction: A Comparative Analysis of Caste," in A. V. S. de Reuck and Julie Knight (eds.), *Caste and Race: Comparative Approaches* (London, 1967), pp. 45–73; Edward Tiryakian, "Sociological Realism: Partition for South Africa?" *Social Forces*, XLVI (1967), 208–221; and Carl J. Friedrich (ed.), *Community*, Vol. II in the Nomos series (New York, 1959).

106. On this point see W. J. M. Mackenzie, *Politics and Social Science* (London, 1967), p. 294.

the United States as well. Such resurgence of pride in ethnicity or social origin can be thought of as one criterion by which the attainment of human dignity is achieved in a given state. Insofar as knowledge of one's own heritage is important in self-understanding, and insofar as every cultural tradition has merit and significance in human development, ethnicity and other components of communality are aspects of self-realization, psychic well-being, and hence human dignity. It is this perspective of the problem which reduces the utility of such expressions as "consensus," "integration," and "community." The contemporary problem is that of reconciling the deliberate encouragement of polycommunality on the one hand with the necessary cohesion of the state by means of suffusion with a fundamental, all-embracing system of values. Thus in Pakistan the problem of Bengali and West Pakistani cannot be reconciled by asking Bengalis to cease calling themselves Bengalis and to think of themselves as East Pakistani. The resolution lies in according Bengali culture and its heroes such as Tagore a parity of esteem with Punjabi culture and its heroes such as Iqbal. The only integrative paramount value, however, may be mutual recognition of parity of diverse communal values, expressed structurally through political competition.

It is probable that even if a temporary dimunution of ethnicity or other components of communality occurs and that at a certain point "integration" appears to be achieved, there may be subsequent resurgences of communality. The bearing of this dimension of ethnicity on maintaining an architectonic integrity can be suggested by thinking of two components: ethos and polity. Ethos is the more inclusive term; it is the total sphere of values held dear by society. The total ethos may embody disintegrative elements derivative from such factors as divergent languages, culture, religions, or stages of development (e.g., tribalism). Polity embraces the constitution and political structures. What is suggested here is that uneven permeation of values in a developing state gives rise to stresses in the whole system, to mediational processes, and points to the crucial need for co-ordinative mechanisms throughout the entire system to give it cohesion. It may be that the scant attention given the evolution of constitutions, the keystone of architectonics, is related to this problem. Sartori comments that constitution-making as "the traditional instrument for political engineering" has fallen into disrepute. He attributes this to the fact that constitutions have governed the behavior of elites, not of mass societies, and that the conjunction of constitutions and universal suffrage makes the former an inadequate "system of channelment of mass society."[107] This observation appears to us to be corroborated by a wealth of data.[108] We do not

107. Sartori, "Political Development and Political Engineering," pp. 272–273.

108. Prewar attention to constitution-making was epitomized by Carl J. Friedrich's influential *Constitutional Government and Politics,* which first appeared (New York: Harper and Bros.) in 1937, reappeared in a second edition in 1941, and in 1950 in a revised edition entitled *Constitutional Government and Democracy.* A revised (fourth) edition under the same title was published by Blaisdell in 1968. Friedrich has been remarkably imaginative in relating the issues of constitutionalism to contemporary idioms of political reform and evolution. Thus the 1950 edition ended with a chapter entitled "Constitutional Dictatorship and Military Government" and the 1968 edition concludes with "Constitutionalism in Emergent Nations." Such insightful contemporary relevancies are continued in his recent series of lectures at Boston University published by the press of that university in 1967 under the title, *The Impact of Constitutionalism Abroad.* This volume deals mostly with the period from 1789 to the Second World War. Friedrich's work and a few other exceptions such as Herbert Spiro's *Government by Constitution* (New York, 1959) are the only major, widely used American works emphasizing constitutions in the evolution of political systems. The current inattention to the writing and interpretation of constitutions is reflected in many other ways as well. Consider, for example, that major constitutions such as those of Ceylon, India, Pakistan, and Malaysia were drafted with no assistance from American scholarship, and only minimal assistance from such British sources as Sir Ivor Jennings. See Sir Ivor Jennings, *Problems of the New Commonwealth* (Durham, N.C., 1958). See also Ralph Braibanti, "The Higher Bureaucracy of Pakistan," in Braibanti and Associates, *Asian Bureaucratic Systems Emergent from the British Imperial Tradition,* esp. n. 150 on pp. 313–314, which analyzes the context of scholarship in comparative law within which Pakistan's second (1962) constitution was written. This is in striking contrast to the direct influence of German, French, British, and American scholarship on the constitutions of China and Japan half a century ago. In contemporary American political science scholarship there is little published analysis of constitution-making and constitutional law of developing states since 1947. There is nothing, for example, as detailed as the series of eight articles by Kenneth Colegrove on the Japanese cabinet, foreign office, privy council, emperor, and Diet which appeared in the *American Political Science Review* from 1931 to 1936 (XXV [1931], 589–614, 881–905; XXVI [1932], 642–659, 828–845; XXVII [1933], 885–898; XXVIII [1934], 23–39; XXX [1936], 585–613, 903–923). These articles were representative of the scholarship of their time in that they were heavily descriptive of law and structure. This kind of formalism is no longer in vogue and we concede that it is not really adequate in political analysis. Yet such description and analysis of the structural-legal base of politics is crucial and must precede analyses which weave structural design with sophisticated constitutional analysis. It is highly unlikely that studies on post-1947 developing states comparable to Colegrove's on Japan would (if they were written) be accepted for publication in American political science journals of today. Much attention was given to constitution-making in the occupation of Japan and Germany beginning in 1945, and this is reflected in the political science writing of that time. But that research, excellent though it is, was

suggest that we should deplore this condition totally, for as Sartori and many others have suggested, the dominant motif of contemporary political development has been mass participation and it cannot be satisfied by constitutions alone. On the other hand, power diffusion must be dealt with in the context of architectonics. The reasons for the neglect of the constitutional component are many. Some of those which relate to dispositions of American social science scholarship have been dealt with

---

narrowly legalistic and focused more on the origins of the constitutions than on the interweaving of subsequent interpretations into the fabric of the whole political process. See, for example, Robert E. Ward, "The Origins of the Present Japanese Constitution," *American Political Science Review,* L (1956), 980–1010, and Justin Williams, "Making the Japanese Constitution: A Further Look," *ibid.,* LIX (1965), 665–679.

There appears to have been a major revolution in thought between the time of the occupation of Germany, Korea, and Japan in 1945 and the two decades of the fifties and sixties following independence actions beginning with India in 1947. This revolution signaled a reliance on extended franchise rather than on legal form in political development. In American political science methodology, this was concomitant with the rise of behavioralism and the waning of institutionalism. The series of six studies on political development published under the aegis of the Committee on Comparative Politics of the Social Science Research Council further suggests this significant contrast in attitudes. These volumes (all published by Princeton University Press) are: Lucian W. Pye (ed.), *Communications and Political Development* (1963); Joseph LaPalombara (ed.), *Bureaucracy and Political Development* (1963); Robert E. Ward and Dankwart A. Rustow (eds.), *Political Modernization in Japan and Turkey* (1964); James S. Coleman (ed.) *Education and Political Development* (1965), Joseph LaPalombara and Myron Weiner, *Political Parties and Political Development* (1966); Leonard Binder *et al., Crises in Political Development* (1967). One is struck by the fact that there is no volume on constitution-making or on law and political development. Similarly, we search in vain for analysis of these subjects in the very valuable series, *Public Policy,* the yearbook of the Kennedy School of Government of Harvard University, where interest in political development and constitutionalism is especially keen. While the 1966 volume has somewhat more than half of its bulk devoted to "Problems of Development," no article treats the subject of law and development (*Public Policy,* Vol. XV [1966], ed. John D. Montgomery and Arthur Smithies). While there is much attention to such constitutional problems as federalism, particularly in Vols. XIII, XIV, and XV (1964, 1965, 1966), there is little attention to such constitutional problems in the new (i.e., post-1947) states. Volumes XVI (1967) and XVII (1968), each of which devotes approximately a quarter of its bulk to development problems, remain similarly silent on developmental aspects of law.

This condition is in contrast to British scholarship, where much attention continues to be given to constitution-making and legal interpretation. See, for example, the series under the general editorship of George W. Keeton, *The British Commonwealth: The Development of Its Laws and Constitutions,* published in London, written largely by University of London faculty, and comprising in 1967 thirteen volumes. See also the twenty-three-page mimeographed "List of Current Legal Studies of the University of London" (15th ed.; London, March, 1967), which lists some 100 (of a total of 354) topics dealing with constitutional developments in new states. Of course, it must also be said that just as American scholarship seems to have neglected legal-structural insights, British political science scholarship seems to be insufficiently cognizant of behavioral insights.

elsewhere.[109] To these reasons and those suggested by Sartori, we might also add the fundamental antagonism between power diffusion—"channelment of mass society," in Sartori's terms—and constitutionalism. Power diffusion has been accomplished in many developing systems largely through community development structures, political parties, or confrontational-agitational politics. These are rooted in an ethos of spontaneity and, often, in extralegal norms. Legal institutions and constitutions spring essentially from norms, structures, and attitudes of mature constitutional systems in the West. Since, in contrast, power diffusion appears to derive from indigenous sources, constitutions can be and are regarded not only as alien but even as impediments to the rapid diffusion of public power. Through the doctrine of popular sovereignty they are, in fact, the source of such diffusion; yet by insisting on an order derived externally, constitutions appear to delay if not block such diffusion. We know too little about the permeative effect of constitutional law as it confronts apparently antagonistic indigenous norms with its own juridical norms derived from Western systems. The nature of this confrontation and the degree to which it is a factor in maintaining architectonic integrity in the face of often overwhelming centrifugal forces is of crucial significance. The recognition of diverse values and their integration into an architectonic embrace can be dealt with partly through spatial allocations of power—a phenomenon commonly referred to as the federal principle. The view expressed by Stein in his review of three books on federalism is consistent with the analysis we have presented here. In his view a federal political system is that form of political system "in which the institutions, values, attitudes and patterns of political action operate to give autonomous expression both to the national political system and political culture and to regional political subsystems and subcultures (defined primarily by ethnic-linguistic factors). The autonomy of these systems and subsystems is counterbalanced by a mutual interdependence. This balance

109. Braibanti, "The Role of Law in Political Development." See also Ralph Braibanti, "Comparative Political Analytics Reconsidered," *Journal of Politics*, XXX (1968), 25–65.

maintains the overall union."[110] In developing systems, this balance is made all the more difficult by institutional and structural weakness and by commitment to recognize and encourage polycommunal differences. The consequent tensions between centripetal and centrifugal forces make prognoses as to the continued existence of the nation-state extremely hazardous. Closely related to this confrontation is the changing pattern of dependence upon indigenous as well as American, British, and other foreign legal precedent. For example, in Pakistan the change to a presidential system and a division of powers into enumerated central and reserved provincial powers requires, and in fact has resulted in, a shift away from British to analogous American precedent.

The importance of architectonics to administrative reform lies in the extent to which the total administrative apparatus is infused with the same values, be they justice, equity, equality, or others. The problem is that of infusing administrative action with the spirit and substance of the architectonics. This involves two kinds of compatibility: compatibility of administrative process with the architectonics—usually a variation of due process of law—and compatibility with the spirit of the statute. This relationship, always difficult to achieve even in mature systems, is much more difficult to attain in new highly unbalanced systems. The bureaucracy, long accustomed to near-paramountcy under imperial rule, relies less on statutory sources for its actions and more on its internal resources and on synaptic relations with extrastatutory sources. Such systems may be tottering on the brink of administrative lawlessness. Ambiguity of function in the whole system, inadequacy of legislative oversight, and other weaknesses allow administrative discretion to flow with minimal reference to the channels—a predicament of which we were well warned in the West as early as 1929 by Lord Hewart of Bury's *The New Despotism.*[111] This kind of despotism is the more dangerous in immature systems. The gap between architectonics and administrative discretion is amenable to determination; it can also be ascertained how the gap can be reduced and administrative ac-

110. Michael B. Stein, "Federal Political Systems and Federal Societies," *World Politics,* XX (1968), 731.
111. (London, 1929).

tion rendered more congruent with architectonics. One is impressed by what a judiciary which has prestige, erudition, and independence can do to regulate this articulation. It is probable that in many developing states the articulation of administrative decisions with architectonics is minimal. Pakistan is one of the few systems where this question has been given much attention, yet even here we find glaring instances of incongruence.[112] Consider the historic "Pan" case of 1964 in which the Ministry of Commerce sought to regulate betel leaf grade without even authority of a statute or ordinance and proceeded to establish administrative rules far exceeding the restraints usually found within the concept of delegated legislation.[113] This kind of problem is closely related to commitment to a rule of law which, as was shown in an earlier part of this chapter, has been given prominence in the Foreign Assistance Act. Rule of law as a component of architectonics recorded in the constitution has little significance if it does not suffuse the entire political order, particularly the administrative system.

Diffusion of power

The second and most important attribute of political development is the involvement of the entire population in political life—the diffusion of power to the periphery of the social order. Ideologically, this derives from concern for enhancement of human dignity, reflected juridically in the concept of popular sovereignty and implemented institutionally and structurally in universal franchise and participative entities such as community development. This attribute has been variously alluded to as participant society (Lerner),[114] social and political mobilization (Deutsch),[115] power-sharing (Lasswell),[116] the participation ex-

112. The first and thus far the only comprehensive study of this in Pakistan is S. M. Haider, *Judicial Review of Administrative Discretion in Pakistan* (Lahore, 1967).

113. *Ghulam Zamin* v. *A. B. Khondkhar*, PLD (Dacca, 1965), 156. See also *Ghulam Sabir* v. *Pan Allotment Committee*, PLD (Dacca, 1967), 607.

114. Daniel Lerner, *The Passing of Traditional Society* (Glencoe, Ill., 1958), pp. 48–50.

115. Karl W. Deutsch, "Social Mobilization and Political Development," *American Political Science Review*, LV (1961), 493–514. See also J. P. Nettl, *Political Mobilization* (New York, 1967).

116. Lasswell, "The Policy Sciences of Development," p. 290.

plosion (Almond and Verba),[117] and channelment of mass society (Sartori).[118] Analysis of the phenomenon of diffusion of power is fraught with some sensitivity in contemporary American (though not British or European) political science. Its delicacy is suggested, for example, by LaPalombara's circumspect qualifications in classifying certain development theorists, some of whom favored a "balanced" political development strategy as being "explicit in their concern for democratic political development" and another who favored an "unbalanced" strategy as one "whose concern with democratic development is equally obvious."[119] Sartori justifiably reflects the same sensitivity: ". . . if one goes ahead and discovers, for instance, that the 'planning of democracy' requires the slowing down of the processes of democratization, it is only to be expected that he will be accused of being a reactionary, if not a fascist."[120] Similarly, Lasswell identifies his concept of development with the "overriding goal of human dignity," which includes "effective general participation in the decision process," and suggests that any other commitment would lead into a reactionary position.[121]

Let it be said immediately that it is abundantly clear to this writer that the rapid involvement of large numbers of people—that is to say, the quantitative aspect of power diffusion—is a necessary aspect of development. Diffusion can bring about that degree of meaningful participation which enlarges choice and experience, develops responsibility, and enhances human dignity. Moreover, efforts to sedate, repress, or delay such diffusion should be regarded with some wariness since they may be subterfuges for authoritarianism.

117. Gabriel A. Almond and Sidney Verba, *The Civic Culture* (Princeton, 1963), pp. 2–3.

118. Sartori, "Political Development and Political Engineering," p. 273.

119. Joseph LaPalombara, "Theory and Practice in Development Administration: Observations on the Role of the Civilian Bureaucracy," in John Plank (ed.), *The Theory and Practice of Political Development* (Washington, 1968).

120. Sartori, "Political Development and Political Engineering," p. 269. Sartori pursues this point perceptively by suggesting that the political scientist's reluctance to propose an "unpopular" measure because it is "undemocratic" even though he considers the measure necessary violates the concept of duty implicit in the ethics of a discipline professing to be scientific (pp. 269–270).

121. Lasswell, "The Policy Sciences of Development," p. 290. See also his extended treatment of values in the works cited in nn. 91–96.

The term "power diffusion" is used here in a sense which subsumes the ancillary concepts of mobilization, participation, and representation. The term does not refer exclusively to the distribution of authoritative actions among loci of power within the institutional arrangements of a political system. Rather, we intend it to mean also the relationship between people outside institutions of government and institutional manifestations of political power. In our view, this relationship embraces three qualities. First, it is embedded in a psychic or attitudinal context which conditions perceptions, expectations, and use of political power and which affects the behavior of persons in relation to government. Second, it includes direct participatory behaviors either in the apparatus of government on a full-time basis or in part-time mediational mechanisms (e.g., interest groups and elections). Here we assume that the mere act of participation, both direct and mediational, enlarges the decisional matrix and serves either immediately or ultimately to diffuse power. Third, most participation is achieved by means of representation. The expansion of the representative concept into all realms of the political system and the notion that representation must produce in institutions of government replications of the polycommunal composition of the whole social order have created new strains on participatory-representational institutions.

The conjunction of power diffusion with new perceptions of participation and representation and with penetration of government to subvillage units is one of the most provocative issues confronted by analysts of political development. An ironic and often overlooked consequence of power diffusion is the ultimate institutionalization of what initially appears as political behavior generated primarily from spontaneity.[122] Accelerated diffusion of power has politicized aspects of life particularly within the village unit. The postindependence diffusion of political power in

122. The methodological problems presented by this condition particularly as they relate to anthropology and political science are discussed in Braibanti, "Comparative Political Analytics Reconsidered," pp. 38–39. For somewhat different but pertinent views see Ronald Cohen, "Anthropology and Political Science, Courtship or Marriage," *American Behavioral Scientist,* XI (1967), 1–8, and Carl J. Friedrich, "Some Thoughts on the Relation of Political Theory to Anthropology," *American Political Science Review,* LXII (1968), 536–546.

the 1950's permeated family, tribal, and village affairs with political actions. The structures for these actions were essentially participative. The more formal were directly related to the franchise: party activity and the voting process itself. The less formal were community development or social uplift activities. The less formal ultimately become more formal if we are to judge from experience of community development in India and Pakistan.[123] There the first stage was focused on substantive program and was generated primarily from a dynamic of spontaneity, effervescence, and informality. But the need for regularity, record-keeping, and consistency in decision-making led inevitably to routinization and to bureaucratization. As this process matured, the impulse to action appears to have been generated less by spontaneity and an effervescent commitment to ideology and more by the formal authority of the orthodox bureaucracy. What is suggested here is that although the early stages of power diffusion may appear to be unrelated to institutionalization, power diffusion quickly leads to a second stage in which political behavior becomes formalized and channeled into institutions and structures. Failure to give attention to this may result in underestimating the role of institutions and thus misinterpreting the progression from unstructured to structured political behavior.

The stress and the crises caused by accelerated power-sharing cannot be overlooked.[124] The problem can be simply put. New

123. A perceptive analysis of this is given in the paper by A. T. R. Rahman, "Theories of Political and Administrative Development and Rural Institutions in India and Pakistan," presented at the SEADAG seminar on administrative development at Carmel, California, November 24, 1967. See also my Foreword to Willard Berry, *Aspects of the Frontier Crimes Regulations in Pakistan* (Durham, N.C., 1966).

124. Sartori has described this condition forcefully:

> . . . it appears that the tempo and the timing of enfranchisement is not merely a matter of "interest" and of class struggle, but also a matter of legitimate "technical" concern. From the point of view of political engineering, no political system can escape overload unless it manages to slow down the outburst of expectations which follows the inauguration of a democracy, and thereby to process the flow of demands according to some kind of gradual sequence. And, at best, overload is conducive to impotence, no matter whether the paralysis of the system is manifest or whether it is camouflaged by spectacular programs of fancy reforms. I would argue, therefore, that the newborn nations of the Third World which have rushed headlong in granting universal enfranchisement have been ill-advised. To be sure, what is done is done. Nonetheless, to refuse to acknowledge a mistake only helps us to repeat the same error the next time.

Sartori, "Political Development and Political Engineering," p. 277.

states often do not have the institutional strength necessary to convert demands into policy or action. More importantly, they do not have a sufficiently even diffusion of norms to ignite the whole political system with the strength of architectonics. This is an important reason for the collapse of new systems—not because of corruption, not because of infiltration, not exclusively because of institutional weakness—because of uneven diffusion of norms, and because of the unnatural straining of stronger institutions (such as the judiciary) to take up the slack of the weaker institutions. The importance of this attribute of power diffusion lies in the fact that rapid diffusion to the periphery of the social order changes the nature and quantum of political demands, thus increasing the strain on the capability of institutions to convert such demand into effective governmental action. Elsewhere this condition has been discussed in terms of "load" and handling of crises. The sequence or timing of institution-building and accelerated power diffusion is crucial. Our attention was earlier directed to "strategic guidance for timing the component elements in sequences of development."[125] More recently, Nordlinger has advanced promising hypotheses emerging from this sequential relationship.[126] His hypotheses point to the need for a rapid rate of government institutionalization preceding mass suffrage and the formation of political parties. This condition is aggravated when demands are escalated by the intervention and massive uncontrolled infusion of foreign norms through technical assistance and international entities bent on dissemination of idiosyncrasies without regard to institutional capacity to handle such demands. The possibility that this demand-conversion crisis could be pushed to the brink of political disintegration by foreign ideological inducements should make us wary of the possible effects in developing states of Title IX as originally stated in the Foreign Assistance Act of 1966. Fortunately the 1967 version with its mention of infrastructure (at least by the House committee, even though not in the text of the statute)[127] provides for both stimulating participation and strengthening institutions of government.

125. Lasswell, "Policy Sciences of Development," p. 295.
126. Eric A. Nordlinger, "Political Development: Sequences and Rates of Change," *World Politics*, XX (1968), 494–521, esp. 507–510.
127. *House Report No. 551*, p. 29.

This would appear to provide a much sounder base for political development. But such strategy presupposes careful analysis of each relevant institution in the system to determine where strength is needed.

Institutions

A third characteristic of political development is the establishment of an institutional apparatus which has the potential for conversion of valid expressions of popular will into actions fairly predictable and consistent with the architectonics of the state. This potential may not always equal present capability; indeed, the gap between potential and capability is one means of determining the effectiveness of this aspect of modernity. Political behavior flows imperceptibly into the interstices created by institutions, and its flow is regulated and conditioned by the locus and effectiveness of institutional power. Although institutionalism as a mode of analysis has been eclipsed by functionalism, this eclipse, like all eclipses, seems to be approaching its end.[128]

128. A need in American political science is the reconsideration of the cruciality of institutions and structures. A functional approach was a necessary corrective to the unrealities of an excessive formalism and served to clear the mind of institutional stereotypes and to free it to look for uncommon, even bizarre, institutional expressions. The operational utility of functionalism seems to this writer to be primarily in an attitude dubious of excessive reliance on the formalism of institutions. That attitude must also recognize that there is always incongruence between actual behavior and institutional intent and that meaningful political analysis not only must examine both but must scrutinize the incongruence as well. Once this intellectual stance is taken, the danger of approaching the study of a political system through its institutions can be minimized. The continuing infusion of social-psychological components in political analysis suggests that, for some time to come, more than adequate attention may be given to the "real behavior" revealed by functionalism. For a review of psychological research pertinent to political science generally, see Henry S. Kariel, "The Political Relevance of Behavioral and Existential Psychology," *American Political Science Review*, LXI (1967), 334–343. See also Fred I. Greenstein, "The Impact of Personality on Politics: An Attempt to Clear Away Underbrush," *ibid.*, pp. 629–642, and "Personality and Politics: Problems of Evidence, Inference and Conceptualization," *American Behavioral Scientist*, XI (1967), 38–54.

One of the earliest evidences of a return to consideration of institutions was the institution-building consortium participated in by scholars from Indiana University, Michigan State University, the University of Pittsburgh, and Syracuse University under the direction of Milton J. Esman. See Milton J. Esman, "A Note on Institution Building in National Development" (Pittsburgh, November 16, 1962, mimeographed); *University of Pittsburgh Inter-University Research Program in Institution Building* (Pittsburgh, 1963?); Milton J. Esman, "Institution-Building and National Development: A Research Note," *International Development Review*, IV (1962), 27–30; Milton J. Esman and Hans C. Blaise, *Institutional Development Research—The Guiding Concept* (Pittsburgh, 1966); Milton J.

The cruciality of institutions in political development has been strikingly brought to our attention by Huntington in the context of the need for balance between the demands or crises of the social order and the capability of institutions for converting these demands into policy or action.[129] Jouvenel reminds us that the political scientist is an expert on institutions and behavior who must "foretell the adjustments suitable to improve the adequacy of the institutional system to cope with changing circumstances."[130] Pennock neatly stated the case: "Whether political and governmental structures are formal or informal, incorporated

Esman and Fred C. Bruhns, *Institution-Building in National Development: An Approach to Induced Change in Transitional Societies* (Pittsburgh, 1965); Milton J. Esman, *The Institution Building Concepts: An Interim Appraisal* (Pittsburgh, 1967). See also the pamphlet published jointly by the Comparative Educational Administration Subcommittee of CAG and the Inter-University Research Program in Institution Building entitled *Institution-Building and Education: Papers and Comments* (Bloomington, Ind., 1967?). For further evidence of this recovery of the political study of institutions see, in addition, Friedrich, Huntington. Jouvenel, Pennock, and Sartori (esp. his n. 6), cited in nn. 87, 46, 130, and 2, respectively, and the following: Fred W. Riggs, "Structure and Function: A Dialectical Approach," a paper prepared for delivery at the 1967 meeting of the American Political Science Association, September, 1967; Joseph LaPalombara, "Parsimony and Empiricism in Comparative Politics: An Anti-Scholastic View," in Robert T. Holt and John Turner (eds.), *The Methodology of Comparative Research* (Glencoe, Ill., 1969). See also William C. Mitchell, "The Shape of Political Theory to Come: From Political Sociology to Political Economy," *American Behavioral Scientist*, XI (1967), 8–38, in which it is asserted that the "institutional structure of the polity is of particular importance because it shapes the public policy-making process, determining which issues and problems are accorded what order of priority, and is itself in part the actual outcome of policy. . . . This being the case the institutional structure of a system is of paramount importance in political life" (p. 17). Eisenstadt expressed a similar view: ". . . the major problem facing [developing] societies is the necessity to develop an institutional structure which is capable of continuously 'absorbing' the various social changes which are inherent in the processes of modernization" (S. N. Eisenstadt, *Modernization: Protest and Change* [Englewood Cliffs, N.J., 1966], p. vi). See also Eisenstadt's "Institutionalization and Change," *American Sociological Review*, XXIX (1964), 235–247, and his "Initial Institutional Patterns of Political Modernization," *Civilizations*, XII (1962), 461–472 and XIII (1963), 15–26. See also Gunnar Myrdal's institutional emphasis in his *Asian Drama: An Inquiry into the Poverty of Nations* (New York, 1968), I, 26, and Riggs's chapter in this volume.

129. Huntington, "Political Development and Political Decay," pp. 386–430.

130. Bertrand de Jouvenel, "Political Science and Prevision," *The American Political Science Review*, LIX (1965), 29, 32. See also Jouvenel, *The Art of Conjecture* (New York, 1967). For a sympathetic critique of Jouvenel's view inspired by his recent writings, see Benjamin Akzin, "On Conjecture in Political Science," *Political Studies*, XIV (1966), 1–14. This and other aspects of political prediction are analyzed in an essay review of six books by Paul T. David on the subject, "The Study of the Future," *Public Administration Review*, XXVIII (1968), 187–194. See also Ortega's essay, "The Forecasting of the Future," in the compilation, José Ortega y Gasset, *The Modern Theme* (New York, 1961), pp. 19–28.

in the legal structure or not, it is of greatest importance that they should be institutionalized; and the process of institutionalization is as surely part of development as are specialization of function and differentiation of structure. It is when certain forms and procedures become the accepted ways of doing things that they become effective instruments of stability and of legitimation."[131]

In discussing institutions and structures we are confronted by difficulties of definition. Much of the political analysis dealing with institutions and structures is derivative from the work of Talcott Parsons,[132] who defines institutions as "generalized patterns of norms which define *categories* of prescribed, permitted and prohibited behavior in social relationships, for people in interaction with each other as members of their society and its various subsystems and groups."[133] Friedrich's definition, which he compares with an earlier (1951) definition by Parsons and implies its consistency with that definition, refers to a political institution as "any stably organized syndrome of political acts or actions having a function and/or purpose in the political system, or to put it another way, a relatively stable collection of roles."[134] Lasswell and Kaplan embrace in their definition the Parsonian aspect of interaction. They regard an institution as "a pattern composed of culture traits specialized to the shaping and distribution of a particular value (or set of values)."[135] For them a culture trait is an act, characteristic of a group, that is recurring under comparable circumstances.

A definition of institution which will facilitate an evaluation

131. Pennock, "Political Development, Political Systems and Political Goods," p. 418.

132. For a survey which integrates Parsonian analysis of institutions into the mainstream of relevant political science doctrine, see chap. 3 aptly titled "The Interdependence of Institution, Decision and Policy" in Friedrich, *Man and His Government*, pp. 70–82. See also Talcott Parsons, "The Principal Structures of Community," in Carl J. Friedrich, (ed.), *Community*, Vol. II in the Nomos series (New York, 1959), pp. 152–199, and William C. Mitchell, *Sociological Analysis and Politics: The Theories of Talcott Parsons* (New York, 1967).

133. Talcott Parsons, *Structure and Process in Modern Societies* (Glencoe, Ill., 1960), p. 177.

134. Friedrich, *Man and His Government*, p. 71. See Friedrich's chapter in this volume, esp. n. 2.

135. Lasswell and Kaplan, *Power and Society*, p. 47. Selznick also regards value as the characteristic distinguishing institution from other organizations (Philip Selznick, *Leadership in Administration: A Sociological Interpretation* [Evanston, Ill., 1957], p. 40).

and measurement of institutional effectiveness must be broad enough to encompass both changing institutional roles in transitional systems and the fact that virtually all institutions in such systems play some part in the use of public power. In the definition of institution here proposed, Parsons' definition of 1960 is accepted as a base. To this we add an emphasis suggested by Lasswell and Kaplan, modified here to suit the needs of developing systems. Those parts of Parsons' and Friedrich's definitions which emphasize the relatively stable and syndromic qualities of a collection of roles are accepted. But to this there is added a quality of dynamism which has both intra- and interinstitutional influence. With respect to such influence the "shaping and distributive" qualities in the definition of Lasswell and Kaplan are approximated. But use of the term "distributive," since it connotes a passivity or at best a routine action, is not completely satisfying. There is need to imply an active, penetrative dynamic which is manifest in the forced recirculation of norms and values within the institution and the propelled rediffusion of norms from one institution to others. These dynamic, shaping, circulating, rediffusing actions are directly related to the phenomenon to be later called "institutional permeability," which is in turn directly related to functional transformation. The suggestion that the dynamism of this shaping-diffusing action is important particularly in developing systems is based on the presupposition that ascribed and perceived roles as well as ascribed and perceived functions are less stable in institutions of developing systems. The very instability increases the incidence of transformational actions and hence accentuates the dynamism of the process. This is an important qualitative distinction for institutions in developing systems. Following this analysis, this definition is proposed: *Institutions are patterns of recurring acts structured to condition behavior of their members both within the institution and in its relationship with other units of the social system and to project a force in the social system in terms of ethos, or action.* Institutions which are relevant to political functions are those which share in any measure in the formation or use of public power. Thus it is conceivable, and indeed likely, that the range of institutions subject to analysis in the political system may be coterminous with those found in the total social system. Certainly, the major institutions would be public civil bureaucracy, public military bureaucracy, non-public commerce and banking, public and non-public education, professions and occupations, interest groups, legislatures, and religious entities.

Use of the term "structure" confronts us with similar definitional perplexities. Almond and Coleman use "structure" in place of "institution" because they feel that the latter term leads them "toward formal norms." They define political structure as "legitimate patterns of interaction by which . . . [internal and external order] is maintained."[136] Almond and Powell regard structure as "the observable activities which make up the political system" and as "particular sets of roles which are related to one another."[137] Riggs uses the term "structure" (which he defines as "a pattern of action of components of a polity") interchangeably with "institution."[138] Lasswell and Kaplan distinguish between structures and institutions. For them structures are "the continuing arrangements . . . by which power is shaped and shared within the community. These can be described according to the form of rule (effective power) and, more generally, the form of polity (both formal and effective)."[139] Friedrich deplores the vagueness and imprecision in use of the term "structure." He implies that structure is a subordinate component of institution:

> "Structure means, generally speaking, that there is a stable and ordered relation of parts, such as characterizes a building, from which the term is derived. . . . [I]t is the static aspect of a system, its 'skeleton.' The structuring of power presupposes its separation into parts. Before power can be structured, it must be stable. The stabilization of power precedes that erecting of a structure which produces institutionalization."[140]

136. Gabriel A. Almond and James S. Coleman, *The Politics of the Developing Areas* (Princeton, 1960), pp. 6, 13.
137. Gabriel A. Almond and G. Bingham Powell, Jr., *Comparative Politics: A Developmental Approach* (Boston, 1966), p. 23.
138. Fred W. Riggs's chapter in this volume, pp. 225 ff.
139. Lasswell and Kaplan, *Power and Society*, p. 200.
140. Friedrich, *Man and His Government*, pp. 181–182.

Miller also emphasizes the static quality of structure, and in his analysis of the use of the term in biology, he points out that when "anatomists study structure they use dead, often fixed, material in which no further activity can be expected to occur."[141] Miller quotes from Leighton, who also stresses the static aspect: "A structure is not something which keeps coming back in a regular flow of movement like a figure in a dance; it is something which just sits there like a chair."[142] Leighton suggests that the term "structure" has been made troublesome by the connotations carried over from contexts in which it has different meaning. Thus, "usage with reference to personality and society is dynamic, while in anatomy, in architecture, and in many other everyday contexts the word refers to the static aspect of things." Miller seeks to avoid this "semantic morass" by defining structure as the "static arrangement of a system's parts at a moment in three-dimensional space."[143] He avoids the difficulty of confusing function with structure by thinking of function primarily as process—process being "dynamic change in the matter-energy or information of that system over time." Here we reject the equation of institution and structure suggested by Almond and Coleman and by Riggs, and the definition of structure by Almond and Powell. Following Friedrich and, especially as regards statics, Miller, and, especially as regards power-shaping, Lasswell and Kaplan, structure is thought of as being static, subordinate, and precedent to institution. Moreover, it is regarded as *relatively* value free, while institutions are highly value laden. Indeed, in our view the explicitness of value retention and projection is a fundamental difference between structure and institution. Structure is usually a component of institution usually preceding institutions and relates to the relatively value-free attributes of allocation of responsibilities, loci of decision-making, assignment of roles to carry out these responsibilities, regulation of flow of work, and an impersonal

141. James G. Miller, "Living Systems: Basic Concepts," *Behavioral Science,* X (1965), 193–237, at 209.
142. Alexander H. Leighton, *My Name is Legion: Foundations for a Theory of Man in Relation to Culture* (New York, 1959), pp. 221–222.
143. Miller, "Living Systems: Basic Concepts," p. 211.

system of related sanctions. It is conceivable that structures can exist outside institutions, but institutions cannot exist without one or more structures within them.

While this view of "structure" may enhance analytical clarity, it is inadequate unless set in the context of "process." Here the work of Miller and Lasswell is illuminating. Much of Lasswell's work is permeated with the concept of the dynamic, hence transformational, nature of process, particularly as regards decision-making. Structure must be viewed as static only for analytical convenience. Moreover, its static aspect is momentary—only when the process which it serves is halted, to use Miller's metaphor, "as when motion is frozen by a high-speed photograph."[144] Thus structures are continually being changed by the process they accommodate. The changes may be slight and extended over a long period of time, or they may be abrupt, episodic, or catastrophic. The reification of structure rather than analysis of it in the dynamic terms of process is an impediment to clear conceptualization.

In addition to institution and structure, we also must identify "sector." Sector is a mini-institution, sharing the same norms and values of the institution of which it is a component part, yet differing from it in some respects. But the differences are not crucial enough to warrant classification as a separate institution. Nor can they be classed as structures since they lack relative neutrality in value projection. Examples of sectors are: officer corps and enlisted cadre in the institution of military bureaucracy. Both share the same norms generally, yet are different in important respects. Sectors are not completely insulated from each other; norms, values, and roles are exchanged and sometimes several roles in various sectors are played by the same person. This identification of three entities—i.e., institution, structure (in the context of process), and sector—is crucial to our subsequent evaluation of institutions in terms of seven indices.

Qualitative differences in institutional performances are bound to exist. Such differences cannot be ascertained without some means of measuring the "quality" of the institution and the scope

144. *Ibid.*, p. 209.

of its functions. Evaluation of the effectiveness of institutional performance in a given system may yield some indication of when and why functions move from one institutional ambit to another. Huntington has suggested four indices—adaptability, complexity, autonomy, and coherence—for the measurement of institutions by which political systems may be compared in terms of their "levels of institutionalization."[145] So little is known about institutional-functional roles in political systems that we cannot here evaluate the adequacy of Huntington's indices. Some of them can be subsumed in a different cast with new indices added and with the new set of seven indices articulated to our immediate purpose in looking at institutions.[146] That purpose, somewhat different from Huntington's, is to attempt an analysis of the performance of institutions relevant to the political system. The functional permutations must be traced and the total performance related to structure, sector, and the total political system. As a consequence it may be possible to plan a strategy for induced political development designed to strengthen institutions in developing systems. Since we are concerned primarily with developing systems, our indices must reflect a disequilibrium of two kinds: sharply fluctuating change in the quantum and the nature of demands reaching institutions for conversion, and oscillation of functions absorbed and rejected by institutions.

In this context, we propose the following seven indices for the appraisal of institutional adequacy. By changing the order in which they are analyzed below and arbitrarily assigning proximate first-letter designations, we can assign the acronym RAB-

145. Samuel P. Huntington, *Political Order in Changing Societies* (New Haven, 1968), pp. 12–24. This view of institutionalization as a primary prerequisite to stability is found also in Eric A. Nordlinger, "Representation, Stability, and Decisional Effectiveness," in J. Roland Pennock and John W. Chapman (eds.), *Representation,* Vol. X in the Nomos series (New York, 1968), p. 115.

146. The present formulation is an elaboration of an earlier, skeletal version proposed in the context of comparative analysis (Braibanti, "Comparative Political Analytics Reconsidered"). The indices proposed are pertinent equally to comparative method and to development. In the former, measurement of institutions enables tracing of function hence comparison of functionality of institutions in different settings. In development theory, the concern is evaluation for the purpose of understanding relative rates of institutional growth instrumental use of which can be made in foreign assistance strategy. The indices are experimental and may have to be further revised or even discarded.

CIRR to this construct of seven indices. RABCIRR is derived from the key words, reception (R), autonomy (A), balance (B), congruence (C), internal (I), reformulation (R), and roles (R). We shall now analyze the indices themselves in an order somewhat more proximate to the flow of events than the listing as demanded by acronymic requirements. (1) The capacity to maintain relative autonomy of ethos and structures while at the same time remaining unantagonistic to and rediffusing the values of the architectonics of the system. The term "unantagonistic" is advisedly used, for it is not implied here that every component of a political system must be a miniaturization of the system as a whole. Thus there may always be military institutions, ecclesiastic entities, and private groups whose organizations may be apparently out of keeping with the whole system. Such incongruence may be more apparent than real; for example, what appears to be highly authoritarian (e.g., military institutions) may actually diffuse non-authoritarian values. Each institution will reflect the architectonics differently. Such reflection must occur within the context of maintaining sufficient autonomy so that a somewhat independent influence can be exerted with vigor and resilience in the whole system. This follows somewhat Huntington's concept of autonomy, but additional emphasis is given to compatibility with architectonics and to maintaining synaptic connections with the total political system so that the advantages of autonomy may find outlets for effective influence. It must be emphasized that this autonomy is relative and that it must be poised delicately in the context of co-ordinative mechanisms capable of extracting the full value of such autonomy while harnessing it to an architectonic whole. In all systems, this balance presents immense difficulties. In the United States, the organization of the Project Camelot episode neatly illustrates the dilemma of attempting to preserve the autonomy of ethos and structure of the academic community, professional diplomacy, and the military establishment while trying to co-ordinate their activities. The fact that each lost its capacity to function autonomously and yet that co-ordination was not achieved suggests the difficulty of attaining this balance. (2) The capacity of the institution to receive new norms from other institutions. Such reception may be in terms of persons or ideas. An example would be the civil bureaucracy receiving into its ranks officers of the military bureaucracy or persons from private commerce, law, or education. In many developing systems there is rigid compartmentalization which prevents or makes uncommon the transfer of persons. New norms may also be received by establishing contact with "mixing" institutions whose primary function may be the reception and distribution of new norms and the mixing of persons in an intellectual context in which such innovation has high prestige. This is the role played by such entities as institutes and administrative staff colleges. The importance of these entities is especially great when participating institutions are hostile to lateral reception of persons. New norms can also be received by use of advisers and consultants who are not an integral part of the system. (3) The capacity to reformulate its own norms in terms of the effect which the reception of new norms has had. This is related to an integrating capacity. The reformulation may be so extreme that it virtually changes the nature of the institution. On the other hand, it may be hardly perceptible. What is important here is not merely the phenomenon of integrating old and new, for such integration will occur in some manner almost spontaneously. The important action is the deliberate reformulation of such integration in a manner which symbolizes and makes real the new institutional objectives and mobilizes the energies and loyalties of personnel in terms of such reformulation. (4) Maintaining internal efficiency and viability. Here we refer to mechanical aspects of doing the work which has been taken on. Examples would be the disposition of cases in the judiciary, timely payment of personnel, decisions in administrative matters, and realistic planning and budget preparation. (5) Maintaining a balance between introverted institutional interests and the public interest. Comprehension of the role of the institution in the context of the political system will probably be characteristic of higher leadership rather than of the total institution. Such comprehension will be manifest principally in co-ordinative relationships with other institutions. This capacity is distinct from index 2 in that the reception of new norms is not a primary characteristic of these co-ordinative relationships but is concomitant and ancillary. In index 5 we seek principally to assess the capacity to adjust to the larger interests of the whole system without sacrificing the objectives of the institution itself. An extreme example of the reformulating behavior of index 3 and the behavior described for index 5 would be the disappearance of the institution as it was previously known and its reconstitution in a completely renovated way. (6) The congruence or incongruence of formally stated institutional objectives and actual behavior related to those objectives. What is sought here is the total institutional behavior as compared with its declared objectives. It is the externality of behavior which is sought, although this is often related to internal changing of roles. Thus, though the formal objectives of a court may be to interpret law, its judges may be called upon to head commissions on matters (such as student's problems, housing, administrative reform) outside that stated objective. In so doing the judge plays a different role and this affects the court internally. But it also affects the court in its relations with other institutions. (7) The degree of congruence among (*a*) roles as perceived by members of the institutions, (*b*) those ascribed by the structure, and (*c*) actual role behavior. This can be determined by role perception analysis, but it presupposes careful structural analysis. We assume the likelihood of a reciprocal interaction between perceived and ascribed roles, that is, the actual role perception will be shaped by prescription but prescription may also be shaped by perception. Role behavior will be shaped by and may in turn affect both. This reciprocal relationship is not unlike the relationship between informal and formal organization so well analyzed by Barnard before the technique of role analysis was developed.[147] Role analysis will yield some clues to the inter-

147. See Chester I. Barnard, *The Functions of the Executive* (Cambridge, Mass., 1947), pp. 114–123. For analyses of the use of role and reference group, see Lionel J. Newman and James W. Hughes, "The problem of the Concept of Role: A Re-Survey of the Literature," *Social Forces,* XXX (1951–52), 141–149; Neal Gross, Ward S. Mason, and Alexander McEachern, *Explorations in Role Analysis* (New York, 1956), pp. 11–18; Theodore Sarbin, "Role Theory," in Gardner Lindzey (ed.), *Handbook of Social Psychology* (Reading, Mass., 1954), I, 223–258; and Frederick Bates, "Position, Role, and Status: A Reformulation of

nal stress of the institution and structural maladjustment, thus suggesting factors bearing on efficiency. The difference between index 6 and index 7 is primarily spatial; the sixth index relates to behavior external to the institution and in relation to other institutions. The seventh index relates primarily to intra-institutional relations of role and structure. The use of indices 6 and 7 presupposes the desirability of bringing into the ambit of institutional action as much relevant behavior as possible. It also presupposes the validity of a hypothesis which has not yet been tested, namely, that the incongruence between formal institutional behavior and actual behavior is greater in disequilibrated than in stable systems. Such incongruence can probably never be removed; it is a problem dealt with at least as early as Aristotle.[148] It is assumed here that the deliberate and effective reduction of such incongruence is a characteristic of a developed system.

The evaluation of institutions and their component structures using the indices suggested above will probably reveal a markedly differential degree of development, which we may call asymmetrical or unbalanced institutional growth. The differential may be noted (1) between institutions, (2) between structures within an institution, (3) between sectors within an institution, and (4) between sectors of different institutions. These differentials are thus intra- as well as interinstitutional.

Let us take an example of analysis in terms of these seven indices. The military bureaucracy as an institution may be divided into sectors (mini-institutions) such as the officer corps and the enlisted ranks. These sectors are not sufficiently distinct to be classed as separate institutions for they are too closely bound together both by structure and the norms of military life.

Concepts," *Social Forces,* XXXIV, 313–321. See also, Muzafer Sherif, "The Concept of Reference Group in Human Relations," in Muzafer Sherif and M. O. Wilson (eds.), *Group Relations at the Crossroads* (New York, 1953), pp. 203–231; Robert K. Merton and Alice Kitt, "Contribution to the Theory of Reference Group Behavior," in Robert K. Merton and Paul Lazarsfeld (eds.), *Continuity in Social Research* (New York, 1950); and Ralph H. Turner, "Role-Taking, Role Standpoint, and Reference-Group Behavior," *American Journal of Sociology,* LXI (1956), 316–328. See also Ilchman's chapter in this volume, esp. pp. 514 ff.

148. This was dealt with in his *Politics*, Book IV, 5, in the context of differences between the constitution established by law and the administration of the constitution.

Neither are they structures, for these, according to our definition, cut across both sectors. The officer sector of the military bureaucracy may be permeated with modern norms (index 2) more thoroughly and may be absorbing such norms faster and more effectively than the enlisted ranks sector. The officer sector may, on the other hand, be less able to maintain its autonomy of ethos and structure (index 1) than the enlisted sector. This may be due to such factors as synaptic relations (familial, linguistic, educational, and other elitist group bonds) between officers and civil bureaucrats or politicians. Such relations may be absent from the enlisted sector, which may in consequence be able to maintain a high degree of autonomy both from the other sectors and from other institutions. Each of the sectors may have differentials in relation to other sectors of other institutions. The whole institution may have differential rates with respect to another institution at variance with those of its sectors. Thus private commerce may have absorbed norms of modernity (index 2) on the whole more than the public bureaucracy. Yet its reformulating (index 3) and balancing (index 5) capacities may be lower than those of public bureaucracy. At the same time in each of these indices, the positions of sectors of the two institutions may be inverted. That is, the reformulating (index 3) and balancing (index 5) capacities of certain sectors of private commerce, such as high level financiers, may be considerably higher than that of lower clerks or even of higher executives in the public bureaucracy. What we are suggesting here is a complex pattern of relationships which might more clearly be illustrated by the use of a series of acetate overlays of various colors rather than by narrative. The relationships are: (1) between sectors within an institution, (2) between sectors of different institutions, (3) between institutions, and (4) each of these three relationships in terms of each of the seven indices. This pattern of relationships we may call substantive differential. We must add to this another consideration, namely, a similar evaluation of structures within each institution in terms of their capacity to carry out the functions suggested by the seven indices. This we call structural differential.

Asymmetrical institutional development is probably inevitable; even in rigidly planned societies control over institutional development seems impossible to achieve. Be that as it may, asymmetrical development poses serious problems not the least of which is the uneven burden assumed by some institutions or their sectors which, by design or default, compensate for the slower development of companion sectors. The implication here is the cruciality of interinstitutional permeability of technology and norms. Institutions may manifest flexibility to absorb from whatever other institutions produce, at any given time, superior, though not necessarily surplus, competences. For example, managerial technology may develop at a faster pace in private commerce than in public bureaucracy, and the technological output of engineering, agricultural, and economic institutions may be superior to those of the orthodox university structure in many transitional systems. It is this kind of permeability which must be assessed in determining the reasons for movement of function among institutions. The transformational process of function and institution analyzed here is closely related to the concept of functional specificity which has been treated widely in the literature on development as a mark of an advanced political system. We are not at all certain that specificity of function is an inevitable progression from a primitive to an advanced system. While some evidence would indicate that it is, there may also be a progression toward functional specificity to a certain level, at which point there is a regression to functional diffuseness. In the United States, the university as an institution has become functionally more diffuse rather than more specific as it responds to activist pressures, develops relationships with public government, and adopts as an ideological goal the responsibility for the immediate rectification of the social order.

Another example is the proliferation of functions of American learned societies. The American Political Science Association and the American Society for Public Administration, to name but two, once fulfilled the single function of bringing into association scholars of a single discipline and publishing a journal for them. Now they serve as lobbies in Washington, insurance agents, travel bureaus, and administer other programs as well. This is certainly not a movement toward functional specificity; rather it is a progression to diffuseness.

Still another example is the institutional collaboration between private business and public government begun on a large scale during the New Deal and continued with respect to such activities as withholding taxes. The very concept now known as "co-operative federalism" is a further diffuseness of function among spatial units of government. In developing states, the "multipurpose" aspect of community development movements strongly indicates diffuseness rather than specificity. What we suggest here is the reversibility of the propensity toward specificity of function. Whether this is a sign of disintegration of a political system we are not yet willing to say. It is conceivable that diffuseness combined with highly developed co-ordinative and integrative techniques may be a more "advanced" form than "functional specificity." Our uncertainty of this leads us to reject the more common designation "functional specificity" in favor of a construct emphasizing permutation and projection of values. It appears that the criterion of autonomy of ethos and structure is essential to collect, formulate, and project values. Yet it may be that autonomy will be lost in the mutations which occur.

What we are here suggesting is a creative association of analysis of institutions and their functional manifestations which would yield not only various permutations of function but also, through measurement of institutional effectiveness, the relationship between effectiveness and such permutations. The "measurement" of such institutional "effectiveness" might then enable us to determine what institutions and structures require strengthening. Ideally—though the difficulties here are enormous—we might be able to suggest structural rectification and the allocation of functions to various institutions in somewhat the same manner as management analysis makes possible in internal administration. This kind of determination would be a necessary prelude to a meaningful strategy implied by Title IX of the Foreign Assistance Act.

Innovation

A fourth element in political development is the institutional and attitudinal capability of creative innovation. The ensuing discussion is limited to institutional rather than to attitudinal aspects. It is assumed that a reciprocal rather than a unidirectional relationship between institutions and attitudes exists. Whether innovation is generated primarily and initially by one aspect or the other is dependent upon the political system and on whether the change being considered emanates from externally induced (foreign assistance) sources or from an internal source. Internal sources are likely to be as much attitudinally as institutionally directed. Most developing systems have an ideological doctrine by which they seek to change popular beliefs as well as render them uniform. But change through institutions is the only means at the disposal of foreign assistance since ideological manipulation is impractical. Moreover, institutional change appears to be increasingly more effective than attitudinal manipulation even as an internal means. While the importance of innovation is implicit in much of the theorizing of political development (for example, change would appear to be essential to maintain legitimacy), it is given explicit recognition by Friedrich and, somewhat less explicitly, by Lasswell. The latter's fifth characteristic calls for a system "capable of creative realistic problem-solving."[149] While this capability is directed qualitatively toward the "pursuit of a rising level of participation in all values," it appears likely that expanded participation as a context for realistic problem-solving will increase rather than diminish the importance of innovation. Friedrich is somewhat more explicit in setting forth as the first feature of this model the capacity of government to cope with "technological requirements of survival."[150] In his chapter in this volume, Friedrich directs attention to a commonly overlooked aspect of innovation, namely, as a dimension of freedom. Innovation may create new alternatives, thus expanding choice and hence personal freedom.[151] This view of political innovation increases its importance, giving it new theoretical cogency and operational force as a characteristic of political development.

It is self-evident that all governments must deal with change.

149. Lasswell, "The Policy Sciences of Development," p. 293.
150. Friedrich, *Man and His Government*, p. 663.
151. Friedrich's chapter in this volume, p. 121.

It is the peculiar intensity of the problem of attitudinal change coupled with the need for drastic institutional renovation—both in the context of acute stress if not crisis—which leads us to delineate innovation as one of four characteristics of political development.

This innovation is of several kinds. First there is adjustment which must be made to the rapidly changing incidence of demands, the substantive content of demands, and the rapidly oscillating roles played by institutions in attempting to fulfil these demands. It is this aspect of innovation—that is, the rapidity, frequency, and severity of incidence, content, and oscillation—which produces what can be called disequilibrium in the system. Such changes perennially occur in all systems; it is rapidity and severity coupled with institutional incapacity which differentiate a stable from an unstable system. Such uncertainty is probably the same quality which Lasswell refers to in the first of his six characteristics of political development, "a sequence of approximations toward a self-sustaining level of power-accumulation."[152]

At the same time that the political system must accommodate to this kind of disequilibrium, and must reduce it to manageable dimensions, it must also move rapidly away from the "law and order" mentality to a "developmental" mentality and must change its institutions accordingly. The bureaucracy, although only one of several institutions, bears the heaviest responsibility for such innovation. The introduction of innovation must occur within the framework of the architectonics as well as in the context of disequilibrium described earlier.

With respect to innovation, we set forth here a series of propositions which might be tested in several developing systems, and which might have relevance to the relationship of administrative to political growth.

A first and overlooked means for introducing needed change in a developing system is vigorous leadership.[153] It might be ad-

152. Lasswell, "The Policy Sciences of Development," pp. 288–289.

153. The present author is indebted to Carl J. Friedrich who, commenting on the first draft of this chapter at the conference at the Villa Serbelloni, called attention to the important role of leadership. The role of personal leadership as a means of keeping a polycommunal state integrated politically is a crucial and

vanced as a self-evident proposition that the need for leadership is greater when institutions are weak. Before the independence movements following the Second World War, it was common to think of great modernizing efforts in terms of dramatic leadership. Thus the Meiji Reform of Japan and the role of Sun Yat-sen in China, Bismarck in Germany, and Kemal Ataturk in Turkey suggest almost immediately a congruence of personality and the substance of reform. The term "great modernizer" was in common currency. For a variety of reasons this congruence is no longer reported; perhaps it no longer exists. One reason may be that the great leadership of many new states, such as Jinnah in Pakistan, Gandhi and Nehru in India, and Sukarno in Indonesia, was primarily a leadership of revolution and independence rather than a modernizing leadership of the type described below. Further, the disenchantment with the role of demagogic leadership in Italy and Germany before and during the Second World War may have directed our attention to other sources of change. Third, misapplications of the concept of charisma to postwar leadership may have deflected our concern from the role of modernizing leadership.[154] Finally, the impact of transnational sources of change, such as foreign aid, make the total process of change far more complicated than in the prewar era and reduce the role of the single great leader correspondingly. Yet the role of leadership remains an important, sometimes a crucial, factor in introducing change in a developing system. The leadership role appears significant in uniting the many strata of the developing

---

primary function antecedent to the innovative role discussed here. The task of political integration has aptly been characterized as "empire-building" rather than "state-building" and the influence of personal leadership in maintaining the "empire" has been developed in Guenther Roth, "Personal Rulership, Patrimonialism and Empire-Building in the New States," *World Politics,* XX (1968), 194–207. See also the extended, illuminating analysis of deficiencies of "tender-minded" leadership in a country such as India in Spengler's chapter in this volume, pp. 602 ff.

154. For analysis of charisma, see Carl J. Friedrich, "Political Leadership and the Problems of the Charismatic Power," *Journal of Politics,* XXIII (1961), 2–24, and Friedrich, *Man and His Government,* pp. 172–179. See also Ann Ruth Willner and Dorothy Willner, "The Rise and Role of Charismatic Leaders," *Annals of the American Academy of Political and Social Science,* CCCLVIII (1965), 77–78; Ann Ruth Willner, *Charismatic Political Leadership: A Theory* (Research Monograph No. 32, Center for International Studies, Princeton University, May 1968); and T. K. Oommen, "Charisma, Social Structure, and Social Change," *Comparative Studies in Society and History,* X (1967), 85–99.

system. There must be profound understanding of the heritage and character of the system and an appreciation of the needs of a modern state. This is essentially what Lasswell means by his felicitous description of the fundamental characteristic of the "leader-follower relation" as appearing to be "the giving and receiving of orientation."[155] Another requisite is the sensitive use of power in a manner which elicits the best of the new yet evokes the old and which regulates the degree of freedom in the system to achieve a balance between the two. Personal leadership is also crucial in inspiring and maintaining the cohesion and relative autonomy of an elite which collectively has the intellectual competence to process change, adjusting it both to architectonics and to externally introduced needs. In contemporary Pakistan, Ayub has been partially successful in this latter activity through interim arrangements such as Manzur Qadir's drafting of the 1962 constitution, and by maintaining the cohesion of the elite cadre (Civil Service of Pakistan) of the civil bureaucracy. The same sort of phenomenon of personal leadership capturing the imagination and loyalty of a modernizing oligarchy has been observed in the case of Meiji Japan[156] and Turkey under Kemal Ataturk.[157] This kind of modernizing leadership is evident in King Zahir of Afghanistan, Reza Pahlevi, Shah of Iran, King Mahendra of Nepal, and Ayub Khan of Pakistan. To some extent it is also evident in Korea, Taiwan, and the Philippines, but in those countries there is a stronger institutional base which somewhat reduces the significance of leadership.

The second proposition is that the generalist elite of the public bureaucracy should be constituted (particularly with respect to recruitment) in a manner facilitating rapid absorption of skills technologically and ideationally relevant to development administration. We assume here the uneven rate of development of skills in various institutions and sectors of the social system,

155. Lasswell, "Conflict and Leadership: The Process of Decision and the Nature of Authority," p. 211.

156. George Ukita, *Foundations of Constitutional Government in Modern Japan 1868–1900* (Cambridge, Mass., 1967), p. 292.

157. Richard D. Robinson, *The First Turkish Republic* (Cambridge, Mass., 1963), pp. 87–92. See also Lord Kinross, *Ataturk, A Biography of Mustafa Kemal, Father of Modern Turkey* (New York, 1965).

described earlier in this chapter. The generalist sector of bureaucratic institutions must be able to absorb superior technological competences from whatever other sectors and institutions are productive of them. This fluidity may thus set up internal tensions and irritants leading to innovation. A correlative proposition is that a delicate balance must be maintained between infusion of new ideas and maintaining a cohesion compatible with architectonics sufficient to permit the bureaucratic system to maintain a high degree of autonomy within the political system. For, as was suggested earlier as an aspect of our first index of institutional "effectiveness," bureaucracy must maintain relative autonomy of ethos and structure while also maintaining synaptic connections with the total social order.

A third proposition concerns the relationship of technical specialists to generalists within the bureaucracy. The specialist should have parity of esteem and perquisities and his role in policy-making should be maximized. Structural devices can enhance this relationship, but ultimately the specialist's status can be improved only when an empirical disposition and technical qualifications are more highly regarded in the whole social order. Nevertheless, the admission of technical expertness into the arena of policy-making is likely to produce a condition of intellectual ferment and tension conducive to innovation. We assume here greater effervescence toward innovation on the part of the specialist. This may be the consequence of close identity with professional norms and professional zeal. Under certain conditions, however, the impetus for change may come from the generalist rather than the specialist. Structures must be built in such a way that the impetus for innovation can be captured from both generalist and specialist sources and so that each can stimulate rather than depress the other.

A fourth proposition is that there must be a delicate balance between the prestige, confidence, and power enjoyed by the bureaucracy on the one hand and the tension and uncertainty produced by the rise of countervailing loci of power within the political system. This is obviously a very difficult balance to achieve because it involves a kind of acrobatic prowess, that is, the creation and maintenance of tension at the brink of instability. This condition also serves to restrain bureaucratic excess, but the consequence we are concerned with here is the creation of a matrix in which there is a facile interchange of ethos, norms, and technology. In such a context the rise of such movements as community or rural development and of government corporations is important. Even though the claims of such movements to a skill or disposition capable of superceding conventional bureaucratic power may be exaggerated, the effervescence of such claims may have an irritating effect and may result in a transfer of norms and skill. The jostling consequent to the movement in transfer may sedate the effervescence sufficiently to enhance ecological adjustment.

Fifth, change may be enhanced by the stimulation of substantive, objective professional standards of performance, the linkage (both institutional and intellectual) of these standards with extranational or international norms, and the continual reinvigoration of these standards by contact with their source. At least three consequences are likely to flow from this linkage system. (1) Professional attitudes of highly developed technical systems such as medicine, engineering, and public health, are likely to make an impact on administrative and political attitudes generally. Insofar as such attitudes reflect respect for erudition, precision, planning, and empiricism, such attitudinal interchange is likely to be beneficial. (2) The rise of professional competences which are superior to the general bureaucratic competence may create new demands of prestige and power capable of producing a response in general bureaucratic competence moving toward improvement. (3) Another effect may be that the ancillary administrative technology which is part of each substantive professional field (such as health administration, educational administration, agricultural administration) may be fused with the larger administrative technology and may accelerate its development. It is often the case that ancillary technologies are more highly developed than the major technology; when there is such disparity, there would be advantage in rediffusing the disparate competences.

Sixth, probably the most important means of stimulating creativity is by institutionalizing an arena in which both learning and adaptation of new technologies occur. While the adaptations may be highly imperfect and a good deal of pedagogical waste may ensue, the ferment of intellectual change within a manageable context may conduce to innovation. In this arena of diffusion, the role of the generalist and the specialist as intellectual and as bureaucratic elites is crucial. The stage is thus set for symbiosis. The generalist's conception of the larger societal values and the specialist's rigor and empirical disposition are elements in that symbiotic process. Again there must be a link between the arena and the radiating source of the new technology and ideas so that the process may be continually invigorated. There should also be links between the newly instructed agent of change and the intellectual sources from which such change emanates. These links can take the form of professional associations, journals, meetings, or manipulation of symbols. When, because of insulation of institutions or sectors owing to caste factors or closed recruitment practices, there is little or no transfer of persons from one to another, the importance of links of this kind is very great. The temporary jostling of people in a planned program of intellectual exchange may well be the exclusive means of transferring norms and values from one institution to another.

A seventh proposition is the deliberate identification of innovation with the traditional sources of bureaucratic power and the establishment of an operating network of procedures and sanctions from which no bureaucratic entity can escape. This appears especially relevant when strata isolation limits effective sources of innovation to upper echelons. Crozier emphasizes this point even for the agencies of the French bureaucracy he studied.[158]

An eighth proposition relates to the strategic use of the capacities of individuals with empathy and creativity. Perhaps we must think in terms of the creative, innovative mind as against the static mind. Some preliminary distinctions are necessary. Empathy refers to the mental characteristic of being able to view the universe from the point of view of someone else and thereby to appreciate new opinions and ideas and to integrate such change

158. Michel Crozier, *The Bureaucratic Phenomenon* (Chicago, 1964), p. 196.

into one's own behavior.[159] Closely related to empathy but perhaps not identical to it is what Inkeles calls individual modernity. A significant study in which he collaborated suggests that "men everywhere have the same structural mechanisms underlying their socio-psychic functioning, despite the enormous variability of the culture content which they embody."[160] The implications of this finding are startling: they suggest that a universal means of testing modernity disposition is now available. Through its use persons amenable to change can be identified and the effect of institutions and planned change on individuals can be measured. These are essential prerequisites to evaluation of effective change through institutions. We now have some evidence from psychology set into a political context by McClelland[161] and by Lerner[162] to suggest qualities of empathy which may conduce to innovation in large structures. McClelland has characterized this quality as the spirit of Hermes, a characterization inspired by the Faustian "will" described by Oswald Spengler.[163]

While these observations may suggest differences of considerable magnitude in the possession of empathy by individuals, the relationship of such personal qualities to organizational change is less than clear. The problem of inducing innovation or change in institutions is more complex. We may assume that persons of empathy and modernity inclination are essential to the process.

159. For a general review of the issues, see Press and Arian (eds.), *Empathy and Ideology.*

160. David Horton Smith and Alex Inkeles, "The OM Scale: A Comparative Socio-Psychological Measure of Individual Modernity," *Sociometry,* XXIX (1966), 353–377, at 377. For a more general survey of personal modernization, see Alex Inkeles, "The Modernization of Man," in Myron Weiner (ed.), *Modernization* (New York, 1966), pp. 138–150. See also Howard Schuman, *Economic Development and Individual Change: A Social-Psychological Study of the Comilla Experiment in Pakistan,* Harvard University Occasional Papers in International Affairs, Number 15 (February, 1967). This significant study suggests that "modernity" attitudes of peasants can, in certain rural social organizations, equal or surpass those of city dwellers.

161. David C. McClelland, *The Achieving Society* (Princeton, 1961).

162. Daniel Lerner, *The Passing of Traditional Society* (Cambridge, 1958).

163. McClelland, *The Achieving Society,* pp. 301–336. The Faustian "soul" described by Spengler is placed in opposition to the Apollinian soul. Spengler associates the Faustian soul with "pure and limitless space . . . ; the art of the fugue . . . ; painting that . . . forms space by means of light and shade . . . ; space . . . a spiritual something rigidly distinct from the momentary sense-present . . ." (Oswald Spengler, *The Decline of the West* [New York, 1939], I, 183–184).

The ability to think imaginatively and creatively is essential. We are by no means certain that empathy, modernity inclination, creativity, and innovation are sufficiently similar phenomena to deal with them collectively. Yet so little is known about them that we risk here dealing with them as a group of closely related emotional- intellectual characteristics. Warshay's study, for example, suggests that the person with intellectual qualities of creativity may not be organic to society in the usual sense, hence his innovative capacity may not be easily translatable into social change.[164] It may be, therefore, that we must think in terms of innovators and managers of innovation distributed strategically in decision-making centers. This notion of the management of innovation is akin to though probably not identical to Crozier's observation that the bureaucratic innovator is "a legislator, a Solon type, rather than a discoverer. He is someone who will once again put everyone in his own place, who will reorder the world in a better way, rather than someone who will launch new patterns, new ways, of doing things."[165] But surely there must be a source for such innovation. It may be, however, that merely locating such persons in an organization is not sufficient. Lasswell has reminded us of the "collective character of creativity" and of its dependence on "context completion."[166] He makes this observation in relation to research, but it may be pertinent as well to innovation in the bureaucracies of developing systems. Friedrich similarly asserts that political innovation is typically a group process presupposing participation: "the wider has been the participation in government, and the wider consequently freedom of participation, the more numerous have become the proposals for innovation, as well as their adoption."[167] What we are suggesting are institutional arrangements designed to facilitate only as much integration and co-ordination as is necessary to enhance creativ-

164. Leon H. Warshay, "Breadth of Perspective and Social Change," in George K. Zollschan and Walter Hirsch (eds.), *Explorations in Social Change* (New York, 1964), pp. 319–345.
165. Crozier, *The Bureaucratic Phenomenon*, p. 201.
166. For a survey of the literature on creativity as well as for a brief analysis of its cultivation, see Harold D. Lasswell, *The Future of Political Science* (New York, 1963), pp. 147–166.
167. Friedrich, *Man and His Government*, p. 375.

ity without stifling it. The achievement of this delicate balance may well be a mark of executive genius.

The ninth and final point is not really a proposition, for we are too uncertain about it to formalize it so. It relates to the effect of crisis on change. It may be that under certain conditions, crisis may conduce to innovation. Leighton, in his analysis of a Japanese Relocation Center in the late 1940's, observed that disarticulation in social organization and disintegration of belief systems conduce to bewilderment and easy acceptance of change. Stress, he asserts, alters social organization; social disorganization increases stress. But he notes also that severe stress and extensive disorganization lead to a violent form of reorganization.[168] Crozier regards crisis as a major source of change in the agencies of the French bureaucracy which he studied:

> The essential rhythm prevalent in bureaucracy is, therefore, an alternation of long periods of stability with very short periods of crisis and change. Most analyses of the bureaucratic phenomenon refer only to periods of routine—put this is a partial image. Crisis is a distinctive and necessary element of the bureaucratic system. During crisis individual initiative prevails and people eventually come to depend on some strategic individual's arbitrary whim. Forgotten, strained dependence relationships reappear. Personal authority supercedes rules.[169]

Crozier relates this only to the French system and does not suggest that it has prescriptive value for other systems. Nevertheless, his perceptive analysis of the French system leads us to raise questions about the role of crisis in change in developing systems. In one sense we can say that developing systems are in a state of chronic crisis: that is, one of the characteristics which makes them "developing" rather than "developed" is disequilibrium. There is violent fluctuation in the quantity and nature of demands. Institutions in the system modify functions, absorbing or at least handling varying categories of demands at unsteadily fluctuating rates. If this is not crisis, at least it is stress. The

168. Alexander Leighton, *The Governing of Men* (Princeton, 1946), pp. 328–340.

169. Crozier, *The Bureaucratic Phenomenon*, p. 196.

experience of Pakistan leads us to observe that the more severe and widespread the stress, the more reliance is placed on the system known best. This might suggest that there are varying levels of crisis—some conducing to greater rigidity, others to innovation.

III. A General Strategy for External Inducement of Political and Administrative Growth

General considerations

The foregoing analysis suggests the inevitability of highly differential growth rates for various institutions relevant to a political system. An issue which has concerned some students of political development is the danger of strengthening the public bureaucracy with the help of foreign assistance to a degree inimical to the growth of other institutions, thereby impeding the maturation of a strong, effective political process. It was with some alarm that several students warned that administrative change without accompanying political reform may have undesirable effects on the larger contextual developmental effort.[170] While there was some argument against too extreme an expression of that view and advocacy of the notion that "administrative reform must proceed irrespective of the maturation of the political proc-

170. Lucian W. Pye, "The Political Content of National Development," in Irving Swerdlow (ed.), *Development Administration: Concepts and Problems* (Syracuse, N.Y., 1963), pp. 25–45. On p. 33 Pye states: "Our analysis suggests, however, that public administration cannot be greatly improved without a parallel strengthening of the representative political processes. In fact, excessive concentration on strengthening the administrative services may be self-defeating because it may lead only to a greater imbalance between the administrative and the political and hence to a greater need of the leaders to exploit politically the administrative services." This point of view is also taken in Fred W. Riggs, "Relearning an Old Lesson: The Political Context of Development Administration," *Public Administration Review*, XXV (1965), 70–79, and in his "Bureaucrats and Political Development: A Paradoxical View," in Joseph LaPalombara (ed.), *Bureaucracy and Political Development* (Princeton, 1963), pp. 120–168. There it is succinctly stated: "premature or too rapid expansion of the bureaucracy when the political system lags behind tends to inhibit the development of effective politics. A corollary thesis holds that separate political institutions have a better chance to grow if bureaucratic institutions are relatively weak" (p. 126). See also Riggs's "Economic Development and Local Administration," *Philippine Journal of Public Administration*, III (1959), 86–145.

ess,"[171] it has been clear that there was disarticulation between doctrine and practice of administrative reform on the one hand and doctrine and practice of political reform on the other. The paradigm implied by the 1967 Foreign Assistance Act is one which permits both an increase of popular participation and the strengthening of institutions. First it should be made clear that we here take the position that the strenghtening of the bureaucratic system is a primary requisite for development. This appears to be self-evident and to require little elaboration. It was put thus by Sir W. Arthur Lewis: "A good Civil Service is thus even to some extent a prerequisite of rapid growth. . . . Development planning is hardly practicable until a country has established a Civil Service capable of implementing plans."[172] The demands of a sovereign political system on the apparatus of public administration appear to increase at a faster pace than does the capability of the total political system. The mere fact of independence and acceptance of external foreign assistance escalates such responsibilities. An expanding capability to convert such demands into administrative action is a fundamental state function. The capacity to act while innovating in the context of technological advance has been suggested in this chapter as a characteristic of development. The acceptance of foreign assistance requires the concentration of the highest bureaucratic, negotiating, and technological skills at the point of impact—in the

171. Ralph Braibanti, "Administrative Reform in the Context of Political Growth," in Riggs (ed.), *Frontiers of Development Administration*. This position is taken also by Ferrel Heady in his "Bureaucracies in Developing Countries: Internal Roles and External Assistance," and by Milton J. Esman, "Development Administration as a Profession," both papers presented at the Brookings Institution conference at Williamsburg in May, 1965. A further expression of these views can be found in Heady's *Public Administration: A Comparative Perspective* (Englewood Cliffs, N.J., 1966), and in Esman's "The Ecological Style in Comparative Administration," *Public Administration Review*, XXVII (1967), 271–278. These views are cogently analyzed and to some extent shared by Joseph LaPalombara in his "Theory and Practice in Development Administration: Observations on the Role of the Civilian Bureaucracy." See also LaPalombara's "Alternative Strategies for Developing Administrative Capabilities in Emerging Nations," in Riggs (ed.), *Frontiers of Development Administration*. The views of the present writer and Riggs are analyzed and presumably "reconciled" by Inayatullah, "Intra-Polity Balance and Bureaucratic and Political Development in the Framework of a Theory of Sub-Systems," a paper presented at the administrative development seminar of the Southeast Asia Development Advisory Group at Carmel, California, November 24, 1967.

172. W. Arthur Lewis, *Development Planning* (New York, 1966), p. 100.

planning, economic, external affairs, and other "nation-building" entities in administration. Foreign technical assistance profoundly aggravates the need for a viable bureaucracy, a fact which has not been widely appreciated.[173] Foreign assistance has been adversely criticized for assisting too much in developing the bureaucracy, but this has been a necessary consequence of solving a problem which the phenomenon of assistance has in itself created. On the other hand, the impact of foreign assistance on the differential rates of growth of institutions has been appreciated; it is this appreciation which is implicit in Title IX and its related provisions.

Our assumption in this chapter is that the strategic strengthening of as many institutions, sectors, and structures as possible is desirable. We suggest that administrative reform is not an autonomous process. It has a permeative effect on other institutions and structures and it may serve as a generant in the growth of those sectors. This is implicit in the analytical construct of seven indices for determining institutional, sectoral, and structural competences elaborated in Section II of this chapter.

A strategy which is suggested by the Title IX challenge and by the analysis of four aspects of political development in Section II of this chapter is based on the peculiar needs and responsibilities of administration in developing systems. It further presupposes the need for balancing the power of bureaucracy with other institutional restraints and the need also of avoiding a demand-conversion crisis.

There are practical limits on the types of institutions which can be strengthened by foreign assistance. Huntington's proposal to assist actively in strengthening political parties and training party

173. The role of foreign relations in internal development has been given too little attention. "It is not unusual," says Lasswell, "in the study of development to give insufficient emphasis to external power relations. . . . It is clear that political modernization is not to be achieved by progressive withdrawal from world politics" ("The Policy Sciences of Development," p. 292). Lasswell does not refer to foreign aid as an aspect of world politics in this analysis. But, certainly, it cannot be excluded. In some instances (e.g., India, Pakistan, Vietnam, Korea) it is the fulcrum in which external power politics is balanced or unbalanced; in any case, it is likely to be a factor in world politics, of varying relevance, to be sure, but a factor to be reckoned with nevertheless. This assumption is the theme of John D. Montgomery, *Foreign Aid in International Politics* (Englewood Cliffs, N.J., 1967).

leaders seems questionable at best.[174] In his testimony before the House committee he used the term "parties." In his earlier advocacy of this point of view, he contended that a single dominant mass party was probably more appropriate for developing systems, but he did not totally rule out a two-party system.[175] If we can extrapolate this presupposition and apply it to his testimony in which his preference of the single mass party or two parties is only inferred, the suggestion that we support a party or perhaps two parties may have some merit. But in new states in which there are more than two parties or in which there are two parties very unevenly balanced in power, active support of party organizations by the United States seems especially dangerous. If all parties were supported equally, this might encourage a proliferation of new parties, the very condition (Huntington warns us) which is conducive to instability. Moreover, indiscriminate support of all valid parties would place the United States in the untenable position of supporting party organizations which actively oppose crucial principles of American foreign policy. Some, ironically, even oppose American foreign assistance. Moreover, we would either have to support Communist parties (as in India, especially Kerala) or discriminate against Communist parties, thus aggravating internal tensions. Certainly the reconciliation of American support of such groups with the foreign policy objectives of American foreign assistance would require remarkable powers of imaginative interpretation on the part of American political leadership. On the other hand, if only certain parties were "certified" by the United States and selected for assistance, difficult situations would arise. The mere act of selection would interfere in the natural evolution of creative, orderly political renovation which can best be provided by unfettered creation of parties arising from legitimate needs for articulating shifting interests. What criteria would be used for "deselecting" parties? The designation "democratic" political parties is hardly adequate to support such

174. See above, nn. 46, 47.

175. See Huntington, "Political Development and Political Decay": "If sufficient resources are available to support more than one well-organized party, that is all to the good. . . . Modernizing states with multiparty systems are much more unstable and prone to military intervention than modernizing states with one party, with one dominant party or with two parties" (p. 427).

a classification. We might refuse to support parties discouraged by the government in power (which would mean all but one party); we might not certify chauvinistic, tradition-oriented groups such as the Jamaat-i-Islami of Pakistan or the Jana Sangh or Akali Dal of India. This might be done on the ground that these parties were "backward looking" and therefore detrimental to modernization. How then could we cope with the problem of transformation in party disposition? One of the characteristics of parties in developing states is the fluidity of coalitions based primarily on personal loyalty groups rather than on ideological issues. Parties change while out of office and when in power, as is clearly shown by the more liberal tone of the Jana Sangh in India in recent years. To deny a party support on the basis of past or present attitudes is to deny it the freedom to transform itself in response to the changing contours of its constituency or simply to changing times. On the other hand, to offer support to parties for specific attitudes would be to tempt all parties to recast their views in the same mold. To discriminate against certain kinds of parties, such as those deemed to be tradition oriented and anti-modern, might upset the ecological balance of the total social order. The existence of tradition-oriented parties is a leavening influence in the process of articulating modernization to tradition. The mere existence of traditional groups with some but not too much power may enforce a restraint and regard for ancient heritage from which a felicitous ecological adaptation might spring. The deliberate support of parties (either all of them or a few "certified" groups) in the manner proposed by Huntington requires probing in the most delicate tissues of the social system. Such probing is not and cannot be consistent with postcolonial sensitivities regarding sovereignty.

Finally, in some instances the support of political parties by foreign sources is clearly prohibited by law. This is the case in Pakistan, where "no person shall form, organise, set up or convene a foreign aided party or in any way be associated with any such party."[176] The phrase "foreign aided political party" is de-

176. Political Parties Act (III of 1962) 3 (2), *Gazette of Pakistan, Extraordinary*, July 16, 1962.

fined as one which has been organized at the instance of or is affiliated with any government or party of a foreign country or receives financial or other aid from any government or political party of a foreign country or a substantial portion of its funds from foreign nationals.[177] Such a statutory provision as this would obviously make foreign help to parties an act promoting illegality.

It is likely that this advocacy of party manipulation arises, as has been suggested, from the assumption that most developing states have two fairly evenly balanced parties of similar competence and sense of responsibility alternating in power at regular intervals. This observation is suggested by the comments of Representative Bradford Morse of Massachusetts, whose vigorous espousal of Title IX in the 1966 Foreign Assistance Act included advocacy of training of foreign parties by the Republican and Democratic parties of the United States.[178]

It is doubtful if the complexities of political life embedded in totally different linguistic, cultural, and religious values can be adequately understood by foreign entities. This would seem particularly true in evaluations made of the viability of various regimes based on such dubious and ethnocentric criteria as "representativeness," "modernizing capability," and "popularity." This has been amply demonstrated by the naïveté manifested in dealing with various regimes in Vietnam.

Having cast doubt on the utility of dealing directly with political parties as a strategy of Title IX, we now propose consideration of specific positive aspects of strategy.

Structural ambiguity

The direct confrontation of newly enfranchised masses with crucial political issues hardly seems possible in systems where elite perceptions and mass perceptions of architectonics are in disparate stages of development, i.e., in a torn or multifurcated society. Such direct confrontation would be likely to result in a demand-conversion crisis. The public bureaucracy is the principal institution for the conversion of such demands after they have

177. *Ibid.*, 1(b).
178. *Congressional Record—House,* July 13, 1966, p. 14776.

been processed by electoral and legislative institutions. Herein lies its relationship with the whole political system. Imbalance can be moderated either by reducing demand incidence, modifying demand content, or by increasing bureaucratic capability to handle the demand crisis.[179] Where bureaucratic strengthening occurs, it must be done within the general restraints imposed by the architectonics and without total retraction of power diffusion if, in fact, diffusion is a commitment. This delicate balance, extraordinarily difficult to achieve, is crucial to the maturation of political systems. In developing systems, spontaneous adjustment to acute imbalance has assumed various forms. In India, we find containment, diversion, and sedation of demands by the spatially diffuse and substantively competent single mass party. In Pakistan, similar consequences are achieved by indirect elections and by near-paramountcy of juridico-administrative norms. Elsewhere we witness total or partial suspension of participative behaviors and dominance of authoritarian oligarchies, usually military. The elaboration of the process of such adjustment, its contextual relevance, and its ultimate political consequences are crucial research objectives for which the disciplines of political science and law are now ready.

We are concerned here with the adjustment the administrative system makes to the political system. Such adjustment may be spontaneous or contrived. We have already mentioned some of the forms such adjustment may assume. Virtually no systematic studies of the adjustment mechanisms have been made. One such adjustment which has intriguing explanatory power is the construct of ambiguity. Structural ambiguity may contribute to the use of power in a manner inconsonant with constitutional or architectonic intent. It permits power to be exercised unpredictably by persons who through deceit, casuistry, or secrecy are the sole possessors of the map with which power can be channeled through labyrinths of darkness. The context created by structural ambiguity can be used positively as a device of control and is

179. The concept of demand-conversion crisis and the notion of "mechanisms" (e.g., structural, cultural, and communication), for regulating "want conversion" is derivative from David Easton, *A Systems Analysis of Political Life* (New York, 1965), pp. 85–149.

commonly used in all administration as a means of power. Uncertainty, unease, ambivalence, diffusion of responsibility through alternate invocation of committee jurisdiction and single officer jurisdiction: these and other variations are common even though ultimately counterproductive devices of power in church, business, university, and public administration. Ambiguity of architectonics and structure is and can be used effectively in regulating the demand-conversion crisis. Consider the case of Pakistan. The new political system is suspended between a parliamentary and a presidential system and is based on an ambiguous distribution of legislative powers as between central and provincial governments. Such ambiguity is neatly illustrated by the 1964 preventive detention cases in Pakistan involving Maulana Maudoudi and the ultra-orthodox Muslim group, the Jamaat-e-Islami. Preventive detention is the concern of two levels of government. The Jamaat-e-Islami was disbanded and certain leaders arrested in two provinces under different laws, both central and provincial. Moreover, the ambiguous powers of the governors acting as agents of the president confused the situation. The mixture of actions made it impossible to focus accountability. It demolished the possibility of legislative oversight, since each legislature ruled out discussion of crucial aspects of the case—aspects which it was impossible to separate. Begum Shamsun Nahar Mahmood, a member of the National Assembly, identified this confusion of responsibility aptly when she said, "if some question about preventive detention is asked . . . the Central Government refer it to the provincial government . . . if provincial authorities are approached they in turn refer it to the Central Government."[180] In the context of such ambiguity, the role of the judiciary is critical simply because it is the only agency in the whole political system capable of dealing with the totality of such actions and thus spreading an umbrella of normative uniformity over an assortment of actions not otherwise amenable to control and crucially at variance with the architectonics of the state. We have suggested that such structural ambiguity can be beneficial in that it regulates demands by putting them through baffles. But this is

180. Pakistan National Assembly *Debates*, July 5, 1962, p. 1066.

probably a short-run benefit. In the long run, excessive ambiguity may damage the social system. A mature political system must be characterized by clarity of policy, focused accountability, courageous acceptance of decision-making by officials, and a high degree of rationality. The dangers of spontaneous, whimsical, or capricious action must be balanced not by structural ambiguity but by countervailing loci of power, each with enough autonomy to be resilient and gently resistant, and each maintaining boundaries of insulation rather than merging ignominiously into a haze of interlocking structures. The effects of ambiguity may appear as a syndrome: frustration, alienation, withdrawal from political life, violence. The quantum of alienation resulting from ambiguity needs to be measured. It is probably a significant source of counterproductivity in the whole political process. The ultimate danger of structural ambiguity as a regulating device lies in the frustration such ambiguity engenders. Frustration leads to repressed and often simmering animosity against power and eventually to violent action, which may then bring crisis to the political system. The evidence for this in political systems is overwhelming. The role of ambiguity both as regulator and as an agitator of crisis has not been studied. Theoretically, there may be an articulated progression—a gradual decrease of ambiguity as a system matures. Perhaps this is what is occurring in Pakistan. We would need to know why such ambiguity decreases. Do law and the judiciary conduce to its decrease, as we suspect they do, or to its increase? This calls for careful microanalysis of legal and administrative structure and of the substance of all public decisions. It calls for measurement of how much and what kind of ambiguity is desirable and at what point it ceases to be an effective regulator of crisis and becomes instead an agitator of crisis. Studies dealing with personal aspects of confrontation with ambiguity rather than its role in a macroinstitutional context as described here are suggestive.[181] Such studies demonstrate (1) the recognition accorded to ambiguity as a variable in manage-

181. Daniel Ellsburg, "Risk, Ambiguity and the Savage Axioms," *Quarterly Journal of Economics,* LXXV (1961), 643–669, and Selwyn W. Becker and Fred O. Brownson, "What Price Ambiguity? or the Role of Ambiguity in Decision-Making," *Journal of Political Economy,* LXXII (1964), 62–73.

ment and (2) the measurability of some of its manifestations. The hypothesis that in personal relations in decision-making some subjects "express an aversion to ambiguity, and under payoff conditions will pay to avoid it" may have potential relevance to our discussion here. For example, it is not inconceivable that this aversion at a personal level may be related to (may even be transferrable as) the frustration syndrome in the institutional context described in this chapter. We are involved here with questionable analogies between individual and social psychology which, of course, require verification before they can be formally stated.

Legislatures

The effect of structural ambiguity may, in the short run, be the dampening or scattering of demands, thus temporarily relieving the strain on overburdened institutions. A more positive means of making participation more effective, rationalizing demands, and at the same time exerting control over bureaucracies which may be too powerful is that of giving attention to legislative bodies. For the sake of perspective, let us consider what little political development doctrine we can cull from the seven-and-a-half-year occupation of Japan starting in 1945.[182] The official political doc-

182. One of the discontinuities of American political science scholarship is the absence in political development theory of reassessments of the induced political development of Japan, Korea, and Okinawa from 1945 to 1952 in terms of subsequent evolution of the quasi-doctrine which has emerged from post-1947 (largely South Asian and African) experience. It may be that the deliberate, rapid strengthening of political institutions in Japan is one of the significant differences between that country's development and that of ex-colonial states. Ordering of the Japanese experience would certainly be a necessary first step in such comparative analysis. The perceptive and systematic treatment by Robert E. Ward, "Political Modernization and Political Culture in Japan," *World Politics,* XV (1963), 569–596, focuses on the Meiji restoration rather than on post-1945 phenomena. In Robert Ward and Dankwart Rustow (eds.), *Political Modernization of Japan and Turkey* (Princeton, 1964), there is no separate, coherent description or analysis of the technique of inducing development in Japan during the seven-and-a-half-year occupation. In Masamichi Inoke's chapter on bureaucracy, one and three-quarters pages out of eighteen pages deal with the post-World War II bureaucracy. Other chapters on Japan give the occupation even less attention. Nor has this condition been remedied by a conference held under auspices of the Committee on Comparative Politics of the Social Science Research Council. For a preliminary account, see Robert E. Ward, "Military Occupations and Political Change: A Conference Held in New York, April 20–22, 1967," Social Science Research Council, *Items,* XXI (1967), 25–29. Some of the papers presented at that conference were published in *Public Policy,* XVII (1968). They are: Carl J.

trine written by General MacArthur's staff states categorically, "A truly representative legislative body, based upon universal adult suffrage, responsible to the electorate, free of domination by the executive, and having full legislative powers, including control over the raising and spending of all public moneys, is a primary requisite of any blueprint for democracy under a representative form of government."[183] Subsequently, the constitution of 1946—still in force two decades later—declared the Diet to be the "highest organ of state power" and the "sole law-making organ of the State."[184] Evidence concerning the actual positions of power of the Diet and bureaucracy is conflicting, but it appears certain that bureaucratic power has been at least partially contained by the strengthening of the Diet. Burks, describing the role of the investigative powers of the special committee on administrative supervision, concludes that the Diet has curbed what had been unlimited bureaucratic power.[185] On the other hand, interviews with Diet members in 1963 reveal that some legislators feel themselves prisoners of the bureaucracy; yet some bureaucrats feel the Diet is meddlesome.[186] There is also a growing co-operation or "connivance" between political parties and bureaucracy, and this may ultimately affect the essential autonomy of the Diet and the administration.[187] In Japan the high legal status of the Diet is indicated by comparison of their salaries with those of civil servants. Members of the Diet in 1967 received a total remuneration of the equivalent of $11,840 annually; the highest ranking civil

---

Friedrich, "The Legacies of the Occupation of Germany"; Leonard Krieger, "The Potential for Democratization in Occupied Germany: A Problem in Historical Projection"; Peter H. Merkl, "Allied Strategies of Effecting Political Change and Their Reception in Occupied Germany"; Hugh Seton-Watson, "Soviet Occupation in Roumania, Bulgaria and Hungary"; Robert E. Ward, "The Potential for Democratization in Prewar Japan"; Richard L. Merritt, "Political Division and Municipal Services in Postwar Berlin." It should be that none of these papers deals with political development in occupied Japan.

183. Government Section, Supreme Commander for the Allied Powers, *Political Reorientation of Japan* (Washington, 1949), I, 145.

184. Constitution of Japan, Art. 41.

185. Ardath Burks, *The Government of Japan* (2nd ed.; New York, 1964), p. 148.

186. Hans H. Baerwald, "Parliament and Parliamentarians in Japan," *Pacific Affairs,* XXXVII (1964), 271–282.

187. Tadao Okada, "The Unchanging Bureaucracy," *Japan Quarterly,* XII (1965), 168–176.

servant (administrative vice-minister) received $10,444.[188] This relationship between legislative and bureaucratic remuneration is almost identical to that which prevails in the United States from which the position of the Diet was adapted.

Little is known of legislative systems in developing states,[189] hence we cannot venture broad comparisons. But the contrast among Japan and India and Pakistan is suggestive. With respect to constitutional elevation of the legislative entity as the "highest organ of the state," there is no comparable provision in the first (1956) or the second (1962) constitution of Pakistan or in the (1949) constitution of India, or in the Constituent Assembly debates of India and Pakistan or in the report of the (1961) Constitution Commission of Pakistan. It may well be that had the legislatures in India and Pakistan been so unequivocally elevated in status without the political preconditions found in Japan, there would have been total disintegration of the system. Perhaps the very ambiguity of the legislative process and the inheritance of a dominant bureaucracy saved the situation. Be that as it may, we submit here that when a certain level of bureaucratic competence and power has been reached, the rapid strengthening of the legislative branch is an effective means of controlling bureaucratic power and linking the bureaucracy with the legislature in a common architectonics. We do not mean to put excessive reliance on the legislative process; it must effectively represent the public

188. I am indebted to Masaru Fukuda, Japanese director of the Asian Development Bank in Manila, for these figures. The same sort of comparison was true in the 1950's as well. See Chitoshi Yanaga, *Japanese People and Politics* (New York, 1956), p. 188.

189. This was noted in Jean Meynaud, "General Study of Parliamentarians," *International Social Science Journal*, XIII (1961). Another effort to present comparative data is *Payments and Privileges of Commonwealth Parliamentarians* published by the Commonwealth Parliamentary Association (London, 1965), compiled and edited by Ian Grey and Louis Marriott.

This condition of scarcity of data on legislatures has been partially remedied by an international conference on legislative bodies held by the Comparative Administration Group of the American Society for Public Administration under contract with the Agency for International Development at Planting Fields, New York, in December, 1967. The objective of this conference was to analyze research needs for study of legislative-bureaucratic relations in developing states. Conference papers will appear in Allan Kornberg and Lloyd Musolf (eds.), *Legislatures in Developmental Perspective* (Durham, N.C., forthcoming).

and must be connected to it by mediating processes—especially parties.[190]

The remuneration in India and Pakistan for the legislative profession also stands in marked contrast to that of Japan and the United States. In Pakistan, a central government legislator receives a little less than one-fourth of the remuneration of the senior-most civil servant. In India, the equivalent remuneration is about one-sixth.[191] This relationship is somewhat closer to that of the United Kingdom, where a member of Parliament receives about 37 per cent of the salary of the highest ranking civil servant (permanent secretary: £8,600; M.P.: £3,250 per year).[192] This situation in the United Kingdom makes it obvious that we cannot establish a correlation between parliamentary prestige and remuneration which is universally valid. Prestige in the British system apparently bears little relationship to remuneration. Yet this prestige derives from circumstances not now duplicated in developing states where prestige must be constructed by the incentives and symbols which have currency in the contemporary scale of values. These are essentially those of remuneration and power reciprocally related. They are not those of artistocratic or landed antecedents in a slowly evolving system. Another indicator of legislative status is the significant transfer of Japanese bureaucrats to the Diet. About 20 per cent of the members of both houses of the Diet are former bureaucrats, and the overwhelming majority of the most influential members are former bureaucrats,[193] in marked contrast to the situation in India and especially in Pakistan. In the latter country, while several former civil servants held ministerial appointments

190. See especially Helio Jaguaribe, *Economic and Political Development: A Theoretical Approach and a Brazilian Case Study* (Cambridge, Mass., 1968), pp. 50 ff.

191. In India, an M.P. receives Rs.500 a month and the highest ranking civil servant Rs.3,000 a month. In Pakistan, the salary of a member of the National Assembly was raised to Rs.700 in 1967; the highest ranking civil servant receives Rs.3,000 per month.

192. *British Imperial Calendar and Civil Service List 1967* (London, 1967), pp. 844, 846.

193. Masamichi Inoki, "The Civil Bureaucracy: Japan," in Ward and Rustow (eds.), *Political Modernization of Japan and Turkey*, p. 298. Beardsley reports that between 1954 and 1961, 35 per cent of the cabinet members were former bureaucrats (Richard K. Beardsley and John W. Hall [eds.], *Twelve Doors to Japan* [New York, 1965], p. 474).

at various times, no member of the elite cadre—the ICS or its successor service, the CSP—has been or is now a member of the National Assembly or the two provincial assemblies. In India, the situation is somewhat but not much different. In the fourth Lok Sabha elected in 1967, four members of the total 521 were former members of the ICS.[194] In the three previous Lok Sabhas, former ICS members numbered one or two in each session.[195] Despite this current situation, the attractiveness of politics as a profession, and thus of legislative work, appears to be increasing in India. Singhvi characterizes legislative politics as "highly prestigious, ranking prominently near the top in the hierarchy of power-oriented social elites,"[196] and Suri asserts that "the social prestige accruing to members of parliament (as to members of the state legislatures) is a strong inducement to the ambitious."[197]

The increase in legislative prestige in India has occurred probably because of rapid politicization. It may be that politics because of its power has gained in status and that legislative work as the natural habitat of successful politicians has simply reflected this. In India, moreover, some effort has been made to improve the prestige of legislators and critical, scholarly attention is directed toward this condition by the establishment of the Institute of Constitutional and Parliamentary Studies in Delhi. The Indian Parliament was roused to a sense of its potential power and its responsibility by the Life Insurance Corporation scandal of 1957 and the subsequent parliamentary inquiry. Certainly it would increase the efficiency of a legislature which had

194. These are N. Dandekar, C. C. Desai, J. M. Lobo Prakhu, of the Swatantra party, and K. K. Nair of the Jana Sangh. This information was secured through interviews by Willard Berry in New Delhi in July 1967. No *Lok Sabha Who's Who* for the 4th Lok Sabha has yet been published.

195. Even if one includes "services" generally, the percentages of former "service" members is low. The *Lok Sabha Souvenir 1962–1967* (New Delhi, 1967) lists the percentages of former service personnel: 1st Lok Sabha (1952–57) 3.7 per cent (N = 499); 2nd Lok Sabha (1957–62) 4.0 per cent (N = 486); 3rd Lok Sabha (1962–67) 0.9 per cent (N = 509). Most of these were from the military services, with a few from the state civil services.

196. L. M. Singhvi, "The Role of Parliament in the Indian Political System" p. 32, and "Legislative Services in India," papers presented at the development administration seminar of the Southeast Asia Development Advisory Group at Carmel, California, November 24, 1967.

197. Surinder S. Suri, "Political Life Cycle of Lok Sabha Members," *Journal of Constitutional and Parliamentary Studies,* I (1967), 30.

been accorded more actual power. In the case of states where the prestige is already high (as in India) structural rectification with or without prestigious remuneration can quickly build on high prestige a political entity of remarkable effectiveness.

The infrastructure of most parliamentary bodies in developing states can be vastly improved. Adequate office staff, committee staff, and a research service comparable to the Legislative Reference Service—all of which have been developed in Japan with American help—are needed. The state of affairs is rather dramatically symbolized in Turkey by the elegant and architecturally awesome legislative building with its superb chambers and luxurious library. Yet members have no offices and use the library as their rendezvous when there is not an actual session in the chambers. The object is to accord the legislature all the facilities necessary to rectify the imbalance which now exists in expertise—an imbalance heavily weighted on the side of the executive. Ultimately the consequence of this structural improvement will be more powerful and more rational control over bureaucracy and the gradual infusion into administrative decision-making of the basic polity reflected in the legislature. Rectification of the practice of delegated legislation, as was mentioned earlier in discussing the "Pan" case of Pakistan, would provide a more effective interplay and tension between the executive and legislative branches. Large segments of administrative action are made immune from legislative inquiry by the statute. A program of institutional strengthening might also include forming a unit for legislative drafting. Even a casual reading of statutes of legislatures in ex-colonial states inheriting the British tradition reveals an appalling state of affairs. The deliberate ambiguity and generality characteristic of an imperial era when it was intended to leave much to administration continues even two decades after independence. To these qualities have been added a certain carelessness of language and vagueness of style which are the consequence of lack of expertise in drafting. This condition invites administrative disorder and strains the judicial system forced to deal with a volume of litigation beyond its endurance, capacity, and in some instances, competence. In some systems drafting is done by ministers of law rather than by the legislature. In such systems help might be provided both the ministry and the legislature. The drafting unit of the latter might serve as a check on the former, thus asserting the expertness as well as the dominance of the legislative process. But there is nothing either in parliamentary or presidential practice to prevent the legislature from organizing large, efficient, competent drafting units staffed by men carefully trained in the technical aspects of drafting. After twenty years of independence, such units should be flourishing. It would only require, let us say, that each major legislature have fifty persons trained in Britain or the United States for three years. This would be a very small expenditure when contrasted with the expenditure for training persons to the A.M. and Ph.D. levels in community development and in other noble but less utilitarian specialties.

The powers given to administrative bodies to "regulate" continue to expand, with the crucial language (e.g., "to regulate") left undefined. The power to convene administrative tribunals without prescribing procedural niceties continues to expand. Ironically, while continuing to accord the executive almost unlimited and undefined discretion in what has become virtually a jungle of administrative lawlessness, the legislatures attack the bureaucracy for "usurpation of powers," "corruption," "inefficiency," and "lawlessness." Part of the problem, of course, is the parliamentary system (in India) or vestigial remnants of parliamentary practice within the presidential system in Pakistan and other states which have converted, wherein legislative drafting has been done by the executive following a tradition of broad and untrammeled executive power. This may have aggravated the demand-conversion crisis rather than contributed to structural rectification and efficiency of the system. Another consequence of the failure of legislatures to control administration is that the party process fills the need. Thus excessive intrusion of party politics in administration, while it does exert control over bureaucracy, may be so irrational that it weakens what little integrity the bureaucracy may possess. This condition may be aggravated in complex "federal" systems like that of India. For even if a central legislature were to exercise control over a cental bureaucracy, state legislatures would also have to be strengthened so that state politics would not enter the vacuum at that crucial level.

It is commonly argued in many developing states that corrupt politicians enter legislative politics and, to enhance their prestige and power would endanger government further; indeed, their power should be curtailed. But this is an argument without hope. Some contrived incentives can be used to entice able men into legislatures; in any event, a strong structure will ultimately be able to minimize the effect of incompetence or corruption. This after all is the essence of government—the mutual support which values, tradition, institutions, and human frailty give each other. This improvement in structure, especially committee structure, would also enhance the supervision of government corporations, which are now almost completely outside the ambit of control. With a more effective structural linkage, the role of the judiciary would be modified and presumably would focus more on broader, fundamental questions of architectonics than on litigation which arises because of the absence of proper legislative controls. Further, a legislative system articulated structurally to the behavior of bureaucracy is the natural and logical institutional fulfilment of mass participation in politics. It is conceivable that its effectiveness may be related to the strength of the party system and even to the use of other means of political expression, particularly agitational-confrontation politics. Finally, the improvement in legislative structure is likely to enhance the possibilities of bureaucratic innovation, an aspect of political development discussed earlier in this chapter. This possibility is related to the notion of interpermeability of norms discussed in connection with indices for evaluating institutional effectiveness. We may recall that in the development of the United States, management and fiscal standards in private commerce were much more advanced than in government and that when the Budget and Accounting Act was passed in 1921 heavy reliance was placed by General Charles G. Dawes, the first budget director, on private businessmen (especially those from Sears, Roebuck, such as Herbert M. Lord).[198] This kind of transfer of attitudes and skills from one institution to another (private commerce and civil bureaucracy) and from one sector to another (military bureaucracy and civil bureaucracy) has been a characteristic of American life. Further relevant examples are the spread of the general staff concept from military to civil public bureaucracy and the transfer of the Planning-Programming-Budgeting System, based on systems analysis, from the RAND Corporation to the Defense Department in 1961 and thence to the entire federal bureaucracy.[199] It is not inconceivable that a strengthened legislature in new states will provide a means for the absorption of skills and attitudes from other institutions and sectors which may be conducive to bureaucratic innovation. Such skills and attitudes if strategically articulated structurally to the bureaucracy may be able to force innovation which is difficult to generate internally. The role of American and British foreign aid in improving legislative capability has, except for meetings of the British Parliamentary Union, been virtually nil. During the Japanese occupation, the leadership exchange program of the Department of State sponsored carefully programmed study tours (not merely trips) of legislators, legislative reference staff, and committee staff from the Diet in the United States. The Legislative Reference Service in the contemporary Diet is almost identical to its counterpart in the United States. Yet of the thousands of people from developing states who have had short study tours under AID auspices in such specialities as administration, agriculture, and community development, few have been parliamentarians or others to study legislative structure and process. Nor have there been any AID contracts or other means whereby the immense experience of parliamentarianism can be systematically transferred to new systems.

198. See Charles G. Dawes, *The First Year of the Budget of the United States* (New York, 1923).

199. See *Public Administration Review*, XXVI (1966), 243–320, devoted to a symposium on "Planning-Programming Budgeting." See also Virginia Held, "PPBS Comes to Washington," *Public Interest*, No. 4 (1966), pp. 102–115, and the symposium, "PPBS: Its Scope and Limits," *ibid.*, No. 8 (1967), 4–49.

Community development

Institutions of community development are another means of increasing participation and relating bureaucratic change to the whole political system.[200] In most developing states these institutions have been the subjects of considerable political attention as well as research and writing. The subject is endowed with Rousseauian overtones of the alleged idyllics of the pastoral. Basic Democracies and panchayats have become cornerstones of the ideologies of Pakistan and India; students have analyzed them to a degree disproportionate to their role as one institution in the political system.[201] The emphasis on rural development has resulted in a neglect of the problems of urban development. In urban development the issue is not so much modernization as it is meaningful, effective participation in the political system by "transitional men" and, most importantly, the drastic overhauling of archaic governmental institutions and structures which are less able to meet urban demands than village government is to meet rural demands.

In part the vigor of community development activities has been the consequence of the existence of a substantial body of doctrine, codified and disseminated by highly organized entities such as the United Nations and the United States foreign assistance program.[202] The codification of doctrine conjoined with

200. The best single reference comparing rural development institutions and putting them into a context blending structural analysis with psychological aspects of participation is Douglas Ashford, *National Development and Local Government Reform* (Princeton, 1966).

201. For example, studies exist relating the text of proceedings of village councils and analyzing details of votes on issues involving the equivalent of five or six dollars. Others present profiles of village councilors in sophisticated manner. Yet for the legislators of Pakistan, no study exists, no profiles of legislators have been made, no study of votes has been made. For India, only the study by W. H. Morris-Jones, *Parliament in India* (London, 1958), exists; no comparable study of the sixteen state legislatures exists, no profiles of legislators, and, except for the promising study by Stanley A. Kochanek, "The Relation between Social Background and attitudes of Indian Legislators," *Journal of Commonwealth Political Studies*, VI (1968), 34–53, and a doctoral dissertation now being written from research in Delhi by Willard Berry of Georgia State College, the study by Morris-Jones has not been updated.

202. United Nations publications on community development number over a hundred. The two most relevant to an expression of doctrine are *Social Progress Through Community Development*, United Nations Document E/CN .5/303/Rev.

newly achieved sovereignty whose principal attribute—power diffusion—appeared to be best achieved by local organization. It also conjoined with older strands of thought in some countries such as India and Pakistan. In the subcontinent before independence we find the rural reconstruction movement of Rabindranath Tagore, starting with Visva-Bharati and Santiniketan in the 1920's. It is worthy of note that the views of Tagore were not as unrealistic as is commonly supposed. He did not advocate an iconoclasm which sought to return all of life to the village; rather, reconstruction was to be achieved by bringing to the village the "new power of man."[203] A more pragmatic genetic strand is the rural uplift movement of F. L. Brayne in Gurgaon district of the Punjab in the twenties. These were given canonical status by Gandhi's movement and became so enmeshed with it that important aspects of the panchayati raj were invariably begun on October 2, Gandhi's birthday. The early developments in India and Pakistan were community development (1952–56) and village AID (1952–59), respectively. These were heavily supported by United States assistance, both financial and consultative,[204] and were more programmatic than structural.

In both India and Pakistan the second post-1947 phase of the movement, panchayati raj in 1956 and Basic Democracies in 1959, had remarkably similar characteristics. Both rejected conceptually Western models and made an effort to adapt to indigenous institutions.[205] Both received little or no financial or advisory

1 (New York, 1955), and *Community Development and National Development*, United Nations Document E/CN .5/370/Rev. 1 (New York, 1963). In the case of Pakistan, the influence of foreign assistance was direct and easily traced. A committee of five agricultural experts headed by M. H. Sufi spent four months in the United States under auspices of the International Cooperation Administration (ICA), which was the predecessor to AID. The resulting report, Government of Pakistan, *Report on Agricultural Extension Work in the U.S.A. and Reorganization of Extension Service in Pakistan* (Karachi, 1952), devoted half of its sixty-four pages to a description of agricultural extension in the United States. For a summary of the origins of the Indian community development program, see United Nations, Department of Economic and Social Affairs, *Report of a Community Development Evaluation Mission in India* (New York, 1959), pp. 7–10.

203. Rabindranath Tagore, "City and Village" (1928) in *Towards Universal Man* (Bombay, 1961), pp. 302–322.

204. Jack D. Mezirow, *Dynamics of Community Development* (New York, 1963), p. 51; Albert Mayer and Associates, *Pilot Project India* (Berkeley and Los Angeles, 1958), p. 367.

205. The Balwantray Mehta study team sought to renovate rural India by "a dispersal of machinery and devolution of authority" (Government of India

support from United States technical assistance, and both emphasized much more integration with their respective political-administrative frameworks. While it is not at all certain that the two community development institutions are performing the rural uplift purposes as effectively as originally contemplated, they are deeply enmeshed in the political consciousness and organization of the two countries. The most recent and most methodologically sophisticated study on panchayats in Rajasthan, the first Indian state to adopt them, was able to say with respect to Jaipur district: "We have found no persons who would recommend to us the scrapping of the panchayati raj institutions altogether; they want to mend them and not to end them. We therefore feel that the establishment of panchayati raj institutions has been a step in the right direction."[206] Chawla similarly reported that "panchayati raj is becoming a way of life in India."[207] Khanna makes essentially the same evaluation for the Punjab.[208] In Pakistan, the acceptance of Basic Democracies is indicated by the fact that the Combined Opposition party (COP) opposing Ayub in the presidential election of 1965 quickly reversed its position of opposition to Basic Democracies when it found that it was losing support because of the earlier stand. The COP supported the institution but not its electoral function. Basic Democracies are a fundamental part of the political system. Even the chief justice of Pakistan, who had not previously taken extensive notice of the institution,

---

Planning Commission, Committee on Planned Projects, *Report of the Team for the Study of Community Projects and National Extension Service,* 3 vols. [New Delhi, 1957]). As Chawla rightly states, "The Report (Balwantray) is a master blue print, a sort of bible for Panchayati Raj. The whole concept of democratic decentralization in India is based on this Report. The existing institutions of Panchayati Raj in India are modelled on this Report" (V. N. Chawla, *Studies in Local Self-Government in India* [Jullundur, India, 1967], p. 50). Addressing a public rally in Lyallpur fifteen days before the introduction of the Basic Democracies system on October 27, 1959, President Ayub said, "The scheme of Basic Democracies has been evolved by us after a careful study of the experience of other countries and the special conditions prevailing in our own. There is no need for us to imitate blindly the type of democracy to be found in other countries. We have to work according to the requirements of our own nation and the genius of our own people" (Syed R. A. Jafri, *Ayub-Soldier and Statesman* [Lahore, 1966], p. 54).

206. M. V. Mathur *et al., Panchayati Raj in Rajasthan* (New Delhi, 1966), p. 298.

207. Chawla, *Local Self-Government in India,* p. 38.

208. R. L. Khanna, *Panchayati Raj in Punjab* (Chandigarh, India, 1966), p. 125.

accorded them an unusual position of prominence in the legal system: "in the derivation of power from the people, the Constitution rests wholly upon the Basic Democracies Order, 1959. . . . the key to the understanding of the Constitution of Pakistan lies in the system of Basic Democrats. A person wishing to understand the full ethos and impact of this new Constitution must acquire a thorough grasp of the actualities and the potential of the Basic Democracies."[209]

Rural (or community) development institutions are predicated on the increased participation from the periphery of the social order inward to the core. It is the directional flow of this participation which is the key to the movement. The style is persuasion and consultation rather than coercion. The mood is one of spontaneity rather than fiat issued by the conventional bureaucracy. The community development programs have typically been explained in terms of socio-economic change and modernity rather than in terms of political power and authority.[210] In the first stage of the movement in both India and Pakistan a deliberate effort was made to dissociate the structure from existing civil administration and local government bodies which were the traditional sources of political power. Viewed retrospectively, it is likely that in this first stage there was too much autonomy and insufficient synaptic connection with bureaucracy. The effervescence of the movement may have increased demands without increasing institutional capability accordingly. This may have been due in part to an insufficient transfer of bureaucratic skills to the movement. The effort to keep the movement autonomous often alienated the traditional bureaucracy and sometimes invited its open hostility. As a consequence, community development workers often encouraged the growth of spurious local groups, and this contributed to factionalism and made co-ordination more difficult. The second phase of the movement met with greater success partly because autonomy was reduced and synaptic connections enlarged. When the movement is connected to administration and at the same time becomes part of the political party system, the

209. Address by Chief Justice A. R. Cornelius, Dacca Centre of Pakistan Council for National Integration, June 15, 1967 (mimeographed).

210. United Nations, *Report of a Community Development Evaluation Mission in India,* p. 48. Similar explanations are given of Basic Democracies.

strains on it may be great enough to disintegrate its original purpose. The Rajasthan study reported that the political impact of panchayats has been overwhelming and that it has "so far shown far greater political potential than economic or sociological results."[211]

Another observation to be made about community development relates to containment and centrality of purpose. The earlier concept of "multipurpose" institution captured the imagination, for it contemplated an institution which reflected the well-established notion that "change," "uplift," and "modernization" involved the whole man and the whole fabric of society. The dramatic simplicity of this truism obscured, however, the possibility that a more productive effort might be more narrowly segmental or concentrated. If the connections between institutions and sectors allowed for sufficient permeability without destroying autonomy such a segmental concentration might have advantages. One would be a relatively easy change of concentration in the event of failure without upsetting the weave of the whole fabric. Second, as a movement of diffuse purposes spreading across the whole social order and based on the idyllics of social improvement (literacy, comprehension of Pasteur's germ theory of disease, etc.) it is likely to become detached from the hard realities of life and to escalate demands to the point of crisis and beyond. The movements in both countries have shifted somewhat away from the emotionally appealing "multipurpose" objective. But the epitome of a recovery of containment and centrality of purpose is the rural works program begun in East Pakistan in 1961.[212] The genius of this program is that it focuses on the specifics of works rather than on the vagueness of social and moral uplift. As a consequence it appears to this writer, who last observed its operation in the summer of 1967, to be an immense improvement over Pakistan's Basic Democracies and India's panchayati raj. The specificity of public works relates the enterprise

211. Mathur *et al.*, *Panchayati Raj in Rajasthan*, p. 282.

212. For analysis of the program, see A. K. M. Mohsen, *Report on Rural Public Works Programme in Comilla Katwali Thana* (Comilla, Pakistan, 1962), *A Manual for Public Works* (Comilla, Pakistan, 1962), and his *An Evaluation of the Rural Public Works Programme, East Pakistan, 1962–63* (Comilla, Pakistan, 1963); and A. T. R. Rahman, *An Evaluation of the Rural Works Programme, East Pakistan, 1963–66* (Comilla, Pakistan, 1965).

to the realities of life; a monetized incentive system slowly assumes form. Social and moral uplift become concomitant results —derivative from actual need. Thus record-keeping, computation, capital formation, sanitary practices, literacy, and a sense of time follow upon need dictated by experience. This is a simple but a crucial distinction. In the earlier community development movements the priorities were reversed. It is possible within this structure to associate more and more activities within the competence of the villagers. Thus Chief Justice Cornelius' proposal for "economic participation" might, along with other types of participation, be progressively folded into the operation.[213] Foreign assistance in this activity can be far more effective than when it is associated with other types of rural uplift. United States counterpart funds can easily be made available for specific works, the nature of which can be determined by the recipient government. But care must be taken to prevent such a program from becoming an activity of the public works department with no participative or uplift features. The ideal community development scheme is poised between the uplift ethos and the public works bureaucracy, partaking of the nature of each but duplicating neither.

Interstitial participation

There are essentially four forms of mass participation in a political system. The first is the franchise and its consequent electoral mechanisms. Whether such mechanism should be direct or indirect or whether it should be based on proportional representation are important issues which, except for Sartori's study,[214] have not been examined in the context of political development. The phenomenon of elections and the party process itself are well known and fairly widely studied components of this first form. The second may be called statutory career participation, by which is meant the legislative and bureaucratic occupations, more or less on a full-time career basis. With respect to the latter

213. The need for greater involvement of the peasantry in economic matters was the central theme of a background paper prepared by Chief Justice Cornelius for the Bellagio conference.

214. Sartori, "Political Development and Political Engineering," cited above in n. 2.

it is often a major form of participation in the total political process, and this fact strains the "rationality" of the bureaucracy, as it responds to severe political strains which become rediffused and reinvigorated internally. The relationship between bureaucratic "representativeness" in the sense meant by Kingsley and "responsiveness" is not precisely known, nor has it been carefully studied in developing societies. It appears doubtful if a bureaucracy whose composition reflects numerically the classes and ethnicities of the whole social order would construct a better mosaic of the public interest than a bureaucracy of different composition.[215] The third is the relatively informal, initially unstructured community development movement rooted in spontaneity and manifest in non-coercive techniques of consultation and education. As has been previously suggested, much reliance is placed on this form of participation in developing states. A fourth form has been paid scant attention. It involves establishing a consultative or advisory relationship between citizenry or particular groups thereof and various entities of the bureaucracy. Because such structures can be found in thousands of, perhaps even numberless, places throughout the bureaucratic system in interstices at all levels, we refer to the phenomenon here as interstitial participation. Certainly it is not a new phenomenon. Appleby alluded to it under the rubric of co-ordination, which he held to be consultation and communication between the bureaucracy and the public.[216] It was characteristic also of the technique of the occupation of Japan, which established citizens' commissions at various levels. Thus, for example, local child welfare boards were

215. J. Donald Kingsley, *Representative Bureaucracy* (Yellow Springs, Ohio, 1944). See Montgomery's chapter in this volume, esp. pp. 444–455, for a critique of Kingsley's concept of representativeness. The difficulties in transferring Kingsley's analysis from the British to other contexts is suggested in V. Subramaniam, "Representative Bureaucracy: A Reassessment," *American Political Science Review*, LXI (1967), 1010–1020. Subramaniam asserts that accessibility of officials (i.e., classlessness) itself changes the importance of representativeness. The present writer would add that the utility of representativeness would vary also with the vigor of other institutions which are intentionally representative, especially legislatures. For a general analysis of this problem see Pennock and Chapman (eds.), *Representation*, especially Joseph W. Witherspoon, "The Bureaucracy as Representatives," pp. 229–259, and David E. Apter, "Notes for a Theory of Nondemocratic Representation," pp. 278–317. See also Hanna F. Pitkin, *The Concept of Representation* (Berkeley and Los Angeles, 1968) and Giovanni Sartori, "Representation: Representational Systems," *International Encyclopedia of the Social Sciences* (New York, 1968), pp. 465–474.

216. Paul H. Appleby, *Big Democracy* (New York, 1949), p. 81.

related to the administration of the Children's Welfare Law;[217] public safety commissions were similarly related to the police power at three levels,[218] and there were election administration commissions as well as inspection commissions. The latter were ideologically derivative from the Chinese censorial system and are akin to the ombudsman which has recently attained considerable prominence.[219] The number of such advisory groups located at centers of policy formulation is limited. Far more numerous are less conspicuous locations. Examples are: councils with members from industry, technical schools and government to guide occupational standards for trade schools, and similar councils to relate the curriculum of such trade schools to industrial needs. Such councils have been proposed for Pakistan and for Turkey.[220] One cannot rely too heavily on such councils. The relationship between them and the responsible bureaucratic entity will no doubt be difficult until the difference between advice and responsibility is understood by both parties. The councils, of course, must also be wary of being used merely as "fronts" to approve policies essentially unpopular and perhaps even wrong. But the educative value in terms of civic training would appear to outweigh these difficulties. The most effective ultimate role of the citizenry is in politics expressed through parties and legislatures, not through political pressure made to impinge on the bureaucracy itself. This was a point Appleby clearly made in protesting a portion of India's Third Five-Year Plan, which asserted that the "day-to-day working" of administration needed the participation of the people.[221] We concur with Appleby that this kind of interference must be avoided. Granted the possibility of such interference

217. Ralph Braibanti, "Executive Power in Japanese Prefectural Government," *Far Eastern Quarterly,* IX (1950), 231–244.

218. Ralph Braibanti, "Japan's New Police Law," *Far Eastern Survey,* XVIII (1949), 17–22.

219. See especially Walter Gellhorn, *Ombudsmen and Others: Citizens' Protectors in Nine Countries* (Cambridge, Mass., 1966) and *When Americans Complain: Governmental Grievance Procedure* (Cambridge, Mass., 1966). See also Roy V. Peel (ed.), *The Ombudsman or Citizen's Defender: A Modern Institution,* published as a symposium issue of the *Annals of the American Academy of Political and Social Science* (May, 1968).

220. On the latter see Yusuf Onertoy, "Advisory Committees" (Ankara, June, 1967, mimeographed).

221. Paul H. Appleby, "Some Thoughts on Decentralized Democracy," *Indian Journal of Public Administration,* VIII (1962), 453.

might be greatly increased with the establishment of advisory councils. Yet, properly organized, such councils may play an important educative role while other institutions such as legislature and parties assume a more effective representative function.

A more subtle advantage of expanded interstitial participation is the facilitation of exchange of values and norms among institutions. Thus the technology of business and industry in the private sector or of private medicine, for example, can penetrate the bureaucracy. Where transfer of persons is difficult or impossible for various reasons, this interchange through advisory entities can be significant.

IV. Summary

The reinforced provisions of Title IX of the Foreign Assistance Act have to some extent crystallized and focused attention on the possibility of systematically engineering viable political systems. The forthrightness of this provision is in contrast to British and French foreign aid, which relies on implicit bonds consequent to imperial relations rather than on explicit models of nation-building. Title IX appears at a time in foreign relations when recipient nations feel a sense of technological competence, are disenchanted with economic and political panaceas of the West, are distrustful of American motives, and are acutely sensitive to intervention in domestic political matters. Whether Title IX can be effectively implemented in this context remains to be seen.

The appearance of Title IX coincides with a period of heightened academic interest in political development, and it has stimulated further interest. The links between AID and the academic community consist of occasional conferences, SEADAG, and particularistic contract research. The continuity of research efforts, change in personnel, and absence of permanent structures have thus far worked against formulating a strategy of political development. Yet this is the context of government-academic relations in the United States, and within this context a beginning has been made from which results may eventually come. French and

British political development practice and theory differ from the American in substance and organization. There would appear to be some advantage in establishing connections among these three important national experiences within the ambit of their foreign assistance operations.

The important problem on which Title IX focuses attention is the formulation of a strategy for inducing political development; a subordinate problem is that of relating administrative growth (in the inducement of which AID has had much experience) to the larger context of political development. To analyze this problem, we have examined four characteristics of political development. Architectonics is important because it calls attention to the need for suffusing the administrative system with the values of the society. This can be accomplished in part by adjusting administrative institutions and by establishing links between the legislatures and the bureaucracy. Diffusion of power must be articulated to a rising institutional capability. The systematic channeling of such diffusion of power in institutions cannot be neglected, especially since institutionalization of what originate as spontaneous behaviors inevitably occur even without being planned. A dominant theme of this chapter is the cruciality of institutions and their development. It is possible to stimulate institutional growth so as to level out to some extent the asymmetrical or unbalanced development of institutions. To do this, institutions must be analyzed in terms of their performance. To accomplish this, seven indices were proposed; institutions and the entities, sector, and structure were defined. When the movement of persons from one institution to another is limited or non-existent, the permeability of norms and values must be accomplished by continued contact with external generants (such as foreign assistance) and by interinstitutional collaboration structured in a manner facilitative of exchange of values and norms. This analysis of institutions is closely related to the fourth characteristic of political development, namely, the innovative capacity of the system, particularly of the bureaucracy. A series of nine propositions relating to innovation is advanced.

A general strategy for political development within the context of Title IX presupposes the strengthening of as many institutions as possible. This does not, however, preclude the further strengthening of already strong bureaucratic institutions, for the existence of a viable bureaucracy is held to be a paramount need of developing states. The problem of accelerating demands at a pace greater than the capability of institutions to process them has been dealt with in the context of negative and positive measures. The deliberate manipulation of political parties by foreign assistance is rejected primarily because of the sensitivities of recipient nations and because of the fluidity of party coalitions. The "demand-conversion" dilemma is adjusted somewhat spontaneously by ambiguity in the system. Such ambiguity can be assessed and evaluated in terms of short-range and long-range effect. One objective of political development strategy is to reduce the ambiguity by institutional and structural rectification. The legislative process is one such institution which has been neglected in the new states. Its strengthening can have several desirable effects. First, it can exercise restraint over bureaucracy; second, it can more adequately reflect the public interest, thus improving the quality of participation; third, its enhanced efficiency and prestige can enable it to function as an architectonic formulator, thus reducing the strain on stronger institutions which have performed that role. Community development organizations can also be effective in deepening the involvement of people in political life. If they are carefully constructed, they can improve the quality of that participation and can keep the scope of participation articulated to the capacity of the participants. The role of law and the judiciary is important as a means of diffusing the administrative system with the architectonics. Interstitial participation is crucial as a means of providing for greater permeability of values, norms, and skills among institutions. A second advantage is the educative value in terms of civic skills and attitudes.

The strategy here proposed is somewhat eclectic rather than narrow. It concentrates on institutional strengthening, thus seeking to improve the quality rather than increase the quantity of civic participation. Finally, it avoids ethnocentric bias and allows for the evolution of indigenous institutions to fit peculiar circumstances. Thus it makes no mention of such entities as co-operatives, labor unions, or women's organizations which are given explicit attention in congressional discussion of Title IX. We do not concede the universal validity of these institutions; on the contrary, we believe their utility will vary from system to system. On the other hand, law, legislative process, community development, interstitial participation, and the construct of ambiguity can be given attention by foreign assistance while still permitting extensive ecological adjustment. A central theme is the manipulation of institutions in a manner facilitating innovation yet preserving a measure of autonomy in each.

·2·

Political Development and the Objectives of Modern Government*

Carl J. Friedrich

I

In their recent and in many ways remarkable *Comparative Politics: A Developmental Approach,* the two authors approach their subject so abstractly and formally that ends, objectives, and purposes are rarely discussed in terms of their content.[1] Not one

* The nature of this paper has not provided convenient opportunity to refer extensively to the fast-growing literature of development politics. Because of the richness and variety of specific cultural background that has to be known to fit a model into a particular situation, much of the general work in this field has appeared in the form of collaborative works. Among these, the author should like to mention the following as having proved helpful to him: Gabriel A. Almond and James B. Coleman (eds.), *The Politics of the Developing Areas* (Princeton, 1960); Ralph Braibanti and Joseph J. Spengler (eds.), *Tradition, Values, and Socio-Economic Development* (Durham, N.C., 1961); John H. Kautsky (ed.), *Political Change in Underdeveloped Countries* (New York, 1962); Karl W. Deutsch and William J. Foltz, *Nation-Building* (New York, 1963); Kurt London (ed.), *New Nations in a Divided World* (New York, 1963); Joseph LaPalombara (ed.), *Bureaucracy and Political Development* (Princeton, 1963); John H. Hallowell (ed.), *Development: For What?* (Durham, N.C., 1964); Ralph Braibanti and Associates, *Asian Bureaucratic Systems Emergent from the British Imperial Tradition* (Durham, N.C., 1966); Herbert J. Spiro (ed.), *Patterns of African Development* (Englewood Cliffs, N.J., 1967); John D. Montgomery and William J. Siffin (eds.), *Approaches to Development: Politics, Administration and Change* (New York, 1966); Paul E. Sigmund (ed.), *The Ideologies of the Developing Nations* (rev. ed.; New York, 1967). Mention may also be made of groups of significant articles in *Public Policy,* the yearbook of the Graduate School of Public Administration of Harvard University, published by Harvard University Press, edited by this author until 1965, and since then by John Montgomery with the assistance of colleagues in economics. Finally, the author should like to mention three works by individual authors from which he has learned much: Rupert Emerson, *From Empire to Nation* (Cambridge, Mass., 1960); Lucian W. Pye, *Politics, Personality and Nation-Building* (New Haven, 1962); and Edward A. Shils, *Political Development in the New States* (The Hague, 1962).

1. Gabriel A. Almond and G. Bingham Powell, Jr., *Comparative Politics: A Developmental Approach* (Boston, 1966), pp. 16 ff.

of these words appears in the index or in the table of contents. They are assumed to be there, as subjective "orientations," whether cognitive, affective, or evaluative, motivating subjective "attitudes" and "actions." That is all. Their entire concern is with operational processes, ongoing functions, and with interests as "inputs and outputs." But what is being put in or put out remains *hors de discussion.* "During the last decade," they write, "an intellectual revolution has been taking place in the study of comparative government," and while they are uncertain about how "the field will be reconstituted," they believe that it is possible to point to the main directions of innovation, and to the dissatisfactions and criticisms which contributed to these changes." Among these criticisms they list the "formalism" of the traditional approach, by which they mean the emphasis on institutions and ideologies "rather than on performance, interaction and behavior." But what are institutions but stabilized behavior patterns? And what are ideologies but thought patterns concerned with the critique and defense of such patterns and the demand for their change? Therefore, if institution and ideology are thus understood, it seems a distinction without much of a difference, except in the more extensive use of quantitative methods.[2] Yet, from another viewpoint, philosophically speaking, it is precisely this supposedly revolutionary and hence exclusive emphasis on operational aspects—admittedly important though they are—which has produced the formalism which abstracts from what all these operations, functions, and interests are all about. In spite of these self-styled revolutionaries, the world of politics, however, goes on bitterly fighting over such elements of content as justice, freedom, order, and believing such content to be the heart of the matter. Not that such presumed foolishness settles it; far from it. But it would be the better part of wisdom, if wisdom is to be grounded in experience, to recognize that such ends, objectives, and purposes are not only worthy of exploration as a

2. Carl J. Friedrich, *Man and His Government* (New York, 1963), esp. p. 71, where a political institution is defined as "any stably organized syndrome of political acts or actions having a function and/or purpose in the political system. . . ." This position may be put in Parsons' terms by saying, "a relatively stable collection of roles." See Braibanti's chapter in this volume, pp. 54 ff.

vital part of comparative politics, but that they are also capable of being so explored.

For gone are the days of the value-agnosticism of a Max Weber or a Vilfredo Pareto who out of the safety of their liberal world would assign the choice of values to individual arbitrariness. On the contrary, like tastes, they are the most worthy objects of careful rational analysis in terms of past experience. For political analysis shapes the values as it proceeds in the study of their workings.[3] No political analysis has ever been undertaken without both assuming and effecting values. Thus the study mentioned above, calling itself a developmental approach, posits that development is good, that it ought to be, that what helps it is good and what does not is bad, that it is fine to be a "revolutionary," but bad to be a "traditionalist." Are any of these basic assumptions mere arbitrary choices? Are they incapable of reasoned exploration and explicit justification? The authors do not tell us whether they are or not. "In speaking of the *developmental aspect* of role and structure, then, we are interested not only in the emergence of new types of roles or the atrophy of old ones, but also in the changing patterns of interaction among roles, structures, subsystems."[4] Again, and quite characteristically, we do not learn what is the direction of the change; in good old American go-getter style, they say: I don't know where they are going, but I know they are on their way. But what does it mean "to be on the way" if there is no specification of the end of the journey? Yet that is all we are told about development, that development is change. Now only a died-in-the-wool rationalist would insist that the "end of the journey" can be stated fully; for we have no map of human evolution and we might as well be willing to say that it is an "immense journey."[5] Yet, for many of the so-called developing countries—a paradoxical expression, to be sure, since some of the most developed countries are among the most decisively developing ones, precisely because the direction of their development has

3. *Ibid.*, esp. pp. 53–56 and 65–69.

4. The authors seem to protest against such an interpretation. See Almond and Powell, *Comparative Politics*, p. 215.

5. Loren C. Eiseley, *The Immense Journey* (New York, 1946); also, Pierre Teilhard de Chardin, *The Phenomenon of Man* (New York, 1959).

been set in grooves that force the wheels to follow them—the question of the direction of their development is most decisive, and the most acerbated struggles revolve around this issue. Should economic development have priority, and if so, should it be agricultural or industrial development, should capitalism or socialism be developed, and so forth and so on. Or should the development of democracy—and if so, constitutional or popular democracy—be given preference? Or should one assume that the course of development to be emulated is that which occurred in Europe, and should therefore strong, sizable national states with a powerful bureaucracy (administration) be developed first? These are questions about which men fight, and reason in the bargain; for who wants to fight for an unreasonable goal?

II

In a sense this range of disputations about priorities involves the issue of the "highest good"—one of the perennials of philosophy and ethics. Before we enter into a discussion of the operative values, the objectives or ends of a political order, it might be well to discuss this hoary issue at least briefly. For it can readily be shown that the arguments over specific developmental goals or objectives can be reduced to this argument over what is the highest good—the assumption that there is such a highest good may actually be that the highest good is development!

The discussion in such writers as Plato, Aristotle, Thomas Aquinas, Machiavelli, Hobbes, Locke, and Kant has run the entire gamut of possible choices: happiness, the state, self-preservation, freedom, and even the "idea of the Good itself" (Plato) have been advanced, whether in terms of transcendent ideas, empirically grounded observation, or something in between. Arnold Brecht has pointed out that each of the claimants, and he reviewed many,[6] had put forward impressive reasons for his choice, but that none was able to "prove scientifically" that his particular value is *the* value. To put it another way, if there is believed to be

6. Arnold Brecht, *Political Theory* (Princeton, 1959), pp. 302–366.

a highest value, one cannot hope to establish in an empirical way, based upon evidence that is transmissible, that this is so. That proposition is true enough, as far as it goes. But empirical evidence further suggests that different persons value different A's most highly, and that even the same person values different A's most highly at different times (e.g., in connection with aging). This evidence forces one to the conclusion that *no rank, no hierarchy of values exists,* no universal preference for one value as against another can be shown to be valid. Politically organized man refuses to make up his mind. He prefers to muddle through on the basis of a plurality of objectives some of which may be so much in conflict as mutually to exclude each other. Political man seems to adjust these value preferences as he goes along, as the situation requires it. Actual communities have been known to jeopardize security for prosperity, or prosperity for security; they have endangered security through lack of diplomacy and excess of pride in prestige, and they have wrecked prosperity by the failure to reduce internal friction and to maintain domestic peace. The political rationalist may bitterly deplore it, but he will have to acknowledge man's willingness to live by plural objectives. Hence neither development, nor rational-legal conduct in the sense meant by Max Weber, nor any other value, high or low, can be said to be the highest good and thereby to shape a set of priorities. In fact, the great statesman presumably is the kind of man who temporarily succeeds in imposing (by persuasion or coercion, usually both) his own value preferences upon a political community thereby shaping its order. He is, in Bertrand de Jouvenel's engaging literary terminology, the *dux* as contrasted with the *rex* who governs in accordance with prevailing values, interests, and beliefs.[7]

But if no *summum bonum* can be shown to have molded the political order, except for brief periods under exceptional leadership, then the problem presents itself anew: what can be the plural "ends of the state"—the several objectives for the realization of which men have striven through their political orders? Two ways of looking at and for such objectives have in the past

7. *On Power* (New York, 1949); *Sovereignty* (Chicago, 1957).

been pursued, and both possess a certain degree of validity. One way is to look for the recurrent objectives, that is to say those objectives which many men in many orders have pursued, or perhaps even all men in all orders. By comparing many political orders such a set of objectives embodying values may be ascertainable. We shall return to them in a moment. The other possibility is to look for particular and specific objectives embodying unique values springing from highly particular beliefs.

It is obvious that the same is true on the individual plane, that if we look at a person in terms of his individual self-development, we shall find something which makes him unique and contrasts him with others; whereas if we look at him in terms of some human ideal shared by many, such as the great religions embody, we shall find something that makes him like others; and if these religions share a common core, a panhumanist aspiration,[8] then persons developing in accordance with that aspiration will resemble each other to the extent to which they live up to it. Now the particular and specific objectives of political communities together constitute what is usually called its culture.[9] Its highest level of creative achievement as much as its lowliest ways—habits of eating, dressing, making love—are distinctive for groups who constitute a community. Such ways spill over into the political arena: Germans debate differently from the French, English, or Americans, all these Europeans differently from Indians or Africans, and the same holds for negotiating and administering. To the extent to which such distinctive ways become valued in a particular community, they become objectives. Education, unfortunately now often called "socialization," is directed toward making members of the community subjectively aware of the new objective, as indeed it is concerned with the transmission of traditional values and beliefs.[10] The existence and role of these

8. Clyde Kluckhohn in *Mirror For Man* (New York, 1949) stated this position for anthropology. For political theory, see C. J. Friedrich, *The New Belief in the Common Man* (Boston, 1942), and its later revision, *The New Image of the Common Man* (Boston, 1950).

9. Not its political culture—a vague concept, particularly if used in a non-valuational sense; the term "political tradition" is much clearer and more appropriate. Cf. contra Gabriel A. Almond and Sidney Verba, *The Civic Culture* (Princeton, 1963).

10. Friedrich, *Man and His Government,* chap. 33, "Tradition and the Role of Education."

particular, not to say parochial, values, beliefs, and objectives is to provide the setting within which the more general objectives may be realized. On the most elementary level: men eat, whether it be meat or fish, bread or rice. There are very general propositions that can be stated about this process of eating, e.g., its limits in terms of underdoing it (hunger) or overdoing it (gluttony) beyond which survival is uncertain. There is no need to spin out this analogy in order to suggest that it is necessary to combine the particular with the general in order to reach a full understanding of the actual process in its ongoing functionality.

Obviously, in discoursing upon "the objectives of modern government" one is primarily concerned with the general component, though restricted to the particularity of "modern" government. Whether "modern" governments—or as some would prefer to put it, the "modern" states—actually have general objectives different from other governments I shall not now discuss. Some would think so, and talk of freedom or human dignity or the classless society. In any case, it is this class of governments with which we are here concerned. The perplexing problem of typology of government implied here we must leave aside, except to note that for many "modern" means "preferable," or at least "preferable now." I should like to avoid this value commitment at this point and suggest that by "modern" we mean government as it has been developing in the West since 1500, and including therefore the absolute monarchies of the seventeenth and eighteenth centuries. For if we exclude them, we are unable to cope with the problems raised by the industrial revolution, and that in turn would mean a good part of what is meant by economic development.[11]

But what about the Soviet Union and similar regimes? Are their objectives to be part of our inquiry? Or are they to be considered "unmodern" governments? To put the question thus is to prejudice it, of course. Intentionally so. For it does not seem to me possible to exclude the Communist objectives from consideration without getting bogged down in ideological commitments which the analysis needs to be concerned with and face. It will in

11. Robert T. Holt and John E. Turner, *The Political Basis of Economic Development* (Princeton, 1966), esp. chap. 7. See also the general works on economic history, such as those of William Cunningham and Max Weber.

fact become apparent that quite a few of the general objectives of modern government, industrialization for example, are shared by the Communist and the Non-Communist world. We are not making our task easier by including the Soviet Union among modern governments, but we will make the results more conclusive by doing it.[12] The equivocal nature of such terms as "democratization" and "popular participation in politics," will thereby be highlighted, and the limits of their applicability to advanced industrial societies forced upon our attention. Is America more democratic now than a hundred years ago? Yes and no. Negroes have greater equality in 1967 than in 1867, but both Negroes and whites have lost in political participation with the agglomeration of ever greater masses in the vast urban combines of our great metropoles. Will the country be more democratic in the year 2000 than it is now? Who would dare to predict? Yet in all kinds of respects it will be further "developed."

A British philosopher writing about "purpose" said recently that "when we turn to consider what can usefully be said about the purpose of the state we are not seeking any single self-evident axiom from which all else can be derived or an all-embracing principle that determines our political obligation." And he adds significantly: "Nor are we reading into the question the assumption that an answer must exist in the form of a comprehensive phrase applicable to all states at all times and solving all practical issues."[13] Yet, he then proceeds, starting from Aristotle, to develop the notion of the "good life" as a sort of introductory answer. He at the same time excludes the idea that the "state" is an end in itself—an idea which is more readily agreed to, when we talk of government rather than the "state." The good life and the related notion of happiness as the ultimate end of government are not really answers to our inquiry; for the further question immediately imposes itself: which life is good? and what makes a person happy? On the answer to these questions the greatest difference of opinion has existed throughout the ages between individuals as

12. C. J. Friedrich and Zbigniew K. Brzezinski, *Totalitarian Dictatorship and Autocracy* (2nd ed. rev.; Cambridge, Mass., 1965).

13. H. R. G. Greaves, *The Foundations of Political Theory* (new ed. rev.; London, 1966), p. 42.

well as groups and nations, so that I am inclined to exclude both the good life and happiness from the objectives of a government; it is more correct to speak of a community's values, interests, beliefs as molding a government's policies, as it pursues the basic and ever-recurrent objectives that will presently be discussed. For if the government helps the community and its members to secure those satisfactions which they seek, they will be happy and leading a good life. Actually, of course, philosophers from Aristotle to Spinoza, and Confucius and Budda not excepted, have insisted that the good life is the life they liked, the life of thought and contemplation and the discussion with men of equal disposition. Where people have achieved some measure of effective self-expression and of participation in the basic decisions of politics, they have rarely, if ever, insisted that their government spend its resources for the purpose of making that kind of good life possible (though, if such introspectionists have been prepared to do some teaching, people have been willing to support them up to a point).

III

If then, the good life and happiness won't do as objectives of modern government, and if it is agreed that no single principle can be said to provide the *summum bonum,* the highest good that men expect from their government, what is the plural congeries of objectives that comparative historical and anthropological inquiry discloses as the recurrent goal of political orders as we know them? Many years ago, I worked out, by comparative analysis, what these purposes or objectives have been for the great national states of the West.[14] I found four such recurrent

14. Carl J. Friedrich, *Constitutional Government and Democracy* (new ed.; Boston, 1968), chaps. 3–4. Karl W. Deutsch has proposed as a first approximation the reduction of these objectives of government to two, i.e., reduction of obstacles to action, and increased capabilities to act. He has emphasized that on further analysis these turn out to imply capacities for learning, self-steering, and self-control. See his *Nationalism and Social Communication* (rev. ed.; Cambridge, Mass., 1966), pp. 72–85, and *The Nerves of Government* (rev. ed.; New York, 1966), pp. 110–113, 124–127, 247–256.

objectives: (1) security and territorial expansion, (2) the reduction of external friction, (3) prosperity, and (4) the reduction of internal friction. It is misleading at best to speak, in line with present usage, of "conflict" instead of "friction," for I believe that the government's objective starts at an earlier phase of divergent individual and group interests, values, and beliefs, and that therefore the term "friction" more accurately reflects the recurrent objective. It will, of course, be observed that these objectives as then demonstrated in terms of the historical record at hand resemble "ends of the state" as expounded by political philosophers in the past, but usually, as already pointed out, in terms of making one of these objectives paramount. Thus Hobbes, in stressing self-preservation and self-defense, insisted upon the priority of the first objective, while St. Augustine and much of the Christian tradition, in focusing on peace, assigned to the second and the fourth, but usually the fourth more than the second, the ruling priority. The fourth objective, more conventionally referred to under the term of "justice" seemed to Plato and a long line of thinkers inspired by him to be the dominant objective. It may seem strange to some that I identify the reduction of internal friction with the search for justice, but as I have explained elsewhere, justice in the political perspective of the just political act is based upon the comparison of alternative courses and the preference of that course of action which provides equal treatment in terms of the values and beliefs prevalent in a particular community. Or, to put it another way: an action may be said to be just, and hence likewise a rule, a judgment, or a decision, when it is based upon a comparative evaluation of the persons affected by the action, and when that comparison accords with the values and beliefs of the community.[15] That community may be as comprehensive as all mankind, or it may be as small as a family or a friendship. If all men acted justly in this sense, or if the government could bring it about that they do, then complete internal peace, that is to say a frictionless community, would be the result.

15. Cf. Friedrich, *Man and His Government*, chap. 15 and pp. 251 ff., where it is shown that this position is not identical to but quite distinct from that of Aristotle. See also C. J. Friedrich, *Transcendent Justice: The Religious Dimension of Constitutionalism* (Durham, N.C., 1964).

To approximate such a halcyon state of affairs is one of the major efforts of all governments. It may be a good thing that they cannot succeed.[16]

Before the analysis of these four basic objectives is carried further, three other ends of a political order which have played a great role in the past discussion of the "ends of the state" need be added: order, equality, and freedom. Why did these not figure as objectives in the general empirical analysis just briefly reported? The answer is easiest in the case of order; for if we speak of the objectives of a political order, as I have done, and thereby avoid the speculative and metaphysical aspects which the term "state" traditionally is associated with, it is evident that to include order among these objectives is a *petitio principii,* as the logicians call it, even a tautology; for an order is presupposed, or seems to be. But could it not be that while the political order is indeed assumed, the term "order" might refer to the social order in general, and then it would be meaningful to say that it is an objective of the political order to extend order to the remainder of the society "framed" by this political order? This is very true. But on closer inspection, it will be found that in this sense "order" largely coincides with what has been called the reduction of internal friction, and the related value of justice in the political sense as described above. For if all are treated justly in the sense of "to the equals equally"—the Roman law stated it in a famous (Troic) triad as *honeste vivere, neminem laedere, suum cuique tribuere* (to live properly, to hurt no one, and to give to everyone what is his)—then perfect order would prevail, provided quality is understood in the sense provided by the community's values and beliefs.[17]

These propositions have already squarely raised the related problem of equality; they have suggested that equality, like order, is a corollary of justice, that is to say of the objective of

16. That point was well made in Harlan Cleveland (ed.), *The Promise of World Tensions* (New York, 1961), especially W. Arthur Lewis, "The Emergence of West Africa," pp. 87–94, and Ralph J. Bunche, "The Emergence of the American Negro," pp. 95–100.

17. Cf. Friedrich, *Man and His Government,* chap. 19, where the value of disorder is demonstrated, and the relevant literature given.

reducing internal friction. But the argument does not end here. For in a community of rapidly changing values and beliefs, such as those the industrializing societies of Europe's eighteenth century were composed of, the issue of equality becomes controversial. The inbuilt dialectics of an equality which depends for its assessment upon what or whom a community considers equal was well put by Orwell's Big Brother Pig who in a famous quip replied to the complaining horse: "We are all equal, but some are more equal than others." The seeming absurdity of the remark hides a profound truth. For the expression "more equal" is paradoxical only if a radical equality of all with all in everything is posited as both possible and desirable.[18] If that chimera is excluded, and to realize equality is seen as the task of "giving to everyone what is his" in terms of the values and beliefs in the actual community, then it is part of the task of rendering justice as defined. To give a concrete illustration, one might take the racial issue in the United States. To give the Negro greater equality with the whites, in the sense of desegregation of schools, restaurants, hotels, and of participation in elections, means to render him justice; for the values and beliefs of many Americans, as well as the rest of the world community having changed dramatically in connection with the liberation of African Negroes from colonial rule,[19] the former treatment of Negroes could no longer be endured. It was, of course, always at variance with the formal law; for the constitution at least since the fourteenth amendment made no distinction between races but provided simply for the equal protection of the laws. The gap between the formal and living law became so glaring after the Second World War—values and beliefs having changed—that quite naturally the highest court of the land found itself obliged to close it. Negroes are not, of course, and will not be for quite some time fully equal to

18. Cf. Carl J. Friedrich and John W. Chapman (eds.), *Justice,* Vol. VI in the Nomos series (New York, 1963), esp. the essays by Richard McKeon, "Justice and Equality," pp. 44–61, and John Rawls, "Constitutional Liberty and the Concept of Justice," pp. 98–125.

19. Among additional factors are the excesses of racial discrimination practiced by Hitler and his regime and the pressure of ideological conflict in the cold war. For an overview, see C. J. Friedrich, "Rights, Liberties, Freedoms: A Reappraisal," *American Political Science Review,* LVII (1963), 841–854.

whites; but they are more equal than before. Similarly women are politically more equal—and not only in the United States, but in many countries—than they formerly were.[20]

These egalitarian trends were not significantly at work, however, in the seventeenth and eighteenth centuries; hence their thrust does not appear and they do not provide a major objective for modern governments until later in the nineteenth century. Yet the monarchs and their mercantilist-cameralist advisers, the Cecils, the Colberts, and others, were egalitarians of sorts, they had to be in their fight against the remnants of a feudal order and the aristocratic privileges of a nobility little interested in the new developments of industry and commerce. Just the same, the egalitarianism of these great ministers of economic development was a secondary motivation, not a primary concern for political equality as such.[21]

There remains the problem of freedom or liberty. For most liberal thinkers on politics from Locke to Kant, the core objective of a political order is to make liberty possible, in the sense of allowing everyone complete freedom, as long as that freedom is compatible with everyone else's freedom.[22] These freedoms of

20. Curiously, the democratic and egalitarian Swiss electorate (in its majority) still refuses to grant women the right to vote; this testifies to the stability of the Swiss social order. See George A. Codding, Jr., *The Federal Government of Switzerland* (Boston, 1961), pp. 58–60.

21. See Friedrich, *Constitutional Government and Democracy,* chap. 5, and Werner Sombart, *Der Moderne Kapitalismus* (5th ed.; Munich and Leipzig, 1922), Part I, Vol. I, pp. 334 ff. Huntington, basing his discussion on the concept of "modernization" which we have avoided here, believes he can distinguish three distinct patterns: Continental, British, and American. See Samuel P. Huntington, "Political Modernization: America *vs.* Europe," *World Poiltics,* XVIII (1966), 378–414.

22. The famous formula of Kant is that the autonomy of the will is the supreme principle of morality, and that hence "every action is right according to whose maxim the freedom of everyone can co-exist with everyone else's freedom according to a general law" (Immanuel Kant, *Metaphysical Elements of Justice,* trans. John Ladd [Indianapolis, 1965], p. 35). This idea is elaborated further in Friedrich's introduction to *The Philosophy of Kant: Immanuel Kant's Moral and Political Writings,* ed. Carl J. Friedrich (New York, 1949 and 1951). Locke, on the other hand, in the great scholastic tradition, stressed reason; in a "state of perfect freedom" men are free "to order their actions and dispose of their possessions and persons as they think fit, within the bounds of the law of nature, without asking leave or depending upon the will of any other man." The last phase suggests, of course, autonomy, but it "is grounded on his having reason, which is able to instruct him in that law he is to govern himself by . . ." (*Second Treatise,* paras. 4 and 63). For practical purposes, the two positions are very similar.

men from interference by others, including their government, are, however, in the longer perspective only a different way of putting the problem of justice and equality. Clearly, the non-compatibility of each man's actions with those of other men is the source of the frictions and tensions which it is the objective of a government to reduce. What therefore appears as justice, when looked at from the point of view of whether men are *treated* in accordance with consensual equality, appears as freedom when the question is focused upon whether they *act* in accordance with their individual preferences. It makes, of course, a good deal of difference whether the task of reducing frictions is primarily looked at in one of these ways or another, but when the problem is that of the objectives, and hence the tasks and functions of a government, this difference is of secondary significance. Here again it is important to recognize that in the political perspective the problem is one of more or less. The question is not, as is so often suggested in political oratory and semantic discourse, whether men are free or not, but rather whether they are more or less free. Related to that is the question of the respects in which they are free. For men are never entirely free, nor do they want to be.[23]

The problem of freedom might at this point be laid aside, but for the challenging issue of the several dimensions of freedom. These dimensions are three: there is the freedom of independence that our preceding remarks were focused upon, the freedom of participation which became of predominant concern in the democratic age, and the creative freedom of political innovation. Innovation based on invention is distinct from choosing and beyond effective prediction. We cannot here go into the many fascinating issues connected with this dimension of freedom; I have done so elsewhere. But it is important, especially for anyone concerned with development, to recognize the distinctiveness of this dimension of freedom. There is obviously a very great differ-

23. Friedrich, *Man and His Government,* chaps. 20–21. See Mortimer J. Adler, *The Idea of Freedom,* Vol. I (New York, 1958), Vol. II (New York, 1961); Michael Polanyi, *The Logic of Liberty* (London, 1951), who overstresses command as an aspect of liberty; Felix E. Oppenheim, *Dimensions of Freedom* (New York, 1961); and Carl J. Friedrich (ed.), *Liberty,* Vol. IV in the Nomos series (New York, 1962).

ence between choosing between alternatives that are known to exist and discovering new alternatives. This dimension cuts across the other two dimensions, as both the freedom of independence and that of participation may involve innovation. But leaving this complex problem aside until later, it seems to me important to face the implications of distinguishing the two freedoms of independence and participation—at times inaccurately referred to as "freedom from" and "freedom to." The freedom of independence which is the freedom of being protected against interference by others, but more particularly the government, has had primary importance for the developing countries in communal terms.[24] Not the freedom of the individual but the freedom of the tribe or native political community has preoccupied the thoughts of these emergent nations. As their independence is achieved, it merges with the first objective, as stated at the outset, namely that of security, as it is their tragedy that in the nuclear age they can only do so within limits. The individual's freedom of independence, on the other hand, is for most of them subject to the kind of paternalism that Plato expressed so dramatically when he declared that "it is better for every man to be ruled by divinity and insight,"[25] and "the principle is this—that no man, and no woman, be ever suffered to live without an officer set over them, and no soul of man to learn the trick of doing one single thing of its own sole motion. . . ."[26] Bills of rights may be included in the constitutions; they are not often part of its living context. In the rising national states of Europe the situation was similar. The main defenders of "rights" were noblemen who sought to protect their traditional privileges against the "state," which certainly was not concerned with such freedom until the Enlightenment. This part of freedom was not an objective at all.

Nor was the freedom of participation which properly belongs to the democratic age. Goethe's quip, "Majority is nonsense; intelligence is the possession of the few," expressed the general

24. On innovation as a characteristic of political development, see Braibanti's chapter in this volume, pp. 66–77.

25. Plato, *The Republic*, trans. A. D. Lindsay (New York, 1950), p. 590; *contra* Sir Isaiah Berlin, *Two Concepts of Liberty* (Oxford, 1958), who suggests the exclusion of external group freedom from the discussion of liberty.

26. Plato, *The Laws*, trans. A. E. Taylor (London, 1960), para. 942.

outlook even among quite a number of the Fathers at Philadelphia, as we all know.[27] But even in the later nineteenth century this freedom of participation was an objective of parties, rather than of the government. It was partly ideologically motivated and partly stimulated by the competition for a majority: the enlargements of the electorate were advocated in the hope of securing additional support for the party promoting such an extension. Since these enlargements had, in the end, to be effectuated by legislation, they can, of course, in this limited sense, be called objectives of the government.

In this connection one final major point needs to be made. There has been a widespread assumption that it is a major, if not *the* major, objective of modern government to "maximize" freedom (including participation). Little thought has been given to the limits which the dialectics of freedom itself imposes. Some of the most bitter controversies of the present time are due to a failure to understand the interdependence of the two kinds of freedom.[28] They cannot be indefinitely expanded at the same time. When the freedom of participation is increased (not by adding to the persons participating, but by adding to the number of fields to be covered and hence of decisions to be taken) the sphere of independence is thereby reduced. The problem of maximizing freedom ought therefore to be seen as that of balancing various freedom claims against each other. The maximizing of freedom is often acclaimed as the self-evident goal of democratic societies. Experience has taught, however, that it is an error to suppose that the majority of citizens in existing real political orders desire a maximum of freedom. Classical liberalism simply assumed it;[29] in point of fact, human beings desire a minimum of freedom, rather than a maximum. All men enjoy making some free choices, but only the unusual man desires to be as autonomous as possible. Most men exhibit a decided preference for values other than freedom. When opportunity for participation is provided, they do not participate, and when chances are given

27. Clinton L. Rossiter, *1787—The Grand Convention* (New York, 1966), esp. pp. 63–64, 242–243, 262–263.

28. This is further developed in Friedrich, *Man and His Government,* pp. 360–362; cf. also Oppenheim, *Dimensions of Freedom,* pp. 163–166.

29. John Stuart Mill, *On Liberty* (London, 1859), *passim.*

for private activity, they do not engage in it.[30] Anatole France, in a well-known barb, commented on the freedom of all rich and poor to sleep under the Seine bridges; what he meant was that bread was more important than freedom to the hungry man. This view is usually contested by the well fed, including labor leaders. Many men seem to prefer to have most decisions made for them, and practically all men prefer to have some decisions made for them. What holds for decisions holds equally for other behavior. There is much empirical evidence to support this proposition. Modern governments whether autocratic or democratic have not had as one of their major objectives to maximize individual freedom, though from time to time the increase of such freedom has been a goal. The extent to which the members of a political community are independently free and participants in its governing is an important question regarding any political order. But it is not possible to say that freedom has been a major objective except in that very general sense in which freedom is identified with power or coincides with the reduction of friction by the guarantee of consensual justice.

We have now cleared the ground for a further consideration of the four primary objectives of modern government: security, reduction of external friction, prosperity, and reduction of internal friction.

IV

The four primary objectives, often spoken of simply in terms of the political processes by which they are pursued, namely the military, diplomacy, legislation, planning, administration, and the judiciary, each constitute a major field of governmental activity.

30. David Riesman, *The Lonely Crowd* (New Haven, 1950). Riesman sets off the autonomous man as the norm of the superior man. His popular distinction is between three kinds of other (lesser?) men into tradition-directed, inner-directed, and other-directed. These are neologisms for men motivated primarily by custom, conviction, or sociability who evidently are less free than the autonomous man who will act on the basis of rational reflection and free choice. See also David Riesman, *Individualism Reconsidered* (Glencoe, Ill., 1954), pp. 287, 311–319, esp. the essay, "The Saving Remnant: An Examination of Character Structure," pp. 99 ff. Kant, contrariwise, made the mistake of assuming that all men seek autonomy; see C. J. Friedrich (ed.), *The Philosophy of Kant* (New York, 1949), pp. 187 ff., 225 ff., xxvi ff.

As we pointed out earlier, it is not admissible to consider one of these objectives as clearly possessing priority over the others, although this has often been done, especially regarding the first. But security (and the territorial expansion which becomes so often associated with the search for security) is often neglected in the search for peace or prosperity, as well as justice. Logic, especially a logic based upon Hobbesian or Freudian psychology, might indeed argue that men are necessarily giving priority to their survival. But the actual facts do not support this logic. Experience shows that humans readily risk survival for all kinds of objectives which are dearer to their hearts than life: give me liberty or give me death or, in modern terms, I'd rather be dead than red are typical.[31]

Since there is then no clearcut precedent for a "hierarchy" among these basic objectives, the problem is for political communities to resolve conflicts between them, when they appear. Each of the rival political orders claims for itself superiority in dealing with such conflicts, and it is evidently not our task here to resolve this problem. It is merely mentioned in order to make clear that a presumption in favor of any one of them, such as parliamentary or constitutional democracy, puts, in a sense, the cart before the horse. The development of modern government does, however, suggest that what Max Weber called a rational-legal order has certain distinct advantages. The regularity which the operation of government according to law provides suits the more highly developed industrial system much better than a arbitrarily discretionary, that is to say, hit-or-miss system. The key instrumentalities of such a rational-legal system are a developed bureaucracy (including a separate judiciary) and a suitable system of representation.[32]

31. Simone Weil, *Oppresion et Liberté* (5th ed.; Paris, 1955), who lived such a choice is very interesting on this point, but in fact all tragedy is built on it.

32. Huntington has pointed out that "rationalization, integration, and democratization . . . commonly appear in definitions of political development," but that "the characteristic . . . most frequently emphasized . . . is *mobilization*, or *participation*." Cf. Samuel P. Huntington, "Political Development and Political Decay," *World Politics*, XVII (1965), 388. In this connection he refers to Daniel Lerner's *The Passing of Traditional Society* (Glencoe, Ill., 1958), for the proposition that modern society will be a "participant society," a view for which Almond and Verba, *The Civic Culture*, also are adduced. It does not seem in keeping with Max Weber's broad conception to contrast the rational-legal bureaucracy with a production rationality; for what Weber had in mind was surely the cameralist bureaucrat who was very much a planner of production.

The experience that security is not necessarily *the* primary objective of a modern government does not mean that it is not *a* primary objective, and one that may have serious consequences for a country's political and economic development. For the cost of adequate security is very high, both in terms of the actual cost of a military establishment and in terms of the danger which such a military establishment on account of modern weapons creates for these emergent nations.[33] How great a handicap these security objectives create can be seen in a number of cases where the need for these expenditures has slowed the development that the preceding colonial regimes were able to foster. We have no adequate comparative figures, but the loss must be quite serious. How great an advantage it therefore can be to have the security taken care of by another government is manifest in the case of Puerto Rico, where that entire cost is borne by the United States; this advantage is, to be sure, counterbalanced by the obligation of Puerto Ricans to serve in the armed forces of the United States—they are, after all, United States citizens. It raises, however, the question whether some developing countries might not be well advised to take care of their security by comparable arrangements. (It might be noted in passing that the German Federal Republic's so-called economic miracle and hence its economic development was to no small extent made possible by the fact that for the crucial first decennium its security needs were largely taken care of by the United States.) The vigorous interest of the developing countries in the United Nations, though admittedly also due to other and even personal considerations of prestige, etc., is no doubt in part motivated by the fact that the United Nations offers an alternative security arrangement very much cheaper than a military establishment. A really effective international police force should be seen in this perspective.[34]

But besides the foregoing, there are other serious dangers

33. John J. Johnson (ed.), *The Role of the Military in Underdeveloped Countries* (Princeton, 1962), especially the studies by Edward Shils, Lucian Pye, Guy Pauker, and Johnson himself. Cf. also Samuel E. Finer, *The Man on Horseback: The Role of the Military in Politics* (New York, 1962); Morris Janowitz, *The Military in the Political Development of New Nations* (Chicago, 1964).

34. Harry Eckstein (ed.), *Internal War: Problems and Approaches* (New York, 1964); see also B. M. Russett and H. R. Alker, Jr., *World Politics in the General Assembly* (New York, 1965).

which an independent military establishment represents in any political community that has not yet acquired any broad consensus on its regime and national loyalty. The large number of military coups and subsequent autocratic and dictatorial governments testify to the reality of this "cost" of security under developmental conditions.[35] It is therefore clear that in this perspective also security arrangements other than military ones would, if they really satisfy this security objective, be highly desirable. In this connection I should like to add that the propensity to expansion which was so markedly a trait of the development of the modern state in the Western world and has been so poignant a feature of the Soviet Union and Red China, if not of the smaller Communist states, would likewise under such arrangements lose some of its trenchancy. The present situation is in this respect anything but reassuring, especially in Africa. In some of the rest of the underdeveloped world (e.g., Indonesia, Egypt, Paraguay) expansionist tendencies have also been manifest and in fact growing.[36]

What has just been said leads immediately to a consideration of the second primary objective, namely the reduction of external frictions, or more conventionally and broadly put, peace.[37] Peace has as much been an objective of the modern state as territorial security and expansion. There have of course been exceptions. Rulers when placed in absolute control have recurrently reverted to war as an intrinsically desirable state of affairs, seeking conquest and glory. But it is characteristic and for our present purposes decisive that such men have been the exception rather than the rule, and that they have found it desirable to wrap up their aggressive actions in arguments which protest their desire for peace and security. No one can read the diplomatic documents of

35. See especially Finer, *The Man on Horseback.*

36. See the works cited in n. 33 above and Nadav Safran, *The United States and Israel* (Cambridge, Mass., 1963), esp. chaps. 15–16. According to *Facts about Israel* (Jerusalem, 1966), 31.6 per cent of the national budget went for "security, special budget and reserve."

37. Friedrich, *Constitutional Government and Democracy*, chap. 3. See also Ludwig Gumplowicz, *Rasse und Staat* (Vienna, 1875), who argued that race conflict was a "law of nature," and Gustav Ratzenhofer, *Wesen und Zweck der Politik* (Leipzig, 1893), who expounded the notion that expansionism was inherent in political organizations (states). See also Raymond Aron, *Paix et Guerre entre les Nations* (Paris, 1962).

the seventeenth and eighteenth, and even more of the nineteenth, centuries without being impressed by the fact that as the particular state becomes modern, as its operations become rationalized and subject to legal rules, the reduction of external friction becomes a primary objective of the government. What stands behind such efforts is of course the realization that a political community has, under modern conditions, more to gain than to lose from the maintenance of peace. This general trend has actually been repeatedly interrupted by atavistic relapses into war. Feudal survivals in outlook and personnel combined with revolutionary thrusts to produce wars as did the intensification of competition for trade and colonies—honor and prestige often being pleaded in extenuation. But the slow evolution of ever more elaborate rules for the conduct of international relations embodied in a law based upon custom and convention testifies to the emergence of this major objective of modern government.[38]

This trend is closely associated with the ever clearer realization of what it takes to achieve prosperity, the third primary objective, under technically advancing conditions such as were associated with the industrial revolution. A very interesting argument has recently been set forth in support of the contention that the government actually has little to contribute to this development; indeed, the argument is to the effect that the "take-off" of industrial development is facilitated by a government which is ill-equipped to play a major role in starting the development. The argument is based upon a comparative evaluation of economic development in France, China, England, and Japan and is presented with all due caution about empirically derived hypotheses.[39] But in spite of this evidence it would seem that such past experience with relatively autonomous systems is apt to

38. Friedrich, *Constitutional Government and Democracy*, chap. 4. See also D. J. Hill, *A History of Diplomacy in the International Development of Europe* (3 vols.; New York, 1914); in Vol. III he gives significant analyses of retrogressions by Louis XIV (pp. 282 ff.) and Frederick II of Prussia (pp. 537 ff.).

39. Holt and Turner, *The Political Basis of Economic Development*, esp. pp. 294 and 307, where they state: "A government (particularly a central government) that does not contribute significantly to the satisfaction of the adaptive functional requisite is a prerequisite for take-off." Sombart's analysis contradicts Holt and Turner; take his striking statement, "modern government emerged from the silver mines of Mexico and Peru and from the gold mines of Brazil."

be misleading. Furthermore, the category of take-off itself is dubious. Economic development in England and France was decisively stimulated by the competition, that is to say the power struggle, precipitated by the discovery of gold and silver by the Spaniards in America. This discovery enabled them to organize and finance professional armies which won the battles that gave the house of Hapsburg predominance. The impact of this development was seen by Werner Sombart as the decisive factor in the development of the modern state.[40] Foreign aid may well be playing a comparable role as the precipitating factor.

The policies associated with mercantilism and cameralism—the increase in wealth as the central goal, the effort to have as large a balance of trade in one's favor as possible, the stimulation of trade and industries through the establishment of monopolies, stable money, acquisition of colonies even—all these were oriented toward achieving maximum prosperity and the fastest possible development. They constituted fairly elaborate plans for such a development of prosperity. I say prosperity, rather than some of the more contemporary terms such as increased standard of living or full employment, because such expressions would be anachronistic for this period. They too were involved, and indeed achieved, but they were not the primary objective.

Now it has been said, and by no less an authority than Eli Heckscher, and on the basis of the contemporary sources, that mercantilism was a system of power and that as such it was primarily a system for "forcing economic policy into the service of power as an end in itself." And he added that "the end was

40. For a general work useful at this point, see Bert F. Hoselitz *et al., Theories of Economic Growth* (Glencoe, Ill., 1960), especially Spengler's chapter, "Mercantilist and Physiocratic Growth Theory," pp. 3–64, and Hoselitz, "Theories of Stages of Economic Growth," pp. 193–238. The concept of "take-off" as a stage of economic development does not appear to have originated with W. W. Rostow, with whose work "The Take-Off into Self-Sustained Growth," *Economic Journal*, LXVI (1956), 25–48, it is commonly genetically linked. The idea of take-off is derivative from the classic literature of economic history, especially from the works of Werner Sombart and William Cunningham. It is especially central to the work of Sombart, who shows much insight into the political dimension. See also Carl J. Friedrich, "Power, Authority, Legitimacy: Political Theory and the Problem of Developing Countries," in Brookings Institution, *Political Theory and the Problems of Developing Countries* (Washington, 1968).

war."[41] This interpretation has been sharply contested by others, and what emerges from this discussion is that these modern governments moved away from "the end of war" as they became modern and that prosperity forged ahead as a primary objective. By the time Adam Smith came to challenge the mercantilist preconceptions, he did it explicitly in terms of economic advantage and industrial growth, in terms, that is, of general prosperity. By the middle of the eighteenth century the rational had won over the irrational urges, one might say.

Such industrial growth presupposed, however, that not only external but internal peace be secure. Hence the long-established concern of all governments with the reduction of internal friction, their fourth major objective, was reinforced by the new preoccupations. In all the developmental political orders it is being increasingly realized that effective adjudication of conflict requires objectivity and that such objectivity presupposes a substantial measure of independence. Hence the movement for an independent judiciary gains ground in the course of these centuries as part and parcel of the development of a modern government. Gone is the feudal dream of a benevolent king sitting under his oak tree and dispensing justice. What had still been accepted by a Locke as "natural," namely that the ruler should control the judges as part of the executive establishment, now is seen as inadequate; judges should be separate and separable. The Act of Settlement (1701) announces that judges shall hold office *quamdiu se bene gesserint,* and the great Montesquieu in the middle of the century, inspired in part also by what he had come to realize was the significant role of the *parlement* or high court in France, rationalized this trend by proclaiming a separate and independent judicial power to be a crucial feature of a "republican," or consti-

41. *Mercantilism* (London, 1935), II, 17. In a critical paper, "Power versus Plenty as Objectives of Foreign Policy in the Seventeenth and Eighteenth Centuries," *World Politics,* I (1948), 1 ff., Jacob Viner has persuasively argued that wealth as well as power was a prime objective of government, but he is wrong in thinking that men like Schmoller, Cunningham, and Heckscher disagree with him; they do, however, incline to think with Cunningham that the mercantile system is concerned solely with the pursuit of national power. See William Cunningham, *The Growth of English Industry and Commerce* (5th ed.; Cambridge, 1915), Vol. I, Sec. 136.

tutional, system. Thus the fourth major objective of modern government, the reduction of internal friction by the objective dispensing of "justice," becomes clearly established. It has remained of decisive importance. What is so often misinterpreted as a "liberal" trend in the totalitarian world is actually an increasing practice of protecting the judicial establishment against arbitrary interference by the executive and all that goes with it.[42]

This rapidly drawn sketch shows what have been and continue to be the major objectives of modern government. In view of the lack of any absolute priorities among the four basic objectives, concrete policy will have to balance the rival claims and thrusts. In this connection, it would be interesting to explore which of these objectives has taken precedence under what conditions over others. For as we noted, the same government has at different times and different governments have at the same time given priority now to security, now to prosperity, now considered internal friction and at another time external friction the more serious and pressing issue. Often an aggressive neighbor has forced the security issue to the fore, or an ideological upheaval has reinforced the desire for territorial expansion. Both in themselves and broadly considered, and when subdivided and elaborated, such objectives of modern government may be (1) spontaneously shared, (2) mutually supplementary, or (3) though conflicting, composed by appropriate fixed procedures. Any study concerned with how priorities are arrived at in specific constellations has to take these alternatives into account. There can be little doubt that the politics of developing countries will be shaped by the same foursome, and that hence the instrumentalities which have served to put them into practice will have to be developed. But that is another story. The preoccupation with such instrumentalities has, as we noted at the outset, characterized much developmental thought. The necessity of continually making choices and establishing priority among the possible major objectives makes it

42. Friedrich and Brzezinski, *Totalitarian Dictatorship and Autocracy,* chap. 10, and Friedrich, *Constitutional Government and Democracy,* chap. 6. Cf. especially Harold J. Berman, *Justice in the U.S.S.R.: An Interpretation of Soviet Law* (rev. ed. enl.; Cambridge, Mass., 1963).

vital that the question of procedures be seen in its relation to the objectives. Space forbids a detailed examination of these procedures and the instrumentalities (institutions) employed to effect them. But it may not be without interest to explore briefly what might be the basic features of a model political order serving the general objectives of modern government. Such a model may properly draw upon the experience of the past and thereby avoid the astigmatic preoccupations with particular orders as they have developed in the West. The developmental pattern is then definable in terms of such a model, rather than the general terms usually employed, such as "rationalization" or "mobilization."[43]

In this general framework, what are the minimal requirements of a good political order as a functioning whole? While the problem is general, let us focus attention upon the national political community. There can be little question that at present none of the existing orders provides these minimal requirements. We are here primarily concerned with the developing countries. But let us not forget that the developed countries have serious difficulties too. Everywhere on earth men are at present dissatisfied with their governments. This widespread dissatisfaction is due to three factors: a drift into misgovernment, an excessive demand (rising expectations), and an unmanageable situation brought on by technological developments. Situations vary, but everywhere there is decline in both authority and legitimacy of governments. Hence the specter of anarchy looms in many countries. In face of this mounting chaos, former systems of government provide no remedy.

Three tasks of an effective political order appear paramount when past experience is taken into account: how to transform a political community by a continuous process of internal renewal, how to plan the actions which the needs of the community require to be taken, how to carry out such plans and policies.

43. That such a possibility exists is vigorously denied by William J. Siffin, when he writes: "Political development *per se* can never be programmed in the real world in a comparable fashion"—comparable, that is, to economic development; see Montgomery and Siffin (eds.), *Approaches to Development: Politics, Administration and Change*, p. 5.

These three core tasks no existing political system is able to fulfil at the present time. This failure is actually not as great as it appears; the false appearance is caused by the ideological claims advanced by both constitutionalism and totalitarianism (popular democracy) on behalf of their systems. While pretending to be optimal solutions, they fail even to be minimal ones. A minimal solution to the problem as stated exhibits the following six features: First, a government that can act effectively, that can take all the measures necessary to cope with the technological requirements of survival, both economically and militarily, including comprehensive planning. Second, some enforcible restraints upon the government's operations which will protect the participant human beings sufficiently to enable them to act as political persons. Third, some operative participation of all adult and sane members of the community in the making of rules. Hence, fourth, general rules to express the more permanent shared values, beliefs, and interests. Furthermore, fifth, a judiciary which will interpret the rules and particularly define the terms of settlement for disputes which may arise. Finally, several voluntary associations (parties) which can as organizations develop alternative policy decisions and put forward alternative candidates for public office, and which will compete with each other in the determination of public business.

Existing political orders exhibit one or more of these six features, but none all of them. Although this assertion cannot be elaborated upon I should like to use the remaining space to make some further comments on two of the features just outlined. To take up the first and the last features jointly, the effective operation of a government under present conditions of a complex industrial society presupposes a great deal of authority and legitimacy; it cannot operate effectively by merely wielding power. The old saying about not being able to sit upon bayonets for long applies with particular poignancy. For if power is largely coercive, it fails to induce the many conforming activities which such an industrial society calls for. It is a formidable task which confronts present-day rulers: to acquire the vast power which industrial society in the more advanced stages of development calls for, and yet to have it remain genuinely consensual. The rulers of developing countries are discovering very rapidly that the very development they seek to promote tends to undermine the rule they wield. Hence the continuous and earnest search for more effectively constituting their institutions of government. To possess the capacity for reasoned elaboration of the grounds upon which the measures are based which economic (and military) development calls for, and to maintain the belief that they are entitled to rule, such rulers must organize voluntary support on a large scale. This kind of support is typically provided by parties, sometimes called movements to suggest a broader canvas; but if only one such party is allowed, both authority and legitimacy are put into jeopardy. The right to rule is then only acknowledged by the members of the party and its sympathizers. Several parties are necessary; what is not necessary is that these several parties alternate in ruling the country, as was the case in the classical British and American systems of constitutional government. It could there be the case, because national integration had already been achieved to a large extent; hence, as Lord Balfour once put it, they "were so fundamentally at one, that they could safely afford to bicker." In the developing countries, the task of integration must be accomplished alongside that of economic modernization. One of the parties may, under such circumstances, predominate over long periods of time and may be replaced by another which did not in fact play a significant role in the past in opposing the ruling party. Indeed the eventual "changing of the guard" may come as a result of a split in the party ranks (as happened in the older systems). The predominance of one party may be the result of the predominance of an individual with great inspirational power; it may be the consequence of great homogeneity in a part of the electorate; or it may be the result of a response to external threats. In any case, as long as competing parties are capable of protecting opposition elements and thus restraining the power-wielders, the second minimal requirement is fulfilled.

V

It would be interesting to pursue this analysis of our model further.[44] Let me conclude, however, by way of a summary. After some general comments on the problems of objectives, goals, and values, and the utopian search for a "highest good," I insisted that the problems of political development do not, in spite of the great variety of cultures, differ basically from the politics in mature societies. "Modernization" is, at least in politics, an equivocal term; for the objectives of modern government are universally (1) security, (2) external peace, (3) prosperity and (4) internal peace. Peace, we noted, is a poetic way of talking about the reduction of frictions and tensions. We tried to show that additional objectives, such as "justice," "freedom," and "equality," are all implied in the four basic objectives stated and are based upon an examination of the actual operations of modern government, as it developed in the West. Some very general observations on the four basic objectives, including more particularly a reminder that developmental planning was at the core of mercantilism and cameralism, recurrently served as a reminder that these four objectives were continually in rivalry as well as interdependence. Only passing note was taken of the instrumentalities, such as the bureaucracy, or the judiciary, except for a concluding sketch of a model political order. Since nations in many of the developing countries have to be built—as once they had to be in Europe—it should be obvious to the historically minded political scientist that leadership is crucial. For all political development a "developer" is needed,[45] but he need not be the formal chief, anymore than Richelieu or Cecil were. The need for such a person highlights the fact that all development, economic or other, is dependent upon political and governmental handling; for without

44. See Friedrich, *Man and His Government*, chap. 35.

45. Weidner has, in this connection, spoken of developmental entrepreneurs (without, however, using this specific term). Edward W. Weidner, "Development Administration: A New Focus for Research," in Ferrel Heady and Sybil L. Stokes (eds.), *Papers in Comparative Public Administration* (Ann Arbor, 1962), esp. p. 113.

power and power-wielders nothing can be done. Taking all the foregoing into account, it seemed advisable to sketch a sober model of political development as a tentative operational plan for the achievement of government's persistent basic objectives. But such a model of procedures and instrumentalities ought not to be confused with the basic objectives themselves. Nor would it be justified to consider such a model, nor indeed its developmental setting, as altogether novel. When Plato wrote his *Republic*, he let Socrates sketch a pattern of communal development, leading from the city of pigs to that of men. When Aristotle, steeped in the developmental problems of biology, wrote the constitution of Athens, he sketched a developmental design for a Greek *polis*.[46] He believed, as had Plato, that he knew what the *telos*, the end or primary objective of man and government, was; hence he could be reasonably sure what the final form, to be achieved through sound development, should be. We are not as fortunate, and therefore all developmental designs are subject to continuing re-evaluation, as a community's values, interests, and beliefs change and as governments must reinterpret their basic objectives in light of the community's evolution.

46. Plato's preoccupation with an ultimately static model has obscured his developmental concern; yet it is also quite apparent in *The Statesman* and *The Laws*, and the task of his Academy was to train "development administrators."

• 3 •

Comment on "Political Development and the Objectives of Modern Government"

Giovanni Sartori

In the opening lines of his chapter Professor Friedrich notes that in the volume by Almond and Powell[1] the subject of developmental comparative politics is approached "so abstractly and formally that ends, objectives, and purposes are rarely discussed in terms of their content"—indeed, "not one of these words appears in the index or in the table of contents" (pp. 107–108). It is readily apparent that the point can be generalized, that much of the current literature gives little place, if any, to a consideration of goals, ends, purposes, or objectives. Furthermore, a number of authors (in addition to Siffin, recalled by Friedrich in note 43) go into considerable pain to explain not only that the ends of political development cannot but also that they should not be stated.

My first reaction is thus to ask: Why? Why is it that we are so inclined, if not eager, to eschew the issue of the objectives of government?

Friedrich sets aside too swiftly, I feel, one of the major reasons for this. He asserts: "For gone are the days of the value-agnosticism of a Max Weber or a Vilfredo Pareto" (p. 109). Granted that the world in which Weber and Pareto lived is foregone, "value-agnosticism" is not. In fact, I would argue that the tide of value-fear and/or of value-phobia is mounting, and that the first reason that "objectives" are ignored, if not refused, is precisely that ends

1. Gabriel A. Almond and G. Bingham Powell, Jr., *Comparative Politics: A Developmental Approach* (Boston, 1966).

are attributed to a normative theory of politics which, in turn, is either considered extra-scientific, or value-biased, or both. The topic on which Friedrich boldly embarks raises, as such, the following preliminary question: is it true that objectives and goals do not belong to the "scientific" study of politics?

In this form my question is hardly manageable and would lead the discussion astray. But the question has at least one important aspect, or sideline, which is very much in keeping with the Friedrich approach and helps us to place his thinking in perspective. If the statement of ends, goals, and targets tends to disappear from the language of the observer (the political scientist), it surely remains central to the discourse of the living actors. Indeed, the living actors do seek and fight for ends that they call justice, freedom, equality, and the like. The query therefore is: how does such language of the observed relate to the language of the observer?

Admittedly the foregoing query solicits the text of Friedrich, even though I hope to remain true to the "spirit" of his paper. In any case it should be acknowledged from the outset that I shall engage in the kind of discussion that Abraham Kaplan calls "reconstructed." After all the real Friedrich can speak for himself; at best, and at most, I can deal with the "reconstructed Friedrich."

Which are *the* "ends of the state," as philosophers would have it? Friedrich (p. 116) brackets the recurrent basic objectives of any and all government (in the modern sense of the term) into four classes: (1) security and territorial expansion, (2) the reduction of external friction, (3) prosperity, (4) the reduction of internal friction. Conceivably there is no end to the number of alternative classificatory schemes one could propose. However, while many scholars are inclined to invent schemes that bear little relation to the way in which the political man perceives politics, the strength of this approach is that Friedrich *is* concerned with deriving his categories from the "questions about which men fight" (p. 110). In fact, Friedrich argues at considerable length that his categories do incorporate and do account for the objectives that the living actors call "order," "equality," and "freedom" (p. 117). And it seems to me that there is a distinct advantage in the "inductive" as against what one may call (for the sake of contrast) the "inventive" method of framing the study of politics.

The inductive method calls upon us to derive the observation of politics (i.e., the language of the observer) from the reality of politics (as expressed by the language of the observed). This is hardly the case with the inventive method, which is dangerously conducive, therefore, to a science of "metapolitics" that loses sight of politics. Differently put, by flying as it were over the head of the inductive method we are exposed to the risk of building for ourselves an ivory tower. One may say that this is for the better, but I imagine that Friedrich would say that this is for the worse.

The distinctive merit of Friedrich's analysis is, then, that he skilfully and judiciously navigates between Scylla and the Charybdis of the profession. He is aware of the danger of retaining the language of the living actors, but he is equally concerned with adopting a vocabulary that *translates* the language of the observed into the language of the observer. Indeed, I would say that Friedrich is prepared only to go as far as the problem of converting the language of action into the language of science allows him to go. Ultimately—as I will suggest—this is why Friedrich refuses much of the structural-functional vocabulary of present-day political science. The extent of his concern with the "translation problem" is readily revealed by his care in showing that the notions of justice and equality can be subsumed under the fourth objective, the reduction of internal friction, and that also the problem of liberty can be reduced to a particular way of looking at justice and equality (pp. 117 ff). One may disagree, of course, with the "translation handling," but what is more important is to note that Friedrich is painfully aware of a problem that is triumphantly neglected in the more recent developments of the discipline.

Having expressed my appreciation for the method, my assignment requires me to express some dissatisfaction as well. When I compare the four objectives of government listed at page 116 with the six features of the existing polities listed at page 132 as a "minimal solution to the problem" of achieving basic objectives of government, it strikes me that the second list contains *more* than a strict inferential derivation from the first list would permit. No doubt many reasons explain the difference between the two schemes. The first is more abstract, more comprehensive, not operational, and drawn from the history of the great national Western states, whereas the second scheme is more operational, elaborates present conditions, and makes particular reference to the developing countries. Yet my feeling remains that all these reasons do not suffice to fill the gap.

Perhaps I part company from Friedrich when he states that he prefers to speak of "political order" to avoid "the speculative and metaphysical aspects which the term 'state' traditionally is associated with" (p. 117). My first comment is to note that, as a matter of fact, most of the time Friedrich speaks of "government." My second comment is, consequently, that while Friedrich is right in pointing to the danger of reification associated with the notion of "state," he is not equally alert to the inherent ambiguity and looseness of the term "government"—if used *alone*. Personally I am inclined to use both state and government in contradistinction to one another—and even so I am still unhappy. In any event, if Friedrich dislikes "state," I would have preferred him to use consistently "political order," for in either case the point can be made that the concept is meant to include *both* the governors and the people who are governed. In this respect "government" is a tricky term, for it easily lends itself to being narrowly associated with those who govern. I am under the impression that Friedrich develops his argument less cogently than one would otherwise expect precisely because there is some oscillation in his exposition between the narrower and the broader meanings of government, that is, between an exclusive "reason of state" and an all-inclusive consideration of the objectives of the whole community.

At least, that is the best explanation I can provide for my inability to relate the initial scheme of page 116 to the "sober model" of pages 132–133. I would say, in fact, that while the first fourfold scheme basically represents the ends of government in the narrower sense (as perceived by the governors, by the power-wielders), in the final scheme the emphasis shifts toward a broader consideration of the ends of government as perceived and desired by the governed, by the power addresses. (Note in this connection: requirement 2, "some enforcible restraints upon the government's operations"; the formulation of requirement 3, which is not satisfied by the mere existence of "rules" but demands "operative participation of all" in their making; and particularly requirement 6, "several . . . parties" which compete, not the single mobilizational party.)

If the foregoing is correct, it also helps to explain why I am reluctant to follow Friedrich throughout in part of his translation handling. To say, for instance, that the "search for justice" can be reduced to the objective of "reducing internal friction" or to imply (as I read Friedrich at page 117) that "justice" corresponds to the activity of the "judges" is fair enough in the perspective of the governors—the narrow meaning. But the reduction is too strong if we are referred to what justice means in the language of the living actors, and thereby with reference to the broader context of the objectives of the governed.

In a similar vein I suggest that while Friedrich is quite right in making the point that "human beings desire a minimum of freedom, rather than a maximum" (p. 122), he is conceding at the same time too much and too little when he concludes that freedom, rather than a maximum" (p. 122), he is conceding at the the sense in which it "coincides with the reduction of friction by the guarantee of consensual justice." Too much in the perspective of governors, for in this narrow context the straightforward argument could be that the freedom of the citizens (freedom of independence) is not an objective. Too little in the perspective of the governed, for it seems to me that on the basis of the aforementioned conclusion the requirements 2 and 6 of his scheme cited above (p. 132) would not be adequately supported.

Returning from some petty details to the essential, the second major contention of Friedrich is that there is "no clearcut precedent for a 'hierarchy' " among the basic objectives of government (p. 111). Since I can only agree with this conclusion, let me suggest that the issue could be developed further by distinguishing between a *hierarchical scale* among ultimate goals on the one hand and, on the other hand, a *procedural precedence* among ends that are also the necessary means for the attainment of ulterior (not superior) ends. For instance, the survival of a state can be said to take precedence over the reduction of internal friction; or it can be argued that liberty of independence is procedurally a *sine qua non* condition of freedom of participation. (This is not to deny the "interdependence" of these two freedoms on which Friedrich rightly lays the stress, but to specify an essential aspect of such interdependence.)

Of course, it is unfair to ask Friedrich for more than he already manages to provide in some thirty pages—indeed a brilliant tour de force, if one is reminded of the range and intricacy of his assignment. Yet I make the suggestion because I feel that his major conclusion that the problems of political development do not differ basically from the politics in mature societies would be reinforced by showing that means-ends relationships and the related procedural priorities are necessarily the same—if these priorities are correctly stated—for all societies at all times. However that may be, I certainly share Friedrich's feeling that we have gone too far in emphasizing the uniqueness, the novelty, and the unpredictability of the ongoing processes of so-called political modernization.

In particular I bow to the masterful manner in which Friedrich makes the point, throughout his chapter, that governments—regardless of whether they are under- or overdeveloped—do pursue persistent, basic objectives, and that these objectives not only are "worthy of exploration as a vital part of comparative politics," but also are "capable of being so explored." The last sentence brings me again to Friedrich's method, and precisely to the question, How can ends be explored?

If I understand Friedrich correctly, ends (and even values) lend themselves to empirical exploration if the historical evidence is subjected to the treatment that John Stuart Mill called "inverse deductive method." It is precisely because Friedrich applies this method that his categories differ from the categories alamode of the so-called structural-functional approach. Indeed the dissatisfaction of Friedrich with the Almond-type vocabulary is a persistent theme of his writings. In the chapter under cross-examination, "political tradition" is preferred to "political culture," declared a vague concept (p. 112 and n. 9); "socialization" is declared a mistaken way, often enough, of speaking of education (p. 112); and Friedrich's dislike for the notions of rationalization, mobilization, value allocation, and in fact for the entire conceptual apparatus of a general systems theory is eloquently testified by his silence no less than by his passes.

My question is: do the new categories of structural-functional analysis replace, and replace advantageously, the more traditional categories of political analysis? More specifically, how does the Parsons-Almond-Easton type of conceptualization compare with the more substantive, concrete, and "inductively translated" categories of analysis that Friedrich draws from the inverse deductive method? This is the problem that Friedrich forcefully poses, and, I suggest, a problem that we should squarely confront.

• 4 •

Goals for Administrative Reform in Developing States: An Open-Ended Design

Henry S. Kariel

> Every habit and faculty is preserved and increased by corresponding actions—as the habit of walking, by walking; or running, by running.
>
> EPICTETUS, *How the Semblances of Things Are To Be Combated*

Much of the current theorizing about political development can be brought into focus if it is assumed to contribute to a general descriptive framework within which the direction, pace, and stages of change can be identified and predicted. There would seem to be a persistent search for the conditions determining development. Even the least sophisticated efforts to accumulate data may be seen as attempts to inventory the relevant variables in what, it is hoped, will ultimately constitute a general descriptive theory—or, more ambitiously, a naturalistic science of means.[1] Whatever the terminological profusion and conceptual confusion, the aim is to minimize ambiguity, rigorously to reduce complexity by abstracting. The imperative is to simplify a linear historical process, to order it and make it manageable. Understandably, the flavor of the literature is technological, the very language putting conventional prose to the test.

The problems which today confront us, if the relevant literature of political science is to be believed, appear to be primarily methodological (insofar as the problems are intramural) and

1. A useful résumé is Robert A. Packenham, "Approaches to the Study of Political Development," *World Politics*, XVII (1964), 108–120.

technological (insofar as the problems pertain to the political terrain outside the universities). It is widely assumed, as LaPalombara has observed in his contribution to this volume, that Western administrative technology, seen as constitutional engineering, is best employed for the realization of generally agreed-on ends—popular participation in politics, personal growth, and, of course, human dignity. Once we discover the right mixture of preconditions, properly balance constraint and freedom, foster habits of civility, and construct the appropriate social, industrial, and economic setting, the common good may be counted on to emerge. The common good is not so much inherent in present activities as in their end product.

To be sure, we occasionally make clear to ourselves that the means-ends distinction on which our scientific preoccupation rests fails to console the mass of men whose days are numbered and who therefore find it hard to muster the patience to wait for the agreeable end results. To deal with our uneasiness, we have found two formulas useful. When facing abroad, we speak of the incredible complexity of phenomena, the unpredictable consequences of all plans, the ultimate hopelessness of all positive intervention in the historical process. Thus Burke is enlisted to answer Machiavelli as well as Marx. On the other hand, when facing the domestic front, we like to imply that the future, all things considered, is virtually here: the ideal is really more or less embodied in that cluster of institutions and mores which we in the Western world have providentially succeeded in developing. Ours is the first new nation. Admittedly, there are residual difficulties: a good number of men remain underemployed, and various managerial elites engage in their administrative routines rather cheerlessly. Yet a sufficiently detached view makes apparent that fundamentally all is well. The system works. It is stable, mature, developed, functional.

I do not mean to intimate that we are so careless as to affirm how impressed we are by our political achievement. On the contrary, we have learned to be cautious and to warn ourselves about the dangers of ethnocentric biases in analysis. Both our prefaces and postscripts explicitly avow that there are many roads and many destinations. Yet as we engage in systematic analysis and assume that functions "really" function, we tacitly close alternatives and relax. Pleased by our own political success story, we come to doubt the present validity of norms defended by orthodox democratic theorists from Rousseau to John Stuart Mill. Somewhat patronizingly, we proceed to appreciate the aims of the orthodox theorists, noting that they may have been realistic enough in their day but that today, surely, it would be foolish to subscribe to Rousseau's sentimental romanticism, Paine's belief in sociability and minimum government, Jefferson's revolutionary rhetoric, Jackson's amateurism in administration, Mill's faith in man's higher faculties, and—it still remains hard to add his name —Marx's utopian society in which the division of labor would not be reified. We insist that today—in view of our own political achievement—there are new issues and new men to formulate them. Thus Friedrich inquires in this volume whether increasing popular participation in politics is really the primary issue of political development. After all, there are other public goods, as the course of modern European history is said to reveal. Modern European history can be made to show not only to what extent men participate in politics but also, and more significantly, to what extent stability has been achieved. Have we not created a system of interest politics which has held public government in check while it promoted private enterprise, protected property rights, and enhanced socio-economic freedom? By the use of actual or threatened violence, in the name of law and order, under such ideological banners as laissez faire, and relying on the powers of the superego which Mill called "the monitor within," relatively stable polities have been established and maintained. It only remained for political scientists to certify them as modern, developed, mature, and legitimate.[2]

2. Thus Gabriel A. Almond and Sidney Verba have made the orthodox democratic model dubious by writing simply: "It might be quite irrational to invest in political activity the time and effort needed to live up to the rationality-activist model. It may just not be worth it to be that good a citizen" (*The Civic Culture: Political Attitudes and Democracy in Five Nations* [Princeton, 1963], pp. 375–376). Also see the critique in my *The Promise of Politics* (Englewood Cliffs, N.J., 1966) and Christian Bay's criticism in "The Cheerful Science of Dismal Politics," mimeographed paper prepared for inclusion in Theodore Roszak (ed.), *The Dissenting Academy* (New York, 1968), pp. 208–230.

One consequence of this contemporary academic posture has been to make the analysis and discussion of goals dispensable: substantive rationality is made to give way to functional rationality. *Knowing* what is functional—identifying functions with forms of behavior that turn out to be, in a word, gentlemanly—we find it sensible and easy to accept our present political condition as healthy. For us the public good is not something to be realized later. Leaving aside a few social accidents at the margins of our political life, ours is the good society in operation. If, then, we still employ a means-ends schema, we do so not in relation to our own political order but in relation to the men who populate the still developing sectors of the world. It is for them that there can be no avoiding an imposed discipline, an externally enforced postponement of gratification. If they can only be made to accept the appropriate sacrifices in life lived fully, they too will experience the pleasures of freedom. There can be no progress without enforced savings, without using men merely as instruments, without a duly disciplined, incorruptible administrative system. And should this posture fail to convince, we add that there is no choice in any event: sacrifices are said to be entailed by "the inner logic of industrialism," "the necessities of economic growth," "inevitable oligarchical tendencies," or "the imperatives of the historical process."

To what extent choices are in fact open to us is of course an empirical question. To raise it so that the very process of answering it constitutes practical political action—producing political change generally or administrative reform specifically—we must postulate testable norms. It should go without saying that such norms cannot be derived from a prevailing state of affairs, not even from conditions which the more organized and articulate members of the community regard as pleasing. But if existing institutions yield no standard, as is widely conceded, where can we possibly turn? The old verities—the great abstractions that were said to conform to natural law—are discredited not only because men have been brutalized in their name but also on epistemological grounds. The problem is to formulate standards justifying change without becoming either positivist or mystical, without (to put the matter simply) departing from the tradition of empiricism.

One promising way to proceed would be to consider the signposts provided by H. L. A. Hart. Wholly within the tradition of British empiricism, he has been concerned with specifying the minimum content for natural law, contending that even for descriptive purposes one must move beyond both definitions and statements of fact to statements "the truth of which is contingent on human beings and the world they live in. . . ."[3] He would have us be oriented by those principles without which social life would not be viable at all, and he regards these as universal characteristics of human nature. Without them, there can be no survival. He specifically lists human vulnerability, approximate equality, limited altruism, limited resources, and limited understanding and strength of will.[4] Stressing that these contingent facts are indispensable to social organization, he postulates no more than man's interest in the maintenance of life. Having put the stress on life, he leads us to open the further question about life so lived that it would incorporate the greatest range and variety of manageable experiences.

This approach has the effect of keeping inquiry into norms within the empirical realm. It also makes it possible to direct attention to the forces which block man's development, arresting his growth or retarding his maturation. Introducing an array of medical metaphors and begging for the use of such terms as health, disease, and pathology, it finally enables us to discuss problems of social therapy.

It is Christian Bay who has most recently embraced the medi-

3. *The Concept of Law* (Oxford, 1961), p. 195. The fruitfulness of Hart's approach has been noted by W. G. Runciman, *Social Science and Political Theory* (Cambridge, 1963), pp. 168–169, and Fred M. Frohock, *The Nature of Political Inquiry* (Homewood, Ill., 1967), pp. 98–99. See also Frederick M. Watkins, "Natural Law and the Problem of Value-Judgment," in Oliver Garceau (ed.), *Political Research and Political Theory* (Cambridge, Mass., 1968), pp. 58–74.

4. Hart, *The Concept of Law*, pp. 190–193. For a summary of the literature dealing with basic needs, see Paul Kurtz, *Decision and the Condition of Man* (Seattle, 1965), chap. 9. James C. Davies has attempted to apply ranked needs to politics; see *Human Nature in Politics* (New York, 1963). For hypotheses about a hierarchy of universal needs, see Abraham H. Maslow, "Theory of Human Motivation," in Philip L. Harriman (ed.), *Twentieth Century Psychology* (New York, 1946), pp. 22–48, and *Motivation and Personality* (New York, 1954).

cal analogy and attempted to welcome a perspective which focuses on man's biological and psychological needs. He would not distinguish between the purposes of political science and medicine. The proper purpose of both is to postpone death and to reduce suffering.

"What is remarkable is that none would be so bold as to say that the overriding purpose of politics ought to be to do away with all avoidable suffering in this world of ours, and that the highest priority for political science should be to study how this can be brought about by means of social organization, including government."

"Political science does not prescribe drugs, for its competence is not in human physiology or body chemistry; but it should aim at prescribing the organizational innovations and social experimentation that will allow us to cultivate, in Albert Schweitzer's term, a 'reverence for life.' "[5] Bay recognizes the problems of dealing with social issues from a therapeutic perspective: he acknowledges that part of life may have to be given to save another part, the problem of establishing priorities and needs, and above all the difficulty of defining health and well-being. But even though one man's misery, as Dostoevski has pointed out, may be another's joy, to formulate our condition and prospects in biopsychological terms can at least give us testable, empirical propositions. The task of determining man's needs empirically, Bay concedes, remains formidable. Yet by defining "human needs" dynamically as any tendency—latent or manifest—whose continual suppression leads to pathology, and by regarding as pathological anything which is not life-facilitating, norms do become accessible to empirical inquiry—without at the same time being reduced to nothing but our immediate wants and desires.[6]

5. Bay, "The Cheerful Science of Dismal Politics," in Roszak (ed.), *The Dissenting Academy*, p. 225.

6. Bay's approach was initially worked out in his *The Structure of Freedom* (Stanford, 1958); he has developed his ideas in the paper cited above as well as in "Behavioral Research and the Theory of Democracy" (November, 1965, mimeographed), and in "Beyond Pluralism: The Problem of Evaluating Political Institution in Terms of Human Needs" (May, 1965, mimeographed). For a comprehensive effort to reduce ethical indeterminancy by providing an empirically grounded valuational base, see Abraham Edel, *Ethical Judgment: The Use of Science in Ethics* (New York, 1955), esp. pp. 143 ff. See also Watkins, cited above in n. 3.

Accepting this approach should free us from the inhibitions imposed by our ideological interests in what has "worked"; it should move us to specify general requisites for optimal human development. Thus freed, we may be able to turn from norms specifically associated with the Western Liberal Tradition (or with the American Way of Life) and consider more universal even if less well supported human needs. Where we tend to associate development with constitutionalism, "rationality" in administration, equality under the law, elite competition, individual acquisitiveness, hierarchical organization, and a highly articulated division of labor, we may be able to expatriate ourselves and become less narrowly "realistic."[7] We might then inquire in psychological terms about the ends of human development—perhaps even reconsider the merits of what Mill called the stationary state[8]—and discuss how we might institutionally accommodate the healthy personality. Although this approach may not yield a blueprint for administrative reform, it may reduce our vague anxieties to specific fears as we face the organizational developments of our times. It is the latter, I should note explicitly, which is my main interest. In pursuing it, I may not specify what appears practicable and realistic to those of my contemporaries who are now under fire (sometimes literally) to make administrative decisions, but my effort should at least reveal our own limitations.

I would in any case concede that I am not oriented by present modes of behavior. If we are persuaded that a certain personality is normatively healthy, we are in no position to argue against our norm on the ground that it is unfulfilled in practice. Kant's advice against taking our bearings by the prevailing forms of human conduct remains relevant:

> A constitution founded on the greatest possible human freedom, according to laws which enable the freedom of each individual to exist by the side of the freedom of others (without any regard to the highest possible human happiness, because that must

7. For a narrowly "realistic" approach which either ignores individual needs or else assimilates them to established institutions, see Lucian W. Pye, *Aspects of Political Development* (Boston, 1966).

8. See John Stuart Mill, *Principles of Political Economy* (London, 1848), Book IV, Sec. 1, where Mill expresses his aversion to interminable growth in population and to a boundless increase in wealth.

> necessarily follow by itself), is, to say the least, a necessary idea, on which not only the first plan of a constitution or a state, but all laws must be based, *it being by no means necessary to take account from the beginning of existing impediments, which may owe their origin not so much to human nature itself as to the actual neglect of true ideas in legislation.* For nothing can be more mischievous and more unworthy of a philosopher than the vulgar appeal to what is called adverse experience, which possibly might never have existed if at the proper time institutions had been framed according to those ideas. . . .[9]

If we desire societies to be well administered; if, furthermore, we realize it is merely question-begging to urge greater administrative efficiency; and if, finally, we know we cannot reasonably speak of administrative reforms without defining the goals we wish to realize, we cannot evade the attempt to define the ideals to be sustained by the machinery of the state.[10] Today, it is not easy to satisfy this imperative. We not only distrust all explicit idealism but are even more distrustful of the specific ideal of human nature which, I would argue, merits general support.

To conceptualize man in the terms of an open-ended system—and I do not believe any alternative conceptualization is finally acceptable—is to arouse understandable resistance. The obstacles to such a conceptualization are familiar: habit, ideology, elites which profit from man's arrested development, and perhaps not least that lazy way of employing forms of the verb "to be" which leads us to claim that man "is" virtuous or depraved, free or determined, selfish or altruistic, competitive or co-operative, one thing or another, but in any case something quite specific. These

9. Immanuel Kant, *Critique of Pure Reason,* trans. F. M. Mueller (New York, 1896), p. 257, emphasis added. The rest of the passage, in which Kant, following Plato and Rousseau, maintains that the punitive aspects of government might be progressively eliminated, is equally relevant; he notes that were man less thwarted by the political system he might serve it (and himself) better.

10. Robert A. Packenham has noted that when scholars writing about development fail to specify the ends of development, the ends tend to be "determined contextually by what 'the people,' 'leaders,' 'institutions,' or 'politically articulate groups' *want.*" And because the question of wants is empirical, normative problems need not be faced. Yet to employ a positivistic approach which focuses on wants is bound to provide normatively conservative answers: only men who are articulate (that is to say, developed personalities) can identify their wants and know how to bring them into balance. Packenham himself concludes that "decision-makers make—and must make—normative decisions about who gets what" ("The Study of Political Development," in Michael Haas and Henry S. Kariel [eds.], *Approaches to the Study of Political Science:* San Francisco, forthcoming]).

blocks to an open-ended conception of man make it hard to find the words which might persuade us to think of the individual as free, or at least as potentially free.[11] Attempting to characterize the free man, we are forever driven to specify what he is free *for*. Given economic scarcity and an ethic of hard work for tangible or at least audible results, it has never seemed enough for a man to be in action; he has to be active in behalf of some good cause, to be good for something. How, then, are we to define man who is free to be himself, who is, to put it bluntly, good for nothing?

For help, I should like initially to enlist the novelist insofar as he has succeeded in dramatizing an engaging image of man I believe to be of general political relevance. Over the last century, the novelist has increasingly crowded the literary landscape with outsiders who are in, with characters who are socially involved but transcend their involvement by being aware of it—that is, with participant-observers. Huck Finn, anticipating legions of anthropologists, takes part in the life and morality of the shore, always interested in the curious rituals of the natives; yet his home remains the raft. Ishmael, the most durable character in *Moby-Dick*, moves easily within every group of that self-contained industrial organization, the "Pequod"; yet he is not so entangled as to go down with it. Lawrence's "man who died," crucified and resurrected, moves on by boat at last; Malamud's Levin, freighted with new academic experiences—a colleague's wife, a bundle of impossible kids—in the end travels lightly toward California in an old car. All depart buoyed up (Ishmael literally so), though all are burdened by knowledge: Mann's Hans Castorp, Camus' Meursault, Silone's Pietro Spina, Hemingway's Nick Adams, and Graham Greene's Mr. Brown, who in *The Comedians* passes the supreme test by being prepared to die for his belief—his belief in nothing more than the desirability of acting out a part in which he permitted himself to be cast, the leader of an utterly futile revolution, dying not for a cause, only for his absurd, comic, deadly role. If these characters die (or pass on to a new life) they die with ease. Their fate is in their own

11. Consider especially the questions raised by Felix Oppenheim, *Dimensions of Freedom* (New York, 1961), and Hannah Arendt, "What Is Freedom?" in *Between Past and Future* (New York, 1961), chap. 4.

hands. Potential suicides, none of them despises life. All seek to make the most of their situation. Castorp welcomes every contact which might extend the range of his perceptions: he deliberately touches cultural polarities. Even Meursault, almost dead to the world, screams in the end that what he desires for eternity is "a life in which I can remember this life on earth." All wish somehow to experience more, and to express what they have experienced. Not satisfied with any specific encounter, forever on the move, they will not permit themselves to become fully involved by playing but one part. Thus Greene's whiskey priest is also the revolutionary, lover, criminal, savior, drunkard, hero, and coward. Silone's Spina embodies the contradictory demands of priest and rebel. And there seems no end to the ways Mann's confidence man, Felix Krull, can present himself to the world. Whatever parts they play, these characters keep their distance from them. Each of them recognizes his manifold affairs as merely human, prone to fail, none so holy as to be worth the whole of one's life.

Their posture, admittedly, is difficult to accept. We certainly do not like to catch ourselves merely at play, only lightly engaged, ready to withdraw from our commitments. We tend to favor those who are true to but one cause, members of but one sex, successful *in* something rather than good *at* something, professional in the civil service system rather than amateurish in what we revealingly call the spoils system. Our concern is with results—getting them as cheaply and quickly as possible. Preoccupied by outputs defined as end products, we embrace a means-ends distinction. We may think of ourselves as enjoying the game of politics, appreciating its give-and-take. We may even speak of science as essentially playful. But we nonetheless want conclusions, decisions, findings. We cherish success, and define it unambiguously.

We scarcely recognize the men who have chosen to fail—or who, knowing there is no way of succeeding, have persisted in communicating that in the end our enterprises must come to nothing. We have yet to see that it is possible to reject Final Rewards or Ultimate Purposes, possible to be devoted to life as an ongoing process, to experience rewards inherent in the act of communicating and not in some final product, in the process of learning and not in the lesson learned. For us there still is something illegitimate about those who fail to graduate and do not wish to come to conclusion. And what is illegitimate—not publicly acceptable—we allow ourselves to play with only in privacy, where it will not matter, where we can afford to indulge our appetite for variety and life.

In the private sector of our lives, seeking mere "entertainment," we welcome secret agents, imposters, picaresque heroes, *Doppelgänger,* confidence men, swindlers, rogues, criminals, and dropouts such as Huck Finn. We who are publicly driven to *be* something, relax privately and marvel at ingratiating characters who can afford to be nothing, who (like James Bond or the spy who came in from the cold) amount to nothing. Unlike us, they are free—free to ignore the calls of Honor, Duty, Destiny, and Country; they are uprooted men whose personality is marvelously split, whose loyalty is divided, whose identity is radically uncertain. We find something intoxicating about their obvious irresponsibility. And given the public burden we labor under—the imperative to succeed—we privately envy them their endless transgressions, their calculated indifference to conventional norms, their illicit affairs. Here are lawless men—or rather men who are laws unto themselves—living in an intriguing world that is fluid and full of surprises, that is dangerous, sinister, forbidden. They are truly opportunists, doing what they must to sustain themselves, but doing no more. They are alert to shifts in their environment, tense from paying attention, weary from too much awareness, hoping in the end to climb the last wall and come in from the cold.

However familiar this type may be to us privately, it annoys us to meet him in the open, for he challenges our beliefs about how public life must be lived, how apolitical the mass of men must remain. He is a disconcertingly *political* being, personally embodying structural complexity and role differentiation. Shying away from politics, we are disquieted by the open-ended personality.[12]

12. I should also like to call attention to a model of man provided by Norman O. Brown's *Hermes the Thief* (Madison, Wisc., 1947); I was introduced to it by David C. McClelland, "The Spirit of Hermes," in *The Achieving Society* (Princeton, 1961), chap. 8.

It is only when we encounter man as a distinctively political being in the literature of social psychology that we give him our approval. Not being aroused by academic designs, we fail to perceive all they offer—and hence find it possible to go along with them. There is little to excite us as we ponder, for example, a portrait of the non-authoritarian personality or Harold Lasswell's dry inventory of the characteristics of what he has called the democratic personality. Yet precisely because the prose of social analysis is dispassionate, it may enable us to review soberly what it means to speak of the developed individual.

Social psychology has by no means constructed a stringently formulated model of man as an open-ended system.[13] Nor is it likely to. The fact is that the very way we use our language impedes precision. Our subject-predicate bifurcation, our saying that something is such-and-such, establishes absolutes.[14] It is our grammar which ineluctably drives us to support a model of man as a closed, homeostatic system possessing various definite attributes. Moreover, a positivistic science which presumes to describe these attributes once and for all impels us to draw a boundary around a settled subject area and express what lies within the boundary in terms of empirical correlations or functional relationships.

When "man" is the object of such a science, he is bound to emerge as a strictly reactive organism. As his past is used as an index to his future, he becomes definable and predictable. What he *can* do comes to be seen as a function of what is manifestly

13. Gordon W. Allport, *Pattern and Growth in Personality* (New York, 1961) and *Becoming* (New Haven, 1955); Harold D. Lasswell, "Democratic Character," in *The Political Writings of Harold D. Lasswell* (New York, 1951), pp. 465–525; Nevitt Sanford, *Self and Society: Social Change and Individual Development* (New York, 1966), chap. 2; Abraham H. Maslow, *Towards a Psychology of Being* (Princeton, 1962); Carl R. Rogers, *On Becoming a Person* (Boston, 1961), and "Toward a Modern Approach to Values: The Valuing Process in the Mature Person," *Journal of Abnormal and Social Psychology*, LXVIII (1964), 160–167; Milton Rokeach, *The Open and Closed Mind* (New York, 1960); Harry Stack Sullivan, *The Interpersonal Theory of Psychiatry* (New York, 1953); Fred I. Greenstein, "Personality and Political Socialization: The Theories of Authoritarian and Democratic Character," *Annals of the American Academy of Political and Social Science*, CCCIXI (1965), 81–95; Robert White, *Lives in Progress: A Study of the Natural Growth of Personality* (New York, 1952, 1966).

14. Nietzsche saw what was involved when he wrote that "we cannot get rid of God because we still believe in grammar" (*Gesammelte Werke* [23 vols.; Munich, 1922–29], XVII, 73).

within him. If he has been thrown off balance because of some external pressure, he can recover, it is assumed, by being induced to use his already available resources. The individual can then be said to have staged a "recovery" in two senses of the term: he has achieved a healthy state and has simultaneously regained something lost. His health is defined in terms of previously accumulated resources; the problem is to provide for their reallocation.

Accepting this model of man as a closed system, we have encouraged a positivistic science to instruct us how much we are in fact victims of our past, how well we behave, how conditioned and personally uncreative we are, how we might be repaired when the mechanism goes wrong. We have learned what we amount to, what we *are*. And because in some measure we undeniably *are* something, namely an organism reacting in predictable ways to external stimuli, the closed model turns out to be potent and attractive.

Its competitor—or better, its complementary model—has hardly been able to hold its own. As I have suggested, it has certainly been difficult to conceptualize persuasively. It cannot be formulated in the unambiguous, denotative terms proper for describing the elements of closed systems. It fails to settle things, for it cannot refer to what men *are*. Thus Gordon Allport has had to speak awkwardly of man as a "being in the process of becoming." From his perspective, we would recognize not a set of substantive character traits but only personal dispositions, not uniform variables but only infinite potentialities. We would see a person as healthy, in Frank Barron's words, "when his awareness includes the broadest possible aspects of human experience, and the deepest possible comprehensions of them, while at the same time he is most simple and direct in his feelings, thoughts, and action."[15] These formulations, it is true, are exasperatingly vague. Moreover, their authors decline to moralize. They express an open-ended conceptualization which frustrates our

15. "What is Psychological Health?" *California Monthly*, LXVIII (1957), 22–25. A promising beginning for a rigorous conceptualization is Nevitt Sanford's discriminating among health, maturity, and development and his suggestion that these be treated as independently variable and not necessarily positively correlated. See *Self and Society*, chap. 2. See also Karl W. Deutsch's formulation of growth in *The Nerves of Government* (New York, 1963), pp. 139–140.

impulse to tell men and women what they ought to do with their lives, to what ends they ought to use them. Although we can still recommend that they are to live their lives fully, we can no longer tell them which roles to play. Assuming that we cannot quite take man's measure and that not all roles have been discovered, we have to let men decide for themselves. They must be left free (or helped to become free) to create and test their own roles, and risk failure. That emphatically does not mean we are morally disarmed. A whole decalogue of formal injunctions remains: keep something in reserve, do not go all the way, do not be taken in, keep an eye out for alternatives, do not put all your eggs in one basket. These conventional warnings, it turns out, ideally guide the conduct of the non-authoritarian, "democratic" person.

Of course such a standard for action seems of no use to the individual whose very survival is threatened, who is forced to use all his power just to hang on. It is said that unless the prerequisites for autonomous action have been met, it is self-defeating (and cruel) to urge him to determine his own future. He must *first* have had the opportunity to develop (1) self-confidence so that he can admit to having made a stultifying decision, (2) a capacity for imagining and theorizing so that he can reflect on alternatives, and (3) enough personal detachment so that he can commit himself to a multiplicity of interests and play a variety of conflicting roles. He must *first* be able to welcome life's contradictory claims, seeing conflict and insecurity not as something to be transcended but as inherently valuable. He must *first* have understood himself as an open-ended system. If I remain skeptical of this approach, this is because of my commitment to a pragmatism which insists that we can learn to act only by acting. To reject this and preserve the means-ends distinction, I would insist, has the practical effect of letting elites continue to live in the realm of ends while the lower orders of society are induced to make sacrifices today so that they may somehow get into the political act tomorrow.

I have taken the long route from novelist to social psychologist in order to expose more than the familiar aspects of the person as an open-ended system. We should now be able to discern the reason for our ambivalence toward him, seeing him as a not always attractive role-player. He opposes outcomes and end products, he endlessly postures and performs, and he finally regards nothing as precious but his act—*and his need to have others join him in it.*

It should prove to be chastening to acknowledge these unfamiliar dimensions of the individual—what I would have us recognize as the fully developed political man. He alone should be posited (in Roland Pennock's phrase) as a political good.[16] Institutionally, he can be fully accommodated only by social organizations which themselves are open-ended, and thus capable of honoring his infinitely varied and never wholly manifest interests.[17] To acknowledge the force of what I am urging may of course make us feel somewhat less optimistic about the feasibility of our own further political development. It might even make some of us ask whether we really should esteem the individual committed to nothing but action, whether we should aim for a pure politics whose practitioners are serious about nothing else. Is it really proper to identify politics with play?

Certainly there is hostility toward taking such a view of man and a reluctance to support the administrative apparatus for which it calls. There are considerable ideological and conceptual impediments. But whatever the feelings of those who remain persuaded that play for its own sake is sinful (or dysfunctional), who believe man must conform to some higher purpose, we might on the most practical of grounds reject the identification of life with play. Thus Rousseau, Joseph de Maistre, and Durkheim believed the restraints imposed by myths to be necessary for

16. J. Roland Pennock, "Political Development, Political Systems, and Political Goods," *World Politics,* XVIII (1965), 415–434. See also Fred W. Riggs, "The Ecology of Development," Comparative Administration Group Occasional Paper (Bloomington, Ind., 1964).

17. The appropriate organizational attributes of development have been variously defined in terms of capability for continuous change—that is, openness. See especially S. N. Eisenstadt, "Bureaucracy and Political Development," in Joseph LaPalombara (ed.), *Bureaucracy and Political Development* (Princeton, 1963), pp. 96–119, and "Modernization and Conditions of Sustained Growth," *World Politics,* XVI (1964), 576–594; Samuel P. Huntington, "Political Development and Political Decay," *World Politics,* XVII (1965), 386–393; Alfred Diamant, "Political Development: Approaches to Theory and Strategy," in John D. Montgomery and William J. Siffin (eds.), *Approaches to Development* (New York, 1966), 15–48.

social cohesion.[18] When the empirical conditions which allow men to become playful do not exist, we tend to conclude that man is not "really" open to becoming a creative, innovative, self-directed actor. If we nevertheless leave room for play, we then define play as merely recuperative and recreational. We grant that play has its uses in a life which is "really" grim: it gives relief and prepares us for what "really" matters.[19] And what is really said to matter is the achievement of some result. We desire not only to travel but also to arrive. We wish not only to carry our burdens—constitutions, voting systems, reform plans, messages, lessons, bombs—but to drop them on target. Our concern for solutions—understandable enough since nature poses genuine problems—compels us to regard human action as properly directed toward some end product. It is then scarcely sufficient for action to be expressive and symbolic: there must be, as we say, some payoff.

What generates this goal-oriented drive is of course the pressure of authentic problems, life-destructive forces which irritate and enrage us until finally we are moved to react. Insofar as our failure to control nature in fact results in nature's controlling and diminishing us it is hard not to be concerned with results. We are then scarcely inclined to play, to consider competing roles, or to entertain conflicting interests. Our interests then easily become singular: to achieve a positive objective, to find relief from an intolerable situation. Under such conditions, we find it hard to stand the strains of role-playing—strains hard to stand in any event.

In view of an ideal which calls for de-emphasizing outputs, I had best concede how difficult it is to remain open to alternatives when decisive action is called for by men whose vision, wealth, and weaponry are not in doubt. We understandably cannot expect men concerned with life and death—military officers, policemen, judges, physicians, or clergymen—to *play* at war-making,

18. See Werner Levi, "Religion and Political Development: A Theoretical Analysis," *Bucknell Review*, XV (1967), 70–95.

19. How thoroughly this view colors Freud's image of man—and therefore ours—has been shown by David Riesman, "The Themes of Work and Play in the Structure of Freud's Thought," in *Individualism Reconsidered* (New York, 1954), pp. 310–331.

law-enforcing, life-saving, or soul-saving. Such activities, we say, are for real; not surprisingly, they are scrupulously separated from politics. They are purposefully and seriously pursued, not to be taken lightly. Battlefields, busy intersections, courtrooms, hospitals, and churches do not strike us as arenas for games. They appear to demand disciplined, controlled behavior by those in charge. They demand full devotion to duty, a fine impartiality toward all who enter—be they soldiers on the field of battle, drivers on city streets, defendants in court, patients in a ward, or worshipers in church. In these enclaves there would seem to be no room for politics; they are not places where we inquire about such matters as party affiliations. Those in charge of them are above politics.[20]

Thus, although we may on reflection prefer an interminable policy-making process, realizing that ultimately nothing else can take full account of our diverse capacities, we may also realize that under some circumstances the choice seems narrowed, hence difficult: we then insist on the singularity of our interest, namely the need to free ourselves and establish a political stage. It is this effort to establish politics which appears to justify the demands by non-political activists for ending debate and putting a stop to what under the circumstances is intolerable conflict. *The empirical question, one which can be finally answered only by staking one's life on the outcome of revolutionary action, is simply whether in fact we do have a choice, whether we can actually afford life as play and politics as a process for the indefinite postponement of conclusions.* To answer this question—assuming our commitment is to ourselves as an open-ended system—we must perennially test reality while at the same time seeking to protect ourselves against destructive responses.

Part of reality is of course so hostile and unyielding that it may be self-destructive to persist in working for an open system of

20. When such men somehow find themselves in politics, in situations where they must play conflicting roles, they experience extraordinary strains. Thus chaplains or physicians in the armed forces, policemen in rehabilitation centers, or judges in political parties resolve their tensions in dramatic ways, making interesting cases histories. See, for example, Waldo W. Burchard, "Role Conflict of Military Chaplains," *American Sociological Review*, XIX (1954), 528–535.

pure politics. Not all obstacles to our further development are in our minds; some of the facts of life are really as cold, hard, and stubborn as the cliché would have it. Our death is certain, however evasively we may treat it. Yet by the same token not all the forces which speed us toward the end are beyond our wit to master, for not all of them are natural, and not all conventional ones are necessary. Individually and collectively, we die by degrees as one after another chance for growth is closed because of conventions to which we have not agreed. Some of us are stillborn not because nature demanded it but because of the structure of a man-made economy. Others never come to life. Variously arrested in our growth, we are enclosed because of an excess of someone else's affection or discipline. Allegedly for our own good, we are administered and institutionalized. Trained and employed only in part, we are constricted by all those conventional devices which serve to limit access first to the economy and then to the public state.[21]

Which of these restrictive devices are natural, which are conventional, and which of the conventional ones actually serve us, we can discover only in action, testing man-made reality, forcing it to yield. Failing to act, we submit to nature without even being aware of the fact. Failing to test possibilities, we accede to convention, or, more accurately, to those in our midst who have the power to play with us, to make and enforce convention, to close the political system and reserve the pleasures of playing the political game for themselves.

Assuming a considerable sector of present-day developmental theory to be preoccupied with the correlates of and requisites for ends which remain implicit, dubious, or unclearly formulated, I have sought to suggest that personality theory may provide empirical norms to orient us as we make history and engage in nation-building. I have not raised specific questions about administrative reforms because it has seemed to me necessary first to reflect on an ideal of man which administrative structures would

21. See Hannah Arendt's account of the attractions of the public stage: *On Revolution* (New York, 1963), pp. 123–124, 127, 258; *Between Past and Future* (New York, 1961), p. 154.

properly accommodate. But for me the issue is not merely one of intellectual priorities. More fundamentally, I do not believe it to be our problem to establish bureaucracies which, when duly functioning, would be capable of bringing about the good society (or the civic culture). Instead, *our problem is to make the administrative arena itself approximate our ideals.*

To the extent the governmental structures are themselves embodiments of our ideals, to the extent that they are not merely instrumental, they must challenge the prevailing means-ends distinction. They must challenge the usual recommendations for administrative reform to achieve purposes external to the administrative organization[22] as well as the administrative techniques in fact employed by what Warren Ilchman has called "rational-productivity bureaucracy."

To formulate the problem of administrative reform in these terms is to raise questions which confront all societies alike, none being truly developed. If we aim at nothing less (and nothing more) than literally self-government—that anarchic condition celebrated by philosophers from Diogenes to Marx, and desired at least for elites by philosophers from Plato to Arendt—we must inquire how to make bureaucratic government compatible with self-government.[23] We must meet the issues vaguely touched on by the phrases "industrial democracy" and "democratization of the administrative process." We must consider the pleas of America's black left (as Michael Miles has called it) for co-operatives, community corporations and independent political units, neighborhood-controlled schools, and civilian review boards—not because paying for these structures in underdeveloped areas will ultimately establish the great society but because the individuals who play roles within such structures have the immediate oppor-

22. The usual formula for reform assumes development to be a process "directed at realizing stated development ends in a prescribed time sequence by optimal means" (Donald C. Stone, "Government Machinery Necessary for Development," in Martin Kriesbert [ed.], *Public Administration in Developing Countries* [Washington, 1965], pp. 54–55).

23. That this issue is central in the United States as an industrially developed nation is made clear in a neglected article: Dwight Waldo, "Development of Theory of Democratic Administration," *American Political Science Review*, XLVI (1952), 81–103.

tunity to make more of their lives and thus more of themselves.[24]

Programs for administrative reforms should not, however, be so much subject of theoretical discussion and exhortation as of practical action—of experimental reality-testing, of determining *in practice* what changes society can support without returning to a state of nature which in turn engenders autocratic rule.[25]

It should accordingly be obvious why we should decline to sketch out abstract organizational plans for the civic culture. We can merely question the metaphysical pathos (to use Alvin Gouldner's phrase) of the fashionable elite theory, putting the bureaucratic and oligarchical tendencies which are said to reside in all large-scale organizations to the test.[26] The imperative—assuming our concern with administrative reform—is both to design life-facilitating, personality-developing social situations and to implement our designs by acting on them. Thus if we have a normative commitment to ourselves as autonomous, purposive beings, our problem is to provide ourselves with settings which de-emphasize our dependence, our specialization, our integration in hierarchical structures.[27] To satisfy developmental needs, it is imperative to create and support organizations which are expressive rather than instrumental, which provide intrinsic rather than extrinsic rewards.[28] Our problem is to provide ourselves with settings sufficiently open to encourage us to become equivocal and multidimensional, which induce us to widen the range of our

24. See the specific cases made by Lucian W. Pye, *Politics, Personality, and Nation Building* (New Haven, 1962), pp. 289–290, and Fred W. Riggs, "Bureaucrats and Political Development," in LaPalombara (ed.), *Bureaucracy and Political Development,* pp. 138–139, 142. Also see Ralph Braibanti's discussion of "diffusion of power" in this volume, pp. 47–52, and more generally the writings of G. D. H. Cole, Ordway Tead, Mary Parker Follett, Peter Drucker, and Paul Goodman.

25. For an example of such reality-testing, see Robert Rubenstein and Harold D. Lasswell, *The Sharing of Power in a Psychiatric Hospital* (New Haven, 1966).

26. For criticisms, see Alvin W. Gouldner, "Metaphysical Pathos and the Theory of Bureaucracy," *American Political Science Review,* XLIX (1955), 496–507; T. B. Bottomore, *Elites and Society* (New York, 1964); and Peter Bachrach, *The Theory of Democratic Elitism: A Critique* (Boston, 1967).

What is being criticized—to cite an extreme example—are such propositions as Ithiel de Sola Pool's that "no society could stand the strain of having more than a small minority among it living *for* politics or could afford the cost of having more than a small minority living *from* politics" ("The Public and the Polity," in Ithiel de Sola Pool [ed.], *Contemporary Political Science* [New York, 1967], p. 40).

27. See "Toward the Year 2000," *Daedalus,* XCVI (1967), 979.

28. This distinction is made in psychological terms by Daniel Katz and Robert L. Kahn, *The Social Psychology of Organizations* (New York, 1966), pp. 117–119.

experience. Our basic concern must be with injecting politics—political procedures and political arenas—into closed administrative systems or, to put this differently, with converting administrative systems into political ones.

Once we explicitly value man as a self-governed agent, we are apt to become sensitive to institutions and procedures which frustrate him. We are led to identify the practices which fail to serve his natural needs—in particular, his need to take a meaningful part within the community so that he might develop his capacity for taking turns to play diverse, mutually incompatible roles.

If men are to be encouraged to identify one another (so that ultimately they can identify *with* one another), each individual must have opportunities to hear his own voice—that is, to assume the positions of others and overhear himself. He therefore needs others, others with the self-assurance, experience, wit, and emotional versatility to appreciate his performance. To get the most out of others, he must be able to treat them as equals however different they obviously are from him. If he is equalitarian in his conduct, this will then not be for their sake, but for his.

It follows that to establish him—to give him command over his impulses—we must foster those habits of mind which enable individuals to identify with others.[29] And here our reform programs, our very language, must be so inconclusive that it can readily include whatever points others have not made, but might still insist on making. Thus our public laws and moral codes cannot properly prescribe some definitive norm of virtuous conduct or meritorious service. Risking good order, they must remain ambiguous, merely formalistic and procedural, granting individuals the freedom to improvise and act—provided we have cleared the space for it.

Such space is of course scarce in underdeveloped areas, wherever men must be disciplined merely to survive. We are familiar enough with situations that seem to justify discipline. At times, it appears, we cannot help but penalize improvisation, playfulness, or halfhearted commitments. We feel we need the fully disci-

29. These conclusions have also been reached by Daniel Lerner; see *The Passing of Traditional Society* (New York, 1958).

plined traffic officer so totally devoted to his calling that he does not have to bother to reflect on it. We have found it economical to free him from the burden of having to play his role self-consciously; we train him so that he does not have to remain continuously aware of himself, of the alternative consequences of his actions, and of his responsibility to others. Untroubled by conflicting interests, he need not see himself from the perspective of others, others who might compromise his dedication to law and order. He is not trained to "play" his role: he is a "natural" for it. Fully absorbed by his job, he truly *is* a cop, the very personification of the type. He is in fact well known even in societies which might tolerate less devotion to duty and more to the individual personality.

Favoring individual development, we cannot ultimately esteem administrative structures designed for such one-dimensional men. We may be unable to control ourselves and proceed to compromise; but in principle we must support the open heterogeneous organization over the closed homogeneous association, the multi-interest over the single-interest group, individual persons who have succeeded in integrating a variety of roles over those who have become the final embodiment of but one role.[30] We must

30. This position is of course opposed to the conventional conception of (1) the *underdeveloped society* as one whose political actors must spend their days doing a great many diverse things—so that the social system as a whole turns out to be "inefficient"—and (2) the *developed society* as one whose political actors are specialized experts in but one job—so that the social system as a whole, enjoying structural differentiation, turns out to be "efficient." (See for example, Fred Riggs, "Agraria and Industria: Toward a Typology of Comparative Administration," in William J. Siffin [ed.], *Toward the Comparative Study of Public Administration* [Bloomington, 1957], pp. 23–110.) It has been recurrently noted that "actors in the political process in Western societies are likely to have more clearly defined and more specific roles than those in non-Western societies. In the latter . . . there is generally a high degree of substitutability of roles. . . ." One may assume that the authors of such statements would regard Western societies as more developed. (The quotation is from George Mct. Kahin, Guy J. Pauker, and Lucian W. Pye, "Comparative Politics of Non-Western Countries," *American Political Science Review*, XLIX [1955], 1026). Presumably individuals in mature, stable democracies (i.e., the United States) properly remain in a state of arrested development while the political system is structurally differentiated. The arrested development of individuals is ultimately acknowledged to be the price that must be paid for a viable democratic regime. (See Bernard Berelson *et al.*, *Voting* [Chicago, 1954], p. 312. See also n. 2 above.) For a different argument casting doubt on functional specificity as a characteristic of highly developed systems, see Braibanti's chapter in this volume, p. 65. See also Landau's chapter in this volume, p. 340.

recognize that a police officer, a judge, a teacher, or even a prison guard is apt to become more civil and less insufferable if he thinks of himself as merely playing a role. Not expecting total fulfilment in their enterprises, men who presume to govern us may thus become more equivocal and less imperious. Admittedly, their signals would turn out to be ambiguous; they would test our capacity for tolerating ambiguity, putting prevailing conventions into jeopardy, opening cracks in the systems run by those who administer our lives and block our growth.

Those in command, I realize, prefer unambiguous communication. They rightly regard indirect and equivocal action as wasteful of their resources. By the same token, however, if laws and institutions were to motivate them to accommodate more ambiguity (and to expect less compliance), the lives of all men would become richer. Our lives would become more risky—whether in prison compounds, in educational establishments, or at traffic intersections. Having space to make unauthorized turns, we might become more venturesome—assuming we have the nerve to stand the strain.

There is in any case no other way to discover if we can bear it, if we can stand politics, than by changing administrative practices experimentally. It remains for political scientists whose sense of injustice is alerted by the prevailing state of affairs to lead the way—or at least to make plausible that only action-oriented methods which substitute self-discipline for an imposed discipline are conducive to individual growth, and that all else is apology.

·5·

Values and Ideologies in the Administrative Evolution of Western Constitutional Systems*

Joseph LaPalombara

I. Introduction

Patterns of administration, even crude technologies of administrative organization and behavior, are discernible wherever we have information about human social organization. Fustel de Coulanges traces the intricate evolution of patterns of authority and responsibility at the dawn of Greek and Roman civilizations.[1] In his harsh and controversial analysis of "total power" in the ancient civilizations of India, China, and the Near East, Wittfogel delineates structures of administrative organization and control that he claims represented for the seventeenth-century Westerner "an intellectual discovery comparable to the great geographical exploits of the period."[2] The kinds of fictions about kinship that underlay political and administrative organization in the earliest municipalities of Greece and Rome are found again in the "primi-

* In the revision of this paper I hope I have benefited not merely from the discussion at Bellagio but particularly from criticisms and suggestions offered by Giovanni Sartori, S. E. Finer, W. J. M. Mackenzie, Fritz Scharpf, Shlomo Avineri, Sidney Tarrow, Leon Lipson, and Henry Parris. Research relating to this paper was facilitated by a grant from the Stimson Fund of Yale University. The present author bears responsibility, however, for the contents of this chapter.

1. N. D. Fustel de Coulanges, *The Ancient City* (New York, n.d.). Although there is much in this brilliant Frenchman's analysis that does not fully square with the Enlightenment's view of the ancient political institutions of classical Rome and Greece, it is significant that Hajo Holborn, in his foreword to the above edition, states that all but perhaps a half-dozen of Fustel's observations turn out to be anthropologically and historically sound.

2. Karl A. Wittfogel, *Oriental Despotism: A Comparative Study of Total Power* (New Haven, 1957), p. i.

tive states" discussed by authors of *African Political Systems.*[3] Apter's work, deeply probing the developmental consequences of primitive social organization that is segmental, on the one hand, or hierarchical, on the other, clearly illustrates that one of the central features we associate with bureaucratic organization (i.e., hierarchy) is deeply rooted in certain ancient African societies.[4] Eisenstadt, in a work encompassing almost thirty "bureaucratic empires," seeks to pull together similarities in administrative development that span the forty-four centuries from ancient Egypt to the absolutist monarchies of Western Europe.[5]

Administrative activity, then, is as old as human organization. Perceptive historians, anthropologists, and other social scientists can describe such activity, infer it from archeological discoveries of societies that left no written histories, order it into theoretical frameworks designed to illuminate the dynamics of social change. For we know that changes in administrative organization and behavior have been intimately involved, as cause and effect, in those major societal transformations over time that we have now come to denominate the process of modernization. As Bertram Gross puts it: "The nature of this close relationship can be stated very simply. Whenever people want to accomplish a difficult social task, they must strengthen existing organizations or build new ones. But organizations do not run themselves. They must be administered. If people want to undertake still more difficult tasks, they must build larger and stronger organizations. This leads to still more administration."[6]

3. M. Fortes and E. E. Evans-Pritchard, *African Political Systems* (London, 1940).

4. See D. E. Apter, *The Politics of Modernization* (Chicago, 1965), pp. 88 ff. Apter's extensive empirical treatment of the relationship between traditional authority structural conditions and subsequent political-administrative development will be found in his *The Political Kingdom of Uganda* (Princeton, 1961).

5. S. N. Eisenstadt, *The Political Systems of Empires* (London, 1963). Whatever reservations one may have about Eisenstadt's bureaucratic developmental "models," the selected bibliography (pp. 473–521) relating to the systems he discusses can be most fruitfully consulted.

6. Bertram M. Gross, *The Managing of Organizations: The Administrative Struggle* (2 vols.; London, 1964), I, 34. I am not certain that Gross would defend as a necessary, rather than a historical, condition the assertion here that the *size* of administrative organization must vary with the complexity of the task to be performed. It seems to me that even the facts of history in the West would challenge this proposition.

Gross correctly cautions that we must distinguish between administrative activity and administrative thought. The activity can, as I say, be discerned by historical or contemporary observation. "Administrative thought—in the sense of specialized, concentrated, continuous, and recorded observation and speculation—is distinctly a modern development."[7] In this sense, administrative thought must be further distinguished from administrative *advice* which can also be identified in written records such as the Old Testament, the books of Plato and Aristotle, and perhaps most pointedly and remarkably in the works of Niccolò Machiavelli. In his fascinating and lighthearted review of such advice, Gross notes that it can be classified as follows: Be wise! Be good! Be bold! Be willing to compromise! Be unscrupulous! Be well advised![8]

It seems to me clear that when we speak of a technology of administration we generally refer to generalizations that grow out of administrative thought. Although such thought may be a priori it is usually based on empirical observation and reflection. This is certainly true of Max Weber, as well as of the more contemporary writers who will be cited below. I believe it equally apparent that very little of administrative thought can be divorced from advice. More than any other branch of the social sciences, the field of administration is one where the scholar is least likely to argue (or to be able to justify, if he does) that his concerns with theory and research of administrative organization and behavior are not necessarily related to concrete or "applied" problems in the management of men or organizations.

My purpose in this chapter is to identify several of the major value commitments and ideological orientations that have characterized the evolution of public administrative arrangements in several of the constitutional political systems of the West. It will be seen that major changes in these arrangements were usually associated with political, social, and economic problems that were certainly not unique to Western countries, even if we must concede that the particular and specific historical circumstances

7. *Ibid.*, p. 32.
8. *Ibid.*, pp. 92–96. The exclamation marks are mine.

of, say, Spain in the fifteenth century, Brandenburg in the seventeenth century, or England in the nineteenth century are not likely to be exactly repeated in any of the so-called developing countries of Asia, Africa, and Latin America today.

Nevertheless, the basic patterns of administrative development that one can detect in Pakistan and Uganda, Chile and the Sudan, or other such countries, as well as the technical assistance activities in administration engaged in by the United Nations Organization and the United States and other so-called advanced countries presuppose that there does exist an administrative technology that is universally applicable—at least insofar as the political unit to which such technology is supposed to apply is the nation-state.

My underlying concern will not be that of suggesting that only one or a few patterns of administrative organization are, so to speak, compatible with certain values or ideologies. Nor do I intend to show that the Western pattern of administrative development is necessarily applicable to all efforts at nation-building, wherever they are found in time and space. It will be my intention to illustrate however that certain values, ends-in-view, or ideologies carry with them implications for administrative organization that would not be relevant or necessary were the values, goals, or ideologies different. Although this observation appears truistic, it seems to me apparent that, like many other truisms about public administration that might be enumerated here, it is not fully understood by contemporary nation-builders, and by those who provide them with "technical assistance."

I should also emphasize that what follows is tentative and exploratory. The discerning reader will quickly detect oversimplifications, as well as the telescoping of decades—sometimes centuries—of Western history that have been treated in minute detail by historians. My effort is not aimed at obscuring historical nuances. It is motivated, rather, by the assumption that where our concern regarding the developing nations is that they may become more constitutional, or less authoritarian, dictatorial, or totalitarian, it may reward us to go back to the histories of Western constitutional systems to ask how it was that they evolved as they did. In so doing, we may find better guidance for the present than is made possible by exercises in abstract theorizing about administration and change.

II. The Bureaucratic State and Its Underlying Values

While we can agree that problems of public administration and alternative arrangements for their solution have been ubiquitous in human history, the same cannot be said for that particular type of administrative organization we denominate bureaucracy. As Hans Rosenberg has rightly noted, "The modern bureaucratic state is a social invention of Western Europe, China's early civil service notwithstanding. Aside from its administrative system, nothing so clearly differentiates the modern state from its predecessor as the legitimate monopoly of physical coercion, the vast extent of the central power, and the distinction between public and private pursuits, interest, rights, and obligations."[9]

Rosenberg's description may be viewed as a definition of the "modern" political system, against which we might presumably measure not merely the relative degree of "modernity" evinced by the more than 120 contemporary nation-states but also the progress (or retrogression) over time registered by any single country as it strove to modernize.[10] It is apparent, for example, in Rosenberg's study of Brandenburg-Prussia that the march toward

9. *Bureaucracy, Aristocracy and Autocracy: The Prussian Experience, 1660–1815* (Boston, 1966), p. 2.

10. Rosenberg's definition of the "modern" state is of course very close to the classical formulation of Max Weber. In its emphasis on centralized power (which is then used to direct purposeful change) the formulation is similar to that suggested by C. E. Black in his recent *The Dynamics of Modernization: A Study in Comparative History* (New York, 1966). It must be noted, however, that Black includes in his definition of "modernity" the concept of societal integration. Judged by this additional standard, it is interesting that countries like Germany and Switzerland, which preceded the United States and the United Kingdom in the achievement of the bureaucratic state, are depicted as having fallen behind the latter countries (and several others) in the achievement of modernization. Whether these different rates of modernizing development imply for Black an ebb and flow—backward steps as well as advances—is unclear. The most useful discussion of the need for such flexibility in one's conception of historical development remains S. Huntington, "Political Development and Political Decay," *World Politics*, XVII (1965), 386–430.

the bureaucratic state was never a long, unbroken one and that, indeed, the Prussian state never succeeded in bringing about the degree of centralized power that rulers from the Great Elector to Frederick William I might have desired. We will have occasion to return later in this chapter to the subject of discontinuous change in the field of public administration.

Although it might be interesting to compare West European national administrative systems since the seventeenth century to certain historical epochs in China, the Middle East, or Rome, I will accept for present purposes the assertion that the system of public administration we denominate bureaucracy is in fact an invention of the West and that reasonably pure examples of it are not to be found before the seventeenth century.[11] The classical formulation of the distinguishing features of bureaucratic administration is Max Weber's. As Alfred Diamant has reminded us,[12] Weber associated bureaucracy with a legal-rational authority system characterized by a consistent set of abstract rules on the basis of which laws are enacted for and applied to all members of a corporate group encompassed by a known territory. Authority in such a system is "impersonal," exercised by those who wield it only on the basis of the "office" they occupy. Authority wielders are restricted to specific spheres of competence; their powers are

11. I recognize that I am begging—better, leaving vague—what "reasonably pure" would mean here. This permits me to avoid having to worry at the moment about certain administrative developments in Spain as early as the fifteenth century or, for that matter, in the court of Frederick II in Sicily as early as the thirteenth century. On the historical evolution of bureaucracies, see: A. Brecht, "How Bureaucracies Develop and Function," *Annals of the American Academy of Political and Social Science*, CCXCII (1954), 1–10; S. N. Eisenstadt, "Bureaucracy, Bureaucratization, Debureaucratization," *Administrative Science Quarterly*, IV (1959), 302–320; A. K. Goshal, *Civil Service in India under the East India Company: A Study in Administrative Development* (Calcutta, 1944); A. H. Lybyer, *The Government of the Ottoman Empire in the Time of Suleiman the Magnificent* (Cambridge, 1913); H. Maine, *Lectures on the Early History of Institutions* (London, 1893); T. F. Tout, *Chapters in the Administrative History of Medieval England* (6 vols.; Manchester, 1920–23).

12. See "The Bureaucratic Model: Max Weber Rejected, Rediscovered, Reformed," in Ferrel Heady and Sybil Stokes, *Papers in Comparative Public Administration* (2nd ed.; Ann Arbor, 1960), pp. 59–96. I should underline here that my conception of the "bureaucratic state" and therefore of "bureaucracy" and "bureaucrats" is in no way pejorative. As von Mises noted years ago, "The abusive implication of the terms in question . . . is a universal phenomenon," including Prussia where "nobody wanted to be called a bureaucrat" (L. von Mises, *Bureaucracy* [New Haven, 1944]).

explicitly specified, and they exercise not only rights but incur obligations as well in the performance of their roles.

Where such administrative organization follows a "monocratic" rather than "collegial" form, Weber notes that

> the whole administrative staff under the supreme authority then consists, in the purest type, of individual officials who are appointed and function according to the following criteria:
>
> (1) They are personally free and subject to authority only with respect to their impersonal official obligations.
>
> (2) They are organized in a clearly defined hierarchy of offices.
>
> (3) Each office has a clearly defined sphere of competence in the legal sense.
>
> (4) The office is filled by a free contractual relationship. Thus, in principle, there is free selection.
>
> (5) Candidates are selected on the basis of technical qualifications. In the most rational case, this is tested by examination or guaranteed by diplomas certifying technical training, or both. They are *appointed,* not elected.
>
> (6) They are remunerated by fixed salaries in money, for the most part with a right to pensions. Only under certain circumstances does the employing authority, especially in private organizations, have a right to terminate the appointment, but the official is always free to resign. The salary scale is primarily graded according to rank in the hierarchy; but in addition to this criterion, the responsibility of the position and the requirements of the incumbent's social status may be taken into account.
>
> (7) The office is treated as the sole, or at least the primary, occupation of the incumbent.
>
> (8) It constitutes a career. There is a system of "promotion" according to seniority or to achievement. Promotion is dependent on the judgment of superiors.
>
> (9) The official works entirely separated from ownership of the means of administration and without appropriation of his position.
>
> (10) He is subject to strict and systematic discipline and control in the conduct of the office.[13]

13. From A. M. Henderson and T. Parsons (trans. and eds.), *The Theory of Social and Economic Organization* (London, 1947), pp. 329–340, and reprinted in R. K. Merton *et al.* (eds.), *Reader in Bureaucracy* (Glencoe, Ill., 1952), pp. 21–22. For more on Weber's views of bureaucratic organization see H. H. Gerth and C. W. Mills (eds.), *From Max Weber: Essays in Sociology* (New York, 1946), pp. 196–244.

Those familiar with the history of Europe will recognize in this consciously idealized decalogue patterns of administrative development discernible in the evolution of Brandenburg-Prussia from the Peace of Westphalia to the defeat of Prussia by Napoleon at Jena in 1806, a defeat tagged by Rosenberg as "the greatest disaster that had ever smitten the Hohenzollern state. . . ."[14] It will also be apparent that somewhere among these criteria expounded by Weber one can find a basis for both the technocratic and the democratic normative prescriptions about public administration that have been incorporated into United Nations manuals, widespread movements for administrative reform in Western and non-Western countries, and the doctrines and programs that characterize United States technical assistance missions. Portions of the Weberian Decalogue, more or less modified or infused with norms and expectations Weber himself may or may not have held, have become rallying points, catechisms or operational codes for institutes of public administration in such varied places as Manila, São Paulo, Caserta, Saigon, and Ankara. In only a few places, to be noted below, do there remain self-conscious attempts to resist aiding and abetting the kind of bureaucratization of the public service that some men insist is incompatible with other, superior values.

It is tempting to assert that the one overriding value that has dominated administrative change (and therefore the emergence of bureaucracy) in the West is power and the desire to maximize and to consolidate it. Whether one thinks of the military and financial magisters sent out by Roman emperors to limit the freewheeling behavior of pretorian prefects, the French *intendants* designed to provide Paris similar control over the provinces, or the eunuchs used by Ottoman rulers to limit the proliferation of competing dynasties, considerations of power appear central in the value systems of administrative innovators.

It should be self-evident that power is only one of the values that can be convincingly associated with the evolution of the bureaucratic state. This seems apparent in European history unless one engages in the kind of dubious reductionism in which it

14. *Bureaucracy, Aristocracy and Autocracy,* p. 203.

is (and can be) argued that any increase in the rationality or efficiency of administrative organization involves considerations of power (i.e., control) as a basic value. Yet it is necessary to note that bureaucratic development, as a particular type of administrative organizational evolution, is frequently, perhaps inevitably, tied to considerations of power. Task orientation invariably suggests that political leadership historically concentrates on the *means* of turning their wishes or policies into concrete realities. When it can be shown that non-bureaucratic, or prebureaucratic systems of administration seriously impeded a nice or efficient fit between ends and means, it is an easy inference that the strengthening of means to meet the policy ends of the "modern" polity requires the bureaucratic form of administrative organization. Several generations of students and advisors in the field of public administration have spoken and written extensively to the dubious point that the power to be effective is inextricably tied to a form of administration such as would emerge from the Weberian characteristics summarized above.

But we should be extremely wary about any uncritical acceptance of the view that administrative power itself is exclusively tied to Weber's ideal-typical constructs. In a brief, brilliantly incisive essay, Carl Friedrich notes how Weber's conceptualization of bureaucracy is neither derived deductively from "higher concepts" nor inferred from careful empirical observation.[15] One consequence of this defect (which Friedrich associates with Weber's normative orientation) is that Weber tends to ignore completely the value or norm of responsibility in the evolution of bureaucracy. Thus, rather than attempt to work through the problem of the interaction between power and responsibility—a

15. Carl J. Friedrich, "Some Observations on Weber's Analysis of Bureaucracy," in R. K. Merton *et al.* (eds.), *Reader in Bureaucracy*, pp. 27–33. In this same vein, it is important to note that values that transcend power, or for which power itself is merely instrumental, may also underlie public administrative transformations. A fascinating depiction of this situation is provided by Dwight Waldo, *The Administrative State* (New York, 1948), chap. 1. I should add here that Michel Crozier insists both that social structures and values will greatly condition patterns of administrative organization and that the bureaucratic form of public administration is not everywhere in time and space the most efficacious means to certain policy ends. See, for example, Crozier's *The Bureaucratic Phenomenon* (Chicago, 1964).

relationship absolutely crucial to a constitutional system—Weber, as Friedrich notes, pushes us to the conclusion that "a bureaucracy is the more fully developed the less responsible it is in its operation."[16] Friedrich then adds:

> It may be an exaggeration to hold that highly authoritarian "norms" have been embodied in this Weberian terminology. It seems to the author nevertheless striking that Weber's fully developed bureaucracy is most nearly represented in three modern organizations: (1) an army, (2) a business concern without any sort of employee or labor participation in management, (3) a totalitarian party and its bureaucratic administration. Is it not revealing that, at the outset of his discussion of the basis of "legitimacy," Weber defines "imperative control" as the probability that certain commands from a given source will be obeyed by a given group of persons?[17]

The European history to which Friedrich refers would certainly have provided a logical rationale for Weber's single-minded concern with power as central to bureaucratic evolution. Most writers associate bureaucratic development with the historical triumph of the absolutist nation-state over the feudal system that preceded it. Although many of the widely applauded norms of administration, such as the separation of the private and public personalities of the rulers, are associated with these monumental struggles, the struggles themselves were generally and correctly perceived as competition for power—and its rewards. This elemental fact cannot and should not be obscured by contemporary references to "nation-building," even if we can agree with Bendix that "the decisive criterion of the Western nation-state is the substantial separation between the social structure and the exercise of judicial and administrative functions."[18] Perhaps this point can be best illustrated by reviewing (all too briefly) the highlights of administrative development in Brandenburg-Prussia.

Writers generally agree that the Great Elector's grand design was to convert the *Territorialstaat* that characterized the Ger-

16. *Ibid.*, p. 31.
17. *Ibid.*
18. Reinhard Bendix, *Nation-Building and Citizenship* (New York, 1964), p. 106.

manic states in the seventeenth century into a *Gesemtstaat* centered in Brandenburg and at Berlin. What was his motivation?

Morstein Marx notes that at the termination of the Thirty Years War the Germanic states were marked by devastation, exhaustion, chaos, and extreme economic depletion. One obvious and overriding need was the restoration of law and order. Another was to forge the kind of political unit that would both preclude another "internal" war and win for Brandenburg a respected place among the political systems of Europe.[19] In similar fashion Dorwart tells us that at no previous stage in the history of Brandenburg was there a greater need for a well-developed, disciplined, professional administrative system that could serve to remove the widespread and rampant confusion.[20]

The idealized conception of the *Gesemtstaat* would have required welding into a single, unified political whole disparate polities consisting of small individual units, dominated by indigenous aristocracies and manifesting considerable diversity in political ideology, religious conviction, economic development, and national interest. In order to achieve this goal, Prussian rulers beginning with the Great Elector and extending through his grandson, Frederick William I, had to overcome concerted opposition which emanated not so much from other major European nation-states as from entrenched, privileged local groups organized in "obstinate corporate bodies."[21]

It is not surprising that Prussian rulers sought to utilize a transformed public administration to achieve national unity. However, it seems to me that statements such as that "it was the common man whom the Great Elector invited to serve as his companion-at-arms in the course of unity"[22] tend to make that extraordinary monarch bigger than life. Such historical myths, I believe, also favor the dubious inference that a concern for the people, and therefore an incipient liberal political ideology, was

19. Fritz Morstein Marx, "Civil Service in Germany," in L. D. White *et al.*, *Civil Service Abroad* (New York, 1935), p. 166.

20. Reinhard A. Dorwart, *The Administrative Reforms of Frederick William I of Prussia* (Cambridge, Mass., 1953), p. 18.

21. This situation is nicely summarized in Morstein Marx, "Civil Service in Germany," pp. 166 ff.

22. *Ibid.*, p. 170.

basic to the Great Elector's ambitions. Much closer to the facts of history, and much more to the point of how radical a break with tradition any ruler can effect, is the evidence offered by Dorwart that prominent members of the nobility—local political dignitaries and military figures—were recruited to the mission, along with middle-class burghers who, in any event, were never permitted to invade the higher echelons of the military bureaucracy in any significant numbers.[23]

The transformations begun by the Great Elector were in a sense completed by Frederick William I in the eighteenth century. As in France, beginning with administrative changes under Louis XIV and culminating in the Napoleonic reforms, the emergence of bureaucratic patterns in Prussia goes hand in hand with the consolidation of the absolutist nation-state. However, in both the French and Prussian cases there emerged important modernizing by-products that in later years facilitated—indeed precipitated—the liberalism of the nineteenth century.

What were these by-products? First, absolutism managed to destroy the local decentralizing pretentions of European feudalism. In the process, the important separation of the public and private personalities and of the personal and public finances of the ruler is established as a cardinal principle of government. Of course this separation was never absolutely achieved. In countries like France where the economic exigencies of the monarch extended the sale of public office into relatively modern times, initial modernizing administrative reforms were considerably watered down. Nevertheless, the separation was a crucial step in challenging and undermining the medieval ascriptive values of privilege, tied as they were to the structure of the family and the legal device of heredity.

I do not intend here to minimize the importance of these breaks with feudal values, or with essentially medieval concepts

23. *The Administrative Reforms of Frederick William I*, pp. 3 ff. To be sure, Dorwart also notes that Frederick William I used burghers against the nobility in the eighteenth century (see, e.g., p. 32). My qualifying remark here is designed to reduce the image of Prussian rulers making *tabula rasa* of the traditional social, economic, and political structures. On the point of the use to which the nobility were put, particularly in the military, see Ernest Barker, *The Development of Public Services in Western Europe, 1660–1930* (London, 1944), pp. 18–21.

of the relationship between rulers and the ruled. It is now fashionable among students of the "developing" nations to speak (pejoratively) about something called "defensive modernization." This concept means, among other things, that the motives of those who advocate or effect change are suspect; it assumes that what is intended is not substantial, and certainly not revolutionary, change but rather that minimum of response or adaptation to changes in demand that will permit an extant elite to survive relatively unscathed. What European history compels us to accept, however, is that responses to impulses toward "defensive modernization" can and do bring about changes that over time have enormously important systemic implications.

Second, therefore, in the critical era of European institutional transformation, the concept of sovereignty as belonging to the centralized nation-state (as opposed to reactionary, medieval corporate bodies) became a hallmark of the absolutist political system. Whether it is a French King declaring that *he* is the state or a Prussian ruler insisting that he is the state's first servant, the implication is clear: that an abstract entity can demand and legitimately receive the first loyalty of citizens and public servants and that the latter can use their monopoly of physical force to limit or to erase the particularistic, disintegrating influence of localized elites. As Brian Chapman and others have observed, the conception of the ruler representing the state and holding power in its name and interests grew out of the late medieval rediscovery of the writings of the Roman lawyers. The same rediscovery applies to the concept of differentiating the public business from the private affairs of the king's household. Thus, on the one hand, Europe's absolutist rulers used Roman law, particularly the fictitious *lex regia,* as a gloss for their naked struggle for territorial power. On the other hand, they also introduced a precondition for later arguments that centralized legitimate power in the hands of the ruler belonged to them, not as a matter of divine right but, rather, as a contractual delegation from the sovereign nation—that is, from a sovereign people. The jargon of modern sociology would describe this result as an unanticipated functional consequence. We need merely note that whatever the nature of the political unit one wishes to endow with autonomous, effective, rational authority, some sort of justification or gloss of this type appears to be necessary.[24]

Third, the monoliths of centralized power, such as Frederick William I was able to make of the Prussian state, accelerated the growth of many of the defining characteristics of modern bureaucracy. In part because growth in state activities requires larger and more rational organization, in part because an emergent bureaucratic elite will tend to develop its own expediential goals and the means to their achievement, the public administrative apparatuses of France and Prussia bore only faint resemblance to the feudal administrative arrangements that had preceded them.[25]

The contribution to public administrative organization and doctrine bequeathed later political leadership by the absolutist state would then include:

1. Great acceleration of the functional differentiation of administrative roles that in the late medieval period was already discernible in the households of Continental princes.

2. The establishment of the principle that at least some sectors of the public service should be open to members of the middle class and that, in any case, those recruited to functional roles should have training and/or qualifications pertaining to those roles.[26] To be sure, the myth-makers of Prussian bureaucracy have

24. See Brian Chapman, *The Profession of Government* (London, 1959), pp. 9–15. Cf. Dorwart, *The Administrative Reforms of Frederick William I*, pp. 5 ff.

25. I do not mean to overstress this point and therefore to suggest that the systems of public administration Brandenburg-Prussia and France devised manifested no heritages at all from Continental feudalism. Rare, indeed, in the West has been the opportunity to create national administrative apparatus largely *de novo*. One such case is the United States, although there is question whether this almost unique situation has been, in the long run, entirely beneficial or salutary. For a most incisive and thoughtful exposition of this ambiguous advantage, see S. E. Finer, "Patronage and the Public Service," *Public Administration*, XXX (1952), 329–358. We might add here that the heritage of medieval practices is nowhere more apparent than, say, in the economic regulations of state-subsidized industry that developed in France in the seventeenth and eighteenth centuries. About these, two recent writers note: "In scope and depth, these government regulations were comparable to the regulations of the guilds which flourished throughout Western Europe during the Middle Ages. In point of fact, the ancient guild rules served as models for the economic regulations handed down by the French government, and one can detect similarity in language and detail" (R. T. Holt and J. E. Turner, *The Political Basis of Economic Development* [Princeton, 1966], p. 103).

26. On the Prussian use of higher education as an instrument of public policy and the creation of chairs of "cameralistics" at Halle and Frankfurt, see Chapman, *The Profession of Government*, pp. 23–24.

tended to overstress these educational reforms, thus ignoring the extent to which the Prussian nobility was able to turn relatively mild qualifications for recruitment to its own ends. In this regard, the Royal Prussian army served as a lifesaver to the aristocracy, many of whom "seized the military job opportunities which gave a fresh lease on life to illiterate noble boys, landless noble bumpkins, unemployed nobles returned from service in foreign armies, and impoverished or bankrupt squires with little or no formal education."[27]

3. The emergence of administrative officials as *public* servants with no proprietary rights to office and for the most part compensated by salary.

4. Establishment of the concept of hierarchical organization, with supreme authority held—monocratically or otherwise—at the center and obedience and loyalty owed office-holders higher up in the hierarchy. Chapman, in his discussion of the evolution of the French *intendants* correctly stresses that the discovery of administrative instruments for keeping field administrators responsible to centralized authorities is one of the more important contributions of this period to modern governmental organization.[28]

5. Finally, we should note that with these structural changes in administration there was diffused the idea not only that administrators would be chosen and governed by a general law, but that law itself would become the basis for the even-handed, non-preferential application of rules to those to whom rules were meant to apply. Here we find that nexus between a legal-rational system of authority and the bureaucratic form of public administration that Weber considered so important.

Such developments, as we shall see, were strictly speaking not directly related to the English concept of the rule of law, which was slow in evolving in England, based on the twin assumptions

27. *Bureaucracy, Aristocracy and Autocracy,* p. 59. Rosenberg stresses not so much the efficacy of educational requirements as he does their limited application and the skill of the Prussian dynastic bureaucrats in evading or ignoring them. See *ibid.,* pp. 58–60, 76–81, 129–130, 180–182, 211–213. But compare Morstein Marx, "Civil Service in Germany," pp. 173–175, who holds that the merit system of Frederick William I brooked of no exceptions.

28. *The Profession of Government,* pp. 20–21.

of inherent general right in the individual and the weight of judicial precedent. Both of these latter assumptions were not acceptable on the Continent and in the case of Brandenburg-Prussia (and, later, Germany) were considered abhorrent. Nevertheless, the Continental developments surrounding administrative change greatly spurred on the Continent the *Rechtsstaat* or *l'Etat de Droit* which, while conceptually and historically different from the rule of law, did indeed engender the idea—and the desirability—of the state based on law and *limited* by it.[29]

However, if we return to our query regarding the values or ideologies that motivated administrative innovators in Europe from the seventeenth to the late eighteenth century, it seems apparent that in the sense of the motives of reformers absolutism had little to contribute to the evolution of the democratic state. In the age of absolutism, power was the prime consideration. The state, and laws willed in its name, became the abstraction around which the raw exercise of power could be rationalized. It is certainly not a matter of mere chance that all over the Continent the earliest administrative reforms were centered in the fields of financial, military, and diplomatic administration. Nationalized armies required a degree of efficiency and effectiveness in the collection of revenue, the conscription of troops, and the enforcement of the center's authority unthought of in the Middle Ages. Absolute monarchs, in their efforts to minimize subversion from within, develop personal secretaries, as opposed to councilors of aristocratic origin who possessed potential countervailing power.

29. I am indebted to Giovanni Sartori for calling my attention to the need for differentiating—conceptually and historically, if not in politically liberalizing consequences—*Rechtsstaat, Etat de Droit,* or *Stato di Diritto,* on the one hand, from rule of law on the other. See G. Sartori, *Democratic Theory* (Detroit, 1962), pp. 288–291, and his "Nota sul rapporto tra stato di diritto e stato di giustizia," *Rivista internazionale di filosofia del diritto,* XLI (January–April, 1964), pp. 310–316.

Sartori's view runs directly counter to that of Otto Kirchheimer who saw rule of law as generic and *Rechtsstaat* and British rule of law (as articulated by A. V. Dicey) as particular cases of it. He would tend in all cases to feel that the individual is better protected "when specific claims can be addressed to institutions counting rules and permanency among their stock in trade . . . ." Kirchheimer insisted that, beyond tradition, procedural safeguards, particularly in a country such as Germany, with police-state traditions, are critically important. See his "The Rechtsstaat as Magic Wall," in Kurt Wolff and Barrington Moore, Jr. (eds.), *The Critical Spirit: Essays in Honor of Herbert Marcuse* (Boston, 1967), pp. 287–312. The quoted phrase is from p. 288.

These personal secretaries later evolve as the first important secretaries of state. The same monarchs grow to be suspicious of the privy councils, great councils, or king's councils and shift administrative responsibilities to new specialized officials or committees. Within these councils themselves, the monarch isolates a chosen few with whom he discusses the most important matters of state and public policy. Thus, while Dorwart's use of "cabinet government" to describe the system of high-level decision-making devised by the Hohenzollerns seems odd, we can certainly see in that arrangement one precursor of what later come to be called in England the "Inner Cabinet."[30]

Europe's absolute monarchs of the seventeenth and eighteenth centuries were thus confronted by and greatly preoccupied primarily with the historical crises of national identity, legitimacy, and penetration. As power-seekers (or nation-builders) they reached out for new patterns of administrative organization that would be instrumental in the resolution of these crises. Where common identification with a Hohenzollern prince was not enough to weld together a Prussian nation-state, military, financial, diplomatic, and judicial means had to be found to coerce the recalcitrants. That the means chosen served to admit middle-class elements to some spheres of power, or that these means should have created new conceptions of law and administration that undermined autocratic rule, is scant reason for viewing this period in Europe as one of conscious democratization "from the top."[31]

Europe's actual or aspiring absolute monarchs then were ex-

30. *The Administrative Reforms of Frederick William I,* pp. 8 ff.

31. Although I do not wish to pursue here what may be essentially semantic problems, it is necessary to note the conceptual distinction between "democracy" and "liberalism" drawn by Sartori. If I read him correctly, he would argue that both the Rule of Law and the *Rechtsstaat* (rule-of-legislators) are to be understood as favoring not democracy but liberalism, as providing as it were two different but related solutions to "the problem of *political* freedom in terms of a dynamic approach to the juridical conception of freedom." Sartori goes on to argue, "This explains why we cannot speak of political freedom without referring to liberalism—liberalism, I repeat, not democracy. The political freedom we enjoy today is the freedom of liberalism, the liberal kind of liberty; not the precarious, and, on the whole, vainly sought liberty of the ancient democracies" (*Democratic Theory,* p. 291). Moreover, it is noteworthy that where, as in Germany, the concept of *Rechtsstaat* developed, that development was greatly complicated by philosophic notions of law emanating from an enlightened despot, found in the writings of Kant and other German writers. See Sartori, "Nota sul rapporto . . . ," pp. 311–313.

posed to salient historical nation-building crises such as those suggested above.[32] To be sure, such crises were not felt with equal intensity in any single country, nor was the "crisis load" the same everywhere across continental space. For example, long before the Great Elector sought to expand the territory over which Brandenburg-Prussia could exercise effective centralized control, a sense of "German" nationality (or identity) was widely diffused in Central Europe. Similarly, a French "national" identity might be traced to the conflict between Philip the Fair and Pope Boniface in the thirteenth century, long before Louis XIV sought to expand the territory over which what was willed at Paris would be translated into conforming behavioral responses in Rouen and Dijon, Bordeaux and Toulouse.

The concept of divine right, or some variation of it, might provide a reasonably effective solution for the problem of legitimacy. The concept was far more effective on the Continent than in an England where the royal prerogative ran continually afoul of such restraining concepts and institutions as the inherent or historical rights of English subjects or the English courts and common law. As I have noted in detail elsewhere,[33] the "crisis of penetration" whenever and wherever it has occurred in the West, and whatever the degree of satisfactory resolution of other nation-building crises, has required that political leadership devote major attention to problems of administrative organization.

By comparison to most of today's developing nations, of course, Western countries did not experience overwhelmingly heavy "crisis loads," or the simultaneous onset of *all* nation-building problems, including identity, legitimacy, penetration, participation, and distribution. It was not after all only England that enjoyed relative leisure in the confrontation of the major historical crises

32. The concept of "salient historical crises" and their relationship to political development is discussed by Joseph LaPalombara and Myron Weiner, *Political Parties and Political Development* (Princeton, 1966), pp. 3–42, 399–435. Cf. Robert E. Ward and Dankwart A. Rustow, *Political Modernization in Japan and Turkey* (Princeton, 1964), concluding chapter. Five such "crises" are treated in detail in L. Binder *et al.*, *Crises of Political Development* (Princeton, 1969). A brief explication of these crises can be gleaned from Lucian Pye, *Aspects of Political Development* (Boston, 1966), pp. 62–66.

33. See my "Penetration: A Crisis of Governmental Capability," in Binder *et al.*, *Crises of Political Development,* chap. 5.

that each nation-state tends to experience.[34] For most European countries, by the time that late-developmental crises such as participation and distribution (associated with the service state rather than the regulatory state) occur, the crises of identity and penetration have been resolved (e.g., Switzerland, England, France, Spain), or central cores of later larger nation-states have had experience in such crisis management and the use of the kind of military or civil administrative apparatus that can provide valuable guides to the handling of additional crises (e.g., Piedmont in Italy, Prussia in Germany).

We must appropriately ask whether there were other values implicit in what the architects of the absolute state undertook in the seventeenth and eighteenth centuries. In Prussia it is certainly possible, as Dorwart claims, that a nation-building genius like Frederick William I was psychologically impelled to win Prussia the grandeur of a great power, as well as the respect of other nation-states with which Prussia would have to compete.[35] This same monarch is generally described as one who in his personal system of values placed the characteristics of probity, discipline, and hard work very high. Thus, even when the Prussian bureaucracy had degenerated into a dynastic citadel, it enjoyed an almost unexcelled reputation of possessing as an institution the very qualities that Frederick William I personified. Moreover, the latter's obviously paternalistic attitude toward his subjects, coupled with the above qualities, must surely have contributed to the development in Prussia of the "guardian" bureaucrat, as opposed to other types.[36]

34. To be sure, we must avoid here either the notion that all of England's nation-building problems were leisurely handled over several centuries or that, once resolved, a crisis never re-emerged there. To cite one example I discuss later in this chapter, the monarchs at London experienced between the eleventh and nineteenth centuries greatly varying success in their efforts to achieve an effective centralized administrative control over the English realm. For an excellent summary discussion of this aspect of English political development, see Holt and Turner, *The Political Basis of Economic Development,* pp. 88–95, 118–126, 147–159, and chap. 5, *passim.*

35. *The Administrative Reforms of Frederick William I,* pp. 32–33.

36. The "guardian" bureaucrat, of course, is not unique to eighteenth-century Prussia. The British bureaucracy, following nineteenth-century reforms, is sometimes described as guardian-like in its management of administrative affairs. More pointed historical examples would involve the dynasties of China up to the Sung period. Fritz Morstein Marx, *The Administrative State* (Chicago, 1957), discusses both the Chinese and Prussian examples, as well as bureaucratic systems of the "caste," "patronage," and "merit" types. See chap. iv.

However, it is also necessary to recognize that conditions on the Continent during the period under discussion were singularly propitious for economic development, and we must assume that a second major value (closely akin to political power) was economic gain or wealth. All over Europe an emergent mercantilist class looked to the state not merely for the non-interference we associate with laissez faire but, more important, for the kind of positive action that would facilitate economic enterprise. "In the age of absolutism," Friedrich reminds us, "public policy was dominated by *mercantilism*—a body of thought which its ablest expositor has called a 'system of power.' Mercantilism, though usually associated with the idea of protectionism, was committed to freedom of trade. Internally, it was an economic corollary of the monarchical policy of centralization and unification."[37] The two goals or desires walked hand in hand.

Thus, men like Colbert in France turned their attention to the problem of administrative innovation in considerable measure because they realized that the guild system of medieval Europe was considerably outdated and that a policy of free trade was not enough to spur the economic growth that he and others sought. He and the extraordinary monarch he served viewed a strong, national administrative system as a critical device that would permit the nation-state to further the growth of industry and commerce. During the seminal years of Colbert, the governors at Paris were perfectly willing to increase state regulation of business and industry, to use public authority to grant commercial and industrial monopolies, and, indeed, to put the state itself directly into entrepreneurial activities. In the seventeenth century, a wide range of administrative arrangements and innovations, ranging from the Conseil des Finances, the Conseil d'Etat, and the *contrôleur général* at the center to the famed *intendants,* and the less-known *lieutenants généreaux de police* and the *inspecteurs des manufactures* in the provinces, can be systematically associated with the impulse to economic growth.[38]

37. Carl J. Friedrich, *Constitutional Government and Democracy* (rev. ed.; Boston, 1946), p. 20.

38. On this important period in French administrative development, see Phillippe Sagnac, "Louis XIV et son administration," *Revue d'histoire politique et constitutionnelle,* III (January, 1939), 23–47; J. E. King, *Science and Rationalism*

Even though reformers and innovators like Colbert were wise enough not to seek to break completely with certain aspects of the medieval guild system,[39] his efforts to create effective administrative control did not go unopposed. The privileges of the clergy were extraordinarily difficult to reduce, and persistent attempts of this character led to antisystem behavior on the part of clerics. Locally based nobility frequently responded negatively to new taxes imposed from Paris, and the *intendants* were often no match against their opposition; the *parlements* of France, even if often cowed by the overpowering majesty and determination of Louis XIV, frequently set legal roadblocks in the way of reform and eventually became a central factor in the ruinous, catastrophic destruction of the *ancien régime.* Nevertheless, many of the organizational innovations introduced in the seventeenth and eighteenth centuries not only spurred economic development in France but remained guides to public administrative reform well into the nineteenth century.

Reflecting no doubt on European experiences such as these, Joseph Spengler delineates a wide range of governmental activity —from the maintenance of law and order and the encouragement of banking to the enforcement of contracts and the investment in social overhead capital—that is not only legitimate but perhaps vital for those developing nations that now seek to find the path to economic modernity.[40] Although, as we shall later note with regard to England, a nation-state can modernize economically given varying degrees of administrative centralization, it is apparent that what the European experience teaches is that laissez faire in its narrowest conceptualization is both historical myth and certainly not the most efficacious road to economic change. Whether it is or is not also the most efficacious route to constitutional government is a matter I will touch on below.

In this period, then, the political interest of a segment of the

in the Government of Louis XIV, 1661–1683 (Baltimore, 1949); Allen Johnson, *The Intendant as a Political Agent under Louis XIV* (Lowell, Mass., 1889); Alfred Cobban, *A History of Modern France* (Baltimore, 1957), Vol. I, chap. 1.

39. See Holt and Turner, *The Political Basis of Economic Development,* pp. 102–103, for a discussion of medieval aspects of French regulation of emergent industries in the seventeenth century.

40. Joseph J. Spengler, "Bureaucracy and Economic Development," in Joseph LaPalombara (ed.), *Bureaucracy and Political Development* (Princeton, 1963), pp. 199–232.

traditional elite and the economic interests of an emergent middle-class elite coincide. Those who sought expanded territorial power quickly understood the importance of economic growth as a means of financing and consolidating such expansion. Those who sought riches similarly realized that they could be best achieved not in the chaos of atomized local political systems tied to the ascriptive, corporative norms of a defunct feudalism but rather through the intervention of a friendly centralized nation-state with sharp administrative and legal teeth.

Given this symbiotic understanding, it is not at all remarkable that a number of the values associated with rational commercial and industrial enterprise should spill over into the public administration sector. It is here that one must look for the modern origins of such Weberian bureaucratic standards as accountability, honesty, efficiency. Thus, when Morstein Marx writes of the German and American "genius" in the management of large-scale organization, his primary measuring rod, indeed the magic word, is "efficiency."[41] Similarly, as one peruses the pages of Dorwart's analysis of the administrative changes effected by Frederick William I, specific reforms such as division of labor, the development of functional specialists, improvement in record-keeping and accountability all center on the value of efficiency, which is so inextricably tied to essentially economic considerations. As Dorwart notes, these changes were greatly spurred by the Hohenzollern ruler's interest in increasing income, national wealth, commerce, industry, and the size of overseas possessions.[42]

Historians record the degeneration of bureaucratic systems in the eighteenth century in both France and Prussia, about whose splendid administrative systems Herman Finer was able to claim that, by comparison, the public services of Great Britain and the United States of that era were barbaric.[43] In France, the degeneration, greatly spurred by the sale of public offices which then

41. "Civil Service in Germany," p. 163.

42. *The Administrative Reforms of Frederick William I,* p. 54.

43. Cited in Morstein Marx, "Civil Service in Germany," p. 173, from Herman Finer, *The Theory and Practice of Modern Government* (London, 1932), II, 1184. The decline of the bureaucratic state of Louis XIV is delineated in Vol. I of Cobban, *A History of Modern France.* For Brandenburg-Prussia, Rosenberg, *Bureaucracy, Aristocracy and Autocracy,* is a useful summary of the ebb and flow of reform and decay in national administration. Cf. K. W. Swart, *Sale of Offices in the Seventeenth Century* (The Hague, 1949).

became hereditary and by a proliferation of essentially uncollectable detested taxes, was dramatically characterized by public identification of a corrupt, arbitrary, and obtuse bureaucracy with the monarch at Paris. Barker insists that the monarchy not only lost its creative dynamic but was much more unsuccessful than England—and, we might add, Prussia—in the co-optation of the emerging professional, commercial, and industrial classes. This neglect toppled French absolutism by revolution.[44]

If the more successful co-optation of the mercantilists in Prussia spared that nation revolution, the later Hohenzollerns were unable to curtail the tendency of the Prussian bureaucracy to become a closed, insensitive, heavy-handed, self-perpetuating, and autocratic caste. So entrenched had that caste become that the system persisted beyond the French Revolution, and Prussia did not take realistic stock of the degeneration until it experienced a resounding defeat at the hands of Napoleon at Jena.[45]

One interpretation of Prussia's response to this crisis emphasizes the movement for reform associated with Baron vom Stein. According to Morstein Marx, vom Stein helped Prussia to adapt to the new conditions (i.e., values and ideology) unleashed by the French Revolution. Disdainful of efficiency, Morstein Marx tells us, vom Stein sought to forge a strong bond between the administration and the people. This would explain the reformer's emphasis on administration devolution, local autonomy, and the need for consultation in administrative decision-making, ideas clearly at odds with Weber's conception of monocratic bureaucracy.[46]

44. See *Public Services in Western Europe,* pp. 10 ff. The Barker view is somewhat oversimplified. Although failure of adequate co-optation was one important factor in disintegration, corruption, arbitrariness, and venality in administration, religious work and clerical opposition to control from Paris, increasing restiveness among French masses (especially in overcrowded rural areas), and the replacement of Louis XIV by lesser monarchs were also contributing factors that should not be obscured.

45. The burden of Rosenberg's excellent study, *Bureaucracy, Aristocracy and Autocracy,* is to trace in detail the persistent survival of aristocratic and authoritarian elements in Prussia's bureaucracy.

46. Morstein Marx, "Civil Service in Germany," pp. 188–191. One of Friedrich's objections to Weber is, of course, that it was precisely the decentralization and consultative aspects of bureaucratic organization that he either ignored or consciously excluded from his ideal-typical formulation. See Friedrich, "Some Observations," p. 31.

A somewhat contrary interpretation of vom Stein's reforms would classify them as an early example of "defensive modernization." To be sure, serfdom was abolished, some new elements were added to the administrative system, new functional ministries were added to the General Directory, and some autonomy and representational arrangements were made in local government. As far as Prussia as a whole was concerned, a national parliament was not introduced until after a second wave of revolutionary liberalism had swept across Europe in 1848. But the 1849 parliament itself indicates how little touched were the Prussian leaders by the ideas of the French Revolution and of the Napoleonic reforms. Absolutist ideas persisted, and the concept of the state (i.e., rulers) as sovereign was carried by German jurists right into the twentieth century.[47] In this philosophical context, limitations on the rulers, be they the monarch or his administrators, was a matter of enlightened despotism, a concession rather than a matter of legal or natural right, or of historical practice. Thus, Barker is quite correct when he declares that the Prussian "revolution" of 1807–10 greatly increased administrative efficiency but did little to mitigate the absolutist ideology that had long underlain Prussian government and administration.[48] Rosenberg puts this view even more pungently: "A strange political bedfellow gave the Prussian bureaucracy the opportunity for bringing to its climax the stuggle to abridge royal prerogatives and to acquire the powers of 'cabinet government.' Napoleon Bonaparte, Emperor of France, '*par la grace de Dieu et les constitutions de la Republique*,' was consolidator of the most effective type of bureaucratized absolutism theretofore known."[49]

Thus, the revitalized Prussian (later German) bureaucratic

47. For reasons of space, I am greatly telescoping this important phase in German administrative development. For an excellent, insightful discussion of this period, see Chapman, *The Profession of Government*, pp. 25–36.

48. *Public Services in Western Europe*, pp. 22–28.

49. *Bureaucracy, Aristocracy and Autocracy*, p. 202. Rosenberg's point requires some qualification. Whatever may have been the philosophical underpinning of the *Rechtsstaat*, it is necessary to acknowledge that the concept itself suggests limitations on rulers and their bureaucratic servants based on legislation. As Sartori correctly notes, *Rechtsstaat*, as it evolved on the Continent, implies the auto-limitation of the state *based on law*. Where such a concept develops, administrative adjudication becomes a crucial consideration. See Sartori, "Nota sul rapporto . . . ," pp. 310–311.

state so widely admired by some Americans in this century (including Woodrow Wilson) was the product of a set of values and ideology which were anything but democratic. Indeed, the persistent assumptions of German jurists, rulers, intellectuals, and public administrators were doggedly opposed to the ideas that emerged from the French Revolution. At best, the German assumptions could support a benevolent paternalistic guardian bureaucracy. At worst, they could be utilized—in pure or perverted form—as the intellectual underpinning for a police state.[50]

Most European states moved in the direction of Napoleonic administrative reforms and French revolutionary assumptions about sovereignty and the relationship between citizen and rulers. As far as Continental Europe is concerned, clearly democratic values relating to administrative organization do not emerge until France has left its indelible imprint on human history.

Ernest Barker suggests that Napoleon served as a bridge between bureaucracy and democracy. Presumably this would mean that Napoleon managed to accept and improve on the Sun King's "bureaucratic state" without permitting it to nullify or to trample on democratic values. The notion that the bureaucratic form of administrative organization is incompatible with freedom and democracy has had many advocates. Von Mises made the idea the fulcrum of his stinging attack on the welfare state and economic planning;[51] almost two decades ago Charles Hyneman, reflecting on his experience in the American federal bureaucracy, sought to underscore both the potential utility of bureaucratic organization and the need for devising effective means of controlling it politically in a democratic society;[52] more recently, a number of writers interested in the development of Pakistan have pointed to the need for trying to reconcile the political goal of

50. On this point, particularly as applied to Weber's reading of the German bureaucratic tradition, see Frederic S. Burin, "Bureaucracy and National Socialism: A Reconsideration of Weberian Theory," in R. K. Merton *et al.* (eds.), *Reader in Bureaucracy*, pp. 33–47.

51. *Bureaucracy.*

52. Charles S. Hyneman, *Bureaucracy in a Democracy* (New York, 1950).

democratic participation with the often non-democratic structures and orientations of bureaucratic agencies.[53]

The notion that such contradictions necessarily exist can be traced to two major sources. The first source would be the kind of history we have summarized thus far, namely, the association over time of the bureaucratic administrative system with an essentially undemocratic Prussian or French state. The second source, which I will discuss below, is another historical tradition —i.e., that of England and the United States—which seems to associate democratic government with a strong antibureaucratic system of values.

Barker himself confirms this apparent contradiction when he notes that "the conjunction of democratic government with bureaucratic administration still marks the political system of France."[54] What, then, we may ask, is the nature of that conjunction? Or, phrased in terms of the topic of this chapter, what *new* values or ideologies are associated with the kind of administrative development that followed in the wake of the French Revolution?

Scrupulousness of historical interpretation requires us to emphasize that Napoleonic concepts such as administrative appointment on the basis of merit and the equality of citizens before the law were not inventions of the Philosophers or Jacobins but, rather, ideas deeply rooted in the evolution of states such as Brandenburg-Prussia. The development of cameralism in that same state compels us to associate with the Hohenzollerns the concept of a professionalized public administration as well. Similarly, the French revolutionary antipathy toward the notion that any secondary, corporative structure could stand between the citizen and the state was already apparent in both prerevolu-

53. Inayatullah (ed.), *Bureaucracy and Development in Pakistan* (Peshawar, 1953). See, especially, the chapters by Masihuzzaman, "Administrative Obstacles to Voluntary Associations in Pakistan," pp. 57–78; Ralph Braibanti, "Philosophical Foundations of Bureaucratic Change," pp. 79–89; Masihuzzaman, "Public Service Tradition in Pakistan: A Case for Revision," pp. 285–298; and A. T. Rafiq Rahman, "Basic Democracies and Rural Development in East Pakistan," pp. 326–352.

54. *Public Services in Western Europe*, p. 14.

tionary French and Prussian attacks on feudal institutions. In the same vein, the administrative characteristics of the Napoleonic unitary state—symbolized by the concepts of duty, hierarchy, functional specialization, and unimpeded central control—had their roots in the absolutist eras of both Prussia and France. Not only the *intendants* of Colbert but also the *steurrat* of Frederick William I were the precursors of the Napoleonic prefect. Thus, when Chapman cites recruitment on the basis of merit rather than class or caste as one of the democratizing influences of the Napoleonic reforms,[55] this statement can be accepted only against the ascriptive dynasty into which Prussian bureaucracy had degenerated and not as an innovative pattern for which there existed no European precedents.

However, Chapman and others have also noted that the critically important *new* value associated with administrative changes effected by Napoleon turns on the concept of sovereignty. With the advent of the Revolution and its aftermath the nation replaces the ruler as the repository of sovereignty. Under this conception, subjects are transformed into citizens, administrators into servants rather than the instruments of an omnipotent state.

This transformation, important as it has been in subsequent administrative evolution on the Continent, has sometimes been incorrectly interpreted to mean that sovereignty was understood to reside in the people and that authority was exercised on the basis of a delegation from the people, whose inherent sovereignty also implied limitations on the exercise of power. But, as Giovanni Sartori points out, the French Revolution enthroned the nation, not the people; deputies represent the will of the nation, not of the people; indeed the concept of "deputy" is misleading in itself for, Sartori tells us, this was the precise moment in French history in which elected legislators ceased being deputies in the strict sense.[56] Thus it is in this sense that we must understand that Napoleonic France, rather than abandon the administrative apparatus that developed under absolutism, replaced *l'état c'est moi*

55. *The Profession of Government*, p. 29.
56. See "Representational Systems," *International Encyclopedia of the Social Sciences*, XIII, 465–474.

with a sovereign "General Will" or, as Barker suggests, with a national *moi.*[57]

This change does not provide a philosophical basis for a democratic, pluralistic conception of the state, which has its roots in popular sovereignty and whose intellectual antecedents can be traced back through the Germanic tribes of the Middle Ages and to the Roman lawyers. The political thought of the French Revolution was overwhelmingly antipluralist, closer to Louis XIV than to English thought of the period. Revolutionary political thought brooked no intervening structures between the nation and the citizen, which might compete for the loyalty or allegiance of the latter.

Nevertheless, we do have here a new value, against which administrative organization and behavior are to be judged. Henceforth administrators are no longer answerable only to the ruler; they can and will be judged against the standard of laws that define—and limit—their behavior. In the name of the overriding value, the nation, rights and obligations would extend to those who administer public policies, as well as to those who are the objects of such administrative activity.

In the administrative sphere, the most important development associated with the change in the concept of sovereignty was the emergence of systems of administrative adjudication. Where, as in England, the rule of law is a matter of historical and philosophical tradition, administrative law and adjudication, as separable fields of attention and activity, seem unessential. Where the *Rechtsstaat* or *l'Etat de Droit* emerges, however, administrative adjudication is inherent in the assumption that legislation will define the limits of bureaucratic behavior. Where such laws proliferate, and are codified, special tribunals to handle litigation arising under them appear as an inexorable development. Napoleon's handling of this problem involved the creation of a power-

57. *Public Services in Western Europe,* p. 13. Fritz Scharpf calls my attention to my usage of "General Will" here, noting that German scholars have tended to link Rousseau with totalitarian ideologies and certainly not with democratic pluralism. This is also my understanding. The French conception I speak of here is incipiently, perhaps inherently, authoritarian. At best, it implies the development of *l'Etat de Droit* or, as Sartori notes, the auto-limitation of the state through law.

ful Conseil d'Etat, which remains today the pride and the major symbol of French democratic administrative justice.[58]

Although similar structures quickly proliferated among European countries (including Germany), the most pertinent question to pose concerning them was and remains the extent to which such judiciary bodies were accorded broad scope and final authority regarding citizens' complaints against the state or its representatives. In those countries where parliaments are viewed as sufficiently geared to the task of holding administrators to the rule of law, separated administrative tribunals are considered unnecessary. In other countries, where the need to be particularly vigilant against the excessive, arbitrary, illegal, or improper use of admittedly essential administrative authority is strongly felt, specialized judicial bodies have come into existence. Even in rule-of-law countries such as England, however, the growth of statutory law alongside the common law has raised serious questions about the need for specialized administrative tribunals.

What this particular development in administration represents is strong emphasis on the service aspect of public administration as a central value. Where such a value is dominant, and where it is conditioned by the limitations implicit in the concept of *Rechtsstaat,* considerations of efficiency, organizational rationality, and professionalization in the bureaucracy will not have the overriding importance that Weberian theory ascribes to these aspects of bureaucracy. In a dramatic fashion that has plagued political theorists for many decades, this development shows the confrontation of technocratic versus humanistic norms. From the standpoint of those who would emphasize the humanistic quality

58. Professor Henry Parris has properly called my attention to a possible ambiguity here. In France, as he correctly notes, administrative law and tribunals grew out of a history in which, even where they tried, the *courts* were little successful in controlling the executive. The *parlements* under Louis XIV, for example, were singularly ineffective in this regard, even if they could sometimes place obstacles in the way of an onrushing, centralizing monarch. In England, on the other hand, the evidence is overwhelming that the courts did succeed in checking the monarch. Parris suggests, therefore, that in England suggestions that there be created separate administrative tribunals appear not merely unnecessary but pernicious.

The French *parlements,* however, were not completely without their effect on public opinion, both during and following the reign of Louis XIV. In this regard, see R. R. Palmer's important discussion of "The Quasi-Revolution in France, 1763–1774" in his *The Age of Democratic Revolution* (Princeton, 1959) I, 86–99.

of organized society, it is no longer sufficient to equate the rule of law with the even-handed application of paternalistically derived rules. Not only is it demanded that those to whom rules apply participate in their formulation; it is demanded as well that structures be erected to assure that the inevitable inequities and other dangers implicit in bureaucratic governance will be corrected. Bendix puts this dilemma quite succinctly: "Impersonal administration provides an indispensable buttress of regularity, detachment, calculability and all of the other positive attributes of order, but these gains are inextricably linked with a studied disregard of personal circumstances and hence of considerations of equity."[59]

Bendix goes on to suggest that the rule of law can prevail as a meaningful concept only if *neither* the concern with equity *nor* the concern with the formal attributes of rule-making predominates within a political system.[60] As I have used "rule of law" in this chapter, Bendix's usage would be incorrect in that the considerations of equity and of procedure implied in this comment would apply to the Continental *Rechtsstaat.* In any event, French and other European political systems have responded to this problem or dilemma by erecting complex and prestigious systems of specialized administrative adjudication. This formula, however, has not been followed by either Britain or the United States, and it is therefore necessary to ask what kinds of values were associated with public administrative development in these Western constitutional systems.

III. The Underlying Values of the Anti-Bureaucratic State

It is well known that England developed many of the characteristics we associate with the bureaucratic state long before the Continental changes discussed above had appeared. For example,

59. *Nation-Building and Citizenship,* p. 111.
60. *Ibid.,* p. 112. Cf. Frederick J. Port, *Administrative Law* (London, 1929), pp. 25–34.

a remarkable degree of centralized administrative control of the country was achieved not long after the Norman Conquest. The administrative genius of the Normans can be seen in part in their decision *not* to try to destroy and replace previously existing "traditional" elites and governmental structures but, rather, to seek to incorporate them into the newly centralized polity.

To be sure, Norman (and later Angevin) rulers did not have an easy time of it, and they therefore could not rely entirely on the local nobility to achieve the desired degree of administrative centralization. Thus, the office of the sheriff came to represent the administrative presence of the king locally. In this sense, the sheriff may be viewed as a historical precursor of the French *intendants* and the Prussian *steurrat,* even if the sheriff's scope of responsibility was much broader than that of the latter when they first appeared on the Continent.

It is unnecessary to detail here the gradual evolution of specialized administration as the diffuse administrative structure of the king's household proved inadequate to deal with new governmental problems and the gradual extension of governmental services.[61] We know that Norman rulers were primarily concerned with the expansion and maintenance of power; that early on they were compelled to accept some limitations on the exercise in favor of locally centered nobility; that over the centuries the Privy Council became an instrument for directing the king's struggles against local interest and nobility; and that a gradual division of labor in the Privy Council moved England from an essentially patrimonial to an essentially bureaucratic type of public administration.

We know too that the evolution of English public administration was not linear and that the ebb and flow of "development" and "decay" persists to the present day. The crisis of legitimacy, for example, was experienced many times between the Norman invasion and the Act of Settlement, and more than one of these crises emanated not merely in dynastic changes but, for a brief period in the seventeenth century, in the abolition of monarchy itself.

61. The still-classic work on administrative evolution in medieval England is Tout's *Chapters in the Administrative History of Medieval England.*

The ebb and flow is more directly apparent regarding the management of the crisis of penetration—the continuing problem of making the center's policies effective throughout the realm, which on many occasions since 1066 took on massive proportions. Institutions such as the sheriff declined as effective instruments of central control; the powers of the monarch often degenerated for a host of reasons including personal qualities of leadership, local and international intrigues, struggles for power among monarchs, parliaments, judicial bodies, and so on. As new territories were added to the English realm, great problems of administrative penetration were created; these new territories also assured that issues of legitimacy and identity, seemingly resolved between the eleventh and fourteenth centuries, re-emerged to challenge and to plague the English rulers at London.[62]

Thus, not only was the evolution spread over many centuries, it was also uneven and subject to retrograde steps. It was indeed retrogression that permitted Finer to describe English administration of the sixteenth and seventeenth centuries as barbaric by comparison with the achievements of France and Prussia.

During the years when strong monarchs were effecting great changes in public administration, the fever of absolutism did not escape the interested attention of English monarchs. The fact that English absolutism was never as pervasive as in Continental countries, and much more short lived, was of enormous importance for later political and administrative development. Of the handful of territories that could reasonably be called nation-states at the beginning of the seventeenth century, all of them lacked effective centralized administrative systems; all of them, as Field notes,[63] still exercised local power and authority through (often tenuous) agreements with local dominant families. It was against such feudal political-administrative arrangements that reform-minded or nation-building monarchs proceeded on the

62. The ebb and flow I refer to here can be gleaned from such sources as these: A. V. Dicey, *The Privy Council* (London, 1860); David Ogg, *England in the Reign of Charles II* (Oxford, 1934); S. B. Chrimes, *English Constitutional History* (London, 1953); Edward R. Turner, *The Privy Council of England in the Seventeenth and Eighteenth Centuries, 1603–1784* (2 vols.; Baltimore, 1927, 1928); R. H. Gretton, *The King's Government: A Study of the Growth of Central Administration* (London, 1913).

63. G. Lowell Field, *Comparative Political Development: The Precedent of the West* (Ithaca, N.Y. 1967), p. 81.

Continent, and in England as well. England was much less successful in centralizing power.

Why was this so? Barker (and others as early as Montesquieu) have noted a number of "ecological" and related reasons for this difference. Thus, while early administrative centralization was facilitated by ease of communications in the British Isles, the security from invasion her insular position provided permitted England not to emphasize a national standing army. Such armies, it will be recalled, were the major instruments used by Continental monarchs to forge absolutist states. Indeed, it was the army that Louis XIV was often compelled to use when his famed *intendants* were unable to collect the taxes his wasteful regime so desperately needed.

Barker goes on to suggest that absolutism in England was also impeded by the absence there of deep class cleavages, by the much weaker system of "estates" that developed under English feudalism, and by the fact that English subjects would have found it difficult to perceive Scottish and Hanovarian monarchs as the incarnation of the deity.[64] Insofar, then, as the absolute state in extreme form does not materialize under Edward IV in the sixteenth or Cromwell in the seventeenth centuries, England is denied or spared historical development that carried with it major administrative changes.

It seems to me, however, that beyond geographic, "ecological," or psychological factors that may have impeded administrative change under English absolutism, certain structural and philosophical phenomena must be noted as well. Structurally, England became a national entity very early, and as I have noted, a reasonable resolution of the crisis of penetration was achieved by the end of the twelfth century. Two extremely important consequences followed from the pattern of attempted hegemony experimented by the Normans and Angevins.

First, the extension of power from the center was characterized by adapting local Saxon institutions to the administrative needs of the center. The sheriff became the king's general agent in the counties. When the sheriff became unreliable, or overburdened in

64. *Public Services in Western Europe,* pp. 29–31.

this role, English monarchs had recourse to justices of the peace who functioned at the parish level, and lords lieutenant who were responsible for managing and supervising the county militias. Administrative innovation rarely involved sending forth magisters, *intendants,* or *steurrats* from the center. Field administrative personnel, even when disposed to be loyal to the monarch, were cross-pressured by their attachments to and identification with local interests. Early in the game, therefore, the monarch was either inclined or compelled to bargain with local centers of power, and to create an administrative control apparatus that sought to integrate rather than to replace or destroy such local centers.

Second, from the infant years of modern England, many administrative changes and institutional arrangements have been spurred by and have appeared as consequences of more or less organized attempts to limit the powers of the central government. Before the Great Elector or Louis XIV could turn his attention to administrative innovation, there was additional territory to conquer, to add to the core nation-states, and to infuse with a new or modified sense of national identity. In England, from the earliest years, English subjects claimed rights, and these rights in turn implied that the powers of the central government would be limited. Such views were articulated as early as the meeting at Runneymede; they were eloquently repeated and elaborated four centuries later in the debates at Putney; they had become so deeply ingrained by the seventeenth and eighteenth centuries that they lay at the center of the Glorious Revolution and the successful American rebellion. Demands to exercise power from the center, then, consistently encountered the counterclaim that power be shared, as well as the insistence that it could and should be limited. It is primarily in the sense of divided and limited power—under a system of rules and understandings that define both the scope of power and the conditions of its exercise —that Carl Friedrich asks us to comprehend the essence of constitutionalism.[65]

65. *Constitutional Government,* pp. 4, 20–21; 116 (on the role of judicial institutions in guaranteeing constitutional restraints); 398 (on the ways of securing responsibility of government).

Other factors served over time to reinforce both of these tendencies and, in turn, to institutionalize anti-bureaucratic tendencies. For example, the English judicial system did serve as a quite effective check on monarchs and central administrative bodies such as the Privy Council. English judges and the common law they created became over time formidable obstacles to the exercise of arbitrary will by the central government. Faced with the opposition of such officials, the power of the monarch became problematical. By the middle of the sixteenth century, there existed approximately two thousand justices, about whom Holt and Turner observe:

> . . . these officials, in contrast with the French intendants, never became the instrument of the central government. The people who were appointed to these posts were landed gentry of the localities, who were largely concerned with their own private interests and the interests of the communities they administered. Since they were the unpaid servants of the crown, they were forced to live on the income from their own estates—a condition that gave them a large degree of independence from the authorities in Westminster.[66]

Given historical developments such as these, it is not so surprising that the doctrine or claims of divine right should have found relatively fewer ready adherents in England than on the Continent. England considered absolutism, flirted with it for a time, and then rejected it with considerable repugnance, along with administrative arrangements that absolutism implied.

Writing of political developments in England in the early seventeenth century, Friedrich nicely summarizes the range of articulated, conflicting values that helped to shape the course of later institutional arrangements. In this period, he says,

> the whole range of political issues, from absolutism in Hobbes to anarchy in the Levellers, was explored, fought over with word and sword, and finally settled in favor of a division of power between king, lords and commons, which, while it sounded medieval and traditionalist, was in fact modern in that the real foundation of this division was the electorate behind the com-

66. *The Political Basis of Economic Development*, pp. 93–94.

mons, rather than the ecclesiastical authorities and feudal land owners behind the Lords.[67]

These claims to share and to limit power persist in all of English history. Such claims might be those of the local aristocracy appealing to feudal practices and institutions; or of religious minorities, demanding the right to be free of centralized religious coercion; or economic, social, and professional groups at Putney and later who insisted on the right to be represented in decisions affecting their well-being.[68] Such ferment and debate could not and did not pass unnoticed in subsequent decisions taken in the governmental sphere.

It was precisely this elemental fact, however, that Charles I failed to understand. As a result, his erroneous belief that the British had restored monarchy and placed it above Parliament cost him his head. The Glorious Revolution of 1688, therefore, enthrones the legislative omnipotence of Parliament at essentially the same time that Prussia and France are enthroning the administrative omnipotence of the centralized ruler. In the critical second half of the seventeenth century, then, it is the British Parliament that consciously seeks to set limits on the executive-administrative power. The Act of Settlement of 1701 is in this sense merely a recognition of the successes scored by the national legislature in restricting the monarch's control in the vital area of finance, limiting his arbitrary behavior toward subjects, and greatly curtailing his ability to govern by prerogative.

Following the Glorious Revolution, we know that British administration degenerated into a morass of nepotism, patronage, corruption, and proliferation of agencies that persisted well into the nineteenth century. The concept of the "gentleman administrator" so persistently dominant in English political culture tended greatly to obscure the fact that "gentlemen" were not

67. *Constitutional Government*, p. 26.

68. Port, *Administrative Law*, pp. 43–44, cites early seventeenth-century demands by Englishmen for even-handed administration. A petition of 1610 to the Stuarts specifically refers to the "rule of law" as a right of an English subject. In this struggle for administrative justice, English common lawyers and legislators played a central and vital role. Henry Parris reminds me that the principle extends much farther back—i.e., *per legem regni nostri vel per judicium parium suorum in curia nostra* (Magna Carta).

necessarily intelligent and that mere intelligence might not be enough to assure the kind of public administration required at the onset of a state's industrialization.

One striking contrast between France and England in the seventeenth century is that the mercantilist fever that affected the former was very mild indeed in the latter country. In contrast with the situation on the Continent, the advocates of mercantilism encountered formidable opposition in England. Efforts by the monarch to grant monopolies, to grant patents and tax exemptions, to regulate existing or nascent industries foundered on the open hostility of the citizenry, and on the successful constitutional objections registered by common-law courts and justices of the peace. Given the very loose linkage between central administrative bodies and local governments, the clumsy structure of crucial bodies such as the Privy Council, and the absence of strong standing armies, Westminster simply could not make many of its efforts in the economic sphere stick.

Moreover, it is reasonably clear that the English monarchs were not so much interested in encouraging economic growth as such, as they were in regulating economic practices and, more important, in increasing the amount of revenue coming to London from the outlying districts of the kingdom. Where such motives became apparent, Parliament itself became a serious roadblock, in the interest of limiting the financial independence of the monarch and assuring itself a continuing power of the purse. Thus, the persistent value or ideology of limited government succeeded in impeding a line of monarchical policy that if implemented would have required substantial administrative change. In this important sense we might note, therefore, that the very corruption and patronage that came to mark English administration may have been quite important for the overriding end-in-view of parliamentary supremacy.

Not until the so-called economic reforms championed by Burke in 1780 did Britain begin to face up to the limitations inherent in a public administration characterized by a multiplicity of boards that had grown up in a crazy-quilt pattern during almost a century of legislative supremacy. Even here, however, the motives or values underlying such reforms were surely not those one associates with a Weberian conception of bureaucracy. As Pares puts this, "When Fox and Burke reformed administration . . . they did so (as they were careful to point out) without any desire to increase efficiency or to save money, but solely to reduce the political influence of the Crown."[69] One indication of the truth of this observation is of course that administrative boards continued to mushroom well into the nineteenth century.

It is only in the last century, then, that we begin to detect administrative changes that are not necessarily associated with the values I have delineated thus far. It is certainly noteworthy that the degree of industrialization, and its associated problems, that compelled attention to reform was not inferior to what the bureaucratic states of France and Prussia had managed to achieve. One possible explanation of this is that Britain's relatively small scale and cheap administration may have freed for economic growth human and financial resources that might otherwise have been drained off by bureaucratic proliferation.[70] This advantage, if such it was, tended to disappear later in the century when nepotism and sinecures abounded and when the cost of British administration became greatly inflated.

In any event, the industrial revolution, as Smellie says, "compelled the state to create a machinery of administration almost as complex as the new machinery of industry itself."[71] However, once again the underlying values are significant, for the accumulation of wealth, while omnipresent as a value of capitalistic society, is superseded by concern for the individual and for protecting him against the inequities, inequalities, and violence associated with the industrial revolution. That such concerns were real and that they did in fact emanate in important administra-

69. Richard Pares, *King George III and the Politicians* (Oxford, 1953), p. 130.

70. I am indebted to Professor Henry Parris for this suggestion. I include it here somewhat skeptically in that the dynamic of the process is far from clear and, in any event, we need more data of a comparative nature in order to arrive at a sound estimate of how expensive British administration was. One such comparison, between Britain and the United States is attempted by S. E. Finer, "Patronage and Public Service" (cited above in n. 25), but, as he himself acknowledges (p. 357) his United States estimates do not include the cost of administering state governments.

71. K. B. Smellie, *A Hundred Years of English Government* (2nd ed.; London, 1950), p. 56.

tive changes is minutely detailed in Parris' fascinating study of the British railroads in that last century. As Parris notes, the notion that Benthamism and classical economics are antithetical is unacceptable. For one thing, Adam Smith insisted that the interest of the consumer is paramount. For another, Bentham himself argued persuasively that there does not exist a "natural right" that immunizes the businessman from state regulation in the interest of the consumer. The conclusion here is apparent: the Benthamite "happiness of the greatest number," as well as Adam Smith's concern for the consumer, might very well imply and require restrictions on free enterprise.[72]

British interpretations of nineteenth-century administrative history are varied, sometimes polar. Smellie tends to abhor the "muddling through," insisting that "it is inevitable that a representative government should suffer from the defective planning of its administrative machinery. For, when government is based upon persuasion, continuity with the past is often a political duty when revolution is an administrative necessity. In England the history of every government department is almost as complex as the history of the constitution itself."[73] Smellie adds that "the growth of English administrative machinery was stunted by the continuity of her political and legal tradition. We paid too big a price in administrative immaturity for our national tradition of gradualism."[74]

The specifics of what Smellie is driving at are not difficult to imagine: chaos, corruption, nepotism, incompetence, inefficiency, and the remainder of a hair-raising roll call of shortcomings. His depiction of changes, when they occur, invariably associates them with complex industrial problems, revelations of administrative madness during the Crimean War, or threats to England's economic hegemony represented by the United States or Continental countries. That England managed to survive at all as a major power and as a democracy seems nothing short of miraculous.

72. Henry Parris, *Government and the Railways in Nineteenth-Century Britain* (London, 1965), pp. 202–203.
73. *A Hundred Years of English Government*, p. 56.
74. *Ibid.*, p. 57.

There are those who argue otherwise, insisting that among other things one must look carefully for the routine and commonplace in administration, and not merely for the sensational and the bizarre. Thus, the Parris volume is a careful explication of the striking degree of professionalism and technical competence that became associated with the government regulation of the railroads after mid-century.

S. E. Finer, in a telling review of British administration in the eighteenth and nineteenth centuries, concedes many of the negative aspects of it identified by historians. For example, he notes laconically that the proliferation of offices and agencies was caused by the fact that "from the Norman Conquest almost no office or department was ever abolished; but functions often were."[75] But Finer's fine eye for the routine and detailed leads him to conclude about the notorious customs system, for example, that it "was not the weltering sink of corruption, immorality and indolence which we have been conditioned to expect."[76] Finer cautions that the low morality or other seemingly negative aspects of British administration should not be inferred from isolated instances of corruption or venality that gain wide public notice. He concludes as well that later in the nineteenth century some of the very conditions that made an earlier British administration the object of opprobrium saved it from evolving in the direction of "spoils" taken by the United States under Jackson.[77]

I have taken this short digression in order to clarify several important aspects of British administrative reform during the last century. First, commitments to abstract concepts of efficiency and rationality associated with Max Weber were rarely paramount in British administrative thought. Second, Smellie and others are undoubtedly correct in suggesting that changes were often motivated by the needs of and the problems created by industrialization, or by international disasters or pressures that threatened Britain's primacy on the world stage. Third, and closely related to the last point, the gradual extension of the suffrage made it

75. "Patronage and Public Service," p. 334.
76. *Ibid.*, p. 343.
77. *Ibid.*, pp. 355–357.

relatively imperative both to reduce the human cost of industrialization and to reaffirm the British tradition of power shared at the local level. Thus, just as the development of the railroads led to administrative changes affecting safety, conditions of labor, and a host of other problems, the Poor Law of 1834 triggered administrative overhauling that eventually led to the creation of a national health administration and the broad regulation of the labor market. In the process of effecting such changes, British administration improved not merely its technical competence but removed many of the organizational defects (e.g., sinecures, multiheadedness) associated with eighteenth-century patterns.

How much reform had actually occurred in Britain prior to the issuing of the Northcote and Trevelyan Report of 1853 cannot be established here with certainty. The document, which Smellie calls "one of the most important state papers ever published," seems to me to represent the first extensive effort on the part of the British to move toward the bureaucratic state. The report's major intention was twin-pronged: first, it sought to reduce the excessive degree of patronage that persisted in British administration; second, it sought to strengthen administration by assuring highly trained candidates for "administrative class" positions. This was to be achieved by the introduction of a classification system that would separate "intellectual" administrative work from other positions and by requiring an entrance examination of entering candidates for the intellectual services.

It should not be thought, however, that the values underlying these reforms were essentially democratic. Far from it. The value of efficiency in administration, learned in part from the reorganization of the Indian Civil Service, was a prominent theme. Benthamite notions regarding administration when reflecting moral indignation could be easily translated into paternalistic reforms that did not greatly affect the administrative system. It is noteworthy that Commons was persuaded to accept the reforms only after its advocates were able to show persuasively that the reforms would not seriously threaten the monopoly over higher administrative office long enjoyed by the British aristocracy. Thus

Smellie notes that "to develop a scientifically planned bureaucracy was impossible because of the opposition of aristocratic prejudice and middle-class parsimony. We were governed," he adds, "by brilliant amateurs with aristocratic prejudices and middle-class paymasters. In spite of the abolition of patronage the leading civil servants were drawn from the same social class and often from the same families as the great political figures they served."[78]

Here it seems to me that Smellie reveals a misunderstanding of the difference between "patronage" and "spoils," as well as his own normative commitment to a particular kind of "scientific administration." Patronage as a guiding principle in the recruitment of administrators at any level need not imply a perpetuation of incompetence or corruption. "Spoils" might not be incompatible with the norm of competence either, except that it does imply frequent turnover of administrative personnel and a corollary impulse to corrupt behavior while administrative office is held. Smellie seems to be objecting not so much to the *quality* of British administration as to the fact that, even after certain reforms, the administrative class continued to be recruited from the aristocracy and the middle class.

Thus, despite the persistence of an aristocratic administration,[79] it is vital to bear in mind that changes effected between 1832 and 1870 had a strong humanitarian cast and, in addition, were spurred by the sense of moral revulsion against human suffering and inequities diffused in England by the Benthamites and their successors. Some of the changes might be said to have been motivated as well, if not by a democratic ideology, then by the fact that the extension of individual liberty and political participation meant that certain mass demands could no longer be casually or callously ignored. In this last regard, however, I be-

78. *A Hundred Years of English Government,* p. 75.

79. William Mackenzie is skeptical about how far one would want to push the "revisionist" view that the notion of a "unified elitist administrative class" was essentially myth. Mackenzie holds that the label of myth will stick only until 1914 when Warren Fisher at the Treasury and a group of "Platonic Guardians" recruited to public service between 1900 and 1914 did indeed constitute an elite. He adds that this generation is now dead and that that succeeding them is now dying out.

lieve Smellie is quite correct[80] in insisting that these reforms, even if impelled by the logic of a democratic ideology, were negatively based, in the sense of improving bad government, rather than positively motivated, in the sense of planning ahead to have the public administrative apparatus capable of responding to the needs of an emerging "service state."[81]

The famous Haldane Report on Machinery of Government (1918) and the rise of a socialist ideology demanding the extension of the "positive" or "service" state account for a third major wave of British administrative reform since 1832. The Haldane Report was based primarily on considerations of efficiency and rationality, and it greatly extended the reforms associated with the Northcote-Trevelyan era. It reflected not so much the rising egalitarian ideology of labor as it did the Utilitarian emphasis on such middle-class values as order and efficiency. Long after such industrially based values had affected the administrative organization of Prussia, they began to make themselves felt among the political leaders of Britain.[82]

A fourth wave of administrative reform, long demanded by Britain's political left, has yet to materialize, although measures of recent years affecting public education and the financing of scientific research may be bellwethers of this. There is little

80. *A Hundred Years of English Government*, p. 172. For a much more detailed history of nineteenth-century administrative reforms, see H. R. G. Greaves, *The Civil Service in the Changing State* (London, 1947). Greaves, as he describes the late eighteenth-century condition of British administration quotes this pointed remark of Burke: ". . . neither the present, nor any other First Lord of the Treasury, has ever been able to make a survey, or make even a tolerable guess of the expenses of government for any one year, so as to enable him with the least degree of certainty, or even probability, to bring his affairs into compass" (p. 12).

81. From this state of affairs, given English traditions, nineteenth-century progress in reform could only be very slow. This point seems to me basic. To be sure, one can turn to the writings of Bentham and find in them the basic format for subsequent administrative reform. The English utilitarians sought to abolish waste, to encourage efficiency; they insisted on a real rather than spurious application of the doctrine of equality before the law; they were outspokenly opposed to political patronage and corruption; and they certainly desired a more streamlined, professionalized public service open to merit. But, as Greaves (*The Civil Service in the Changing State*, p. 20) correctly emphasizes, agreeing with Smellie, these men were primarily concerned with alleviating the abuses of the past, not in anticipating the needs of the future.

82. Thus Greaves (*ibid.*, p. 26) argues that public service careers open to talent were seen by the nineteenth-century reformers not as an end in themselves but rather as a means of increasing efficiency and economy in the management of governmental affairs.

question that the motives of humanitarianism, efficiency, economy, and reducing social tension associated with the reforms of the last century produced in Britain a model system of administration—one that in some ways rivaled the Prussian model in its organizational attributes. But it remains a highly elitist administrative system, dominated by men who make a fetish of the value of the intelligent amateur in administration and who continue to insist that the British system needs no radical transformation—particularly in the areas of training for the public service and administrative adjudication.

Typical of many British attitudes toward the bureaucratic state modeled along French or Prussian lines is the stinging, lively attack of Sisson on the concept of *régime administratif.*[83] Sisson clearly does not care for the Weberian-type bureaucratic system. He insists that the excessive codification associated with Napoleonic reforms, as well as the Conseil d'Etat, means "no doubt that people confronted with a somewhat high-handed bureaucracy feel the need for some re-assurance and that, while administrative officials could not be tied down to so rigid a procedure as the courts, there could be a declaration that they would conduct themselves in a manner which would give the citizen of the new republic every chance of getting his rights."[84]

Chapman puts this latter point more neatly when he suggests that "a country's view of public administration reflects its underlying philosophy of society and the state."[85] Thus, in countries such as Germany with a monarchical tradition, Chapman finds that people will manifest trust in the competence and probity of public officials. In republican-tradition countries such as France and Switzerland, on the other hand, administrators are considered overbearing and corrupt.[86] Presumably the monarchical tra-

83. C. H. Sisson, *The Spirit of British Administration* (London, 1959). Henry Parris suggests that Sisson's book may in fact be a subtle and bitter attack on British administration. This seems plausible, given the grotesque way in which Sisson characterizes the bureaucratic state.

84. *Ibid.*, p. 69. But cf. Port, *Administrative Law*, p. 330, another British scholar, who in 1929 could write, "So far from administrative law in France unduly favoring Government officials, it is true to say that in no other country is the ordinary citizen so well protected against the consequences of acts of State servants, as he is in France at the present time."

85. *The Profession of Government*, p. 303.

86. *Ibid.*, pp. 308–309.

dition accords the bureaucrat the kind of high status that breeds mutual confidence; the republican tradition leads to an extensively articulated administrative adjudicative system designed to compel otherwise untrustworthy bureaucrats to adhere to the principles and disciplines of constitutionalism.[87]

By these standards, it would be difficult to place Britain and the United States neatly in either the "monarchical" or "republican" traditions. American distrust of administrative elites, unleashed in the Jacksonian era but apparent under colonialism, did not lead to institutions of administrative adjuciation anything like the Conseil d'Etat. The British "monarchical" tradition may help explain the persistent deference toward public officials that one associates with that country but that does not in turn completely square with the distrust of centralized authority and the centuries of trying to limit it which I have reviewed above. For that matter, Germany itself might be a "deviant case" in that German administrative courts really grew out of internal administrative review boards and have as a central purpose the tying of field administrative units to central authority. That they might also serve to protect the citizen against bureaucratic excesses seems an "unintended" or "unanticipated" consequence.[88]

We do know, however, that the administrative reforms of the United States were influenced by factors similar to those that characterized England in the nineteenth and twentieth centuries. The Jacksonian effort to democratize a hitherto elite national government led to the kind of patronage that was also typical of England, although the "spoils" system went far beyond anything

87. On the critical importance of the *status* accorded the higher bureaucracy by a social system, see Fritz Morstein Marx, "The Higher Civil Service as an Action Group in Western Political Development," in LaPalombara (ed.) *Bureaucracy and Political Development,* pp. 63–95. Cf. Chapman, *The Profession of Government,* p. 315, who states, "The public official is naturally affected by the way the public regards him. He inevitably acquires characteristics which the public expects of him. If he is treated with respect, he will carry himself with conscious dignity; if with distrust he will become defensively aggressive."

88. I am indebted to Fritz Scharpf for this observation. He adds the point that the centralizing function of German administrative courts remains basically important in West Germany today, and that one must remember that giving meaning to *Rechtsstaat* through such tribunals may mean nothing more than that the individual must be treated by administrators "according to the rules," no matter how arbitrary or authoritarian or undemocratic the rules themselves might be. (The last phrase is my inference, not Professor Scharpf's statement.)

that Britain experienced in the eighteenth and nineteenth centuries. Efforts at reform later in the century were strongly influenced by the implicit values of an emergent industrial society. Between these two periods, administrative change was associated with cataclysmic events such as civil war, just as the earliest period in the evolution of American national administration was influenced by the need for welding together a nation-state.

If the history of public administrative development in the United States has any distinctive features, they seem to lie in this: that American national history begins at a time when Europe had already completed a variety of experiences in the organization and management of government. These experiences were not lost on American nation-builders, who enjoyed the luxury of being able to approach problems of public administration almost *de novo.* Just as we are able to identify nation-building crises and values or ideologies with which major choices or transformations in European administration were associated, so were Federalists and Republicans able to do the same thing. As a result, administrative evolution in the United States is early influenced by active, self-conscious debate. The debate begins with the critically important Federalist-Republican confrontation on the nature of national power and extends right through the era of scientific management and the onset of the positive state. Even a cursory look at American history will reveal that canons of administrative law and organization have been borrowed both from England and from the Continent. The hybrid pattern the United States has evolved manifests an unwillingness to rely exclusively on the common law and philosophical assumptions that undergird the rule of law and a commitment to rely as well on constitutional and statutory limitations I have associated with *l'Etat de Droit.*

Thus, queries about whether a Conseil d'Etat is desirable, or how far up or down the Weberian principle of merit should extend, or how much delegated authority or emergency power should be accorded the executive branch, or what special rights and obligations accrue to the public servant as opposed to the ordinary citizen—all questions such as these cannot be settled merely by reference to an administrative "technology" plus a legal system that is presumably universally applicable. Unlike the rose of Gertrude Stein, an organization is not simply that. It exists within a particular cultural setting and will be influenced by and in turn will influence that setting. Where the organization is governmental (in the sense of being endowed with the powers of the state), seemingly technical questions about it will always be tied to feelings the governors and governed have about the meaning and mission of government itself. Thus, questions about public administration are almost always in part ideological.

IV. Bureaucracy, Democracy, Constitutionalism

As my brief review of administrative developments in several Western countries suggests, changes invariably were associated with certain ends-in-view (values, ideologies) held by those who sought to bring about change, or to impede it. For the Great Elector, Frederick William I, Louis XIV, and the early Norman kings, the overriding value appears to be the extension of territorial power. Where such extensions occurred, they required some administrative reorganization in advance, so to speak, in sectors of defense and the military. They also required, after the fact of extended jurisdiction, the creation of new administrative arrangements to make effective control of enlarged nation-states possible. Thus, in these countries at least, the reasons why earliest administrative reforms occurred in the military and financial sectors appear self-evident.

In these same countries and others, however, a new catalytic value—wealth, economic development—recurs throughout their histories, but takes on particularly significant importance when the opportunities of trade, commerce, and industrialization are viewed as requiring governmental intervention for their maximum achievement. Thus the European mercantilists became the advocates of the absolutist state—and of a system of administration that would provide the internal (sometimes external) conditions that would help make men rich. Monarchs and their advisers pursuing their own interest in maximizing political power found it relatively easy to work with those whose interests, particularly in colonial exploitation, were so congruent with their own.

In these periods, one might say that there were no independent doctrines of administration but that public administrative arrangements were seen primarily (perhaps strictly) as instrumentally related to goal attainment. However, with the advent of industrialization certain aspects of administrative organization began to take on the trappings of absolute values in themselves. The kinds of canons of human organization and behavior that appeared "natural" to industrial enterprise were generalized for all organizations and particularly for public administrative organization.[89] Similar canons were derived from transformations in military organization and applied to both private and public administration. Even more significantly, the canons were derived from the Roman Catholic church, dominant in Europe for several centuries and endowed with a system of administrative organization which would have influenced secular governments even if "princes of the Church" had not been so prominent as administrators of the latter. These are the root sources of such concepts as hierarchy, command, obedience, discipline, accountability, specialization of labor, professional qualifications, order, efficiency, and economy. They clearly represent the technocratic side of public administration, and no end of debate, as well as mischief, has been caused by assumptions that such aspects of administra-

89. This view of the transformations I treat here was expressed by a critic of my paper at Bellagio. As I recall the position there expressed by Michel Crozier, it might be summarized as follows: (1) the Napoleonic state did not introduce administrative changes that represented radical breaks with patterns of previous centuries; (2) the "bureaucratic state" may be neither a "great" Western discovery nor, in itself, a new method for governing men; (3) what makes the important difference over time are not the objectives of governments but new ideas about center-local relations, the citizen and the state, etc.; (4) the discovery that man can be governed "rationally," so closely associated with Weber, inevitably leads to rigidities of organizational patterns, which in turn influence even the *kind* of objectives a society can seriously contemplate.

I can agree with much of this, but must defer in part from Crozier's conclusion that the critical question must be how one can administer given a range of existential conditions—such as changes in political participation, technologies of communication, etc. Differently put, the question is how rulers can move men when they seek to realize something. I assume that such questions have been posed from time immemorial but that choices are always limited by what is inherited from the past. This inheritance includes institutions, values, perceptions, and even systems of rationality. It is these variables that I have in part sought to identify and gauge in this chapter.

tion, meritorious though they may be in the abstract, can be uncritically applied to any public service, wherever found in space and time.

Those who would stress the technocratic or "scientific" side of Western administrative doctrine often ignore a second strain of values or ideology that influenced political and administrative development. In a word, that value is the individual. Whether concern for him is derived from early Christian thought, the writings of the Roman lawyers, social-contract or natural-law theorists, or Utilitarians, it is clear that this value has also served to condition the development of public administrative systems. Indeed, even the absolute monarchs, who presumably rarely drew a democratic breath, indirectly acknowledged this value when, for other reasons, they insisted on even-handed treatment of subjects by administrators, according to law.

Where, as in England, the concept of the individual's rights received articulation early, attempts emerged not to aggrandize but to define restrictively, and to limit, the exercise of power. This remains true throughout British history and is therefore a central goal of those Englishmen who, after political power had been tamed, sought to limit the alleged excesses in the exercise of economic power. On the other hand, where the value of the individual was not strongly articulated prior to the consolidation of national power, absolutism took hold, and only violent revolution was in some cases able to modify patterns of administration. Indeed, in such situations locally based resistance was almost always considered nefarious for the nation's well-being—as incidentally such resistance is generally viewed today in the developing nations. Neither *Rechtsstaat* nor *l'Etat de Droit* provides a strong protection for the individual in that these concepts, unlike the rule of law, imply only that, whether by tradition or statutes, the state and its servants will govern not arbitrarily but by the rules.

As many view the history of the West, it appears that the most efficient and effective administrative systems have been associated with despotic power. That such power would quickly be seen as stemming from a highly technocratized public bureaucracy was inevitable. That such technocratic public bureaucracies often stressed expediency as opposed to principled values and sometimes succeeded in establishing overpowering dynasties in opposition to both people and monarch seemed to some to be equally inevitable. It therefore seems perfectly logical that a British people accustomed to stress the individual as a central value appear to prefer to be administered by "amateurs" rather than experts. How else explain Sisson's comment that "the high official faced with an awkward question feels for a specialist as Goering felt for his revolver when he heard the word 'culture'? The passion for specialization, so characteristic of the Germans and betraying their desperate hope for certainty and their basic wobbling, may increase the size but certainly cannot increase the homogeneity of the service or the facility of communications within it."[90]

Mr. Sisson's view of the British public servant is of course patently naive and empirically false, particularly when he suggests that "it is the absolute nonentity of the British administrator that is his chief merit."[91] However, it is noteworthy that his principal target is Max Weber and that, in striking contrast to scholars like Morstein Marx, he prefers that members of the administrative class be strictly rather than judiciously neutral politically.[92] To be more than a nonentity or to be more politically committed would constitute for the British administrator a violation of the constitution, "for it would make the administrator a man who mattered, competing in his own right for public attention and support, instead of his being, as he is at present, the mere servant of a Minister of the Crown."[93]

90. *The Spirit of British Administration,* p. 117. Two observations might be added here: First, it is not entirely clear that despotic systems are more "effective" or "efficient" if the test is, roughly, the ratio of resources utilized to the ends-in-view. Despotic systems have drained off many human and material resources to maintain order. Relatively liberal regimes, such as England in the eighteenth century, could keep disorder at a bearable minimum with relatively few resources and thus free men and materials to the tasks of economic development. Second, one must be wary about accepting stereotypes such as the "passion for specialization" in German administration. German administration—like that in Italy and a host of other countries—is plagued by the overwhelming presence of non-specialist lawyers in administrative positions.

91. *Ibid.,* p. 127.

92. Morstein Marx, "The Higher Civil Service."

93. Sisson, *The Spirit of British Administration,* p. 146.

Of course, it is the "nonentities" Mr. Sisson refers to who have made the British public service the envy of many nations. I cite him here not to engage in polemics but merely to illustrate how deeply ingrained is the Englishman's suspicion of the Weberian-type bureaucrat and how insistent are the British that the only reliable "guardian" bureaucrat is one who has not made a specialization or a fetish of administration.

Briefs for the administrative generalist on the one side and claims for the specialist on the other are simply another way of phrasing the presumed tension or antipathy between bureaucracy and democracy. Although all administrative systems require both specialists and generalists, the fear is that increased emphasis on functional specialization will lead to the destruction of democracy by the technocrats. The problem and the debate are of course greatly complicated in the era of the service state, which followed on the heels of universal suffrage and the growth of socialist ideology in the West. One of the supreme ironies of socialist thought, of course, is that it simultaneously anticipates enormous growth in public services *and* the withering away of bureaucracy. However, in the face of concrete experiences ranging from Lenin's discovery that not every citizen can administer to more recent Western experiences with the administration of national economic planning, socialist ideologies have returned to the question how bureaucratic administration, which appears essential to modern government, can be kept responsible.

This is, of course, the appropriate question, as Carl Friedrich has been insisting for more than thirty years.[94] It is clear that limitations on bureaucratic behavior that are self-imposed by benevolent guardians will not do for those who are unwilling to sacrifice the dignity and the freedom of the individual for the benefits that derive from a technocratically splendid Weberian bureaucratic system. But it is also self-evident, as Friedrich has insisted, that before there can be constitutionalism there must exist a state whose government and governors can then be sub-

94. See C. J. Friedrich and R. T. Cole, *Responsible Bureaucracy* (Cambridge, Mass., 1932), and C. J. Friedrich (ed.), *Responsibility,* Vol. III in the Nomos Series (New York, 1960), pp. 189–202.

jected to a division of powers, careful definition of spheres in which power can be exercised, rules regarding the circumstances and conditions under which power is legitimately used, and finally, the means of peaceful redress and correction when the rulers exceed constitutional bonds.

Alvin Gouldner has written eloquently to this problem.[95] He laments polemics among social scientists about whether Max Weber's writings on bureaucracy were antisocialist or procapitalist, suggesting that Weber's view may well have been "a plague on both your houses." However, he adds that "if Weber is to be regarded as an 'ideologist,' he is an ideologist not of counter-revolution but of quiescence and neutralism. For many intellectuals who have erected a theory of group organization on Weberian foundations, the world has been emptied of choice, leaving them disoriented and despairing."[96]

Rather than have us despair, Gouldner would have us be courageous and inventive in our search for public administrative arrangements that do not do violence to humanitarian democratic values. Thus he says about social scientists who have elaborated the dynamics of pathology in organizations,

> Instead of telling men how bureaucracy might be mitigated, they insist that it is inevitable. Instead of explaining how democratic patterns may, to some extent, be fortified and extended, they warn us that democracy cannot be perfect. Instead of controlling the disease, they suggest that we are deluded, or more politely, incurably romantic, for hoping to control it. Instead of assuming responsibilities as realistic clinicians, striving to further democratic potentialities wherever they can, many social scientists have become morticians, all too eager to bury men's hopes.[97]

For the so-called developed countries, most of which have resolved crises of identity, penetration, legitimacy, and participation, Gouldner's prescriptions would call for exploring a range of modified institutional arrangements or the creation of some new

95. Alvin W. Gouldner, "Metaphysical Pathos and the Theory of Bureaucracy," *American Political Science Review,* XLIX (1955), 496–507.
96. *Ibid.,* p. 498.
97. *Ibid.,* p. 507. For Gouldner's attempt to spell out how the clinician would proceed, see his *Patterns of Industrial Bureaucracy* (Glencoe, Ill., 1954).

structures. To some extent, the research of recent years on legislative-executive relations, legislative oversight, and the creation of institutions like the ombudsman suggest that some at least are in search of solutions.

For the developing nations, with the heaviest kinds of "crisis loads," the situation is manifestly much more complicated. To what extent, for example, can the development of bureaucracy within the context of democratic institutions that marks Switzerland's experience be extrapolated to the developing nations?[98]

Is Friedrich correct in suggesting that the cart of parliamentary government should not be put before the horse of a well-developed bureaucracy?[99] In the public administrative literature on the developing nations, the chorus of voices accepting "mobilization regimes" or essentially bureaucratically run systems as the only logical direction that these nations can take grows louder and more insistent.[100]

I confess to skepticism about such views, particularly when we seem now to have reached the point where we are able to define the concepts of administrative capability and political development in ways that free these concepts from Western bias.[101] Purifying our concepts, however, should not lead us to obscure the patterns of Western administrative development or the conflicting systems of values that were incidental to them. To do so would involve not merely the possibility of an irresponsible social engineering. It might mean as well that prescriptions drawn for many of the developing nations would be unworkable. Whatever calculus is developed, then, must take into consideration what I have said above. In addition, prescriptions will have to take into account the fact that in most of the developing countries *all* of

98. The burden of the Friedrich-Cole study, *Responsible Bureaucracy,* is to delineate how such development occurred.

99. *Ibid.,* p. 5.

100. See, for example, Milton J. Esman, "The Politics of Development Administration," Comparative Administration Group Occasional Paper (Bloomington, Ind., 1963). Cf. my "Alternative Strategies for Developing Administrative Capabilities in Emerging Nations," Comparative Administration Group Occasional Paper (Bloomington, Ind., 1965).

101. Alfred Diamant, "Political Development: Approaches to Theory and Strategy," in J. D. Montgomery and W. J. Siffin (eds.), *Approaches to Development: Politics, Administration and Change* (New York, 1966), pp. 15–58.

the demands or crises that were periodized in the West over several centuries are simultaneously present. Unless this is done, we will be forced to conclude pessimistically with C. E. Black that there is little reason to believe that the development of the newer nations will involve less crime, war, murder, and economic upheaval than it did in the West.[102]

102. *The Dynamics of Modernization,* pp. 150 ff.

·6·

The Structures of Government and Administrative Reform*

Fred W. Riggs

I. Introduction

Writers on public administration tend to focus their attention on bureaucratic structures and behaviors, taking their political context for granted. In relatively developed countries of the West such a constriction of attention is understandable and probably served a useful purpose during the first stages of an effort to understand and describe administrative phenomena. It can be taken for granted that in each of these countries a governmental framework exists within which career officials work responsibly. Among the key elements of this framework is a system of political parties, elections, legislative bodies, and independent tribunals. Bureaucratic behavior in this context can be examined essentially in terms of administrative and managerial norms, in terms of criteria for maximizing outputs and minimizing inputs, in terms of efficiency and effectiveness.

But where, as in many countries of Asia, Africa, and Latin America, the governmental institutions within which bureaucracy operates do not provide either effective policy direction or enforcible sanctions, bureaucratic behavior has a different meaning. In

* The author is indebted to the Center for Advanced Study in the Behavioral Sciences, Stanford, California, where the original draft of this chapter was written, and to the Social Science Research Institute of the University of Hawaii, which provided support for its revision. The author is grateful to Samuel E. Finer, discussant of this paper at the Bellagio conference, to Giovanni Sartori for comments reflected in the revision, and to Ralph Braibanti, who organized the conference.

this chapter I propose to examine some diverse governmental contexts of bureaucracy in order to theorize about political change and administrative reform in transitional societies. How are parties, elections, and legislatures related to bureaucracy? How are the structures of government related to administrative development? Does modernization of governmental institutions assure democratization, or the strengthening of administrative capabilities?

Bureaucracy: Politics and administration

To answer these questions we must use a concept which embraces all the positions falling hierarchically under the authority of an executive. While granting that the word bureaucracy often refers only to some portion of this hierarchy rather than the whole, I ask indulgence for the modified usage employed here in preference to coining a new word for the concept.

Let us distinguish between the office of executive to whom bureaucrats, by definition, are formally responsible and the hierarchy of all positions subordinated to an executive. The word "bureaucracy," then, as used in this paper will refer to all offices formally subordinated to an executive who exercises authority over a polity. This definition, when used without qualification, makes bureaucracy include all the officials, military and civil, of a state, of a politically organized society. Other organizations, including local governments, corporations, trade unions, political parties, and churches, may also have administrative staffs that are formally organized into hierarchies. They are also bureaucracies, but to avoid confusion, they are in this chapter spoken of only with appropriate qualifying adjectives, such as a party bureaucracy, a city bureaucracy, corporation bureaucracy, church bureaucracy. If any ambiguity arises, the phrase state bureaucracy may be used in place of bureaucracy, it being understood that state does not refer here to one of the fifty American states but to an independent nation-state.

Some readers will object that the military services of a country are not, properly speaking, a part of the bureaucracy. They may prefer to limit the term to civilian public offices. Since the word bureaucracy clearly has a variety of meanings in ordinary usage, I shall not dispute the question what the word really means. I do want to use a concept which includes the hierarchy of all offices formally subordinated to an executive. If it seems inappropriate to use bureaucracy for this concept, then the critic is free to propose and use another word. Perhaps he would prefer officialdom, for example, but my concept refers not to the officials, the incumbents of these offices, but to the offices or roles. The word "officialdom" is used for the body of office-holders, and therefore I cannot accept it as a term for the concept defined above. In some contexts the military may be contrasted with the bureaucracy, but in this context the military is part of the bureaucracy. Non-military offices in a bureaucracy may be referred to as the civil bureaucracy. The foregoing objection arises because the concept developed here embraces more public offices than might be included under the heading bureaucracy. Other objections may be raised because it does not cover all public offices in a given domain. Clearly there are many offices, such as those of legislators and judges and of cities, authorities, boards, and other self-governing entities, which are not formally subject to the authority of the executive. Thus there are not only private bureaucracies but also public bureaucracies which are not included in this concept of the bureaucracy of a state. Since valid statements about a state bureaucracy may not apply to other public and private bureaucracies, the distinction is essential. If we wish to generalize about bureaucratic behavior in general, we can simply refer to "all kinds of bureaucracies," and non-state bureaucracies can be separately discussed by using appropriate qualifying adjectives.

It may still be objected that even so, the term is too restrictive because there are public offices excluded by my definition which should be included. For example, it is often said that party offices in a Communist state, such as the Soviet Union, form part of the bureaucracy, and hence this kind of regime constitutes a bureaucratic state. By contrast, it is also sometimes said that since a single party dominates the state such a regime should be known as a party-state.

Both terms are inappropriate to the usage proposed here, as will become apparent below. It is my understanding of party offices, even in the Communist party, that they rest formally on election by party members. No doubt, in practice, top office-holders of the party can manipulate the elections to their own advantage, but in principle, authority rests with the membership, not the office-holders or the executive. Thus, leaving aside the question how control is actually exercised, the formal structure of authority in a Communist system makes the executive responsible to the party, whereas the bureaucracy is responsible to the executive. I want to limit the concept of bureaucracy to those offices which are formally subject to the executive's authority as executive, regardless of the strength or weakness of control actually exercised. Moreover, the concept does not include offices which are not subject to this formal authority, regardless of the extent to which the executive may actually exercise control over these offices, nor does it include offices in a party bureaucracy which may be subject to the authority of the same man, but in his role as party leader, not as executive.

This structural distinction makes it possible to discuss the various institutional settings which affect bureaucratic behavior, and hence administrative performance. These institutional settings bring to mind interest groups, political parties, courts of law, legislatures, executives, and other forms of organization. Not all of these structures have existed in every state possessing a bureaucracy, although, by definition, every state with a bureaucracy must have an executive. Many polities have existed in which there were no political parties and elective legislative bodies. Familiar examples come to mind, such as ancient Egypt, China, and Persia; until relatively modern times, France and other European kingdoms; and even, in quite recent times, such states as Siam and Ethiopia.[1] The existence of such polities makes it possible to study, largely from historical records, political and administrative behavior in governments lacking parties, elections, and legislative assemblies. Such analysis might provide a framework for under-

1. A sustained analysis of these bureaucracies is contained in S. N. Eisenstadt, *The Political Systems of Empires* (New York, 1963).

standing better how administrative reform has or can occur as the characteristically modern institutions of government are superimposed on older executive and bureaucratic structures.

The bureaucracies in premodern states, lacking parties, elections, and legislative bodies, were sharply limited in their political and administrative capabilities. As a body of royal servants, bureaucrats were obliged to serve their rulers, but kings and emperors had a limited ability to exercise effective control over their subordinates. Many ingenious devices were evolved by traditional monarchies to help them maintain their authority over the officials nominally responsible to them. In practice, bureaucrats tended, insofar as they could, to make use of whatever powers they could grasp to serve their own self-interests and the interests of their relatives and friends. If possible, they would build a power base for themselves and seek to perpetuate this power as a family privilege.

The inherent conflict between ruler and bureaucracy, therefore, was one between the centralizing tendencies of the former and the localizing propensities of the latter, between the pressures for increased discipline and co-ordination of action against the forces for greater laxity, permissiveness, and official autonomy. These contradictory pressures can be found in the governments of any traditional civilization. When the centralizing demands of the rulers were most successful, a political system emerged which could be called an oriental despotism, to use Wittfogel's trenchant phrase, or perhaps better, a bureaucratic empire. When localizing tendencies prevailed, the resulting political system might be termed feudal, resembling a type of government which prevailed in medieval Europe. Unfortunately, this terminology is so ambiguous that clarity of statement is difficult, but in the present context further refinement is unnecessary.[2]

What needs to be pointed out here is rather the changing functions of bureaucrats. In traditional political systems, their political functions varied with the degree of centralization and

2. For a more extended discussion of this point see my essay, "The Ambivalence of Feudalism and Bureaucracy in Traditional Societies," Comparative Administration Group Occasional Paper (Bloomington, Ind., 1966).

royal control exercised over the bureaucracy, as did their administrative functions. Bureaucratic structures, then, even traditionally, did not determine the political and administrative functions performed by officials, but they provided settings within which a considerable range of variation in functions was possible. The addition of modern institutions of government to the traditional executive and bureaucracy has changed the limits within which functional variation is possible. Although bureaucracies have persisted from ancient into modern governments, their functions have tended to become more administrative and less political, but even in modern governments a considerable range of variation in bureaucratic performance can be found.

Before we can discuss this subject, which goes to the heart of the problem of administrative reform, we need first to clarify the way in which the concepts of structure and function are used in this essay.

The need to distinguish structure from function

In ordinary usage, the effective consequences of a structure for the political system in which it is lodged are included among the connotations of the words used to name the structures. It is difficult to find words to use for governmental structures, defined as patterns of action independent of their system consequences. I cannot pretend that it is easy or even possible, in an exploratory essay such as this one, to make the distinction clearly and consistently. Nevertheless, I shall try to use words in such a way as to separate concepts of governmental structure from related concepts of political and administrative function.

There is so much confusion and ambiguity connected with the use of the terms "structure" and "function" that explanation of their use in this chapter is warranted.[3] Let us think of an organization, such as a government, and of its components, such as legislatures, courts, executives, bureaucracies, and the like. These components are structures, and the ways in which the components affect the government are functions.

3. No attempt is made here to reconcile this definition of structure with that developed by Braibanti in his chapter in this volume, esp. p. 54.

In other words, I am using the word "function" as it is used in mathematics and economics to designate a relationship between two or more variables. In political science there has been a tendency to use function for another meaning, such as intent, purpose, or program. In that sense a function is an intention on the part of an actor or a collectivity to accomplish some result, whether or not this result is actually accomplished.

In separating manifest and latent functions, one is asked to distinguish between what an actor or collectivity states to be its intent and what actually happens that is different from this intent. This is not a distinction I wish to make here. I would not regard a declaration of intent or of program objectives as a function at all, although this is what writers usually mean by manifest function. I treat as a function only actual relationships between two items, where a change in one affects the other. In this sense the activity of a bureaucracy affecting the political system of which it is a part is a function.

Some such relationships correspond to formally authorized statements about what the relationship should be, but many empirical interactions are not so authorized and may even be regarded as improper or illegitimate. The former might be called overt functions and the latter covert. What is called a latent function in the sociological usage mentioned above is probably the same as a covert function. However, an overt function is not the same as a manifest function because it refers to an actual authorized consequence and not just to what is said to be the intended consequence of action. Clearly, statements about intended consequences may or may not lead to actual consequences. From the point of view proposed here, a manifest function—declaration of intent—is thought of not as a function but as part of a pattern of action and hence of a structure. The word function will be limited to meanings in which a relationship between two items is specified such that one has a systematic effect on the other.

In terms of this distinction, I have attempted above to define a bureaucracy structurally, as a formal pattern of action, without implying in the terminology used what the functions of a bureaucracy might be, whether administrative, political, economic, ceremonial, or what not. Thus, by defining bureaucracy in terms of a hierarchy of authority we can leave open the question of how much actual control is exercised within the hierarchy. In these terms, a feudal system is a type of bureaucracy in which actual control of superior over subordinate offices is highly attenuated. Indeed, this functional change leads us in ordinary usage to say that a feudal system is not bureaucratic and to reserve the term for those bureaucracies in which a substantial degree of actual control corresponds to the structure of formal authority.

The point may be illustrated by a simple analogy. A coat may be defined in terms of its shape and its use, but we then face the difficulty of not knowing whether a coat used for an unusual purpose—such as to walk on—is still a coat or has been transformed into a rug. The difficulty is purely definitional, for if we define coats by their shape (i.e., structurally) we can then hypothesize about their uses (i.e., their functions). A coat used for an unusual purpose then still remains a coat, and the definition is not violated.

The commonsense view of bureaucracy makes the same error when it attributes functions to the structure by definition. If we say that a feudal bureaucracy cannot be a bureaucracy because it does not perform as bureaucracies normally do, we overlook two key considerations. First, there is probably never, in any bureaucracy, full correspondence between actual control and formal authority. Thus the behavioral differences between a localized feudal hierarchy of authority and a centralized royal bureaucracy is a matter of degree, not of kind. Second, the structure of authority in a feudal system contrasts markedly with that in a primitive tribal society which lacks a hierarchy of offices. The hierarchy of offices in medieval Europe, as in traditional Japan and other feudalistic systems, was clearly patterned on the bureaucratic structures of imperial Rome and China, respectively. Thus the functional modification of borrowed structures of government is a familiar historical phenomenon, taking the emergence of feudalism as prototype.

In similar fashion, in our times, structures of government first invented in the West have been widely adopted in non-Western countries. But whereas these structures served one set of functions in their original settings, they have often been adapted to quite different functions after being transplanted. If this is true, then clearly it is only by distinguishing between formal sturctures and the functions they perform that we can see what has happened. Otherwise, when a familiar structure is used for quite novel functions we are unlikely to recognize it as the same structure, and hence fall into considerable perplexity to describe or perceive what has happened.

Among the important new structures of government to emerge in relatively modern times have been the institution of popular elections, elected national assemblies, and political parties. These institutions have profoundly affected not only the role of monarchs but also of bureaucracies. Moreover, just as the formal structure of bureaucracy spread in the past from the classical empires to surrounding hinterlands and succession states, so parties, elections, and legislative bodies have also diffused in our time from the Western to the non-Western world. But with paradoxical results, for the functional impact of these structures on government in general, and on executives and bureaucracy in particular, has often been quite different from what it was in the countries which invented these institutions.

Functional transformations in the executive role are more familiar than those of bureaucracies. In the Western democracies the new structures of government drastically curtailed the effective power of hereditary monarchs, in some instances reducing their role to that of ceremonial head of state and in others displacing them completely by elected executives. In general, the role of executive in most Western polities, whether hereditary or elective, became ceremonial or constitutional, rather than that of effective head of government. The major exception is found in those few polities which use the presidential form of government, as manifested in the United States.

In the modernizing countries which have borrowed these institutions from the West, however, the role of the executive has often not changed in the same way. Hereditary monarchs, for example, though embattled, have sought, sometimes with success, to use these institutions to enhance their personal power. Where kings have been replaced by elective executives, they have often also sought to capture the new institutions to buttress their own authority.

Similar paradoxes have occurred in the impact of these modern institutions on the functions previously performed by bureaucracies, or perhaps better, by leading state officials (military and civil). In the Western homeland of these new structures of government, the political influence and role of bureaucrats has largely been curtailed and their administrative function enhanced. By contrast, it seems probable, at least in many of the new states, that the borrowing of these novel legislative, electoral, and partisan structures of government has enhanced the political role of bureaucrats—especially those near the top, and those engaged in military operations—often at the expense of their administrative efficiency and capabilities.

If there is any truth to these sweeping generalizations, impressionistic as they seem, then a variety of questions arises. We might ask, for example, for hypotheses to explain these paradoxical effects of the borrowing of Western political institutions. We might look at various ecological relationships, the influence of geography, demography, culture, technology, economy, and other environmental factors to help us understand what happened. Important and interesting as such an inquiry might be, it must be put aside, except for a few passing remarks, as beyond the limited scope of this preliminary essay. Instead, let us inquire more narrowly into some of the possible consequences, rather than the causes, of these political and administrative transformations. The structure and performance of evolving bureaucracies as forces affecting the behavior of legislative, elective, and partisan institutions in the new states might be examined.[4] Rather, taking the opposite side of the coin, let us ask how the new structures of government have affected the behavior of bureauc-

4. This has been discussed in Fred W. Riggs, "Bureaucrats and Political Development: A Paradoxical View," in Joseph LaPalombara (ed.), *Bureaucracy and Political Development* (Princeton, 1963), pp. 120–167.

racies and bureaucrats, especially in the performance of their administrative functions. First, to clarify several dimensions of ecological change which are closely related to changes in the institutions and performance of governments; then, to turn to an examination of patterns of governmental change, and their relation to administrative reform.

II. Types of Ecological Change: Development, Democratization, and Modernization

Changes in the structure of government, in bureaucracies, political parties, elections, and legislatures are not regarded here as subjects of intrinsic interest. The significance of these changes derives from their relation to the far-reaching social and economic transformations through which contemporary societies are passing, transformations which go by such names as modernization, the industrial revolution, political and economic development, and democratization. It is in the context of these great transformations, which I shall call ecological change, that the governmental changes to be discussed in this chapter must be seen. By ecology I refer to environmental forces which both influence and are influenced by polities, by the political system.

Unfortunately, many ambiguities interfere with clarity of thought about these ecological transformations. The available words have been widely and often indiscriminately used, sometimes almost as synonyms, frequently for quite different concepts. Let us therefore distinguish between three dimensions of change which are immediately relevant. Other important types of change, such as population growth, urbanization, religious conversion, international violence, etc., can also be identified, but it is unnecessary to deal with them here.

Developmental revolutions

One type of change is frequently meant when the term "development" is used. This involves such related phenomena as the industrial and scientific revolution and increased use of non-human energy and advanced technology in the production of manufactured goods and the provision of services. Associated with this economic revolution is an increase in the specialization of labor and the differentiation of roles, both individual and institutional, a rise in per capita income, an increase in the functional specificity of social structures, and higher levels of social mobilization. Let us refer to this extensive transformation of society and economy in modern times as the developmental revolution.

The developmental revolution has profound implications for government. Two of these implications, which are closely interrelated, are particularly relevant to the theme of this chapter.

First, because of the developmental revolution, differentiated roles and institutions must be consciously integrated with each other by devising and enforcing ever more complicated rules and regulations. Machinery is needed to determine what norms should be invoked and also to make sure that they are applied. This means that in societies experiencing the developmental revolution there is need for a great increase in the magnitude of large-scale decision-making, far beyond the capabilities of a single ruler and his advisers, no matter how enlightened and altruistic they might be. Moreover, the enforcement of these decisions requires a governmental apparatus far more precise and reliable as an instrument of administration than the bureaucracies of traditional civilizations. The new structures of government invented in the West are widely perceived as a necessary means for achieving these functional benefits.

Second, territorial boundaries have to be set for the making and enforcement of policy if the operations of government in a society experiencing the developmental revolution are to succeed. This was not true in traditional civilizations where royal governments had minimal needs to penetrate the societies over which they reigned. As one moved away from a capital city, one found local princes and magnates, self-governing corporations, autonomous tribes, clans, castes, monasteries, shrines, and guilds, each of which could survive without need for governmental intervention. Thus, if the boundaries of a traditional realm were diffuse and unmarked, little harm was done, nor was there any need for the subjects of a king to think of themselves as citizens, as members of a body politic. Their identifications were with parochial social structures and the primary groups of everyday social experience.

But these identifications are no longer sufficient in societies experiencing the developmental revolution. The territorial and membership boundaries of the polity need to be sharply drawn in order to specify where the new policies and statutory enactments of government apply and where they do not.

Moreover, insofar as populations are drawn ever more closely into a net of obligations and services created by government, they also demand to be heard in the making of these policies. In other words, the governmental changes which accompany the developmental revolution are matched by changes in popular attitudes and identifications which we may call politicization or secularization. This is the process of nation-building, the establishment of a body politic to correspond to the territorial domain and citizen provenance of the state.

To summarize, at the governmental level the developmental revolution provokes institutional transformations in the organization of government intended to enable it to formulate and implement increasingly complex policies and to integrate more and more differentiated structures. To accomplish this result governments need machinery which is both politically responsible and administratively capable. At the popular level, the developmental revolution generates increasing politicization of populations. This is not to say that the two processes must proceed at the same rate —indeed, it is typical to find imbalances and lags. Our hypothesis, rather, is that the developmental revolution will tend to be impeded in societies which fail to strengthen certain governmental institutions and where the population does not become secularized or politicized. Conversely, it is also unlikely that governmental transformations of the sort indicated will take place in societies which are not also undergoing a developmental revolution. Neither process is a prerequisite of the other, but the two are associated with each other in a process of circular causation or reciprocal reinforcement.

Democratization

These interdependent processes of social change are related to a different dimension of ecological transformation which is often spoken of as democratization. What is at issue here is the extent to which access to the values prized in a society are equally shared. Basic also is the right to challenge accepted policies and to seek to replace them. This dimension of transformation may not be closely correlated with the developmental revolution, even though there are social thinkers who say, perhaps wishfully, that the developmental revolution is necessarily accompanied by increasing democratization. Perhaps the coincidence between the industrial revolution in the West and the rise there of democratic regimes generated a natural association of ideas. Moreover, even in the single-party regimes which appear to Westerners to be least democratic, the norms of social justice and equalitarianism are widely held in the name of true democracy. If we look at traditional civilizations and folk societies, we will see also a considerable variation in the distribution of power and wealth, and in the openness of these societies. The clash between democratic and aristocratic values has been a recurrent theme in political philosophy since the time of Aristotle. The success of the Soviet Union in carrying out a developmental revolution should, by itself, be a clear enough proof of the lack of necessary correlation between the developmental revolution and democratization. In short, we find democratic tendencies without development, and development without democracy.

Certainly we would be well advised, in thinking about governmental changes, to dissociate the idea of popular participation in decision-making and equalitarianism in governmental administration from the types of political and administrative change spoken of above as a necessary concomitant of the developmental revolution. Let us think of democracy as a constraint on development: if the governmental changes associated with the developmental revolution are to be made compatible with democratic values, then what implications follow for politics and administration? It is in this sense that I shall attempt to draw a distinction between types of governmental structure which are compatible with the developmental revolution and with democracy and others which are favorable for development but not for democracy.

Modernization

A third type of ecological transformation in the cultural sphere is taking place in the world today. It is sometimes spoken of as Westernization, but I prefer to call it modernization. Unfortunately, this word has other meanings, including both of the ideas discussed above under development and democratization. The reader is free to use another term, but I mean by modernization a type of emulative acculturation in which cultural practices, institutional forms, and technologies are consciously borrowed or adapted by one society from another. The process of acculturation is more general than modernization. It occurs whenever cultural traits diffuse from one area to another. Acculturation is modernization only when the borrowing group looks on the source of its borrowed traits as more advanced. In our industrial era, the Western powers are widely regarded as advanced, which means that their specific institutions and practices are being extensively emulated throughout the world. In this sense, contemporary modernization involves Westernization.

Yet the two terms should not be used as synonyms. Preindustrial modernization was engaged in by Japanese emulating Chinese and by Bulgarians emulating Greeks. Intra-Occidental modernization takes place when Germany tries to catch up with England or the Russians try to surpass the Americans.

Modernization, strangely, also involves emulating the past, seeking to revive and purify the best of one's historical traditions. This type of modernization, which looks to history rather than to contemporaries for the best models, is often referred to as neotraditionalism. In commonsense usage, neotraditionalism is thought of as the antithesis of modernization, yet empirically neotraditionalism is probably always associated with Westernization in the contemporary modernizing countries. It is important to be aware of the syncretism between traditional and Western models in the third world, especially in the field of government, because here we find archaic and indigenous institutions mixed in various combinations with imported forms.

It has been widely and, I believe, erroneously said that the process of Westernization, the introduction of modernizing innovations, would destroy and replace traditional institutions. One of the concerns expressed by spokesmen for some non-Western societies has been the fear that Westernization would involve the loss of cultural identity, the sacrifice of prized traditional values, as non-Western countries were made over in the image of the West. Yet surely this fear rests on a basic misconception of the process of modernization. It is true that certain functional changes are necessary if old societies wish to accomodate themselves to the requirements of an industrialized and increasingly interdependent world. I think it is also necessary, if they are to succeed in this functional adaptation, for them to make use of new structures of government and new technologies invented in the West. But old institutions can also survive and ancient practices may even be revived and revitalized at the same time. We have already mentioned the survival of kingship, one of the most archaic of institutions, in the face of new parliamentary, electoral, and political party institutions. The survival of bureaucracy, itself scarcely a Western invention, is another example of the same phenomenon, the persistence of institutions. Our concern here may be viewed, in part at least, as a study of the functional changes in the role of an ancient institution, bureaucracy, as it is confronted by new governmental institutions, namely parties, elections, and elected assemblies.

Just as democratization needs to be distinguished from the developmental revolution as a possible but not a necessary concomitant, so one must see the transformation of modernization as probably a necessary but not a sufficient condition for both the developmental revolution and democratization. Modernization involves structural innovation. Structural innovation may make functional transformations possible, but it offers no assurance that they will take place. This is a matter of everyday observation, yet we frequently overlook its significance.

The proverbial slum-dweller who stores coal in his bathtub may be taken as a prototype of the society which adopts a new constitutional form of government but uses it only to mask the persistence of a patrimonial mode of governance. Lest we be smug, think also of the American tourist who brings home from Japan or China an abacus, one of the most sophisticated and efficient desk-top instruments for calculation, and can think of nothing better to do with it than use it for a lamp stand. Clearly political parties, elections, and elected assemblies can be used to decorate a polity as well as to guide or control it. There is no reason, let me repeat, why new structures of government must drive out old ones. Kings persist long after parties and parliaments come into being. We still walk in a jet age, and we still talk to each other in an era of television. The most primitive savages walked and talked, as do the most civilized of men. Thus contemporary modernization (or emulative acculturation, if you prefer) has to do with the introduction of borrowed structures, both Western and neotraditional, but not with the way in which they are used, or how they affect pre-existing structures.

With this in mind, we can watch structures of government spreading by emulation to societies that have not experienced the developmental revolution. We have to understand how these structures are used where the developmental revolution has taken place, and we must also see how they are used where this revolution has not occurred or is only starting, i.e., in places that have modernized but not developed. Our problem, then, is to understand the relation of bureaucratic performance to new structures of government—notably political parties, popular elections, and elected assemblies—in countries where the developmental revolution has taken place and also in countries where it has not. We also examine the differences between governmental systems—whether modernized or not, and whether developed or not—where power is more widely (democratically) distributed and those in which it is more narrowly (despotically) concentrated.

III. Traditional and Modern Patterns of Government

When we examine the phenomenon of governmental modernization—as defined here in terms of the spread by emulative acculturation of new structures and technologies—we discover that striking institutional changes have been diffused throughout the world in the twentieth century. It matters not how developed a society or economy may be as measured by indices of economic and social performance, nor how democratic or autocratic. With but few exceptions the key structures of Western government have been superimposed on whatever patterns of governance previously existed. Thus modernization has frequently occurred without either development or democratization. Governmental behavior, the functioning of politics and administration, however, can only be understood in terms of the composite outcome of interactions between the old and new, the traditional and modern.[5]

Some of the elements of the superimposed Western pattern of government can readily be identified. Among the most familiar are the legal elements, including the spread of international law, the idea of having a written constitution, the adoption of new

5. In another context, I have suggested the prismatic model as a useful way to try to conceptualize and analyze this curious mixture of often contradictory elements in contemporary transitional societies (*Administration in Developing Countries: The Theory of Prismatic Society* [Boston, 1964]). Anyone who looks through a prism may discover a composite scene in which the upper half is inverted and superimposed in a non-integrated fashion upon the lower half. The structures of modernizing government are similarly fashioned of dysrhythmically interlaced neotraditional and Western elements. For the concept of dysrhythmic change, see C. S. Whitaker, Jr., "A Dysrhythmic Process of Political Change," *World Politics*, XIX (1967), 190–217. In quoting from my own work, Whitaker seems to think that I argue for the complete penetration and displacement of traditional by Western forms, whereas my view, as indicated above, is that modernization has neotraditional as well as Westernizing consequences, and that old institutions persist with functional adaptations in modernizing societies. The challenges posed by the developmental revolution in the West create problems which can scarcely be avoided in every sector and in every country, but the pace of change varies within wide limits, and the particular solutions adopted in one setting may be strikingly different from those embraced elsewhere. What is similar everywhere is the challenge of the West, but the universality of response does not imply that all responses are identical.

legal codes, and the establishment of courts of law based on this jurisprudence. On the political side, the organization of political parties, elected assemblies, and popular elections has spread to virtually every contemporary state, as already noted. This is the main subject to which I shall return for a detailed analysis.

But first let us focus attention on some changes which affect bureaucratic structure. Here it is not easy to identify the distinctively modern. Unlike political parties and elected legislatures, bureaucracies are an ancient form of government. We have already mentioned bureaucracy in traditional civilizations, pointing to the antinomy between the centralizing drive of rulers to institutionalize responsibility and the localizing counterdrive of officials to protect their self-interests. These countervailing pressures continue to affect contemporary bureaucracies, but their operation is affected by new forms of organization.

Administrative reformers see themselves as carriers of an innovative social technology particularly applicable to bureaucratic organization. Yet some items in their tool kit are ancient indeed. It is as though foreign advisers were to start teaching the Chinese how to print books, forgetting that it was the Chinese who first invented this particular gadget, using it to create the greatest the Chinese about civil service examinations, the Chinese can justifiably protest that, after all, they were the ones who first invented this particular gadget, using it to create the greatest bureaucratic machine of any traditional civilization. Examinations and a career service, in other words, are not distinctive structures of modern bureaucracies. Like the printing of books, they have become essential ingredients of modern life without being distinctively modern, just as walking and talking are also universal elements of modern living, but scarcely distinctive.

Bureaucracies: Simple and complex

What, then, are the distinctive institutional components of modern bureaucracies which set them apart from all traditional bureaucracies? Weber thought of rational-legal authority as distinctively modern and, in terms of Parsonian pattern-variables, modern bureaucracies are perhaps more achievement oriented, universalistic, and functionally specific than traditional bureaucracies. But these are all functional attributes, and to some degree they are also found in ancient bureaucracies. They do not provide a clear-cut basis for distinguishing between modern and premodern institutions. Moreover, there are clearly great variations in the degree to which these presumed touchstones of modernity are found in different contemporary societies, in Iran or Eire, in Britain or Bulgaria, in Canada or Ethiopia.

The point may be illustrated by using a readily measured variable, such as size. In general, comparing primitive tribes with the United States and the Soviet Union, we can hypothesize that modern states are larger than traditional polities. But when we compare Denmark with imperial China we have to recognize that, however valid the statistical correlation, size is not a distinctive test of modernity. And neither is universalism or legal-rationalism.

On the premise that key structures of government have already been widely disseminated by emulative acculturation (or modernization), we can look for any structural characteristics of bureaucracy which might be found equally in Thailand and Belgium, in Nigeria and Mexico, in Poland and Egypt, but not in the Ottoman Empire, in Tokugawa Japan, or in medieval France. It may not be possible to find such characteristics at all, in which case we would conclude that modern bureaucracies are no different, structurally, from traditional bureaucracies. If they work differently or better, it might be only because they are larger, have more resources, are more honest, or have more regulations. A more reasonable hypothesis might be that modern bureaucracies function differently from traditional ones, not because their internal structures are different but because something new has been added to the political environment of bureaucracies—political parties, popular elections, and elective assemblies. There is much to be said on behalf of this hypothesis, which will be discussed later.

But first let us look a bit further for any specifically modern structural characteristic of contemporary bureaucracies. The characteristics mentioned here can be found, at least in embryonic form, in several traditional bureaucracies, but perhaps the elaboration of these forms does constitute something distinctive about modern bureaucracy.

A salient element in every standard textbook on public administration is the distinction between staff and line. This pattern of organization is usually attributed to the German army, but it has spread to civilian bureaucracy and to many countries within the last century. What is the significance of this distinction?

The simplest kind of bureaucracy clearly embodies one of the classical rules of administration: unity of command. This means that subordinates in a bureaucracy report to one and only one superior. At the head of the hierarchy is a ruler, the executive. Under the ruler may be many officials, each reporting only to the ruler. Each of these officials in turn has a number of subordinates who report only to that official, and so on down the line. A bureaucracy of this type is termed a simple bureaucracy. It may well have considerable specialization of labor, but this specialization is not very penetrative. Every official, for example, may have a scribe who specializes in writing letters, but there is no central ministry of scribes which recruits, transfers, and sets standards for the secretarial function. Similarly, magistrates may have a treasurer who keeps and distributes treasure, but who does not belong to a national ministry of finance. Superiors pay their own subordinates, insofar as they are paid, but there is no paymaster to perform this task.

Many traditional bureaucracies were probably simple in this sense. Each local magistrate and provincial governor might duplicate, at his territorial level and in miniature, an entourage of specialists parallel in nature to the court of the king or emperor, but these specialists were not linked together in separate networks having a functionally specific mandate. Bureaucracies of this type are peculiarly susceptible to disintegration. Any local official who wants to defy the ruler and go it alone has within his own domain and under his control all the requisites for autonomy. If he can make his office hereditary and consolidate his control locally, he can defy the central domain and become an independent feudality.

To counteract this danger, the larger and more successful traditional bureaucracies usually constructed supplementary bureaucracies to check the first. A leading example is the Chinese Censorate, an auxiliary apparatus whose members had independent access to the throne and were widely distributed throughout the empire. They had no administrative responsibility but had the authority to investigate and impeach regular officials. We find in most of the bureaucratic empires one or more auxiliary bureaucracies whose mission was to keep the primary bureaucracy loyal. The structure of both the original and the auxiliary bureaucracies is simple, but when the two are combined into one system, we may speak of the composite whole as a compound bureaucracy. Sometimes a cosmological principle of organization is employed, having a right and left bureaucracy, a green and a blue, a north and a south. Sometimes these countervailing bureaucracies become functionally specialized, for example as a military and civilian bureaucracy.

A normal characteristic of compound bureaucracy is the emergence of a succession of councils, courts, or prefectures, with names which indicate status, rank, or topological position, but not function. Privy Council, Lord of the Seal, Star Chamber, State Department, Grand Secretariat, Pretorian Prefect, Sublime Porte, Fisc, Chancery: such are the typically noncommittal names assigned to the highest organs of a compound bureaucracy. They are often collegial in character; their assigned duties tend to shift; they rise and fall in power and prestige; and one can, historically, trace a succession of such offices gradually replacing each other and taking over the duties of their predecessors.

The essential idea of a staff unit, by contrast, is the abstraction of a relatively specific function from the regular chain of command and the designation of a specialized office to supervise this function. Officers responsible to a staff unit are also often assigned to work as subordinates in a line unit. Although the polite fiction that a staff unit advises but does not command is used, operationally a staff member in a line unit is responsible to two superiors. Unity of command is replaced by the principle of multiplicity of command, which seems to be the operational practice of modern bureaucracies, even though the standard textbooks still call nostalgically for the inoperative principle of unity of command. A bureaucracy in which multiplicity of command is widely institutionalized can therefore be called complex bureaucracy.

This means, in practice, that one bureaucratic network collects and distributes funds for other networks; another network takes responsibility for the selection, placement, and rotation of personnel; a third system collects information on plans and seeks to reconcile them with each other; and another network specializes in information services. The number of staff and auxiliary units in a bureaucracy is not so decisive as recognition of the proposition that a man can serve more than one master simultaneously, that he can discriminate functionally discrete spheres of action and can rely on A to provide the premises for action in one sphere while B provides the premises in another sphere.[6]

The basic organizational principle of a complex bureaucracy applies at all geographic levels. Territorial administrators—governors, prefects, and district commissioners—are responsible not only to a home office or interior department but also to central ministries of agriculture, industry, transport and communications, labor, and education. Overlapping these program-oriented missions are the staff units concerned with such administrative processes as finance, personnel, information, adjudication, and planning. Historical investigations will show that these structures of complex bureaucracy were invented in Europe and spread within the last century to every continent and almost every country of the world.

It is not specialization that spread. In traditional compound bureaucracies there was always a good deal of specialization of role. What spread was the organizational pattern of complex bureaucracy, which made it possible—though not necessary—for

6. In another context I have used the term "introjection" to describe the ability of officials and offices to internalize a set of functionally specific norms prescribed by another official or office as an authoritative guide to action. In this sense, modern bureaucracies require a high degree of introjection of norms ("Administrative Development: An Elusive Concept," in John D. Montgomery and William J. Siffin [eds.], *Approaches to Development: Politics, Administration, and Change* [New York, 1966], pp. 225–256).

the degree of functional specificity in bureaucracies also to increase dramatically. That staff units came into being, in other words, did not mean that they would behave as we think staff units should behave.

Constitutive systems: Political parties, popular elections, and elected assemblies

More or less concurrently, several important new institutions of government came into being in Europe during the last two hundred years—largely, indeed, within the last hundred years—political parties, popular elections, and elected assemblies. Each of these structures of governance has its own history, and can and should be analyzed separately. Elected assemblies, for example, clearly originated before political parties, which evolved from a parliamentary seed bed in order to mobilize voters and nominate candidates for legislative seats.

However, it is also useful to look at this composite of related structures as itself a single complex structure taking a variety of forms. The fact that we lack a term for this composite whole may mean that there is no need for such a concept, or it may simply be the case that, having never thought of the system as a whole, we lack a term for it and have suffered in our analysis as a result.

Two common phrases for this structural complex might be considered. One is the political system. Yet there clearly were political systems before parties, elections, and elected assemblies were invented. Moreover, we need a term which suggests the structural characteristics of this complex of institutions, not the (political) functions it performs. Just as I cannot accept administrative system as a synonym for bureaucracy even though the main function of bureaucracies is administrative, so I cannot agree that this complex of governmental structures should be called a political system even though its main functions are political.

Another possibility would be to call it a party system. The connotations of this term are clearly much closer to what I have in mind, but even here, as a review of the literature will show, the concept of a party system is usually handled in such a way as to leave out the related parliamentary or legislative structures, except by indirect inference, and usually also to leave out the electoral system. I have reluctantly come to the conclusion, therefore, that a new term is needed for this complex of institutions, and I call it a constitutive system.[7]

A constitutive system is defined by its component structures, not by its functions. Its functions are undoubtedly largely political in most governments, but it also has administrative functions. More importantly, for our present purposes, constitutive systems affect the behavior of public officials, of bureaucracies. In terms of the central concerns of this chapter, the problem of administrative reform, I shall argue that the functional transformation of bureaucracies from mixed politico-administrative into primarily administrative systems requires as a necessary condition the establishment of a constitutive system capable of exercising substantial power and of imposing effective controls over the bureaucracy.

To say that a constitutive system is a necessary condition does not, of course, imply that it is a sufficient condition. My general orientation is ecological, and there are many other environmental factors in a society, in its culture, geography, economy, and demography whose combined influences shape political and administrative outcomes. The focus here is on the governmental structures which affect administrative development. Let us, therefore, try to pin down more precisely the structural components of constitutive systems, without using terminology that suggests the functional performance of these structures as components of government or of the polity.

7. This is the structure of government which typically receives most of the attention of the founding fathers in constituent assemblies, and we can scarcely conceive of a modern constitution or constitutional government without the presence of a constitutive system. I admit that in premodern times, constitutions of government existed without constitutive systems, and they may even have been constitutional, in a technical sense. Perhaps in time a better term may be found, if the idea is interesting and useful. Meanwhile I propose to use "constitutive system" to save the trouble of writing out, every time, "the complex structure of government which includes one or more political parties, an electoral system, and an elected assembly." The term is explained and used in my "Comparative Politics and the Study of Political Parties: A Structural Approach," in William J. Crotty (ed.), *Approaches to the Study of Party Organization* (Boston, 1967), pp. 45–104.

To avoid misunderstanding, let us now define and discuss the terms used in defining a constitutive system, remembering that our aim is to identify structures independently of the functions they perform. Assemblies of men to debate public policies, to advise kings, and to implement decisions are among the oldest of governmental structures. We find them in tribal societies, and quite elaborately in the Greek city states, the Roman Republic, and in some Eastern as well as Western traditional societies. But elected assemblies are a relatively recent phenomenon. The English House of Lords is clearly not an elected assembly, its members belonging by virtue of their ascriptive status as peers of the realm, but the House of Commons is an elected assembly and, despite earlier precedents elsewhere, became the leading model for emulation by other polities.

In order for members of an elected assembly to be elected, there must, by definition, be a method of voting and someone to vote. Those who are eligible to vote are the voters. There is nothing in the concept of voter which specifies who has the right to vote. If everyone in a given polity has the right to vote, we speak of universal suffrage, but even then, children, the insane, criminals, and other categories of people are not permitted to vote. In some constitutive systems, only a small part of the population affected by the system are its voters.

For an elected assembly to exist, there must clearly also be a procedure whereby voters register their support for or opposition to candidates for seats in an assembly. This procedure is known as an electoral system, and each time when candidates are selected by this procedure is known as an election. If voters in an election are typically given a choice between two or more candidates for the same office, we may speak of a free election; if they are only offered an option to vote yes or no for a single candidate, then we can speak of a legitimizing election.

The existence of legislatures need not involve the existence of political parties. Historically, however, the obvious need for procedures to nominate candidates for seats in legislatures led to the emergence of organizations which carried out this operation. Any organization which nominates candidates for seats in a legislature will therefore be called a political party, or more simply a party. Note that this is a structural definition which leaves open what functions parties perform and what other structures they possess.

What is often called a parliamentary party is not a party by this definition but a group of members of a legislature who also belong to a party. Greater clarity of thought would be secured if we could avoid using the word party in contexts where the reference is to a part of a party or to an organization which does not nominate candidates for elections. For example, what is often called a parliamentary party might preferably be called a parliamentary group, or if this seemed ambiguous, a party's parliamentary group, or a party group in parliament.

A nationalist movement seeking independence is sometimes called a party, but I would call it a political movement unless or until it nominates candidates for an assembly, at which time it becomes a party. A given organization may become a party and then stop being a party, as when it is legally prohibited from nominating candidates. It may then become again a movement, club, association, or conspiracy.

Executives and tonic polities

We have already referred to the executive as the role which exercises authority over a polity. As in the case of bureaucracies, there are roles which exercise authority over collectivities other than polities, such as corporations, trade unions, churches, cities, associations. The word "executive" is often used to refer to a leading role in such organizations. Here, however, the word will not be used with such meanings, unless with a qualifying adjective such as corporation executive, trade union executive, church executive, etc. But other words such as governor, manager, board chairman, mayor, bishop, are preferable for these roles.

The executive is no doubt the oldest structure of government. Thus, the presence of an executive, while characteristic of all modern forms of government, is not a distinctive feature of modernity. If we try to characterize modern executives structurally, we cannot even say that they have a distinctive form. It would not be true to say, for example, that all modern executives are elective, for hereditary monarchs continue to serve as executives, notably in the United Kingdom and in most of the more stable Continental European democracies.

Statistically, of course, one might point out that more modern executives are elective than hereditary, whereas in traditional societies more executives were hereditary than elective, but this does not give us a distinctive criterion of modernity. The difference between monarchic and republican forms of government, in other words, is not a distinction between traditional and modern structures but a difference to be found in the structure of executives, ancient and modern. This illustrates both the persistence of ancient structures and the inadequacy of terms based on premodern structures of government for the analysis of modern structures which contain constitutive systems.

This brings us to the heart of the problem of classifying modern executives. What is distinctive is not the structure of the office but its functioning, and this change in function arises from the invention of constitutive systems and new patterns of relationship between executives and constitutive systems. This point is related to the idea of constitutional government. No doubt the idea of constitutionalism, of the formal accountability of executives to human collectivities rather than to supernatural entities, long antedates the appearance of constitutive systems. But the earlier forms of constitutionalism appear to have been relatively rare, precarious, and difficult to enforce. It was the appearance of constitutive systems which made possible the effective institutionalization and maintenance of constitutional government.

However, to say that constitutive systems made stable consitutionalism possible is by no means to say that the adoption of constitutive systems assures constitutionalism. As we have seen before, structures are functionally ambiguous, and we must consider the possibility that executives can exploit a constitutive system to help them exercise arbitrary power. Such a possibility must seem paradoxical because to most of us it has been taken for granted that constitutive systems always impose limits on the exercise of executive power. Yet this is clearly a possible and perhaps likely outcome, although not the only outcome imaginable.

In order to examine these possible outcomes more closely we need to have a simple way to refer to political systems which have constitutive systems. Since it would distort the meaning of established terms, such as modern, contemporary, Western, and developed, to ascribe this structural meaning to them, I see no good option except to coin a new term, therefore I propose to use the phrase "tonic polity" for this purpose.[8]

If a polity has a constitutive system, let us assume it also has an executive and a bureaucracy. These more ancient institutions not only can but in fact do persist after constitutive systems are established. Consequently let us add to our definition of tonic polities the structures of an executive and a bureaucracy. I cannot imagine a polity with a constitutive system and without an executive and a bureaucracy, but let us screen out that possibility by defining tonic polities as polities which contain a constitutive system, an executive, and a state bureaucracy.

Dictionary users will find a wealth of meanings attached to the word "tonic" in several fields, including a condition of tone or tonicity—a healthy state of tension or vigor, involving partial contraction of muscle fibers while at rest. In this borrowed usage I wish to emphasize not the functional aspect of tonicity but the structural condition involving a pairing of tensor muscles in relation to joints. One type of muscle consists of flexors which contract a moving part, and the other of extensors which open the same part.

The metaphor applies quite aptly, I think, to governmental systems in which the executive serves as a kind of joint or fulcrum, the bureaucracy as flexor, and the constitutive system as extensor. Even if the metaphor be not well chosen, the validity of the concept rests on political analysis, not anatomy. The word "tonic" is short and familiar and readily lends itself to typological

8. The term was introduced in my "The Comparison of Whole Political Systems," in Robert T. Holt and John Turner (eds.) *The Methodology of Comparative Research* (Glencoe, Ill., publication scheduled for 1969).

analysis by the use of prefixes, as will be shown below. I hope the term can be evaluated on its merits as a mnemonic and heuristic device to help us keep a particular concept in mind, not in terms of the degree to which the analogy implied is correct or incorrect.

Focusing on the relation between executive and constitutive system, we can now distinguish between two major types of tonic polity. In the normal type, the type with which we are most familiar in the Western democracies, the exercise of power by the executive is qualified by the executive's responsibility to the constitutive system. For example, the executive may be chosen by the constitutive system and subject to replacement from time to time, as in republican tonic polities. Alternatively, if the executive is hereditary, a separate office which exercises effective control over the bureaucracy is established, and the executive becomes a ceremonial figurehead as head of state rather than of government. This is the situation in monarchic tonic polities.

We need to recognize, though, that while both the republican and the monarchic form of executive can be adapted to the requirements of constitutionalism in tonic polities—namely to hold the executive accountable to the consitutive system—there is no assurance that either structure will assure constitutionalism. Since the older form of tonic polity is typically one in which an absolute monarch agrees to the establishment of a constitutive system without surrendering power to it, I propose to refer to this type of system as protonic. By contrast, a tonic polity in which the executive is held accountable to the constitutive systems or, as we shall see, to the bureaucracy, may be called a neotonic polity. This distinction clearly cuts across the older dichotomy of monarchic/republican forms. Neotonic polities may have hereditary or non-hereditary executives, and the same is true for protonic polities. However, neotonic polities are constitutional in form by definition, whereas protonic polities are not constitutional—even if they have written characters.

As the analysis below will show, most contemporary states have neotonic polities, even though a number of protonic polities can also be found in the world today. We shall find neotonic polities not only in the modern and democratic countries, but also in modernizing and totalitarian states. In other words, the mere fact of constitutionalism by no means assures a high degree of development or of democratization in a polity, any more than does republicanism as contrasted with monarchism. I believe that we can make significant progress toward understanding the necessary conditions for development and democratization only by shifting the focus of our analysis from the executive structure to bureaucracy. How are the various types of polity related to bureaucratic structure and administrative performance? This, of course, is the basic question of this chapter. The ground has been cleared for examination of the question by identifying some structural characteristics of the governmental environment which seem likely to be relevant. Note that we are deliberately omitting a discussion of other ecological variables which are also important. The argument is therefore at the level of *ceteris paribus* for the analysis of governmental structures affecting administrative development or reform.

IV. Complex Bureaucracies in Tonic Polities

How are bureaucracies related to government in tonic polities? The answer requires an examination of the relation between bureaucracies and constitutive systems and a study of how executives play their mediating or hinge role between these two major components of modern governance. To make such an analysis, we shall first have to examine the structure of bureaucracies. This will enable us to be more specific about a variety of executive and mediatory roles which will pave the way, finally, for some hypotheses about the relation of these various structures to administrative modernization, development, and democratization.

Differential rates of bureaucratic diffusion

Considering the structure of bureaucracies first, then, let us recall the distinction between forms of simple, compound, and complex bureaucracy. It is probably true that the pattern of complex bureaucracy was invented in Continental Europe before the structures of a constitutive system had been invented in England. Certainly in the non-Western world the structures of complex bureaucracy were diffused to many countries, notably under colonial rule, before the adoption of constitutive systems, and this happened also under the leadership of native modernizing elites as well as of European colonial rulers.[9]

It is quite possible, therefore, to have a complex bureaucracy in a polity that is not tonic. Although I recognize several different types of governmental structure which are not tonic, it is sometimes useful to group them all together as non-tonic polities.[10] They might also be referred to as pretonic polities, but this term carries teleological overtones which I wish to avoid here, so I shall not use it. We may therefore hypothesize that complex bureaucracies are highly correlated with tonic polities, but we can find complex bureaucracies in some non-tonic polities, and we may find tonic polities which do not contain complex bureaucracies. The interest of this hypothesis is primarily historical and helps to explain the developmental dynamics of several varieties of tonic polities. There seems to be some evidence, for example, that democratic orthotonic polities appeared in countries where the constitutive system took shape before the appearance of complex bureaucracy. By contrast, many of the polities which have become orthotonic but not democratic, or which are homotonic today, introduced complex bureaucracy before they did constitutive systems. The first hypothesis applies to many countries in Western Europe and North America, the second to Eastern Europe, Asia, and Africa, with notable exceptions in each case.

By distinguishing between the rate of penetration of complex bureaucracy and the diffusion of constitutive systems we are able to refine the idea of modernization. Emulative acculturation tends to be selective, some institutions of the foreign model being regarded as more useful or more worthy of borrowing than others. If we study the differential rate of selective borrowings by

9. This process is described in some detail in Fred W. Riggs, *Thailand: The Modernization of a Bureaucratic Polity* (Honolulu, 1966).

10. A proposed classification of non-tonic polities is presented in Riggs, "The Comparison of Whole Political Systems."

modernizing countries we shall gain a better understanding of the dynamics of change involved.

In this instance, it is not difficult to see that native elites and European colonial rulers alike were quick to grasp the probable advantages to themselves of the introduction of the forms of complex bureaucracy as a governmental technology which would enhance their own power, enable them to consolidate their control, penetrate the subject society, and defend their domains from foreign attack. Indeed, it may well be that the structures of complex bureaucracy were first introduced through the military services, as they were first invented for these services in Continental Europe. By contrast they perhaps feared—at least in most instances—the introduction of constitutive systems as likely to undermine their power. This was especially true of European colonial rulers, even though, or perhaps precisely because, constitutive systems had already been established at home. In some instances indigenous rulers may have thought that they could capture control over a constitutive system and use it to enhance their power and authority, but Japan seems to be the only important non-Western instance of this phenomenon. American rule in the Philippines was also exceptional in its early stress on constitutive structures, perhaps because colonial administration was handled through Congress rather than the executive branch, and perhaps also because of the deep ambivalences in American public life about policy toward the Philippines.

What native and foreign rulers both failed to perceive was that complex bureaucracies could enhance their power only if they (the bureaucrats) were kept under effective control. Before long it became apparent that executives, unaided, could not permanently master and discipline complex bureaucracies which, Frankenstein-like, tended to seize power on their own. But whereas a simple or compound bureaucracy out of control tended to change in the direction of hereditary office-holding and localization of power, a complex bureaucracy can maintain itself autonomously as a relatively centralized and independent structure of power.

Under these circumstances both rulers and ruled began to see the structures of a constitutive system as a possible solution for their problems, as a means of holding bureaucrats accountable. Indeed, within the limitations of currently available governmental technology, we can scarcely think of any other means for controlling complex bureaucracies. This is not to say that the adoption of a constitutive system assures a polity control over its bureaucracy; rather it may be a necessary but not a sufficient condition for establishing such control.

Types of complex bureaucracy

What are the types of complex bureaucracy? How are they related to constitutive systems? How do these variations affect the functional relation between these structures? There are undoubtedly many ways in which we might try to classify bureaucratic systems. We have used an organizational principle to distinguish between simple, compound, and complex bureaucracies. Is there any other organizational principle which might be used to distinguish among several varieties of complex bureaucracy?

Let us consider the possibility of using the territorial arrangement of offices as a criterion. In virtually all contemporary polities the national domain is divided into a set of territories which are variously known as provinces, states, counties, departments, etc. Let us call them all provinces regardless of what actual name is used in a particular country. We can then recognize the head of a province as the provincial executive regardless of the title he bears, whether governor, prefect, commissioner, or mayor.

The first point to make is that the provincial executive may or may not be a member of the bureaucracy. In some countries—those with a federal form of government, for example—the provincial executive is selected by a separate constitutive system which operates autonomously at the provincial level. Various federal departments and ministries have field offices at the local level, but they do not constitute, formally, part of the provincial bureaucracy responsible to the provincial executive.

By contrast, we often, perhaps more frequently, find systems in which the office of provincial executive belongs to the bureaucracy of the polity. In such cases it is usual to find that these offices belong to one ministry, and the field offices of other ministries and departments are formally responsible to the provincial executive as well as to their own central offices. Let us call the latter type of bureaucracy prefectural and the former type non-prefectural. The French type of field administration, in which prefects employed by the Ministry of Interior serve as provincial executives, best illustrates the structure of prefectural bureaucracies, and the American federal system of elected governors illustrates a non-prefectural bureaucracy. The significant differences between these two patterns and some reflections on their historical origins and functional consequences have been perceptively examined by James Fesler.[11]

It may be that there are significant differences in the functional implications and capabilities of prefectural as contrasted with non-prefectural complex bureaucracies, and in their relation with constitutive systems, but I have not been able to discover them. Consequently I have concluded, at least for the present, that no useful purpose would be served by pushing the analysis further in terms of this organizational criterion of classification.

Are there other criteria which might be used? Consider what happens when we use the basis of recruitment of incumbents to offices. This is a subject which is frequently discussed in the literature of public administration. Distinctions are often made between career men and appointees, between generalists and specialists, between the merit principle and patronage or spoils. Similar distinctions may be found in the writings on Communist polities where, for example, a contrast is drawn between the expert and the red, the former being essentially a career man within the state bureaucracy and the latter a party stalwart assigned to work in the bureaucracy.

The most general distincton to be made here is between the practice of filling offices with men who work their way up from within the bureaucracy, and the opposite practice of filling offices by appointing men from outside the bureaucracy concerned. One

11. See James W. Fesler, "The Political Role of Field Administration," in Ferrel Heady and Sybil L. Stokes (eds.), *Papers in Comparative Public Administration* (Ann Arbor, Mich., 1962), pp. 117–144.

might call the first recruitment of career men and the latter the recruitment of appointees. These terms are ambiguous, however, since the outside appointee may also be a career man in his party or in some other organizational bureaucracy and the career man appointed from within is also, no doubt, an appointee. Other words, such as "merit" and "patronage," carry both invidious connotations and functional implications for performance which we wish to avoid in this context.

Let us therefore use the somewhat more neutral and less conventional terms "insider" and "outsider." In this special usage an insider is not someone with special access to the elite or someone privy to secrets, but is specifically a person appointed to a bureaucratic office whose previous career has largely been within the bureaucracy of which that office is a part. The concept can be operationalized by specifying an absolute number of years, or a proportion of working years, required to consider a man's career as largely within a given bureaucracy. By contrast an outsider is not someone without influence or knowledge but someone whose previous career has largely built on experience outside a given bureaucracy who is named to an office in that bureaucracy.

It seems probable that some insiders and some outsiders are appointed in every bureaucracy, modern and traditional, simple, compound, and complex, but the ratio of the two kinds of appointments varies within wide limits. We often think of a merit system as a bureaucracy in which most positions are filled by insiders and a spoils system as one staffed by outsiders. But this does not carry us very far. Although the merit principle may be necessary for administrative efficiency and effectiveness, the spoils principle may also be necessary, at least at some levels, if a bureaucracy is to be subjected to control by a constitutive system. This gives us a clue to an additional principle of classification with which the insider-outsider criterion can be combined. If we examine the distribution of insiders and outsiders in a bureaucracy, we may arrive at a useful basis of classification for our present purposes.

Bureaucratic offices may be distinguished from each other by their level or echelon. Organization charts typically show a pyramid of authority. At the top level or echelon there may be one or a few positions. At a second level several positions will be represented as responsible to the post shown on the first echelon. Similarly, the third echelon represents positions responsible to offices of the second level. In complex bureaucracies, there will also be a set of staff offices, with dotted horizontal lines signifying advisory relationships, but for present purposes we can ignore them. Note also that we are speaking here of formal lines of authority, not effective relations of influence, and actual flows of communication, which may or may not follow the formal lines.

In contemporary polities the first echelon of bureaucrats (those below the executive) includes the heads of ministries, the major organizational structures into which government is divided. Not counting staff positions, the first echelon typically constitutes a cabinet. It should not be difficult to identify the first echelon positions in most bureaucracies. Let us call the organizational structures headed by first echelon offices ministries.

The major components of a ministry are often called bureaus, agencies, departments, offices, or divisions, each of which is charged with responsibility for a major program of the ministry. For ease of reference, let us define the word department to mean any such component, and the head of a department will be treated as a third echelon position. (This terminology does not conform to American governmental practice, where a ministry is called a department, and a department is usually called a bureau. The practice in most countries fits the proposed terminology better than American usage does.)

Second echelon positions may be defined as those considered to lie between the first and third echelon. They normally carry such titles as undersecretary, deputy secretary, assistant secretary, parliamentary secretary, etc.

It is unnecessary, for present purposes, to attempt to distinguish any other echelons. The three which have been defined are enough to give us a fivefold classification scheme when combined with the insider-outsider dichotomy, as shown in Table 1. Note that this table defines several types of complex bureaucracy by

Table 1. ***Types of Complex Bureaucracy, Classified Structurally by Echelon Staffing***

	I	II	III	IV	V
First echelon	+	−	−	−	±
Second echelon	+	+	−	−	±
Third echelon	+	+	+	−	±

structural criteria. It does not contain hypotheses, nor does it refer to functional relationships.

In Table 1 the sign + means that positions at this echelon are predominantly staffed by insiders, and the sign − means that positions are chiefly staffed by outsiders. The sign ± suggests either a mixture of insiders and outsiders, or frequent changes, with insiders replacing outsiders, and the reverse. If more than two-thirds of the available positions at an echelon are staffed in a given way, this is the predominant way. Interpreting this table, Type I complex bureaucracies are those in which positions at all echelons are predominantly staffed by insiders—military officers being included as well as civil servants. By contrast, Type IV is a bureaucracy in which most positions at all echelons are filled by outsiders. The intermediate Type II is a bureaucracy in which the first echelon is filled by outsiders and the other two by insiders. Intermediate Type III is a bureaucracy in which the first two echelons are mainly filled by outsiders but the third level is largely staffed by insiders. Type V is a residual category of indeterminate or rapidly changing staffing patterns.

It may make it easier to remember the several types of complex bureaucracy as structurally defined by this scheme if we think of the type number as indicating the highest echelon normally filled by the appointment of insiders: that is, the first echelon for Type I, the second echelon for Type II, the Third echelon for Type III, and the fourth echelon—positions below the third echelon—for Type IV. This mnemonic rule does not hold for Type V, which is a residual category for bureaucracies in which insiders may be appointed, spasmodically, at all echelons, as may outsiders.[12]

12. In an earlier draft of this chapter I called Type I bureaucracies autonomic, Type II generalist, Type III specialist, and Type IV workhorse. I am indebted to

A special problem in this typology needs to be considered. Among the various branches of a state bureaucracy, there is one in which the propensity for insiders to staff all echelons is undoubtedly greater than in others, namely the military branches. We find, therefore, regimes in which first echelon positions of the defense or war ministries are filled by career military officers rather than by outsiders, even though other positions at this level are staffed by outsiders. Since the power potential of military officers is greater than that of other bureaucrats when a bureaucracy becomes highly politicized, I would classify under Type V a bureaucracy in which career military officers hold cabinet positions exercising authority over the armed forces, and other cabinet posts are held by outsiders. An admitted limitation of this chapter is the need for more detailed analysis of this type of bureaucracy.

Several other hypothetical types of bureaucracy are possible, if a matrix for all possible combinations of the variables used in this classification is employed. We can, however, disregard them as empirically unlikely since they would consist of systems in which insiders predominated at higher echelons than outsiders. Arguing from the proposition that insiders will typically appoint other insiders to all positions under their jurisdiction, we can even regard these possibilities as unimportant, if not impossible. Should they be discovered, however, they could be added to the residual Type V category.

Functional relations of complex bureaucracies

There seems to be a significant relation between types of tonic polity and types of complex bureaucracy when the latter are classified according to recruitment patterns. At least, the relation seems to be more interesting than when the organizational classification based on the prefectural–non-prefectural distinction is used.

Professor Samuel Finer for pointing out some of the logical and semantic difficulties raised by this terminology. His arguments are convincing, but I regret that I cannot think of any better substantive terms. For the time being, at least, the numerical typing may do, but suggestions of better names for these bureaucratic types will be welcome.

One of the key structures in constituent systems (a component, by definition, of all tonic polities) is one or more political parties. Clearly, therefore, one of the considerations that arises in naming persons to fill bureaucratic offices in tonic polities is whether or not they belong to a political party or are identified with its aims and candidates. Thus the political orientations of public officials measure a functional relation between bureaucracies and tonic polities.

Whether bureaucrats are insiders or outsiders seems to have a close relation to their political (or partisan) tendencies. In general, we think of insiders as predominantly administrative in orientation and outsiders as more politically oriented. Closer scrutiny, however, shows that this hypothesis oversimplifies a more complicated pattern of relationships.

A distinction can be made between two different, though related, senses in which people often speak of the political orientations of bureaucrats. In one sense, they refer to orientations toward a political party; in a different sense, to orientations toward intrabureaucratic struggles for power and conflict between various components of the bureaucracy, such as between its military and civilian arms.

A bureaucrat, therefore, is partisan to the extent that he is simultaneously active in a political party or allows favoritism toward members of a party to affect his decisions as a public official. Among the operational criteria of partisanship which might be employed we could list recruitment and promotion within the bureaucracy as a result of party support and/or simultaneous party work as at least an activist, if not a leader.

By contrast, a bureaucrat is politicized to the extent that his basic interests and activities within a bureaucracy concern the acquisition of power rather than the implementation of governmental decisions. Clearly, there may be a correlation in the sense that those bureaucrats who are most partisan may also be highly politicized. But this is not a correlation by definition, and one would need empirical research to demonstrate its extent. Moreover, one can imagine situations in which partisan bureaucrats, recruited under a party spoils system of appointment, would nevertheless handle their assignments in a routine way without becoming politicized. Postal employees in the United States may sometimes come under this heading.

Alternatively, we can think of bureaucrats who are highly politicized but not partisan. This could readily occur in a polity where officials constitute a ruling caste and political parties have little or no influence. Here intrabureaucratic rivalry may be the most important form of politics, but without parties there would be no partisanship. The significance of partisanship, therefore, varies with the nature of the polity. In a one-party state, all or most officials might be members of the ruling party, many playing an active party role. In this sense the level of partisanship would be high. Yet insofar as the bureaucracy is firmly guided by the party in terms of administrative norms, serving as a politically neutral apparatus for the implementation of public policies, the level of politicization may be low. Such a bureaucracy would be high in partisanship, low in politicization.

A simple four-cell matrix, in which one dimension of variation represents degrees of bureaucratic politicization and the other dimension represents degrees of bureaucratic partisanship, illustrates these possibilities. A plausible example of each condition is mentioned.

Without taking time to discuss the situation in each of the

Table 2. ***Degrees of Bureaucratic Politicization and Partisanship***

Degree of Bureaucratic Partisanship	Degree of Bureaucratic Politicization: *High*	Degree of Bureaucratic Politicization: *Low*
High	*Partisan and politicized* Ghana under Nkrumah	*Non-partisan and politicized* Thailand
Low	*Partisan and non-politicized* Israel	*Non-partisan and non-politicized* United Kingdom

countries mentioned as possible illustrations of these various combinations, let us try to probe some underlying dynamics by speculating about possible relationships between degrees of partisanship and politicization in bureaucracies, the character of the polity concerned, and the type of bureaucracy. Rather surprisingly, I think, we will discover no simple correlation between the functions of partisanship and political development when the latter is measured by the structural distinction between neotonic and protonic polities. If one makes the conventional assumption that the more advanced a political system, the more likely it is that its bureaucracy will be based on merit rather than spoils, then one is apt to infer that the degree of partisanship in bureaucratic appointments will vary inversely with the level of development. What we will learn is rather that the degree of partisanship in a bureaucracy is typically greater in neotonic than in protonic polities. By contrast, I suspect that the degree of politicization is more highly correlated with levels of political development. I believe the structure of bureaucracy gives a basis for elaborating this hypothesis.

Let us consider the five types defined above and the political and party orientation of officials. It is correct to say that two important functional relationships affecting the bureaucracy are called for in the government of any well-developed political system. One of these functional requisites is political responsiveness, and the other is administrative capability. Political responsiveness refers to the propensity of a bureaucracy to internalize the norms and rules formulated by political institutions outside the bureaucracy itself.[13] Administrative capability refers to the ability of a bureaucracy to implement policies with efficiency and effectiveness.

As already indicated, I regard governmental structures as necessary though not sufficient conditions for the accomplishment of political and administrative functions. In this sense, the only

13. Elsewhere I have proposed that the term "introjection" be used in a technical sense to refer to this process of internalizing and implementing externally formulated norms, and I have argued that increasing introjection accompanies administrative development. See my "Administrative Development: An Elusive Concept," pp. 251–252.

structure capable of enforcing political responsiveness on a complex bureaucracy is a constitutive system, although the mere presence of a constitutive system by no means guarantees political responsiveness. In order for the constitutive system to enforce responsiveness on the bureaucracy it must utilize a variety of controls. Of these, the structure which seems most likely to be effective is the practice of designating through the constitutive system the occupants of all or most first echelon positions in the bureaucracy. In other words, a structure in which cabinet members are chosen by the constitutive system, and are therefore outsiders so far as the bureaucracy is concerned, seems to be a necessary (though again not a sufficient) condition for imposing political responsiveness on a bureaucracy. This rule applies with particular force to military offices and implies the appointment of civilians to cabinet positions in authority over the armed forces.

The implication of this proposition is that we will find outsiders at the first echelon in politically responsive polities, and consequently that we will not find bureaucracies of Type I in such polities. Let us also hypothesize that a bureaucracy can scarcely attain high standards of efficiency and effectiveness unless most of the positions at its third echelon are staffed by individuals with considerable experience in carrying out the kind of work called for in that department. This requirement is most likely to be met if career men (insiders) are appointed to these positions. In other words, we will scarcely find Type IV bureaucracies in polities which are administratively capable.

Note that the prevalence of insiders at the third echelon of a bureaucracy may be a necessary but not a sufficient condition for administrative capability. We can imagine a bureaucracy in which all insiders are incompetent rascals. I find it difficult, however, to imagine a complex bureaucracy in which administrative duties are efficiently and effectively carried out even though most posts at the third echelon are staffed by outsiders. Note also that the criterion of recruitment of insiders is a structural characteristic of bureaucracy, whereas the criterion of administrative capability is a functional relationship between the bureaucracy and the polity.

Tonic polities redefined structurally by bureaucratic types

Our discussion of political development has suggested that the machinery of government in a developed political system should be not only politically responsive but also administratively capable. What structural characteristic is likely to make a bureaucracy administratively effective and efficient, and also politically responsive? I suggest it is the prevalence of outsiders at the first level, and of insiders at the third level, in other words, of a Type II or III bureaucracy.

It may be useful to have a general term to refer to both Type II and Type III bureaucracies. Let us use the word "compensate" in its mechanical meaning of counteracting variations. In this sense a bureaucracy is compensated if it recruits mainly outsiders at the first echelon while recruiting largely insiders at its third echelon. This terminology enables us to identify a new concept: any neotonic polity with a compensated bureaucracy. Such a polity may be called "orthotonic." By contrast a neotonic polity whose bureaucracy is not compensated may be called "heterotonic."

It is important to recognize the great difference between two types of heterotonic polity: those with Type I bureaucracy and those with Type IV. Let us call the former "homotonic" and the latter "syntonic." The prefix "homo-" suggests identity or similarity, hence the political domination of a bureaucracy by career bureaucrats. The prefix "syn-" carries such meanings as associated, like, along with, at the same time. The word "syntonic" has been used in electronics with the sense of resonance. Let us think of it in a governmental sense as referring to a form of government resembling the orthotonic in structures designed to subject the bureaucracy to political control by the constitutive system, but differing as regards the structures thought to enhance administrative capability.

Empirically and historically we find syntonic polities in two quite different settings. A fair number of contemporary new states which have come to power under the leadership of a revolutionary movement for national independence have systematically replaced experienced public officials with outsiders in the name of nationalization. For the most part, these outsiders have been friends and supporters of the new ruling party. In bringing the government under political control they have sacrificed administrative values, with adverse results so far as the implementation of public policies is concerned. In some cases popular dissatisfaction with these regimes has already manifested itself in support for a coup d'état staged by military officers who have overpowered the constitutive system and established a homotonic regime with a Type I bureaucracy.

Historically speaking, however, we find other examples of syntonic polities, notably in the United States and England, where patronage and spoils prevailed in the bureaucracy during portions of the nineteenth century when the government had already been brought under political control by an electoral (constitutive) system. In these historical instances popular dissatisfaction with governmental inefficiency manifested itself in reform movements which led to the introduction of civil service examinations, more systematic military training, and regularization of the career services in the name of the merit principle. Thus syntonic (premodern) polities led, through administrative reform, to the emergence of orthotonic (modern) polities. By contrast, in contemporary syntonic (modernizing) polities, widespread discontent has more frequently led, through military violence, to the appearance of homotonic (bureaucratic) polities. This formulation supplements the hypotheses stated above about the differential rate of introduction of complex bureaucracy and constitutive systems in nontonic polities.

Let us now return to the propositions which provoked this discussion, namely the degree of partisanship and politicization associated with various kinds of bureaucracies, considering first differing degrees of partisanship. The first echelon positions in orthotonic polities are staffed by outsiders, normally leaders or active adherents of at least one political party. By contrast, a large body of insiders in these bureaucracies depend on their experience and expertise more than party affiliation for their professional success; hence they need not weight partisanship highly or may even strive for non-partisanship. My conclusion is that within a fairly broad range of variation—to be explored in more detail below—bureaucracies of orthotonic polities are simultaneously moderately partisan and moderately non-partisan.

By contrast, if we look at a syntonic polity where outsiders secure appointments far down in the bureaucracy, we must conclude that a high degree of partisanship prevails. But if we look at homotonic polities, we will be struck by the unimportance of party labels and the high degree of non-partisanship possible in these systems, where career men (military and civil) are promoted within the bureaucracy itself to the top echelon. Thus heterotonic polities are marked by great variability in their level of partisanship.

If we assume that orthotonic polities are largely found in politically developed systems, then political development is not correlated with either increase or decrease in partisanship. The degree of bureaucratic partisanship varies between extremes of non-partisanship in homotonic polities and partisanship in syntonic polities. Development is probably associated, therefore, with an increase in partisanship in some cases, a decrease in others. A more general statement would be that development is associated with an increase in moderation of partisanship as contrasted with extremism in either direction. This is based on the assumption that heterotonic (both homotonic and syntonic) polities are found more often in less developed countries and orthotonic more often in developed countries.

If we look at politicization as a separate dimension of variation, distinguished from partisanship, a more interesting and significant pattern emerges. Clearly in the case of a homotonic polity, the very fact that first echelon positions are filled by insiders means that the competition for these offices must be very keen. Moreover, since basic decisions affecting public policy are made at this (cabinet) level, we can infer that the level of politicization in Type I bureaucracies will be very high. Moreover, insofar as the constitutive system is unable to place its candidates in these positions, it lacks power; hence political action in the constitutive system may be considered more formalistic than effective.

If we consider syntonic polities having a Type IV bureaucracy, we will also find that the level of politicization in the bureaucracy is high, as well as the level of partisanship. Here most higher officials are, by definition, outsiders, and therefore politically oriented to start with. Moreover, conditions of service are likely to be such as to generate anxieties and insecurities, leading to a keen struggle for extrabureaucratic support as a necessary condition for retaining office and for securing promotions.

If we consider orthotonic polities, we will surely discover a significant degree of politicization also, but not a high degree. Competition for office and promotions is a universal characteristic of any bureaucracy, but such competition can be regarded as political only when it is concerned primarily with the determination of policy goals and looks to alliances as its main means of success. It is non-political to the extent that it is primarily concerned with instrumental means for the implementation of previously established (introjected) norms and relies on successful accomplishment and expertise as a basis for career success. In this sense, I suspect that the level of politicization in the compensated bureaucracies of orthotonic polities will be substantially lower than in the uncompensated bureaucracies of heterotonic polities. My conclusion, therefore, is the hypothesis that the degree of bureaucratic politicization tends to decline to moderate levels—never to disappear—as political development increases. A corollary would be that administrative capability and political sensitivity rise from moderate to high levels as political development occurs.

An analysis of Type V bureaucracies has been deliberately omitted from the foregoing discussion. In part this is because this type is a residual category for unclear and marginal cases, and further study is needed before anything more definite can be said. Let me hazard the guess that we will find that generalizations which hold for uncompensated bureaucracies in general hold also for Type V bureaucracies. Moreover, I think we will probably find Type V bureaucracies to be typical of protonic, rather than neotonic, polities.

The foregoing hypotheses can be summarized in schematic

form, as shown in Table 3. Note that whereas Table 1 gives structural criteria for defining several types of bureaucracy, Table 3 summarizes several hypotheses about probable functional relationships between these bureaucracies and the whole political system of which they are a part.

These hypotheses may be formulated as follows:

1. Type II, III, and IV bureaucracies (in orthotonic and syntonic polities) are more likely to be politically responsive to a constitutive system than Type I bureaucracies (in homotonic polities).

2. Type I, II, and III bureaucracies (in orthotonic and homotonic polities) are more likely to be administratively capable than Type IV bureaucracies (in syntonic polities).

Table 3: ***Hypothesized Functions of Complex Bureaucracies for Their Polities***

Degrees of:	*Type I*	*Type II*	*Type III*	*Type IV*	*Type V*
Political responsiveness	L	H	H	H	H/L
Administrative capability	M	H	H	L	M/L
Politicization	H	M	M	H	H
Partisanship	L	M	M	H	H/L
Balance	L	H	H	L	L

Note: H = high, M = medium, L = low, / = or.

3. The degree of partisanship is likely to be moderate in compensated bureaucracies (Type II or III in orthotonic polities) as contrasted with relative extremes on this scale for uncompensated bureaucracies: highly partisan for Type IV (in syntonic polities) and highly non-partisan for Type I (in homotonic polities).

4. The degree of politicization is likely to be relatively high in uncompensated bureaucracies (I and IV in heterotonic polities) as contrasted with relatively moderate in compensated bureaucracies (II or III in orthotonic polities).

5. The ability to achieve both political responsiveness and administrative capability (i.e., balance) is likely to be high in compensated bureaucracies (II and III in orthotonic polities), whereas one or other of these functions is likely to be poorly

performed, hence unbalanced, in uncompensated bureaucracies (I and IV in heterotonic polities). Note that the term "balance" is introduced here for a functional relation of bureaucracy to polity involving political responsiveness and administrative capability, whereas the term "compensated" refers to a structural characteristic of bureaucracies, namely predominant recruitment of outsiders at the first echelon and insiders at the third echelon.

6. Characteristics of Type V bureaucracies and the type of polity in which they are to be found remain to be determined more precisely, but it may be guessed that for most purposes their functional behavior will resemble that of Type I or Type IV (uncompensated) bureaucracies, rather than Type II or Type III (compensated).

We have so far tried to speculate about several types of complex bureaucracy and to relate them functionally to a variety of polities, classified structurally. Several major gaps remain to be filled. For example, it is not clear what the differences are between Type II and Type III bureaucracies, functionally speaking. Perhaps if we classified constitutive systems structurally, we could shed additional light on the differential behavior of bureaucracies and therefore on administrative development and reform. Let us turn to this subject.

V. Constitutive Systems in Tonic Polities

The normal procedure in a comparative discussion of political institutions is to start with the components of constitutive systems and to formulate a typology based on the mode of selecting heads of government—as reflected in the presidential-parliamentary-Communist trichotomy—or to use a major component of constitutive systems, the party system, as a basis for classification. This leads to a one-party, two-party, and multiparty scheme. Such classifications have, of course, been refined and extended for the analysis of European polities.

When these schemes have been applied to the new states of the non-Western world, however, their inherent limitations have been starkly revealed. Several responses to these difficulties have become popular within the last twenty years. Efforts to utilize structural or institutional criteria for studying comparative politics have been discarded in favor of functional schemes based on various models of the functional requisites of any political system. The difficulty with this approach is that, although it has greatly increased our understanding of the functions performed by components in relation to polities, it has tended to block systematic inquiry into the structural characteristics of government in the new states.

An alternative response has been to move from comparative institutional analysis to what has been called an area approach. Essentially this is an ecological framework in which political behavior is treated as dependent on a considerable variety of environmental forces, cultural systems, and social, economic, geographic, historical, demographic, and other variables. Two inherent difficulties arise from this mode of analysis. The ecological criteria are so open-ended and unlimited, and their relations to governmental performance so vaguely specified, that area studies have frequently resulted in the accumulation of huge quantities of data which do not shed much light on political and administrative behavior.

A second weakness of the area approach for our purposes has been its antitheoretical emphasis. Fascinated by the uniqueness of each historical and cultural entity, area specialists have been reluctant to give serious consideration to cross-cultural generalizations, whether they concerned structures or functions. Thus the area approach—ironically because area studies have generated much of the new knowledge required for comparative studies of politics and administration—may well have had the latent function of holding back progress in the study of comparative government.

I am inclined to think that the source of our original difficulty lay in the use of political classifications based on the components of constitutive systems (parties and parliaments) as the primary criteria for institutional analysis. No doubt the relatively greater interest, the public excitement, generated by politics as contrasted with administration led to this selective perception. It was reflected in the predominance of political analysis in political science and the relegation of public administration to minor status as a subfield of political science, if, indeed, it even belonged in the discipline. Administrative specialists have themselves reinforced this misperception by attempting, often enough, to withdraw from political science in the name of professionalism and the training needs of candidates for the public service, which naturally enough are not limited to the study of political science.

What would happen if we turned this priority of criteria upside down? Let us suppose that we first classified polities in terms of the characteristic structures of their bureaucracies and executives rather than of their constitutive systems? I suspect that both of the tendencies mentioned above—functionalism and the area approach—would not have prevailed but would have been seen as contributory to the central thrust of political science, a thrust more in harmony, interestingly enough, with the traditional interests of the discipline.

In this essay I propose to experiment with such an approach to see whether or not the results would be interesting. Having already set forth a typology of complex bureaucracies, and having used them for the structural definition of polities, we have paved the way for an experiment of this sort.

Let us first make clear that the analysis is limited to tonic polities. A universal framework of analysis for all political systems would have to include non-tonic polities as well. It will be easier to make such an expansion of our frame of reference, however, after we have grappled successfully with the more limited, yet surely gigantic, task of classifying and theorizing about tonic polities. Some of the difficulties encountered by the functionalists in comparative politics have arisen from their effort to generalize too soon about ancient city-states, feudal and bureaucratic societies, and primitive tribal societies as well as contemporary nation-states. Because they were fascinated by the concept of the functional requisites of any society, they thought they could jump quickly to an analysis of shared functional attributes of all political systems.

While the concept of a tonic polity excludes most premodern political systems, it includes almost all contemporary independent states. Thus it makes possible a structural analysis of governments in the non-Western world. Had it been thought possible to do this, the influence of area studies on comparative government might not have been so overpowering. Instead of trying to learn everything about selected societies, political scientists might have concentrated on what was particularly relevant to an understanding of political and administrative behavior in these countries.

This is not to suggest that I take it as already demonstrated that all contemporary states can be readily and usefully classified in terms of type of bureaucracy. However, it may prove to be possible pending a better procedure. Moreover, I think the presence of constitutive systems in almost all contemporary states makes it possible to classify them as tonic polities. This at least takes us the first step forward in our undertaking.

Let us begin the experiment, therefore, by looking first at orthotonic polities, that is at tonic polities with compensated bureaucracies. We will find such polities not only in most or all of the Western democracies but also in some of the Communist countries, notably the Soviet Union and several of the East European states, and also in some countries of Asia, Africa, and Latin America. These include Japan, and probably the Philippines, Malaysia, Singapore, India, Lebanon, Israel, South Africa and Rhodesia, Mexico, Chile, Costa Rica, Uruguay, Jamaica, Trinidad-Tobago, and no doubt others. There will probably be debates about some of these, revolving in some instances about substantive problems, in others about matters of definition.

For instance, it will be argued that since party membership is an important criterion for advancement in the Soviet Union and other Communist states, their bureaucracies should be classified as Type IV rather than as II or III. Alternatively, if the party bureaucracy is considered part of the state bureaucracy, it will be said that everyone in the government is an insider, and hence a Communist bureaucracy is of Type I.

The Chinese experience with a recently organized Communist state provides an interesting test case. There the contrast between expert and red has been sharply drawn in polemical debates—as already noted. In an analysis of this subject, based on interviews with refugees, Doak Barnett states that in a government division from which his informants came, "the most highly qualified specialists in the unit were non-Party cadres, and the general level of expertise was considerably higher among this group than among the Party personnel."[14] It is not possible to learn from Barnett's data whether most of the positions at the third echelon in the Chinese bureaucracy are filled by non-party cadres (insiders) or by party personnel (outsiders); consequently we cannot tell from this evidence whether to classify the Chinese Communist bureaucracy today as Type IV or Type III, assuming the first and second echelon positions are predominantly filled by outsiders (reds). More significantly, Barnett's interview data tell us that in the perceptions of Chinese state officials under Communist party rule the distinction between insider and outsider (between expert and red) is a real one.

It should be possible to make similar discriminations quite generally. We should be able to determine on the one hand whether first echelon (cabinet) positions are filled by insiders (such as army officers) or by outsiders (such as party stalwarts). We should also be able to determine whether third echelon positions are predominantly staffed by insiders (career men) or by outsiders (spoilsmen, party cadres, political protégés, etc.). We may not be able to identify every position at these echelons, or determine the background of every incumbent, and we must not expect that all of the posts at any level will be staffed only by insiders or by outsiders. But if we can determine the prevailing tendency, we will be able to make our structural classification.

If we grant the possibility of making such a general classification of bureaucracies in most contemporary states, and if we

14. "Mechanisms for Party Control in Government Bureaucracy in China," *Asian Survey,* VI (1966), 669.

grant that they also have constitutive systems and executives, then we can not only classify them as tonic or non-tonic, but we can also subclassify the tonic polities into orthotonic, homotonic, and syntonic varieties. In doing this, it will of course be important to attach dates because a polity can be transformed very quickly from one kind into another. One advantage of starting with orthotonic polities lies in the fact that they seem to be relatively stable—once established, they seem to perpetuate themselves in a fairly continuous fashion. By contrast, homotonic and, even more, syntonic polities seem to be unstable and likely to change their forms more frequently.

Three types of orthotonic polities

Remembering that positions at the first echelon of an orthotonic polity are filled by outsiders selected through the constitutive system, we can now ask how this selection process is carried out. If we find a number of distinctively different ways, we can then classify orthotonic polities accordingly.

It will be recalled that a constitutive system has three major components: one or more political parties, an electoral system, and an elective assembly. As a first approximation, let us think about the possibility that each of these components may play a dominant role in the designation of first echelon (cabinet) members. We may, in other words, find some systems dominated by party selection, some by voter selection, and some by assembly selection. In fact, these three modes of selection correspond very well to one of the best-established trichotomies of political systems: the Communist party, the presidential, and the parliamentary. Can we confirm or modify this classification by using rigorous criteria? I suspect that we can, and that the important objections that have been raised to the scheme will be found to stem largely from the effort to apply it to heterotonic polities. The reasons will become more apparent later when we look at constitutive systems in homotonic and syntonic polities.

Here let us look more carefully at the way in which constitutive systems select first echelon officials in orthotonic polities. Two different criteria will be used. First, constitutive systems may or may not be competitive. If opposition candidates are permitted to run for office and to be seated in the elected assembly the constitutive system is competitive. They may or may not have a good chance to win control of the government. If they do, the constitutive system permits turnover, but if not, a single dominant party may exercise continuous hegemony in a competitive constitutive system. We can recognize, in other words, both turnover and hegemonic types of competitive constitutive systems.[15] The electoral system in any competitive constitutive system is free, not just legitimizing.

It is clear that in any non-competitive constitutive system, where elections are not free, effective decisions concerning the occupants of first echelon positions are made within the ruling party and not by the electoral system or the elected assembly. (Note that the term "ruling party" is used here for the single party in a non-competitive constitutive system, whereas the term "hegemonic party" is used of a dominant party in a competitive constitutive system. The Communist party in the Soviet Union is a ruling party, but the Congress party of India is hegemonic.)

Although in polities where the Communist party rules it is a ruling party, the concept is more inclusive than the particular Marxist ideology of communism. In other words, non-Communist parties may also be ruling parties and have the same structure for selecting officials as that used by Communist parties. Let us therefore refer to any orthotonic polity with a non-competitive constitutive system as an anatonic polity. The prefix "ana-" has a variety of meanings, including excessively and greatly. We might interpret this new term to refer to an orthotonic polity in which a single ruling party plays an excessively great role. Clearly most anatonic polities in the world today are dominated by Communist parties. But the two terms are not synonyms. All Communist

15. Joseph LaPalombara and Myron Weiner, in "The Origin and Development of Political Parties," in LaPalombara and Weiner (eds.), *Political Parties and Political Development* (Princeton, 1966), pp. 35–36, make the distinction between turnover and hegemonic parties, but they apply it to party systems rather than to constitutive systems, and they try to apply it to all polities rather than just to orthotonic polities. I believe the distinction is not germane to heterotonic polities, and in orthotonic polities it is secondary in importance to the distinction between competitive and non-competitive parties.

states do not necessarily have anatonic polities. If most of the third echelon positions in their state bureaucracies (excluding party offices as such) are filled by outsiders (i.e., by reds, by party cadres) the polity is not anatonic, by definition. Moreover, all anatonic polities do not necessarily have Communist ruling parties. I do not know if there is an example of such a system; perhaps Tunisia might qualify, but it would contain a ruling party with a non-Communist ideological orientation. By definition the constitutive system would be non-competitive and the bureaucracy compensated.

Let us turn now to competitive constitutive systems in orthotonic polities. Here we can make a second distinction. Competitive orthotonic polities are either assembly-oriented or not. Noncompetitive constitutive systems cannot be assembly-oriented because, under a ruling party, the elective assembly can legitimize decisions of the party but lacks the power to name or unseat its candidates for first echelon posts in the bureaucracy. In competitive orthotonic polities, by contrast, the elective assembly always plays an important role. The designation of outsiders for first echelon posts involves a combination of action by parties, voters, and the elected assembly. The role of the assembly in this process varies. A competitive orthotonic polity may be said to be assembly-oriented if its elected assembly has two powers: if it has the authority to unseat a government by a regular majority vote, thereby compelling a new cabinet to be formed; and if it can require most cabinet (first echelon) members to be recruited from the membership of the assembly itself. A polity of this type is normally called a parliamentary system, and the elected assembly in such a polity is called a parliament.

It would be convenient, therefore, to refer to an assembly-oriented competitive orthotonic polity as a parliamentary system except for one drawback. In the process of modernization many of the new states have adopted parliamentary forms of government, but they do not necessarily have orthotonic polities—in other words, their bureaucracies may be uncompensated, of either Type I or Type IV. We can find parliamentary homotonic and syntonic polities as well as parliamentary orthotonic polities.

Much difficulty will be caused in efforts to theorize about parliamentary government if true statements about parliamentary orthotonic polities are applied to parliamentary heterotonic polities, where they may be untrue.

We could use the compound form parliamentary orthotonic polities to meet this situation or, alternatively, coin a new and simpler expression. Since we have already learned how easy it is to add prefixes to the root "tonic," let us use the term "monotonic polity" to refer to any competitive, assembly-oriented (parliamentary) orthotonic polity. The prefix "mono-" is selected because the cabinet in a monotonic polity is at the same time a party group or coalition in parliament, a parliamentary committee, and the first echelon of the bureaucracy. Thus cabinet members unite three crucial roles in their persons, creating a unity of partisan, parliamentary, and bureaucratic leadership which justifies the idea of unity or singleness expressed by the prefix "mono-."

A competitive orthotonic polity which is not assembly-oriented is one in which the assembly lacks the authority to unseat the government by a regular vote and in which it cannot require cabinet members to be members of the assembly. It may be able to unseat the government by a special majority, as in the congressional impeachment proceedings authorized by the American constitution. It may permit or require cabinet members to attend meetings of the assembly or its committees, and its consent may be required in the appointment of the first and even second echelon officials. Thus the distinction between a polity which is assembly-oriented and one which is not may be regarded as merely a matter of degree. But the degree is important and creates a threshold on either side of which an important qualitative distinction can be made.

Competitive non-assembly-oriented orthotonic polities are normally referred to as presidential systems. However, as in the case of parliamentary systems this term is ambiguous. Monotonic polities may, and frequently do, call their executives presidents, and they are elected in a variety of ways, usually by the assembly itself. Thus many parliamentary as well as non-parliamentary orthotonic systems are presidential. Moreover, in the process of modernization, many of the new states have adopted presidential forms of government so far as the election of their executives is concerned. We therefore have presidential syntonic and homotonic as well as presidential orthotonic polities.

In order to refer unambiguously and simply to competitive orthotonic polities which are not assembly-oriented (presidential), it is again useful to coin a special term. I propose to call systems of this type, of which the United States is a leading example, isotonic polities. The prefix "iso-" is proposed because it suggests the idea of equality or similarity which may be applied to the traditional idea of a separation of powers to be found in isotonic polities. More exactly, the fact that an orthotonic polity is not assembly-oriented generates a necessary duality and tension between the leadership role of the elected executive (president), and his cabinet-level appointees outside the assembly, and the leading party groups or elements within the assembly.

We can now formulate a hypothesis about the difference between bureaucracies in monotonic and isotonic polities. I think we will find that monotonic polities tend to have bureaucracies of Type II (where second echelon posts are predominantly filled by insiders), and isotonic polities tend to have bureaucracies of Type III (where second echelon posts are filled by outsiders). Certainly hypotheses of this kind permit exceptions where countervailing ecological forces may lead to deviations from the pattern predicted by the hypotheses. If the pattern prevails in most instances, the hypothesis should be considered reasonable.

Having formulated this hypothesis, I do not want to engage in further discussion of it because it takes us too far from our central theme of administrative reform. Reform implies development and requires us to devote most of our attention to the study of heterotonic polities. However, there are those who think in terms of the superiority of merit systems over spoils and therefore regard any change which leads to the appointment of more insiders at higher bureaucratic levels as a desirable reform. By excluding first echelon (cabinet-level) positions from their concept of a bureaucracy, they are able to think in terms of an idealized all-merit bureaucracy.[16]

Having characterized the difference between monotonic and isotonic polities, one might go on to add further variables and discuss differences among them. For example, in regard to monotonic (parliamentary) polities, very interesting distinctions can be made as to the number of parties to be found in their constitutive systems. We can distinguish not only between two-party systems and those having more than two parties but also between highly polarized multiparty systems—having six or more parties, for example—and those which are not so polarized, having three to five parties. This distinction has been worked out with a wealth of detail and great analytic skill by Giovanni Sartori.[17]

It would be irrelevant and redundant to try to add to or modify Sartori's scheme here. I have, in an earlier essay, speculated on the variety of political party systems, and some ideas presented there might usefully supplement his formulations.[18] More to the point in the present context would be a study of variations in bureaucratic structure accompanying the various types of monotonic (parliamentary, party) systems. If the hypothesis formulated above is correct, they would all tend to be of Type II, although there could well be variations among them. For exam-

16. This point of view seems to be implicit in a recent book review by D. N. Chester, *Public Administration*, XLIV (1966), 493. After describing the difference between top level staffing patterns in the United Kingdom and the United States, he asks, "Here is an interesting problem in comparative administration. Which is the better system: The American or the British?" The question is posed as though it were possible, in either system, to make a drastic change in favor of the practices followed in the other as regards second echelon appointments. If my hypothesis is correct, such a change would not be possible without a more fundamental change toward isotonic government in the British case, or toward monotonic government in the American case. Actually, I believe both systems are orthotonic and permit a high level of political responsiveness and administrative capability. Which is better probably cannot be determined, and I doubt that the issue is properly one of administrative reform.

17. "European Political Parties: The Case of Polarized Pluralism," in LaPalombara and Weiner (eds.), *Political Parties and Political Development*, pp. 137–176. Sartori has expanded on these ideas in *Parties and Party Systems* (New York, forthcoming).

18. "Comparative Politics and the Study of Political Parties," in Crotty (ed.), *Approaches to the Study of Party Organization*, pp. 45–104.

ple, it seems reasonable to expect that the more polarized a monotonic polity, the more partisan would its bureaucracy become. If a small number of pro-system parties habitually divide cabinet posts among themselves in shifting coalitions, whereas members of antisystem parties rarely or never are given cabinet posts, then we can also expect some continuity of party tenure of particular posts. Party X will normally take ministry M and party Y usually gets ministry N. When this happens, we expect positions in ministry M to be staffed to a high degree by supporters of party X, and supports of Y to be appointed in N. However, these appointees might all be experienced insiders, and the level of politicization in the bureaucracy might remain low. Israel might be a case in point and perhaps Italy. Certain rigidities in interdepartmental communication and co-operation might arise from such a structure, but perhaps no more so than where a high degree of professional specialization prevails among appointees in different departments.

If we consider monotonic polities in which a single party is dominant, although opposition parties are successful in securing the election of their candidates to the national assembly, we may find a similar phenomenon, namely a preference for partisans of the dominant party in bureaucratic appointments at all levels. It seems to be but a small qualitative jump from the dominant or hegemonic party in a competitive orthotonic system to the ruling party anatonic type of polity. Here party identifications may be universally expected of public officials, and in the absence of any opposition parties formal requirements of party membership may even be imposed. A relatively high level of non-partisanship in bureaucratic appointments may be expected chiefly in two-party systems, whether monotonic or isotonic, in which the turnover rate is sufficiently high that alternating parties name the cabinet several times during a single career generation, that is, from the time of cadet recruitment to retirement, or about forty years.

In speaking of ruling and hegemonic party systems, we begin to deal with societies whose polities lie on the border between orthotonic and syntonic. Let us turn our attention, therefore, to an examination of the varieties of heterotonic polities, subclassified with reference to their constitutive systems.

Two types of syntonic polities

We have defined syntonic polities as tonic polities with a Type IV bureaucracy. This means that, by definition, third echelon positions in the bureaucracy, in addition to first and second echelon posts, are staffed by outsiders. Since, by definition, such a polity also has a constitutive system, we may add that these outsiders are presumably recruited through the dominant party or parties of the constitutive system. These are, in other words, party-dominated regimes in which political spoils prevail in bureaucratic recruitment. The leading contemporary examples of such polities are probably to be found in Africa where ruling parties have emerged out of nationalist political movements which fought for independence from colonial rule. Following independence, under the guise of indigenization and the elimination of expatriate and hence unreliable officials, party stalwarts and their friends and relatives have been placed in governmental positions at all levels. This is not to say that the forms of recruitment through a merit system have not been followed, but it is clearly possible to manipulate these forms in such a way as to secure the appointment of party followers in preference to others who might be more highly qualified technically. We shall also find historical examples of syntonic polities, as already mentioned, in those Western countries, notably the United States and the United Kingdom, where patronage and spoils prevailed under party rule prior to the establishment of examination systems for the public services.

Is it useful to distinguish several varieties of syntonic polities in terms of characteristics of their constitutive system? Since the constitutive system is politically decisive, by definition, in a syntonic polity, we may expect variations in the structure of the constitutive system to parallel those found in orthotonic polities. Let us therefore consider first the distinction between competitive and non-competitive constitutive systems. As defined above, opposition parties are permitted to nominate candidates for elections in the former but not in the latter. I think we will, in fact, find contemporary examples of both types of systems in syntonic polities. The non-competitive type gives us a political system having characteristics described by David Apter as those of a "mobilization regime," and the competitive type resembles Apter's "reconciliation regime."[19]

It might seem reasonable to adopt Apter's terminology to characterize these two types of syntonic polity, except for a logical difficulty. The criteria used by Apter are essentially functional. They refer to attitudes or policies of dominant parties and the impact they have on the governed political system. Moreover, there is no mention in his discussion of bureaucratic types as defined here. The relationship between his characterization and mine becomes therefore one of hypothesis, not of definitional equivalence. In other words, one may hypothesize that governments having the structural form which I call competitive syntonic are likely to have the functional characteristics of a reconciliation regime, and non-competitive syntonic polities are likely to be movement regimes. This confirms our need for distinctive terms to refer to structurally defined polities, as contrasted with concepts for political systems which are functionally defined.

We could, of course, use the phrases given above, competitive syntonic and non-competitive syntonic. However, given the ease with which tonic combines with prefixes, let us consider the possibility of coining two new words which would somewhat simplify reference to these two types of syntonic polities. I propose that we call competitive syntonic polities atonic and non-competitive syntonic polities hypotonic. The prefix "a-" denotes not only without but also less. I think of competitive syntonic polities as lesser in the sense that they are probably quite unstable, tending to change and give way either to the non-competitive syntonic form, to a homotonic form, or to an orthotonic system. I judge this to be true because if the bureaucracy is of Type IV its administrative performance will be very poor, and

19. David E. Apter, *The Politics of Modernization* (Chicago, 1965), pp. 357–390.

this in turn will not only provoke opposition to the regime but will make it relatively easy for resistance groups to organize and carry out revolutionary and subversive activities and also to run candidates in elections. The tendency of the party in power to regard political opposition as inherently disloyal or treasonous in character is likely, therefore, to lead to mounting pressure to restrict the freedom of opposition parties, to control nominations, and perhaps to transform the polity into a non-competitive form in which opposition parties are made illegal.

Since the other patterns of change for an atonic polity involve transformations into non-syntonic systems, let us discuss them later, while considering here the alternative (non-competitive) syntonic form which I called hypotonic above. The prefix "hypo-" also carries a meaning of lesser, as well as below or beneath. The combined form happens to be used in physiology for a condition of less than normal tone. Let us assume that a non-competitive ruling party which insists on placing party activism above administrative competence and experience in recruiting personnel for third echelon positions in the bureaucracy will find that it cannot carry out its plans and policies efficiently. In this sense it may be thought of as lacking administrative capability, or as having less than normal tone. We may hypothesize that mobilization regimes are typically less capable in this sense than totalitarian regimes and that the difference can be explained in large part by administrative ability, the former being hypotonic and the latter anatonic systems.

We might well study the cultural revolution in China as a possible example of the crisis of hypotonic polity on the verge of becoming an anatonic system. One reasonable interpretation of the revolution seems to be that it results from a determined drive by reds to reduce the influence and power of experts who had, within the previous decade, become increasingly prevalent at, shall we imagine, the third echelon. From Barnett's and other data, it seems clear that reds prevailed at the first and no doubt the second echelon. Some party leaders must have seen the rising influence of experienced state officials in the non-party bureaucracy as a threat; accordingly, they moved to oust or humble these officials and also their leading supporters at the highest levels of the government and party. In this sense it is clearly not a simple question of the party versus the bureaucracy, but it may well be a question of where to strike the balance between insiders (experts) and outsiders (reds) in bureaucratic recruitment, and hence how to draw the line between the spheres of influence of party and bureaucracy, and how to weight the relative importance of political responsiveness and administrative capability.

Undoubtedly many other ideological and policy issues, and the circumstantial play of conflicting personalities and interests, cover such an underlying clash, if indeed this is the underlying clash. But if there is any truth in this view, then we might regard the cultural revolution as a countermovement likely to throw the Chinese regime back into a hypotonic stage just as it was on the verge of self-transformation into an anatonic polity.

The second distinguishing criterion of orthotonic polities we were able to identify above was whether or not competitive systems were assembly-oriented. Returning to the consideration of competitive syntonic (atonic) polities, we can now ask whether or not a similar distinction would make sense here. Does it matter whether the parliamentary or presidential form of government is used in a regime having a Type IV bureaucracy? This is probably a question worthy of investigation, but intuitively I feel that the significance of this distinction in atonic polities is probably very limited. An important reason for this feeling is the proposition that legislative bodies in all these systems are extremely weak and are therefore so amenable to manipulation by the party in power that it makes little difference whether, formally speaking, cabinet members belong to the assembly and the assembly has the authority to dissolve a government.

What may be far more decisive is a different though related distinction. We may observe, if we take a historical perspective, a considerable range of variation between atonic polities in which the elected assembly has considerable power and those in which it does not. If the assembly has power, it will also have an interest in maintaining party competition, because the only way in which most assemblymen in the ruling party can preserve a sphere of personal power and influence for themselves is to perpetuate the assembly as a power-holding body. They must realize that if they support measures designed to suppress opposition parties power will gravitate to the leaders of the ruling party, and they will become mere pawns. The result would be to transform the assembly into a rubber stamp body, and to deprive assemblymen who belong to the ruling party but not to its central elite of a significant and interesting role. In other words, the existence of an opposition in an assembly may well be a necessary condition for non-elite members of the government party (or parties) to exercise any significant influence.

Historically speaking, it seems to me unlikely that any elected assembly can gain significant power if it is created after a party system has gained power over the bureaucracy by naming members to its first echelon positions. But if the elected assembly comes into existence before the party system gains power, the assembly has a much greater chance of exercising effective power in its own right. This happened only in premodern, not in modernizing, countries. Let us call an atonic polity in which the assembly exercises decisive power—whether in a parliamentary or presidential form of government—assembly-based. Thus an assembly-based system may be assembly-oriented or not. We can then say that assembly-based atonic polities are probably found mainly in premodern societies, such as the United States and the United Kingdom during the first half of the nineteenth century. By contrast all contemporary atonic polities are likely not to be assembly-based.

Considering the problem of administrative reform in hypotonic (non-competitive) polities, we can see several interesting possibilities. As the Chinese case illustrates, the rise of experts under the control of a ruling party might convert a hypotonic into an anatonic polity. It is suggestive to compare the difficulties experienced by the Soviet Union during the prewar Stalinist years with the current cultural revolution in China. The great purge in Russia was perhaps symptomatic of a similar crisis in relationships between reds and experts. By the time of Khrushchev a balance had been established which generated an anatonic polity. Whether or not a similar pattern of development will occur in China remains to be seen.

In this sense administrative reform can have the effect of changing a non-competitive syntonic polity into a non-competitive orthotonic polity. As a result political development may occur without democratization. Indeed, I find it hard to see how democratization could take place when development occurs in this way.

By contrast, what are the prospects of administrative reform in atonic (competitive) regimes? If the regime is assembly-based, opposition parties will be provided an opportunity to harass the government continuously for its administrative incompetence and abuse of power. The basis will be laid for reform movements designed to expand the merit principle at the expense of patronage and spoils. An assembly-based atonic polity, then, may have a good chance of transforming itself into a competitive orthotonic polity, whether of the assembly-oriented (monotonic) or of the non-assembly-oriented (isotonic) variety.

However, if the atonic polity is not assembly-based, the prospects for administrative reform seem much poorer. Without the open forum of a powerful assembly interested in preserving the right of opposition, the temptation will be continuously faced by leaders of the hegemonic party to co-opt and suppress rival parties rather than to sacrifice the privileges of a spoils system. Indeed, one of the most effective means of overcoming the opposition of competing parties may well be to offer choice posts in the bureaucracy to its leaders. When this happens, the effect of party competition may be to reinforce spoils and expand its effects in the bureaucracy rather than to curtail them on behalf of a merit system.

There are interesting examples in the new states of competitive systems which might well be studied from this point of view. The Philippines is perhaps an atypical case of a contemporary atonic polity which is assembly-based. There are historical reasons why the Congress in this country is particularly powerful. Moreover, a basis for recruitment by civil service examinations of civil servants had been laid prior to independence, under colonial administration. An empirical question to be raised today is whether most of the third echelon officials are insiders with administrative experience and ability or outsiders brought in through political patronage and manipulation of the formal rules. It may well be that the Philippine government is already an orthotonic polity of the isotonic type, or it may be an atonic polity on the verge of making this transformation.

There are a number of countries that were formerly under British administration which have relatively powerful parliamentary bodies, including India, Jamaica, Trinidad-Tobago, Malaysia, Singapore. Are they, then, not also examples of atonic polities? Certainly their first echelon officials are predominantly outsiders recruited through their constitutive systems. But what about positions in the third echelon of their bureaucracies? Are these not filled predominantly by insiders? If so, these polities would meet the minimum requirements for orthopolities of the monotonic variety.

The critical differences between these and many other new states appear to include two elements: on the bureaucratic side the creation of a career system in which the process of indigenization had made very substantial progress prior to independence, so that the nationalist party could not readily replace third echelon officials with outsiders in the name of nationalization; and on the constitutive side, the emergence of a relatively well-established system of party organization and an elective assembly with substantial experience of parliamentary government. By contrast, in states such as Indonesia, Burma, Pakistan, Ghana, and Nigeria, in which military officers have taken power, the constitutive system was much less well established at the time of independence, and indigenization had made far less progress in the bureaucracy.

In order to shed more light on these military transformations, let us turn now to an examination of types of homotonic polities.

Two types of homotonic polities

We have defined homotonic polities as tonic polities with Type I bureaucracies. If career officials themselves fill the first echelon posts in the bureaucracy of a tonic polity, two related characteristics may be postulated.

First, there is no legitimate way of recruiting a prime minister or president if the choice is not made outside the bureaucracy. The only way in which it can be made therefore is by an intrabureaucratic struggle for power culminating in a coup d'état. Whereas decisions in a constitutive system are made by counting votes, winners are typically men of persuasive power and organizational ability; winners in an intrabureaucratic struggle for power are typically men who control the means of violence, namely military officers. Thus the access to supreme power of military officers in a tonic polity is probably always a sign of the emergence of a homotonic polity.

In many discussions of military regimes the armed forces are treated as an organization equivalent to political parties and, like them, standing outside the bureaucracy. Implicit in this model is an unclear conception of bureaucracy, except that it usually limits the notion to civilian offices and does not include first echelon positions. The issue is then posed as one between military and civil power, thereby lumping civilian bureaucrats in the same category as the civilian leaders of the constitutive system. No doubt it is possible to describe what has happened in many of the new states in these terms. I believe, however, that a much more precise picture and more predictive hypotheses can be formulated if we use the framework provided by the concept of a homotonic polity.

In accordance with this concept, a military coup is perceived not as a victory by a military organization over a civilian but as the outcome of an intrabureaucratic struggle among highly placed public officials. The victors in such a struggle are normally led by military officers, but the winning group or coalition of groups normally also includes civilian officials, and a civilian may even be given the leading position of premier or president as a result of a coup. This has been the normal practice in Thailand, for example.[20]

20. For details see my *Thailand: The Modernization of a Bureaucratic Polity*, pp. 211–241.

Moreover, it is not typically the army, or the armed forces as an organization, which seizes power, but a political group composed of military officers which mobilizes enough support within the armed forces to make a show of force capable of overwhelming the previous government, which may be, and often is, also composed of military officers. This is the normal way of changing governments in a homotonic polity.[21]

There are perhaps two reasons military officers play such a dominant role in intrabureaucratic power struggles. One is the obvious reason that where a decision is made by the exercise of naked power, capacity to use violence counts for more than other means of securing power, and military officers are professionally expert in the use of violence. In addition, however, it is probably also true that among the various services constituting a bureaucracy the career principle is most highly prized within the military services, and the claims of career officers usually are also recognized outside these services. In other words, even in political systems where civilian positions are being widely filled by political protégés (i.e., by outsiders), military offices may be filled by career officers (i.e., by insiders). This means that in terms of intrabureaucratic values and experience, even in a Type IV bureaucracy, the military components may have a Type II or even a Type I form of organization.

Insofar as this proposition is true, it follows that when the ability of the constitutive system to control the government is in doubt the units within the bureaucracy which are most likely to be able to act in a co-ordinated fashion are military units, provided a group or clique of military officers comes into being capable of commanding a decisively superior set of these military units. In other words, it is not merely the use of the means of violence which sets military officials apart from their civilian opposite numbers, it is also their superior organizational skills based on the longer experience of these officers as career men inside the bureaucracy.

A second major characteristic of homotonic polities follows

21. Samuel E. Finer, *The Man on Horseback: The Role of the Military in Politics* (London, 1962).

from the inability of the constitutive system, by definition, to name the incumbents of first echelon posts in the bureaucracy. If the constitutive system is ineffective in this fashion, then surely the formal structure of that constitutive system will be irrelevant as a defining characteristic of the polity. In other words, constitutive systems in homotonic polities may be competitive or non-competitive in form, assembly-oriented (parliamentary) or not assembly-oriented (presidential). But these differences will make no significant difference in the operation of the polity.

Here we see most clearly why a typology of political systems that starts from the form of the party system and/or the presidential-parliamentary dichotomy runs into difficulties. In Thailand, for example, the formal structure of the constitutive system for much of the time since 1932 has been parliamentary with competing parties and free elections. Except for a brief period after the war when the constitutive system began to increase its political influence, effective power has rested with a ruling group of military and civilian officials. If, because of the formal structure of its constitutive system, this polity were classified with European parliamentary (monotonic) polities, everyone would instinctively recognize the imprecise, not to say misleading, character of such a classification. Indeed, so obviously wide of the mark would such a typology be that specialists in comparative politics have in effect given up the effort to classify the structure of government in countries like Thailand except in terms of such imprecise categories as traditional, transitional, or modernizing oligarchy. However, if the primary criterion for classifying tonic polities were a typology of bureaucracies and executives rather than of constitutive systems, it would be possible to establish parameters within which the differences between constitutive systems would be significant. In homotonic polities, however, these differences are not significant.

Can we, nevertheless, discover any criteria affecting the constitutive system by which different types of homotonic polities might usefully be distinguished? Let us turn to the distinction we made in discussing syntonic polities between systems which are assembly-based and those which are not. Perhaps a comparable distinction might be made among homotonic polities between those in which the constitutive system plays no important political role and those in which the constitutive system, while subordinated to the bureaucracy, nevertheless does play an important political role.

An operational criterion might be the ability of the constitutive system, from time to time, to succeed in designating some first echelon officials, including the chairman or prime minister of the cabinet. Actual selection of such officials would have to be distinguished from the mere ratification of selections previously made by a ruling group of officials. Normally such a cabinet would contain a majority of outsiders, but the cabinet posts responsible for military affairs would be retained by career military officers.

Another characteristic of regimes with influential but not decisive constitutive systems would be their intermittent character. Short periods during which the cabinet is predominantly named by the constitutive system would be followed by periods in which the government would be formed by a coup d'état. During the periods of rule by a military junta, the constitutive system would survive despite any efforts of the new government to suppress political parties, suspend the constitution, and delay elections. The vigor of the constitutive system would be revealed by its ability in due time to compel the military junta to permit elections, to restore the constitution, and to turn the reins of government over to a cabinet predominantly selected by the constitutive system.

Perhaps the best structural test for distinguishing varieties of homotonic polities, then, would be the ability of the constitutive system, intermittently, to name outsiders as first echelon bureaucrats. Such a homotonic polity could be distinguished from an orthotonic polity by the presence of career military officers in the cabinet. As has been indicated above, an orthotonic polity must not only name outsiders to most positions at the first echelon but the direction of military ministries in particular must be in the hands of outsiders.

It is not easy to make the distinction described above in simple terms. We want to distinguish homotonic polities in which the constitutive system persists only as a means of legitimizing the authority of a ruling bureaucratic group from those polities in which the constitutive system exercises some significant power as shown by its ability from time to time to name outsiders to most first echelon positions, but not to the military command positions. We might call the latter type constitutive-system-influenced and the former type not constitutive-system-influenced. A more succinct formulation involves the coining of new terms for two subtypes of homotonic polities. We may, for example, refer to homotonic polities which are constitutive-system-influenced as antitonic and those which are not constitutive-system-influenced as autotonic. Interpreting these neologisms, consider that the prefix "auto-" refers to the self and suggests the idea of self-directed. In this sense an autotonic polity is one in which the bureaucracy is continuously self-directed, even though it has a constitutive system. The prefix "anti-" is defined as signifying against, counter, rivalry, or supplanting. We may therefore think of an antitonic polity as a homotonic polity in which the constitutive system nevertheless puts up a brave fight, seeking to control the bureaucracy but never quite succeeding.

We may expect the general political style in an antitonic polity to be much more controversial and exciting than in an autotonic regime. There will be much talk of revolution and much turmoil, heated elections being succeeded by military coups, and public officials will tend to become highly politicized. By contrast, in an autotonic polity the general political temperature will be much lower, and the level of bureaucratic politicization will also be lower. Only higher officials will be engaged in the struggle for power, and the public will tend to be apathetic. Elections may be run off as routine affairs, without much excitement, because everyone understands that the outcome of elections has little real impact on the structure of power.

This hypothetical and speculative discussion may be given more empirical content by looking at recent events in Ghana, where, I would judge, a syntonic polity was replaced by a homotonic polity, following the coup d'état of February 24, 1966. A seven-man National Liberation Council composed of army officers deposed Kwame Nkrumah and his government based on the ruling-party regime of the Convention People's party. The role of the bureaucracy in this overturn is indicated in the following quotation from a recent report:

> At the Army's request, senior civil servants took charge of all the ministries and the provincial administrations. On their own volition, eight of the most prominent members of the civil service issued a statement in support of the new regime.
>
> Quite strikingly, all of the members of the National Liberation Council were careerists—in the sense of having, early in their lives, been primarily concerned with personal professional advancement, and of having succeeded. . . .[22]

Not only were civil servants linked with key military officers in this transformation, but the constitutive system was immediately put under pressure. We read that "one of the first acts of the military leaders was to outlaw the CPP. The prohibition, however, was quickly extended to all other political parties, and political activities."[23] Dr. Kofi Busia, previous leader in exile of the suppressed opposition to the CPP, declared that the new government would not automatically bring about democracy. General Ankrah, chairman of the NLC, sharply criticized Dr. Busia, then later named him to a prominent official position. It would appear that political leaders, even those opposed to Nkrumah's regime, could not operate through party mechanisims but might be co-opted into governmental posts. We read that the "National Liberation Council did not distinguish between corrupt and non-corrupt politicians and parties. They held it necessary to ban all parties. . . ."[24] At the same time political protégés of the CPP were systematically rooted out of the bureaucracy, to be replaced by insiders. "Allegedly incompetent party functionaries of the old regime were replaced as regional and district commissioners by 'committees of administration.' The Civil Service Commission was recreated to ensure fair play and security for

22. Irvin G. Markewitz, "Ghana Ten Years after Independence: The Development of Technocracy-Capitalism," in *Africa Today*, XIV (1967), 6.
23. *Ibid.*, p. 8.
24. *Ibid.*, p. 9.

all civil servants. . . . Civil servants were among the foremost of those who applauded these reforms."[25]

Whether or not the economy and society of Ghana will be transformed at the functional level as much as this reporter suggests, there can be little doubt that the structure of government has been profoundly reshaped. It is clearly today a homotonic polity. Whether it is autotonic or antitonic perhaps remains to be determined. If the party and constitutional system can survive and make a comeback, leading in due time to new elections, it may qualify as an antitonic polity. If the constitutive system remains completely dormant, it becomes autotonic.

Protonic polities and the role of the executive

In an early section of this chapter we considered briefly the changing roles of executives in tonic polities and found that the traditional distinction between hereditary (monarchic) and elective (republican) forms of government did not enable us to discriminate significantly between various kinds of contemporary polities. We also saw that the role of the executive varied significantly in relation to different types of polities. Now that we have formulated a scheme for classifying tonic polities in terms of the characteristics of their bureaucracies and constitutive systems, we can return usefully to a consideration of the structure of the executive as a distinguishing criterion of different polities.

Let us review the possibilities available. The familiar distinction between hereditary and non-hereditary executives, between kings and presidents, has already been mentioned. A second distinction may be considered, between effective and ceremonial executives. We think of absolute and constitutional monarchs on the one hand, and of presidents who rule contrasted with those who merely preside. If we think about these four possible types of executives in relation to tonic polities, we will see that three of them are compatible but one is not, namely the absolute monarch. Constitutional monarchs are compatible with monotonic and homotonic polities on the assumption that the ruling constitutive and bureaucratic systems, respectively, designate the

25. *Ibid.*, p. 10.

effective head of government but choose to leave the king as a ceremonial figurehead. We will find presidents who rule in isotonic and some syntonic polities where the executive is chosen by and responsible to the constitutive system. Presidents who merely preside may be found in monotonic, anatonic, syntonic, and homotonic polities also.

Shall we then eliminate the absolute monarch as a type of executive found only in non-tonic polities and bound to disappear with the rise of tonic polities? If we think of countries such as Iran, Ethiopia, Nepal, Jordan, Greece, and a few others, where absolute monarchs have but recently disappeared, we will perhaps reach the paradoxical conclusion that politically strong kings may indeed survive despite the establishment of constitutive systems in their countries. How can this unusual structure of government fit into our typology? Under what heading should we classify it?

Or should we devise a new category of political systems to take into account these abnormal cases? One possibility would be to consider the executive as an independent variable, not in terms of the two criteria used above but perhaps by introducing a third dimension of variation. Can we perhaps think of types of tonic executives which are not held accountable to either the constitutive system or the bureaucracy? Let us make a distinction between accountable and non-accountable executives. Surely a ruling president is accountable insofar as he is subject to election. Even the leader of a military junta is accountable to the bureaucracy which is liable to overthrow him by another coup. It would seem that all the types of executives found in the tonic polities examined so far are accountable. The distinctions made regarding the variety of executive structures, in other words, apply to accountable executives. Do they also apply to non-accountable executives? And is there reason for considering the non-accountable executive an independent variable?

We have already seen how the political power of bureaucracy may increase rather than decrease as a result of the addition of a constitutive system, leading to the appearance of homotonic polities. Is it possible for a similar phenomenon to occur with the office of executive? Could the addition of a constitutive system be used by a ruler to enhance the power of his office? Let us at least consider this possibility and inquire into the possible outcome in situations where the executive somehow is able to exercise independent power, not subject to control by either the constitutive system or the bureaucracy. Clearly a hereditary monarch may exercise such power, as we can tell from the few cases mentioned above.

We have already touched briefly on this subject, referring to tonic polities with non-accountable executives as protonic, and those with accountable executives as neotonic. We have been considering neotonic polities, in their orthotonic and heterotonic forms. Let us now think about protonic polities.

Are we now to consider the persistence of strong monarchs as the only form of protonic polities? Or are there other non-hereditary executives who might also qualify for the designation? What about elective or appointive executives who seize or acquire relatively independent power in relation to both the constitutive system and the bureaucracy? Such might well include those contemporary rulers who build around themselves some kind of leadership cult or charisma. The personality cults of Hitler, Stalin, Mussolini, Ataturk, Chiang Kai-shek, Sukarno, Peron, and others come to mind. These were not hereditary monarchs, yet they exercised a degree of power similar to that possessed by powerful kings. Perhaps a structural criterion might be the decision of a polity to give its executive lifelong tenure in office. Many charismatic leaders, even though elected by the constitutive system or brought to power by a military coup, have been able to secure an independent political role by having their personal positions institutionalized on a lifetime basis.[26]

If we think of the variety of polities which have constitutive systems it may suddenly occur to us that we have been overlooking an important category, namely dependent territories. Clearly, countries such as India, the Philippines, Nigeria, and others had

26. The criteria for recognizing a non-accountable elected executive are given in more detail in my "Bureaucratic Politics in Comparative Perspective," *Journal of Comparative Administration,* I (1969).

constitutive systems before independence. Shall we disregard these areas under colonial rule or try to bring them within our frame of reference? We could disregard them by saying that, as dependencies, they were not separate polities but subnational regions or provinces of the imperial power. Admittedly we are dealing here with a marginal case, but what would happen if we were to accord dependent territories the status of a political system, a polity, even though not formally independent? Or rather, what happens to the executive position in this case? We might regard the executive as the chief of state of the imperial power, for example, the King of England in relation to India. Or we could treat the governor-general, as the king's surrogate, as the executive. On the assumption that it is the governor who exercises independent power in a country under colonial administration, it might be more useful to regard the governor of a dependent territory as its executive. Such territories, I believe, always have a bureaucracy, but many in addition acquired a constitutive system, especially during the few years preceding independence. After they have acquired such a constitutive system we might treat them as protonic polities with an independently powerful, and appointive, executive. If we recognized this type of political system, we could then formulate more clearly theories about the transition from dependence to independence through hypotheses relating to the transformation of protonic polities.

But we have now identified three distinctly different kinds of protonic polities, varying in their executive structure. In order to distinguish among them we shall need separate terminology. I propose, therefore, to call protonic polities paratonic if their executives are hereditary monarchs, hypertonic if their executives are elective on a lifetime tenure basis, and antetonic if they are appointive.

The prefix "para-" signifies beside, alongside of, or beyond. In this sense a paratonic polity is a protonic polity which also contains, alongside of the constitutive system and bureaucracy, an independently powerful monarchy. A criterion of such power is the ability of the monarch to dissolve a parliamentary government, even though it still has sufficient support in the constitutive system to continue in office, and to create a government although it lacks such support. Alternatively, the polity is paratonic if the king can create a government despite opposition among high officials and overthrow a government which has such support. The former criterion is relevant when the constitutive system is more powerful than the bureaucracy, the latter when the bureaucracy is more important. Thus the former case resembles a syntonic polity, the latter, homotonic.

The concept of a paratonic polity might help to explain a concrete political situation such as that of contemporary Greece, where a system of government prevailed which had all the earmarks of a regular parliamentary system with a constitutional monarchy. However, closer scrutiny would show that the king regularly intervened in the political process to make and unmake governments over the heads of the parliamentarians. As a result of the military coup it may be thought that the new government has become a homotonic polity. Still, the kingship survives, although probably weakened politically. It remains to be seen whether and to what extent the king can intervene in the political process under bureaucratic domination. If he can, the system will remain paratonic in character.[27]

A comparative study of Greece and Iran would be interesting in this connection because Iran apparently has another paratonic system, but one in which bureaucratic forces on the whole have been stronger than the constitutive system. Except for the Mossadegh period, when parliamentary power severely challenged royal supremacy, the country has had a paratonic system in which the Shah has maintained his personal power by manipulating the appointments of high officials and using the Majlis as a pawn rather than submitting to its rule.

A very similar pattern of governance may be found in hypertonic polities with charismatic elective leaders. Indonesia under Sukarno during the Guided Democracy period might be taken as

27. This was written before the abortive attempt of the Greek king to overthrow the military regime. The king's subsequent flight and self-exile showed the Greek regime to have become homotonic.

a good example. Here, however, it was the Communist party, rather than parliament, which the ruler systematically manipulated against the military bureaucracy. As a result of the abortive effort of party forces to smash the military, we now see a government of military officers in Indonesia, following the destruction of the party. But it is significant that, although Sukarno has been shorn of power and position, he remains very much on the scene. What has now emerged may well be a homotonic polity of the antitonic type, as indicated by the resurgence of non-Communist political parties and a restive parliament. However, if Sukarno can ever stage a comeback, or if someone else takes over his former role, the polity might well revert to a hypertonic system.

The prefix "hyper-" means something which is over, above, or beyond the ordinary. In this sense, a hypertonic polity is one in which an elective executive nevertheless exercises powers well beyond those ordinarily vested in this office. Other rulers who might well be compared with Sukarno as hypertonic executives are Peron, Chiang Kai-shek, Syngman Rhee, and Stalin. Recognizing the great ideological differences between these men and their regimes, we can yet see how, as non-accountable rulers, they manipulated party forces against military-bureaucratic cliques to perpetuate and build up their own power. The sequel to Stalin's regime was a triumph of the ruling party rather than of military leaders, but it may be that this is the exceptional rather than the more usual pattern in hypertonic polities.

The power struggle in a hypertonic polity should not be expected to fit a simple model. The ruler, who lives in perpetual danger of assassination, military uprisings, and political intrigue, may survive only by deftly playing one force off against another, first building up one clique at the expense of another, then trying to strengthen the constitutive system and weaken the military, or relying on the secret police, organized labor, militant youth and student groups, to curtail the power of threateningly powerful elements.

Characteristically, hypertonic polities are short-lived. They can scarcely survive the lifetime of their founders, and they do not begin with his election to office but emerge gradually as he builds up his image as a charismatic leader and adds new official titles until it becomes apparent that he has made himself führer for life.

By contrast with paratonic and hypertonic polities, the antetonic polity is likely to appear a rather tame affair, since appointive executives under colonial administration are more likely to behave like ceremonious bureaucrats than like aggressive and dramatic leaders. The prefix "ante-" has been chosen because it means before, preceding, anticipatory. Thus an antetonic polity normally paves the way for the establishment of a different kind of tonic polity, whether protonic or neotonic.

The relation between antetonic executives and the constitutive system is quite different from that found in paratonic and hypertonic polities. Here the struggle for power is almost completely an intrabureaucratic affair, and the executive succeeds to the extent that he can effectively balance off pressures generated by the officials under his authority against those emanating from his home office, namely the headquarters of colonial administration in the imperial power overseas. Although a struggle between military and civil officials falls under this general heading, it is the civil servants rather than military officers who normally play a dominant role in antetonic polities.

In this setting the rise of a constitutive system is typically seen either as a set of preparatory steps leading toward eventual independence or as a series of concessions to demands made by an increasingly restive and unruly native population. We might usefully study the phasing of the introduction of constitutive systems in antetonic polities as a clue to the subsequent history of the new states. If an elective assembly is introduced rather early, then there is probably a good chance for the new state to evolve toward an assembly-based syntonic polity and, eventually, toward an orthotonic system. The Philippines might be taken as a good case study of this pattern. By contrast, if an assembly is not established until very late in the game, then a revolutionary movement lacking experience as a political party may well become quite strong before independence and may rely more on violence than on negotiation to secure victory. Such a movement is likely to become a ruling party after independence and to give short shrift to any elective assembly that may have been created during the last days of the colonial regime. This is a familiar pattern, and examples may be found in Vietnam, Burma, Congo, Ghana, and other new states.

India under imperial rule clearly fell between these extremes, for it had a relatively long experience with parliamentary institutions, but they were granted reluctantly, and the Congress party itself vacillated between postures of co-operation and resistance to them. Thus in postindependence India the Congress party became hegemonic, but a competitive free electoral system and a moderately effective Parliament were also established.

Note that the definition of a protonic polity does not specify what type of bureaucracy it has. Each of the neotonic polities was defined by reference to the type of bureaucracy found in it. By contrast, we can leave open for empirical inquiry determination of the type of bureaucracy to be found in protonic polities, although I suspect that they will resemble Type I, but in a rather peculiar sense. That is, protonic executives, in their effort to enhance their own power, will select personal protégés for appointment to first echelon posts, but in doing so they will recruit from the ranks of career officials. In this sense it may be that bureaucracies in protonic polities have atypical characteristics for Type I systems and should be classified as Type V bureaucracies.

However, I do not want to suggest that we define protonic polities as having Type V bureaucracies. Rather, although I am not fully persuaded of this, I suspect that a better procedure would be to say that the classification of bureaucracies into the five types offered above applies only to bureaucracies in neotonic systems. Type V is probably found, then, mainly in homotonic polities and in some syntonic polities. We could add a sixth type of bureaucracy, which is defined ecologically rather than structurally, namely the type found in protonic polities. This type would resemble Type I and Type V but would also have some distinctive characteristics of its own.

At this point it may be useful to summarize the foregoing discussion and perhaps clarify the argument in tabular form. Readers of earlier drafts of this essay and earlier essays of mine should be warned that the terminology proposed here differs in several minor respects from previous statements, and replaces them, so far as I am concerned.

Table 4. ***Types of Tonic Polities***

(Tonic polities all have executives, bureaucracies, and constitutive systems.)
PROTONIC: with non-accountable executives, Type VI bureaucracy
- *Paratonic:* with hereditary executives
- *Hypertonic:* with elective executives
- *Antetonic:* with appointive executives

NEOTONIC: with accountable executives, Types I to V
- *Orthotonic:* with compensated bureaucracies, Types II and III
  - Anatonic: with non-competitive constitutive systems (ruling party)
  - Monotonic: with competitive, assembly-oriented constitutive systems, probably Type II (parliamentary)
  - Isotonic: with competitive, not assembly-oriented constitutive systems, probably Type III (presidential)
- *Heterotonic:* with Types I, IV, or V bureaucracies
- *Syntonic:* with Type IV bureaucracies, perhaps Type V; constitutive system dominant
  - Hypotonic: non-competitive constitutive systems (mobilization)
  - Atonic: competitive constitutive systems (reconciliation)
- *Homotonic:* with Type I bureaucracies, perhaps Type V; bureaucracy dominant
  - Autotonic: constitutive system no influence (pure bureaucratic polity)
  - Antitonic: constitutive system intermittently influential (marginal bureaucratic polity)

As this table should make clear, the approach to structural classification of political systems proposed here rank-orders the criteria as follows: (1) executive system, (2) bureaucratic system, and (3) constitutive system. This contrasts with more conventional classification schemes primarily in that it uses differences among constitutive systems as a basis for third-order sub-classification, rather than for first-order classification. It also differs, of course, by using criteria for the classification of executive systems and bureaucratic systems that have not to my knowledge been hitherto employed.

VI. Conclusion

To present a typology of political systems is not, of course, to justify its use. Whether or not this typology should be employed in the study of comparative politics or administrative development will depend on its utility, and utility depends on several criteria. Is the scheme logically coherent? This can be determined by internal analysis of the scheme itself. Is it operational? This can only be determined by subsequent efforts to code political systems in terms of the scheme, an exercise which has not yet been done.

There are two other ways in which the scheme can be evaluated in a preliminary way. First, we can look at some of the other proposed schemes for classification. If we find that they include categories which have been omitted from the present scheme, then possible holes or gaps will be called to our attention. Such an exercise should also help us to understand and clarify methodological problems involved in the construction of such a typology.

A second procedure involves the construction of hypotheses in which the typology is used. Does the classification suggest promising hypotheses? Is it easier to formulate fruitful hypotheses when this typology is available? Will hypotheses utilizing these categories turn out to be more predictive than others on the same subject which do not use these categories? Obviously a great deal of work is necessary before definite answers can be given to such questions, but perhaps a few first steps can be taken, especially to relate the scheme to modernization, development, democratization, and administrative reform.

In terms of these two procedures, then, let us first look at some other classification schemes. It should be clear that the logical basis of classification is distinctively different. Most available schemes combine structural and functional criteria in their definitions. They also frequently mix definitions with hypotheses in ideal types. These take the form of statements that Type A tends to have characteristics M, N, Q, T, etc. If these are hypotheses, they cannot be tested because Type A is not otherwise defined. If they are definitions, they are logically defective because a definition should assert what is always present, by definition, in order for Type A to be present.

The point may be illustrated by looking at Apter's concepts of "mobilization," "reconciliation," and "neo-mercantilist" regimes. The "mobilization regime" is described as combining hierarchy and consummatory values. It is not clear to me whether these are hypothetical statements about mobilization regimes or a definition. They also combine structural and functional elements: hierarchy being a structural category and consummatory values probably referring to a functional relationship between components of government and their system consequences. I have already suggested that hypotonic polities are likely to have the characteristics attributed to a "mobilization regime." So do anatonic polities. However, Apter's interest is clearly in hypotonic rather than anatonic regimes. This suggests that his conception covers a larger range of phenomena than he actually treats in his discussion, and hence that his definition needs to be given a sharper focus, as by distinguishing different kinds of "mobilization regimes."

Similarly Apter's definition of a "reconciliation system" combines pyramidal structure and instrumental value orientations. I think it likely that atonic polities will be found to be reconciliation systems, as will isotonic and monotonic polities. This parallels, in other words, the position as regards mobilization regimes.

What Apter calls "neo-mercantilist systems," modernizing autocracies, and military oligarchies are described as hierarchical and instrumental. I imagine that modernizing autocracies are largely paratonic and military oligarchies are autotonic. The category "neo-mercantile" is more difficult to place, but may cover characteristics of a range of homotonic and protonic polities.

Making the comparison from the other side, I do not find in Apter's scheme any place to classify regimes which I have categorized as antetonic and antitonic, nor does his scheme, being primarily concerned with modernizing rather than modern government, have any explicit place for orthotonic polities.[28]

Shils's regime types and tonic polities

Perhaps the best known and most influential of the typologies of political systems in current discussions of political development and modernization is one which was proposed by Edward Shils in 1959. Although Shils himself has subsequently modified his scheme in various respects, the fullest statement of the classification and the criteria used to establish it is contained in his original formulation.[29] In that essay he proposed classifying alternative courses of political development under five headings: political democracy, tutelary democracy, modernizing oligarchies, totalitarian oligarchy, and traditional oligarchy.

Under each of these headings Shils specified "components" and "preconditions." By components he meant a combination of structural conditions and behavioral patterns thought to be typical of the proposed type, and by preconditions he specified various circumstances likely to produce such regimes or to perpetuate them. It may be instructive to compare these categories in summary fashion with the classification scheme proposed in this chapter.

By political democracy, Shils writes, is meant a "regime of civilian rule through representative institutions and public liberties."[30] He specifies that it has a legislative body at its center, that this body is periodically elected by universal suffrage, that it can initiate legislation and enact measures proposed by the leadership of the executive branch. The executive branch may be either separately elected or selected from members of the legislature. He says that the executive "carries out its policies through a hierarchically organized bureaucracy which is ultimately answerable to its political head or minister . . . who is answerable to the legislature." Candidates for seats in the legislature are nominated for election by one of several contending parties. Shils specifies

28. Apter, *The Politics of Modernization,* pp. 357–421, esp. p. 397.
29. *Political Development in the New States* (The Hague, 1962).
30. *Ibid.,* pp. 51, 52.

the existence of a written or traditional constitution and the need for an independent judiciary.

The discussion of preconditions for each type falls under a standard set of five headings which includes the ruling elite, opposition, machinery of authority, public opinion, and civil order. According to Shils, political democracy requires, under machinery of authority, "a competent civil service well enough trained and organized to carry out the measures taken by the legislature (or the executive leadership). He states the need for a respected and impartial judiciary and for machinery to protect the constitutional order, including a police force, intelligence system, and loyal military officers.[31]

Clearly the type of system specified here has the structural characteristics designated by my category of competitive orthotonic polity, including both the monotonic and isotonic subtypes.[32] Let us note the differences in treatment, however. Shils attributes to his model not only a few minimal structures needed for a definition but a considerable list of additional structures, such as an independent judiciary, and also fairly detailed prescriptions about the behavior of legislators, the need for universal suffrage, etc. Moreover, what I have defined as a bureaucracy is broken down into several components, each treated separately, including the executive branch (which covers more than my concept of the executive), the civil service, the military, the police, and an intelligence system. Functional relationships are built into the model by definition, as when Shils specifies that "a hierarchically organized bureaucracy" carries out policies of the executive, and the executive is answerable to the legislature. Apparently Shils conceives of bureaucracy as not necessarily hierarchic but does not imagine that it could exercise political or non-administrative functions. In other words, he seems to be thinking of bureaucracy functionally, as an apparatus that performs civilian administrative functions. Thus, when he says that the civil service

31. *Ibid.*, pp. 55–56.

32. Elsewhere I have proposed that the term contratonic be used for orthotonic polities with competitive constitutive systems, including both monotonic and isotonic polities. See "Some Problems with System Theory" in Michael Haas and Henry Kariel (eds.), *Approaches to the Study of Political Science* (San Francisco, in press).

must be "competent" and "well enough trained and organized" to implement legislative and executive policies, he is specifying functional relationships, not structures likely to make these functions possible.

To clarify the difference in approach, let me restate the definition of monotonic and isotonic polities: they are tonic polities in which the executive system is accountable, the constitutive system competitive, and the bureaucracy compensated. All of the other structural features specified by Shils may be given as hypotheses rather than as part of the definition or the model. For example, we might then hypothesize that most, though not all, orthotonic polities have universal suffrage. We can hypothesize that bureaucracies in such polities are typically well enough trained and organized to carry out public policies, but this functional attribute is not ascribed by definition. If we found a political system meeting the formal criteria for an isotonic polity, but whose civil service was not notably competent, or where the president failed to "work in collaboration with the majority party in the legislature," we would not be required on these grounds to say that this was not an isotonic polity.

The difficulties raised by the considerable list of characteristics posited for the Shils model become apparent when he writes, "No existing states really fulfill all the preconditions for the effective working of the regime of political democracy."[33] I would formulate the underlying idea rather differently. Having identified a set of polities which meet the formal criteria for a competitive orthotonic system, we could then compare members of this set with each other in terms of the relative degree of effectiveness of their administrative machinery, their relative responsiveness to political forces, relative degrees of centralization and of protection for opposition parties, levels of civility, etc. Shils's procedure has been, rather, to construct an elaborate idealized model whose standards are fully met by no state.

A further difficulty arises from the general context within which Shils presents his typology. He is dealing, essentially, with the new states, by which he means only those states which have

33. *Ibid.*, p. 59

secured their formal independence in recent decades. This includes many, but not all, of the countries of Africa and Asia. It excludes Latin America, which is described as an intermediate zone between the modern and unmodern states. It excludes old states of Asia and Africa, such as Japan, China, Iran, Thailand, Ethiopia, and of course all the countries of the West and of Eastern Europe, including the Soviet Union. Since most of the political democracies clearly fall within these excluded categories, Shils can scarcely point to a new state to illustrate his model. He does, however, indicate that India's regime is "as close to political democracy as a large inheritance of cultural, economic, and political obstacles permits."[34]

By contrast, the typology of tonic polities is designed to refer to all political systems which have the specified structures: a constitutive system, executive, and bureaucracy. Since this includes almost all the countries of the contemporary world, it provides a more general basis for comparison. The category of competitive orthotonic polity, moreover, includes not only most of the Western countries but also, I would guess, more of the new states than India.

Let us look next at Shils's fourth category, totalitarian oligarchy. He first discusses totalitarianism, mentioning the bolshevist and the traditionalist (German, Italian, Japanese) examples, and indicates that it is the former model which has the greater appeal in the new states. However, he writes, "no new state has yet become communist, so the picture of totalitarian oligarchy which we present will be drawn from doctrine rather than from practice."[35] This self-denying restriction seems remarkably unnecessary. Both North Korea and North Vietnam had Communist regimes when Shils published his essay, and there are certainly old but not developed states, such as China, Cuba, and Albania, which might have been used to illustrate practice rather than doctrine.

The central feature of the totalitarian oligarchy is said to be "a single party rather than a clique, with its own powerful bureauc-

34. *Ibid.*
35. *Ibid.*, p. 75.

racy, which controls the party and, through the party, the bureaucracy of the state." The ruling (Communist) party possesses a monopoly of power, "tolerating the independent existence of no other party." These polities dispense with parliamentary institutions "except for acclamatory and ceremonial purposes." There are popular elections, Shils says, but they do not determine the composition of the elite.

In discussing the machinery of authority in totalitarian oligarchies, Shils writes that these regimes require "a vast administrative apparatus." Since this apparatus is subject to numerous deficiencies, it "will require supplementary controls, such as party supervision over the governmental bureaucracy. Partly to control this bureaucracy, partly to control the citizenry, partly to control the elite itself (outside the governing clique), an elaborate, dense, and intense police apparatus is a necessity for such a regime."[36]

This description largely fits our definition of an anatonic polity, i.e., an orthotonic polity in which the constitutive system is not competitive, and in which the bureaucracy is compensated. But Shils cannot specify that the bureaucracy be compensated, and therefore his description will also apply to polities having uncompensated bureaucracies of Type IV, namely hypotonic polities, that is, syntonic polities with non-competitive constitutive systems. The Shils classification is shown here to be both too broad and too narrow. It is too broad in that it lumps together two types of polities which need to be distinguished structurally if we are to understand why some states with a ruling ideologically oriented party are more developed than others. It is too narrow in that, while including most polities with a ruling party, it excludes those which permit competition, namely atonic polities. Nor does the classification provide any clearly defined category for this rather important type of competitive hegemonic party regime.

The relation between ruling party and bureaucracy in the Shils category of totalitarian oligarchy is also obscured by an unnecessarily complex formulation. As described, we can visualize a ruling (party) bureaucracy controlling a party which in turn

36. *Ibid.*, pp. 75–78.

controls a vast (state) bureaucracy which in turn is controlled by an elaborate police apparatus. If, instead, we think of the structure of anatonic and hypotonic polities as consisting of a noncompetitive constitutive system and a bureaucracy, the model becomes easier to understand. Large parties normally have their own bureaucracy, and ruling parties even more so than competitive parties. Moreover, all bureaucracies need to be controlled if they are to work effectively to implement policies. In a ruling party regime, competing parties and associations are suppressed, as are independant courts, which means that full responsibility for control over the (state) bureaucracy falls on the party (including its bureaucracy).

All complex bureaucracies also contain internal divisions among competing units, some of which may be charged with responsibility for inspecting and controlling other units. It seems natural to hypothesize, therefore, that in these ruling party regimes—where the bureaucracy has to be inflated to take over functions performed in competitive regimes by private organizations—the specialized agencies of the bureaucracy with investigatory and police functions should also become inflated. It is not claimed that one way of describing the structure of these regimes is correct, the other incorrect, but rather that one is simpler than the other and also facilitates comparison with other types of polities.

It is interesting that although these two categories of political systems described by Shils include all orthotonic polities and therefore a considerable number of contemporary states, they apply to very few of the new states, the limiting set of polities examined by Shils. It looks as though, in essence, he has simply taken the conventional idea of democratic and totalitarian systems, based primarily on European experience, and tried to extend it, even though marginally, to the countries of Asia and Africa.

Are there, perhaps, in his other categories concepts which would more appropriately characterize the polities of the new states? Let us consider the third category, modernizing oligarchies, which seems to come closest to meeting this criterion.

Shils indicates that a modernizing oligarchy has a well-organized cliquelike elite. It eliminates parliament as an autonomous power, reducing it to "acclamatory and ratifying roles," and may dissolve all political parties or all but one party, or interfere with election results and procedures to safeguard its power. "Modernizing oligarchies," Shils writes,

> must depend on an elaborate machinery of bureaucratic administration. Civilian oligarchical elites, even when they claim to reform the obtaining structure of government, are likely to compromise with their inherited civil service and retain most of the old personnel, installing a few of the "new men" in crucial positions, and sometimes even recruiting certain senior civil servants of the old regime for posts in the cabinet. Military oligarchies, too, must utilize most of the civilian civil service, since they are not in a position to replace it by their own military bureaucracy. The desire of the oligarchies to modernize will force them to depend on the civil service to a large extent.[37]

Here, surely, we have a description of the usual characteristics of homotonic polities. Shils asserts that the new states have shown a tendency toward oligarchy, citing Pakistan, Sudan, the United Arab Republic, and Iraq as examples. Among the functional characteristics of these regimes, we are told, are their drive against corruption and disorder and their desire to modernize.

It is interesting that Shils thinks a modernizing oligarchy can consist of a civilian elite. He does not recognize the bureaucratic basis of such elites—they seem to appear from nowhere and then impose their will on both the party system, the bureaucratic administration, and the military forces. He mixes together two characteristics which seem to me to contradict each other. On the one hand, parliament is reduced to ceremonial and advisory roles, but on the other the oligarchy struggles against political parties and strives to manipulate elections. It will be recalled that homotonic polities were divided into two types according to the power position of the constitutive system. If the legislature is fully under control, then I infer that a single official party monopolizes most of the seats, and presumably either co-opts the legislators who are freely elected or controls the nomination of all candidates for

37. *Ibid.*, p. 69.

election. This is the structure we have identified as autotonic. By contrast, where the regime finds itself struggling with parties and elections, we find polities in which the constitutive system is down but not out, and where elected legislators may still hope to influence the composition of the elite in some significant way: in a word, these are antitonic polities.

The basic distinction between the concept of a modernizing oligarchy and my notion of a homotonic polity is that the latter idea indicates the source of the ruling elite as a group of higher officials in a bureaucracy capable of naming its own members, for the most part, to first echelon posts. Such a ruling clique, in my opinion, would almost always consist primarily of military officers, not civilians, but it would also have to co-opt experienced civil servants to fill important posts in the bureaucracy. But this is a matter of hypothesis, not of definition.

Moreover, the concept of a homotonic polity is free of assumptions about how the system performs, whether or not it is modernizing, administratively effective, or honest. Indeed, these are all dimensions on which homotonic polities display a considerable range of variation. As tonic polities, they would all by definition have constitutive systems and therefore would have engaged in some modernization. The extent to which a homotonic polity would engage in further modernization might well be left open for empirical investigation rather than asserted as a matter of definition. In other words, bureaucratic polities may vary between wide limits in the degree to which they are modernizing.

The second category used in Shil's classification is somewhat more confusing and confused. He calls it tutelary democracy and describes it as a system similar to that of political democracy, but it involves greater executive power, more discipline by a ruling party, and "the peaks of the executive branch of the government of the dominant party move closer to identity than they do in a regime of political democracy." A strong personality is needed to maintain discipline, and parliament, if it is retained, is much weakened.

> The elite in a tutelary democracy must be attached to the idea of democracy and sincerely hope, in the course of time and ultimately, to see it flourish. It will, when it coincides with the

> plans of the executive, permit certain institutions of political democracy to continue to operate effectively, such as parliamentary and journalistic criticism, university autonomy, etc. . . . It will, therefore, as the occasion arises, reinstate or establish anew some of the institutions of political democracy.[38]

Among the preconditions for a tutelary democracy are said to be a competent civil service, an independent judiciary, and "the leadership of the armed forces must accept the supremacy of the civilian political elite."[39]

The nearest convergence between this description and my typology is the atonic polity, in which a hegemonic party nevertheless permits opposition parties. Non-competitive ruling party systems of the hypotonic type are excluded, so that a tutelary democracy does not cover the same concept as syntonic polity. Although it may be true that a tutelary democracy requires a competent civil service, it seems doubtful whether, in practice, it often has one. If it did, then it would probably also have to rely on experienced insiders to staff its third echelon positions, which means that it might qualify for classification as an orthotonic polity. Perhaps what Shils has in mind is something that might be classified on the margin between atonic polities and competitive orthotonic polities.

Some of the characteristics of a tutelary democracy are to be found in those colonial regimes which I have classified as antetonic polities. By limiting the scope of his work to the new states, Shils deliberately excludes from his scheme regimes in which foreign rulers might actually have been interested in promoting democratic structures and practices as long-term but not immediately practicable goals. Certainly if one were to look concretely at India or the Philippines before independence, one might have found many of the functional and structural characteristics attributed by Shils to the tutelary democracies.

Perhaps more significantly, these characteristics could also be found in hypertonic polities, systems with non-accountable elected executives. Such charismatic leaders, as we have seen, are capable of converting the executive office into an independently

38. *Ibid.*, p. 62.
39. *Ibid.*, p. 65.

powerful organ, and they maintain their personal rule by playing the bureaucracy and the constitutive system against each other. I suspect that such leaders frequently espouse the idea of democratic tutelage as a long-term goal to justify their own roles as tutors.

Our third type of protonic polity, marked by non-accountable hereditary executives, may also have many of the characteristics of tutelary democracies. Shils, however, scarcely finds any monarchies in his collection of new states. To the extent that he does find traditional structures of government, he refers to them as traditional oligarchies, the fifth term in his scheme. Apter's term, "modernizing autocracy," would perhaps come closer to my idea of a paratonic polity, for we have here not truly traditional (i.e., non-tonic) monarchies, but kingdoms in which modernization has gone far enough to generate a constitutive system.

For Shils, traditional oligarchy centers on an ascriptively recruited ruler, whose basis of legitimation is religious, who is surrounded by a palace retinue or court, who has no need for legislative bodies, and whose civil service is limited in size and patrimonial in character, rather than bureaucratic. Not surprisingly, Shils does not find traditional oligarchies in control of government in any of the new states, but he suggests that "traces of traditional oligarchy" will be found in all of them because "it is the proper polity of the traditional society."[40]

In the sense that older institutions of government survive the addition of new ones, it is no doubt true that monarchic forms of executive persist, not only in some transitional societies but even more notably in some of the most successful Western democracies. It is, indeed, precisely in the new states that kingships have been most thoroughly discredited. Monarchic institutions in which royal power persists are mainly found not in the modern or in the new states but in some of the old and modernizing polities of Asia and Africa, such as Iran, Ethiopia, Morocco, Jordan, Nepal, Kuwait, and recently, in Greece. But it greatly oversimplifies these regimes to think of them merely as modernizing autocracies. They do have constitutive systems which, somewhat fitfully and intermittently, can exercise decisive power. Nor are their

40. *Ibid.*, pp. 80–82.

bureaucracies the rudimentary, patrimonial establishments suggested by Shils. Indeed, some traditional monarchies, long before the invention of constitutive systems, had generated large-scale bureaucracies, as in the Chinese, Roman, Byzantine, and Ottoman empires and in post-medieval Europe. I suspect that one reason Shils views traditional oligarchies only in terms of modest, feudalistic, and patrimonial institutions is because he tends to look on large-scale bureaucracy as a typically modern phenomenon. This is a view shared by many experts in public administration who have given little thought to bureaucratic phenomena outside the contemporary West. A more comparative and historical view will see bureaucracy itself, as well as monarchy, as a survival in modern times of a traditional institution.

This comparative analysis and summary of the typology for new states proposed by Edward Shils has been presented in the hope that it would test the comprehensivness and utility of the scheme presented in this chapter. It is also hoped that this exercise will relate the new classification to some of the existing literature of comparative politics. Table 5 should aid the visualization of the comparisons discussed above. The second column

Table 5. ***Classificatory Equivalents—Riggs, Shils, Apter***

Tonic Polities After Riggs	*Regime Types* After Shils	*Regime Types* After Apter
ORTHOTONIC	Political democracy	No equivalent
Monotonic	Political democracy	Parliamentary democracy
Isotonic	Political democracy	Presidential democracy
Anatonic	Totalitarian oligarchy	Totalitarian
SYNTONIC	No equivalent	No equivalent
Hypotonic	Totalitarian oligarchy	Mobilization system
Atonic	Tutelary democracy	Reconciliation system
HOMOTONIC	Modernizing oligarchy	No equivalent
Autotonic	No equivalent	Military oligarchy
Antitonic	No equivalent	Neo-mercantilist society
PROTONIC	No equivalent	No equivalent
Hypertonic	Tutelary democracy	Charismatic
Antetonic	No equivalent	Colonial
Paratonic	Traditional oligarchy	Modernizing autocracy

gives the terms used by Shils, and the third column combines Apter's terms with other familiar descriptive words.

Causes and consequences: Some hypotheses

Most of this chapter has consisted of a rather extended discussion of structural criteria which can be used to classify a wide variety of contemporary political systems. The construction of typologies is often deplored as an idle exercise likely to postpone the time when truly fruitful theory about political and administrative behavior can be formulated. We are urged to forget about models and classificatory schemes and proceed directly to the important task, which is to explain and predict behaviors.

I fully agree that our primary objective should indeed be the development of fruitful theory and that classification as such is not theory in this sense. But fruitful theory must wait upon the formulation of helpful classifications because it is otherwise unable to specify the context within which propositions are valid. Duverger's theories about the relations between political parties and voting systems, for example, may hold with relatively little need for modification in orthotonic polities, yet be quite untrue for heterotonic polities. If so, it becomes a simple matter to state the conditions to which these theories apply. Otherwise one becomes entangled in endless debate, either rejecting the theories out of hand because of the many countries in which they do not work, or introducing a long list of qualifications to explain the exceptions. Similarly, I find Sartori's propositions about political parties to be extremely fruitful in the analysis of variant behavior within monotonic polities, but they are much more difficult to use fruitfully for other types of systems.

The same kind of statement may be made with reference to problems of administrative reform. Doctrines propounded in the American literature on administrative reform seem to me to be highly relevant and useful for work in an isotonic polity, and much of the British doctrine in this field is very helpful when applied to a monotonic polity. But both varieties of administrative theory tend to produce paradoxical and perverse results when applied to syntonic, homotonic, and protonic polities.

Classification schemes propounded in the past have not been more helpful because they were not clearly based on structural principles of analysis. They mixed functional with structural criteria in such a fashion that they were difficult to operationalize and illogical to apply and they confused definitions with hypotheses. There is no advantage in attempting to classify political systems by functional criteria. Consider such terms as "effectiveness" and "centralization." Reformers are naturally interested in administrative effectiveness, and it might seem useful, therefore, to classify governments in terms of the degree of effectiveness of their administrations. Degrees of centralization might also be used. When we talk about more and less developed systems we are, of course, doing the same kind of thing.

Where a functional variable is concerned, we should not use it as a basis of classification, but we can well use it for purposes of comparison. In other words, several items of the same structural class can be compared with each other in terms of a functional variable, but it is probably not useful to try to classify them by the same functional criterion. I would, for example, hypothesize that the level of development in orthotonic polities is generally higher than in heterotonic systems, and that the degree of concentration of power is generally greater in anatonic than in isotonic polities. If we can make such statements, then we can next formulate propositions about why such relationships should hold, and we can test them empirically with comparative data. This would enable us to seek means to change systems to enhance the functional goals we prize.

This brings us to the problem of explanation. The typology of polities presented above does not in itself explain change or development. The dynamics of change from one type of polity to another are not contained within the structural characteristics of the polity itself. Each system, indeed, may be regarded as a self-perpetuating structure of government likely to maintain itself unless changed by the intrusion of some external influence. Thus it provides a framework for discussing problems of developmental change but is not intended by itself to account for either the causes or the consequences of such change.

For explanation, therefore, I look to ecological theory and to the political process as such. By ecological theory I mean the need to understand how external forces—such as population change, technological innovation, foreign invasion and military threats, the spread of ideologies and religions, and economic growth or decline—influence political systems. By political processes I understand the conscious decisions made by human beings acting in organized collectivities to achieve common purposes. Such decisions may, of course, be imposed by one or a few upon many, or they may reflect the outcome of widespread participation in bargaining processes and efforts to arrive at a consensus. Our structural typology explains neither ecological constraints nor political decisions affecting processes of change. But it does provide a framework for examining these processes.

For example, I submit that large-scale collectivities can formulate and implement decisions far more effectively if these decisions are processed through the structures of an orthotonic polity than if they are processed by heterotonic polities, and I suspect that any tonic polity can also make and implement decisions better than any, or certainly most, non-tonic polities. Such decisions include schemes to modify the physical and human environment of a polity.

Taking economic growth as an outcome of efforts to manipulate the non-human environment of a society, a politically developed system would be able to do more to promote economic growth than a less developed system. Accordingly I would expect orthotonic polities to be found, for the most part, in the more economically developed societies, and I would expect heterotonic polities to prevail in the less developed economies.

I am indebted to Professor Samuel Finer for suggesting the use of the Yale indicators to check this hypothesis. Among these indicators, the most obvious one is per capita GNP. As of 1957 there were thirty-four countries with a per capita income over $U.S. 400.[41]

41. Bruce M. Russett *et al., World Handbook of Political and Social Indicators* (New Haven, 1964), p. 155. The list follows:

1. Kuwait	$2,900	3. Canada	1,947
2. United States	2,577	4. Switzerland	1,428

The countries of the world have not yet been coded in terms of the criteria used in the classification of tonic polities. However, my impressionistic coding of the list of thirty-four countries having per capita GNP above $400 gives a list of twenty-nine, or 85 per cent, which probably have orthotonic polities. Eighty-nine countries are listed as having per capita GNP below $400, of which, by the most favorable estimate, 11 or 12 per cent might be classified as having orthotonic polities. If we considered only the countries having per capita income below $200, of which there are sixty-two, only one, India, appears to have an orthotonic polity, giving 1.2 per cent.

On this showing most of the more economically developed countries have orthotonic polities, and most of the less developed ones do not. Although there are exceptions on both sides of the line, which is to be expected in any statistical association of this sort, they provide opportunities for additional hypothesizing. The country with the highest per capita income, Kuwait, happens to have fabulous natural resources in relation to its population in the form of underground oil which has been exploited by foreign companies who have paid great royalties to the Kuwait government. Obviously the ratio of natural resources to population provides a basis for predicting that some countries will do well economically despite the lack of an orthotonic polity, and others will do poorly, even though they have an orthotonic polity. Thus, at the other extreme, we might feel that India has an orthotonic polity even though its per capita income is at the $73 level, but it is burdened with a vast population in relation to its resources, as

5.	Luxembourg	1,388
6.	Sweden	1,380
7.	Australia	1,316
8.	New Zealand	1,310
9.	Belgium	1,196
10.	United Kingdom	1,189
11.	Norway	1,130
12.	Denmark	1,057
13.	France	943
14.	West Germany	927
15.	Netherlands	836
16.	Finland	794
17.	Israel	726
18.	Czechoslovakia	680
19.	Austria	670
20.	Venezuela	648
21.	Soviet Union	600
22.	East Germany	600
23.	Iceland	572
24.	Puerto Rico	563
25.	Ireland	550
26.	Italy	516
27.	Argentina	490
28.	Hungary	490
29.	Uruguay	478
30.	Poland	475
31.	Cyprus	467
32.	Cuba	431
33.	Trinidad and Tobago	423
34.	Singapore	400

is China at about the same economic level, with a polity that is probably atonic but possibly could become anatonic without any great increase of per capita production. Japan, clearly a highly industrialized country with a monotonic polity still has a relatively low per capita income, $306, attributable in great measure to its high population in relation to resources.

This exercise does not by itself indicate causal relationships. One could argue that economic growth favors the establishment of orthotonic polities or that the creation of an orthotonic polity favors economic growth. The truth is probably a combination of both views; there are feedback effects such that economic growth makes it easier to create an orthotonic polity, and the establishment of such a polity makes it easier to adopt and carry out policies favoring economic growth. In this way an improvement in the ecology aids decision-making, and increased ability to make political decisions reinforces desired ecological transformations.

These considerations relate to one of the dimensions of ecological variation discussed in the opening portion of this chapter, namely development. What about democratization? Can anything be said about the prospects for democracy in relation to types of political systems? The prospects for democratic decision-making and social justice are greater if the constitutive system is competitive than if it is non-competitive in any tonic polity.

There will perhaps be no great disagreement with this proposition so far as orthotonic polities are concerned. We have defined non-competitive orthotonic polities as anatonic, and the competitive variety includes both monotonic and isotonic polities. The Soviet Union and several East European states are probably the leading examples of anatonic polities; the West European, North American, a few Latin-American and Commonwealth countries and Japan are the isotonic and monotonic (i.e. contratonic) polities.

More difficulty arises in relation to the heterotonic polities, the remainder of the modernizing states. Among these the homotonic polities do not have dominant constitutive systems, even though they may hold open elections. Among the syntonic polities, the atonic variety has a competitive constitutive system, but one which is precariously liable to dissolution. Paratonic polities may also contain a significant potential for democratization, under somewhat unstable and unpredictable circumstances. Impressionistically, the prospects for democratization are better in atonic, antitonic, and antetonic polities than they are in hypotonic, autotonic, and paratonic polities, but again, we would no doubt find considerable variation from and exceptions to this hypothesis in an empirical analysis, after coding all contemporary governments.

Let us now relate what has been said above to the process of modernization, which involves emulative acculturation of foreign models, and in our times this includes the adoption of material technology, scientific knowledge, governmental institutions, and other cultural traits evolved in the West. As part of this modernization process, constitutive systems and the structures of complex bureaucracy have diffused throughout the world so that there is scarcely a country today that does not have a tonic polity.

Technical assistance programs are systematically designed to accelerate this process of modernization by helping recipient countries adopt the structural features of contributing countries. They do this in the name of development, although often with the concurrent expectation that democratization will also be an outcome. As we have seen before, however, structures are functionally ambiguous. Paradoxically, structures which have served one function in their original homes may serve quite contrary functions elsewhere. In orthotonic polities, for example, measures of administrative reform which involve increasing the complexity and strengthening the career orientation of the bureaucracy serve to enhance the capacity of the government to carry out public policies. But if the constitutive system of a polity is incapable of controlling the government, then the same structural changes, made in the name of administrative reform, may well have the different consequence of strengthening tendencies toward the establishment of a homotonic polity. Military dictatorships, in other words, are a likely outcome of administrative reform in countries with weak constitutive systems, including atonic and paratonic polities.

If the regime is hypotonic, the same administrative reforms could lead to development, but surely in the non-democratic direction of establishing an anatonic polity. If the regime is antetonic, then the probable consequence of administrative reform will be to speed up the growth of revolutionary discontent and the eventual overthrow of the antetonic regime itself.

If the goal of administrative reform were the establishment of polities likely to be capable of sustaining both political development and democratization, then the aim of public policy would presumably be to encourage activities likely to lead to the creation of monotonic or isotonic polities. If this were so, the reforms to be promoted in any particular case would be designed in light of its type of polity.

For example, if one were dealing with a homotonic polity, priority might be given to strengthening the constitutive system in the hope that it would secure control over the bureaucracy and make it more politically responsive. Projects of reform which involved working directly with the bureaucracy would be thought of in terms of their indirect impact on the prospects of the constitutive system.[42] By contrast, if one were dealing with an atonic polity, efforts to stabilize and strengthen the career system might directly enhance the prospects of democratic development, but if the polity were hypotonic, the likely outcome of administrative reform might well be the establishment of an anatonic system, developed but not democratic.

In conclusion, then, the theory of administrative reform is likely to be improved if it takes into account the governmental context of reform, and a structurally based classification of political systems seems to be necessary for this purpose. The precise criteria used for the classification proposed in this chapter may need to be revised, but the approach taken is one which should enable us to deal more intelligently with the whole question of administrative reform.

42. My essay "Bureaucrats and Political Development: A Paradoxical View," further develops this subject.

Glossary of Terms Defined and Given a Technical Meaning in this Chapter

accountable executive: an executive subject to replacement by authority of the constitutive system or bureaucracy in a tonic polity

administrative capability: a functional relation between a polity and its bureaucracy involving effective and efficient implementation of policies and programs

anatonic polity: an orthotonic polity with a non-competitive constitutive system

antetonic polity: a protonic polity with an appointive executive

antitonic polity: an homotonic polity with an intermittently influential constitutive system

assembly-based: ability of the elected assembly of a syntonic polity to designate first echelon bureaucrats or control governmental expenditures

assembly-oriented: authority of the elected assembly in an orthotonic polity to dissolve the government, and the practice of appointing assembly members to first echelon positions

atonic polity: a syntonic polity with a competitive constitutive system

autotonic polity: an homotonic polity with an uninfluential constitutive system

balance: a functional relationship between bureaucracy and polity characterized by simultaneous presence of political responsiveness and administrative capability

bureaucracy: a hierarchy of offices subject to the authority of an executive

compensated bureaucracy: a bureaucracy in a neotonic polity with a predominance of outsiders holding first echelon posts and of insiders holding third echelon posts

competitive constitutive system: a constitutive system in which opposition parties nominate candidates for elections

complex bureaucracy: line- and staff-type organization having multiplicity of command

compound bureaucracy: two or more simple bureaucracies superimposed

constitutive system: a component of polities, containing an elected assembly, an electoral system, and one or more political parties contratonic polity: an orthotonic polity with a competitive constitutive system, i.e. an isotonic or orthotonic polity

democratization: a function of political systems involving expanded popular participation in decision-making and access to the outputs of government

development: a function of political systems involving increased ability to shape and reshape their environment

elected assembly: a collegial organization most of whose members are elected

elections: a procedure whereby voters cast ballots for one or more candidates for public offices

executive: an office which asserts authority over a polity

free election: an election in which voters choose between two or more candidates for the key positions to be filled by the election

function: a relation between a structure and a system involving mutual influence or interaction

heterotonic polity: a neotonic polity with a non-compensated constitutive system

homotonic polity: a neotonic polity with a Type I bureaucracy. The meaning assigned to the prefix "homo-" here refers to identity or similarity. In this context it means that political direction of bureaucracy is provided by bureaucrats not by extra-bureaucratic institutions.

hypertonic polity: a protonic polity with an elective executive on life tenure

hypotonic polity: a syntonic polity with a non-competitive constitutive system

isotonic polity: an orthotonic polity with a competitive but not assembly-oriented constitutive system

legitimizing election: an election in which voters are normally given a choice only between yes and no for a single candidate for each office

modernization: a function involving the emulative acculturation of structures, institutions, and practices

monotonic polity: an orthotonic polity with a competitive, assembly-oriented constitutive system

neotonic polity: a tonic polity with an accountable executive

non-orthotonic polities: include heterotonic, protonic, and non-tonic polities

non-tonic polity: a polity without a constitutive system

orthotonic polity: a neotonic polity with a compensated bureaucracy
paratonic polity: a protonic polity with an hereditary executive
partisan: degree of identification of bureaucrats with a party
party: an organization which nominates candidates for election to an assembly
political responsiveness: a functional relation between a bureaucracy and its polity involving willingness to internalize and implement norms and policies formulated by the constitutive system
politicization: degree of involvement of bureaucrats in struggles for power and in the shaping of key governmental policies
polity: political system at the societal level
protonic polity: a tonic polity with a non-accountable executive
simple bureaucracy: a bureaucracy with unity of command
structure: a pattern of action of components of a polity
syntonic polity: a neotonic polity with Type IV bureaucracy
tonic polity: a polity with an executive, complex bureaucracy, and constitutive system
Type I bureaucracy: a bureaucracy in a neotonic polity in which first, second, and third echelon posts are predominantly filled by insiders
Type II bureaucracy: a bureaucracy in a neotonic polity in which first echelon posts are predominantly filled by outsiders, second and third echelon posts by insiders
Type III bureaucracy: a bureaucracy in a neotonic polity in which first and second echelon posts are predominantly filled by outsiders, third echelon posts by insiders
Type IV bureaucracy: a bureaucracy in a neotonic polity in which first, second, and third echelon posts are all predominantly filled by outsiders
Type V bureaucracy: a bureaucracy in a neotonic polity which is not of Type I to IV
Type VI bureaucracy: a bureaucracy in a protonic polity

·7·

Political and Administrative Development: General Commentary

Martin Landau

The chapters in this volume turn on theoretical problems of administrative reform in developing states. The issues raised have to do with the logic of inquiry, the theory of development, and the substance of development administration. Because, however, so rich a variety of analysis is presented I have chosen to limit attention to two rather important and persistent problems in development analysis: names and concepts and the use of persuasive terms in theoretical analysis. In so doing, I shall give most of my attention to Chapter 6 by Fred W. Riggs and shall refer in an ancillary way to Chapters 1, 2, 4, and 5, by Ralph Braibanti, Carl J. Friedrich, Henry S. Kariel, and Joseph LaPalombara, respectively. The commentary is concluded by a general analysis of distinctions between ends and means, in which the primary referrent is Friedrich's chapter. The net effect of this decision is an imbalance of treatment, but this is not to suggest that those chapters which are only minimally referred to, if at all, are unimportant contributions. On the contrary. I hasten to add, too, that I can make no comment on Joseph J. Spengler's chapter for reasons that have to do with limitations of my own competence in economics. The critique which follows is offered on the understanding that the building of knowledge is a process that must be indifferent to personality and motivation and that such a process rests always and exclusively upon argument and evidence.

I. Names and Concepts

In the initial stages of any inquiry, concepts are rarely defined so as to permit a determination of their extension with any appreciable degree of precision. What this means is that we are often not sure of what it is we are talking about, looking at, or looking for. Ominous as this may sound, it is not necessarily a cause for alarm. If we had certainty with respect to the object at issue, there would be no reason to enter upon its study. Inquiry thus always begins with vague notions which, by a process of successive definition, sometimes lead to formulations of great power.

But it is to be emphasized that in its early stages, systematic investigation must employ lexical terms—those with conventional meanings. These frequently, if not always, result in paradox: their denotations are much clearer than their designations. By custom and convention, that which they point to is recognizable, the things they denote are relatively clear, but the *grounds* upon which identification is made remain quite implicit. Investigation, therefore, appears to be loose and ambiguous, shifting and imprecise, and loaded with bias. Once the ground itself is opened to question, the process of redefinition has begun.

With this in mind, I wish to discuss first the matter of naming and conceptualization as it emerges in the chapter by Fred Riggs. I shall be direct in my comment if only because Riggs is, in my view, one of the foremost theoreticians in the area of political and administrative development. No one at work in this domain is without obligation to him—which is the same as saying that the entire field is in his intellectual debt. What troubles me, however, is that his formulations have not generated the research they warrant.

It may well be that this is the result of a rather large volume of writing which appears sprawling and unorganized. And, to be sure, the Parsonian output of Riggs is in need of a similar codification if the basic structure of his theory is to be exposed. Although this is a weakness, the major problem turns on the use of a vocabulary that is at once esoteric and alien and which, contrary to its intention, obscures the theory. The continuous, almost relentless, introduction of new names makes it extremely difficult to order Riggs's work and serves, in addition, as an obstacle to the development of a standardized vocabulary. Accordingly, I want to offer some comment on names and concepts.

There is appended to Riggs's essay a glossary of some fifty-odd terms, each of which is defined by stipulation; that is, each is assigned a definite meaning by Riggs. A general exposition in a technical domain often carries a similar glossary, but the definitions are lexical: i.e., the glossary is a list of the names of important concepts in the field and the more or less standardized meanings of these concepts as they are used in that field.[1] The glossary itself is a convenient reference for readers since they can always turn to it should they be puzzled about the meaning of a term. Such a glossary is especially helpful to the lay reader or the untrained student, who, not too familiar with the usual or standard terms of discourse, can there ease his difficulties. For the professional reader, no such glossary is necessary since it is assumed that he possesses the same working vocabulary. On occasion, of course, a new term will be introduced and its author will both explain and demonstrate its need.

But the fact that a new concept is offered does not mean that it will be accepted. Standard vocabularies are marks of considerable development in any field and are built, as all knowledge is built, rather slowly and carefully. In this process, a great many terms are volunteered but only a few are retained. Some, presented with the appearance of authority—say, from a highly reputed scholar—may enter a technical vocabulary easily, only to be discarded as their promise fails to materialize. Those that do remain, that become standard terms of discourse, are not and cannot be legislated from on high. They are employed because they do their job—they name concepts that possess a demonstrated power. In such a field, research is organized on the basis of these concepts.

1. See, for example, Colin Cherry, *On Human Communication* (New York, 1957).

One can, therefore, understand Riggs's effort to provide a technical vocabulary. In one sense it is quite salutary. For it is true that our locutions in this field vary widely, that many of our key terms are ambiguous, that we often use the same name for different concepts and different names for the same concept. With a considerable integrity, Riggs seeks to avoid such confusions by making his usage as exact as he can. In this effort, he invents a rather large number of new concepts, so many in fact that any reader is transformed into a novice. The glossary is really necessary.

It is one thing, however, to seek to clarify an existing concept, and another to invent one. Moreover, it is often not clear whether we are inventing a new concept or a new name, a neologism. For a name and a concept are by no means identical. A concept is a class term and it consists of a set of properties or attributes. The set of characteristics which define the concept (its intension) provide the criteria by which we assign things to the class (its extension). The name of the concept is a tag we append to it for purposes of convenience.

In his chapter, Riggs employs the term "tonic" polity. Originally, this was presented in a discussion of "whole political systems," but there it was subordinate to a naming system based upon the root form "cephal" which was used to tag such systems.[2] Here, however, the focus is more restricted and tonic anchors the analysis.

Tonic polity is given a formal definition—one which is stipulated. Stipulative definitions are crucial, absolutely necessary, when a new term is introduced; otherwise one is lost as to its meaning. Nor is it required that the definition be wholly original. It suffices that it be novel in the domain of discourse in which it is introduced. Once presented, however, it constitutes a proposal for adoption. The receiver may accept or reject the proposal. If we find that it has advantage, that it reduces surplus meaning, eliminates emotive connotations, and organizes the intended

2. Fred W. Riggs, "The Comparison of Whole Political Systems," in Robert T. Holt and John Turner (eds.), *The Methodology of Comparative Research* (New York, 1969). Here the classification system includes such terms as metacephalies, heterocephalies, orthocephalies, procephalies, acephalies, and supracephaly.

sphere of application more effectively than any other concept, we will undoubtedly accept it. We may do so on any one of these grounds, depending upon the nature of the problem which confronts us. If there are too many sets of meanings assigned to one name, we may find it helpful to narrow this down by using one term for one set. If the term has persuasive force where we wish a purely cognitive construct, we may again create a new term for the concept. But if none of these factors weighs heavily, and if it cannot be shown that they do interfere with our understanding of the problem, then the new terms may confuse more than enlighten. Coining new terms cannot be wholly arbitrary; the minter must take due account of existing linguistic practice and the problem at hand. It suffices to note that many of the fundamental terms in physics—force, field, wave, particle, mass, friction—were drawn from the vernacular.

To return to tonic polity, we find that it consists of an executive, a complex bureaucracy, and a constitutive system. To proceed further, a polity is a political system at the societal level. Riggs does not define political and allows it to remain primitive. An executive is an office (used interchangeably with role) which asserts authority (undefined) over a polity. A complex bureaucracy (bureaucracy itself is defined as a hierarchy of offices subject to the authority of an executive) is one in which there is a multiplicity of command as represented by a line-staff type organization. And a constitutive system consists of an elected assembly, an electoral system, and one or more political parties. In turn, an elected assembly is a collegial organization most of whose members are elected, and electoral system (elections) is a procedure whereby voters cast ballots for one or more candidates for public offices. And, finally, a party is an organization which nominates candidates for election to public office. Needless to say, all definitions are Riggs's.

We can now say that a tonic polity is one which consists of an office which asserts authority over a political system, a hierarchy of subordinate offices, a collegial organization most of whose members are elected, a procedure whereby voters cast ballots for such public offices, and an organization which nominates candidates for these offices. Alternatively, we may say that a tonic polity is one which possesses an executive, a bureaucracy, an assembly, an election system, and parties—what we usually refer to as a governmental system. Indeed, we even have terms (concepts) which indicate the logic of relations (structure) which obtain among these components, as when we say separation of powers, presidential system, party government, and the like. To be sure, this form of address is not very precise, but it may nevertheless be superior to the notion of tonic with all its "precision." It is, after all, a relational (and, therefore, a structural) construct while tonic is merely a collection of components.

In any case, it is difficult if not impossible to determine or to appreciate what is new about this concept. Ordinarily, the appearance of a new term in the analysis of a problem signals a new concept, a new category of analysis, a new system of classification. But this is not so here. A tonic polity is a very familiar notion to me, although I did not know its name.

There is, however, a special utility in fixing a name on a concept, even an old one. Frequently we allow concepts to slip by us because they are not labeled. When they are named, they can more easily be called to mind and put to use. It may, therefore, be helpful to accept the name tonic. If I hesitate, however, my doubt has to do with the fact that Riggs uses the three major properties of a tonic polity to form a vast classification system—further complicated by the fact that each of these properties is itself subdivided. The result is a bewildering number of names, each standing for a particular subclass: orthotonic polity, homotonic, syntonic, anatonic, antetonic, antitonic, protonic, paratonic, heterotonic, neotonic, montonic, isotonic, hypotonic, hypertonic, atonic, and non-tonic. Interestingly enough, the intention of this effort is very well placed. In establishing a set of constant reference points, a typology of formal structures, a basis for charting change is set down: by distinguishing between formal structures and the functions they perform we can see what has happened.[3]

It follows, then, that the tonic formula is not simply "a mne-

3. Riggs's chapter in this volume, p. 223.

monic and heuristic device," as Riggs suggests,[4] designed to help keep the basic concepts in view. Far more is involved: a theory, however incomplete. Riggs may see his formulations as only a framework for the treatment of "developmental change" and may look to enlarge it by means of what he calls "ecological" factors.[5] But his definitions are all within a stated theoretical context, informed by the basic concept of structure. He is, therefore, raising a hypothesis, as do all classifications the moment we raise inquiry about their extension. What he is saying is that his concepts, all presented as sets of structural properties, will permit us to predict the behavior of those polities which the class term covers. Thus, the level of development in orthotonic polities is generally higher than in heterotonic systems, and the degree of concentration of power is generally greater in anatonic than in isotonic polities.[6]

To fix the point, let us look at the latter hypothesis somewhat more carefully. Both classes are tonic (having an executive, a complex bureaucracy, and a constitutive system). Both have accountable executives and a compensated bureaucracy, but the isotonic polity has a competitive but not assembly-oriented constitutive system, and the anatonic a non-competitive system. A competitive system is one in which opposition parties nominate candidates for election.[7]

Now I am not sure whether we have a hypothesis before us or a tautology, but let us assume the former. The distinguishing feature here, as nearly as I can follow, seems to be opposition politics or party competition. Suppose, then, that we have two countries, A and B. A falls into the class isotonic and B is anatonic. In placing them in their respective classes, we are stating that each possesses the requisite class properties. Suppose, again, that while I knew Riggs's classification system well, I had never encountered these countries in any way. All that I knew was that one, B, was anatonic and the other was isotonic. Would I not then claim

4. *Ibid.*, p. 249.
5. *Ibid.*, p. 317.
6. See p. 265.
7. *Ibid.*, p. 322.

(predict) that B would evidence in its operations a much greater degree of concentration of power? In fact, I would go further and state categorically that A has at least two parties and B has only one. Were I to find the opposite, I would immediately wonder whether we have classified these countries properly. And if I had a classification system, the extension of which permitted the prediction of only the most obvious behaviors, its value would be quite debatable.

But I do not wish to question the value of Riggs's system. The more immediate trouble is that the typology itself is elusive. It is so hard to work with. It would be one thing if it consisted of a few well-chosen basic properties divided into a few subclasses, each with a name. Logically speaking, Riggs's system could be easily reduced without any damage and with much profit. A reader could keep in mind four or five simple terms and follow the discussion with relative ease, even to the point of internal consistency. With fifteen or more neologisms, however, all rather tortuous, it becomes almost impossible to read his formulations. The names get in the way. To check the proposal about anatonic and isotonic polities, I had to swing back and forth: first to tonic, then to isotonic and anatonic, then to orthotonic, to anatonic again, and then to neotonic, to compensated bureaucracy, back to isotonic and anatonic, and I am still not sure I have it. One has the double task of keeping track of the name of each type and what it stands for, and the result is simply the loss of the line of analysis. The central question—the relationship between types of governmental structures and administrative operations—is all but obscured. One concludes Riggs's chapter not with a clear set of concepts, not with a clear statement of their interrelationships, but with a long list of names. And names do not provide any basis for research.

Finally, I wish also to point to one special irony revealed by Riggs's essay. If there is any concept that we have tried to move to the point of standardization, it is bureaucracy. As LaPalombara points out, the "classical formulation of the distinguishing features" (defining properties) of bureaucracy is Max Weber's.[8]

8. LaPalombara's chapter in this volume, pp. 171 ff. Cf. below, p. 221.

And elsewhere I have argued that the formulation is so classic as to have reached the status of a paradigm, in Kuhn's sense.[9] Apparently, although I may misread Riggs here, he does not wish to use this concept because it contains functional properties.[10] Instead, he selects "hierarchy of offices" under an executive and proceeds to call this bureaucracy. Since this usage, however, is different from the usual, and is in fact a different concept, why retain the original name?

By way of contrast, Braibanti's procedure in the introduction of new terms and the assignment of new meanings to old terms is rather striking. Seeking to identify characteristics of political development that are germane to administrative reform, he transfers the term "architectonic" to stand for "an overarching purpose which gives form, cohesion, and direction to all public action within a sensed community." In doing so, he reviews the usage of several terms which roughly express the whole or parts of this concept. In one case, the instance of "polity," he states that earlier published formulations of his paper employed this term but with its meaning changed—narrowed from its original Aristotelian usage. This, however, "appears now to be somewhat of an impertinence as well as perplexing, since 'polity,' so ancient a term and with little change in connotation, fulfils an important expository and conceptual need, and is comfortably seated in the literature."[11] Hence the need for "architectonics."

In not following this rule, which is so sensible precisely because it is economic, Riggs, despite an expressed doubt as to the wisdom of using bureaucracy to name hierarchy of offices,[12] contributes much to the ambiguity he strives to reduce. One patent illustration should suffice: employing the classical for-

9. See "Sociology and the Study of Formal Organization" in Dwight Waldo *et al.*, *The Study of Organizational Behavior,* Papers in Comparative Public Administration, Special Series No. 8 (Washington, 1966). The concept of paradigm, central to Thomas S. Kuhn's *The Structure of Scientific Revolutions* (Chicago, 1962), cannot briefly be defined; in a sense Kuhn's entire book is its definition. It embraces a widely shared commitment to the same rules and standards for scientific practice, a consensus about the nature of problems to be solved, yet an open-endedness for redefinition by succeeding groups of practitioners (pp. 10–11).

10. Riggs, pp. 221, 227, above.

11. Braibanti's chapter in this volume, p. 37.

12. Riggs, p. 221 above.

mulation, LaPalombara accepts bureaucracy to be a product of the West, not to be found before the seventeenth century; for Riggs, however, it is scarcely to be taken as a Western invention.[13]

It might appear to the uninitiated reader that this is an empirical difference, to be resolved by further research. In fact, however, it constitutes a semantic difference—there are two distinct concepts involved and each denotes a different institution.

Terminology is thus a problem of telling proportions in any empirical domain. If we seek a knowledge that is publicly accessible to all, that is independent of personality, then our working vocabularies must possess clear and standard meanings. It is worth emphasizing that this rule is at the base of proposals which call for operational definitions, the goal of which is to develop concepts (and terms) that have identical meanings for all who use them. If standard vocabularies can be had, the power of our theories and concepts can be put to effective test. But if we employ vocabularies that are idiosyncratic, that disregard conventional disciplinary usage, the net effect must be a semantic confusion that restricts effective exchange of experience as it promotes unnecessary research. It behooves all of us at work in an empirical domain to treat our language with great care.

II. Theoretical Analysis and Persuasive Discourse

Among the many methodological problems that beset students of politics, none is more vexing than the subtle but powerful tendency to employ "persuasive" definitions in theoretical discourse. The significance of this difficulty is to be seen in the fact that such definitions are essentially evocative in character and are to be distinguished from other types of definitions by their appeal to interests, to dearly held values, and to emotion.[14]

The presence of persuasive definitions is always to be observed when there is a conflict of interest or a difference in ideology. An

13. LaPalombara, pp. 170 ff, and Riggs, p. 223, above.

14. Charles Leslie Stevenson, "Persuasive Definitions," *Mind,* XLVII (1938), 331–350. See also Irving M. Copi, *Introduction to Logic* (New York, 1961), pp. 99–107.

election campaign, a protest meeting, the summation of a trial attorney, a legislative debate, a session of the Security Council—all these situations will be replete with the familiar device of shifting the conceptual meaning of a term without in any way changing its emotive content. In such circumstances, this may be a sensible propagandist procedure; for the special purpose or rhetorical function of a persuasive definition is to move people, to effect a change in their attitudes, not to classify, delimit, or differentiate. But it is not to be assumed that their appearance is limited to exhortation. Any definition—theoretical, stipulative, lexical—can become persuasive: it does so the moment evocative elements override cognitive elements. There is always the risk, then, that persuasive definitions will intrude quite implicitly—an intrusion which is traceable to the value-laden connotations of the definiendum. And there is the further risk that such intrusion will not be recognized for what it is, thereby contributing to considerable confusion. Needless to say, as we have noted earlier, this is a primary ground for the introduction of neologisms in scientific discourse.

In political science, we have an additional difficulty. As an empirical discipline, our concern is with matters of fact and the relations which obtain among them. I trust, of course, that it is not necessary to defend this statement—a trust, incidentally, which is sustained by the efforts of both Carl J. Friedrich and Henry S. Kariel to ground their discussion of ends on empirical foundations in their respective chapters in this volume.

Yet many of our terms, those in widest use, are patently ethical constructs. They are, as Friedrich says, elements which the world "goes on bitterly fighting over."[15] To be sure, such concepts as freedom, justice, democracy, representation, responsibility, and participation have considerable cognitive content. But they carry enormous valuational connotations. This is immediately to be seen when we couch them in the negative, for the negation here is not simply a contrary cognitive assertion. It is far more. What, indeed, is the character of the meaning involved when we say of something that it is undemocratic, or unrepresentative, or irre-

15. Friedrich's chapter in this volume, p. 108.

sponsible? Responsible government, democratic government, representative government—is it clear that these are good governments and the contrary are bad?

Now, in using terms like responsible or representative, we assume that because we have stipulated definitions that are nowise preferential, we have transformed them into cold, precise, and technical concepts. We therefore operate as if this process has neutralized their ethical or emotive connotations. But the plain fact seems to be that for all our efforts to establish these terms as descriptive concepts, their meaning is essentially emotive or evocative in character. If so, theoretical analysis which turns on such concepts will oscillate between the demands of theory and those of desire. The net result is bound to be a confusion which helps neither. I suspect that this is one difficulty that confounds us in the analysis of political development. Perhaps I can demonstrate this, but a few comments on the concept itself may be in order before doing so.

Political development is, as we all know, neither a new concept nor a distinctive one from the standpoint of program. It was absorbed into the methodology of American political science at the very time that the empirical discipline was established.[16] No one who reads the work of Woodrow Wilson, A. Lawrence Lowell, Frank Goodnow, or Henry Jones Ford can escape the evolutionary thrust of their analysis. Indeed, it was precisely the concept of development and change that prompted their revolt against a moral Newtonianism that had controlled for so long. They rejected the existing "vocabulary of our constitutional language," holding that it constituted a "literary theory" (model) which had obscured the reality of development. Names, Wilson cautioned, "are much more persistent than the functions upon which they were originally bestowed; . . . institutions constantly undergo essential alterations of character, whilst retaining the names conferred upon them in their first estate; and the history

16. I may also add that as a mode of analysis it was generally misunderstood by those who rejected it as traditional or formalistic. See Martin Landau, "The Myth of Hyperfactualism in the Study of American Politics," *Political Science Quarterly*, LXXIII (1968), 378–399.

of our own Constitution is but another illustration of this universal principle of institutional change."[17] At about the same time, Lowell proposed that a political system "is an organism, and in order to appreciate its possible forms and the causes of its development, stability or decay, it is necessary to investigate the laws of its organic life." This was the "fresh and original approach" that was the hallmark of the new political science.[18]

What, then, is distinctive about the contemporary effort? The answer lies in the difference between a metaphor and a model.[19] Whereas the early pragmatists proclaimed an atheoretic bias—seeking to avoid the "temptations of the deductive method," pursuing their research "unclouded by theory," and, in general, adopting, as Goodnow put it, a "policy of opportunism"—we have reversed this procedure, eschewing opportunistic *ad hoc* formulations as we seek, deliberately and consciously, to build appropriate and effective models.

Partly, this is a product of our intellectual climate. But it may also be said that the exasperating problem of the new states has assigned a new priority to theory-building. Interest in these countries was originally stimulated by matters of practical concern, which is the way most inquiry begins. Quite apart from practical considerations—or rather because of our early involvements—it has become obvious that such countries actually constitute a new set of phenomena for us: they defied our usual classification systems and presented, therefore, a vast uncharted area. Hence we have been prompted to review our formulas and have thereby been forced into the construction of models by which to represent this phenomenon. Moreover, the opening of a vast new research area which provides a laboratory-like setting for the study of institutional change permits us to raise formulations whose range of application can be tested against the universe of

17. Woodrow Wilson, *Congressional Government* (New York, 1956), p. 28.

18. See Martin Landau, "On the Use of Metaphor in Political Analysis," *Social Research*, XXVIII (1961), 331–353, and "The Myth of Hyperfactualism in the Study of American Politics," *Political Science Quarterly*, LXXIII, 378–399.

19. See Martin Landau, "Due Process of Inquiry," *American Behavioral Scientist*, IX (1965), 4–10.

states. This is one time, as George Washington Plunkett might say, that "we seen our opportunity and took it."

Accordingly, we have become preoccupied with our first major theoretical problem—the invention of a classification system that would simplify (order) our object of inquiry. Heretofore, however, our basic class terms, many of which are contained in the constitution where they appear as state descriptions that are to last indefinitely, were largely employed on the assumption that the data they organized were discrete in character. And, indeed, a good deal of it is. But we have met with increasing difficulty in assigning behavior to a particular class. There are too many borderline cases, there is a vast twilight zone or penumbra—which terms are employed because we cannot precisely distinguish a strong executive, a party government, a responsible bureaucracy, or a developed polity.[20] This inability to mark off clearly the class of behavior involved may be the result of faulty definition in the first place. But it is more likely that this difficulty will be greeted with a firm declaration that politics does not lend itself to clean, precise, and mutually exclusive boundary markers. This has often been used as an excuse to avoid the arduous task of definition—leaving us with a set of disjunctive classes (either-or) which we use as we violate them.

Difficulties in assignment, however, may very well suggest that "those characteristics of the subject matter which are to provide the defining basis of classification cannot fruitfully be construed as simple property concepts determining, as their extensions, classes with neatly demarcated boundaries."[21] That is, our subject matter is continuous in character, hence we had best approach it in terms of more or less, not either-or, and on the basis of graduations, not inclusion and exclusion. In the area of political development, this posture is mandated by definition.

20. For pertinent discussion of the problem of classification as it relates to difficulties in comparison, see Ralph Braibanti, "Comparative Political Analytics Reconsidered," *Journal of Politics*, XXX (1968), 25–66, esp. 40–44.

21. Carl G. Hempel, "Typological Methods in the Social Sciences," in Maurice A. Natanson (ed.), *Philosophy of the Social Sciences: A Reader* (New York, 1963), p. 213.

Accordingly, the sphere of comparative politics and administration has been struggling to create a classification system which forces recognition of the continuous character of its problem area. It is in this context that Riggs's original formulations are so impressive. Tackling the thorny problem of traditional, transitional or modern systems, Riggs's fundamental point of departure is the principle of structural differentiation and functional specialization which he has coupled to several Parsonian pattern variables. These dichtomous variables, interestingly enough, provide the polar points of a scale of differentiation which marks the range of variation within which societies can be ordered in terms of degree. It is thus possible, in principle, to plot (describe) any society on this scale, thereby permitting movement "from the classificatory, qualitative level of concept formation to the quantitative one."[22] In this respect Riggs's work is truly comparative; not because of its coverage of numerous countries but because it provides an orderly framework for both diachronic and synchronic analysis.

This venture is not unique. It can be observed that the concept of development, defined in terms of structural differentiation and functional specificity, seems to have attained the status of a paradigm in this sphere of interest. There are some variations on the theme, but these are either minor or derivative.

Pye, in one estimate of the state of inquiry, distinguishes some ten basic formulations and then proceeds to extract a "developmental syndrome" consisting of three basic properties: equality, capacity, and differentiation. Equality as a definitive factor is immediately persuasive, but I do not wish to dwell upon it. It involves participation ("active citizens or at least the pretense of popular rule are necessary"), laws which are universalistic (the rule of law), and recruitment on the basis of achievement (the well-known merit principle). Capacity, a more neutral term, has to do with the ability of the government to affect society and economy and thus is associated with performance and scale of operations. Differentiation, of course, refers to the specialization

22. *Ibid.*, p. 216.

of structures: distinct offices, limited functions, and division of labor within government. There is an added note here that differentiation entails an ultimate integration.[23]

Upon analysis, however, differentiation emerges as the critical property of development, if not the only one. That is, capacity is conjoined to differentiation so closely that it may be no more than a logical extension thereof. Structural differentiation means an increase in the scale of performance, an observation which we may make more easily by noting that Pye states, "with differentiation there is also, of course, increased functional specificity of the various political roles in the system."[24] Specification of role, needless to say, entails a fixed domain of operations. So far as equality is concerned, universalistic law is implicit in functional specificity; otherwise neither the merit system (the achievement principle) nor the substitutability of actors could obtain. As regards participation—mass participation, that is—it seems to me to be theoretically irrelevant. If Pye were to suggest pluralism as we usually understand it, it could be shown that this too is entailed by differentiation and specialization. It does appear that we will not find differentiation and capacity as defined here to vary inversely anywhere. But one always remains open to correction. It can be noted thus that Braibanti, generally silent with respect to differentiation as a necessary aspect of development, strongly suggests its reversibility.[25]

To continue, LaPalombara marks out four major properties: structural differentiation, magnitude, achievement, and secularization.[26] Magnitude is not defined with any appreciable clarity and is therefore a difficult variable to work with. But it seems to be employed in a manner similar to Pye's use of capacity. It stands as a "ratio of political activity to all other activity that takes place in a society." By definition, then, it can only be

23. Lucian W. Pye, "The Concept of Political Development," *Annals of the American Academy of Political and Social Science*, CCCLVIII (1965), 1–14.

24. *Ibid.*, p. 12.

25. Braibanti, p. 65 above. See also Kariel's chapter in this volume, p. 164, n. 30.

26. Joseph LaPalombara, "An Overview of Bureaucracy and Political Development," in LaPalombara (ed.), *Bureaucracy and Political Development* (Princeton, 1963), pp. 39–48. See also Martin Landau, "On the Use of Functional Analysis in American Political Science," *Social Research*, XXXV (1968), 48–76.

observed upon the appearance of differentiation and, as LaPalombara notes, "will increase as greater structural specialization evolves." We need not deal with "achievement orientation" again, and with respect to secularization, it too is implicit in differentiation.[27] If we turn to Almond's work,[28] he also builds upon differentiation and specificity. For Eisenstadt, "the first characteristic of political modernization is a high degree of differentiation. . . ."[29] The list could be extended at great length.

From this brief exercise, it should be clear that scholars have assumed the defining property of development to be structural differentiation and functional specificity. Those additional properties which are usually stipulated are either redundant or they have the status of accompanying characteristics. What remains in bold relief is the proposal that rates and levels of development are to be addressed as rates and levels of differentiation.

It is well to remember, however, that what we have been puzzling over is the concept of "development," not that of "political." In the latter case, the variety of locutions to be found in this volume, as in the literature, do not obscure the fact that this term is taken as a primitive. There are occasional references to something like the authoritative allocation of values, but the concept itself invariably remains non-problematical. Its meaning is intuitive; that is to say, it is employed quite conventionally. Its denotation, therefore, presents no mystery since it is *known by custom and usage.* We all know that it refers to a system of government.

Now it would appear that our line of reasoning from this point on should be rather simple. To determine the extent of development, all we need to do is treat governmental systems in accordance with the rule of differentiation. To be sure, there are some difficult technical problems to be overcome, but these do not in principle bar us from plotting governmental systems in terms of

27. For a discussion of secularization in this context see Martin Landau, "Decision Theory and Development Administration," in Edward Weidner (ed.), *Development Administration in Asia* (Durham, N.C., forthcoming).

28. Gabriel A. Almond and G. Bingham Powell, *Comparative Politics* (Boston, 1966), and Fred W. Riggs, *Administration in Developing Countries* (Boston, 1964).

29. S. N. Eisenstadt, "Bureaucracy and Political Development," in LaPalombara (ed.), *Bureaucracy and Political Development,* p. 99.

the dimension specified. Just as economists may use per capita income as a rough indicator of economic development, as Spengler does in this volume, so we might use, in Max Weber's phrasing, "the quantitative extension of administrative tasks." This, or the extension of the merit system (recruitment on the basis of skill qualifications) may in fact provide us with a "simple and generalizable index of political development,"[30] but it is a fair suggestion that such a proposal would be opposed by the comment, "*That* isn't political development."

Such objection may be offered because it is felt that the index itself (contained in the principle of structural differentiation and functional specificity) is faulty. But it is more likely that the objection is more *persuasive* than otherwise. For, as can be seen in the chapters by Braibanti, Friedrich, Kariel, and LaPalombara, politics is a term that is richly laden in values and, therefore, emotion. Mixed emotion, more precisely, because the emotive meaning of this word varies in accordance with the approved value system of different groups. I cannot extend upon this here, but to contemporary scholars, politics does not connote graft, cynicism, chicane, and sheer opportunism as it may for the man in the street when he declares, "That's politics." It was so in the days when political scientists joined with civic movements to take politics out of government, but in our time it is, rather, the goodness of democracy, constitutionalism, participation, and the sharing of power that is meant.

Hence it is that in retaining "political" as a primitive term to be understood conventionally, its fairly stable emotive meaning is maintained even when its conceptual elements are rearranged (by means of a stipulative definition) in the interests of purity. As a result, the tacit element of persuasion works to transform analysis and argument into advocacy and debate. The process is subtle but is to be observed in the widespread tendency to react negatively to formulations that do not include such "good" attributes. On the positive side, Braibanti's brief review of prevailing definitions serves to illustrate conceptualizations which are quite evocative.[31] Or better still, the following: "political development

30. Spengler's chapter in this volume, p. 589.
31. Braibanti, pp. 34–36 above.

is in quintessence the ordering of the affairs of men into a polity more or less commonly agreed upon, clearly known, capable of rational adjustment, the whole being infused with qualities of freedom ennobling the puny lives of those who have formed the state." Morever, it "can be viewed as a series of ultimate progressions (with periodic regressions and even oscillations) from ascription to personal achievement, from ambiguity to certainty in the use of public power, from alienation and withdrawal to enlightened participation . . . , from coarseness and coercion to refinement and sensitivity in public action, from contraction to expansion of free choice." This moving language need now only be reinforced by the magnificent statement from the encyclical *Populorum Progressio* "to do more, know more and have more in order to be more."[32] Against such persuasive rhetoric, who can stand? I, for one, am ready to toss my index to the fires below.

Before doing so, however, let me illustrate this phenomenon another way. The institutional manifestation of either index is, of course, bureaucracy. We can, therefore, return to Max Weber's original proposals, as we invariably do. What is interesting here is the way we repeat them and the way we resist them.

We repeat them because we have to. But frequently discussions of the bureaucratic paradigm transform it into a checklist of simple class properties, against which bureaucracies themselves are measured. What emerges, of course, is the "finding" that the paradigm has much less than universal application, that there are rather sharp variations in actual bureaucracies, many of which are quite irrational. Thus, one case after another is produced to demonstrate the weakness of the model.

What is often lost sight of, however, and we owe this observation to Carl Hempel, is the fact that Weber was not defining bureaucracy by genus and difference, under which specific cases could be covered.[33] On the contrary, Weber thought it was "nonsense" to even try, and he used this word.[34] What he thought he was constructing was a genuinely comparative typology—a limiting concept—against which one could determine the *extent* to

32. *Ibid.*, p. 34.
33. "Typological Methods in the Social Sciences," p. 211.
34. Max Weber, "Objectivity in Social Science and Social Policy," in Natanson (ed.), *Philosophy of the Social Sciences*, p. 399.

which a given concrete situation "approximates to or diverges from" the model.[35] This is entirely consistent with his fundamental formulas, built upon painstaking analysis of historical change, which establish a direction of movement from Kadi-justice to a legal rational order. The latter is to be understood as a system founded upon the *principle of substantiation* where "the presentation of facts is decisive." Hence the pre-eminence of the trained expert, the informing principle of differentiation, which not only establishes bureaucracy as the major institutional form of modern society and government but makes the latter "absolutely dependent upon a bureaucratic basis." Indeed, "the larger the state, and the more it is or the more it becomes a great power state, the more unconditionally is this the case."[36] The proposal here is not for a classification bureaucracy which permits sharp and precise coverage of discrete cases but for a polar point bureaucracy which permits concrete institutions to be ordered in terms of "the extent to which." The closer a system approaches this point, the more is it "modern."

If we understand this logic, it is pointless to suggest that systems are mixed no matter how modern. Nor need we be surprised that particularism, spontaneity, ascription, traditionalism, nepotism, are also to be found; on the contrary, they should be anticipated. But it is also to be anticipated that as institutions assume a bureaucratic form, "action orientations" based on kinship, tradition, and personal sympathy weaken to the point of displacement. Not without great tension, however, as Abueva's chapter demonstrates. For in this process, one cultural mode is being replaced by another—sometimes quite abruptly.

Nevertheless, Weber is unequivocal in the statement that the "peculiarities" of modern society demand an absolute and unconditional dependence upon bureaucracy. These transform the "quantitative extension of administrative tasks" into "qualitative changes of administrative tasks." Rules, matter-of-factness, and the means-end calculus, "dominate the bearing" of the mature

35. *Ibid.*, p. 396.
36. *From Max Weber,* trans. and ed. H. H. Gerth and C. Wright Mills (New York, 1958), p. 211.

bureaucracy. It is rational, precise, technical, and ordered, and the "more complicated and specialized [we would say structurally differentiated and functionally specific] modern culture becomes, the more its external supporting apparatus demands the personally detached and strictly 'objective' *expert*."[37]

There is thus predicted a new order of social relations, a new "style of life," a new set of cultural rules for the pursuit of any social objective. These give rise to an action orientation unlike any known in the past, the summation of which Ilchman refers to as "rational productivity bureaucracy."[38] So powerful is this phenomenon that it tends increasingly to characterize the whole of governmental operations, let alone those of the external sectors. All we need do is to look about us to see its penetrating effects. There is little doubt that the primary institutional characteristic of highly complex and differentiated societies is bureaucracy.

Yet such a conclusion is troubling: not because of any logical or empirical weakness but because, as Merton put it, bureaucracy is a *Schimpfwort*.[39] It is pertinent to note that "bureacuracy" entered the English language about 1848 and soon after was stamped by Carlyle as that "continental nuisance." It is invariably tied to the rise of Prussia and Germany, thus enabling the caution that it was the product of a set of values and an ideology which were anything but democratic.[40] Indeed, if we follow Laski, it is more: it is a profound threat to public liberty. And from Kariel, after Marcuse, we learn that it is a breeder of "one-dimensional man." And such men may be "ritualists," exhibit the "insolence of office," and if not this, then a "trained incapacity to think." We have a long way to go in purifying this concept of its persuasive power, but it should be clear that a large part of its meaning is emotive.

It is one thing, however, to evaluate the phenomena a theoretical proposal directs us to and quite another to evaluate the proposal itself. In the former case a value judgment is expressed,

37. *Ibid.*, pp. 212–219, 244. Emphasis in original.
38. Ilchman's chapter in this volume, pp. 474 ff.
39. Robert K. Merton, "Bureaucratic Structure and Personality," in Merton *et al.*, *Reader in Bureaucracy* (Glencoe, Ill., 1952), p. 364.
40. LaPalombara, p. 173 above.

and in the latter the worth of the proposal depends upon empirical demonstration. It appears, however, that many of our criticisms of Weber are not so much directed to his theory as to the phenomenon which he predicted. By a subtle stroke, antipathy to the phenomenon of bureaucracy is transferred to the theory itself. There is then a tendency to inquire into the motivation of the theorist, the values that prompt—so to speak—the theory itself. Thereafter, the test of the theory can easily become the ethics of its father. When this occurs, the theory has been transformed into ideology and the universe of discourse has changed.

With respect to Max Weber, this has been done in many ways, two of which are immediately relevant—the assignment of a "metaphysical pathos" and the selected use of rhetoric. Originally, it was Alvin Gouldner who urged that the metaphysical pathos of the theory of bureaucracy was "pessimism and fatalism."[41] And it is on the foundation of this pathos that both Kariel and LaPalombara erect their caveats, warning us about the dangers inherent in the acceptance of Weber's theories. But when Arthur O. Lovejoy introduced this term, his primary concern was to establish "the ultimate objects" of interest for the historian of ideas. "Of what sort . . . are the elements, the primary and persistent or recurrent dynamic units, of the history of thought, of which he is in quest?" Among these elements, Lovejoy included metaphysical pathos—"exemplified in any description of the nature of things, any characterization of the world to which one belongs, *in terms which, like the words of a poem, awaken through their associations, and through a sort of empathy which they engender, a congenial mood or tone of feeling* on the part of the philosopher or his readers."[42] The point of this, however, was not to assert, as Gouldner does, that "those who have committed themselves to a theory always get more than they have bargained for";[43] rather, Lovejoy suggests, there exist susceptibilities to various types of pathos, and this plays a part both in the formation of

41. "Metaphysical Pathos and the Theory of Bureaucracy," *American Political Science Review*, XLIX (1955), 496–507.

42. *The Great Chain of Being*, Harper Torchbook, (New York, 1960), pp. 7, 11. Emphasis added.

43. "Metaphysical Pathos," p. 498.

"philosophical systems" and in their public reception. And this he adds, "has nothing to do with philosophy as a science," we may say with theory as theory; it has "to do with philosophy as a factor in history."[44]

Suppose, however, that we allow a metaphysical pathos in the case of a theory. It would still have nothing to do with the power of the theory, or with its range of application. The test of a theory must always stand independent of the personality, the values, the motives of the theorist. Otherwise, criticism reduces to the *ad hominem,* and we have blocked the way of inquiry.

Assume, nevertheless, that we cannot escape a metaphysical susceptibility and that Weber's theory is bathed in pathos of necessity. Then it follows that Friedrich, Kariel, and LaPalombara must respond in accordance with their own moods. For the metaphysical pathos which they exhibit is most pronounced and rarely disguised, and it is not at all congenial to such proposals as those which Weber offers. This, in good measure, accounts for the tendency to transform theoretical problems into ideological contests. But even more, it begets a selective use of rhetoric which is frankly persuasive and designed to elicit an emotive response.

Thus, Friedrich, in commenting on Weber's discussion of election and appointment, hierarchy, control, and discipline, writes: "The very words vibrate with something of the Prussian enthusiasm for the military type organization. . . ." Now I have never felt such vibration despite the fact that I have been told this many times. Should I persist in my position, however, there may be added to the discussion the assertion that "Weber's fully developed bureaucracy is most nearly represented by three modern organizations: (1) an army, (2) a business concern without any sort of employee or labor participation in management, (3) a totalitarian party and its bureaucratic administration." With this imagery, the conclusion is indeed inescapable that the more fully developed a bureaucracy, the less responsible it is.[45] But if one notes that "precision, speed, unambiguity, knowledge of the files,

44. *The Great Chain of Being,* pp. 13–14.

45. Carl J. Friedrich, "Some Observations on Weber's Analysis of Bureaucracy," in Merton *et al., Reader in Bureaucracy,* p. 31. See also LaPalombara, pp. 175 ff. above.

continuity, discretion, unity, strict subordination [read strict accountability]";[46] that "specializing administrative functions according to purely objective considerations"; that calculable rules and the "personally detached and strictly objective expert"—that these are the marks of full development,[47] then it is a fair hypothesis that it is "most nearly represented" by a rational-productivity bureaucracy (to use Ilchman's term).

Such, then, are the devices by which we tend to transform theoretical questions into ideological problems. By resorting to persuasive definitions, by allowing the implicit ethical connotations of so fundamental a concept as "political" to intrude, by assigning a metaphysical pathos, and by using a directive rhetoric, we all fall prey to this tendency. When this happens we are more likely to legislate preferred ends than engage in systematic analysis. We will, therefore, opt for political solutions to problems as against bureaucratic solutions. We will, of necessity, seek to enlarge the ratio of political activity to administrative activity on the assumption that politics is intrinsically superior to administration. This is so fundamental an ethic that we do not hestiate to export it. It appears to me, incidentally, that this is one reason why, as Montgomery puts it, "administrative reform has lost its grip on the imagination of political scientists."[48]

There was a time, however, when American political scientists —fully cognizant of the German experience—were not all that fearful of bureaucracy. This was a time when the ratio of political activity to administrative activity was very large. It was the time of the long ballot, the Black Horse Cavalry, and the "shame of the cities." Bosses, rings, courthouse and gashouse gangs, nepotism, favoritism, and chicane—this was "politics." It was all very personal, and if there were protected islands of objectivity, it was always possible to buy personal attention. This, incidentally, is the function of a bribe.

When, in this circumstance, the pragmatic political scientist came to offer solutions, it was bureaucracy that was to provide

46. Gerth and Mills (eds.), *From Max Weber,* p. 214.
47. *Ibid.,* pp. 214–216.
48. Montgomery's chapter in this volume, p. 427.

the correction. Along with a host of devices to depoliticalize many of the affairs of government, to reduce the ratio, the bureaucratic mode of operation—objective, efficient, technical, and achievement oriented—became a paramount preferred end. Constitutions and charters were rewritten, the short ballot was introduced, the system of public administration was extended, and its organizational form, under a strong executive, became monocratic. The highest priorities were assigned to the minimization of "political" interference, the establishment of technical qualifications for appointment, and the assignment of increasing authority, as Weber would say, to the personally detached and strictly objective expert. And all of this was under the banner of "democracy": *for it was then assumed that the primary tension derived from the relationship between democracy and "politics," not democracy and "bureaucracy."* There were, to be sure, cries of "administrative absolutism," resistance to an "administrative law," and dire predictions that the constitutional system was itself being undone. But again, as Weber would say, the external apparatus of an emerging industrial society demanded the action orientation most favorably offered by bureaucracy. It is not often observed that Frank Goodnow's celebrated *Politics and Administration* provides a theoretical basis for the "structual differentiation and functional specificity" which informed the praexiology of this period.

None of this is to suggest that there is no strain between politics and bureaucracy at the present time. But if the implicit ethical connotations of politics are as favorable as they seem to be, then this attitude may be attributed to the remarkable achievements of the American passion for administrative reform. The ideological implications of this page in history merit fully as much attention as does the German or the English experience. Theoretically, however, these variations serve to sustain Montgomery's general rule that bureaucracy is not to be presented as a constant surrounded by a set of dependent variables, but is itself a variable factor.[49]

49. *Ibid.*, p. 470.

III. Ends and Means

This rule can be stated alternatively following LaPalombara: an organization "exists within a particular cultural setting and will be influenced by and in turn influence that setting."[50] When phrased this way, we can recognize it as an expression of the familiar principle of "mutual interdependence." Drawn from the classic model of an energy-transfer system, it specifies that a statement about a system, or any part of it, takes in the environment as well.[51]

There are several implications of this rule, but the most immediate instructs that an organization will influence and be influenced to the extent that its distinguishing properties are distributed throughout the system of which it is a member. In the social sphere such properties are, in their fundamental form, existential and evaluative premises. When they are widely distributed, when there is a congruence between the organization and its task environment, the situation is rendered less uncertain; when there is not, it is fraught with hazard. Recognition that some degree of congruence is necessary for effective, mutually effective action, lies at the base of the caveat that Western canons of public administration cannot be automatically or uncritically applied in developing states. To do so is, indeed, to court mischief.

Existential and evaluative premises, however, are another way of speaking of fact and value and, thus, of means and ends.[52] Means-end relationships are problem-solving devices, and all societies have their own trusted recipes for meeting trouble. But trouble is precisely the loss of correlation between means and ends. When there is a good fit between the two, things run smoothly or at least predictably. If, however, there should arise anomalies, discrepancies between normal expectations and actual outcomes, the fit has been broken. If the break persists, an or-

50. LaPalombara, pp. 166–170 above.
51. See Landau, "Due Process of Inquiry." For discussion of an energy-transfer model, see Landau, "On the Use of Functional Analysis."
52. See Landau, "Decision Theory and Development Administration."

dered situation has become random and a reassessment of some kind must occur. The usual things (means) do not work any more and there is trouble. Whatever conflict and tension ensue, the stage has been set for the deliberate introduction of a change agent. For the overwhelming tendency of the twentieth century is not to leave such conditions to chance.

In general, therefore, and a fortiori as regards developing states, governments are brought into play in these troublesome situations. Their task, regardless of whether their jurisdictions are total or partial, is to act upon a set of conditions that are deemed unsatisfactory, and their goal is to produce outcomes which alter the existent condition in such manner as to constitute a solution to those problems which originally called forth their deployment. Hence, all governments are instrumental in character; they are, in Dewey's words, "intermediate between an existing situation and a situation that is to be brought into existence" by their own actions.[53]

This does not mean, however, that specific governmental or administrative or political arrangements cannot be valued. In fact, they must be. As Dewey puts it: "For every condition that has to be brought into existence in order to serve as a means is, *in that connection,* an object of desire and an end-in-view, while the end actually reached is a means to future ends as well as a test of valuations previously held."[54]

Now it should be clear that the principle of "mutual interdependence" mandates the *field-determined* character of the instruments we choose to solve problems with. And, in fact, we have come to understand this, which is why we are insistent in pointing to the transactional relationship between culture and instrument. Thus, we do not rush to apply the formidable technology of Western administration to developing states without considerable modification. We know full well that the epistemological premises which sustain this technology are not widely enough distributed in the environment and that any indiscriminate appli-

53. John Dewey, "Theory of Validation," *International Encyclopedia of Unified Science* (Chicago, 1939), II, Part IV, 27–33.

54. *Ibid.*, p. 43. Emphasis in the original. See also Herbert Simon, *Administrative Behavior* (New York, 1947).

cation is foolhardy. If we hesitate, therefore, it is because we recognize that the choice of means in any problem-solving situation is a crucial factor and is *to be valued only to the extent that it contributes to a solution.* Indeed, when a means arrangement continuously contributes the solution to a problem, we elevate it to the status of a process law and adopt it as the *best* means at our disposal. But the word "best" is to be understood as such only in a strictly defined field.

But what of ends. How are they to be regarded? The answer is partly given to us by Friedrich, in voicing his complaint that ends, objectives, and purposes are rarely discussed in terms of their content by students of development. In illustrating such ends, Friedrich asks, "Should economic development have priority . . . should it be agricultural or industrial, should capitalism or socialism be developed . . . should the development of democracy be given preference . . . or should strong, sizeable national states with a powerful bureaucracy (administration) be developed first."[55] Each of these alternatives, however, can easily be viewed not as *ends* but as *means,* for whether a condition is to be regarded as an end or a means can be determined only by the place it occupies in a means-ends chain. This is the essence of Dewey's quotation above. Such alternatives are not, therefore, ends in themselves for they presuppose even further ends—as the very form of Friedrich's question indicates. They are neither final nor ultimate and can only be regarded as intermediate. As intermediates, however, they necessarily become *means.* In this regard, our difficulties arise because we simply do not know which alternative is the best and which, accordingly, to value. There may come a time, however, when the state of our knowledge is such that we will be able to establish on empirical grounds that one or another of these alternatives is to be valued. What this will mean is that we have established a particular program of operation as the *means* which contributes most to the solution of a problem. In the absence of such knowledge, however, what we invariably do, what we have to do, is to cut the continuum at some point and establish this point as an *end.* Thereafter, we

55. Friedrich, p. 110 above.

quarrel over these ends on ideological grounds. But it should be clear that along the length of a means-end chain, knowledge and ideology bear an inverse relationship to each other.

Where, however, should we cut the chain? Here again the decision must be field determined. Relevant, important, valued, ends are only relevant, important, and valued in a cultural context. Ends are never "independent of the structure and requirements of some concrete empirical situation"[56] and cannot be treated as such. The logic which applies to a consideration of means applies to ends as well; for ends as outcomes can be anticipated "only in terms of the conditions by which they are brought into existence."[57] It follows, then, that an indiscriminate legislation of ends is as foolhardy as the indiscriminate application of means. Unless we understand the field-determined character of both means and ends we run the risk of maintaining a dreamworld even as we watch it collapse. It must be remembered that a means-ends relationship is a proposition, a hypothesis. If we break its contextual limits, we not only transform a hypothesis into sheer speculation, but we rob ourselves of the opportunity to observe consequences and, hence, to build knowledge. Effective development strategies depend, therefore, upon accurate appraisal of systematic conditions and upon the construction of means-ends continua that are contextually or systemically relevant. Thus, the existence of a one-dimensional bureaucrat may be a problem in the United States. In Vietnam, the problem may be to bring the one-dimensional bureaucrat into existence.

56. Dewey, "Theory of Validation," p. 55.
57. *Ibid.*, p. 35.

•8•

Toward a General Theory of Directed Value Accumulation and Institutional Development

Harold D. Lasswell and Allan R. Holmberg

The present chapter is a sketch of the criteria of a general theory of directed social change and a provisional outline of a theory that meets these specifications. Given the enormous scope of the task it is perhaps unnecessary to say more by way of disclaimer than to underscore the words "sketch" and "provisional outline."

The fundamental criterion of a general theory is contextuality. It must be inclusive enough to take into consideration all significant interactions in the social context of change. Because of the importance of the nation-state as the unit of decision in the contemporary world, we give prominence to the national frame of reference. However, a general theory must be formulated in ways that can be adapted to the world community as a whole, to transnational regions or to subnational communities.

Contextuality includes the requirement of versatility in regard to the goals of directed change, since development can be conceived in many different, even incompatible, terms. The general theory is basically a systematic model of social change whose primary categories provide an inventory of the most relevant variables in the process, and whose rules of interaction allow for the statement of static and dynamic equilibria confirmable by empirical observation. The theory must be equal to the challenge of studying the salient features of the past and of incorporating modifications of detail in the light of accumulating knowledge. A suitable theory is also required to provide guidance for the projection of past and present trends and conditioning factors into the future. A satisfactory theoretical system will, in addition, guide the policy-adviser or decision-maker in inventing and evaluating the net advantages of policy options.

The criteria may be summarized as principles of guidance in performing the intellectual tasks of problem-solving in reference to directed social change. The intellectual tasks are clarification of goal, discovery of salient trends, progressive analysis of conditioning factors, projection of futures, and invention, evaluation, and commitment to value maximizing policies.

Preference models

It may be worth emphasizing the point that social change can be directed toward terminal states that differ from one another in fundamental characteristics. Some preference models are inclusive of the value-institution processes of the community, while others are limited to a single sector. We are accustomed to thinking of economic models, and to an increasing extent preference models are gaining definition in terms of politics, health, education, and related sectors. Inclusive goals can be formulated in reference to human dignity or indignity, the former expressing aspirations toward a free society, the latter giving voice to the ideology of caste. Preference models differ in time span, extending from long-range through middle-range to immediate periods. In general, when we speak of goal values, we have in mind the overriding distribution pattern of power, wealth, and other values; less long-range and more particular objectives emerge in the context of immediate policy urgencies.

Social change generalized

We introduce at this point in the discussion a highly generalized mode of characterizing the process of social change. Change is social since it is interactive, involving in varying frequency and intensity all participants. Social change is a process, since it is not chaotic. As human beings are involved, valued outcomes are sought to be maximized (such valued outcomes are often called needs, desires, wants, preferences). The collective process of interaction is pursued by relatively stable patterns of practice which are somewhat specialized to particular value outcomes, which we call institutions. Institutions that prepare the outcomes are chiefly concerned with value-shaping (production); institutions functioning at the outcome and post-outcome level are concerned for the most part with value-sharing. In a phrase, social change is a process in which participants seek to maximize net value outcomes (values) by employing practices (institutions) affecting resources.

The choice of value-institution groupings

The general model we propose uses eight categories to distinguish the principal value-institution groupings in social process. These eight values are power (P), enlightenment (E), wealth (W), well-being (B), skill (S), affection (A), respect (R), rectitude (D). By using the letters assigned to each we can hereafter refer to the group by the acronym PEWBSARD. It need scarcely be said that there is no magic about the number eight. The choice was made with several considerations in mind. First, an inclusive list of terms is required in order to foster the comparative study equivalencies among observational fields or among equally inclusive, though different, lists. Second, a short list is required, since the number of specific outcomes sought is an unwieldy total. For instance, thousands of words are necessary to designate the articles on sale in a supermarket or the items of food and clothing in a given culture.

A third point is that the principal value-institution categories are especially convenient if they can be closely related to the several branches of specialized knowledge in the sciences relating to social process. It is evident that our terms refer to sectors of society that are investigated by readily discernible groups of scholars. The power value and the institutions of government are the province of political scientists, students of international relations, and jurists. The enlightenment value and institutions of communication and inquiry are studied by professors of journalism and others. The wealth value and economic institutions are the economists' concern. The well-being value and institutions of safety, health, and comfort are investigated by social biologists and specialists in public health. The skill value and institutions of pedagogy and of occupational and professional standards are objects of research by educators and occupational sociologists. The affection value and institutions of friendship, family, and loyalty come within the domain of anthropologists and sociologists of family and kinship structures. The respect value and institutions of caste and class fall within the scope of anthropologists and sociologists who deal with social structure. The rectitude value and institutions are the province of scholars of comparative religion and ethics.

Value outcomes are culminating events in the never ceasing interplay among participants in the social process. Power outcomes are the giving (and receiving) and the withholding (and rejection) of support in matters of community-wide concern. Enlightenment outcomes are the giving (and receiving) and withholding (and rejecting) of information about the social and natural context. Wealth outcomes are the giving (and receiving) and the withholding (and rejecting) of claims to processed and unprocessed resources. Well-being outcomes are the giving (and receiving) and the withholding (and rejecting) of opportunities directly affecting safety, health, and comfort. Skill outcomes are the giving (and receiving) and the withholding (and rejecting) of opportunities directly affecting the acquisition and exercise of proficiency in the performance of teachable, and learnable, operations. Affection outcomes are the giving (and receiving) and the withholding (and rejecting) of intimacy and loyalty. Respect is the giving (and receiving) and the withholding (and rejecting) of recognition. Rectitude is the giving (and receiving) and the withholding (and rejecting) of characterizations of conduct in terms of responsibility (religious, ethical).

Value-shaping and value-sharing

In these culminating situations, participants in the social process are seeking to maximize their net value position. A value indulgence is a positive gain or an avoided loss; a value deprivation is a positive loss or a blocked gain. To maximize net values is to use available values (base values) to influence outcomes in ways that leave the participant or participants relatively well off in terms of indulgences and deprivations of scope values (preferred values). Obviously any value may be a base for itself as a scope value (power for power, enlightenment for enlightenment, wealth for wealth, etc.) or as a base for another value as the scope value (power for enlightenment, power for wealth, etc.). The maximization postulate may be given a strict or a loose interpretation by the social analyst. A loose interpretation calls for a result that is relatively advantageous, though not the best possible.

The flow of preparatory events prior to the culminating outcome is value-shaping; outcome events of value-sharing foster value accumulation or value enjoyment, the former referring to the potential use of a value to shape more of itself, the latter referring to the potential use of value to obtain other values.

Functional and conventional meaning

The social scientist equipped with a value model who approaches a specific social context employs it to scan the interactions occurring therein for the purpose of identifying institutions that perform a functionally equivalent role. The practices that are relatively specialized to power outcomes (decisions), pre-outcomes and post-outcomes are the governmental, legal, or political institutions. Similarly, the institutions of enlightenment, wealth, well-being, and the other values can be located.

The distinction between functional and conventional categories is to be emphasized. The terms introduced in the scientific model are defined to serve the purposes of comparative research on all social contexts, regardless of inclusiveness or location in the time-space manifold of events. There are, however, rough equivalents current in the usage of most cultures. The investigator must, as a rule, begin his study of strange social contexts by identifying the situations that are conventionally regarded as approximations to power and other institutions.

The initial classification of situations may be drastically modified as research discloses the finer structure of the total process. At first, "medicine men" and their activities may be assigned to the category of well-being. In the end, some of these persons and operations may be reassigned to power, as it becomes clear that they are deeply involved in the making of community-wide decisions which are supported by the use of what are recognized to be severe value deprivations. It is a commonplace of scientific inquiry on a cross-cultural scale to find that conventional institutions, when functionally considered, play roles that differ from the local label. Private monopolists of land, for instance, may belong to the power elite, not only to the elite of wealth.

A comprehensive value model makes it possible to select any institutional pattern to explore its significance in the shaping and sharing of all values, not simply the one or two on which it has the heaviest impact.

In using the generalized value map in relation to concrete circumstances it is ultimately desirable to choose operational indices of each conceptual term. These indices must refer to institutional patterns even though they are selected with value categories in mind.

The flow of gross and net outcomes

One task of any value model is to guide investigators in the search for convenient ways of describing the flow of outcome events during any selected period, whether we speak of years or of multiples or fractions of years. Since the present frame of reference gives prominence to value accumulation and institutional development, the scientific investigator must define the change he assumes to be the goal model. It is not necessary that the preference model gives expression to his personal demands. In his strictly scientific role, the specialist may go no further than adopt a model as a point of departure for research.

An inclusive preference model prescribes (1) a pattern of participation in value-shaping and value-sharing and (2) a pattern of basic, institutional structures. Such a model defines the system of public (or civic) order which it is proposed to achieve or maintain. For convenience we label as "preferred" the patterns that conform to the goal (others are "non-preferred"). The term "preferred" is not to be understood as expressing a personal judgment by the investigator, unless this is specified.

During any given period value outcomes can be described to bring out the relationship between current indulgences and deprivations. All participants in the social process who identify themselves with preferred patterns are value-indulged when these are approximated and value-deprived when they are not. The gross outcome is the sum of indulgences; the net income is the sum when deprivations have been deducted.

The first step in examining power outcomes is to identify all changes that have occurred in the given period in the structure of the decision process (the constitutive process). Some of these changes are issues, since they reach a specified minimum of attention. Even preferred innovations carry deprivations (costs) with them, and a balance sheet must take costs into account. At this stage of research it is not necessary to insist on a sole method of measurement. Let us assume that specific costs are the base values required to neutralize or overcome non-support on issues. It is not unreasonable to assume that cost varies inversely with the margin of success or failure, which implies that the narrower the margin, the more opposing or noncommittal elements are neutralized. Non-issue changes involve non-specific costs or gains. (Issue and non-issue changes can be considered as equal, or weighted according to scope.)

Power outcomes (P) (during select period)
gross = marginal support on successful preferred issues
+ preferred non-issue changes
net = gross outcome
− marginal support on unsuccessful preferred issues
− non-preferred non-issue changes

The preferred model of enlightenment prescribes criteria for the content of communication, characterizing the degree to which community members are exposed to (or have access to) intelligible, comprehensive, and realistic statements about past and future events. The techniques of content analysis are available for the task, whether the media are oral or documentary, and whether information is disseminated or stored.

Enlightenment outcomes (E)

gross = exposure to preferred communication (news reports, research reports, forecasts, storage of potential information; exposure to media and to educational presentations)

net = gross exposure
− exposure to unpreferred communication

The preferred wealth model prescribes the level of aggregate income sought, and the volume and composition of the products resulting from production. The latter specification may be in such vague terms as "increase" in products requiring impersonal technology, or in explicit objectives expressed in money units. The aggregate result may be formulated in terms of the resource characteristics of products (animals, plants, minerals, clothing, shelter, etc.). The preferred model prescribes a pattern of income-sharing (distribution).

Wealth outcomes (W)

National income

gross (in money units)
= preferred level sought
− (or +)* gross national income (income received by all production units, less materials and service payments made by production units)

net (in money units)
= (above)
− net national income (depreciation on plant and equipment, indirect business taxes)

gross (in resource characteristics)
= preferred level of product (animals, etc.)
− (or +) gross level of product

net (in resource characteristics)
= (above)
− products utilized in production

* The gross outcome usually falls short of the goal; however, the plus sign indicates the possibility that a goal may be exceeded.

Personal incomes
gross (pattern of distribution)
= preferred pattern of distribution
− (or +) pattern of aggregate personal income payments
net (pattern of aggregate disposable income expenditure)
= (above)
− personal taxes and savings

The preferred well-being value goal prescribes the aggregate level sought, particularized as to safety, health, and comfort category, and the pattern of incidence (sharing)

Well-being outcomes (B)
gross = preferred level sought
− (or +) population additions (births, immigrants)
+ positive vigor (health, injury-free, defect-free, anxiety-free, comfort)
net = (above)
− population subtractions (deaths, emigrants)
− negative vigor (injuries, illnesses, defects, anxieties, discomforts)
− care (time in activities specialized to custody, treatment, preventive measures)
− destructiveness (time in activities specialized to killing, maiming, etc.)

The preferred affection goal prescribes the desired level of individual congeniality. For example, the objective may be to eliminate quarrelsomeness. However, some models may conceivably aim at maintaining attitudes of indifference or even dislike among individuals. The preferred goal also prescribes loyalty activities toward the symbols of the whole (as when a national goal requires expressions of loyalty to the flag). The goal model also prescribes collective congeniality (or uncongeniality), emphasizing affirmative (or negative) expressions among groups inside or outside the context. This differs from the first objective mentioned above in that it concerns interactions among individuals in terms of their group identities rather than simply as human beings who belong to the nation. (The accent may be on sectional, ethnic, or other groupings.)

As a matter of convenience in examining a social context, we assign such conventional institutions as the family to the affection category. In complex societies, the family does appear to be divested of the economic, power, and other value-shaping and value-sharing functions with which it is so highly implicated in folk or peasant societies. If kinship and immediate family institutions are functionally studied in a peasant society, the initial classification as an affection-oriented institution is almost sure to be drastically revised. This is a typical instance of the end result of exploring any institution contextually with a multivalued model.

Affection outcomes (A)
- gross = preferred level sought
  - − (or +)* individual congeniality (positive activities towards and by others)
  - + loyalty (own group identity; positive activities)
  - + collective congeniality (positive activities toward other groups)
- net = (above)
  - − individual uncongeniality (negative activities toward others and by others)
  - − disloyalty (negative activities)
  - − collective uncongeniality (negative activities toward other groups and by other groups)

The preferred respect model prescribes the level and pattern of recognitions (or discriminations) among individuals. If the goal is an open society, the aim is to abolish discriminations that depend on race, sex, and other characteristics beyond the control of the individual, and to insist on a minimum base level of respect for all persons as human beings. Beyond this, the goal is for respect to be accorded on the basis of merit. In societies that are concerned with maintaining or achieving a self-perpetuating caste, the allocations of recognition and discrimination are appropriately stratified. We classify outcomes according to the individ-

* The minus sign indicates not only that positive activities may fall short of the goal but that they may not be included in it.

ual-to-individual pattern sought, and according to the collective pattern (group identity to group identity) sought.

Respect outcomes (R)
gross = preferred level sought
− (or +) individual indulgences (individual recognitions of others by others)
+ collective indulgences (recognitions of groups by groups)
net = (above)
− individual deprivations
− collective deprivations

The preferred rectitude goal prescribes the level of conformity to uniform standards of responsible conduct, including religious or metaphysical rites and articulated beliefs. In some circumstances the preferred objective is to achieve a state religion and to tolerate no others. The open society seeks to develop individuals who demand of themselves and others that they take the common good into account. The open society also condemns moral and religious denunciations of individuals or groups who worship in their own way, and who otherwise impose no unwarranted deprivations on others.

Rectitude outcomes (D)
gross = preferred level sought
− (or +) conformity to standards
net = (above)
− non-conformity

Value accumulation and enjoyment

Values are accumulated when the level at the beginning of an outcome period is heightened by the end of the period. Disaccumulation is also possible when the total situation is appraised in reference to a given preference model. It is to be stressed that any assessment of values at a cross-section in time is largely a characterization of potential responses to a future set of specified environmental circumstances. Inferences are based on overt responses observed in the recent or remote past. We do not at present express a judgment on whether a single comprehensive model that employs all values, and summarizes a situation in quantitiative terms, is worth attempting.

The only solid conclusion that we presently recommend is that a generalized inclusive model provides a frame of reference in which a great many partial models can be explicitly perceived in relation to one another.

Value accumulation, as has been indicated, is change or addition of predisposition among individuals and change of resource capabilities. Power accumulation is positive when the predispositions in support of the preferred system of public and civic order at the outset have been maintained without loss or intensified, and when the resource capabilities at the beginning of the outcome period have been replenished in case of depletion or have been added to. In regard to the perspectives of the participants in the social process, the inference is that initial responses were able to obtain net indulgences sufficient to sustain or intensify themselves, and that these perspectives were effective in influencing capabilities to maintain or expand the total stock. Such a theoretical model, at least, is suggested by the maximization postulate. Its relevance to concrete circumstances depends on the results of empirical inquiry.

We have called attention to the fact that participants who obtain a value indulgence may employ the indulgence to influence the future of the value immediately involved or may use the indulgence to obtain another value. The former is value accumulation; the latter is value enjoyment. The participant who receives a value indulgence in return for providing participant A with enjoyment may regard this input as part of his gross income as a value-shaper and make various setoffs against it before arriving at his net. The net value claim may be accumulated (used as a base for the same value) or enjoyed. It need not be assumed that all or even a high proportion of value indulgences are deliberately classified by a participant in social interaction as a value input, or as a gross or net input, or that his disposal responses are self-appraised as accumulation or enjoyment.

In the aggregate outline, note that the power model is restricted to constitutive changes in a nation-state. Hence it does not deal with the power position of the state in the world arena except to the extent required to complete the constitutive specification. For example, the preferred constitutive model presumably includes enough independence of external control to maintain the role of a nation-state. But the present preferred models do not include, for instance, a demand to dominate the states in a given region, or to conquer and include them within an expanded nation-state. Such models, however, can be explored within the comprehensive map of social process in which we are operating.

Accumulation:

power (P) = initial support of preferred constitutive pattern sought
+ net outcomes

enlightenment (E) = initial level of preferred knowledge stored, or reporting, of forecasting, of exposure to media, of exposure to educational presentations
+ net outcomes

wealth (W) = initial level of preferred assets (reproducible tangibles) for production, land (surface), net foreign balance, consumers' semidurables and perishables, subsoil, and pattern of income distribution
+ net income (in terms of resource characteristics) and pattern of aggregate disposable income expenditures

well-being (B) = initial level of preferred population and vigor (expectation of death, injury, illness, defect, anxiety, discomfort), care, and destructiveness
+ net outcome (expectations at terminal date)

skill (S) = initial level of preferred training and experience
+ net outcome

affection (A) = initial level of preferred patterns of individual congeniality, of loyalty, of collective congeniality
+ net outcome

respect (R) = initial level of preferred patterns of recognition and discrimination, individual and collective
+ net outcome

rectitude (D) = initial level of preferred patterns of responsible conduct
+ net outcome

Although the data required for an enjoyment model have not been called for in the preceding outlines, the theoretical model is clear:

Enjoyment = net power indulgences used to indulge or deprive others in obtaining enlightenment, wealth, well-being, skill, affection, respect, rectitude (appraised according to preferred patterns)
net indulgences of each other value (enlightenment, etc.) used to indulge or deprive other participants in obtaining other values (appraised according to preferred patterns)

Assuming that the comprehensive value model can be applied to a national context, it becomes possible to characterize the relative significance of accumulation or enjoyment for each value, and the significance of each value for every other. Input-output analysis among the sectors will reveal the ratios of interchange among them. The shaping of each value calls for inputs from other value sectors which typically are costs that take the form of outputs to all other value sectors; and the enjoyment of each value also calls for outputs to all other sectors.

According to the maximization postulate, the allocation of values is carried on in ways that are expected to achieve or maintain net value indulgences. Let us assume that the relevant perspectives of demand and expectation can be measured by such relatively direct procedures as interviewing. It is therefore possible to examine the allocation of values to discover the degree to which the aggregate pattern realizes net expectations or, on account of error or chance, deviates from them.

If the allocation does, in fact, conform to the pattern sought, it may be static or dynamic. In the former case, the expected net advantage calls for no structural changes in the system. In the latter case, structural changes are required. Since we are concerned with value accumulation and institutional development, the preferred models are likely to be dynamic and to call for structural changes of demand and expectation.

When events conform to a static model, changes in the rate of value accumulation do not occur, since no change is expected to yield a net advantage. The situation is parallel to the indifference model employed in describing situations in which economic change is perceived as culminating in no net advantage.

We have a national context in view in the present discussion but have given little explicit attention to the interaction between one nation and its neighbors. It is feasible to apply contextual analysis to this interplay. Similarly, it is pertinent to describe the balance of interaction between a subnational community and its environment.

Value units

If the inclusive model is to be related to concrete events, appropriate value units must be devised and applied. The fundamental units must be formulated in terms that refer to the elementary components of an interaction. Two categories of elementary components are patterned in every such interplay: the subjective events (the moods and images) of each participant and the non-subjective events. A scientific observer can obtain direct access only to his own subjectivities. He can, however, make inferences about the subjective events of others by examining non-subjective patterns. If we call the non-subjective patterns the mass and energy events that can be indexed by physiochemical measures, attention can be focused on somatic happenings in the body, on body movement, and on any implicated resource features of the environment.

An interaction is any sequence of events among participants in a social process whose relationship to value outcomes can be conveniently characterized. Such a sequence, we have indicated, can be described as a pattern of subjectivities, of somatic events, of body movements, and of resource changes.

An interaction can be summarized as a sequence of communication and collaboration. The distinctive mark of communication is the use of signs, which are somatic events, body movements, or resources that are specialized mediators between the subjectivities of participants. The collaborative dimension of an act is composed of non-sign events. As indicated in the definition of an interaction, communication and collaboration are implicated in every act, though in varying degree. To say that a sign mediates is to underline the point that in addition to physiochemical dimensions, to which it refers, its referents are the interpretations by those who initiate a sign sequence or are exposed to signs.

Since value events are defined as interactions, they can in principle be designated by the use of three kinds of elementary units which can be combined into patterns of any degree of complexity. The units are symbols, signs, and resources. The interactions specialized to any value can be described during any period as frequencies of symbol references, of signs, and of resource changes appropriate to the value.

A power unit must be a fundamental unit of support (non-support) in a decision. If a distinctive term for the unit is desired, we may borrow the word "vote" from conventional usage. Recall that the universe of decision events during a time interval may be a peaceful election or a battle. The number of votes is the number of decisions and decision-makers. The unit of support is partially defined as a symbol reference indicating who is supporting (non-supporting) in the context. In addition to the directional reference, a vote has an intensity dimension. In a free election, the intensity of a vote can be described according to the hours spent in seeking to influence the outcome, and the resources devoted to this objective. (Resources can be summarized according to the voter's proportion of all the resources mobilized in the election.) In a battle, the direction may be articulated ("Long live the King!"); intensities include the man-hours and resources committed (a proportion of all the man-hours and resources mobilized for the struggle). Not all decisions become issues, and observers may discover that the culminating events are spread over time rather than bunched in an election or battle. These culminating events must be located before the alignment of votes can be identified and measured. Power interactions obviously vary in the degree of awareness among participants, as well as in the expectations in regard to the character of the commitment events themselves (whether the ballots of a civil arena or the victories or defeats of a military arena).

An enlightenment unit is an act directing an informational communication during a stipulated time period, with a degree of intensity that is describable by the time and resources involved in pre-outcome activities. The scientific observer must identify the culminating events, noting the total flow of relevant communications and the number of participants. As implied above, he must also describe pre-outcome hours and resources. Although there is no agreement on a basic unit of enlightenment, communication content is often described in terms of statements, or of signs (information bits). It may be useful to generalize the term "vote" and to define the fundamental unit of enlightenment as the enlightenment vote, meaning an act of disclosure (or non-disclosure) of information.

A wealth unit (or vote) is a claim over resources, whose intensity can be described according to the time and resources involved in pre-outcome and outcome activities. The scientific observer of the social process must identify the culminating events, taking account of the transfer of claims, the number of participants, the pre-outcome hours and resources involved, and the resources referred to by the claims at the outcome phase. When participants in the outcome phase calculate the net advantage of transferring their claim in return for a claim to a common medium of exchange (money), a pricing institution is involved. If the participants calculate claims in kind, barter is used. When a claim is transferred without an explicitly negotiated agreement to receive an equivalent, though with the expectation of sooner or later obtaining an equivalent in accord with customary expectations, we speak of reciprocity. Mutuality is a relationship in which the transfer of a claim is unreflective, and hence not accompanied by expectations of obtaining any explicit equivalent; however, the implicit expectation is that the claim of mutuality will continue indefinitely.

A well-being unit (or vote) is a claim to opportunity for safety, health, and comfort, or for the limitation or destruction of such opportunity. The claim can be described as a communication (explicit, implicit) whose intensity can be gauged by the pre-outcome and outcome time and resources involved. The scientific observer of the social process must identify the culminating events of realized or damaged opportunity and the number of participants. Some interactions can be located as episodes that are rather narrowly delimited in time and space, such as giving or receiving life (birth) or a mortal blow. Some outcome events are spread through time and may be described according to the units of time during which they continue and the magnitude and character of the resource involved (a mental or physical defect, for example).

A skill unit (or vote) is a claim of opportunity to acquire or exercise proficiency. The scientific observer must identify the culminating events, the numbers involved, the time and resources implicated at pre-outcome and outcome phases. Proficiency is the arrangement of component elements in an operation. The terminal event that calls for skill may be a value other than skill, as in proficiencies connected with obtaining political and other results. If the outcome event is an arrangement of elements as an exercise for its own sake, the skill is aesthetic, as in the case of "pure music" rather than military band music, where effects are disciplined by the impact sought on soldiers and civilians.

An affection unit (or vote) is a claim of opportunity involving love or loyalty. The scientific observer must identify the outcomes, the number of participants, and the time and resources involved at pre-outcome phases.

The respect unit (or vote) is a claim to opportunity for recognition. The scientific observer must identify the outcome events, the number of participants, the time and resources involved.

The rectitude unit (or vote) is a claim of opportunity to act responsibly. The scientific observer must identify the outcome events, the participants, the time and the resources employed.

The foregoing analysis outlines the possibility of devising value units by the use of composite indices that relate to communication (or communication equivalents) in selected time intervals. The operational indices are the scientific observer's bases of inference about the direction and intensity of demands (claims) made by participants at the outcome phase of interaction. The scientific observer takes responsibility for identifying the aggregate flow of outcome events during chosen periods and categorizes them according to the values available for transfer and the number of participants involved. An available value is indexed according to the message content of communication (or communication equivalents): "I vote . . ." (power). A value unit is a participant's direction of commitment; this too, is indexed by message content: "I vote for or against; I don't vote." The intensity dimension of a value unit is indexed by the participant's proportion of all the resources mobilized in the context at pre-outcome and outcome phases and by his proportion of activity in symbol and sign manipulation during the pre-outcome phase.

Indices are adapted to the shaping or sharing roles performed by the participants described, since every participant functions to some extent both as a shaper and sharer of every value. Participants act as individual personalities or as members of organized and unorganized collectivities.

Value-shaping and value-sharing roles, with some examples:

Power-shapers	= officials, leaders
Power-sharers	= participants in a domain
Enlightenment-shapers	= reporters, researchers, forecasters, storers (librarians, etc.)
Enlightenment-sharers	= learners (of accumulated knowledge), viewers, readers, or listeners to news
Wealth-shapers	= producers (controllers of production factors)
Wealth-sharers	= income receivers, consumers
Well-being–shapers	= caretakers, therapists, preventers, destroyers

Well-being–sharers	= experiencers of safety, health, and comfort
Skill-shapers	= practitioners (levels of training and experience, of performance), apprentices, masters (trainers)
Skill-sharers	= evaluators (critics, connoisseurs)
Affection-shapers	= projectors of affection (friends, parents, loyalty models)
Affection-sharers	= experiencers of love and loyalty (of indifference, dislike)
Respect-shapers	= formulators of respect standards and appliers (etiquette models)
Respect-sharers	= recipients of recognition (or discrimination)
Rectitude-shapers	= formulators and appliers of religious and ethical standards of responsibility
Rectitude-sharers	= recipients of evaluation

If we examine the value distribution at any cross-section in time, the participants in any social context can be classified by each value, or in terms of all values, as elite, mid-elite, rank and file, or in any convenient number of classes (or castes).

***Institutions: Sub-outcomes** (**prescription, intelligence, promotion, invocation, application, appraisal, termination**)*

The value map of social process, though providing a contextual guide for the examination of any matrix of interaction, must be brought into close relationship to the institutional patterns current in any particular situation. This can be accomplished by successive breakdowns of the fundamental pre-outcome, outcome, and post-outcome phases of the value-shaping and value-sharing process. It is, for example, useful to describe the various culminations as components of a pattern whose interrelationships are viewed as a system. Some collective movements may pass through every conceivable outcome phase in any imaginable sequence; many collective operations, however, are focused around a single phase.

We begin with prescription (chiefly because of its obvious

importance). To establish a prescription is to formulate expectations about a general norm of conduct. Every prescription is analyzable into three components: norms, contingencies, sanctions. The norms refer to the required standard, contingencies to the circumstances in which the norm is appropriate, and sanctions to the indulgencies or deprivations expected to achieve and maintain conformity. Prescriptions are sometimes "issues" that are explicitly resolved by a specialized formal structure (e.g., legislatures), or they are "non-issues" whose crystallization is dispersed (e.g., changing customs about family formation) and typically must be discovered by specialized research. We define prescription to include more than words; it is necessary to demonstrate a minimum frequency of conformity in appropriate situations. Since programs of development involve new prescriptions, it is important to identify the time when articulated prescriptions become effective prescriptions. Prescriptions define the role of any organized policy institutions specialized to the value in question. Constitutive prescriptions make explicit how the policy structures are set up and operated. Supervisory prescriptions cover private controversies regarding the value which are referred to policy-makers for settlement. These prescriptions indicate how the controversies are to be brought to the attention of the judges or arbitrators and how they are to be disposed of. Regulatory standards deal with activities that are left to private participants, yet may require intervention by the policy-makers concerned with the value in question if conformity to collective norms is to be maintained. Enterprisory prescriptions, though perceived as distinct from the constitutive process, are administered by structures that act for all the participants in the value process involved. Corrective prescriptions, strictly defined, do not cover all sanctions (although it is often convenient to consider all sanctions together). Corrective measures refer to individuals who require personality reconstruction or permanent exclusion from full participation in the value process. During the transitional phases of development, rigid personalities may require special methods of re-education or control. In folk or peasant societies, as well as in civilizations, corrective measures are used to cope with the young, the defective, the chronic offender, and related challengers of the established order.

By public order of a nation we mean the pattern of value distribution and of basic institutions which need to be protected by the use of power, if necessary. Power relations involve the expectation that decisions, if defied, will be enforceable against defiers by extreme value deprivations. It is also assumed in the context that defiance rarely, if ever, achieves the level of civil war. The civic order of a nation is the protection of basic value and institutional patterns by the use of relatively mild, rather than severe, sanctions. The scientific observer must take responsibility for specifying the context the prescriptions he classifies as inclusive of the nation and as involving severe or mild deprivations.

It is pertinent to bear in mind the distinction between functional and conventional categories in the study of public and civic order. From the conventional point of view, legislative statutes are commonly assumed to be part of the public order. Research may, however, show that some of them belong to the civic order (functionally defined). Many statutes are not expected to be, and are not, enforced; many others involve only mild deprivational sanctions against offenders. Note also that from the conventional point of view many ecclesiastical, business, and other prescriptions are not part of the national system of statutes. They are perceived as part of the civic order. Research may nevertheless demonstrate that some of these prescriptions have important value consequences throughout the nation and that they are enforced against nonconformers by severe sanctions. Hence, in the functional sense, they belong to the public order. The scientific observer must take responsibility for specifying the minimum level of value consequences in the community which are important, and the meaning of severity. Since the aim of contextual analysis is to exhibit the full richness of interaction in a social process, it is far less helpful to draw lines in a continuing gradation of events than to make sure that the entire gradation is covered. The gradation from public through civic order poses problems of great relevance to development policies, since a major strategic question is when to proceed on a nationwide or a smaller territorial or pluralistic program, and when to employ severe or mild sanctioning measures.

It is also useful to employ concepts of public and civic order within other than national social contexts. The public order of a business, for example, includes patterns which are supported against deviants by sanctions that, within the business setting, are severe rather than mild. If all interactions in the social process are included within the power process, the society would be entirely politicized.

For convenience, the following comments will often refer to conventionally perceived institutions. It is, however, to be understood that functional findings must ultimately be obtained to locate their true significance.

Enlightenment prescriptions that refer to the constitutive structure of policy formulate the norms concerning who, using what base values, for what objectives, in what manner, is authorized to make what policy choices. In societies where mass media exist, the main policy-makers are a blend of government and private organizations and individuals. Hence, some constitutive policies are also part of the power process. Supervisory prescriptions provide guidance for policy-makers, such as those who are asked to settle the complaints of two newspapers or television stations concerning violations of an agreement about the retention or dissemination of information. The regulatory prescriptions of a private code of broadcasters may set standards which authorize action by the administrators of the private code. Enterprisory prescriptions cover the scope of the activities undertaken by a joint agency of research, storage, or dissemination. Corrective prescriptions deal with the enforcement measures at the disposal of policy-makers.

Prescriptions in regard to the constitutive processes of wealth may depend considerably on agreements made in a market that is largely free of government control. The supervisory code may provide for mediation, arbitration, or private adjuciation of controversies arising under formal or informal codes. Regulatory prescriptions may authorize trade associations to step in to alter practices that violate the code. Enterprisory activities, such as a co-operative purchasing organization, may be run according to a prescriptive code. Corrective prescriptions cover various enforcement instruments at the disposal of policy-makers.

The code of well-being prescriptions contains constitutive arrangements concerning policy-makers, such as who is authorized to define disease or defect. The supervisory code prescribes for the handling of disagreements, including those referred to health associations for settlement. (Also there are regulatory, enterprisory, and corrective prescriptions.)

Skill prescriptions that set forth the constitutive code cover such questions as who is authorized to set standards of excellence for occupational, professional, and artistic operations. Affection prescriptions that deal with constitutive relations prescribe who is authorized to formulate norms of love and loyalty. Respect prescriptions relating to constitutive matters indicate who can legitimately formulate norms of recognition (or discrimination). Rectitude prescriptions of the constitutive code specify the policy-makers who may prescribe norms of responsible behavior (religious, ethical). Skill, affection, respect, and rectitude codes also include supervisory regulatory, enterprisory, and corrective standards.

Although the outcome events specialized to prescription have been considered first, they are preceded by intelligence and promotional outcomes in a typical social movement. Intelligence outcomes that relate to power are decisions to disseminate or withhold information of possible concern to public policy (e.g., to release a report on official planning or to defer publication). Intelligence outcomes, when specialized to enlightenment activities, pertain to policies regarding the acquisition and dissemination of knowledge. Included is the choice of information about news, research, and forecasting operations at home and abroad. Intelligence outcomes, when related to wealth, include choices to publish or withhold information about economic trends, conditions, projections, goals, and objectives. Similarly, intelligence choices pertaining to other values concern information about the appropriate trends, conditions, projections, goals, and objectives (skill, affection, respect, rectitude).

Promotional outcomes, if specialized to power, are decisions to advocate or refrain from advocating public policies. Thus, governments sometimes forbid themselves to engage in specific propaganda campaigns, or decide to co-operate in them. Enlightenment promotions are commitments to advocate (or abstain from advocating) specific news, research, storage, and related operations. The type of promotion particularized to other values is fairly clear.

Power invocations are decisions that provisionally characterize concrete cases in prescriptive terms (as when a police officer alleges a violation or a grand jury returns an indictment). Parallel operations occur in other value institutions.

Power applications are decisions that finally characterize concrete cases in terms of prescriptions. The decisions of most administrative organs are covered. Other institutions engage in parallel activities.

Power appraisals are decisions in which official activities are characterized according to their effectiveness in the implementation of policy objectives. Legislative committees, for example, may vote to censor officials for failure or inefficiency.

The terminating outcome in the power process is a decision to end a prescription and to deal with the expectations raised during the period when the prescription was in effect. Development programs typically entail the obsolescence and final termination of older norms. Compensation or failure to compensate affects the smoothness of transition. Whole areas of human interaction, previously subject to customary claims, are forcibly moved by the state into zones of negotiated agreement. The transformation "from status to contract," in Sir Henry Maine's phrase, does not necessarily provide compensation, for example, to the holders of previous claims to the use of communal lands. The termination function, like appraisal, is performed in all value institutions.

Institutions: Interaction situations (arenas, etc.)

In fitting generalized value maps to institutional detail, attention must go to interaction situations where the boundaries of any social context are, in fact, defined. The nation's arena of power is the locus of interaction among nation members. For convenience it is conventionally delimited by boundaries. There are many lesser arenas in which participants recognize that power is a dominant value. Many of these situations are explicitly organized as part of governmental, political party, or pressure group structures.

Political parties and pressure groups are among the distinctive structures evolved by modern, large-scale popular governments. A political party is organized to obtain votes in elections by presenting both candidates and an inclusive platform of issues. A pressure group focuses on particular issues; in elections it may or may not try to obtain votes in its own name. In a functional sense, it may be noted, some conventionally labeled parties are pressure groups (the Prohibition party in the United States, for example). Recent totalitarian movements have partially incorporated the practices of popular governments, such as elections and political parties. Because authority and control are monopolized by a single organization, the Nazi, Fascist, and Communist "parties" are not true parties. They may be called "political orders"; and power-seeking groups which coercively pursue specific outcomes are "gangs."

Organized arenas are territorially centralized or decentralized (with many intermediate steps between the most and the least inclusive units). At any territorial level policy organizations are concentrated or deconcentrated, depending on the number of co-ordinate organs involved. In the United States body politic, for instance, the legislative, executive, and judicial branches are independent; in a system of formal and effective kingship, the monarchy exercises concentrated authority at the top. At any territorial level organizations may be monopolistic or pluralistic. We speak of a national society as highly governmentalized when interactions are formally and effectively monopolized by government (relative to the role of private organizations). The degree to which individual activities are regimented or individualized is also to be noted, whether the regimentation is by governmental or pluralistic associations.

We underline the point that an organization is to be understood as a pattern of situations which are interconnected by communicative and collaborative activity. An official agency exists (whether official for power or some other value) when a stable routine of formal and informal messages reaches the attention of officials (and other significant participants), and when messages are interpreted by common criteria. The message flow must be managed in a way that permits the overt collaborative operations of the organization to be stabilized. The personnel, equipment, and other facilities of the total enterprise are assembled, processed, and released as a stream of outputs. Each situational component of an organization is appropriately structured when it mobilizes the value expectations, demands, and identifications which are necessary to lead the participants in the situation to expect to be better off by performing the operations required than by failing to do so, or by acting inefficiently.

Value institutions: Myth (doctrine, formula, miranda)

The participants in every social process act in the frame of reference of the myth. The subjective events of individuals (perspectives) can be classified according to the symbols of identity (I, we, you, they), of demand (value preference or volition), and of expectation (matter-of-fact reference to past, present, and future events). The myth is the pattern of stable perspectives among the members of a collectivity. The myth clarifies goal, provides a historical panorama of trend, formulates assumptions about conditioning factors, projects the future course of events, and fosters the invention and evaluation of policy.

A myth comprises doctrinal statements (the high-level abstractions or philosophy), statements of the formula (prescriptions of public and civic order), and miranda (popular versions of past, present, and future). In isolated folk societies the myth is unchallenged. Attempts at development are likely to introduce a novel set of conflict experiences in which the traditional myth becomes the ideology of the established order (or one section of the elite), while new perspectives become a counterideology propagated by some members of the elite (or non-elite).

For comparative purposes it is essential to describe the intensity with which myths, and myth components, are held by representative participants in a social context. (Methods of varying depth are available.) In complex societies it is not difficult to distinguish somewhat distinctive value myths from one another. Among the current myths of power are liberal democracy, totalitarianism, racism. The principal enlightenment myth presents a scientific view of man and nature, and a demand for freedom of information. Among the ideologies of wealth are private capitalism, socialism, and consumers' co-operation. Well-being myths differ in their degree of reliance on scientific methods of inquiry and on the inclusion or exclusion of subjective events as significant factors in disease. Skill myths glorify various forms of excellence as ends in themselves ("art for art's sake"), or as indispensable contributors to other social outcomes. Affection myths magnify the importance of love and loyalty in individual and group relations, often seeking to direct love along the conventional channels provided by the established patterns of sex and family relations. Respect myths characteristically glorify individual human beings and meritorious achievement or claim recognition for racial or other castes. Rectitude myths include the many religious and ethical systems of the globe.

In folk societies the differentiations of myth may be lacking, or require subtle observation.

Institutions: Strategies

The level of development of any society is directly reflected in the strategies in use for manipulating the base values of the community. These strategies can be variously classified to highlight distinctive operations. There is, for example, the distinction between assembling and processing. The objective of strategies specialized to assembling is to bring together the personnel and facilities essential to complete the preparation of impacts at the outcome phase. In an industrialized society, where popular government prevails, the exercise of influence on decision calls for the establishment of a party or pressure group organization tooled to manage campaigns. Enlightenment operations need personnel and equipment if they are to engage in gathering and dissemination of news and in other functions appropriate to the obtaining and circulation of knowledge. Production activities require the assembling of units of personnel and facilities capable of manufacturing or otherwise processing commodities for the market. Parallel operations are required in connection with all the other values, as suggested by referring to hospitals and well-being, schools and skill, family formation and affection, ecclesiastical organization and rectitude.

Strategies can be classified according to the degree to which reliance is put on communication and collaboration. More precisely, the distinction is according to the relative position of elements (symbols or signs, resources). When power is used, we commonly refer to diplomacy and propaganda, or to economic and military instruments. (Diplomacy is elite to elite negotiation; propaganda is elite to rank and file communication.) Enlightenment includes scientific and informative statements; such statements can be used for influencing purposes as part of diplomacy or of a general program of enlightenment. Resources specialized to research or dissemination can be employed productively (or destructively). Wealth instruments include the statements, specialized to production and consumption, which enter into negotiation and advertising. Economic means also comprise the goods withheld in boycott of or supplied for weapon manufacture. Well-being instruments are statements from elite to elite or are public communications about safety, health, and comfort. Also included are specialized physical resources (infectious agents, etc.) and facilities relating to health. Parallel distinctions apply to skill, affection, respect, and rectitude.

A fundamental dimension of strategy is the management of indulgences and deprivations (positive gains, avoided losses; losses, blocked gains). The most complex problems in this connection appear when the base values manipulated by the strategist are not perceived in the same terms by the targets of influence. The trading beads of the early explorers and adventurers were viewed as worthless by the explorers but not by the targets of negotiation, until they gained more enlightenment about the larger world.

Another important dimension of strategy is along the continuum of persuasion and coercion. In the former case, the participants have several choices which they regard as yielding favorable results; in the latter, some participants have few if any options, and all are perceived as severely deprivational.

We distinguish further between strategies of isolation and joint action (in general, strategies of coalition). In this connection, we comment on the aggregate pattern formed by the flow of strategic activity in an arena, or in any other situation. If a single participant were to exercise a predominant role over the others, the pattern would be unipolar. Other combinations are bi-, tri-, pluri-, and multipolar; and each seems to exhibit somewhat distinctive features.

Innovation, diffusion, and restriction

The social process of any nation is in perpetual interaction, whether casual or intensive, with other nations. Viewed in the global setting, institutional patterns identifiable during a given period can be classified as innovations or as instances of the diffusion or restriction of previous patterns. A comprehensive model of social process must point to the relations that account for the occurrence of these three responses. The maximization postulate is a guide to the formation of realistic hypotheses, since it suggests that innovation, for instance, occurs when alternative responses are expected to yield not disadvantages, hence the search for new patterns is favorably viewed. In modern industrial societies, the deliberate pursuit of innovation is a built-in characteristic. It is exhibited in the pursuit of new political tactics, new scientific and scholarly knowledge, new commodities and modes of production, new means of diagnosis and therapy, novel forms of skilled expression, novel experiences of love, novel modes of fashionable distinction, novel experiences of responsibility. A theoretical model of an extremely static society emphasizes the severity of the sanctions imposed on deviation from established norms. The entire web of institutional practice is comprehended within the public order of such a society. To adopt a novel pattern is to perform an act whose significance can be faintly communicated to a modern man by characterizing it as an act of treason, of sacrilege, of immorality; it is shameful, villainous, stupid, disloyal. The adjectives that evoke some sense of what is involved come from the sectors of power and rectitude, as a rule, with some embellishment from other components (such as respect—"shameful," enlightenment—"stupid," affection—"disloyal"). In the static model, personalities are so deeply molded by socialization that the punitive superego may actually impose self-destruction on the violator of the common norm. The specialists on the transempirical forces that are perceived as determining the fate of the community are beneficiaries of the sacred myth; they are often the power elite, superior to chiefs and specialists on such limited forces as those connected with individual worries about love, disease, or craftsmanship.

The theoretical model of a wholly static society (of the savage "caked with custom") is in varying degree inapplicable to the facts of folk and peasant society. After all, innovations did occur in folk societies and did spread from one society to another. In principle, there is nothing new about the spread of modern science, technology, and its accompanying patterns; distinctiveness resides in speed and depth of change.

If our theoretical models are to be disciplined by the results of prediction, it is desirable to map the zones of culture distribution throughout the globe, with particular attention to the lines that delimit equality of access to competing institutional patterns. From the present evidence, it seems that the spread of science and technology is far from uniform along the radii of potential diffusion from the centers in Western Europe or North America, or the subcenters outside Europe and North America. The same observation applies to associated institutional patterns, such as "socialism" from the Soviet Union and "capitalism" from the Western powers. Social scientists have scarcely begun to chart the "zones of equi-deprivation," the localities where available patterns are perceived as affording net disadvantages.

In this connection, insufficient scientific attention has been given to the latent (the repressed and suppressed) rebelliousness of primitive and peasant societies against their cultures. The potential intensity of these responses is suggested by the alacrity with which features of the universalizing pattern of scientific technology are partially incorporated in many areas. The image of the self as faintly ridiculous ("naked" savage; "quaint" costumes) and also as more than a little unenlightened is probably much more general among underdeveloped peoples than is usually assumed. The static model of society may underplay the intensity of the unacknowledged internal conflicts generated by the deprivations of curiosity (enlightenment) which are inseparable from small group living. As latent tendencies are stirred, many defensive mechanisms of the individual psychic system come into action (boredom, for example).

The value-institution model

The preceding discussion has suggested how to adapt the highly generalized social process model to the finer details of a social context. The figure restates the social process the social

Figure. *The Value-institution Model*

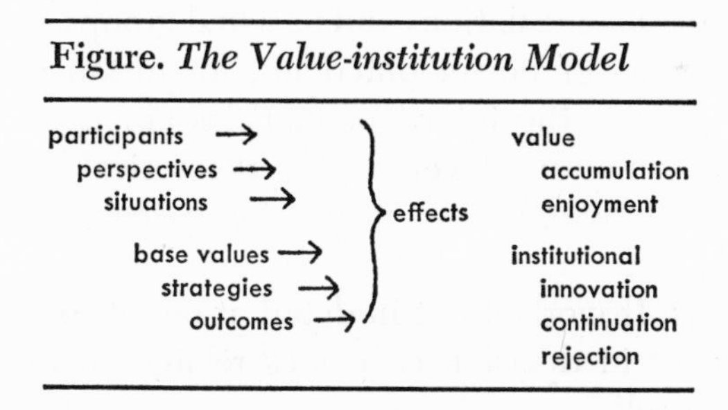

process as participants interacting in situations, controlling base values, employing strategies to influence outcomes, with effects on value accumulation and enjoyment, and also institutional innovation, continuation, and rejection.

We suggest that the conception of development as growth, if somewhat reformulated, is a satisfactory model of the process. The conception must be generalized beyond one value (wealth) to all values in the social process. In order to remove the ambiguities of a model that is exclusively stated in value terms, it is important to complete the preference map in institutional terms. As indicated above, our recommended goal is widespread participation in all preferred values; furthermore, we stipulated some of the principal institutional features of such a model. It is only when a value-institution pattern is clarified that it becomes possible to pinpoint the predispositions and the resource capabilities that are required to achieve the goal.

The theory of definite stages of value accumulation and institutional development is misleading and ought to be dropped. The idea of "self-sustaining" growth is serviceable only if it is understood to mean that the preferred model, once established, can perpetuate itself as a system of public and civic order. Goals are most likely to be approximated at different tempos, in different sectors of a nation, and in various nations.

Although it is theoretically possible to quantify the dimensions of a preferred system of public and civic order, the data required for such a model, or for approximating toward it, are not presently available. No doubt it will be possible to move toward inclusive quantification by a series of partial models, adapted to the contours of specific nations and national groups.

A partial model of power outcomes, for instance, can be devised to summarize the interdependencies among sub-outcomes within the nation at any level. Such a theoretical image must be able to predict how any flow of decision outcomes (intelligence decisions, for instance) will influence (and be influenced by) all other decisions. If worked out in detail, it ought to be possible to predict changes in decision outcomes related to the process of development itself.

The predictive role of a model that refers strictly to outcomes is less satisfactory than a model that includes more features of the social context. Suppose we enlarge the model to cover changes in the number of participants in the decision process. If the voting population increases, the demand to modernize may become more urgent.

The image can be further refined by including information

about the predispositions of newcomers into the arena. Survey research may show that the younger generation at all levels is pro-modernization.

Further modifications may introduce data about arenas, base values, and strategies. The model may allow for enlargements of the franchise for increased funds at the disposal of modernizing parties, or for new political propaganda methods.

Each of these categories of the power process can be dealt with in great detail. To choose a single example: the perspectives of power participants can be described in ways that disclose the direction and intensity of their support for, or rejection of, established myths. Distinctions can be drawn between perspectives relevant to doctrine, formula, and miranda. The model may include stipulations about the routines of influence, indicating which changes in doctrine, for instance, bring about changes in formula and miranda. Or—to choose another example of elaboration—power structures can be dealt with in detail. Perhaps any shift from centralization to decentralization will immediately precipitate movement in the opposite direction or changes from concentration to deconcentration.

In the formation of explanatory theories of development, it is important to give prominence to the role of significant participants (communities, classes, interests, personalities). The present discussion, of course, gives prominence to national communities. However, the model can be extended to cover any territorially oriented group (transnational, national, subnational). A key scientific question is how nations function as factors in development; and this calls for the identification and assessment of factor combinations that characterize a nation's potential.

Since the response to be explained is acceptance or rejection of changes which are partially modeled in other nations, predispositions in regard to such changes are pertinent factors. There is the delicate problem of matching readiness to perceive with the presented configuration. In extreme cases of cultural discrepancy, novel patterns are seen as confusion, not as a pattern. An image of the self as a past beneficiary of change—as in the Japanese case—is a favorably disposing propensity. Estimates of past experience with innovation operate as significant selective elements in the present. The application of the total model to dynamic situations can be expected to bring out the distinctive combination of pertinent factors.

We are concerned with class interactions as they relate to development. The term "class," it will be realized, refers to the upper, middle, or lower position of individuals in reference to one or all values. The class structure of any stable community is a set of social environments that affect the predispositions of each member. At any given moment the significant question is whether and to what extent the active elite perceives itself as threatened from within, or without, by novel patterns. If indigneous elites have been subordinated by foreign empires (though permitted to continue), their predispositions are deeply affected by the strategies of the imperial rule to which they are subject. If modernizing patterns have been partially incorporated by the indigenous elites, it is probable that a split will eventually occur, in which dissenting elements break away from accommodation with the colonial master and join a coalition of middle- and lower-class elements who strive to secede from the empire and achieve independent statehood. Since Japan, Turkey, and Thailand were not formally colonialized, their evolution diverges from that of India, Pakistan, Burma, or much of Africa. The generalization that appears to account for the pecularities of "innovation from above" is the principle of minimum power loss or risk, which means that political elites seek to make as few changes in power as they expect to be able to get away with.

In addition to the role of communities and classes, it is relevant to examine interest groups, that is, groups that are less inclusive than the former categories (of community and class) or cut across them. Every value, value phase, and institution can provide an experience of identity, demand, and expectation that functions as in interest factor in relation to growth. In some feudal societies the "lead" as against the "lag" role is taken by military specialists when they see traditional weapons and tactics collapse before the products and strategy of industry. Crucial initiatives may germinate in the minds of top officials or diplomats who see the handwriting on the wall; or initiatives may originate with traders and go-betweens who recognize how to exploit novelty for gain. A new class of scholars may appear in connection with translation, journalism, teaching, and eventually research. Contrasting roles may be played by intellectuals of skill and of enlightenment. A skill specialist is prone to act like Pye's civil servants in Burma who hold tenaciously in postindependence years to a laboriously acquired set of operations which they used to obtain such personal objectives as economic security, respect, and shreds of power. An enlightenment-oriented intellectual, on the contrary, is concerned with an inclusive version of man and nature which is at once innovative and realistic, meditative yet compatible with active participation in life. (Interests can be conveniently classed according to value-institution category.) Collective roles furnish us with many clues to the dynamics of growth. It is, nevertheless, important to look at human beings as whole personalities and to explore the significance of their interplay in growth process. Personalities differ from one another in value orientation, in balance of conscious and unconscious components, and in reliance on mechanisms of integration. Scientific interest has been brought to bear on these factors by McClelland's emphasis on the demand for achievement, Hagen's analysis of the deeper motivations and mechanisms of enterprisers, and Lerner's evidence of the place of empathy in enabling individuals to entertain a wide and rather accurate image of the perspectives of other human beings.

In commenting on subjective events, we mentioned images (which refer to particular events) and moods (which are suffuse experience—euphoria, depression, and so on). As acts move from unconscious levels to conscious awareness and expression, the psychic systems of individuals and groups appear to maintain characteristic patterns of equilibrium. These patterns are often described in terms of "temperament" and provide relatively stable subjective features of culture. The moods are classifiable according to the values that are indulged or deprived if the acts are permitted to run to completion (e.g., imperiousness, intellectual curiosity, acquisitiveness, anxiety, aesthetic absorption, love, pride, righteousness).

When act systems conflict with one another they generate a mood of anxiety (negative well-being); and other moods, images, or somatic activities are employed as defenses against anxiety. The mechanisms of repression and resistance operate to stabilize a mechanism of continued exclusion from conscious awareness. However, if intense conflicts are restored, these mechanisms can be overcome.

Since culture transformation invariably involves personality reorientation, it is important to encourage intensive inquiry into the sequences of acceptance or rejection of novelty. Some successions are well known: individuals in culture A, after early nonattention and rejection, idealize culture B, and either desert A or seek to revolutionize it. At a later phase of partial incorporation of myth and technique from B, B becomes a target of active rejection. Ultimately, a complex blend of elements from A and B becomes relatively stable and acceptable. In these several sequences we distinguish between the patterns of A and B and the identities of the cultures involved. A often rejects B as an entity at the same time A is incorporating many of B's principal institutions.

In refining the analysis, we may consider the factor of crisis level, meaning that responses are affected by the intensity of conflict between the nation and other national or subnational groups and among and within classes, interest groups, and personalities. If power elites, for instance, are in internal conflict (or engaged with other power classes), coalitions may bring external individuals and groups into the national picture. Conflicts of interest may aid in weakening the hold of traditional identifications by criss-crossing tribal, ceremonial, and related drives.

We especially note the significance of crises in the course of national growth. They are characterized by changing levels of mood among participants in the social process and by the competition of strategies to give direction to collective expression. Crises range from near-total disorganization to reaffirmation of solidarity and co-operation with the emerging frame of public and civil order.

Directional and lateral dimensions

The contextual model of social process, modified to emphasize the problems of value accumulation and economic development, can be variously applied for the purpose of giving prominence to particular frames of reference whose significance emerges as research and policy considerations change. One advantage of the inclusive model is that it can be rotated or turned on its side as an aid to theory formation and investigation.

By underlining the arrow of time—the directional flow of events, the model directs attention to the sequence of shaping and sharing of every value. When the value categories are applied to the sequence of events in any situation, it is possible to describe the extent to which activities are passing through the same or different phases at the same time. By moving back and forth between the directional and the lateral dimensions of process, the context gains intelligibility.

The institutional categories refer to directional phases of the shaping and sharing model (pre-outcome, outcome, post-outcome). At any cross-section of time the institutional categories give finer visibility to the lateral sequence of events in each value sector.

Because of the relative novelty of some of the distinctions employed, it may be clarifying to comment on the relationship between the value-institution model outlined here and some topics of interest as phrased in more conventional language.

Assume, for example, that we are interested in socialization, the induction of newcomers into roles appropriate to a mature participant in a given political and civic order. All career lines are conceived as interacting sequences of events; hence, the socialization of the infant begins as soon as he is exposed to, and capable of interacting with, the social environment. The traditional emphasis is on the face-to-face relations between the target of socialization and all who influence him (the socializers), especially family, school, and neighborhood members. This image is inadequate to deal with the facts in a society in which mass media of communication supplement, or in some matters supplant, the models of conduct presented to the growing individual in primary relationships. Whatever and whoever influences the formation of predispositions in the pre-adult are components of the socialization process.

Since our general model emphasizes the interactive character of society, it suggests that any conception of socialization is inadequate that deals solely with changes on the part of pre-adults and ignores the impact of socialization on adults. Where mass markets and mass communication exist, the changing perspectives of the young influence the perspectives of adults, inside and outside the family circle. These effects can be traced in every value-institution sector. In developing societies it is particularly pertinent to inquire into, and to devise strategies for, managing and training and selection of personnel for common and specialized roles in every institutional context, whether arenas of power or the situations in which affection, rectitude, wealth, or some other value predominates. To study socialization is to investigate a lateral feature of all social interaction, a feature defined by the presence of pre-adult participants.

Activities relating to development are no exception to the generalization that a specialized elite begins to emerge in connection with every continuing policy problem. Specialists on social development, especially transnational development, have come into existence to face the challenges and opportunities of assistance programs. All the usual questions arise with this new generation of specialists. From what sources in the society are they drawn? How do their predispositions influence the perspectives they bring to the arena of politics? What assets and liabilities (base values) do they start with? What strategies are they disposed to use in seeking to affect outcomes? What impact do they have? How are they modified by the situations, formal and informal, in which they find themselves? What is the probable future of these new occupations and professions?

It will be of great interest to assess in detail the diffusion, restriction, and innovation process. How does the new elite of developers conform to or deviate from the roles previously evolved by foreign investors and enterprisers, missionaries, advisors of governments, and private foundations devoted to medical, educational, and scientific purposes?

Another frame of reference related to the whole process of development is the reciprocal impact of participation in these operations on the assisting nations. At the outset of programs connected with transnational development, the effective initiative may be taken by a few, notably by small cliques of important political, military, and financial figures. As the policy becomes stabilized, more elements in the assisting country are involved, either by direct participation in specific programs or as opponents of the policy. Latent predispositions in the body politic set limits on which is sought to be done, and how.

Goal models reconsidered: A power sketch

Having come this far, it may be clarifying to consider some of the implications for a political model of value accumulation and institution development. A power model must be far more explicit than an economic model in referring to the total society.

1. We accept the conception of political development as a sequence of approximations toward a self-sustaining level of power accumulation. This means that when the structural characteristics of the preferred goal have been made articulate, attention will be directed to the predispositions and capabilities in terms of which value accumulation can be assessed.

2. We join with those who wish to achieve an ideology of progress, of commitments to wide participation in power as a long-run goal. A primary function of any policy model is to provide a guide for taking sides in controversies over basic objectives. We concur in recommending the conception of human dignity as an overriding goal. We understand this to include effective (and formal) participation in the decision process. Such a position implies the willingness to make sacrifices of economic growth, if necessary to sustain progress toward popular government. We accept as problematic—and therefore as an appropriate topic of continuing research—the frequent assumption that

economic growth automatically guarantees the attainment of political development. The motivations and instruments of control available to modern garrison-police states are so formidable that it is no foregone conclusion that they will be insufficient to perpetuate an oligarchical or even a caste system.

3. An adequate model of political development emphasizes the importance of obtaining sufficient power to maintain national independence, and therefore includes effective political demands not only for economic developments but for growth in all the value-institution sectors of the body politic.

Since effective independence is a collective demand to function as a nation-state, it carries recognition of the necessity for control over the base values on which effective power depends. In this frame of reference it is obvious that political development calls for economic growth, and that lagging economic growth is at least a partial consequence of political underdevelopment. If the past decision process had been more realistic in planning for the future, many states would not have lagged behind states which eventually infringed their independence, after first attaining economic superiority. As we look back at the expansion of Europe, a fascinating question is why the elites of the European world failed to estimate the significance of the then present for the future. Equally impressive are the examples of effective acceleration which power elites have often been able to give to economic growth. For present purposes, the significance of the record is that it draws attention to the reality-orienting task that faces the decision process of every political unit in world politics and underlines the significance of political realism for development.

4. Political development includes willingness and capacity to play a responsible role in world politics. In paragraph 2 above we emphasized the cruciality of power for the task of maintaining an independent role in the world arena. The present criterion makes the related point that unrestricted pursuit of power is not an acceptable component of the objectives of a developed national state. Political modernization is not to be achieved by withdrawal from world politics; withdrawal is not permitted. A developed nation-state expects, and is expected by most other members of

the world arena, to conform to an inclusive body of authoritative prescription; and this expectation implies an internal system of public order both willing and able to comply.

In a political sense, every nation-state must remain somewhat underdeveloped so long as the arena of world politics falls short of inclusive public order in which transnational responsibilities are effectively defined in terms of human dignity. There are, of course, great differences among nations in the levels of responsible participation in world affairs. Among contemporary states, no one doubts that Great Britain sustains a relatively high level. On the other hand, the states of the Soviet bloc that have depended on the Kremlin are only beginning to move toward a sufficient breadth of contact with other states to gain the cumulative experience and discipline needed for full acceptance as internationally responsible.

The following indices are among those that show the accumulation or disaccumulation of predispositions to act responsibly in external affairs: universality of formal recognition by other states, exchange of diplomatic officials, membership in transnational organizations, acceptance of third-party assistance in the persuasive settlement of disputes, participation as a third party in the persuasive settlement of disputes, acceptance of obligation to aid in the sanctioning activities of transnational bodies, maintenance of impartial legal protection of aliens in harmony with transnational norms.

5. It is implied in the foregoing, but must be made explicit, that political development calls for an internal process of decision whose structures—both formal and informal, organized and unorganized—constitute a system of public order capable of creative, realistic problem-solving in pursuit of a rising level of participation in all values.

We characterize briefly (and incompletely) the seven phases of the decision process. The intelligence phase functions appropriately when it supplies a flow of realistic information about trends, conditions, and projections which foster the clarification of overriding goals, and the invention and evaluation of policy alternatives. As technology advances, it becomes both necessary and possible to rely heavily on mass media and research agencies to supply current intelligence and, in conjunction with schools, to shape the socialization process.

The promotional phase of decision is in some ways the most distinctive mark of advanced polities. Promotions must include diverse demands and expectations which are non-coercively pursued for the purpose of affecting the course of decision. In caste-bound societies it is unthinkable that the political process operates on the basis of authoritative and controlling expectations that the non-power castes will have anything to say about what goes on. Under conditions of vast distress they may erupt into the arena of politics; but this is a sign of chaos, not of orderly participation. Political party systems (not one-party dictatorships, political orders), pressure groups, and public commentary are fundamental features of power-sharing in big-scale states, and they are substantially missing from "village plus oligarchy" or "village plus monocracy" at the inclusive level.

The prescribing function in modern societies must be able and willing to foster the growth of expectations in regard to appropriate norms by means of explicit legislation, rather than by relying on unacknowledged legislation (customary usage). It is often alleged—though research is meager on the point—that the discipline of rule-writing, resented and evaded as it may be at first, spreads the expectation that controversies will be impartially resolved and that traditional loyalties to family, neighborhood, and tribe will be undermined for the ultimate benefit of state loyalty. The prescribing function as an instrument of development takes the lead in clarifying and repeating the aims of the body politic and the practice of justifying specific measures in these terms.

The phases of invocation and application are focalized in administrative organs, civil and military. A detailed specification of relevant criteria must be included in a full model. The same point applies to appraisal and termination.

6. Adequate political models provide strategic guidance for timing and placing the factors that are estimated to contribute to the terminal result. Programs of national development must keep

transnational trends and prospects in view if favorable opportunities are to be seized and adverse circumstances nullified. The developers often operate across national lines from a national base or in the framework of an intergovernmental organization. Whatever their geographical situs, developers are active agents of innovation, diffusion, and restriction. A growing country responds selectively to the models in its international environment at different times. Policy and science are both concerned with identifying the contexts in which innovations come to the notice of individuals who are located at various geographical and social distances from where the activities occur. Who perceives himself better off by directing attention to them? By ignoring them? Among those who hear of change, who sees himself as better off (in terms of all values) by facilitating or blocking diffusion? As a result, what patterns of route and zone are followed if innovations spread?

As a means of stimulating further inquiry, we formulate a few principles addressed to advisers or final decision-makers who are responsible for programs of value accumulation and institutional development:

1. Think contextually; keep policy questions related to the goal values of all whose effective support is required for success.

Part of the problem is to invent policies and to devise programs of policy presentation that elicit the coalitions needed to obtain an effective demand to innovate. Expectations that affect value demands and self-identification must be strengthened or modified.

2. Among more particularized guides is the principle of decisiveness. It affirms the importance of avoiding confusion or paralysis during nation-building by maintaining a decision process that produces realistic and timely commitments. As Karl Deutsch has emphasized, communication networks may be overloaded; but indecisiveness may be a consequence of poor collaborative as well as poor communicative synchronizations.

The principle must be disregarded when the effective elite of a nation is largely hostile to the innovations it feels constrained to make. The strategy of development calls for measures that increase the strength of whatever factors make for indecisiveness in the official process of decision, while simultaneously giving aid and comfort to a modern-minded alternative.

3. Although external assistance in development programs is likely to be welcomed by important elite and non-elite elements, dependence is also resented. Hence, outside assistance ought to be given tactfully, which means giving respect to nationals of the receiving country.

4. The devolution of effective power to recipients of aid needs to be a reward for responsible performance by the elite elements which it is proposed to encourage on a long-term basis.

National elites can be expected, as part of the ordinary power-balancing process, to seek to dilute their dependence on one foreign source by multiplying these sources. As far as possible, the relinquishment of whatever effective power results from providing assistance should be used to strengthen modern-minded elements who are willing and growingly competent to act responsibly. The problem is to avoid the use of aid as blackmail by archaic or incompetent social formations.

5. Sound strategy requires the ideological incorporation of the entire nation into the challenging task of development and the encouragement of self-awareness of the process. Doctrine, formula, and miranda gain impact, elaboration, and stability as a by-product of collective problem-solving. If economic development is an attractive ideal, it should be integrated with the demand to achieve a nation that is truly modern in all dimensions of life.

6. National development requires simultaneous emphasis on a universal minimum of literacy and education, and on the rapid preparation of highly expert personnel. This is a warning against unbalanced skill and enlightenment policies; more concretely, it is a warning against the neglect of universal education or the overproduction of university-trained students without a future.

7. A general principle for the institutions of decision-making is to encourage administrative competence without precluding the growth of responsible legislatures, parties, and other plural associations. One implication of this principle is that administrative

inefficiency and corruption are not to be treated with too much alarm if they contribute to the growth of leaders and organizations who develop a new set of identities, expectations, and demands that crosscut and supersede older social formations.

8. International organizations should be used as far as possible to assist in strengthening ideological and organizational adherence to civil order, including the protection of basic human rights.

Since underdeveloped nations are often power vacuums, they provide an occasion for consolidating the institutions of transnational order while aiding the process of national growth.

• 9 •

Bureaucratic Development and the Psychology of Institutionalization

Lucian W. Pye

In the history of the social sciences there are many examples of new developments claiming intellectual advancement while simply ignoring the old and intractable problems which were holding up progress. Once the need to prove progress has receded, new methods and old problems may at last confront each other. There are two such examples in the history of the study of institutions. The first instance occurred when historians still dominated the field and there was growing dissatisfaction over the focus of historical analysis because of a lack of dynamic dimensions. The result was the rise of the institutional approach—instead of dealing with particular men, the scholar was expected to place the larger and more impersonal forces of institutions at the center of his analysis.[1] Very quickly the institutional approach was proclaimed to be a significant advance, but over the decades as it became more rigidly legalistic the analysis of institutions all too easily took on the quality of glorifying particular arrangements in terms of either ideal models or particular descriptions at different sequences in time. The result was in such cases a static form of analysis that lacked even the dynamic thrust of the method of merely telling a tale. Also, in inept hands the tradition

1. The institutional approach began in the middle of the last century with the study of legal and constitutional institutions by such scholars as Leopold Ranke and Thomas Stubbs. See Edward Fueter, *A History of Modern Historiography* (Paris, 1914), and G. P. Gooch, *History and Historians in the 19th Century* (2nd ed.; London and New York, 1952).

of institutional analysis became one of indulging in grand abstractions, of attributing potency to impersonal forces that were no more than analytical abstractions.

The second turn in the road toward progress occurred when dissatisfaction with the institutional approach encouraged the advent of behavioralism. The prime thrust of behavioralism was the reassertion of the simple fact that decisions happen in the minds of specific individuals and, therefore, institutions are composed of the acts of individuals.[2] Thus analysis should concentrate on the behavior of individuals if the results are to be dynamic and precise. As the focus of analysis shifted from the abstractions of institutions to the concreteness of individuals the basis was established for integrating psychology with the more politically and historically oriented social sciences. As Lasswell made the general study of politics the answering of the question who gets what, when, and how, so others have made the more particular study of organizations revolve around the question who influences whom, either formally or informally, in the making of collective decisions?[3]

The return to concreteness has, however, tended to favor a concern for precision and measurement over the need for a more dynamic understanding of the history of institutions. The static character of the institutional approach was thus replaced by the equally static emphasis of much of behavioralism.[4] What seems to have happened is that political scientists have learned to be profoundly dissatisfied with explicitly employing grand abstractions which cannot be readily tested empirically. Yet on the other hand, we have been slow to focus behavioral analysis on the questions which compelled the grand abstractions in the first

2. The rise of behavioralism and the controversies over its merits are so near at hand that it is hardly necessary to document its history. An interesting approach, however, to its history is to be found in such accounts of the development of American political science as Albert Somit and Joseph Tanenbaum, *The Development of Political Science* (Boston, 1967), and Harold D. Lasswell, *The Future of Political Science* (New York, 1963).

3. The classic study of bureaucracies in such terms is Chester Barnard, *The Functions of the Executive* (Cambridge, Mass., 1938). See also Amitai Etzioni, *A Comparative Analysis of Complex Organizations* (New York, 1961).

4. For a statement of how modern social science is as static and descriptive as the earlier formal, legalistic studies see Dankwart A. Rustow, "New Horizons for Comparative Politics," *World Politics*, IX, (1957), 530–549.

instance. As a consequence we can claim progress while not facing up to the original problems which inspired the search for new methods.

I. Institutions

These reflections on the transitions from the chronological to the institutional and then to the behavior approaches were inspired by reflections on how little the social sciences have to say about the question of institution-building, which has become a major policy concern in the developing nations. For some time scholars and policy-makers have sensed that the future development of the countries of Africa and Asia calls for the building of new and stronger institutions.[5] It is striking, however, how little we have to say that is constructive about what in actual fact must take place when what we call "institutionalization" takes place.

Political scientists have long used this awkward term as a shorthand expression for what remain the mystical if not magical processes by which all manner of activities take on sufficient form to be recognized as structures.

In moving from the chronological to the institutional approach it became possible to talk casually about how this or that government was becoming more or less institutionalized without feeling compelled to elaborate precisely what this would mean in behavioral terms. How stable, predictable, and orderly does group behavior have to be before we can say that institutionalization has taken place? How does behavior change when any process becomes institutionalized? What changes must occur in individuals for institutionalization to take place? What changes must take place in the society or community as a whole for it to be recognized that institutionalization has occurred? What is substance and what is form in all the actions that might be related to

5. A recent and forceful statement of this need is Samuel P. Huntington's "Political Development and Political Decay," *World Politics*, XVII (1965), 386–430.

institutionalization? These are the questions one might have thought would have been raised when behavioralism tended to replace the institutional approach. Strangely enough the overwhelming burden of behavioral studies of institutions and organizations has been on trying to explain how the individual adapts his behavior when he joins or acts within an established institution, and we have done almost nothing on the problem of how behavior can create an institution in the first instance. As with the earlier institutional approach we have tended thus to contrive to take most institutions as constituted givens and to treat behavior in either formal or informal terms.

With respect to the problem of institution-building we have in some respects been retrogressive. For example, Max Weber's great concern was with precisely how different forms of authority came into existence and the relationship between different types of authority and social, cultural, religious, and economic factors.[6] Later social scientists have turned Weber's categories into static, idealized models largely divorced from their historical and developmental context.[7]

Once we acknowledge that we can and should ask more direct and precise questions about what is involved in such a broad concept as institutionalization, it does become disturbingly "unscientific" to use the concept in a loose and sweeping fashion. If we accept the behavioral assumptions that the act is the prime unit of analysis, the use of such a term as "institutionalization" can easily retard rather than aid the advancement of understanding. Indeed, once we do examine explicitly the underlying elements or components of the general concept of institutionalization it becomes embarrassingly evident that we have often found it useful because it helped us to reason in a circle. For example, to define political development in terms of institutionalization is to be tautological unless we are prepared to spell out

6. See Max Weber, *The Theory of Social and Economic Organization*, trans. A. M. Henderson and Talcott Parsons, Parsons (ed.) (New York, 1947), and *The Protestant Ethic and the Spirit of Capitalism*, trans. Talcott Parsons (New York, 1930).

7. See Joseph LaPalombara's chapter in this volume.

exactly what we mean by political development and by institutionalization and show that there are some especially relevant differences between the two.

Although it has been commonplace to talk of different patterns of bureaucratic behavior becoming institutionalized or of the need to institutionalize modern administrative practices without being any more precise about what this may mean, we do at times assume we are being more specific when we suggest that institutionalization involves accepting and internalizing norms of action. But what in fact is involved if people internalize norms? What is it that they are learning, and how does learning that produces institutionalized behavior differ from that which produces, say, learned people?[8]

If it is correct that the process of institutionalization basically involves the internalizing of norms, then it must be essentially a psychological process. Is the process a quite specific one which demands that the individual incorporate into his daily behavior certain habits of action until they become "routinized," whatever that equally evasive term may mean? Or is the process essentially a negative one, in the sense that it involves losing the capacity to conceive of alternatives, i.e., non-institutionalized ways of doing things. How much does the process depend upon people putting on psychological and cognitive blinders? What is the relationship between internalizing norms and inhibiting imagination? To what extent is it true that creativity can again blossom once the struggle to internalize norms has been completed?[9]

The question of institutionalization involves both social and individual psychology. The development of such institutions as bureaucracies calls for quite particular forms of group behavior, and thus the acts of individuals must be placed in the larger context. But what makes up this context? It certainly involves more than the particular individuals and their experiences of recruitment and training. The perspective of social psychology must give way to a historical point of view. Whatever is meant by institution-

8. See, for example, Gordon W. Allport, *Personality and Social Encounter* (Boston, 1960), esp. Part III, "Normative Problems in Personality."

9. See Calvin W. Taylor and Frank Barron, *Scientific Creativity: Its Recognition and Development* (New York, 1963).

alization, it cannot happen when only a few people adjust their actions; it calls for much broader changes that must be anchored in the historical continuity of the community.

If these assumptions about the importance of social psychological considerations for institutionalization are acceptable, we should be asking rather precise questions about the limits to kinds of institutionalization that may be set by the conditions of the society. Is it true that societies tend to get the institutions they deserve? To what extent can a society achieve institutionalization at levels of performance in, say, efficiency and dependability that are above the general norm of behavior of the culture? How far can different types of institutions move ahead of the cultural level of the society? What forms of institutionalization are easier to achieve, and which ones are more difficult for societies that are still close to the traditional order? How far can a society actually go in trying to improve upon its existing institutions by consciously attempting new forms of institution-building?

Finally, to understand the behavioral dimensions of what we commonly mean by the general term institutionalization, we need to know more about what must happen to change a system of human interaction so that what we tend to call a "process" becomes so regularized that it also becomes a "structure." What is it in people's expectations and perceptions that makes it seem reasonable to attribute to some processes the general quality of being stable enough to be structures? A bureaucracy is certainly a process, yet we are inclined to recognize it as a structure. In a well-established political system it is perfectly clear that process and structure represent only different analytical perspectives for viewing the same phenomena—and thus we can speak of the legislative (or bureaucratic) processes or the legislative (or bureaucratic) structures and institutions. But in transitional societies can there not be processes that are lacking some element of orderliness so that they are not yet structures? Conversely, can there not also be in such societies some structures that are either so artificial or so moribund that they lack enough significant life to contain processes? Therefore, is not the problem of institution-building in such societies to a large degree one of relating structures and processes?[10]

II. Precolonial and Postcolonial Institutionalization

From the foregoing remarks it should be apparent that we may open a Pandora's box when we begin to ask detailed and specific questions about the actual behavior that lies behind our commonplace generalization about the institutionalization of bureaucracies. We can appreciate again why life would be so much easier in political science if we could only go on employing grand concepts and terms in place of actual descriptions and explanations. Yet the advancement of knowledge apparently demands that we try to isolate the behavioral elements that can give greater empirical content to such concepts. Presumably we should proceed in this effort sustained by a faith, which unfortunately is becoming increasingly daunted, that a commitment to clarifying detailed and precise problems should eventually make us better prepared to return to the discussion of grand issues. The sad truth seems to be that all too often the concern for precision in empirical analysis leads into an endless bog of details of ever more trivial dimensions so that we never seem able to come out again on the side of excitement and bold generalizations. Honesty also compels us to admit that at times the effort at achieving precision by way of behavior analysis can result only in the restatement of conventional wisdom in an unintelligible language. However, in spite of these pitfalls we can at least hope that the exercise will leave us a bit more sensitive to the subtleties contained in the grand concepts that we will probably have to continue to rely on in most of our discourses about bureaucratic development.

Our task would be considerably easier and less uncertain if the

10. It is this problem which is particularly well highlighted by the structural-functional approach. See Gabriel A. Almond, "Introduction: A Functional Approach to Comparative Politics," in Gabriel A. Almond and James S. Coleman (eds.), *The Politics of the Developing Areas* (Princeton, 1960).

specialists of individual and group behavior, the psychologists, had already broken ground on studying the psychology of institutionalization. Unfortunately the considerable body of work on psychology and organizations has been almost entirely premised upon the prior existence of the organizations; thus the emphasis has been upon how individuals are socialized to particular structures and how they adapt their behavior to the requirements of organizational life. For psychologists the tendency has been to accept as hard realities all institutional matters which they see as falling within the domain of such disciplines as sociology and political science. In this perspective the psychological problems of organizations are mainly variations on the theme of differences between private motives and institutional necessities.[11]

With these introductory thoughts in mind, we shall in this chapter examine the psychological and behavioral dimensions of two quite different patterns of institutionalization in the building of bureaucracies in two historical periods. The first period was that of colonialism when rather rapidly numerous civil bureaucracies were created in still highly traditional societies. The second is that of the postindependence period when there has been great desire for bureaucratic development but also great difficulty in actually establishing new institutions.

11. This same tradition was built into psychologically oriented political science when Harold D. Lasswell in his pioneering book, *Psychopathology and Politics* (Chicago, 1930; paperbound ed., 1960), pp. 75–76, suggested a formula for expressing the developmental aspects of political man: $p\}d\}r = P$, in which p stands for private motives, d is displacement onto a public object, r is rationalized in terms of public interest, P is the political man, and $\}$ symbolizes "transformed into." In his approach Lasswell was firm in suggesting that personality and political institutions were quite separate, that each had its distinctive dynamics, and thus that the one could hardly shape the other.

It has been only with the students of personality and culture that we have had the view that characterological considerations can be decisive in structuring public institutions, and that once such institutions have been established they can reshape the modal personality of a culture. An example of such a characterological approach to political behavior is Nathan Leites, *A Study of Bolshevism* (New York, 1953). The theory of the interrelationship of personality and public institutions can be found in Everett E. Hagen, *On the Theory of Social Change* (Homewood, Ill., 1962).

The problem we are facing here goes beyond these approaches in that we are asking about the relationship of personality to the initial establishment of institutions—what compels individuals to build institutions in the first instance, and since personal motivations generally conflict with established institutions how can weak and as yet uninstitutionalized organizations gain the support necessary for historical continuity?

The spirit of the clerk: Ritualization and the power of the word

The first pattern of the institutionalization of a bureaucracy that is relevant to understanding the problem of political development occurred with the establishment of colonial administrations. To date social scientists have tended to focus on the end of empire and on the heritages of colonialism, and beyond historical narratives we have had little systematic analysis of how it was possible for Europeans so readily to implant themselves in control of what could be for them only exotic and mysterious societies.[12] The ideologues of history have asked why colonialism took place, not how did it happen, or why did it "take" so easily and so completely for so long. Aside from making vivid what was supposedly good and bad, these moralizers of imperialism tended mainly to strengthen the impression that if colonialism was not inevitable it was at least remarkably solid and substantial almost from inception.

It is true that the full establishment of colonies was often so slow as to be almost imperceptible; it took the Dutch nearly three hundred years to complete their eventual domination of all of contemporary Indonesia, and the spread of British control throughout the states of India was nearly as slow.[13] Yet what is significant is how rapidly, almost instantaneously, authority could be established in any locale once the decision was made to practice governance. More often than not, the process depended upon a local traditional authority welcoming European support, for it is important to keep in mind that colonialism did not generally begin as an adversary relationship.

The mystery is still why was it so easy to achieve what were considered to be respectable administrative systems, according to

12. For example, in his classic study of nationalism as the natural response to colonialism Rupert Emerson found it unnecessary to treat in any detail the initial establishment of colonial rule. See his *From Empire to Nation* (Cambridge, Mass., 1960).

13. For an excellent account of the early years of Dutch penetration of India see George Masselman, *The Cradle of Colonialism* (New Haven, 1963). The story of the British involvement in India is told in A. B. Keith, *A Constitutional History of India, 1600–1935* (London, 1936), and Sir Percival Joseph Griffiths, *The British Impact on India* (London, 1952).

the highest standards of that day, when we recognize how difficult it has been in the postcolonial era to achieve workable systems of administration according even to past standards, to say nothing of contemporary standards. True, changes in standards have meant that we expect a great deal more of government now than in the days when the British East India Company first began to practice civil rule. Still, if the first generation of postindependence leaders could have come as close to establishing in as short a time the appearances of permanent institutions as did Hastings and Raffles our current problems would be quite different. Our point is that while the capacities of those administrations were limited, at least within their context, they very rapidly became what we would call institutionalized.

For example, what is striking is that within a couple of decades after British rule was established in Burma we find Burmese writing about their own lives and careers as if the British institutions were permanent and fully understood. In India, well before the Mutiny, the culture of colonial administration was taken as much as a predictable given as, say, the differences between Hindu and Muslim. Let us be clear: we are not suggesting that colonial administrations were liked or disliked, only that the processes of administration were somehow acknowledged as having the qualities of institutions in a reasonably brief period of time.[14]

We cannot examine all the strands in the story of why colonial authority was generally so quickly institutionalized. Common to the pattern was a strange blending of emphasis upon massive grandeur and minute detail. For the community at large the stress was upon inordinate size in all symbols of authority. In contrast with all that had existed before, colonial architecture strove to be outlandishly huge. In some cases this was easily but dramatically achieved, as in Singapore, Manila, and Djakarta, but

14. It is true that these colonial administrations did not penetrate deeply into the societies, and in this sense colonial rule was a very limited form of rule since it did not touch the basics of social life. The fact, however, that the majority of the people could ignore or treat lightly the colonial administrative system does not alter our thesis that within the colonial services institutionalization did occur rather rapidly, especially in light of the fact that the system was essentially a foreign one which did not reflect the values of the indigenous culture.

elsewhere it took considerable striving to overshadow previous imperial symbols, as in India.

For the individuals involved, however, the process of colonial administrative institutionalization demanded infinite attention to details, concentration on the smallest matters, and the inhibition of imagination. The speed with which it was possible to create the spirit of the clerk in traditional societies from Asia to Africa was matched only by the remarkable uniformity of the product in spite of great initial cultural differences. Whether it was done by the British East India Company in Bengal or the Dutch East Indies Company in Java or by the British authorities in Nigeria and the Gold Coast, the training of local civil servants had much the same outcome.[15]

In these cases institutionalization had some very powerful psychological overtones, for the individual was supposed to be radically and thoroughly transformed, shedding his original personality and adopting a new one. The change was as great as expected when civilians became soldiers or in a later era when sentimentalists became hardcore Communists. We can only briefly enumerate what apparently was involved in this process of psychological adjustment basic to creating new institutions.

Above all, the training of potential civil service employees dwelt on instilling anxieties about the unimaginably dangerous consequences that can follow from the slightest error in behavior. The sensitizing of individuals to the notion that mistakes are bad and indeed evil generally took the form of a sharp and unambiguous system of rewards and punishments which was enveloped in considerable emotion. When a clerk made a mistake it invariably tended to produce outrageous anger on the part of superiors. There was also, but with less certitude, the possibility for some

15. Unfortunately we do not have any systematic comparative studies of the training of early civil servants in different parts of the British and French empires. Although there are formal studies of these early civil services, an interesting basis for a comparative study of attitudes and sentiments might be found in the rich tradition of novels about life in such societies. See especially Philip Woodruff, *Call the Next Witness* (London, 1945) and *The Wild Sweet Witch* (London, 1947); John Masters, *Lotus and Wind* (New York, 1953); Maurice Collis, *Trials in Burma* (London, 1947); George Orwell, *Burmese Days* (London, 1934); and for Africa there is of course the classic, Joyce Cary's, *Mister Johnson* (London, 1939).

show of human warmth and even praise when all was done with exactness. The style of training tended however in most colonial situations to stress the unlimited potential of authority to lose its temper over any mistake regardless of its significance.[16]

Institutionalization that involved learning roles was based upon great fears and anxieties. Actions thus became ritualized and the rituals were heavily shrouded in affect. Things could not be casual, for the judgment of the worth of the self in the eyes of all others depended upon one's careful attention to details. For superiors it was the details within the office routine, for outsiders it was the details that went with the habits of dress, of speech, and of daily routine that were associated with public impressions of what the civil service was all about.

When the system is placed under close scrutiny, what seems to have been involved was that people were taught a set of role relationships which were expected to evoke tremendous emotional reactions but also demanded the complete control of behavior. The relationships themselves were on the surface largely devoid of affect, or at least only the superior could give expression to his emotions; the trainee had to contain within himself anxieties and feelings which heightened the significance of what he did without, however, allowing him truly to express himself. Consequently he tended to ascribe almost magical powers to the substance of what he dealt with, and this substance was words. The words of the administrative codes then had all the potency which essentially sacred texts are capable of having for the human mind.[17]

There were thus, on the one hand, all the mysterious powers that the human imagination is prepared to imbue in written symbols; on the other hand there was a sharply limiting scope for the expression of affect that occurs whenever human relationships are defined solely in role terms. The relationships within colonial

16. For a discussion of the emotional and psychological dimensions of the training experience in the Burmese civil service see Lucian W. Pye, *Politics, Personality and Nation Building* (New Haven, 1962).

17. For an insightful analysis of the psychology of the power of the word and the book, see Erik H. Erikson, *Young Man Luther: A Study in Psychoanalysis and History* (New York, 1958).

administrations were not complete ones in that they did not give scope to the full range of sentiments appropriate to human relationships. The contrast between the dehumanizing aspects of rigid and limited role relationships and the evocation of intense emotions about the potency of written words seemingly produced a psychological set of attitudes in which it was possible to maintain remarkably disciplined and enduring habits of behavior.

Indeed one of the gloomiest pictures of the human potential for enduring routinized activities is that of the careers of men trained under colonial administrations. What apparently made these lives endurable and unfaltering were the emotions that supported and gave deep meaning to essentially ritualized routines. The power of this psychological process is to be seen in the lives of the thousands of Africans and Asians who early moved from their traditional settings through a few years of Westernized schooling to what would appear to be painfully restricted and inhibiting careers, and who at every stage rejoiced over what they conceived of as their good fortune to be among the elect.[18]

In the larger context colonial institutionalization was reinforced by the responsiveness of the societies in giving status and respect to all who entered the civil service. These were societies that found it easy to give deference to clerks. In large measure this deference was extracted from the public by the behavior of the clerks whenever they had to deal with outsiders. No clerk was too lowly not to be able to treat mere civilians with proper scorn. The public would have to wait on the slow pace of movement of junior officials just as these officials had to adjust their pace to the whims of their superiors.

It would be hard to underestimate the psychic satisfaction that members of these civil services derived from the manner in which they treated mere citizens. In a sense this was the escape valve for people who had to control so much of their emotions in their relations with superiors.

18. Much has been made over the status- and deference-oriented qualities of colonial administrations and of the desire of young people in these societies to follow careers in government because of their elite quality and their promise of security. What has been generally overlooked is the psychic satisfaction that people in such societies can derive from the drama of ritual and from being knowledgeable about esoteric routines. See, for example, U Ba U, *My Burma: The Autobiography of a President* (New York, 1958).

For the society at large it was also possible to ascribe rather quickly high status to those working with the ruling authorities because there were so few alternative claimants to authority. Within the still highly traditional societies there were authority figures, such as fathers, headmen, landowners, priests, and the like, but none of these could in any sense be compared with, or seen as competing with, governmental authority. Thus all the emotional meaning that traditional people attach to the myths of authority could be easily transferred to those who served within the civil administration.

Out of these considerations of individual and collective experiences we can find the ingredients for the building of quite new but also stable institutions. The model for the institution, however, was a static one. For the Europeans the model was that of the machine, as conceived in the nineteenth century, which had rigidly fixed and interchangeable parts.[19] For those recruited the model was more that of a disciplined life such as would be expected of soldiers in an army or priests in an order. Above all, the pattern of rewards and punishments conspired to strengthen the basic notion that all other forms of behavior were inconceivable. The emotions involved in the magic of ritualization and reverence for the word of the law were sufficient to set sharp boundaries on the imagination. Security and well-being could be adequately realized by focusing all attention on what had to be done in the daily round of events.

Historically the colonial environment was thus unique, for it provided a setting in which it was possible to introduce the model of a new role, that of the clerk, which was adequately exciting, easily enough learned, sufficiently rewarded, and devoid of any significant competitors. For those who were motivated to try their hands at playing the role there were few temptations to seek other roles. The circumstances were thus right to achieve rather readily a particular form of institutionalization.

19. Although as individuals the British colonial officials tended often to be extraordinarily idiosyncratic, each universally committed to the notion that only he really understood the people, the sum effect of all their efforts was to create an impersonal system, insensitive to favoritism, and thus a mere machine. For a nice illumination of this contrast between individuals and systems see Philip Woodruff, *The Men Who Ruled India,* Vol. I: *The Founders* and Vol. II: *The Guardians* (New York, 1954).

The spirit of the adversary process: The limits of structuring controlled aggression

With the end of colonialism the problem of bureaucratic development took a radically new turn. The old pattern of institutionalized behavior had to give way, and a new basis for the psychology of institutionalization had to be found. When nationalist politicians replaced foreign superiors as the authority figures in the hierarchical system, the highly constricting quality of role relationships disappeared, and subordinates quickly came to expect the legitimacy of much more complete human relationships. The colonial superiors had been foreigners, but now the politicians were from their own society, so communication and associations should have been more intimate and less restraining, or so many civil servants expected when independence came to their countries.

Also with independence there has usually been enough confusion and uncertainty to destroy any lingering mystique about the potency of legal codes and the written word in administrative decisions. Thus the contradictory pressures of grandeur and detail on the civil servants were each in their way undermined. At the same time, new roles of authority began to appear in these societies. The status of the official was no longer supreme. New skills could be recognized and new forms of rewards and punishments were available for the ambitious.

In short, with independence most civil servants found that their world had changed so that they were suddenly compelled to adjust not to a disciplined order of role relationships but to the tensions of a political arena. Power relationships have replaced ritualized ones. Civil servants found that they now had a new source of danger and new fears and anxieties. Whereas the transition from traditional social relationships to ritualized bureaucratic life had involved the continuity of highly structured and relatively unambiguous situations, the political realities in most former colonies have tended to be much more in flux; consequently there has generally been considerable uncertainty about what should be taken as the proper cues for guiding behavior.

This uncertainty about power relationships has been at the basis of most of the difficulties in institutionalizing new administrative authorities.

It would be impossible to enumerate here all the various specific problems and difficulties which have complicated the process of organizational development in the emerging areas during the last decades. Almost without exception, however, a key problem has been that of achieving the institutionalization of essentially *political* relationships. The relationships are political not only between the civil servants and the political leaders but also among the civil servants. As long as these conflicts are open and unresolved it is difficult for such vigorous political processes to become structures.

More specifically, the basic problem in such societies is that of containing and making potentially constructive adversary relationships. The new bureaucracies must be built around conflict and competition. Psychologically this will call for the institutionalization of apparently aggressive forms of behavior. Instead of suppressing intensely held emotions according to the dictates of discipline and ritualized lines of behavior, the task now is to establish order and predictability in conflict as gamelike situations. The prospect for such a change is complicated by the memories of those involved in the former colonial civil services, which often lead them to try to recapture the pattern of behavior which once had significance and once provided the security they associated with that form of institutionalization. Thus it is clear that the practices and training methods which once produced apparently dramatic results are no longer relevant.

It is not just that the conditions which once readily yielded institutionalized behavior no longer exist, but behavior within the bureaucracies must now be quite different. Under colonialism the training that produced institutions did not extend to training in decision-making. The purposes of the bureaucracies created were largely to enforce decisions, insure that information was accurately transmitted, and preserve precise records of what was being done. At present the first task of civil administration is still to preserve law and order, but it is necessary for bureaucracies to be able to do a great deal more.[20] The capacities of governments must be much greater if there is to be development.[21] To the extent that there has been a revolution of rising expectations in the new states, it has been largely one of assuming governments should be capable of doing much more than in the past. And once bureaucracies are assigned unreasonable tasks, it soon becomes generally expected that they will probably fail in most of what they seek to accomplish. In thinking big, some of the new regimes have felt that they no longer need to do what were once the routine tasks of government. Yet if these governments are ever to raise their capabilities they will have to achieve, on quite new terms, the institutionalization of their bureaucracies.

The basic change, however, is that bureaucracies must now be built around conflict situations. The ending of colonial rule not only provided power for nationalist political leaders who could threaten the status of the administrators trained earlier. In addition the ending of government by static law and the introduction of rule by politics meant that all manner of communal and regional groups found themselves in competitive situations. To understand the psychology of civil servants it is necessary to note the extent to which independence brought about a structural change in social relations which inevitably produced a sharp rise in internal tensions and competition in most former colonial countries. The intensity of these general conflicts and the resulting rise in social insecurity and tension have been carried over to relations within the transformed bureaucracies. Thus, before analyzing the problem of institutionalizing adversary relationships, we must first appreciate the general problem of conflict in former colonial societies.

One of the most significant by-products of the confrontation of cultures under colonialism was a sharpening awareness of communal realities. As a step in the process of nation-building coloni-

20. For a contrast of colonial and postcolonial bureaucratic practices see Joseph LaPalombara (ed.), *Bureaucracy and Political Development* (Princeton, 1963), and Ralph Braibanti and Joseph J. Spengler (eds.), *Administration and Economic Development in India* (Durham, N.C., 1963).

21. For a theory of capabilities as the key measure of political development see Gabriel A. Almond and G. Bingham Powell, *Comparative Politics: A Developmental Approach* (Boston, 1966).

alism encouraged identification not with the total community but with significant segments of it. Everyone under the colonial system belonged to some subcommunity; race and religion provided the most common basis of identification, but all manner of clan, tribal, regional, and religious distinctions were acknowledged and tolerated.[22]

These distinctions of identity were usually part of a highly elaborate division of labor which did far more than just provide integration for the economy. The division of labor under colonialism had the quality of attributing to each community a sense of its unique and often, but not always, valued characteristics. That is to say, those who made up the elements of the division of labor tended to be acutely aware of being members of viable subcommunities, each of which was recognized as having a dynamic and spirit of its own. The changes in the economy brought about by colonialism created the need for new roles which in turn were filled not by random individuals but by members of specific communities. In part this cellular development of subcommunities was possible because colonialism, even though in an absolute sense it brought a sharp break with traditional patterns, was based on a relatively static technology. Once Europeans introduced the plantation economies and the urban trading and shipping industries, those who learned the new roles found that there was little threat of change or obsolescence. Each community that was identified with a role in the system could be confident that further change was not likely, and thus the notion that there was legitimacy in the ways in which tasks and rewards were divided was easily accepted. The lack of rapid technological change also meant that changes in the state of the economy tended to affect everyone in much the same way. With the world depression all groups went down; and the fluctuations in the prices of raw material exports tended to be felt in much the same degree by all. This meant that there were few changes which raised questions about how the economic pie should be divided, for it was exceed-

22. See, for example, Cora Du Bois, *Social Forces in Southeast Asia* (Minneapolis, 1949), and Norton Ginsburg (ed.), *The Pattern of Asia* (Englewood Cliffs, N.J., 1958).

ingly rare that one community would prosper while another suffered.[23]

With the end of colonialism a new model of politics immediately developed in which all the cellular communities of the previous period sensed insecurity in varying degrees and thus sought to expand their power. All groups had to readjust their relationships to each other because some groups appeared to be advancing their positions in a competitive and threatening fashion. With uncertainty and competition there was in nearly all the countries a rising sense of suspicion among communities.[24]

In fact, this increase in suspicion was a direct consequence of the ethos of anticolonialism which had proclaimed that the foreign rulers had exploited the country and that with the ending of colonialism people should be better off since the presumed profits of colonialism could be redistributed among the people. When independence did not bring an improvement of living standards for most people the suspicion immediately developed that somebody else must be benefiting from independence. According to the logic of anticolonialist propaganda there should have been a new "cutting of a larger pie," and everyone became more sensitive to questions of relative benefits.[25]

The tragedy of many former colonial countries is that even the most sincere politicians could not avoid seeming to be a threat to elements of their society. For example, U Nu as soon as he became prime minister and tried to champion the aspirations of Burmese Buddhism as part of an expression of Burmese national-

23. For descriptions of the connections between economic roles and communal groups see F. G. Bailey, *Caste and the Economic Frontier* (Manchester, 1957); Fred R. von der Mehden, *Religion and Nationalism in Southeast Asia* (Madison, Wis., 1963); T. H. Silcock. *The Commonwealth Economy in Southeast Asia* (Durham, N.C., 1959); and T. Scarlett Epstein, *Economic Development and Social Change in South India* (New York, 1962).

24. For descriptions of this rise in communal tensions see W. Howard Wriggins, *Ceylon: Dilemma of a New Nation* (Princeton, 1960); Myron Weiner, *Party Politics in India* (Princeton, 1959); and Richard L. Sklar, *Nigerian Political Parties* (Princeton, 1963).

25. The most extreme example of this tendency, as with so many others, was the Congo. See Crawford Young, *Politics in the Congo: Decolonization and Independence* (Princeton, 1965). But the problem of unequal gains and losses and general disappointment also occurred even in the more sophisticated India. See George Rosen, *Democracy and Economic Change in India* (Berkeley and Los Angeles, 1966).

ism was seen as a threat first by the Karens and then by nearly all the minority peoples, ranging from the Shans to the Chins, Kachins, Mons, and even the Arakanese. Once politics became competitive in Burma all the people suddenly began to appreciate the relative insecurity of their particular communal grouping.[26]

In Indonesia the early attempt to expand party organizations into the countryside had a similar effect by heightening the anxieties of the various subcommunities. Party organizations were seen at the village level as giving greater strength to particular groupings and thus as a threat to others. People could be readily mobilized because of the prior communal or cellular structure of their society, but once mobilized they tended only to heighten the level of intercommunity tension.[27]

Once power was open for competition the cellular character of former colonial societies lost its remarkably stable quality and rapidly became charged with tension. As groups realized that they would have to tend to their own security they became aware of their status as minority groups. Much of the dynamic drive in the basic pattern of politics in many Afro-Asian states is to be found in the approaches and strategies of the various groups and communal leaders in coping with the realities of minority status. Even the national leaders have gradually had to accommodate their styles to the fact that they represented less of the nation than they initially assumed they did.

In this general environment of politicized tension the members of bureaucracies often see themselves as a specific community, like many of the others, whose status has been threatened by the universal search for power. But for the leading civil administrators the situation has been somewhat different from that of the leaders of the other communal groups, for they have responsibilities for governing. The task of government, however, has become more complex, and this means that within bureaucracies conflicts inevitably arise. Such clashes have been novel and disturbing experiences.

26. Richard Butwell, *U Nu of Burma* (Stanford, 1963).

27. Herbert Feith, *The Decline of Constitutional Democracy in Indonesia* (Ithaca, N.Y., 1962), and Clifford Geertz, *The Social History of an Indonesian Town* (Cambridge, Mass., 1965).

Under the more static conditions of foreign rule and with foreigners themselves making the decisions that affected allocations among the various ministries, departments, and bureaus, the old civil services were institutionalized without their members feeling that competition and conflict should be a serious or proper matter of government. Since independence civil servants have had to discover that when they were not in conflict with their political masters they were likely to be in conflict among themselves. They now have to confront decisions for which there are no automatic technical or value-free answers; thus they must turn to power conflicts and controversy in order to resolve prevailing issues.[28]

Consequently a basic problem in institutionalizing numerous new bureaucracies has been that of learning how to handle adversary relationships in an orderly fashion. The difficulty is that conflict tends to produce aggressive and threatening behavior, particularly in cultures in which the traditional emphasis was upon denying all appearances of conflict among friends. The fact that in many transitional societies there have been great difficulties in introducing competitive party politics is well appreciated, but it is less generally realized that much the same problem with competition has plagued bureaucratic development.

Learning how to deal in an undisruptive manner with adversary relationships in government offices has been complicated by the earlier traditions which suggested that there was magic in precision and in the appearances of grandeur. The old pattern called for subordinates to control their emotions and for superiors to display their displeasure. Now the adversary situation calls for intense control of emotions, and superiors must learn to inspire and mobilize support. Skill in discovering how far it is possible and worthwhile to attack and defend initial positions, how to arrive at compromises that do not destroy the effectiveness of programs, how to appeal for support of others without becoming the object of greater hostilities must all be learned with little support from either past bureaucratic experiences or general cul-

28. Pye, *Politics, Personality and Nation Building*; Richard L. Park and Irene Tinker (eds.), *Leadership and Political Institutions in India* (Princeton, 1959).

tural practices. In most transitional cultures people have long believed that it was healthy to suppress or deny conflicts in face-to-face relationships.[29] Yet if the new bureaucracies are to become institutionalized it will be necessary for their participants to learn patterns of behavior which will make it possible for them to routinize adversary relationships and to extract benefits from controversy.

The change from ritualized procedures and hierarchical role relationships to adversary relationships requires the actors to reduce their inhibitions and to become more imaginative about what is conceivable. Conflicts call for strategies and the inventiveness inherent in "game" situations. The key behavioral question now is what distinguishes the integrative potential of conflicts from their disruptive potential? What is it that makes it possible for some societies to contain and benefit from such dynamic clashes while others tend to disintegrate as the level of aggression rises?

Because of the urgent need for rapid bureaucratic development in so many Afro-Asian states it is disturbing that the training for competitive relationships is difficult, and this training is deeply and diffusely imbedded in those societies that have been more successful in achieving integration from conflict. Cultures that train people to deal explicitly with manifestations of aggressive behavior are more likely to succeed in using conflict integratively than cultures that stress the need to sublimate and deny any manifestations of aggression. Experience is critical because the vital difference is that people in competitive cultures have learned that conflicts need not be terminal, that there will always be another chance.

Unfortunately, in many of the developing countries the basic human expectation is that conflicts will be terminal. Politicians have little confidence that they will have another chance to gain power if they are ever defeated. This ethos easily carries over to the conflicts within the bureaucracies. The expectations of

29. For India see G. Morris Carstairs, *The Twice Born* (London, 1957); for Indonesia see Clifford Geertz, *The Religions of Java* (Glencoe, Ill., 1960); for West Africa see M. J. Field, *Search for Security* (London, 1960).

officials is that if their relations should become even a contained political process, it would be impossible for them to make that process appear to be a structure.

At present the problem of training administrators is above all that of teaching the art of adversary relationships. Since civil servants also need technical skills of ever higher levels, it is understandable that most efforts at technical assistance in public administration have focused on the non-controversial aspects of professional techniques and knowledge and little has been done to prepare people for adversary situations.

In Western countries the legal profession has done the most to train people to understand adversary relationships and to appreciate the advantages of controlled aggression and conflict in helping to establish orderly relations. Law, however, in most colonial societies was taught not as adversary conflicts but as codifying procedures concerned with ultimate justice. Therefore in many ex-colonial societies the need is to transform an exaggerated but highly formalistic appreciation of legal training into an understanding that this should mean an appreciation for institutionalized conflict.

III. The Search for Authority and Creativity

Quite different psychological considerations are involved in a process of institutionalization based upon ritual—one of detail and anxiety about words and the law—and in a process of institutionalization based upon adversary relations and the manipulation of controlled aggression. Each is rooted in a different form of the mystique of authority. Behind the concept of ritual and of the importance of correctness in details there is almost always a psychological sense of dependency upon a greater authority so that the self feels that it is gaining potency and self-realization by surrendering to the spirit of that higher authority.[30] Thus the

30. Although it is central to much of psychoanalytical theory, there has been little systematic study of the links between personality and culture on the one hand and types of ethos of authority on the other. See Gregory Bateson, *Naven*

dynamics that provided the thrust for continuity and repetition, which are essential for the phenomonen of institutionalization, was closely associated psychologically with feelings for authority which are equally essential for the bureaucratic phenomenon. Concern for ritual, detail, the word and the book, has its origin in the earliest sense of hierarchical relationships. Once the link between dependency and authority was established the individual could find enough sense of security to engage at times in countermores behavior, and out of this process of restrained challenges to the ethos of the system it was possible to realize an element of creativity. The clerk, like the child in an authoritarian family, could at times seek to be honored by being clever.[31]

In the new situation of more open competition for power and influence there is no longer the same direct psychological linkage between a sense for authority and the need to maintain a continuous pattern of role relationships. Indeed, if the adversary relationships get out of hand there may seem to be no basis whatsoever for any form of continuous authority. Whereas the security of dependency provided a substantial rationale for accepting and rejoicing in hierarchical relationships, the stress of competition tends to accentuate the importance not of authority but of sheer power.

It is only when such competition takes on the structured form of controlled adversary relations that it becomes universally apparent that the necessary conditions for the continuation of such relations provide a firm basis for a new concept of authority. Instead of authority being associated with hierarchical considerations and the superiority of age and experience, the sense of authority associated with adversary relations is connected with the spirit of civility and the dictates of collective survival that underlie peer relations and that have their origins in effective

(2nd ed.; Stanford, 1958), chaps. 16, 17. The form of authority which accompanied the spirit of the clerk in colonial societies was one step removed from the concept of the traditional mind as described in such studies as Robert Redfield, *Peasant Society and Culture* (Chicago, 1956), and Hagen, *On the Theory of Social Change*.

31. On the possibilities of creativity out of counterethos behavior in a rigid system see Gardner Murphy, *Personality: A Biosocial Approach to Origins and Structure* (New York, 1947), chaps. 19 and 35.

sibling relations. "The rules of the game" as both abstractions and functional necessities thus become an ultimate form of authority, for there cannot be a sense of the rules of the game unless there is a meaningful game.

There is then a fine line between the disorder and paralysis that can come from unchecked aggression and the sense of discipline and respect for ultimate or constitutional rules that is central to effective adversary relationships. This same fine line exists for not only the question of authority but also that of creativity. The prevalence of uninhibited aggression can be paralyzing, but on the other hand creativity seems to depend upon some forms of regulated competition and conflict.[32]

In most of the new states it will be necessary for members of the civil bureaucracies to learn how to cope with debate, argument, and confrontation without reacting either with paralysis or with deep emotional resentments before they can realize creativity. The increasing uncertainty of life and the lack of career stability in these countries makes it, of course, peculiarly difficult for people to perceive conflicts in anything but personal terms.[33] People need a high degree of basic ego security if they are to be successful in coping with frequent expressions of aggression. When people lack such ego security they are likely to be overly imaginative of the danger in conflict and fail to appreciate the authority of the rules of the game or display much creativity. This problem is frequently dramatized when foreign advisers have sought to raise the level of creativity of civil servants by encouraging them to conceive of a wider range of choices for their actions—an approach that would have been highly appropriate if the institutionalization were still based in the colonial pattern of ritualized and constrained behavior. Yet such an approach can be self-defeating when civil servants, confronted with conflicts, tend to be overly sensitive to the possibility that nothing is predictable. In short, the lack of creativity among some civil servants in

32. "It seems that in every process of creation the gradual emergence from conflict plays its part" (E. Kris, "Psychoanalysis and the Study of Creative Imagination," *Bulletin of the New York Academy of Medicine*, XXIX [1953], 51).

33. See Leon Festinger, *Conflict, Decision and Dissonance* (Stanford, 1964).

these situations is caused by too much rather than too little imagination. Or more precisely, too much imagination about the dangers of adversary relationships and little appreciation that regulated conflict can be the basis for both order and authority.

The difficulties of institutionalizing bureaucratic relations around the dynamics of adversary relations contribute to another phenomenon in the new states, the excessive tendency to pass all decision-making to the higher levels of authority. In any bureaucracy one of the most effective means of managing conflicts is to arrange for appropriate systems of appeal to higher authorities.[34] Yet the need to refer all matters to higher authorities for independent judgment suggests that there is little spontaneous appreciation of the logic of adversary clashes in which the participants can judge among themselves the reasonable outcome. The constant need in many of the new states to appeal for any decision means that civil servants are still looking for the direct hierarchical forms of authority of the colonial system.[35]

IV. Conclusion

As we return to the questions posed at the beginning about the psychology of institutionalization, it is apparent that the mechanisms at work in creating the colonial services produced a more direct match between personal, psychological motivation and the logic of the administration system than can be the case today in most developing societies. The organizational patterns of today that call for conflict, adversary confrontation, adaptation, and going beyond all rule books do not have direct links to patterns of positive personal behavior. Although in all organizations there are gaps between personal motivations and the purposes of the organization as a whole,[36] this gap seems to be peculiarly great in

34. William G. Scott, *The Management of Conflict: Appeal System in Organization* (Homewood, Ill., 1965).
35. Robert L. Kahn and Elise Boulding (eds.), *Power and Conflicts in Organizations* (New York, 1964).
36. For an interesting analysis of the relationships between personal motivations and organizational purposes see David Katz and Robert L. Kahn, *The Social Psychology of Organizations* (New York, 1966).

situations which call for uncertain change in the rationale of postcolonial administrations. Under the colonial pattern there was a much smaller gap between the system's need for order, predictability, adherence to regulations, and precision in recording and the individual's need for dependence, ordered hierarchy, security, and the sense of efficacy from mastering the written word. Today the much more sophisticated concept that wisdom and justice can best be insured by adversary relationships has little psychological support in the cultural predisposition of most of the people now trying to create the postcolonial administrative services.

Alternatively, what must occur is for more people to discover how to combine effectively psychic satisfaction from mastering some forms of technical skills and the satisfactions of competitive game situations. When this is done the necessary psychological basis for achieving the subtle combinations of technical and political skills which are the hallmark of the skilled modern administrator can exist. When more people in the new administrative services begin to find that they achieve great personal satisfaction from this combination of skills we can at last expect to see the institutionalization of truly modern administrative systems.

• 10 •

Sources of Bureaucratic Reform: A Typology of Purpose and Politics

John D. Montgomery

For reasons unrelated to the urgency or intrinsic interest of its subject matter, administrative reform has lost its grip on the imagination of political scientists. Specialists have concentrated more on the processes and even the mechanics of reform than on its political purposes and interactions. The current literature on the subject, such as it is, consists largely of manuals, handbooks, a few case studies, and monographs on ideal types. It all but ignores the conceptual problems of adapting static models of administrative perfection to dynamic political reality, leaving them instead to advisers, practitioners, and politicians. Administrative reform is, of course, a political process in that it must adjust the relationships between a bureaucracy and other elements in a society, or within the bureaucracy itself, in order to change the behavior of the public service. But it is an intellectual problem as well, in that accepted principles and theories of administration find their ultimate test in the many unexpected consequences of their application.

I. Introduction: Administrative Reform and the Political Order

Actual and desired relations between bureaucracy and society, or within the bureaucracy itself, are not constants. Some societies seek to reform conditions which others would consider desirable. Both the purposes of reform and the evils to which it is addressed vary with their political circumstances. Most administrative reforms are undertaken by one of three actors: by the rulers, policy-makers, and other power sources in a government; by other elements in the social order, external to the government; or by the bureaucracy itself, in its search for an adequate degree of internal cohesion and discipline. From its own vantage point, the bureaucracy perceives the sources of these reforms as representing its upward, lateral, and internal relationships. All three relationships depend upon the nature of the political and social order of which the bureaucracy is a part. A personal ruler who is seeking to use the bureaucracy to support his own position tends to attack as evils certain modes of behavior that might not be objectionable at all in an impersonal, more complex state. And the leaders of contemporary postcolonial modernizing states may undertake reforms against evils that both of the other systems could easily tolerate. Reforms in each of these three situations possess distinctive characteristics because they are addressed to different modes of undesirable bureaucratic behavior. Reforms may thus be classified according to an "annoyance principle": they are as much negative as positive within their own political context.

An analytical matrix may be constructed out of these two sets of dimensions, enabling us to distinguish among the perceived upward, lateral, and internal sources of reform as they emerge in a given system. For illustrative purposes, it may suffice to start with the three conventional classifications of political systems mentioned above—personal rulerships, democracies, and modernizing states—and to draw at random upon well-known historical examples of reforms characteristic of each. This approach will present at least the appearance of order, restrain the temptation to devise new ideal type forms as a substitute for reality, postpone problems of terminology, and permit us to make use of a few dramatic incidents to illustrate the contrasting interrelationships between administrative reform and political purpose.

Only later will we return to some of the methodological reservations enjoined by this approach.

This analytical approach differs somewhat from the widespread preoccupation with class struggle as the most useful means of interpreting these social relationships.[1] It accepts, however, the proposition that administrative reformers must consider change more as a social phenomenon than as a mere legal or procedural problem. In states where the bureaucracy appears as a social force possessing a degree of internal coherence and institutional self-consciousness, efforts at reform can indeed be seen as reflecting the competition for power and privilege, and it is quite possible to interpret such events as an expression of the class struggle. Louis XIV, archetype of the monarchic despot, provides evidence for this view, since he consciously tried to protect himself from his own bureaucratic Frankenstein's monster by appointing humble and obscure men to public office. As he himself said, commoners were preferable to "men of more eminent station because . . . it was important that the public should know, from the rank of those whom I chose to serve me, that I had no intention of sharing my power with them. . . . They themselves, conscious of what they were, should conceive no higher aspirations than those which I chose to permit."[2] For this reason he introduced reforms of a class-related character: he forced noblemen and other feudal relics holding public office to compete with a new professionalized bureaucracy of humbler origins. Similar attempts account for many of the "reforms" introduced in France and Germany in the seventeenth, eighteenth, and nineteenth centuries.[3] In the class struggles of eighteenth-century Prussia, the rising bourgeoisie outthought and outperformed the nobility, and reforms were instituted that, as President Von Schön put it, permitted the former to do "work for which high-born councillors

1. Karl A. Wittfogel, *Oriental Despotism: A Comparative Study of Total Power* (New Haven, 1957); S. N. Eisenstadt, *The Political Systems of Empires* (New York, 1963).

2. *Memoirs de Louis XIV,* quoted in Franklin L. Ford, *Robe and Sword* (Cambridge, Mass., 1953), p. 7.

3. Hans Rosenberg, *Bureaucracy, Aristocracy, and Autocracy: The Prussian Experience, 1660–1815* (Cambridge, Mass., 1958), pp. 16–17 and chap. 3.

were unqualified." But it is interesting to note that there was no revolutionary intention in such use of the lower classes to fill public offices: commoners were not expected to take the nominal responsibility for their decisions. "Middle-class people know only how to work, not how to govern. . . . It is not unusual, therefore, to appoint bourgeois councillors so that the upper-class bureaucrats will have time for more important matters."[4] Drawing on similar evidence from an impressive number of historic bureaucratic empires, Eisenstadt[5] interprets almost all reform in class terms: it is seen as an effort either to prevent the subjugation of the bureaucracy to "any strong group within the society," or to strengthen the bureaucracy as a weapon against "the monopolistic position of various status groups."

The "class struggle" interpretation of administrative reform does not apply with equal force in all societies, however. The centralized dynastic autocracies have provided sociologists with much impressive evidence, but the bureaucracies did not often constitute a single homogeneous class. It is well known, for example, that bureaucratic factions in ancient China actually struggled against each other. Adherents of the class struggle interpretation offer no explanation of the mystical equilibrium among the contending forces that mobilize the bureaucracy into a single coherent class.[6] When bureaucratic officials struggle for better pay, improved status, and more security, they do not often unite for these purposes. They do not become a class; and it is hard to accept Eisenstadt's argument that these common elements are

4. *Ibid.*, p. 181.
5. Eisenstadt, *The Political Systems of Empires*, pp. 169–170.
6. *Ibid.*, p. 166, citing Y. C. Wang, "An Outline of the Central Government of the Former Han Dynasty," *Harvard Journal of Asiatic Studies*, XII (1949), 134–185; R. Des Routours, "Traité des fonctionnaires et traité de l'armée," traduit de la *Nouvelle historie des T'ang* (Leiden, 1947–48), Vol. VI, Tomes I–II, chaps. 44–46, Introduction; E. G. Pulleyblank, *The Background of the Rebellion of An Lu-shan* (London, 1955); W. Eberhard, "Wie wunden Dynastien gegründet? Ein Problem der chinesischen Geschichte," *Dil ve Tarih-Cografya Fakültesi Derigesi* (Ankara, 1945), III, 361–376, *A History of China* (London, 1948), and *Conquerors and Rulers: Social Forces in Medieval China* (Leiden, 1952), chaps. 2–3; S. Runciman, *Byzantine Civilization* (London, 1933); Ford, *Robe and Sword;* P. Sagnac, *La societé et la monarchie absolue, 1661–1715* (Paris, 1945), p. 41; L. E. Fisher, *Viceregal Administration in the Spanish-American Colonies* (Berkeley, 1926) and "Colonial Government," in A. Curtis Wilgus (ed.), *Colonial Hispanic America* (Washington, 1936), chap. 7; C. H. Haring, *The Spanish Empire in America* (New York, 1947).

important enough to create political and social unity within their ranks. It is even more difficult to agree that divergent social origin and outlook contribute to an autonomous point of view rather than the reverse.[7] And finally, the irrelevance of the traditional class struggle interpretation becomes the more marked as the content and tactics of administrative reforms are placed in a wider perspective of historical experience than that of the traditional autocracies. The "annoyance principle" provides, I believe, a more adequate explanation of the complexity of the relationships involved in administrative reform. It can be applied not only in autocracies but also in democracies and modernizing states. It permits us to examine the sources of reform in several interacting layers, and it provides an analytical means for explaining the diverse consequences of reform efforts in different situations.

II. Traditional Autocracies

A system where political leadership is concentrated in the hands of a single ruler provides a relatively simple means of classifying the annoyances that make reform necessary. In these cases, the ruler is taken to be the sole reformer, although the levels of reform include all three relationships defined above. Thus from the traditional ruler's point of view, the greatest threats from the bureaucracy are usually to his own person, and the steps he takes to protect his position constitute the upward relationships of administrative reforms. The lateral or social relationships of the bureaucracy in an autocratic government involve revenue for the ruler's household. And the internal relationships governing bureaucratic discipline are perceived in terms of the ruler's prestige. In a personal domain of a size and structure capable of responding to the influence of a single ruler, then, the evils ("annoyances") most commonly attacked through reform may therefore be described on the three levels as disloyalty, inadequacy (in terms of resource-producing capacity), and dis-

7. Eisenstadt, *The Political Systems of Empires*, p. 167.

honor. These evils seem to be feared by most dynastic rulers, emperors, and in slightly modified form by charismatic dictators who have attempted to impose their personal authority upon the governed and have chosen to use bureaucratic intermediaries to do so.

Upward relationships

History offers an extraordinary range of autocratic efforts to reform the bureaucracy by weeding out sources of disloyalty. Such instances are most dramatic, of course, where no concept of "public" service has developed, where no distinction exists between a royal household and a government, and where loyalty itself is definable as blind, selfless obedience to the will of the ruler. Frederick William I's statement is classic: "One must serve the king with life and limb, with goods and chattels, with honor and conscience and surrender everything except salvation. The latter is reserved for God, but everything else must be mine."[8] Some absolute monarchs seemed to regard their servants as automatons. This condition found almost proverbial expression in Prussia, where detailed *règlements* were repeatedly produced for each official and each office, where rules of conduct, terms of employment, and functional duties were minutely defined, and where civil servants were treated like "valets, naughty school boys, and prospective criminals," yet "were constantly reminded of their special status as a distinctive and superior occupational group."[9] Such reforms, although subsequently hailed as instruments of efficiency, originally aimed at creating upward relationships of loyalty. Loyalty was also promoted by means of rotation, which permitted the ruler to treat civil servants as pawns, to be moved about at will. "Frederick William I [of Prussia] would never station an official in his native province, lest he should forget his primary loyalty."[10] The *Bakufu* government of Tokugawa Japan also used a complex system of rotation to keep feudal

8. Reinhold August Dorwart, *The Administrative Reforms of Frederick William I of Prussia* (Cambridge, Mass., 1953), p. 36.
9. Rosenberg, *Bureaucracy, Aristocracy, and Autocracy*, p. 92.
10. E. Barker, *The Development of Public Services in Western Europe, 1660–1930* (New York, 1944), p. 20.

retainers both impoverished and subject to the will of the autocrat.[11] One of the most bizarre techniques for maintaining loyalty was the use of eunuchs in important posts (including espionage) in Persia, China, Rome, and Byzantium. This practice was based on the proposition that the humble origins and lack of family prospects of these unfortunates would increase their dependence on the ruler and weaken the temptation to disloyalty and self-service.[12] Such reforms seem to echo Plato's advice for avoiding conflict of interests: eliminate the rights of private property ownership and of family to avoid loyalties outside the guardian's interests. Slaves could be, and were, used with similar intentions.

There are, of course, less drastic means of producing upward loyalty by weakening possible diversionary interests of the bureaucracy. Among these devices, the most fundamental was the effort to recruit civil servants from classes that supported the ruler's interests against those of potential rivals. The civil service examination, for example, was often used to permit the entrance of commoners and destroy the monopolistic position of privileged classes. Over centuries of such usages in ancient China, the numbers of commoners among the mandarins rose appreciably. The increase was only token, however; it never constituted a serious threat to the nobility (see Table 1).

The creation of other bases of merit entry into the bureaucracy also served to weaken monopolistic expectations of the privileged classes. Thus, in Rome, Byzantium, and China, titles were awarded not only on a class basis but also to those who performed designated functions, regardless of class.[13] Many states, in

11. See, for other examples, L. Bréhier, *Les institutions de l'Empire byzantin* (Paris, 1949), chaps. 1–2; C. Diehl, "The Government and Administration of the Byzantine Empire," in *Cambridge Medieval History* (Cambridge, 1927), Vol. IV, chap. 23; A. E. R. Boak and J. Dunlap, *Two Studies in Later Roman and Byzantine Administration* (New York, 1924); R. Guilland, "Etudes sur l'histoire administrative de Byzance," *Byzantina-Metabyzantina*, I (1946), 165–179, and "Sur les dignitaires du Palais et sur les dignités de la Grande Eglise, du Pseudo-Codinos: chaps. 1–4, 8–13," *Byzantino-slavica*, XV (1954), 214–229; Haring, *The Spanish Empire in America*, chaps. 4–6.

12. Wittfogel, *Oriental Despotism*, pp. 354–358.

13. Eisenstadt, *The Political Systems of Empires*, pp. 132–133, citing, among others, R. Des Routours, "Le traité des examens," traduit de la *Nouvelle histoire des T'ang* (Paris, 1932), Vol. II, chaps. 44–45; Sagnac, *La societé et la monarchie absolue* and *La révolution des idées et des moeurs et le déclin de l'ancien régime, 1715–1778* (Paris, 1946); M. Beloff, *The Age of Absolutism* (London, 1954).

Table 1. *Increase in Commoners among Chinese Officials (percentage)*

Class background of mandarinate dynasty	*T'ang (618–907)*	*Sung (960–1279)*	*Mongol (1234–1368)*	*Ming (1368–1644)*
Officials with				
upper-class background	83	85	85	77
officials' families	70	72	74	63
ruling house or nobles	13	13	11	14
Barbarians	7	—	—	—
Commoners	under 10	15	15	23

Source: Compiled from data in Karl Wittfogel, *Oriental Despotism: A Comparative Study in Total Power* (New Haven, 1957), pp. 351–354.

fact, created special administrative cadres as a means of controlling feudal power,[14] often filling them with middle-class and urban groups.[15] These efforts to create a professional bureaucracy and secure its loyalty often included reforms resembling modern administrative "improvements." (Even the Chinese practice of employing eunuchs finds a recent parallel in the Hatch Act and the less formal political emasculations of the McCarthy era in the United States. The expectation of personal loyalty and efforts to secure it through administrative reforms are, however, much more visible in autocratic than in democratic states.)

A more positive effort to restrain disloyalty has been the encouragement of bureaucratic interests complementary to those of the ruler. In Prussia, individual deviations from the common loyalty were discouraged as the sense of professionalism rose within the bureaucracy. The "collegial principle," among other

14. Eisenstadt, *The Political Systems of Empires*, pp. 133–137, citing also Ford, *Robe and Sword;* J. B. Black, *Reign of Elizabeth* (Oxford, 1936); R. W. Davies, *The Early Stuarts, 1603–1660* (Oxford, 1937); J. A. Williamson, *The Tudor Age* (London, 1953); G. Clark, *The Later Stuarts, 1660–1714* (Oxford, 1955); Diehl, "The Government and Administration of the Byzantine Empire"; C. Diehl, *Les grands problèmes de l'histoire byzantine* (Paris, 1943); G. Ostrogorsky, *History of the Byzantine State* (Oxford, 1956); A. Christensen, *L'Iran sous les Sassanides* (Copenhagen, 1936), chaps. 1–2.

15. Eisenstadt, *The Political Systems of Empires*, pp. 133–137, citing Guilland, "La collation et la perte ou déchéance des titres nobilaires à Byzance," *Revue des études byzantines*, IV (1946), 24–69; L. Bréhier, *Les populations rurales au IXième siècle, Byzantion*, I (1924), 177–190; Diehl, "The Government and Administration of the Byzantine Empire."

things, used committees and professional groups of civil servants to criticize the work of individual members of the departments and review extraordinary cases.[16] Drastic means of restraining excessive individualism (i.e., disloyalty) among bureaucrats have been widespread. Inspectors to check disloyal acts have been known in different settings as spies, commissaries, intendants, censors, or visitores.[17] To insure their loyalty to the monarch (*Quis custodiet . . .* ?), spies were usually not posted to their home districts.[18] Intense punishments and rewards within the system have also been used to encourage civil servants to focus on the virtues of loyalty. Punishments (transfers, denial of promotion, fines, salary cuts, suspension, dismissal, jail, and even hanging) were administered very severely in Prussia, for example.[19] At least once the corpse of a petty embezzler was put on public display as an example by Frederick William I.[20] In the Abbassid empire, punishments included expropriation after death, so that an offender's family could be posthumously penalized for his

16. Rosenberg, *Bureaucracy, Aristocracy, and Autocracy,* p. 97.

17. *Ibid.*, pp. 99–100; M. N. Prokovsky, *History of Russia* (New York, 1931), pp. 398 ff.

18. O. Hintze, "Geist und Epochen der preussischen Geschichte," *Hohenzollern-Jahrbuch,* VII (1903), 76–90, "Die Entstehung der modernen Staatsministerien," *Historische Zeitschrift,* XCIII (1907), 53–111, and "Die Hohenzollern und der Adel," *Historische Zeitschrift,* CXII (1914), 494–524; W. Dorn, "The Prussian Bureaucracy in the Eighteenth Century," *Political Science Quarterly,* XVLI (1931), 403–423; Dorwart, *Administrative Reforms of Frederick William I;* G. Pagès, "Essai sur l'évolution des institutions administratives en France," *Revue d'histoire modern,* VII (1932), 113–137; G. Zeller, "Gouverneurs de province au XVIième siecle," *Revue historique,* CLXXXV (1939), 225, "De quelques institutions mal connues du XVIième siècle," *Revue historique,* CXCIV (1944), 193–289, and "L'administration monarchique avant les intendants; parlements et gouverneurs," *Revue historique,* CXCVII (1947), 180–215; Fisher, *Viceregal Administration in the Spanish-American Colonies,* p. 29; W. W. Pierson, "La intendencia de Venezuela en el régimen colonial," *Boletin de la academia nacional de la historia,* XXIV (1941), 259–275; J. H. Parry, *The Audiencia of New Galicia in the Sixteenth Century* (Cambridge, 1948); C. H. Haring, "The Genesis of Royal Government in the Spanish Indies," *Hispanic American Historical Review,* VII (1927), 141–191; Des Routours, "Le traité des examens" and "Traité des fonctionnaires et traité de l'armée"; C. O. Hucker, "The Chinese Censorate of the Ming Dynasty" (doctoral dissertation, University of Chicago, 1950, available on microfilm from University of Chicago Library), "Confucianism and the Chinese Censorial System," in L. B. Nivison and A. F. Wright (eds.), *Confucianism in Action* (Stanford, 1959), pp. 182–208, and "Statecraft and Censorship in Ming China," in "Conference on Political Power in Traditional China" (Laconia, N.H., 1959, mimeographed); H. Li, *Les censeurs sous la dynastie Mandchoue, 1644–1911, en Chine* (Paris, 1936).

19. Rosenberg, *Bureaucracy, Aristocracy, and Autocracy,* pp. 99–100.

20. *Ibid.*

misdeeds.[21] Usually in such systems rewards were also of a high order. Prussian office-holding nobles were well paid: indeed, the privileged classes did not find it necessary to invoke myths of austerity and self-sacrifice justifying their position until liberal and democratic forces had begun to challenge their claims to power.[22]

Characteristically, reforms that were aimed at reducing disloyalty inevitably introduced other consequences as well. In spite of the lack of competing class loyalties, slaves and eunuchs provided potential kingmakers from their own humble ranks; "collegial" administration produced plotting and factionalism as well as fear of disloyalty to the crown; the use of committees and subcommittees to determine and review major policies increased the bureaucratic desire to act on rational decisions rather than simply accept authority. Indeed, almost any reform that aimed at creating a systematic response to new problems weakened the mythology of instant obedience. The search for facts "raised the level of trained mediocrity" and thus threatened the principle of blindly following the king.[23] Similarly, civil service examinations could be used not only to reduce automatic claims to office but also to deny the king the privilege of appointment. They did not always weaken the claims of the rich and noble: they theoretically opened public office to the lower classes, but they still kept out commoners who could not afford the high fees. And even commoners who could pay were not necessarily considered suitable or socially acceptable unless during their youth they had engaged in politically socializing activities resembling those of the nobles.[24] Whatever classes benefited from these reforms posed problems eventually. In Prussia, the kings used local *Landräte* and nobles to offset the central bureaucracy's increasing power, but they soon found that the latter also began to display unwonted independence. A General Directory was established to reduce the feudalistic proliferation of administrative bodies,[25] but eventually its power, too, had

21. Wittfogel, *Oriental Despotism*, p. 76.
22. Rosenberg, *Bureaucracy, Aristocracy, and Autocracy*, p. 102.
23. *Ibid.*, p. 96.
24. *Ibid.*, pp. 97, 180.
25. Dorwart, *Administrative Reforms of Frederick William I*, chap. 8.

to be weakened through the creation of functional ministries such as Trade and Industry, Army, Mining and Smelting, and Foreign Affairs, all of which were responsible directly to the crown. In 1766 the king established budgetary controls over these departments by creating the *règie* under French fiscal experts who presumably had no local loyalties except upward. Yet in spite of these efforts, the crown's power declined relatively in the eighteenth century and the bureaucracy became an ever more important oligarchy.[26] Strong personal dynasties were nearly all subject in their periods of decline to increasing bureaucratic disloyalty.[27] Administrative reforms in the name of loyalty were not enough to offset political developments that attracted loyalties outside the desired channels.

Lateral relationships

The second range of administrative reforms in an autocracy deals with the relationships between the bureaucracy and society (or the part of it that counts). A bureaucracy must at a minimum produce adequate revenues from the society. Even in feudal societies governed out of a prince's domestic household, financial problems become increasingly important as the ruler's obligations increase.[28] Where there is no professional civil service or system of general taxation, the bureaucracy itself is widely used as a source of revenue. Rulers have often had to raise funds by exchanging their patronage for cold cash. In France, after the fifteenth century, "most rulers were more anxious to exploit medieval forms of government for their own profit than to abolish them."[29] It was expected that noble office-holders would benefit financially from a royal appointment, and one means of recogniz-

26. Rosenberg, *Bureaucracy, Aristocracy, and Autocracy,* pp. 165–174.
27. Eisenstadt, *The Political Systems of Empires,* pp. 286–287, citing E. Stein, "Introduction à l'histoire et aux institutions byzantines," *Traditio,* LXXIV (1954), 95–168; Ostrogorsky, *History of the Byzantine State;* Ford, *Robe and Sword;* G. Pagès, *La monarchie de l'Ancien Régime en France* (Paris, 1928); E. G. Barber, *The Bourgeoisie in Eighteenth Century France* (Princeton, 1955); H. O. H. Stange, "Geschichte Chinas vom Urbeginn bis auf zur Gegenwart," in E. Waldschmidt *et al., Geschichte Asiens* (Munich, 1950), pp. 363–542.
28. Dorwart, *Administrative Reforms of Frederick William I,* p. 8.
29. K. W. Swart, *Sale of Offices in the Seventeenth Century* (The Hague, 1949), p. 7.

ing and legitimizing the practice was to extract from them a portion of the proceeds. French kings permitted officials to sell their offices on condition that a portion of the sales price (one-tenth to one-fourth) went to the royal treasury.[30] Montesquieu indorsed the sale of public office, believing that "chance will furnish better subjects [as civil servants] than the prince's choice."[31] Such "skimming" practices were used in China, India, Byzantium, Egypt, and the Inca empires: all took courtly advantage of the fact that impoverished nobles used public office to restore family wealth.[32] Part-time officials were paid by fee (they were allowed to keep 5–10 per cent of all the taxes they collected in Ptolemaic Egypt, 1–5 per cent in Byzantium, 10 per cent in Muslim Egypt). Sometimes, they took too much: one study found that the Manchu bureaucracy arrogated 30 per cent of the government revenue.[33] But such losses had to be serious indeed to warrant administrative reforms that might attenuate this form of revenue; and when they did occur they seldom changed the system very much. Frederick William I undertook extensive reforms in financial administration,[34] but he still required "kick-backs" from all appointees and promotees.[35] Later efforts to eliminate the petty corruption that this system encouraged were evidently less satisfactory than taxing it, as Frederick II found when he tried to abolish "fees" only to have them replaced with "service charges."[36] The outright sale of offices, sometimes under a bidding system, was regularized in France under a decree of 1604 conceived by the financier Paulet, who made office a "legal privilege, a secure base of personal power, and often also a means of acquiring prestige titles and noble status." Capital outlays for public office were much more rewarding than other likely investments.[37] The payment of an annual fee, called the *Paulette*, guar-

30. *Ibid.*, p. 8.
31. *The Spirit of the Laws*, V:19 quest. 4, discussed in Bert F. Hoselitz, "Levels of Economic Performance and Bureaucratic Structures," in Joseph LaPalombara (ed.), *Bureaucracy and Political Development* (Princeton, 1963), p. 194 n.
32. Wittfogel, *Oriental Despotism*, p. 316.
33. Cited in *ibid.*, p. 335.
34. Dorwart, *Administrative Reforms of Frederick William I*, chap. 5.
35. Rosenberg, *Bureaucracy, Aristocracy, and Autocracy*, p. 77.
36. *Ibid.*, p. 104.
37. *Ibid.*, p. 16.

anteed the privilege of inheriting offices without paying a full purchase price.[38] British *rentiers* also bought offices and drew their profits from the investment.[39] Unfortunately, this revenue-seeking device lowered the "professional ability, dignity, and industry of the bureaucracy"[40] and beclouded the will of the king, which now had to be filtered through the "opaque density" of the expanding civil service. The result was the growth of a "new feudalism."[41] Royal sharecropping with noble and bourgeois office-holders tended to weaken the loyalties of the latter, and in the last analysis did not provide a satisfactory source of revenue either. The most sophisticated institutional reforms of Frederick William I were addressed to this problem. "Each college [a forerunner of the modern functional ministry] was concerned with one great objective, viz., to collect as much money for the king as possible, and consequently every source of income was claimed that could be drawn within its jurisdiction."[42] But once again, reforms designed to overcome the revenue-producing inadequacies of the bureaucracy as seen by the personal ruler tended to set new forces in motion and further weakened the responsiveness of the administrative system to other demands upon it.

Internal relationships

In traditional autocracies, there is little concern over internal bureaucratic relationships (i.e., values and doctrines) until the behavior of individuals in the service of the personal ruler begins to affect the prestige and honor of his government. Reforms in these interests are necessarily more diffuse and less purposeful than those addressed to loyalty and adequacy. Offenses against "honor" are vague annoyances; they call forth an incoherent and bewildering variety of reforms.

Bureaucratic honor was supposedly achieved through the nobles who held office and provided their own myths of service. When Prussian nobles were replaced by professional civil servants

38. Swart, *Sales of Offices in the Seventeenth Century*, p. 10.
39. Barker, *The Development of Public Services*, p. 32.
40. Ford, *Robe and Sword*, p. 115 and chap. 6.
41. Barker, *The Development of Public Services*, pp. 9, 11.
42. Dorwart, *Administrative Reforms of Frederick William I*, p. 163.

under the Stein reforms of the nineteenth century, the government continued to rely upon the historical association of ideas of honor and privilege with official appointments.[43] The Prussian collegial principle was also seen as the "surest guarantee of honest, efficient management of office in the interests of the king. One official would always be a check upon the other if he had to be responsible for the other's actions."[44] Personal leadership by the three great Hohenzollerns provided the example of "the high moral character of the Prussian bureaucracy."[45] Even in the tradition of British amateur government, administration through *rentiers*[46] carried strong class overtones thought to support the dignity of the state. The Chinese civil service examinations, based on the classics, provided "excellent means for thoroughly indoctrinating ambitious commoners and for compelling the talented sons of officials and bureaucratic gentry families to submit to a most comprehensive professional ideological training."[47] Prussia achieved the apotheosis of the mystical pride in royal service, the bureaucratic creed, and the ideology of self-sacrifice, as equated with the public interest.[48] The proverbial devotion to work and expectation of "unstinted sacrifice" were consciously molded by Frederick William I and Frederick II.[49] Similar conditions were found in other contemporary societies possessing a powerful bureaucracy.[50] In general, the creation of a "public law" system as contrasted with the private law rule of a king's household enhanced the prestige and dignity of the state, often by giving it an impersonal, mystical embodiment.[51]

On the whole, reforms addressed to the state of mind of the

43. Barker, *The Development of Public Services*, pp. 22–23.
44. Dorwart, *Administrative Reforms of Frederick William I*, p. 190.
45. *Ibid.*, p. 192.
46. Barker, *The Development of Public Services*, p. 32.
47. Wittfogel, *Oriental Despotism*, p. 351.
48. Rosenberg, *Bureaucracy, Aristocracy, and Autocracy*, pp. 92–94; cf. Alfred Weber, *Ideen zur Staatz- und Kultursoziologie* (Karlsruhe, 1927), pp. 93 ff.
49. Dorwart, *Administrative Reforms of Frederick William I*, pp. 192–193.
50. Cf. B. J. Hovde, *The Scandinavian Countries* (Boston, 1943), I, 206 ff., 328; V, 512 ff.
51. Rosenberg, *Bureaucracy, Aristocracy, and Autocracy*, p. 9 and chap. 3; Barker, *The Development of Public Services*, pp. 4–5; Christensen, *L'Iran sous les Sassanides;* A. Christensen, "Die Iranier," in A. Alt *et al., Kulturgeschichte des alten Orients* (Munich, 1933), Vol. III.

bureaucracy, as might be expected, were much less effective than those concerned with mere behavior. And when they were successful, the effort to enhance the dignity and prestige of the public service produced only an excess of arrogant pride and thus weakened the infinitely more desirable quality (to the personal ruler) of loyalty. Administrative reform achieves outward manifestations of bureaucratic behavior more easily than the inner qualities of a bureaucratic creed.

The argument presented so far relates the negative purposes of administrative change to the will of a personal ruler. These purposes seem to apply both to small feudal estates and to large dynastic empires. Totalitarian dictatorships resemble the traditional autocracies in these respects, since the sovereign uses the bureaucracy here, as well, as an instrument of his personal will. The differences in size among these polities are essentially technical problems of communication; they can be overcome as new modes of travel and transmission are developed. In spite of striking differences in purpose, organization, and political behavior among these governments, the existence of a personal sovereign seems to bring to the surface recurring and ubiquitous annoyances of governing and to introduce similar uses of administrative reform to deal with them.

Administrative reform does not, of course, arrest the processes of political decay at work in personal autocracies. Indeed, achieving the desired bureaucratic qualities in a personalized autocratic state can be the prelude to disaster. Beyer observes that the Roman bureaucracy became "oppressive and burdensome to the people," thus weakening their civic virtue and contributing to their ultimate defeat.[52] The Nazi German example affords contemporary confirmation of the dangers that may attend the state in which policy-making is paralyzed by an excess of blind loyalty, single-minded concern with adequate performance in exploiting the public, and the mythology of nationalism developed in the civil service. The symptoms of acedia often anticipate decline in

52. W. C. Beyer, "The Civil Service of the Ancient World," *Public Administration Review*, XIX (1959), 243–249.

autocracies that have succeeded too well in eliminating personal annoyances to the ruler, and have contained too well the moving forces of change.

III. Western Democracies

The annoyances that lead to reform in the large, complex, polyarchic democratic states of recent history reveal at once the differences of purpose and style between personal and constitutional rule. Constitutional democracies do not, of course, make politics impersonal, but they discourage the overt and systematic use of governmental instruments for personal purposes. Objections to disloyal actions on the part of the bureaucracy in these circumstances tend to become functional and institutional rather than ritualistic and personal; elected rulers who might be tempted to purge the bureaucracy for their own purposes succeed each other too rapidly to develop real cults of personality. Annoyances about the inadequacies of revenue-producing services likewise tend in a democracy to be diffused into concerns about the efficiency of action-related services. And offensive bureaucratic actions are not here thought of as dishonoring the state so much as failing to serve it. On all three levels of relationship, the range of bureaucratic annoyances in a pluralistic government is of an altogether different political order from those that beset a personal ruler.

Upward relationships

Bureaucratic loyalty is relatively detached from personalities in a large, complex democratic state. F. M. Marx notes that "although committed to loyal service of the government of the day, the civil servant [under democratic rule] is expected to place still higher his loyalty to lawful government as such, in its essential continuity, government after government."[53] In France, where

53. Fritz Morstein Marx, *The Administrative State: An Introduction to Bureaucracy* (Chicago, 1957), p. 154.

constitutions have changed as rapidly as once monarchs did, the civil service earned praise for the flexibility of its loyalties:

> The persons that the July monarchy had developed in the grand imperial tradition, temporarily driven out by the February revolution [of 1848], re-entered the administrative service under the Prince-President; thus was perpetuated down to 1870, and even as late as 1890, by division and bureau chiefs, the tradition of an administration vigilant, honest, and conscientious of its duties toward the public, even if too much imbued with the notion of the sovereign rights of the State.[54]

Hyneman echoes the proposition that a sense of duty to the public is the supreme loyalty demanded of bureaucracy in a democratic state,[55] noting that "the feeble character of the lines of communication and the weakness of the bonds of loyalty [among] different parts of the public services make it difficult for any leader . . . to change the course of the federal bureaucracy as a whole. . . ."[56] In the United States, neither Congress nor the President has readily permitted the other to impose its will on the structure of bureaucracy.[57] Fiscal accountability and adherence to statute have been achieved through a slow process of reform. In England, the instruments of reform used to maintain the structure of loyalty include continuous controls that were developed in the Treasury.[58] Loyalties in these circumstances are institutionalized: in rare cases where personal or political loyalties have been found essential, an appointment may be exempted from the requirements of a professional civil service. But when demands for political loyalty penetrate the career service too far, the results can be devastating. In 1937 a British civil servant was found guilty of a technical security violation. His conviction was based on evidence obtained in a highly dubious burglary of his property, but he was nevertheless dismissed from the British public

54. F. Masson, in *L'echo de Paris*, July 24, 1911, quoted in Walter R. Sharp, *The French Civil Service: Bureaucracy in Transition* (New York, 1931), p. 7.
55. Charles S. Hyneman, *Bureaucracy in a Democracy* (New York, 1950), pp. 10–17.
56. *Ibid.*, p. 23.
57. Richard Polenberg, *Reorganizing Roosevelt's Government* (Cambridge, Mass., 1966), pp. 3–6.
58. Samuel H. Beer, *Treasury Control: The Coordination of Financial and Economic Policy in Great Britain* (London, 1956).

service in a strikingly disproportionate penalty probably explained by his left-wing views. The consequences were a public uproar and a decline in morale.[59] In the United States, extreme abuses of the disloyalty issue have been commonplace in wartime, but, as in Britain, they seldom affected the morale and self-confidence of the bureaucracy. The McCarthy era was an exception which paralyzed whole sectors of the public service. Dramatic "loyalty" reforms can be much more disruptive in democracies than in states which can generate a personal or other specific focus for loyalty.

Far from requiring loyal political activities of their civil servants, democracies have increasingly discountenanced any political participation at all in that quarter. Loyalty to the party in power is no defense against a charge of political misconduct. As Judge Holmes told a free speech plaintiff from his Massachusetts bench in 1892, a man "may have a constitutional right to talk politics, but he has no constitutional right to be a policeman."[60] A neutral civil service is of course considered desirable in any modern state where professionalism has risen to protect public careers against political vicissitudes. But an autocracy demands more support even from supposedly neutral civil servants than a democracy does, as the examples of Nazi Germany and the Soviet Union show. Democracies not only tend to free civil servants from the obligations of supporting the current government politically, but they even require tolerance of unfavorable activity. In Britain the civil service was permitted to take sides against the government in the railway strike of 1919, when the Union of Post Office Workers refused to act as "strikebreakers"; and many civil servants joined in the Sinn Fein strike of 1920. In 1921, when the British government was considering the possibility of war against the Soviet Union, the Union of Post Office Workers joined the Trades Union Congress and Labour party in threatening to call a general strike "if such a war were declared." As Kingsley wryly

59. J. Donald Kingsley, *Representative Bureaucracy: An Interpretation of the British Civil Service* (Yellow Springs, Ohio, 1944), pp. 224–226; National Council for Civil Liberties, *The Strange Case of Major Vernon* (London, 1938). See also Braibanti's chapter in this volume, pp. 100 ff. and n. 215.

60. Marx, *The Administrative State*, p. 127.

points out, "the doctrine of Civil Service neutrality was relevant only in a stable social environment."[61] In a democracy, the doctrines of neutrality require the political leadership to tolerate marked degrees of disloyalty.

As a democratic state's operations and policies become more complex and the power and influence of the bureaucracy increase, ordinary tests of loyalty in fact become meaningless. They offer no adequate basis for administrative reform. The civil servant must be loyal simultaneously to the constitution, the laws he seeks to enforce, and the public interest as conceived within the entire political culture. He owes allegiance to the civil service as a whole, the agency and division in which he works, and his supervisor. These divided loyalties require the bureaucracy to be generally representative of the nation, not of a class, and thus able to harmonize its increasingly pluralistic functions. Kingsley offers a mystical interpretation of the meaning of loyalty to the state: ". . . the essence of bureaucratic responsibility in the modern state is to be sought, not in the presumed and largely fictitious impartiality of the officials, but in the strength of their commitment to the purposes that State is undertaking to serve."[62] Kingsley surely overstated the importance of class representation in a bureaucracy; he even doubted at all that the upper-middle-class British civil service could function effectively under a Labour government at all.[63] It is this class interpretation that forces Kingsley to propose some vague higher loyalty as the only protector of the general public interest. Clement Attlee himself offered the best evidence against this narrow view of representativeness:

> The first thing a Minister finds on entering office is that he can depend absolutely on the loyalty of his staff, and, on leaving office, he will seldom be able to say what the private political views are even of those with whom he has worked very closely. The second thing that he will discover is that the civil servant is prepared to put up every possible objection to his policy, not from a desire to thwart him, but because it is his duty to see that

61. *Representative Bureaucracy*, pp. 107–110.
62. *Ibid.*, p. 274 and chap. 12.
63. *Ibid.*, p. 280.

the Minister understands all the difficulties and dangers of the course which he wishes to adopt.[64]

Kingsley's historical study of British bureaucracy suggests, perhaps extravagantly, that abuses of class privilege were among the most important causes of reform. It could certainly be argued that the most urgent reform-mongers there were the successively rising classes rather than the retreating privileged orders. In the eighteenth century, the aristocratic tradition was perhaps waning, but the process was certainly gradual enough to avoid open threat to the system. As late as 1806 Cobbett—a polemicist, to be sure—sarcastically considered public office as a means "of upholding and cherishing those amongst the ancient nobility and gentry, who otherwise might fall into a state that would inevitably bring disgrace upon rank."[65] It is important to note that reformers did not at first object to this use of the public service on the grounds of the illiteracy and incompetence of occasional appointees; they saw no need to remove clerks, for example, merely because (as one observer reported) some of them could not count above ten.[66] The reforms of the nineteenth century were rather a recognition of the value of introducing increasingly broader sectors of the elite into the public service. By the end of the first quarter of the nineteenth century, appointments were officially tied to partisanship, and the patronage secretary in the Treasury had the function of clearing nominees.[67] Patronage now became a means of broadening the representative character of the civil service. This reform replaced a system of appointments which, according to one only half-humorous summation, denied office to anyone who "lacked family influence or had been born in lawful wedlock."[68] Unlike parallel developments in autocratic

64. "Civil Servants, Ministry, Parliament, and the Public," *Political Quarterly,* XXV (1954), 308, quoted in Marx, *The Administrative State,* p. 131.

65. William Cobbett in *Political Register,* March 1, 1806, quoted in Kingsley, *Representative Bureaucracy,* p. 27.

66. *Ibid.,* p. 38.

67. *Ibid.,* pp. 33–34. The best description of patronage as a means of enlarging the representativeness of the civil service appears in S. E. Finer, "Patronage and the Public Service," *Public Administration,* XXX (1952), 329–360.

68. Kingsley, *Representative Bureaucracy,* p. 27. Cf. S. E. Finer, *The Life and Times of Sir Edwin Chadwick* (London, 1952), pp. 65–68, 108–109, 152, 198, 276.

states, patronage of the civil service neither increased loyalty to the crown nor provided financial gain for the rulers. It broadened the base of the civil service, using neither adequacy nor loyalty as the basis of appointment. Offices were no longer sold as in Germany, France, and England in earlier periods. Similar class changes in the American bureaucracy are identified with the Jacksonian era, when the principle of rotation was introduced to end both superannuation and the idea of property in public office-holding, and to discourage the development of an office-holding class.[69] "Rotation was imposed because it was demanded from below, not merely because it was advocated from above."[70] Although relatively few offices were involved, the flavor of the whole period was a rejection of class rule and nepotism. It might be argued that the purpose of patronage in Britain as well as in the United States was to encourage loyalty to the party, since the process of clearing appointments with members of Parliament was used to increase the popular appeal and influence of party members who stood for election.[71] But such loyalty is itself an influence toward representativeness. At any rate, patronage was not a means of creating personal empires within the administration. Its purpose and effect were to change the composition and attitudes of the civil servants. It thus made them not so much *loyal*, in our special personal sense, as *representative*. As the ruler is pluralized in a democratic state, so are the upward loyalties of its bureaucratic elements.

Lateral Relationships

In lateral as well as upward relationships, administrative reforms in democracies have broadened the purpose and outlook of the bureaucracy. Just as the new uses of patronage and other class-related reforms made the civil service nationally representa-

69. Leonard D. White, *The Jacksonians: A Study in Administrative History, 1829–1861* (New York, 1954), p. 5.
70. *Ibid.*, p. 301.
71. *Ibid.*, pp. 316–324. Finer, "Patronage and the Public Service," p. 355, points out that Jackson's purge—somewhere between 950 and 2,000 of a total civil service of 11,000 or 12,000—"established the spoils system formally as an institution of American Government" because of the rapid rotation of parties in office thereafter. He also notes that patronage had long before begun to serve the purposes of party (as opposed to class) loyalty in Britain.

tive rather than merely upwardly loyal, similarly, in the relationship between the bureaucracy and the society, reforms seem to be aimed at producing efficiency rather than mere adequacy. Middle-class complaints about aristocratic monopoly of public office in Britain, for example, have been based less on the desire of commoners to gain preferment than on the need for better performance of the duties of office. The compromise that had terminated the Glorious Revolution continued to protect the claims of the aristocracy so long as the public officials themselves seemed competent to administer public affairs;[72] but as humiliating military defeats in America and on the Continent demonstrated the national incompetence, and as the economy progressed and made greater demands on the government, the administrative capacities proved increasingly inadequate. Repeated evidence of bureaucratic unfitness, rather than middle-class aspirations to power, finally destroyed the value of the original compromise. Administrative ineptness in the American colonies led Burke to campaign for "Economical Reform" in 1780, demanding parliamentary controls over sinecures, changes in civil service pay, and administrative reforms in the exchequer, customs, and other operating departments. As industry developed, the population moved away from farming, which occupied less than half the people by the 1820's;[73] and the proletariat became increasingly active partisans of a positive governmental role in the economy. In the 1830's, when local government reforms began, the state was expanding its service to commercial and industrial classes and the proletariat, and competition began to replace patronage in civil service recruitment. In 1823, 1828, and 1836, General Orders specifically sought to eliminate "influence" as a factor in merit promotions in Customs, and in 1831 in the Excise office.[74]

The need for efficient, and professional, administration now became a current political topic. In 1853 the Trevelyan-Northcote recommendations provided the basis for the present civil service by recognizing established age limits for career entrance and

72. Kingsley, *Representative Bureaucracy*, p. 21.
73. *Ibid.*, pp. 44, 46.
74. *Ibid.*, p. 50.

limiting admission to civil service to those passing "literary examinations" administered by a central board. Civil service work was to be divided into two categories, routine and intellectual, with distinguishing examinations fixed for entrance to each. The principle of promotion by merit was established soon thereafter. True, the qualifying examinations, like the educational system itself, continued to emphasize classical learning and thus consciously favored the leisure classes. Even so, the reform was especially unpopular in the House of Lords, and it took fifteen years of pressure from without before it became effective. When the Civil Service Commission began operations in 1855, it was obvious that its attentions were needed. In that year over half of the 1,686 individuals nominated by the department for civil service appointments were rejected for "gross ignorance." But rejection by the Civil Service Commission did not necessarily deny an unsuitable candidate his post: not until 1859 did the Superannuation Act give teeth to the rejection procedure by barring pensions to those not admitted to employment by the Civil Service Commission.[75] In 1860, the principle of certifying three qualified candidates was established, thus permitting "limited competition," and in 1870 an Order in Council provided for open competition. The possibility of receiving promotion from lower to higher class in the Civil Service was recognized in 1876,[76] and the three-class system—administrative, clerical, and routine—with separate education tests based on recruitment from different educational levels, was introduced by the MacDonnell Commission in 1912–14.[77] These reforms not only implied changes in the class basis of the civil service; they also constituted a continuous and cumulative effort to improve efficiency. Such efforts, like nearly all presidential initiatives for administrative reform in the United States before the time of Franklin Roosevelt,[78] were addressed to issues of economy and efficiency.

75. *Ibid.*, pp. 50–74.
76. *Ibid.*, pp. 78–84.
77. *Ibid.*, pp. 97–98.
78. Barry Dean Karl, *Executive Reorganization and Reform in the New Deal: The Genesis of Administrative Management, 1900–1939* (Cambridge, Mass., 1963), pp. 15–28, 184–186: Polenberg, *Reorganizing Roosevelt's Government*, p. 7.

Internal relationships

In democracies, reforms touching the internal dynamics of the civil service are seldom undertaken in the name of honor. Perhaps the closest democratic parallel to the autocratic reforms designed to enhance the prestige or honor of the state through those of its bureaucracy are the retention of status symbols and the use of class preferment. The examinations established for entrance to the Administrative Class of the British Civil Service, for example, include a viva voce element permitting the examiners to insure that candidates have a presentable accent and an adequate capacity for small talk. At first, face-to-face interviews accounted for one-third to one-fourth of the total qualifying grade.[79] There still remains in the British Civil Service a mythology that places "constant emphasis upon the necessity of reputability. Standards of propriety are erected into commandments." The written code prohibits a Civil Servant from engaging in any "undertaking which might in any way . . . be inconsistent with his position. . . . [T]he sphere of activity of the Civil Servant is much more restricted than that of the ordinary citizen."[80] A board of inquiry on the subject once stated that "the surest guide (of social conduct) will, we hope, always be found in the nice and jealous honor of the Civil Servants themselves."[81] Democratic America was not above such class orientations: the United States began as a government of gentlemen. George Washington made character and reputation his primary qualifications for appointments to major public office, hoping to add "dignity and lustre to our National character,"[82] but also believing that personal integrity would be the best guarantee of future public service. Government under the Federalists was for the people, if not of or by the people.[83] The decline of the "gentleman" class basis of public service orientation required the development of other ethical

79. Kingsley, *Representative Bureaucracy,* pp. 198–201.
80. *Ibid.,* pp. 209–213.
81. *Ibid.,* p. 212.
82. Leonard D. White, *The Federalists: A Study in Administrative History* (New York, 1948), p. 259.
83. *Ibid.,* p. 508.

bases of bureaucratic behavior.[84] For the French Third Republic the ideal could be similarly described: "The duty of the civil servant consists essentially in devoting his work to the public service. He cannot content himself with going through the motions of work like an ordinary worker. . . . The civil servant is attached body and soul to the public service. The status of the civil servant does not leave him for a single instant even when distant from his office."[85] Similar German views are expressed in terms of a "pride of outfit," which allows the civil servants to judge their peers' performance, and thus protects the professional honor of the service as a whole.[86]

Expressions of this sort still survive as relics of an earlier, aristocratic age, but they take on new meaning in modern democracies. Although politicians make rhetorical appeals to traditional codes of behavior, they have undertaken few actual reforms in democracies to reintroduce the spirit of *noblesse oblige* or the myths of honor as a controlling principle in the civil service. In most European nations, the civil servants long ago established their own courts to maintain surveillance over internal disciplinary problems. But their present activities seem little more than bureaucratic self-protection. They do not aggressively seek to develop and preserve a sense of administrative honor. It would seem more appropriate to consider these activities in the light of the general tendency of bureaucracies to substitute "internal for external controls over service affairs." Administrative courts follow a natural inclination to "become states within states, perfecting elaborate machinery for their governance and reducing to a minimum the area of detailed supervision by the political organs." They do not really affect the quality of internal relations in a bureaucracy. Kingsley regards this desire for independence from political control as "inevitable."[87] It is doubtless true, as F. M. Marx suggests, that administrative courts do indirectly protect

84. White, *The Jacksonians,* pp. 418–420.
85. Aubert Lefas in Leonard D. White (ed.), *The Civil Service in the Modern State* (Chicago, 1930), p. 238.
86. Carl J. Friedrich in White (ed.), *The Civil Service in the Modern State,* pp. 417 ff.
87. Kingsley, *Representative Bureaucracy,* p. 186.

the state against scandal and perhaps express some "sense of propriety" on the part of the civil service.[88] But as one examines the nature and focus of more recent democratic reforms of the administrative tribunals, it becomes apparent that the concern is less with protecting bureaucratic, self-enforcing principles of honor than with providing a sense of professionalism and public service. The ombudsman first introduced in Sweden 150 years ago is a deliberate effort to keep the bureaucracy responsible to public needs. His activities may seem slight and even petty, but the institution itself and the growing interest in it in New Zealand and the United States provide a symbol of the need for a service-oriented sense of professionalism.[89]

The modern professional responsibilities of a democratic civil service do not correspond very closely to the notions of honor fostered by monarchic and aristocratic states. The substantive issue in the famous Friedrich-Finer debate, for example, is not whether career civil servants are held together by a sense of honor, but whether their professional consciousness alone is sufficient to insure a continuous posture of public service.[90] The presence of conflicting pressures in a democracy provides at least some protection against favoritism, partiality, and neglect.[91] Bureaucratic evils in a democracy are usually blamed on inattentions to the public interest rather than on internal codes of behavior or insufficient prestige. Hyneman's catalog of bureaucratic ailments[92] lists prejudicing elections, misinforming the public, inaugurating policies contrary to public will, failing to take initiative where necessary, and inefficiency: all of which, apart from the first, result from inadequate performance of the service role of a public bureaucracy. Nigro's list[93] is longer and more specific,

88. Marx, *The Administrative State*, pp. 117–125.
89. William A. Robson, *The Governors and the Governed* (Baton Rouge, 1964), pp. 22–23.
90. Carl J. Friedrich, "Public Policy and the Nature of Administrative Responsibility," in Carl J. Friedrich and Edward S. Mason (eds.), *Public Policy* (Cambridge, 1940), I, 3–24; Herman Finer, "Administrative Responsibility in Democratic Government," *Public Administration Review*, I (1941), 4.
91. S. N. Eisenstadt, "Bureaucracy and Political Development," in LaPalombara (ed.), *Bureaucracy and Political Development*, p. 109.
92. *Bureaucracy and Political Development*, p. 109.
93. Felix A. Nigro, *Modern Public Administration* (New York, 1965), pp. 446–456.

though sometimes overlapping: dishonesty, unethical behavior, overriding the law, treating subordinates unfairly, violating procedural due process, showing partiality to private interests in defiance of legislative intention, gross inefficiency, covering up mistakes, and failure to show initiative. It is significant that the extensive remedies he proposes[94] call in almost every case for legislative action of some sort; but clearly such laws must be accompanied by increased responsibility for institutional self-discipline and a public service orientation.

An interesting question about reforms of this category is whether reliance upon legislative action—upon resolutions, investigations, and laws—can produce the desired service orientation. As Crozier discovered in his analysis of French bureaucracies, civil servants develop a resistance to change, becoming more rigid as they perceive a threat to themselves, and thus in the end making the change all the more urgent. His conclusion is that "change in a bureaucratic organization must come from the top down and must be universalistic, i.e., encompass the whole organization *en bloc.* Change will not come gradually on a piecemeal basis. It will wait until a serious question pertaining to an important dysfunction can be raised."[95] In the examples studied by Crozier, the French administration responded to change by maintaining an equilibrium among three patterns of behavior: "(1) The alternation of periods of routine and crisis and the need for crisis for breaking up the daily routine order; (2) the will and passion for planning, ordering, and equalizing all situations; (3) the opposition between the negative and conservative behavior of all formal groupings, and the effervescence and intellectual irresponsible creativity of individuals."[96] His conclusion from the French experience is that "reform can be brought about only by sweeping revolution."[97] This judgment seems to rule out piecemeal reform as an effective means of improving the internal relations of a bureaucracy. Yet melioristic reorganizations in the United States have introduced reforms sweeping enough to sat-

94. *Ibid.*, pp. 457–480.
95. Michel Crozier, *The Bureaucratic Phenomenon* (Chicago, 1964), p. 196.
96. *Ibid.*, p. 286.
97. *Ibid.*, p. 287.

isfy even Crozier, bringing the bureaucratic structure in line with changing functions, and thus contributing to a programmatic service orientation. Reorganization can also become a fairly routine matter. The American Congress has often permitted the President to make reforms piecemeal. The Overman Act of 1918, a law of 1932 giving President Hoover reorganization authority and another in 1933 for Franklin Delano Roosevelt, and the Reorganization Acts of 1945 and 1949 all authorized the President to use executive orders to reorganize and even abolish agencies, subject to congressional vetoes of various kinds.[98] The piecemeal approach has prevailed even in France, where legalistic approaches to administration reign supreme, although the civil service was never governed by a common code. "Every attempt to enact *statut des fontionnaires* by parliamentary action has ended either in partial or in complete failure."[99] Civil servants desired protection against arbitrary treatment, but the government so feared radical unionism that efforts to encourage and permit it in 1846, 1848, 1888, 1891, 1895, and 1897 all failed, as did a central commission after two years of work in 1909. The French solution, like the American, was a series of acts, both legislative and administrative, rather than a general Civil Service Code. The legislature acted, but no revolutions occurred.[100]

In recent years, however, important (and perhaps revolutionary) changes in administrative behavior have been introduced by changing procedures rather than organization. Performance budgeting, planning-programming-budgeting systems, and other such devices bring about a kind of artificial self-discipline by focusing on the larger purposes of an agency. Simon[101] and other students of administrative behavior have also shown that organizations possess many informal resources for influencing the individual decisions and behavior of employees. These include, for example, assertion of authority over areas of activity that lie in the individual civil servant's zones of acquiescence or "indiffer-

98. Hyneman, *Bureaucracy in a Democracy*, pp. 108–114.
99. Sharp, *The French Civil Service*, p. 50.
100. Cf. *ibid.*, chap. 3.
101. Herbert A. Simon, *Administrative Behavior* (rev. ed.; New York, 1957), pp. 12–16.

ence";[102] encouraging individual self-identification with the organization, usually by harmonizing the interests of each; gradually making use of criteria of efficiency and rationality; constantly engaging in persuasive communications of advice and information; and finally, through training or "preprogramming" bureaucratic actions. These devices are less than revolutionary, and more than legislative. But they are often effective, and even these gentle techniques for introducing behavioral change therefore meet with resistance. Practically all experiments with modern techniques in human relations and participative management have produced some uncertainty and unexpected employee resistance.[103]

Both revolutionary and routine reforms find their greatest difficulty in dealing with the internal dynamics of bureaucratic behavior. This difficulty is perhaps greatest in a democracy, which seeks to induce a self-renewing public service orientation. Paradoxically, the bureaucratic systems themselves nearly always seem to derive the strength to resist change most directly from reforms aimed at internal relationships. They either absorb the reforms into their own goal-sets and thus divert further action against their behavior, or they gain from them increased responsibility for self-discipline. The more democracies demand from the bureaucracy, the more important it becomes to make use of self-generating professional standards as a means of improving internal relationships.

IV. Modernizing Polities

Most postcolonial countries emerge from a political context of ostensibly democratic ideology and aspiration with a national leadership that is highly personal, if not autocratic. Other mod-

102. Chester I. Barnard, *The Functions of the Executive* (Cambridge, Mass., 1938), p. 169.

103. E. A. Fleishman, E. F. Harris, and H. E. Burtt, *Leadership and Supervision in Industry* (Columbus, Ohio, 1955); Rensis Likert, *New Patterns of Management* (New York, 1961); Nancy Morse and Everett Reiner, "Experimental Change of the Major Organizational Variable," *Journal of Abnormal and Social Psychology*, LII (1955), 120–219.

ernizing polities display a similar mixture of political forces even when they have been spared the benefits and costs of colonialism. Yet few of these states are either traditional autocracies or Western democracies. Although they have points of resemblance to both forms of government, their political requirements of modernization and national self-assertion are distinctive and unique. Unfortunately, however, there are few data upon which to examine the nature of administrative reform in these polities.

The position of the bureaucracy (both civilian and military) in such countries is of unique importance. Its social and political coherence and its proficiency nearly always outreach those of other potentially competing or controlling groups, and its relative political strength in the society makes it resistant to control. Thus where national independence is recent, or where the desire for economic modernization has been suppressed, there has been little history of administrative reform. Some nominal reforms may have taken place, but they have often had little effect because the rulers have lacked the political power to introduce any measures not solicited by the bureaucracy itself. Even so, it is possible to extrapolate from recent experiences in developing countries the desired upward, lateral, and internal bureaucratic relationships that give rise to reform efforts. In a few such countries, some gestures of reform are visible, or at least predictable. In still others, however, only the more unpleasant consequences of inaction are on display, and one can only speculate about the extent to which administrative reform might have been able to avert or mitigate political disaster.

In these modernizing countries, the bureaucratic failings of greatest moment are those concerned with nation-building and economic development, two goals generally pre-eminent in the political consciousness of the rulers and elites.[104] Failure to deal with these weaknesses has often had serious political consequences, resulting not only in the fall of governments and constitutions, but also in the substitution of mystical, non-rational goals

104. Milton J. Esman, "The Politics of Development Administration," in John D. Montgomery and William Siffin (eds.), *Approaches to Development: Politics, Administration and Change* (New York, 1966).

for the original aspirations of the new statehood.[105] The three levels of bureaucratic relationships examined previously can all be interpreted in terms of these twin aspirations. The bureaucracy's upward relationships to the political leaders are not merely those of loyalty, as in the traditional autocracies, or of representativeness, as in the Western democracies, but of polycommunality,[106] a much more explosive matter. Failure to achieve ethnic balance in the bureaucracy was one of the leading causes of the present Nigerian civil war. The lateral relationships of the bureaucracies in these countries are even more fundamental than those of adequacy in producing revenue or efficiency in performing public functions. They become the ultimate tests of a government's survival: effectiveness in establishing the basis of social order and economic growth. Finally, the internal coherence of the public service is not based either on honor or on a creed of public service but on its political contributions to national development. Independence from an external colonizer or from traditional rulers makes the bureaucracy an essential element in political mobilization and popular socialization. Its internal logic must therefore be some combination of these two elements, and administrative reforms directed internally represent an effort at what we usually call politicization (see Table 2).

The elemental forces released in the processes of political and economic modernization are those of violence as well as pride. The bureaucracy has great responsibilities in these countries. As a favored elite it is often far removed from the way of life of the "upstart" politicians on the one hand, or the traditional landlords and peasantry on the other. It is a distinct force in its own right. It is not only the guardian of public safety, inheriting the functions of the colonial or traditional past, but it is also the primary agent of economic and social development. Moreover, it is also

105. Joseph J. Spengler, "Theory, Ideology, Non-economic Values, and Politico-Economic Development," in Ralph Braibanti and Joseph J. Spengler (eds.), *Tradition, Values, and Socio-Economic Development* (Durham, N.C., 1961); John D. Montgomery, "Public Interest in the Ideologies of National Development," in Carl J. Friedrich (ed.), *The Public Interest* (New York, 1962), pp. 218–236; Paul E. Sigmund, Jr. (ed.), *The Ideologies of the Developing Countries: The Theory of Prismatic Society* (Boston, 1964), p. 160.

106. Fred W. Riggs, *Administration in Developing Countries: The Failure of Prismatic Society* (Boston, 1964), p. 160.

Table 2. *Political Forms and Administrative Reform*

Administrative relationships	Forms of Polity: Traditional autocracies	Western democracies	Modernizing states
Upward	Loyalty	Representa-tiveness	Polycommunality
Lateral	Adequacy	Efficiency	Effectiveness
Internal	Honor	Service	Politicization

called upon to play new political roles of building a nation and creating a civic culture. Its upward relations to the tribal and other ethnic groups are essential to nation-building; its lateral duties to the society are necessary elements in economic development; its internal beliefs and attitudes, drawing from both the political and the economic aspirations of the nation, are symbols of a civic culture that must still be created in the society as a whole. In whatever direction the bureaucracy looks, it finds its own role enlarged and expanded. For these reasons, adequate administrative reforms seem both more essential and more difficult in the new states than in other polities: essential because these societies cannot achieve the conditions of survival unless their governments can perform as demanded; more difficult because neither the knowledge nor the controls exist to convert a makeshift civil service into the powerful and even saintly self-denying force that seems necessary. The consequences of this paradox are to be seen in the wreckages of democratic institutions and hopes on three continents. Conventional approaches to reform are tragically inadequate in these instances.

Upward relationships

"Polycommunality" describes an upward relationship not to a personal ruler or governmental institution or even a social or economic class, but rather toward the sources of power that must be integrated in order to establish a nation-state. Nearly every colony, for example, was artificially created for the convenience of Westerners who sat in distant country houses or elegant conference rooms and drew impressionistic boundaries on sketchy and inaccurate maps. Linguistic consistencies and tribal loyalties were not the bases of creating many of these colonies, which were never conceived of as nations even in embryo. They were to be governed by a foreign bureaucracy with the assistance of whatever native leaders could be found. The notion of creating political unity for affirmative collective action was seldom useful for imperial purposes, and it was not until the independence movements succeeded in creating or taking over central governments that the administrative structure began to reflect the divisive separatisms known loosely among Westerners as tribalism. When local forces began to compete for position and power in a larger political context, the bureaucracy also began to reflect these new ethnic factors. Modernizing states that have not had recent colonial experiences, from Guatemala to Ethiopia and Thailand, often display similar communal multiplicities that have to be recognized in the bureaucratic composition.

Ethnicity in the first instance meant little more than replacing colonial administrators with local personnel. Kingsley found that this process usually took the first one to five years after independence.[107] A Nigerian commission quoted the Malayan government approvingly in citing the dictum that "one of the fundamental rights and privileges of a self-governing colony is that it must have control of its public service."[108] This process had to include district local officers so that the people could see the fruits of independence.[109] At the governmental centers, too, the process of localization had to be visible and, often, sudden. Only 451 of the 1,064 members of the Indian civil service in 1947 remained after the partition.[110] Younger's survey showed the dramatic change that took place in Ghana and Malaya in the first years of independence (see Tables 3 and 4).

107. J. Donald Kingsley, "Bureaucracy and Political Development with Particular Reference to Nigeria," in LaPalombara (ed.), *Bureaucracy and Political Development,* pp. 301–317, esp. p. 308.

108. *Ibid.,* p. 309; Kenneth Younger, *The Public Service in New States* (London, 1960), p. 34.

109. Kingsley, "Bureaucracy and Political Development," p. 309.

110. S. P. Jagota, "Training of Public Servants in India," in Ralph Braibanti and Joseph J. Spengler (eds.), *Administration and Economic Development in India* (Durham, N.C., 1963), p. 74.

Table 3. *Localization of the Public Service in Ghana, 1952–58*

	June 1952	*December 1958*
Ghanian officials	544 (29%)	1,984 (69%)
Overseas officials	1,322 (71%)	880 (31%)

Source: Kenneth Younger, *The Public Services in New States* (London, 1960), p. 53.

Table 4. *Localization of the Public Service in Malaya, 1956–58*

	August 1956	*January 1958*
Malayans	781 (26%)	1,185 (38%)
Overseas	1,721 (58%)	1,185 (38%) [*sic*]
Vacancies	468 (16%)	751 (24%)
Total	2,970	3,121

Source: Younger, *The Public Services in New States,* p. 62.

In Sudan, British officials serving in the civil service dropped from 1,180 in 1954 to 160 in December, 1955.[111] Sudan represented, in Younger's view, an "extreme form of the familiar experience. . . ."[112] But even so, "there was no administrative collapse. There was, however, a general drop in efficiency and a real threat to future development. . . ."[113] The demand for localization was not, of course, for a complete turnover in the public service: of the 300,000 members of the British colonial service in 1949, only 4 per cent had been "recruited externally." The problem was that nearly all of these expatriate administrators (as they were called after independence) occupied the higher and controlling posts.[114]

In some cases the process was gradual and planned. Cole's discussion of Nigerianization notes that preparations for replacing British bureaucrats began with a scholarship scheme before World War II; then in 1952–53 a commission was appointed to study Nigerianization, and in 1957 a Nigerianization officer was

111. *Ibid.,* p. 68.
112. *Ibid.,* p. 70.
113. *Ibid.,* p. 72.
114. *Ibid.,* p. 1 n. Cf. John D. Montgomery, "The Role of Induced Elite Change in Political Development," in John D. Montgomery and Arthur Smithies (eds.), *Public Policy* (Cambridge, 1964), XIII, 133–151.

directed to report annually on the progress of localization. A special parliamentary commission in 1958 urged greater speed even at the cost of "some deterioration of standards."[115] Fainsod notes that some countries (Pakistan, Nigeria, India) tried to make the transition smooth by keeping expatriates in selected posts temporarily, while others (Burma, Congo, and Indonesia), which had been led by independence "freedom fighters," expelled foreign civil servants en masse, thereby creating an administrative vacuum.[116]

But polycommunality in the public service did not mean merely expelling Western colonial officials in favor of local administration. It also meant choosing nationals from the right ethnic or tribal groups. Thus Younger[117] observed that in one case "the object of the government [is] not merely Nigerianization but Northernization," and Cole[118] noted that "Northernization has been directed much more vigorously against Southern Nigerians than against Expatriates." Tilman's study of the Malayan bureaucracy took special note of the communal problems following independence. Between 1956 and 1962, the number of British and other Western civil servants dropped from 2,060 to about 200.[119] But in filling these posts the different ethnic groups increased their strength disproportionately: the numbers of Chinese in Division I posts grew from 13.2 per cent in 1957 to 34 per cent in 1962, while the Malays increased only from 14.1 per cent to 29.3 per cent and the Indians from 7 per cent to 15.9 per cent.[120] Thereafter a substantial preference—as high as four to one—was given to Malays in the quotas established for recruitment into the most prestigious levels of the civil service. The ethnic balance desired in the Malayan civil service was not proportionate representation of various population groups but the

115. Taylor Cole, "Bureaucracy in Transition: Independent Nigeria," *Public Administration*, XXXVIII (1960), p. 332.
116. Merle Fainsod, "The Structure of Development Administration," in Irving Swerdlow (ed.), *Development Administration: Concepts and Problems* (Syracuse, 1963), pp. 4–5.
117. *The Public Service in New States*, p. 23.
118. "Bureaucracy in Transition," p. 334.
119. Robert O. Tilman, *Bureaucratic Transition in Malaya* (Durham, N.C., 1964), p. 68.
120. *Ibid.*, p. 70.

protection of a political power base for the Malays. This base had been established under the British in order to protect the natives against the urban, educated, and more aggressive Chinese and Indian communities that already dominated professional and commercial life. Similarly, the disproportionate role of Northern and Central Vietnamese in the governmental structures of South Vietnam was a source of serious discontent with the Diem regime, which used not only ethnicity, but its most extreme form—kinship—in making key administrative appointments.[121] The partition of Pakistan and India also arose from ethnic causes. Before partition only 9 per cent of the Indian civil service had been Muslims, nearly all of whom transferred to Pakistan thereafter.[122] Few Hindus were in secretaryships in Pakistan after independence.[123] President Ayub admitted in 1961: "We are inclined towards provincialism, parochialism, tribalism, and selfishness":[124] an ethnicized civil service became a welfare device for providing employment for unnecessary and incompetent help.[125] Ethnic and communal specialization in the bureaucracy has also been noted in Burma and Ceylon.[126] The administrative reforms demanded in the name of polycommunality are as urgent and necessary as those called forth by the ruler's demand for loyalty or class demands for representativeness. But ethnicity or polycommunality is not a single factor, and judgments about timing and proportions are among the most tortuous political decisions that have to be made in the nation-building phases of independence.

Lateral relationships

It is ironic that in the underdeveloped countries economic development demands more of the bureaucracy than adequacy in

121. John T. Dorsey, "The Bureaucracy and Political Development in Vietnam," in LaPalombara (ed.), *Bureaucracy and Political Development,* pp. 336–337.

122. Ralph Braibanti, "Public Bureaucracy and Judiciary in Pakistan," in LaPalombara (ed.), *Bureaucracy and Political Development,* pp. 364–366.

123. *Ibid.,* p. 368.

124. *Ibid.,* p. 389 n.

125. *Ibid.,* p. 384.

126. James F. Guyot, "Bureaucratic Transformation in Burma," in Ralph Braibanti and Associates, *Asian Bureaucratic Systems Emergent from the British Imperial Tradition* (Durham, N.C., 1966), pp. 379–381; Robert N. Kearney, "Ceylon: The Contemporary Bureaucracy," in *ibid.,* pp. 505–506.

supplying resources for the state's operations, but it does not require as much as efficiency in performance. What is required is rather the more immediate goal of effectiveness.[127] At whatever cost in corruption or mismanagement, the government must collect the taxes and fees needed, and it must actually carry out at least most of the programs that have been planned and promised. It would be going too far to say that efficiency is not desired, and even urged, but few governmental functions can be radically altered merely because they were too costly or too slow. Even legal responsibility is a secondary consideration. Western legal codes designed to keep the bureaucracy responsive to law do not seem to have this effect in underdeveloped countries because there, administrative performance is paramount. "[J]udged by their political consequences, the courts would appear to have heightened bureaucratic irresponsibility rather than reduced it."[128] Relatively few of the reforms that have taken place in the underdeveloped countries have really aimed at reducing costs, speeding performance, improving quality, or enhancing legal responsibility. New governments do not have to be efficient; but they have to do in actuality most of what they declare must be done. There is little room in the scope of government operations in these countries to permit the luxury of non-performance.

One reason why postcolonial governments have to settle for so little is the sheer burden of the demands placed upon them by independence. In Malaya, as elsewhere, "independence and the expanded development schemes of the Federation have imposed upon these officials more responsibility than their British guardians ever had to bear."[129] In general, development administration, as the "carrier of innovating values . . . embraces the array of new functions assumed by developing countries embarked on the path of modernization and industrialization."[130] To fulfil the enormous expectations of independence, the new governments have had few alternative instruments of social action beside their own

127. Riggs, *Administration in Developing Countries*, pp. 263–265.
128. Riggs, "Bureaucrats and Political Development: A Paradoxical View," in LaPalombara (ed.), *Bureaucracy and Political Development*, p. 156.
129. Tilman, *Bureaucratic Transition in Malaya*, p. 89.
130. Fainsod, "The Structure of Development Administration," p. 2.

civil service.[131] Few students of administration could predict other than difficulty, as Kingsley did for the government of Ghana, when the bureaucracy was impelled into "complex economic areas [such as detailed import and export controls]."[132] The relative youth and inexperience of the civil service as a result of ethnicity reforms[133] often tend to induce feelings of inferiority and inadequacy, which, in turn, lead many civil servants to rely heavily on outworn procedures, ritualized into a form of security, and to adopt arrogant, face-saving attitudes in dealing with a dissatisfied public.[134]

The reforms that are called forth by these conditions are less those of streamlining and efficiency than those which permit the government to do its tasks at all. Performance budgeting in the Philippines did not improve the use of the budget as an instrument of cost control; it was introduced as a substitute for political reform so that the government could appear to respond to Western techniques without interrupting the normal course of events.[135] Western conventions of the merit system are also sometimes disappointing when practiced in the undeveloped countries: no civil service that is based on ethnic representativeness can be recruited by universal competition.[136] Indeed, it could be argued that too much bureaucratic efficiency would be a source of weakness in the political development of states lacking other countervailing sources of power.[137] The most acceptable of the administrative reforms brought in by Western technical advisers are technical rather than managerial in nature. They occur as a result of suggestions made on a program basis, involving the introduction of professional standards to insure competent per-

131. Joseph LaPalombara, "An Overview of Bureaucracy and Political Development," in LaPalombara (ed.), *Bureaucracy and Political Development,* pp. ix, 4–5.

132. Kingsley, "Bureaucracy and Political Development," pp. 313–314.

133. *Ibid.*, p. 311.

134. Riggs, *The Ecology of Public Administration* (Bombay and New York, 1961), pp. 100–117; Riggs, *Administration in Developing Countries,* pp. 15–19, 176–179.

135. Malcolm B. Parsons, "Performance Budgeting in the Philippines," *Public Administration Review,* XVI (1957), 173–179.

136. Riggs, "Bureaucrats and Political Development," p. 128.

137. *Ibid.*, pp. 126–127.

formance. When such approaches are taken, programs in public health, agriculture, and other professional fields become more effective than before, though often at costs that appear exorbitant to any observer except the government that installed the programs in the first place.

There are, of course, routine operations in which the introduction of more efficient methods will be welcomed and even demanded, especially if the misused funds or personnel are needed elsewhere. But these purposes are usually secondary in the newly developing countries where the government's main problem is to establish itself, to fulfil the political and economic promises of independence, to provide ethnic balance within the national community, to protect a few bastions of privilege, and perhaps to make use of public employment as spoils or a substitute for traditional welfare activities. Quite apart from the readily perceived dangers of making a bureaucracy so efficient as to threaten the political leadership, too much efficiency may endanger the effectiveness of certain government programs that are more important than the saving of time or money. Perhaps the norms of efficiency may be safely installed only when they do not threaten other more important values.

Internal relationships

Even if reforms in the cause of polycommunality succeed in dominating the selection process in the civil service, and the administrative performance is sufficient to move governmental programs forward satisfactorily, the potentials of the bureaucracy for nation-building may still be unfulfilled. The requirements of independence involve mass responses not known in colonial times. And the administrative elite, although considered a primary instrument of modernization, is almost by definition far removed from the population in education, outlook, and style of living. Both the necessity of building national consciousness and the need for mobilizing public co-operation for economic development, especially in agriculture, call on the bureaucracy to serve as popular teachers and leaders. When the bureaucracy is temperamentally unfitted to participate in the political socialization of the public, it must be internally mobilized for the purpose. It becomes itself a prime target of political socialization.

Many observers have identified the politicization of the civil service as one of the first consequences of independence. The plenary powers of the local district officer give way to new specialized functions as the new officials are organized along political lines and lose their magisterial functions to the police.[138] The new civil servants become less concerned with maintaining order and supplying resources than with representing "their respective movements, parties, or sectors," seeing their role as one of "accommodating various groups to the framework of the centralized polity."[139] Their work must now transcend local concerns, since regional and national programs now become "potent instrument[s] of unification," binding together new nations which were no more than "historical accidents in the first place."[140] Politics rather than law becomes the root of successful administration. Riggs, observing an imbalance between policy-making and policy-implementing structures in new nations, also notes that the political function is gradually "appropriated" by bureaucrats. Since elections in these countries are not seen as necessarily a reflection of popular will, and since the courts do not serve as restraining "bulwarks of the rule of law," the consequences are that chief executives and their administrators tend to become arbitrary, authoritarian, and even charismatic—in a word, political but unresponsive.[141] Pye is not really dissenting from this judgment in his complaint that the bureaucracy is too legalistic and not politicized enough. "In many of the new countries administration would be far more effective if administrators were to adopt more aggressive measures and seek to be more political."[142] The difference between Pye and Riggs on this point is not whether the bureaucracy in the new states tends to become politicized, but whether it is politicized enough.

138. Kingsley, "Bureaucracy and Political Development," p. 313.
139. Eisenstadt, "Bureaucracy and Political Development," pp. 107, 110.
140. Kingsley, "Bureaucracy and Political Development," p. 313.
141. Riggs, "Bureaucrats and Political Development," pp. 120–122.
142. Lucian W. Pye, "The Political Context of National Development," in Swerdlow (ed.), *Development Administration*, p. 34.

Efforts to use the bureaucracy as a first step in the political socialization of the public often begin with a recruitment campaign to enlist the support of hitherto disadvantaged groups. Ethnicity reforms, already discussed, are part of this process. In Malaya during the guerrilla emergency, one-quarter of the higher civil service posts were opened by quota to Chinese and other non-Malays, "to demonstrate to the urbanized Chinese [who might have otherwise been tempted to support the guerrillas] that they were to be given official status in the Peninsula."[143] The Chinese needed special opportunities to participate in government positions because as immigrants to Malaya they had received their political socialization from clans and extended families, unlike the Indian immigrants who had merely moved from one paternalistic colony to another and were already familiar with relevant political processes and values.[144] Bureaucratic recruitment based on ethnicity only recognizes the importance of ethnic groups in the composition of the state, however. Strengthening the political capability of the bureaucracy requires changing traditional ethnic behavior and attitudes as well. The next stage of reform in Malaya may well include some effort to use the Chinese element in the bureaucracy to strengthen the national self-consciousness.

Internal reforms are required if the bureaucracy is to communicate effectively with the citizens they are to activate and mobilize. The civil service belongs to, and represents, "the values, prejudices, and ambitions of a very definite and limited stratum of the total society—the more established, Westernized, and educated families. Generally, the politicians do not belong to this social class. . . ."[145] In India, the "governmental leadership is recruited from the 2 per cent of the population which speaks English. . . ."[146] The language of the planners is usually remote from the people, often assuming a widespread demand for immediate improvement in standards of living: a form of "xenophilia"

143. Tilman, *Bureaucratic Transition in Malaya,* p. 35.
144. *Ibid.,* p. 31.
145. Pye, "The Political Context of National Development," p. 36.
146. Wilfred Malenbaum, "Leadership Tasks in India's Economy," in Braibanti and Spengler (eds.), *Administration and Economic Development in India,* p. 163.

that betrays a "severely deficient empathy for the state of mind of one's fellow-countrymen."[147] In an eloquent essay, Sovani speaks of the relics of the Hindu tradition that impede development in India, ranging from the caste system to the sterile ways used by individuals to escape from the immobility of their own past. The solution to these attitudes calls for national moral leadership[148] that will almost certainly involve the civil service in finding new ways of releasing national and individual energies. But securing the desired attitudes and actions from the civil service calls for reforms not listed in the handbooks of public administration. What is needed is not only the assignment of new roles to the bureaucracy and reorganization of the government's instruments of action, but also, within the bureaucracy itself, new perceptions of society and the state. These perceptions cannot be developed through training programs alone, which may soon become routine and legalistic, especially when designed by, and left to, the experts. The kind of moral leadership called for by Sovani requires not merely the exhortations of political figures but more especially the example provided by the most trusted and respected members of the civil service itself. As experiences in the Western democracy have suggested, many of the most important administrative reforms involving codes of behavior have to be introduced from within.

V. Conclusion: A Note of Caution

Before drawing conclusions from the evidence presented thus far, it is time to invoke some of the caution that has been momentarily suspended for the sake of this rather unconventional argument. The present analysis has deliberately fused bureaucratic reform with constitutional and political factors that students of public administration usually consider irrelevant. It has not considered the problem of governments that need reform but seek

147. *Ibid.*, p. 169.
148. N. V. Sovani, "Non-economic Aspects of India's Economic Development," in Braibanti and Spengler (eds.), *Administration and Economic Development in India*, pp. 277–280.

instead to perpetuate static traditional values, or those whose political condition is too unstable to consider reform at all. Finally, it has overemphasized modal differences in administrative behavior and reform in the three forms of government in order to clarify their relationship to other political circumstances. Overemphasis introduces oversimplification, a risk especially dangerous for the literal-minded who may be inclined to substitute historical generalizations for a specific political reality. It is probably unnecessary to state that few personal-rule states can really make all political decisions flow from a single source; that democracies do not always seek to control the arbitrariness of administrative actions but may tolerate them for long periods of time; and that postcolonial states do not necessarily give nation-building socio-economic modernization the highest political priorities. The assumption that these things are more or less true is only a convenience for classifying what reforms they do undertake. By the same token, reforms in the interest of loyalty are no monopoly of the traditional autocracy, and the politicizing role of the bureaucracy may sometimes be assigned, with appropriate alterations, in personal autocracies as well as in the modernizing states. Nor does this catalogue of reforms cover all possible motives of individual reformers. What I am attempting to do is to counteract the effects of one set of oversimplifications (those that attempt to divorce administrative reform from politics or equate reform with some objective natural-law virtue) with what seems to be a less distorted set. These generalizations do not eliminate the need for analyzing interrelationships among the three levels of possible administrative reform and their respective political settings.

Such an analysis would have to acknowledge the existence of tensions and ambiguities among these levels of administrative interaction. The dimensions "upward," "lateral," and "internal" do not mean the same things in different polities where the focus of the relationship varies. In traditional autocracy, the upward focus is upon a single figure or symbol, as contrasted with that in a democracy, where a diffused sovereignty of the people is assumed. In newly developing states, the upward relationships may be tied into symbolic leaders, but are often obscured by responsibility to ethnic groups that are less than a whole nation but more than a ruling class. Similarly, the lateral relations of the bureaucracy in the traditional autocracies look only to the noble and moneyed classes, while in the democracies and modernizing states they include the citizens and beneficiaries of government programs. The internal self-discipline of the bureaucracy also reflects (and perhaps in the form presented here, exaggerates) the different perspectives in which the civil service is expected to perceive its role. Finally, the bureaucracy is not presented as a constant surrounded by a set of dependent variables but as itself a changing quantity. These facts call attention to errors arising from the convention that portrays a nation's bureaucracy as a static resource to be allocated according to rational political and economic criteria.

The administrative specialist as reformer is also tempted to overlook the fact that little is currently known about the detailed consequences of past reform measures. In the absence of guaranteed results, he is tempted, following the famous "Hawthorne" experiments of a few generations ago,[149] to take the view that any reform is better than none. Just as a patent medicine that does not deal with the causes of a sickness may improve the psychosomatic conditions that produce the symptoms, attention to the need for better administrative performance may bring it about. The proposed approach does not challenge the potential therapeutic value of such witchcraft. It may, however, aid the diagnostician to make use of political folk medicine instead of ignoring it.

Bureaucracies are not easily mobilized by external forces. Even when the public does make its demands known, the bureaucracy may lack the empathy necessary to develop a sense of urgency in its response. In most underdeveloped countries, both sides of the demand-response formula are weak; the public possesses scanty resources for expressing its interests, and the bureaucracy has little sympathy for the conditions under which most citizens live. The forces that compel or induce bureaucracies to follow a desired rationale in these circumstances are much more complicated

149. Elton Mayo, *The Social Problems of an Industrial Civilization* (Cambridge, Mass., 1945), pp. 75–82.

than the legal relationships, the prestigious hierarchies, and the popular demands that have supported reforms in autocracies or Western democracies. Because of the greater difficulty of using reform as a means of changing bureaucratic behavior in the newly independent countries, a wider range of sanctions, and especially those invoking the participation of competing subsystems, is called for.

In the last analysis, the behavioral sources of administrative reform cannot be seen as standardized faults in a bureaucracy or as the caprice of a ruling group. Just as it takes two to make a quarrel, so two parties are necessary—and, indeed, several more are usually involved—before a bureaucratic annoyance leads to action. Inappropriate behavior becomes so only in terms of political requirements of a society's leadership. Thus the conventional wisdom of Western public administration often fails to provide adequate standards for prescribing reform in the new states. The leaders of these governments may find comfort in the knowledge that the challenge and the range of experimental alternatives available to them far transcend those available in the West at any time in its history. It is perhaps less comforting to them to discover that this fact greatly reduces the immediate relevance of Western doctrines to their current problems.

• 11 •

Productivity, Administrative Reform, and Antipolitics: Dilemmas for Developing States*

Warren F. Ilchman

Politicians at the top, then the military, and the real brains at the bottom. . . . We're living in a society that contains a monstrous contradiction, modern in technology but archaic in its social organization. . . . We [scientists] do the thinking for an archaic crowd of nitwits and allow ourselves to be pushed around by 'em in the bargain.

FRED HOYLE, *The Black Cloud*

Instead of a rigid hierarchy of status and authority there tends to be what is roughly, in formal status, a "company of equals," an equalization of status which ignores the inevitable gradation of distinction and achievement to be found in any considerable group of technical competent persons.

TALCOTT PARSONS, Introduction to Max Weber's *The Theory of Social and Economic Organization*

Ironically, the last outpost of colonialism may be the university. There, otherwise humane and tolerant men, such as we,

* This study was made possible initially by a grant from the Rockefeller Foundation for the study of planners and political problems of economic development in South Asia and the Middle East. My wife, Dr. Alice Stone Ilchman, and Professor Philip K. Hastings of the Roper Center for Public Opinion Research, assisted me in the research and with an early formulation of the argument. See Warren F. Ilchman, Alice Stone Ilchman, and Philip K. Hastings, *The New Men*

stratify the world for the purposes of analysis and invariably place those who ruled at the top of the rank order and those recently liberated at the bottom. In all things deemed relevant in modern social science, they who were least remain so. Where schoolboys' maps were once colored to indicate empires, they are now marked to show the industrially advanced and backward, the overpopulated and properly populated, the politically stable and unstable. Even the white man's burden is curiously rediscovered when we define the course of change, the relative merits of technologies, and the readiness of others to absorb our advanced ways.

But in this act of stratifying nations for scholarly purposes we often reveal ourselves in unintended fashions. For instance, we assume that intellectual technologies, whether they are social work or public administration or economics, are "natural" to our societies and deeply rooted in our problems, values, and styles of productive activity. Elsewhere, especially in "developing states," we further assume that these technologies are "unnatural," that their importation must be prepared for, that values must be changed and peoples equipped to accommodate the exported complexity and sophistication.

This latter proposition may be true. The intellectual technologies we export contain a host of values and orientations that may find little nurture in the host developing nations. But it may also be true that among those technologies are some which are scant socialized even by the donors. The purpose of this chapter is to explore one of those technologies and to point out that in nations, "advanced" and "less advanced," a problem is shared. The problem relates to the rise of a group of public servants advancing an administrative and program technology and the potential political consequences of that development.

---

of Knowledge and Developing States (Berkeley, 1968). I am grateful also to Miss Carolyn Clark of the Department of Economics of the University of California at Berkeley for the content analysis of the planners' responses, to Mrs. Joyce Munns, Allan Samson, Theodore M. Smith, and Stephen Zwerling for research assistance, and to Miss Margali Sarfatti, Miss Helen Rudy, Professor Robert P. Biller, Mrs. Kay Lawson, Professor Michael Brenner, Norman Uphoff, and Guy Benveniste for critical comments. The author remains solely responsible for facts and analysis in this chapter.

I

The appearance of what might be a new ideal type for social analysis should be treated in the same manner as additions to the periodic table are treated. The discovery provides an occasion to reconfirm a mode of research and to expand the possible combinations in the analytic universe. Not only may previously identified elements be compared in new light, but scholarship is advanced through the necessity of cataloguing the ideal type's attributes and relationships. Such an opportunity is provided by the emergence of rational-productivity bureaucracy which constitutes the new general administrative and program technology and poses political problems for "developed" and "developing" states alike.

Emergence implies a swift appearance, essentially unheralded. This is inaccurate in the present case. The likelihood of rational-productivity bureaucracy was foretold by Saint-Simon, Comte, and Veblen and kept alive by sociologists and social critics, especially French, with the interim and imprecise conception of "technocracy."[1] But interim and imprecise was the earlier concept. A clearer referent can now be identified. It imputes no more autonomy, scope, or science fiction-like attributes than empirically exist or are logically necessary. Moreover, the newer ideal type is largely free of the obloquy, fears, and inflated aspirations that mark technocracy.

Rational-productivity bureaucracy as an orientation toward action and a form of social organization can be associated with specific episodes and major on-going developments. Many events, in various parts of the world, chronicle the emergence of activity approximating rational-productivity bureaucracy: the 1909 social budget in Great Britain;[2] the development of permanent military planning staffs in Western Europe in the nineteenth and early

1. See, for example, Maurice Druesne, *Les Problems Economiques et la Technocratie* (Paris, 1933), and Jean Meynaud, *Technocratie et Politique* (Lausanne, 1960).
2. Sidney Pollard, *The Development of the British Economy, 1914–1950* (London, 1962), chap. 1.

twentieth centuries;[3] the first five-year plan in the Soviet Union in 1928;[4] the overturning in the late 1930's of constitutional restraints on United States' governmental managing of the economy;[5] the Beveridge Reports of 1942 and 1945 and later Labour party social and economic planning;[6] the Employment Act of 1946 and subsequent establishment of the Council of Economic Advisers;[7] the Monnet Plan in 1944 and the first French plan in 1947;[8] general national and regional planning occasioned by the European Recovery Program and later the European Common Market;[9] the development of national and international technical assistance programs,[10] the creation of the Policy Planning Staff in the United States Department of State in 1947;[11] large-scale public subsidization of basic and applied scientific research in the post-1945 period;[12] the first five-year plan in India in 1951;[13] the beginning of the National Economic Development Council in Great Britain in 1961;[14] the application of Program Planning Budgeting System in the American Federal Executive in the

3. Samuel P. Huntington, *The Soldier and the State* (New York, 1964), pp. 19–59, 222–269; Ernest Barker, "The Development of Administration, Conscription, Taxation, Social Services, and Education," in Edward Eyre (ed.), *European Civilization: Its Origin and Development* (London, 1937), V, 1031–1045.

4. Abram Bergson, *The Economics of Soviet Planning* (New Haven, 1964).

5. C. Herman Pritchett, *The Roosevelt Court: A Study in Judicial Politics and Values* (New York, 1948), chap. 8; Bernard Schwartz, *The Supreme Court: Constitutional Revolution in Retrospect* (New York, 1957), chap. 2.

6. William Beveridge, *Social Insurance and Allied Services* (London, 1942) and *Full Employment in a Free Society* (London, 1945); Pollard, *The Development of the British Economy,* chaps. 6–7.

7. Stephen K. Bailey, *Congress Makes a Law: The Story Behind the Employment Act of 1946* (New York, 1950); Edward S. Flash, *Economic Advice and Presidential Leadership* (New York, 1965).

8. John Hackett and Anne-Marie Hackett, *Economic Planning in France* (Cambridge, Mass., 1963); Andrew Shonfield, *Modern Capitalism* (London, 1965), pp. 121–175.

9. See, for example, Achille Albonetti, *Prehistoire des Etat-Unis de L'Europe* (Paris, 1963), pp. 46–80, and Shonfield, *Modern Capitalism,* pp. 71–238.

10. Ralph Braibanti, "Transnational Inducement of Administrative Reform: A Survey of Scope and Critique of Issues," in John D. Montgomery and William J. Siffin (eds.), *Approaches to Development* (New York, 1966), pp. 133–184.

11. Robert E. Elder, *The Policy Machine: The Department of State and American Foreign Policy* (Syracuse, N.Y., 1960), pp. 71–92.

12. A. Hunter Dupree, *Science in the Federal Government* (rev. ed.; New York, 1964), pp. 369–382; Don K. Price, *The Scientific Estate* (Cambridge, Mass., 1965), *passim.*

13. A. H. Hanson, *The Process of Planning: A Study of India's Five-Year Plans* (Oxford, 1966), pp. 27–234.

14. Samuel Brittain, *The Treasury Under the Tories, 1951–1964* (London, 1964), chaps. 7–9.

1960's.[15] From these landmark events, major continuing developments began or were accelerated: for example, the rise of continuous professional military planning and later civilian national security analysis;[16] professional diplomatists with increasing area and functional specialization;[17] the mounting role of economists in welfare planning and later in managing whole economies;[18] the enlarging significance of professional management specialists in and out of government;[19] the emergence of communications and computer scientists in the public and private sectors;[20] the enhanced activity and number of scientists and engineers in weapons research and in government and private research and development activities.[21] Few existing studies even indicate the changing total of people so engaged; none as yet can indicate qualitatively their importance to various social, political, and economic ends.[22]

Many of the reasons adduced by Weber—both "conditions" and "predeterminants"—for the rise of legal-rational bureaucracy apply to rational-productivity bureaucracy as well.[23] While I can-

15. Charles J. Hitch, *Decision-Making for Defense* (Berkeley, 1965).

16. Bruce L. R. Smith, *The RAND Corporation* (Cambridge, Mass., 1966); Charles J. Hitch and Roland N. McKean, *The Economics of Defense in the Nuclear Age* (Cambridge, Mass., 1960); Bernard Brodie, *Strategy in the Missile Age* (Princeton, 1959).

17. Warren F. Ilchman, *Professional Diplomacy in the United States* (Chicago, 1961); James L. McCamy, *Conduct of the New Diplomacy* (New York, 1964).

18. Examples are Flash, *Economic Advice and Presidential Leadership,* and Shonfield, *Modern Capitalism.* See also Walter W. Heller, *New Dimensions of Political Economy* (Cambridge, Mass., 1966).

19. See, for example, Reinhard Bendix, *Work and Authority in Industry* (New York, 1956), and Dwight C. Waldo, *The Administrative State* (New York, 1948).

20. Robert Boguslaw, *The New Utopians: A Study of Systems Design and Social Change* (Englewood Cliffs, N.J., 1965); Smith, *The RAND Corporation.*

21. For example, William Kornhauser, *Scientists in Industry* (Berkeley, 1962).

22. An exception, perhaps, for one variant is Price, *The Scientific Estate,* cited above in n. 12.

23. H. H. Gerth and C. Wright Mills (eds.), *From Max Weber: Essays in Sociology* (New York, 1958), pp. 196–244. Carl J. Friedrich has pointed out to the author that Max Weber subsumed "rational-productivity" in his conception of "legal-rationality." It is only, he adds, the Anglo-American interpretation that necessitates the second formulation. From the American translations of Weber, however, it seems clear that the concept of legal-rationality does not fully comprehend economic planning and similar activity. Moreover, the abuses Weber feared from German bureaucrats are not of the same order or kind as the potential abuses of rational-productivity bureaucrats. Finally, "efficiency" and "productivity" are not necessarily synonymous.

not attribute approximate weight to them, several seem, a priori, to have relevance. Among them, undoubtedly, are the continued social and economic policy consequences of legal and political equality—achieved and aspired to. These have thrust the state, almost everywhere in the world, into an active continuous role to maintain or improve incomes and to insure health, safety, and education of whole populations.[24] "Expert" skills in large numbers are required for this not only in government but also in interest associations; flexible, goal-defined policies give scope to those with these skills.

Simultaneously, the needs to induce changes in the modes of production or to sustain a highly diverse and interdependent economy necessitate rational productive skills in the public and private sectors alike. They are used to insure the supply of the factors of production at predictable and plannable levels, to preserve, extend, or project the parameters of foreign commerce, and to foster industrial innovation through research and development activities.

These changes and the skills required to exploit their opportunities have been accelerated by transformations occurring in the international system. For the last generation at least, national security has been defined in global and functionally total terms. Events everywhere are of relevance to regimes somewhere. In this context, there is demand for skills to formulate national security strategies, advance weapons development, and participate in the international exchange of productive skills and capital to employ these skills that are now part of modern "defense."

There are other factors: the modernization of the university, the social emphasis on education and fitness influenced by the spread of legal-rational bureaucracy, the growing size of the political community, changing technologies in communications and transportation, etc. In varying combinations, all of them contributed to the emergence and maintenance of rational-productivity bureaucracy.

The persons fulfilling these functions brought about by identi-

24. Reinhard Bendix, *National-Building and Citizenship* (New York, 1964), pp. 55–144.

fied and other forces are rational-productivity bureaucrats. Despite obvious differences in their education and in the problems on which they work, they share a common orientation toward action, source of authority and legitimacy, and criterion for choice. The social organizations in which they act are usually rational-productivity bureaucracies which, regardless of their different goals and subordination to other types of bureaucracy, share similar structural attributes. Occasionally, a rational-productivity bureaucrat is assigned to conventional bureaucracy and is denied the shelter of common orientations and hospitable structure.

What are these common orientations and structures and how do they differ from those more closely akin to the ideal type of legal-rational bureaucracy? This can best be seen typologically:

Structure and orientation	*Legal-rational bureaucracy*	*Rational-productivity bureaucracy*
Degree and importance of hierarchy	High (many-levels); great importance	Low (few levels); little importance
Monocratic authority	Formally, yes; substantively, yes	Formally, often; substantively, seldom
Formal communication channels	Great importance	Little importance
Centralization	Great; criterion is uniformity of decisions	Ambivalent; criterion is productivity
Role attainment	Achieved	Achieved-dependent on considerably longer educational period
Relevance of pre-entry education to position	Generally low	High
Training experience	Mostly post-entry	Substantially prior to entry
Dominant resource for internal compliance	Coercive-utilitarian	Normative
Career orientation	Intra-bureaucracy mobility; lifetime in general position	Inter-public-private-university-sector mobility; lifetime in profession
Promotional opportunities of decision-making echelons	Varied, but common	High
Reference group	Intra-organizational	Extra-organizational and intra-organizational
Instruments of action	Laws, with low autonomy for agent	Broad directives with great autonomy of choice for agent
Source of legitimacy	Law	Knowledge
Power means	Office	Expertise

Structure and orientation	*Legal-rational bureaucracy*	*Rational-productivity bureaucracy*
Functional specifity	High	Low
Loyalty	Organization	Profession or program
Time orientation	Present (immediate past and future)	Future
Criterion for choice	Efficiency	Productivity (effectiveness and efficiency)
Goals	Administration without "regard to persons"	Maximum output of goods and services
Ability to change	Low	High

A final common bond joins rational-productivity bureaucrats across nations and "levels of development" and makes the ideal type a useful category for analysis and for identifying problems of administrative reform. This bond derives largely from their legitimating source in knowledge, their loyalty to substantive programs, and their value commitment to productivity. In essence, these three factors combine to predispose the rational-productivity bureaucrats to be against conventional politics—regardless of whether the politics are liberal pluralistic or authoritarian. Unlike their legal-rational predecessors and colleagues, for whom politics was the source of law, the rational-productivity bureaucrat claims a knowledge superior to that of the politician or statesman, a clearer sense of program needs than what emerges as a demand from the clash of political forces or leaders, and a feeling that politics is antithetical to productivity. What is political, they argue, is inherently unproductive. To transform what is politically contested into administrative discretion, not routine, is their common objective. With a mandate higher than law—whether it is "national security," "population control," "economic development," "cost effectiveness," "pure science," "planned organizational change," etc.—the rational productivity bureaucrat engages, tacitly or actively, in the politics of antipolitics.

II

Rational-productivity bureaucrats and rational-productivity bureaucracies are increasing in number throughout much of the world. The actual number and mix varies from nation to nation. The criticalness of the contribution they make also varies, and with it their political importance as well. While we may only assume temporarily that the actual number is greater—absolutely and relatively—in the industrially more advanced nations, we can be certain that the intellectual technologies that undergird this activity are heavily influenced by the practice of the same industrially advanced nations. Moreover, these nations are the chief exporters of the various rational-productive technologies—and, alas, importers.[25] Even the attempts in developing nations at "intellectual import substitution" bear the identity of the originals.

But no one should assume that rational productive technologies and their exponents are firmly grounded in and supported by the institutions and values of the industrially advanced. Three types of evidence support this contention. First, there is by now a considerable body of literature—either garbed by "science" or frankly exhortative—that argues that conventional bureaucracy is inadequate for the new intellectual technologies and that there should be structural changes to meet this change and increase in responsibility.[26] Second, several exponents of rational-productive values have sought to convince a wider public of the imperatives of their view.[27] In either case, a widespread acceptance of these forms and values would not require such a volume of literature. But, finally, in many regimes of the industrially advanced category, there is considerable political and intellectual opposition to the spread of rational-productivity values and ways.[28] Indeed, Professor David Apter believes that a coalition of the tech-

25. John C. Shearer, *Intra- and International Movements of High-Level Human Resources* (Bloomington, Ind., 1967).

26. Examples are Victor A. Thompson, *Modern Organization* (New York, 1961); Robert Presthus, *The Organizational Society* (New York, 1962); Warren G. Bennis, *Changing Organizations* (New York, 1966); and Michel Crozier, *The Bureaucratic Phenomenon* (Chicago, 1964), chaps. 7, 11.

27. Such as Heller, *New Dimensions of Political Economy;* Marshall E. Dimock, *Administrative Vitality* (New York, 1959); Pierre Massé, *Le Plan ou l'anti-hasard* (Paris, 1965); François Bloch-Laine, *Pour une reforme de l'enterprise* (Paris, 1963).

28. Michael Young, *The Rise of the Meritocracy* (London, 1961); Price, *The Scientific Estate;* Jacques Ellul, "The Technological Order," in Carl F. Stover (ed.), *The Technological Order* (Detroit, 1963), pp. 10–37.

nologically obsolescent and status-deprived constitutes the major political threat in the future of the developed nations.[29]

How have rational-productivity bureaucrats fared in developing countries? Here my research and competence limit the argument to one variety—the economic planner in the public service. And, then, the perspective from which I have chosen to view the planners is one that will tell us more about how they feel about relationships with society and politics than how their technologies have been absorbed. On the other hand, this will permit a subsequent discussion of the predeterminants and conditions for these feelings, their potential administrative and political consequences, and some suggestions about administrative reform.

Public advisers on increasing the wealth of a nation are not new. They had predecessors, for instance, among the mercantilists of the late seventeenth and eighteenth centuries. But it is in the period since the Russian Revolution for Eastern Europe and since the Great Depression and the Second World War for Western Europe and the United States that the economic planner has become an increasingly permanent feature of public bureaucracies. Regimes—capitalist and socialist, totalitarian and democratic, rich and poor—all have their contingent, and their numbers are swelled by professional economists in the bureaucracies of the United Nations and functional international organizations.

One might cavil at the phrase "economic planner" as too narrow to include the broad range of responsibilities of these men. Many are not formally involved in planning ministries or commissions. They have responsibility for analyzing and projecting trends and even implementive authority in such diverse fields as exchange controls, taxation, imports, transportation and basic industries, population, small savings, co-operatives, ad infinitum. They are nevertheless concerned with the impact of programs on the growth potential of the nation, they seek to improve decisions in the present by holding constant some desired state in the future, and they use common assumptions and techniques derived from the discipline of economics. They may not call them-

29. David E. Apter, "Introduction: Ideology and Discontent," in Apter (ed.), *Ideology and Discontent* (New York, 1964), pp. 30–34.

selves economic planners, but instead "economic public servants," "economists," or "economic advisers." But across regimes they share a concern with the economic planner for the future, and their knowledge is legitimated by its claim to predictive ability. For this reason, the category "economic planner" is used to describe the public role of the rational-productivity bureaucrat with this range of responsibility.

Little is known of these people in industrial countries, except their good works, their short- and long-term projections, and their failures.[30] Even less is known about their colleagues in industrially backward nations. This situation, of course, is true to the state of knowledge on political elites generally in the non-Western world. What is known is anecdotal, impressionistic, idiographic, often derived from the compulsions of structural-functional theory, and concerned largely with the views and actions of a handful of charismatic political figures or combative opposition parties. Too much is generalized from the attitudes of too few. Above all, the studies are not substantially quantitative and only infrequently comparative. The specific studies on economic development either assume away the political relationships of planners or are too institutional and polemical to be of value in this problem.

Nevertheless, it is commonly agreed that the planner and his counterparts in other professions are crucial not only to the economic growth of low-income countries but to their political development as well. Edward Shils unequivocally argues:

> There is a new sector of the intellectual class beginning to grow up . . . who do not share in the older political traditions of their countries' intellectuals, and who resemble the "new intellectual class" of the more advanced countries. . . . It is on the growth and influence of these two latter groups (the technical and executive intelligentsia) that the emergence of a stable and progressive civil society depends.[31]

30. An exception is Michel Crozier, "Pour une analyse sociologique de la planification Française," *Revue Française de Sociologie*, VI (1965), 147–163; Jacques Lautman and Jean-Claude Thoenig, *Planification et Administrations Centrales* (Paris, 1966); Guy Benveniste, "On Inductive Planning" (Stanford, 1967, mimeographed); Bertram M. Gross, *Action Under Planning* (New York, 1967), especially chapters by Wiles and Crozier.

31. *Political Development in the New States* (The Hague, 1962), p. 24.

Proceeding from different assumptions, Apter arrives at the same position. In *The Politics of Modernization* he asserts that "perhaps the most important elite modernization roles are the technical and civil services of a country." He later adds, "In Latin America today, the economist has displaced the lawyer as the key figure of modernity."[32] Whether judged more "philistine" than conventional intellectuals or called "middle-level elites," the economic planners are the agents of science and technology, bureaucracy and the rational administration of affairs, achievement and universalistic values, and perhaps even civility.[33]

For this reason, it would seem valuable to enter into the theoretical consciousness of economic planners in low-income countries and to understand their conceptions of society, its politics, and its possibilities for the future. It is important to penetrate their understanding of the process, value, and costs of economic development and how this dictates certain of their judgments on their civil service colleagues, their political regimes, and the various strata and sectors of society. What should be sought is the "ideology of economic development," in the planners' own terms, that impels certain choices. Otherwise we cannot judge whether the economic planners are a force for stable and progressive societies or what are some likely problems of administrative reform. This, however, cannot be done without testing as well these attitudes against other variables in the role of economic planner. Are planners modally similar on all issues, or do their views vary depending on their specific responsibility within the public bureaucracy, the source of their education, the level of economic development of their society, the political regime for which they work, and the social strata from which they are recruited?

Economic planners are difficult to interview in their own countries. Not only are they too busy for extensive interviewing but the political constraints weigh heavily on them. No matter how open-ended or abstract the questions, their political implications are too sensitive when it is known that the interviewer will

32. David E. Apter, *The Politics of Modernization* (Chicago, 1965), pp. 166, 175.

33. See Leonard Binder, "National Integration and Political Development," *American Political Science Review*, LVIII (1964), 630–631.

remain in the country for some time and undoubtedly will speak to other civil servants and political leaders. Much—perhaps too much—must be inferred from innuendo and chance remarks. Despite this the author was able to discuss at length the political context of economic development with a large number of planners in six countries in South Asia and the Middle East. But the assumption that there is a concrete role for planners that has considerable cross-national comparability required a broader sample. For this objective it was decided that mid-career planners from low-income countries studying in the United States at institutes of economic development would test the comparability hypothesis. These planners would be freer for extensive interviewing both in terms of time and the relative absence of political constraints.

Over a period of two years, thirty-three mid-career planners from eighteen countries were interviewed at length.[34] Six served regimes in Southeast Asia, eight in South Asia, six in the Middle East, five in Africa, six in Latin America, and two in the Communist world. Each agreed to a two-hour plus interview; and though percentages without tests for significance are used, the size of the sample must be kept in mind. Each was studying advanced economic techniques—input-output analysis, linear programming, etc.—at a graduate institute of economic development. Al-

34. The sample is composed of members of two one-year graduate training programs in development economics. The regional and functional distributions are those of the admitting institution. In the first group, five members of the total class preferred not to be interviewed, though only one implied that political reasons constrained him. Those who refused came from different regions, served different categories of regimes, and held different bureaucratic assignments. All of the second group consented to interviews. The interviews were conducted by trained social scientists and included a lengthy open-ended questionnaire, two short survey instruments, and the projective stories from Morroe Berger's *Bureaucracy and Society in Modern Egypt* (Princeton, 1957), pp. 200–211. The two short questionnaires are not relevant to the problem raised by this essay, and the planners refused to answer most of the questions in the Berger study on the grounds that they were pointless and "picky." All of the responses were categorized by an economist and later by a political scientist, neither of whom was aware of my intentions.

There are many problems with the sample. Chief among them, of course, is the lack of randomness. I have no data to compare this group with other populations, both in the industrially advanced and developing states. Much of this rests on conjecture and speculation. Moreover, I recognize the misuse of percentages for such a small sample. My defense is simply to argue that comparisons are easier with percentages. To use levels of significance would only demonstrate my statistical talent and fail to illuminate the issues further.

though all considered themselves economists, their range of responsibilities extended from long-range "perspective" planning to the implementation of programs in small-scale industries. More specifically, seventeen defined their work as planning, five in line development implementation, and eleven in finance, budgeting, or central banking. The sample had an average of eight years of experience in their countries' bureaucracies. Each had been identified by economic planners in his country as a planner with promise of considerable responsibility in the future. Already this promise has begun to be demonstrated. Since returning to their home countries, one planner has written the major section for the fourth five-year plan in a large North Indian state, another is the chief author of the development plan in a country of Southeast Asia, a third is now responsible for projections of export promotion in another Southeast Asian country, a fourth is chief educational planner in a nation in West Africa, a fifth is responsible for programs to increase small savings in a major Latin-American country, and so the record goes. Indeed, it might be argued that the views expressed on economic development by these planners might easily be the prevailing views for the next generation.

In most cases, their life profiles suggest that they are men in the middle, between conditions conventionally described as traditional and those considered as modern. For many, little existed in their family structure, educational pattern of the family, and place of residence to buttress their professional careers. Several indicators support this, though the same indicators illustrate the extremes in backgrounds. Fathers' education is one. Thirty per cent of the fathers had little or no education; another 23 per cent received a college degree or had completed some postgraduate education. A Middle Eastern planner claimed he was the first in his family to receive a "proper education" and indicated that his father could only "read the Koran." All the planners but one had finished the Bachelor of Arts or its equivalent, half had M.A.'s, and many had diplomas in short courses in the various institutes of the economic commissions of the United Nations. The decline of traditionality can be more graphically seen by comparing mothers' education with that of wives. Sixty per cent of the mothers had little or no formal education, 12 per cent had been to middle school, 21 per cent had been to high school, and 6 per cent had been to university or had completed some postgraduate work. Among wives, on the other hand, 40 per cent had been to high school, another 40 per cent had attended or received degrees from universities, and 20 per cent had received postgraduate education. Marriage patterns are another indicator. Although the median age is thirty-one, only 58 per cent had married. Of those, only 25 per cent had this marriage arranged. A third indicator is family size. Only three planners were raised in a nuclear two-generation family; 51 per cent lived in a family with between five and nine members, and 36 per cent lived in large joint families with over ten members. Of those married, 20 per cent had no children, 70 per cent had one or two children, and only two planners had more than three. All the planners indicated a preference for controlling family size.

A further indicator is participation in family decisions. Sixty-six per cent indicated that they seldom or never participated in family decisions when they were children, and only 33 per cent suggested that they had. When asked about career choices for their sons, most indicated that they would prefer that their sons went into economics or other professions, but the choice was entirely the sons'. In terms of fathers setting the pattern or reinforcing the career choices of the sons, the career pattern of the fathers is interesting. Again the extremes are present. With more than one category common, 45 per cent were civil servants, military officers, or professional men, but 51 per cent were small traders, moneylenders, peasants, or primary school teachers. Nine per cent were politicians and another 9 per cent were landlords. Another indicator of "between-ness" is their contact with other cultures. Forty-eight per cent had been educated abroad, while only 10 per cent of the fathers had. They spoke, on an average, two world languages, while their wives, on an average, spoke one and two-thirds world languages. All but one had read newspapers and periodicals, especially from Western Europe and the United States, before they left their countries to begin their mid-career graduate studies. In describing the places where they grew up, 79 per cent claimed urban status, with many insisting upon describing this as "the capital" or "the major city." Finally, assuming the commonness of ascriptive features in their countries' personnel policies, 72 per cent insisted that "ability" be the major criterion for promotion, 12 per cent suggested "education," and 9 per cent ranked "experience" as the major item. As they distinguished between "experience" and "seniority," it is interesting that only one planner ranked "seniority" as the major factor that governments ought to follow for promotions.[35] Finally, while the planners live in countries where few voluntary associations exist, it is interesting to note that 72 per cent of the sample belong to professional associations of economists or civil servants, only 12 per cent did not belong in countries where there were these associations, and a final 15 per cent lived in countries where these associations did not exist. While many indicated they were not active, several described themselves as "intensely active" or "I am one of the leaders."

In summary, then, the planners can be seen as coming, in varying degrees, from more traditional backgrounds, but they are constructing their own lives along more modern lines in terms of free choices of marriage partners, family size, and career, and they indorse achievement values in their work above all other criteria. When their backgrounds and accomplishments are measured against the education, spatial mobility, and social practices of the countries in which they live, it is clear that they share more with professionals in industrially advanced countries than with the great mass of their fellow citizens.

What is the planners' ideology of economic development? Ideologies must be rejected because the similarities and views on the most crucial questions suggest that a central belief system exists. While the regimes and cultural contexts in which these planners

35. "What is the most important factor which you feel should be taken into account when the government decides to promote a person?" "Next most important?" "Next?" Responses below are given in percentages.

	Ability	*Experience*	*Education*	*Seniority*	*Other*
1st	72	9	12	3	3
2nd	18	27	18	12	18
3rd	—	3	9	18	15

serve differ greatly, the ideology of economic development reduces these differences, positing a course from a stage of backwardness to a stage of modernity. This system is an amalgam of values, perceptions, judgments on sectors of the society, and guides to action. As an ideology, this system of beliefs simplifies reality by identifying the essential mechanics of desired change, the heroes and villains of the process, and the appropriate paths.

That the planners valued the component processes of "modernization" and "industrialization" is hardly surprising. Ninety-four per cent thought modernization a desirable process, and the entire sample felt industrialization desirable.[36] What is interesting is that, on open-ended questions with considerable encouragement to expand upon any answer, only 28 per cent suggested that there are human costs to modernization and only 32 per cent felt that there are human costs to industrialization. Each process was described as essentially bringing desirable objectives. As one Indian planner claimed for industrialization, "It doesn't mean the loss of anything; only gains for my nation." When asked to describe modernization, each respondent enumerated many aspects. Chiefly, the replies can be summarized in a few categories. The modern society is thought to be one in which innovation and change become routinized. As a planner from Pakistan succinctly put the case, "It is a changing dynamic state where the emphasis is on progress rather than security." The chief virtue claimed for modernization is that it expands human choice. This is accomplished, according to a Turkish planner, "by eliminating many things that should be destroyed, such as the hold of religion on the people" and by eliminating poverty. A Mexican planner, using the idiom of his "economic science," claimed "it would bring higher standards of living for all members of the society and would bring groups presently outside of the income stream into that stream." Moreover, modernization meant to the planners a society marked by high social mobility, especially for youth, and status determined by achievement. Another Pakistani plan-

36. Percentages are expressed in round numbers; disparities exist where fewer than the entire sample responded to a question. For tabulated responses and the questionnaire, see Ilchman, Ilchman, and Hastings, *The New Men of Knowledge and Developing States.*

ner argued that "modernization permitted the individual to have an opportunity to organize his life—to choose anything if he is capable." But the chief definition of expanded choice is not in the self-actualizing sense; the materialistic basis of choice was stressed. An Egyptian planner summarized what he and his colleagues felt when he said, "Modernization allows you to live at a higher standard."

Another theme sounded by the planners is the connection of modernization with productivity and productivity values. Modernization, according to a South American planner, is "rationality and scientific analysis as goals of life." A South Asian added, "It is a reduction of fatalistic attitudes, the reorganization of values to the productive role of the human mind." To scientific analysis, rationality, and the use of modern technology is added organization. A Mexican planner stressed the criticalness of organization "to achieve a permanent state of change." While other factors are identified, such as breaking down of barriers and participation in a world culture, these two themes of expanding choice and the increase of productivity values are dominant.

Many also see modernization as a prerequisite to economic development. A Sudanese insisted, "If it could be attained it would enhance economic development and eliminate poverty." An Indian planner argued, "It is a process by which a whole society can take its proper place in the world—by being equal to other nations and other peoples in the levels of economic wealth." He added that "it is natural." This theme of inevitability "with assistance" frequently appears in the responses. To summarize the general attitude, another Sudanese planner confidently insisted, "Modernization is inevitable and welcome."

One further point should be made about "modernization." When the planners were asked if it was the same as Westernization, 18 per cent said yes, 21 per cent said not necessarily, and 61 per cent said no. Even among the yeses, when an elaboration was offered, the argument is in terms of the historical primacy of modernization in the West, but that the value changes are derivative from a neutral technology. One could accept the technology and its values without the undesirable features of the West. On the latter, the planners are both more specific and unconsciously ironic. Eighty-seven per cent claimed there are characteristics of the West which they "hoped their country would avoid in its development." Forty-three per cent identified too much individualism, 21 per cent too much materialism, 27 per cent indicated various social problems, such as child and female labor, and 11 per cent identified capitalism. The virtues of modernization from their responses to an earlier question become many of the vices when confronted with the Westernization question.

Responses generally to the modernization question suggest that in the planners' minds this process is wider than and subsumes industrialization. This may partly be accounted for by the different priority in the various development programs industrialization (usually thought of as heavy industry) has. To the question, "What does industrialization entail for your country?" several common themes are sounded. The values—already adduced for modernization—of education, science, rationality, productivity, new technologies, and organization are also stressed for industrialization. A South Asian planner summed up the process: "Old systems will have to be discarded—more naturally integrated communities instead of self-contained villages must arise; there will be more organization—from simple to complex life." Above all, industrialization represents a movement away from agriculture with accompanying change of residence, skills, and values. Those who identified costs usually did so in terms of foregoing current consumption for future gains. A Turk maintained, "We must limit consumption to provide capital for development, to increase savings and avoid the 'demonstration effect' —that's a necessity."

But, as in their responses to the modernization question, they stressed the need for industrialization. A Malaysian insisted, "It is the road we must take if we want development." A Nigerian recognized that there "would be lots of sacrifice and destruction of traditional values," but added, "It is a good thing and the sooner the better." More sympathetic is a Thai planner who admitted, "I feel it is painful but necessary—someone must be hurt; it is unavoidable." Many also evinced impatience. An Indonesian complained, "We have started, but I am not satisfied; it could have been done better." In quantitative terms, the answers to the industrialization question found 72 per cent of the planners identifying the changes in skills as necessary; 40 per cent identified the movement from the countryside to the city; and 59 per cent identified the specific values that needed to be changed. For all the wrenching of human conditions, it is surprising that only 9 per cent ever mentioned the likelihood of greater government coercion to maintain political stability.

Modernization and industrialization are highly valued both as objectives of collective efforts and as processes. In the responses to the general questions, however, few specific perceptions were included. Until one leaves the plane of abstraction and possible rhetoric, it is impossible to see the political implications of the planners' ideology. As objectives, how are modernization and industrialization reached? As processes, what do they constitute? Answers to both of these questions were given by the planners in the context of problems of economic development.

The central question for both processes and objectives is the cause of "backwardness," the explanation as to why the countries represented in the sample are less productive than those in Western and Eastern Europe. When asked "What or who in your country constitutes the greatest impediments to economic development," the planners agreed largely that the impediments are internal. Only 18 per cent in a question where more than one factor is usually identified claimed that among the major impediments are external factors, such as foreign exchange problems or insufficient economic assistance. No planner identified the legacy of colonialism and the impact of neocolonialism as factors; though on another level of explanation, several would probably have done so. For them the failure to develop could be explained by internal factors essentially. On internal factors, 36 per cent of the planners indicated structural economic problems, such as low savings rates and bottlenecks in transportation. Thirty-nine per cent identified political and administrative factors. For instance, a West African planner claimed that "the present generation of politicians constituted the greatest impediment" and that "they must be put out"; a Middle Eastern planner impiously argued that his country's prime minister was the chief impediment; a Southeast Asian planner maintained that "extremist leftist groups were hampering legitimate programs in order to get control over the country and not because of the efficiency of the existing government." However, the most common factors of backwardness in terms of impeding economic development are seen to be cultural and traditional. An Indonesian identified the cultural value placed on work as the chief impediment; a Malaysian claimed the impeding factor is "the uneducated agricultural part of society." But even the political and economic factors for backwardness, while not stated in these terms, would originate in a set of cultural values labeled traditional. Underlying many of the responses is the tautology implicit in economic development: in order to be modern, a nation must cease to be backward. As a Colombian tersely put it, "the major impediment is the 'underdeveloped syndrome'—it is everything."

While the sample includes countries of great differences in industrial complexity, only one planner claimed his society did not have an important traditional sector. For the large majority of planners, then, backwardness is due to the prevalence of traditional values. When asked what these were in detail and if any of them are compatible with economic development, the following breakdown occurred (with more than one factor identified):

	(a) Percentage	(b) Percentage of (a) feeling value compatible
Religious values	49	6
Ascriptive values (importance of family, respect for elders, caste and class values)	66	9
Conservatism	26	0
Respect for law and authority	21	71
Regional and local identity	10	0

Others identified "ego-centeredness," "leisure," and "destructive opposition," finding all of these incompatible. Of all the planners only eight found a value in their traditional sector at all compatible with economic development, and of these only four found the values of traditional society ultimately compatible.

But the extent of support of these values is equally important in estimating the political implications of the claims of the economic planners. Excluding the Latin-American planner who felt that his society could not be classified as traditional, the question, "Who in your country, if any, support traditional values?" yielded these results (with more than one answer given by many respondents): whole population, 12 per cent; low-income group, 9 per cent; rural groups, 47 per cent; landlords, 15 per cent; government, 21 per cent; others, 9 per cent. Considering the fact that the distribution of the income and the mode of production in the countries of the sample would include the great majority of the population in categories "low-income" or "rural," it is apparent that 57 per cent (excluding those who found traditional values as compatible with economic development) of the planners must contend with a very large unsympathetic population. Further, assuming a high influence of landlords on government, it is apparent that another 36 per cent of the planners serve regimes officially or indirectly supporting sectors which hold incompatible views on economic development.

Thus, from the perceptions of the planners on the causes of backwardness, two points have emerged. First, to overcome the impediments to economic development it is necessary to push beyond the economic sphere to the underlying cultural values of the society. Second, these values are widely and often officially held and are thought by the planners to be largely incompatible with economic development.

There is inherent in these perceptions a potential for support of a non-Western variant of the "New Soviet Man" ideology and the need for revolutionary transformation of much of society. But what partly moderate the intensity of their feelings are the relative recentness of development programs, the signs that the impediments are being overcome, and growing elite support of development. Evidence for these more optimistic perceptions is clear though seldom unqualified. All of the planners see sectors in their societies contributing to modernization and industrialization. These sectors differ among the sample. In questions involving extended responses, 55 per cent identified "government" as the chief contributor to overcoming the impediments to economic development. Of these, over half specified the public bureaucracy and state enterprise. Nineteen per cent felt that modernizing intellectuals are the chief contributors; 26 per cent indicated the private business sector; another 21 per cent claimed "modernizing entrepreneurs"; and 10 per cent argued that agriculturalists, especially farmers with large holdings, are the chief contributors. In the spirit of Yugoslav and Arab socialism, two planners claimed "the people," while 19 per cent noted external forces—foreign aid givers and foreign businessmen. It is clear from the responses, however, that the planners generally see the forces to overcome backwardness as either themselves and their bureaucratic colleagues or elites in other fields willing to break away from the prevailing values and modes of traditionality. Economic development for most is an elite process.

But islands of diffuse support also reduce the intensity of the planners' concerns. From where does the support and awareness come for the development programs the planners formulate, finance, and implement? From those holding political office or politicians generally, the planners perceive different degrees of support. Although a distinction was made in the interview schedule between office-holders and politicians, it is clear from the responses that many of the planners perceive those holding political office and politicians in general as the same category. When asked whether office-holders understood the problems and needs of economic development, the planners' responses yield the following results: 51 per cent said yes and 48 per cent said little or not at all. Among those who said yes a distinction was made between levels. A Southeast Asian planner found "the most encouraging aspect" is that "the top echelon does support us." A Latin-American likewise felt that "leaders in higher positions, especially some individuals do"; but he added that it is not so at "the base; there the concern is with the short run only; economic development is long run." Those answering "little or not at all" explained their answer in two ways; it was either a question of ignorance or venality on the part of office-holders or a question of political constraints. Typical of the former explanation is a response of a West African planner: "Some just don't understand. Those who do are indifferent and selfish—ignorant in some cases." A South Asian insisted, "They never had training and are still too interested in the status quo." Two planners from military regimes argued that "development is not grasped by the military leaders." More indignantly, a Southeast Asian claimed that office-holders demonstrate "a pure ignorance of the things we have experienced and indifference or complacency to them." A Middle Eastern planner tersely revealed, "I don't like politicians." Many argued political constraints, such as regional interests, as interfering with the office-holders' support of development programs. A South Asian claimed that office-holders were "unable to shoulder the costs and sacrifices which development entails." A Southeast Asian claimed that the office-holders supported programs until "they conflicted with political problems." With a tone of despair, a Middle Eastern planner added, "Understanding does not result in action."

Although the percentages changed slightly, the responses to the same question using politicians revealed similar distinctions and explanations. The results of the general responses are: yes, 36 per cent; little or not at all, 60 per cent; don't know, 3 per cent. An insight into the degree of hostility which some planners feel in relation to politics can be found in the negative responses, such as: "Only a minority understand. Most don't want to understand because of their economic and social backgrounds. The support is verbal; they interpret it in different ways" (Middle East). "None have disagreed, but that is because they don't understand. It is fashionable to support development" (South Asia). "The people who don't understand shouldn't count" (South Asia). "Politicians don't support development because they are personally sufficiently prosperous and don't care about the rest" (South Asia). "They are mostly political position-seekers. Their interests are local and they do not worry about the nation" (Southeast Asia). "They don't want to pay the cost of development" (Latin America). "Military types are essentially uneducated; they mistrust intellectuals and don't use us" (Middle East). "There are too many landlords in parliament; they want development but don't want to pay for it" (Middle East).

If many of the planners felt the political system as unsupportive of their efforts, they found relatively greater support among their civil service colleagues. While the question in the interview asked whether "the civil servants are aware of the problems and needs of economic development," the respondents assumed "aware" as synonomous with "support." The results are: yes (unqualified), 53 per cent; yes (upper echelons), 7 per cent; most, 13 per cent; little or not at all, 27 per cent. On the other hand, the degree of support is seen wanting in many cases. It was common for respondents to add phrases such as "not as much as they ought to be" to their affirmative judgments. Furthermore, when asked if civil servants should be required to take some training in development economics, the planners implied that such knowledge was lacking in the majority of instances. The results on this question are: yes (for all), 51 per cent; yes (for higher civil servants only), 30 per cent; some (for all), 9 per cent; no, 9 per cent. Training, it would seem, would universalize the value norms of development and improve the quality of civil servants' support.

To what extent do university-based intellectuals support their development efforts? The question asked "whether universities were included in the planning process" and was not squarely on the point. But if the responses to this question can be used as an indicator of the planners' perception of sympathetic and useful people in the intellectual sector, then 48 per cent of the planners felt university intellectuals were supportive, while the remainder thought that they were minimally supportive or not at all. The reasons given for the latter judgment included: "the creative persons are all in the government," "the universities are too isolated from real problems," and "the professors are too abstract."

In some cases, such as with the Latin-American planners, the planners also taught in the universities.

How do the planners feel about the participation of the private sector and trade unions in their development efforts? Already it has been pointed out that a total of 48 per cent indicated that private sector business and modernizing entrepreneurs are the chief contributors to economic development and presumably the planners would find them generally supportive of their efforts. On the other hand, trade unions are not included by any planner in his responses to that question. While in a later question 84 per cent argued that trade unions played an important role politically and economically in their countries, only 48 per cent felt that trade union activities, as they perceived them, are useful in development. The grounds for this judgment varied. These responses indicate the different perceptions: "They can help overthrow conservative elements in government" (Latin America); "By not asking too much of government and industry and also rallying support of workers for government and economic development" (West Africa); "They help convince workers that hard work is important and that wages should be increased only if productivity increases" (Southeast Asia). In other words, trade unions are useful only if they do not perform the functions of economic unionism. If they act politically or if they can be controlled for economic development purposes, they are useful. The negative responses of the remainder of planners on the usefulness of trade unions are similar when amplified. The unions are too political or do not mobilize the workers for productivity and sacrifice. Two negative responses indicate these positions: "Unions are used by some political parties mainly for agitation" (South Asia); "Unions are not enough concerned with productivity increases or the larger aspects of industrial growth" (South Asia).

Finally, do the planners perceive the "people" as supportive? Answers to this type of question are invariably rhetorical. Already answers to other questions indicate that for most of the countries the great majority of the population entertains traditional values and practices that are thought to be incompatible with economic development. Nonetheless, when asked the general question, 54 per cent indicated that "most are," although about half of these indicated that the people are unaware of the sacrifices. Another 39 per cent claimed that the people are little or not at all aware of development plans.

The whole question of support can be turned around, and an equally revealing question is: "Which groups try to secure advantages from the government for their members and is this harmful to your development effort?" A summary of the responses follows (with more than one group identified by many planners):

	(a)	(b) Percentage of (a)		
Group	Percentage	Harmful	Harmful to some extent	Not Harmful
Military	21	86	14	—
Agriculture	27	78	11	11
Businessmen	27	55	22	22
Workers	42	36	36	28
Civil Servants	18	50	33	17
Everyone	24	75	—	25
Politicians	15	60	20	20
Others	6	—	—	100
No one	9	—	—	—

From the answers to these questions, it seems apparent that planners find major sectors of the population—officeholders, politicians, civil servants, university-based intellectuals, trade unions, and the people—unsupportive and/or positively detrimental in the development effort. Planners in the affirmative in relation to one sector are in the negative in others. Many planners responded negatively to all the sectors included. Coupled with their highly valued objectives of modernization and industrialization and the explanation of the causes of backwardness, the planners' perception of the varying degrees of support and hostility add up potentially to a polity-sized political problem for these new men of knowledge.

But the ideology of economic development is more than values, explanations of backwardness, and perceptions of support and hostility. It is a set of guides to action as well. The objectives of action are implicit in the values and perceptions. The guides include methods of altering the structure of society, criteria for decisions, and time horizons. The general methods for dealing with the impediments to economic development are revealing. In response to a question inquiring into the best method for overcoming backwardness, the planners divided as follows (with more than one answer given by many):

	Percentage
External means (foreign public and private capital and skills)	10
Spontaneous generation (backwardness is eliminated through the spillover of economic development)	26
Political unity and leadership	7
Programmatic action by government	57
Comprehensive planning	23

While the chief impediments to development are cultural and political, the chief methods of achieving it are seen to be economic. While political co-operation is required for programmatic action and comprehensive planning, only 7 per cent advocate the need for political unity and leadership. Finally, behind 36 per cent of the answers (external means and spontaneous generation) is a conception of economic and technological determinism that sees cultural and political backwardness overcome through the values and institutions created by economic change.

The fact that 80 per cent feel programmatic action and comprehensive planning as the best methods requires further analysis. Later in the interview the planners were asked, "Is development possible without government planning?" Twenty-one per cent said yes without adding a qualification; 36 per cent said yes but qualified this by suggesting that it would be too slow or, though possible elsewhere, not in their country; 42 per cent said no. When asked "How comprehensive must planning be?" the following responses were given:

	Percentage
Very comprehensive (without qualification)	39
Very comprehensive (qualified by skills, analytic tools and data)	29
Limited to activity which private sector is unable or unwilling to undertake	13
Primarily only to provide incentive for private sector	19

Finally, when asked if it is possible to plan adequately if there is a strong private sector, 85 per cent of the planners said yes, though many qualified this with caveats about bribery and speed of development. Thus, the chief methods are more concretely linked with comprehensive planning, limited only by skills and data, while the existence of a strong private sector is felt to be no match for or so intertwined with government that backwardness can be overcome within a mixed economy.

The specific measures for the agricultural sector also show considerable agreement. When asked, "What can be done to improve the rate of adoptions of innovations in the agricultural sector of your country?" only one planner argued that there was no problem in his country in agriculture. Among responses that permitted several preferences, 78 per cent of the planners indicated education. This phrase meant different things to each. In some cases it meant rural extension, and in others it meant getting at the older generation by educating the younger generation in productivity values. Twenty-four per cent argued that research is indispensable, especially to provide seeds and fertilizers more adaptable to their environment. Forty-eight per cent preferred structural changes in the rural economy: the abolition of intermediaries, development of markets, monetization, land redistribution or consolidation, consumer and producer co-operatives, etc. A final 24 per cent advocated explicit measures of force, such as removing people from the land and replacing government farms by the ownership of agricultural land.

In some respects the categories are misleading. Behind the preference for force is undoubtedly the first strategy of incentives and persuasion. Behind the preference for structural change is the possibility of force. And the term "education" can embrace a variety of mildly coercive to outright coercive measures. While no planner advocated force alone, it was interesting to see a form of "planners' escalation" underlying their answers—education first, structural reform if education fails, and ultimately force if structural reform fails. Though this appeared in only 24 per cent of the responses, it would not be incautious to speculate that the number would have been higher had the planners developed their answers to the question more fully.

Criteria of choice is another area that reveals the planners' guides for action. Two questions were posed about the allocation of its resources by government. The first asked, "On what basis should your government make its decisions regarding the allocation of resources?" Each respondent was encouraged to expand his answer; thus more than one criterion is possible. The overwhelming majority, 75 per cent of the planners, argued that "maximizing growth" should be the basis. Typical responses are: "to produce a progressive and continued rise in GNP" (Southeast Asia); "the maximum rate of growth" (South Asia); "emphasis must be on directly productive investment" (South Asia); "on the basis of the strategy and priorities of economic planning" (South Asia); "eliminate the bottlenecks to productivity" (Southeast Asia); "to see that resources go to the right projects which bring most to the national income" (Middle East). Those allocations that are more specifically political, such as regional equality, programs for redistribution of income, and politically stabilizing investments, are indicated by 27 per cent of the planners, although only 9 per cent indicate them alone. A Middle Eastern planner, for example, preferred a criterion for allocating public resources that "provides political structures capable of preserving the development effort." Six per cent had no opinion.

It is possible of course to argue that "growth" will ultimately allow higher real incomes and contribute to political ends. Nevertheless, it is also equally appropriate to argue that programs of "maximum growth" are politically counterproductive in the short run and that the long run may be beyond the lifetime of the planners. Thus there is apparent in these responses a prevailing downgrading of allocations that are thought to be politically necessary or just. This can be seen in the responses to the question, "What would you consider to be an irrational allocation of public resources?" While it is impossible here to give percentages on political versus economic responses, the flavor of responses suggests that attempts at distribution, regional equality, and prestige expenditures are felt to be wasteful and irrational. For example: "anything short-run and non-productive like defense or consumer goods" (Southeast Asia); "political bribery of the people" (Middle East); "too much emphasis on equitable distribution" (South Asia); "defense" (Southeast Asia); "If you have a plan, any deviation other than improvement is irrational. Don't appease groups. Don't give up the plan for individuals" (South Asia); "money spent on social security or prestige projects" (East Africa); "Market efficiency should not be deviated from" (Latin America); "any regional allocation that is not on grounds of economic productivity" (Latin America); "extremely primitive productive techniques, like cottage industry" (South Asia); "anything inconsistent with planned priorities like the influence of particular groups in the country" (Southeast Asia); "compromise expenditures and politicians" (Middle East); "any resources going to the military, luxury building, or industry with excess capacity" (Middle East). Stadiums, television, capital cities, monumental buildings, embassies, and universities that specialize in the liberal arts are mentioned by different planners as irrational. One omnibus category was mentioned by a Latin American—"anything that leads to waste." Waste presumably is defined as anything that does not meet the criterion of growth, which in turn does not advance the objectives of industrialization and modernization as these planners conceive of it and value it.

This pronounced antipolitical bias can be seen in the planners' attitudes toward foreign economic and technical assistance. Among the responses to the several questions asked, those relating to the grounds for rejecting aid and the most desirable conditions for accepting aid are to this point. A distinction is made in scoring the responses; anything that enhances national prestige, involves the distribution of power and status in the society, and supports the power or claims to power of a particular group, affects foreign policy, etc., is called "political"; any response that refers to economic utilization of assistance is labeled "technical." In response to the question, "Under what conditions would you think your country ought to refuse aid?" the planners divided as follows (with more than one answer possible): political conditions, 42 per cent; technical conditions, 63 per cent; don't know, 6 per cent. The response to the second question reinforces the technical propensity. The question, "What would you consider the most desirable conditions under which your country might be given such aid?" produced the following results (with more than one answer possible): political conditions, 12 per cent; technical conditions, 93 per cent. The political conditions included bringing about political stability, reinforcing progressive forces, helping a country to find its rightful place in the world. Technical conditions included untied loans, lump sums to be used as the plan dictates, greater heed paid to experts on development, more control over the choices of technical assistance, etc.

While the question in the pretest schedule inquiring into the length of time envisioned for the objectives of industrialization and modernization proved meaningless, it was possible to probe the planners' time horizons by asking, "How long will foreign assistance or economic and technical assistance be required?" Here the assumption is that foreign economic and technical assistance will be needed until the processes of industrialization and modernization become self-sustaining. While many of the responses are clearly outrageous from external observer's point of view, the responses are as follows: within ten years, 10 per cent; ten to twenty years, 26 per cent; over twenty years, 29 per cent; "a long time" or "indefinitely," 35 per cent. Thus, well over 60 per cent believed that continuous external assistance will be required through their political generation and into the next. As a guide to action, their time horizon implies that many of the planners see the process of induced change as one stretching into the very distant future.

Finally, a suggestion of the planners' preferences for action can be found in the countries to which they look as models. To the question, "Which countries if any do you look towards as the models for your country's development?" the planners divided as follows (with more than one answer possible):

	Percentage
United States	27
Western Europe	27
Communist bloc	6
Japan	30
Developing nations, (such as Israel, Yugoslavia, and Egypt)	18
Best from all	12
None	18

From the responses, it appears that an unintended distinction was made. "Development" in the question meant the public policies and processes adopted to achieve the objectives. Many planners interpreted the question in terms of the level of living or industrialization to which they aspired. Furthermore, the planners were studying in the United States and were being interviewed by American social scientists. Both factors probably skew the results in favor of the United States.

Eighty-five per cent of the planners claimed that this model had not changed. Among those who identified a specific country, 27 per cent did so on the basis of the level of industrialization the model country had achieved. Twelve per cent did so for historical reasons (colonial legacy, in particular); one planner admired France for its "world position"; only 12 per cent looked to other countries because they had similar cultural and economic features and had still achieved or were achieving growth. What is inferred from these responses is that many planners sought to emulate nations that used highly centralized and coercive measures, such as Japan, for their development and that very few included in their model factors of political freedom. The United States and Western Europe are admired for their standards of living and levels of industrialization.

Considerable commonalities mark the planners' attitudes. Industrialization and modernization are deeply held values, and the costs of these processes tend to be minimized by the planners. Their explanations of causes of backwardness stress the pervasiveness of values hostile to development and imply the need for substantial transformation before the processes can become self-sustaining. The planners see the agents for change among themselves primarily and certain elite sectors willing to break away from traditional methods. Although varying in source, the planners find certain key sectors unaware and unsupportive of their efforts and many other sectors detrimentally taking advantage of development programs. Despite problems defined in cultural and political terms, the planners feel that economic programs and planning—the more comprehensive the better—are the most trustworthy guides for action. The agricultural sector must be "educated" for innovations, though structural reform and force are also advocated. Both the desired increases in resources of foreign aid and the desired allocation of resources by the government are defined largely in technical terms with an explicit rejection of premises that might be labeled "political." Most planners feel that the achievement of a self-sustaining industrialization and modernization process is a long-run task, stretching into the next generation. And many planners hope to emulate regimes which achieved industrialization in a hurry, through the use of centralization and coercive mechanisms, and few planners include their political structures among the characteristics of the countries to admire in their development.

III

If what has just been summarized can be taken as a composite ideology of development, it seems appropriate to see how different variables affect the ideology on various issues. Five variables are thought to be especially relevant.[37] The first is the regime in which the planner works, whether it is military, one-party, or competitive party. The comparative level of economic develop-

37. It was found that "region" explained little. While there was some variance by regions on problems, there was little on important political issues discussed here. The comparative data on which the section is based can be found in *ibid.*

ment is a second variable. The third is "bureaucratic function" or the relationship between particular responsibilities of development and attitudes. A fourth is the source of education, whether it was received abroad or at a domestic university. Finally, the social status of the planners should be considered, that is, whether they can be classified as part of the continuous or new elites.

The first independent variable is the political regime in which the planner works. Here the assumption is that some types of regimes are more compatible to development than others and that compatibility derives from their ideological sympathy for development, their acceptance of technical definitions of planning problems, and their capacity to mobilize resources and assure compliance. While Apter's categories of reconciliation, mobilization, and modernizing autocratic regimes might have been more revealing, they are foregone in favor of categories with fewer judgments implicit in them.[38] A sample is divided into three categories: military, monopoly-party, and competitive-party regimes.

Two subsidiary assumptions are made at the outset that are akin to the Apter classification: that military regimes are more sympathetic to technical definitions and that monopoly-party regimes are more ideologically oriented toward development. While the appropriateness of some of these categories has changed since the interviews (the Sudanese are no longer ruled by the military and the Nigerians and Indonesians now are), the attitudes toward the then-prevailing regime are measured. Thirty-six per cent of the planners served competitive-party regimes, another 36 per cent served monopoly-party regimes, and 27 per cent served military regimes. Despite every attempt to insure the respondent's own perceptions and judgments, the answers to the interview questions occasionally expressed an official view. There is, however, no way of separating official from individual attitudes.

It seems apparent that the monopoly-party regime is felt by the planners to be most conducive to their values and methods. This

38. Apter, *Politics of Modernization*, pp. 22–42.

is seen in many ways. In expressing their values for modernization and industrialization, planners in monopoly-party regimes are less likely to identify costs of any sort. They also conceive of both processes in more complete terms, arguing that cultural-traditional factors are the sources of backwardness, that comprehensive planning and political leadership are the best methods to overcome them, and that it is a long-term and more thorough process than thought by planners of other regimes. An example of this can be found in their recommendations for improving the rate of agricultural innovation. Here they more frequently advocate force and structural reorganization. Like the ideologues they serve, the planners conceive of development in more group-focused terms; they seek to avoid the "individualism" and "materialism" of modern industrial countries and maintain a love-hate relationship with the "people." While they find the "people" less supportive, they are inclined to say that no one takes advantage of their development efforts. To remedy this lack of support, the government and modernizing intellectuals are the chief contributors to economic development. Office-holders and politicians are thought to be highly supportive. Generally they have greater confidence in their nations' capacity, as evidenced by their greater eclecticism in choosing external models to emulate. On the assumption that the political regime has settled the broader issues of development, the planners seem to be able to define their work in more technical terms, a proposition supported by their views on the grounds for acceptance and rejection of foreign assistance.

It is difficult to rank the other categories of regimes in terms of their hospitality to the planners. Their problems seem to be different. The planners in competitive-party regimes emphasize the constraints created by the political structure of the regime and its need to maximize support. Costs of industrialization and modernization are more frequently cited by planners in competitive-party regimes, and they find more specific sectors of the society harmful to development. They stress education for improving innovation in the rural sector and are low on recommending force and structural reorganization. While government is seen as the chief contributor to economic development, the planners find office-holders and politicians less supportive than do their colleagues in other regimes. It would seem that the abstract "people" are more supportive than political forces, and this may contribute to the planners' advocacy of very comprehensive planning as an attempt to limit the bargaining propensities of their political masters. Their external models are more unrealizable and are perhaps a reflection of the political objectives of the regimes more than their own standards. A paradoxical statement of resignation may inform their judgment that "spontaneous generation" is the most likely means of overcoming backwardness.

Planners in military regimes, on the other hand, suffer from the inability of their military rulers to mobilize resources and to conceive of development programs in their economic terms. This category of planners looks to civil servants and the private sector for the major thrust of development. The military is thought to be harmful to their efforts and unsupportive. Linked with this lack of support is their perception that the "people" are unaware of the development program. From their isolation, planners seem to de-emphasize the likelihood of comprehensive planning. Programmatic efforts and private development are upgraded. Finally, they look to as external models those regimes which have been more capable in mobilizing resources. Japan and the monopoly-party regimes of the low-income world are particularly seen as models.

The second variable is the level of economic development of the nation which is served. The hypothesis is that level of economic development determines some responses of the planners to the composite ideology. Here the underlying assumption is that the higher the level of economic development the more widely diffused are productivity values. In addition, the level of development also covaries with the ease of mobilizing resources. While there are many measurements of economic development, only one can be found for all the countries in the sample—per capita income. There are many objections to the use of this index, but until a more telling one arises this may have to serve the purpose. The arbitrary point of $250 is taken to indicate two clusters of the sample. As 72 per cent of the planners come from regimes with less than $250 per capita, it must be stressed that the composite ideology is heavily weighted in their favor.

It would seem that the hypothesis is true and the underlying assumption finds empirical confirmation. Planners in countries of higher per capita income find the public and office-holders more sympathetic to development efforts. Furthermore, their explanation of backwardness includes more economic and external factors. For this reason, development is seen as more possible without formal planning. As more widely diffused values of productivity conduce to a technical definition of their work, planners in higher income countries would reject aid more on technical than on political grounds and look to research more frequently for improving the rate of agricultural innovation. At the same time, continued increases in growth depend on thrusts from modernizing entrepreneurs in government, and in the backward areas of agriculture there is greater willingness to use force.

For planners in lower income countries, the lack of widely spread productivity values and the capacity to mobilize resources lead them to define backwardness more in cultural-traditional terms. Politicians, office-holders, and the "people" are less aware and supportive of their efforts, and for their colleagues in the civil service they are more wont to recommend training in economic development. In the process of the development, the planners look to a modernizing intellectual elite as the major contributor and think that development is less possible without formal planning. As the lower income countries are most recently and less firmly established, the planners feel that aid should be rejected if political conditions are imposed, though they are willing to accept aid with "progressive" political intentions.

The composite ideology should also be compared with the responses based on three more personal variables: bureaucratic function, source of education, and social status. For this study, the planners are divided into three categories of bureaucratic functions—formal economic planning, finance planning, and line development implementation. Involved in planning commissions, ministries, and departments are 51 per cent in the sample.

Thirty-three per cent have planning responsibilities in ministries of finance, budget offices, and central banks. A final 15 per cent have direct responsibility for implementing development programs, ranging in the sample from small industry programs to rural credit projects. While it is true that the composite ideology is heavily weighted in favor of the formal economic planners, nevertheless it is assumed that the three categories vary on certain issues in ways that can be explained in terms of their "bureaucratic functions." Underlying this assumption is a further assumption that each bureaucratic responsibility perceives the problems and opportunities of development in somewhat different ways. This perspective derives from structural differences, clienteles served, definition of the development problem, degrees of authority, data utilized, and formal bureaucratic structure. Financial planners, for instance, usually work in more routinized and stable authority situations, while formal economic planners usually work in more recently created structures with ambiguous authority patterns. While development bureaucrats are dependent on direct personal support, support is defined more abstractly by members of the other two categories. Similarly, a perspective cannot help but be affected if the bureaucrat deals directly with the public or with other planners, foreign technicians, and high ministerial officials, or if he is concerned essentially with foreign exchange problems as opposed to integrating these in an overall plan.

How do bureaucratic functions affect the ideology of development in certain of its components? Only a tentative answer can be given on account of the sample, especially in view of the preponderance of formal economic planners in it. The following generalizations, among many possible generalizations, emerge:

1. The more directly the bureaucrat deals with the public (i.e., line development personnel) the more he is aware of the costs of change.

2. Those who identify the problems most broadly (formal economic planners) see more encompassing impediments, such as cultural and traditional factors, in backwardness, while those

who conceive of their functions most narrowly (finance planners) see impediments as economic.

3. In specifying values prevailing in the traditional sectors, those who deal least frequently with the public (formal economic planners) cite more abstract values, such as conservatism and religious values, and find them more incompatible, while those who deal directly with the public cite values more concretely linked with people, such as respect for family, and find them less incompatible. Furthermore, the former see support for these values more broadly based than do the line development bureaucrats.

4. Those who are most dependent on diffuse support (formal economic planners) find government and intellectuals the major agents of development, while those with specific clienteles see the clients as major contributors.

5. The more institutionalized the bureaucratic function (line development implementation and finance planning) the greater the support one feels forthcoming from the civil service.

6. The more directly sensitive the bureaucratic function is to public corruption the more unsupportive the political sector is thought to be.

7. The more abstract the level on which the bureaucrat operates (formal economic planning) the longer he feels the process of development will take.

8. The closer one's function is to that of another category (finance planning to formal economic planning) the less critical the latter's contribution is felt to be.

9. The more technically the function is defined (formal economic planning) the more likely the acceptance or rejection of foreign aid is justified on technical grounds.

10. The country which excels in the appropriate bureaucratic function is more likely to be looked to as a model by its counterpart in low-income countries.

The second more personal variable is the source of education of the planners. A little less than half of the planners were educated at universities abroad, while the remainder attended universities in their own countries. The hypothesis is that the source of education is a determinant of attitudes. Underlying this is the assumption that planners educated in other countries receive both a more accurate picture of the development process and a greater sense of backwardness of their own society. Also the experience of "uprootedness" affects values and perceptions.

In most of the cases the planners educated abroad received their education in Western and Eastern Europe or in the United States. In two cases, however, the planners went to more advanced countries in their own region.

Some salient differences exist on several points that might be explained tentatively by the hypothesis, though on most issues there is considerable agreement of the two categories' responses with the composite ideology. Those educated abroad reveal a more unqualified support of modernization and see it less clearly identified with "Westernization." What they wish to avoid in their development is more concrete. As they have presumably witnessed the public affirmation of productivity values in the countries of their education, they find the "people" in their own countries less aware of development plans and needs than do planners educated domestically. For those educated abroad, the whole process is seen as taking longer than their colleagues see it, and their de-emphasis on comprehensive planning may derive from a belief that wide-scale participation is a necessary part of the process. This may also account for a greater hesitancy to use force to increase the adoption of innovations in the rural sector. At the same time, they stress an explanation of backwardness that limits it essentially to economic factors; this perhaps can be understood in terms of their recognition that cultural-traditional factors survive the industrialization and modernization of the West. It also could be argued that their comparatively high rejection of foreign aid on technical grounds stems in part from their education in nations where the political system is more supportive of technical values. On a more personal level, they stress what they know as exemplary in models for economic development. Most had been educated in Western Europe. Also, when identifying the values of traditional society, such ascriptive features as respect for family are less seldom cited, owing probably to the opportunity to leave the family system to go abroad for education.

The final variable is social status. While it was impossible to get an attributional response on relative status for the planners, it was possible to divide them on other criteria into two categories: continuous elites and new elites. Members of the first category are planners whose fathers occupied positions of high status: civil servants, landlords, military officers, and professionals. In the second category are planners whose fathers had lower status: peasants, primary school teachers, moneylenders, and traders. Little over half of the sample are members of the new elite. Education abroad and continuous eliteness are not synonymous. The hypothesis behind this distinction is that continuing elites will value the processes, perceive the problems, and judge the sectors of society differently from new elites. The latter are engaged in social mobility, often of a rather dramatic sort, while the former have links with those ruling the country.

The mobility variable may partly account for the new elites' unqualified indorsement of modernization, a more pervasive definition of backwardness linked to cultural-traditional factors, and an emphasis on ascriptive values as prevalent in the traditional sectors. Perhaps their own advance in status assures them of the general possibility and thus encourages them to downgrade the use of force in agricultural improvement. On the other hand, continuous elites see backwardness arising from economic factors, for which the use of force in agriculture is more necessary. Their allies they find in modernizing intellectuals rather than the lower status business sector. The civil service is felt to be less aware, a judgment which may stem from the increase of new elites in its ranks. Continuous elites are more confident in their external models and conceive of the aid problem in more technical terms. Not surprisingly, religious values are thought to be more characteristic of the traditional sector than ascriptive values.

The major variable in this study has been the role of planners in economic development. It has been argued so far that considerable agreement exists on general attitudes toward politics and society and that this makes it meaningful to talk about planners as a category for social analysis of developing countries. The five subsidiary values—regime, level of development, bureaucratic function, source of education, and social status—were found to have merit in explaining variations from composite ideology. Other variables not analyzed here might also have been revealing, such as more sophisticated measurements of economic and social complexity or the relationship of the responses within the ideology to each other. But the central task of understanding the political implications of the role of planners has not yet been discharged. To that task we now turn.

IV

An understanding of role theory is useful as an entree to the question of variable political attitudes. A conventional definition of the concept of "role" illustrates its utility.

> The role is that organized sector of an actor's orientation which constitutes and defines his participation in an interactive process. It involves a set of complementary expectations concerning his own actions and those of others with whom he interacts. *Both the actor and those with whom he interacts possess these expectations. Roles are institutionalized when they are fully congruous with the prevailing cultural patterns and are organized around expectations of conformity with morally sanctioned patterns of value-orientation shared by the members of the collectivity in which the role functions.*[39]

There are two elements of relevance in the definition. First, there is a mutuality of expectations between those who are in the role and those with whom they interact. And, second, the role is not institutionalized until it is congruous with prevailing cultural patterns and value orientations.

Already I have argued that both elements are only partially achieved for rational productivity bureaucrats in the industrially

39. Talcott Parsons *et al.* (eds.), *Toward a General Theory of Action* (New York, 1964), p. 23. See also Braibanti's chapter in this volume, p. 62 and esp. n. 147. See also the concept of role in Kariel's chapter in this volume, esp. pp. 163 ff.

advanced nations. But this is especially true for those who inhabit less-developed nations. The role of economic planner, for instance, arose in the public and private sectors of industrial nations, a mutuality of expectations more or less exists between the planners and those with whom they interact, the role partakes of the professional norms of the larger cultural pattern, and its values of productivity and increase in national wealth are shared more widely in industrial society. The relevant fact about economic planners in low-income countries is that their role is developed elsewhere and is congruent with the expectations, cultural patterns, and value systems of the societies of its origin. When the role is diffused to other societies with different cultural patterns toward professionalism and widely diffused values unsympathetic to productivity, however, there is a lack of integration. The more incongruent the role is the greater the need for the planner to transform society so that it will be consistent with his expectations and values.

Three aspects of the role of economic planner give content to the political attitudes. The first derives from the fact that economic planners came largely from the profession of economics, usually university-based. As a profession, economics shares with many other professions a basis in systematic and generalized knowledge that is taught by members of the profession, a loyalty to an abstract public interest, an operating assumption that clients do not know best, and a desire for autonomy in insuring standards.[40] The university origins of the profession especially devalue a client orientation and contribute to the acceptance of colleagues as the qualified judges of competence.[41] That professionalism reinforces the antipolitical propensity of economic knowledge cannot be doubted. Finally, the empirical evidence on professions adds value to this ideal type in the explanation of the planners' attitudes. Professors S. M. Lipset and Mildred Schwartz have found in the literature on professionals that it is common for

40. Everett Hughes, "The Professions in Society," *Canadian Journal of Economics and Political Science,* XXVI (February, 1960), 54–61; Ernest Greenwood, "Attributes of a Profession," *Social Work,* II (July, 1957), 44–55.

41. Harold L. Wilensky, "The Professionalization of Everyone?" *American Journal of Sociology,* LXX (1964), 155.

radical protest and political activity to stem from otherwise conservative professions when there are "limited job opportunities" and discrepancies between traditional values and the realities of the work situation. In relation to professionals in countries similar to those in the sample, they argue, "The chief exceptions to this generalization [the essential conservatism of professionals] occur in nations in which political conservatism is identified with traditionalism or religion and in which certain types of higher education are associated with anti-clericalism or anti-traditionalism. . . ."[42] All three conditions exist in the countries of the sample.

A second aspect is the underlying character of the knowledge that legitimates their authority. Modern economic theory cannot be summarized in a paragraph. Elsewhere the author has shown that deeply imbedded in at least "development theory" is a clear antipolitical bias.[43] The regime is assumed and when specified in concrete examples it is clear that highly authoritarian structures, heavy expenditures on coercion, and presumed compliant peasants and workers underlie the "big push" in all its varieties, "unbalanced growth," and other theories. When something is assumed in theory it is given ultimately zero value.

Even a perceptive economist-cum-social scientist, Everett Hagen, recommended an ideal curriculum for teaching institute of economic development to include instruction in anthropology, sociology, and personality theory. The impact of development programs on politics and the need for political leadership found no place in his curriculum.[44] Furthermore, there is a prevailing view in economics that what is political is ultimately unproductive and perhaps irrational. Indeed, if the analogy can be used, economics is concerned with productivity (the altering of variables to achieve a desired future state), while politics is thought to be essentially distributive. In the planners' operating assumptions

42. S. M. Lipset and Mildred A. Schwartz, "The Politics of Professionals," in Howard M. Vollmer and Donald L. Mills (eds.), *Professionalization* (Englewood Cliffs, N.J., 1966), pp. 299–310, at p. 301.

43. Warren F. Ilchman and Ravindra C. Bhargava, "Balanced Thought and Economic Growth," *Economic Development and Cultural Change*, XIV (1966), 385–399.

44. Everett E. Hagen, "The Role of Different Sciences in the Teaching Curricula of the Institutes" (Paris, 1964, mimeographed).

what is distributive today is counterproductive for the future. All of this is shrouded in the guise of value neutrality, or science.

Explanations of this bias in economics are varied. The ancestors of modern economists saw a function of their political economy in delimiting the economic role of the state and expanding the province for private self-interested choice. Later the concentration on the firm meant an isolation of economic theory in the period of much of its conceptual development from political problems. The Marxist variant of political economy conceived of the state as an instrument to maintain the form of ownership of the means of production which will one day wither away. Moreover, economics as a science arose in societies where the fundamental political problems of nation-building had been more or less solved, and this allowed the luxury of abstracting an autonomous economic sphere that still prevails in analysis. The hedonistic definition of economic man transfigured the political actor and permitted the downgrading of public choices as dominated by self-interest and ultimately and probably unproductive of more wealth. All of this has been buttressed by the structure of the modern university and its fragmentation into specialized departments.

The third aspect assumes the relevance of a recurring pattern in social history. There is evidence that "experts" arise at a time when common sense is called into question either by an alteration in the environment that cannot be comprehended by common sense or by a new definition of the existing situation with new standards of failure and success.[45] The function of experts, whether priests or economic planners, is to use the ability to divine the future, to make intelligible to the statesman choices based on specialized knowledge that will minimize chance. Cicero argued that "there is no nation, whether the most learned and enlightened or the most grossly barbarous, that does not believe that the future can be revealed and does not recognize in certain people the power of foretelling it."[46]

45. Florian Znaniecki, *The Social Role of the Man of Knowledge* (New York, 1940), pp. 23–91.
46. Robert Flacelere, *Greek Oracles* (New York, 1965), p. 1.

For the planners, this requires reproducing conditions in which the desired change has taken place elsewhere "by either introducing into the changed conditions whatever is needed to realize the cause; or counteracting whatever interferes with realization of the effect, or both."[47] This mode gives the man of knowledge both his manipulative propensity and an internalized tension with existing society. The latter is exacerbated by the fact that the experts' utility depends on recognized success. The planner can maintain this by fulfilling the promise of the plan; to avoid failure is as important as to exceed the plan. Indeed, to exceed the plan calls into question his expertise. His success is further jeopardized by the proponents of common sense, who resist his choices and his vision of a new society, and by politicians who ultimately define the problem and decide the political cost of the conditions necessary for the planners' predictions to come true. All of these —a new definition of the situation, the supposed inability of common sense to comprehend it, the residue of the proponents of the old common sense, the basis of status and power in new knowledge, and the inherent conflict between politics and the men of knowledge—mark the low-income world.

Elsewhere there is theoretical and empirical support for the argument in this chapter. Apter has shown in *The Politics of Modernization* the likelihood of conflict between the planners and the politicians, especially in the late modernization and early industrialization phases. He argues, "When the functional significance of both the career and non-career roles is large, one can expect a direct confrontation between these two groups and a struggle for power."[48] Later he adds, "If political entrepreneurs . . . attempt to acquire all elite functions for themselves at the expense of civil servants, we may expect constant conflict between the two groups."[49] He has shown the basis for these conflicts in terms of roles and the problems of self-definition. He has also demonstrated the comparative efficiency of different regimes

47. Znaniecki, *The Social Role of the Man of Knowledge*, p. 44.
48. P. 166.
49. *Ibid.*, p. 169.

for "growth," the sacral quality economic development assumes, and the clash of nationalism and modernity as seen in the conflict between politicians and scientists.[50]

Although fragmentary and anecdotal, there is also evidence in the literature of comparative analysis to support these propositions and in turn verify the soundness of this essay's argument.[51] In relation to another rational productivity role—that of professional soldier—Janowitz has shown propensities similar to those of the planners. He writes:

> While it is impossible to identify a military ideology in new nations, common ideological themes are found which help to explain the professional officer's political behavior. These include a strong sense of nationalism, a puritanical outlook, acceptance of extensive government control of social and economic change, and a deep distrust of organized and civilian politics. As a result of social background, education, and career experiences, military personnel of the new nations become interested in politics, but they maintain a strong distrust of organized politics and civilian political leaders.[52]

He also suggests that one of the factors impelling political intervention is the need to protect the "career" from political debasement.[53]

Furthermore, the problem of "unrootedness" and of closer functional linkages with their counterparts in industrial countries is illustrated by such facts as the National Institute of Planning in

50. *Ibid., passim.*

51. See, for example, Richard P. Taub, "Bureaucracy in the Context of Social Change: A Case Study of the Indian Administrative Service" (unpublished Ph.D. dissertation, Harvard University, 1966); Moshe Lissak, "Social Exchange, Mobilization and Exchange of Services between the Military Establishment and the Civil Society: The Burmese Case," *Economic Development and Cultural Change*, XIII (1964), 1–20; F. G. Bailey, *Politics and Social Change: Orissa in 1959* (Berkeley, 1963); Fatma Mansur, *Process of Independence* (London, 1962); David E. Apter and Robert R. Lystad, "Bureaucracy, Party and Constitutional Democracy: An Examination of the Political Role Systems in Ghana," in Gwendolyn M. Carter and William O. Brown (eds.), *Transition in Africa* (Boston, 1958), pp. 16–43; Lucian W. Pye, *Politics, Personality and Nation Building* (New Haven, 1962); T. B. Bottomore, *Elites and Society* (New York, 1964); Peter Clark, "Economic Planning for a Country in Transition: Nigeria," in Everett E. Hagen (ed.), *Planning Economic Development* (Homewood, Ill., 1963), pp. 252–293.

52. Morris Janowitz, *The Military in the Political Development of New Nations* (Chicago, 1964), pp. 28–29.

53. *Ibid., passim.*

Cairo using English as its medium and the recent Iranian development plan being written by Iranians in English and then translated into Farsi. It is also apparent that the "sages" of the profession are external. Consulting with foreign economists is an important legitimating function of various planning commissions; under the prodding of the United Nations, IBRD and AID, many nations have engaged foreign planners in preference to their own economists or in the absence of their own. This, of course, further raises the status of the role in the eyes of the native neoprofessionals. Finally, the antipolitical bias of economic planners and their career orientation seem to be indirectly corroborated by two studies of political socialization of university students. A survey conducted by Professor K. H. Silvert in Latin America showed, among many things, that economists had lower national identification than other students in the sample.[54] And Professor Dwaine Marvick's study on West African students shows a high propensity for economists to define their education in career terms.[55]

How are conflicts between planners and the polity resolved? First, there seems to be an unwritten Plutarch's *Lives* of planners that they apparently know well. It is replete with episodes of the fate of planners who engaged political forces directly. It includes the fate of Ebtehaj and the purge of the Plan Organization in Iran; it also includes the experience of a South Asian planner who objected to the level of military expenditures and suddenly found himself advising for the United Nations in a Middle Eastern sheikdom. Discretion, then, becomes the better part of survival, especially in that planners have fewer resources than the military to threaten politicians.

There are other ways as well. In many countries, the planners are trying to get a separate economic service in order to protect themselves and to insure purity among their members. In Iran, for instance, it has been customary to try to finish plans before

54. "National Values, Development, and Leaders and Followers," *International Social Science Journal*, XV (1963), 560–570, at 566.

55. "African University Students: A Presumptive Elite," in James S. Coleman (ed.), *Education and Political Development* (Princeton, 1965), pp. 463–497, at p. 479.

the Majlis meets in order to forestall political bargaining. Elsewhere there is a constant campaign to "educate" political leaders of the need for technical definitions of problems and technical solutions. AID and IBRD give considerable support to this view and provide incentives. Often planners have to struggle against other technicians. In Egypt, economic planners must struggle with the engineers, and this, too, dictates continuous education of the political leadership as to the relative merits of the two fields of knowledge. After the 1961 Turkish coup, the newly appointed planners took it upon themselves to visit the provinces to convince the "people" of the rightness of the plan. This strategy is fully political and only one step away from the planners in Iran who founded the Progressive Center in order to gain more power through political means. A more dramatic gesture, which ultimately could not resolve the conflict, occurred when the Turkish planners resigned over the failure of the coalition government of Inonu to support their recommended structural reforms. The compromises for the reforms required them to work within a largely unsupportive regime, and this was intolerable.

There are also more subtle and informal ways. For instance, a Middle Eastern planner admitted to the existence of a progressive network of like-minded people in strategic ministries which kept "the projects moving." Another planner suggested that in the next generation there would be a working alliance between planners and young military officers. He added that the alliance was already in its formative stages.[56] In a sense, of course, these are less examples of resolving conflict than going about one's tasks in spite of politics.

V

There are many questions, of course, which this analysis has not touched. Indeed, its results can only be considered as preliminary to a wider study. Among the unaddressed subjects is how

56. These observations are derived from field interviews.

widely these values are shared among elites in the public and private sectors. It was suggested earlier in this chapter that the ideal type embraced a large number of activities and those responsible for these activities had similar outlooks, especially toward politics. This has not yet been proved. Other ministries and professions would have to be surveyed to see if their members could be subsumed in the larger category. Moreover, it is important to ask if the results would have been different in significant ways if the interviews were conducted in the home countries. Although I have argued earlier that the mode adopted produced more genuine results, the issue is an empirical one and not yet resolved. Finally, the explanation I have chosen does not identify the origins of this ideology, except by implication. What is needed is a longitudinal study revealing changes in attitudes over the space of the career of the rational-productivity bureaucrat.[57]

Implicit in the explanation so far has been the "colonial" assumption about "levels of development" and "readiness for progress." Although I earlier argued that rational-productivity bureaucrats have difficulty everywhere, I chose the conventional model for explaining the planners' attitudes because of its efficiency and currency. All that is required is positing a "congruence" of institutions and values for the benchmark nations and treating the attitudes found elsewhere as the product of "incongruence" or as a "strain toward congruence." Unfortunately, however, this mode of analysis misses many interesting possibilities —especially for questions of administrative reform.[58]

It would be useful to speculate, without the attribution of level of development, on the conditions that correlate with different political attitudes and behavior of rational-productivity bureaucrats in various regimes. Here again I will use economic planners and enter at the outset any disclaimer to empirical foundations for the speculations which follow. There are as yet none. But if

57. The author is grateful to R. Taylor Cole, who was discussant of this paper at the Bellagio conference, for calling attention to the observations made in this paragraph.

58. See, for example, Warren F. Ilchman and Norman T. Uphoff, *The Political Economy of Change* (forthcoming).

there were, I suspect several propositions might be favorably tested.

If economic planners as a group in any regime could be arrayed along a continuum on the basis of the frequency of certain sorts of political behavior or outcomes, they might be seen in this fashion:

[	1	2	3	4	5	6	7	8	9	]

Legend

1 Antigovernment collaboration
2 Resignation
3 Formal participation only
4 Major conflict and losses on policy matters
5 Gains equal losses
6 Major conflict and gains on policy matters
7 Shared authority on policy allocations
8 Policy dominance by planners; formal participation by other political organs
9 Policy control by planners without need of conventional legitimation

The more the planners move toward the right of the continuum the more control they exercise in policy matters and probably the more engaged and productive they are in their work; the more they move to the left the more impotent they are in relation to policy and probably the more alienated and antigovernment in their behavior. Any regimes—rich or poor, developed and developing, sophisticated in the modes of production or not—could thus be compared.

What independent variables affect movement in one direction or another? Four, among many possible ones, seem especially salient: (1) the degree of significant support for productivity values; (2) the extent of significant belief that government is the major catalyst for social and economic change; (3) the incidence of public compliance with planners' policies (or, perhaps, the availability of "free-floating resources" for pursuing policy ends);[59] and (4) the number of elites outside government claiming expertise similar to that of the planners. Each can be more or less measured.

59. S. N. Eisenstadt, *The Political Systems of Empires* (New York, 1963), pp. 27 ff.

Perhaps the relationships can best be seen visually:

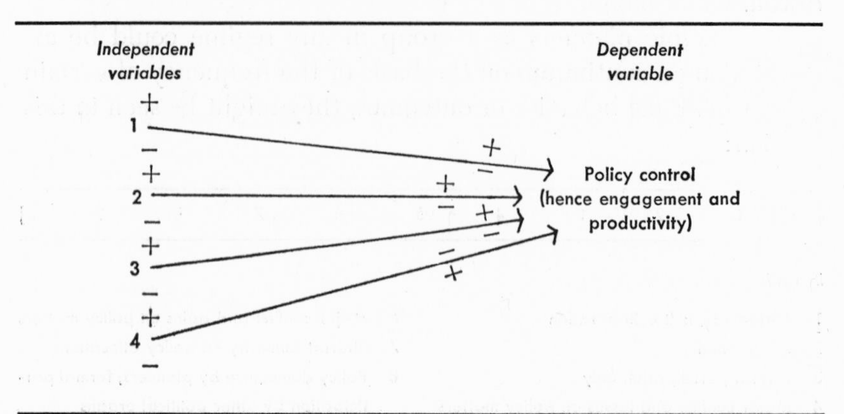

From these, several propositions arise. One might be: the greater the degree of significant support for productivity values the greater the policy control possessed by planners and hence their engagement and productivity. A second is: the greater the extent of significant support for the government as the major catalyst for social and economic change the greater the policy control possessed by planners and hence their engagement and productivity. Third, the greater the incidence of public compliance with planners' policies (or resources for attaining planners' goals) the greater the policy control possessed by planners and hence their engagement and productivity. Finally, the greater the number of elites outside government claiming expertise similar to that of the planners the less policy control planners have, hence their engagement and productivity are less.

As the above formulation is not part of the tradition of "functionalism," the derivative propositions may be tested without concern for issues such as subsystem adequacy or effects on system development. Moreover, one may speculate on different combinations of the independent variables and their impact on planners, e.g., planners in regimes that are high on significant support of productivity values but low on significant belief that government is the major catalyst for change. This, above all, permits a political-administrative study of, say, the Soviet Union and India without the Trojan horse problem of the conventional development model.

VI

What can be learned about administrative reform from this chapter? Can choices made by statesmen and others be improved by the concepts and conclusions advanced here? Three ideas seem to have potential.

First, if a statesman assumes that imported intellectual technology, either through foreign economic advisers or his own staff of planners, is an instrument to be used as he and his regime please, he is essentially wrong. There is a propensity on the planners' part to downgrade the outcomes and costs of politics that might make them a political force of some consequence. *Caveat emptor!*

Second, when advocates of administrative reform seek to induce reform in developing nations, they must be explicit about the type of organization and orientation toward action they mean. Often advocates use the idiom of conventional bureaucracy when they intend to recommend rational-productivity bureaucracy. This is especially important because many programs can be better discharged by conventional bureaucracy than by its more recent kin.[60]

Third, experience with rational-productivity bureaucracies in various parts of the world suggests that there is a relationship between structure and forms of authority and effectiveness. This relationship indicates the need for rational-productive activity to be carried out in less hierarchical structures with more informal channels of communication than normally obtain. Moreover, the means used by executives to secure compliance on the part of participants should become more normative in their content.[61]

60. This confusion can be seen in Victor A. Thompson, "Administrative Objectives for Development Administration," *Administrative Science Quarterly,* V (1964), 91–108.

61. For example, Amitai Etzioni, *A Comparative Analysis of Complex Organizations* (New York, 1961), pp. 248–262; Bennis, *Changing Organizations,* pp. 3–78; Tom Burns and G. M. Stalker, *The Management of Innovation* (Chicago, 1962); F. E. Emery and E. L. Trist, "The Causal Texture of Organizational Environ-

At the heart of these suggestions and the entire chapter is a fourth point of possible value. It is the aspiration to see, without the constrictions of models predicating direction or "congruence," emerging forces in all their political variety. From this a more fruitful and comparative discussion of the theoretical problems of administrative reform in developing nations might arise.

---

ments," *Human Relations*, XVIII (1965), pp. 21–32; William Delany, "The Development and Decline of Patrimonial and Bureaucratic Administrations," *Administrative Science Quarterly*, VII (1963), 458–501; Todd R. LaPorte, "Conditions of Strain and Accommodation in Industrial Research Organizations," *Administrative Science Quarterly*, X (1965), 21–38; Max Pages, "The Socio-therapy of the Enterprise: The Conditions of Psycho-Social Change in Industrial Concerns and the Role of the Social Psychologist as an Agent of Social Change," *Human Relations*, XII (1959), 317–334; and Cyril Sofer, "The Assessment of Organization Change," *Journal of Management Studies*, II (1965), pp. 128–142.

This literature makes, in different ways and for different types of organizations, the point about structure and effectiveness. Unfortunately, most of it is couched in the context of debureaucratization (not in the sense it is used by Eisenstadt). The ideal type employed here is more useful, for it is clear that a new kind of organization is emerging that is suited for some but not all purposes and that it will coexist with its predecessor. To suggest a trend in the direction of the destruction of hierarchy is not supported by data, only pious hopes.

• 12 •

Comment on "Productivity, Administrative Reform, and Antipolitics: Dilemmas for Developing States"

R. Taylor Cole

Warren F. Ilchman's stimulating, thoughtful, and provocative study of "rational-productivity bureaucrats" makes certain initial assumptions. One of them is that rational-productivity bureaucrats constitute a group of individuals with such clearly definable features as to permit a study of these special characteristics. These distinctive features, as outlined on pages 478–479 distinguish them from other subgroups within the bureaucracy and from the "legal-rational" bureaucrats in particular. The bond of the ideal type of rational-productivity bureaucrats consists primarily in their "legitimating source in knowledge, their loyalty to substantive programs, and their value commitment to productivity" (p. 479). Specifically, special attention is directed to the economic planners among the rational-productivity bureaucrats and to their conceptions of society, its politics, and its possibilities for the future, or, more succinctly stated, to the ideology of economic planners.

With this general purpose of the author before us, several questions can be posed for the sake of discussion. In so doing, occasional reference will be made to bureaucrats and planners in two developing countries of Africa, namely, Nigeria and Tanzania.

First, a somewhat more limited title for this chapter might be justified. It is devoted primarily to an examination of the characteristics of economic planners in the public services of certain developing countries and to the ideology of these economic planners. The author gives little more than passing attention to administrative reform as such and that in the two brief concluding sections. One of these sections (pp. 495 ff.) is devoted to an analysis of the political behavior of the bureaucrat, in which certain tentative propositions regarding the degree of engagement or involvement in "policy control" are outlined. The final section consists of a brief presentation of three ideas which are pertinent to administrative reform. The first suggests that planners will minimize the "outcomes and costs of politics" where "statesmen" import "intellectual technology." The second suggests that advocates of administrative reform, who seek to induce reform in developing nations, be explicit "about the type of organization and orientation toward action" in their programs. Many programs, it is believed, can be better discharged by conventional bureaucracy than by its "more recent kin." Third, the experience with economic planners indicates the need "for rational-productive activity to be carried out in less hierarchical structures with more informal channels of communication than normally obtain." These three "ideas," or hints, would seem to merit careful but independent consideration, but their direct relevance to the main theme of this chapter is not apparent.

Second, questions may be raised about the author's methodology. How were the members of the group selected for study and what was the nature of the sample which resulted? The author states that he has contacted "a large number of planners in six countries in South Asia and the Middle East" but, for the purpose of procuring a broader sample, selected and interviewed over a period of two years some "thirty-three mid-career planners from eighteen countries" who were studying in the United States "advanced economic techniques . . . at a graduate institute of economic development" (pp. 484–485). The sample showed an average of eight years' experience in the bureaucracies of the home countries. The author recognized that the sample consisted of advanced students, or "planners," resident in American institutions and interviewed by American social scientists (p. 484). The rationale for the choices is clearly stated and provides practical justification for the selections made. But would alternative selections have been worthy of consideration?

The first alternative would have called for a more specific definition of "rational-productivity planning" and a delineation of the many types of bureaucrats—from differing public service classes and groups and with varying disciplinary backgrounds—engaged in such planning. Would not educational officials in the ministries of education, engineers in the departments of public works, officers in the military services in the ministries of defense, and political scientists and sociologists in the ministries of interior and local government be as vitally engaged in rational-productivity planning as are those who have had training in economics? If the main emphasis is on rational *productivity*, can one really differentiate between the economics-trained bureaucratic planner and the non-economics-trained bureaucratic (i.e., conventional) planner? In this connection, I have noted the statement by the author (p. 515) that "as a profession, economics *shares with many other professions* (italics mine) a basis in systematic and generalized knowledge that is taught by members of the profession, a loyalty to an abstract public interest, an operating assumption that clients do not know best, and a desire for autonomy in insuring standards." This alternative suggests a wider area for choice of the sample on the basis of clearer definitions of planning than has been made. I am also indicating, by implication at least, some skepticism of certain of the distinctions drawn in the table on pages 478–479 on such points as the "relevance of pre-entry education to position" ("high" vs. "generally low"), "training experience" ("substantially prior to entry" vs. "mostly post-entry"), etc.

A second alternative approach might have been to select for examination all economists in the higher public services, on the assumption that all such economists are by definition engaged in some way in rational-productivity planning. The assumption that all these economists might be included finds support in the activities of those covered in the actual sample chosen, for, in the author's words, these ranged from "long-range 'perspective' planning to the implementation of programs in small-scale industries" (p. 485). If all such economists in the higher public services are in the group from which the sample is chosen, then the size of the group will be substantially larger than the one originally utilized. It is to be noted, to digress for the moment, that in Nigeria in 1964–65 over 80 per cent of those persons with "high level skills," to borrow terminology used in the International Bank for Reconstruction and Development survey of 1966, were employed in the public services. The public servants trained in economics in the Nigerian universities probably exceeded in number those trained in the other social sciences. (At the University of Ibadan in 1964–65, there were ninety majors in economics and seven in political science after the division of the Social Science Department into separate departments.) In sum, it is appropriate to ask first if the qualifications or characteristics of rational-productivity planners can be more specifically outlined; second, if all university-trained economists in the upper ranks of the public services should not be included in the group of public servants from which the sample is chosen; and third, if these rational-productivity planners can be differentiated as clearly as the author indicates from the high-ranking conventional civil servants who are concerned with goals, strategies, and techniques of implementation.

Third, is the evidence presented by the author convincing that the rational-productivity bureaucrat is "antipolitical" in a unique and distinctive way? Is the author clear in the use of such terms as "political," "politics," "antipolitical," "political conditions," "political forces," "political system"? Just what does he mean by such expressions as the "politician or statesman" and the "clash of political forces or leaders," the "degree of hostility which some planners feel in relation to politics," "politicians, office-holders, and the 'people', " etc.? Are the "conventional bureaucrats," from whom the rational-productivity bureaucrats are differentiated, and the members of the "government" included among the "political forces" and "politicians"? If so, how can one explain that 55 per cent of the respondents "identified 'government' as the chief contributor to overcoming the impediments to economic development" (p. 494), or that most civil servants "are aware of the problems and needs of economic development" and are "supportive" of the efforts of the planners (p. 496)? If so, how can one explain that in monopoly-party regimes, which planners consider to be "most conducive to their values and methods" (p. 506), the "office-holders and politicians are thought to be highly supportive" of economic development (p. 507); that, in competitive-party regimes, while "office-holders and politicians" are less supportive, the "government" is seen as the "chief contributor to economic development" (p. 508); and that, in military regimes, while there is skepticism of the capacity and willingness of the military rulers to "mobilize resources and to conceive of development programs in their economic terms," the planners still look both to the civil servants and to the "private sector for the major thrust of development" (p. 508)? To support his thesis, the author cites as "theoretical and empirical support" works by Apter[1] along with selected references from the literature of comparative analysis where the citations include mention of a volume by Lucian Pye.[2] The "antipolitical bias of economic planners" is indirectly corroborated, it is further contended, by Silvert's studies in Latin America[3] showing that economists evidenced less national identification than students in other disciplines, and by Marvick[4] in his researches on West African students indicating the high propensity of majors in economics to "define their education in career terms" (p. 520). This literature merits more careful examination than I have been able to give it. But, on balance, I find the terminology on "politics" and the "antipolitical" to be vaguely defined, and in partial consequence the evidence submitted in support of the author's main argument to be somewhat unsatisfying.

Fourth, if there were the possibility of a choice, should the examination of the characteristics and attitudes of the economic planners among the rational-productivity bureaucrats have been

1. David E. Apter, *The Politics of Modernization* (Chicago, 1965), pp. 166, 175.

2. Lucian W. Pye, *Politics, Personality and Nation Building* (New Haven, 1962).

3. K. M. Silvert, "National Values, Development, and Leaders and Followers," *International Social Science Journal*, XV (1963), 560–570, at 566.

4. Dwaine Marvick, "African University Students: A Presumptive Elite," in James S. Coleman (ed.), *Education and Political Development* (Princeton, 1965), p. 492.

done in the institutional setting of the home countries represented in order to elicit the type of data which would be most pertinent for a study of administrative reform? The assumption underlying this query is consonant with the position taken by Braibanti on the "cruciality" of institutions in political development and in comparative political analyses.[5] The variations in the organization, intragovernmental relationships, and *functions* of planning agencies and boards, including the ones which are called by those names, vary so widely in African states as almost to defy classification. At the minimum, would there not be present a number of factors and considerations which would affect the responses of the rational-productivity bureaucrats in ways different from those factors and considerations which affected their responses as graduate students in American institutions of higher learning? Reference may be made to the history of the planning ministries and directorates from 1960 to date in Tanganyika and, later, Tanzania (Ministry of Finance, Ministry of Development Planning, Directorate of Planning and Development, and after 1965, Ministry for Economic Affairs and Development Planning) to illustrate the point for one country.[6] During the period of the three-member directorate, the differences between these members were largely ideological and jurisdictional; the bonds between the French, German, British, Tanzanian, and American economists and social scientists were possibly more institutional, "administrative," and personal than professional and antipolitical. Indeed, one of the basic agreements among those rational-productivity bureaucrats involved in the preparation of the five-year plan, 1964–69, and in its early implementation, was that their work was being encouraged and heavily supported by President Nyerere.[7] To make the point again, I am doubtful if the

5. Ralph Braibanti, "Comparative Political Analytics Reconsidered," *Journal of Politics*, XXX (1968), 25–66, and his chapter in this volume.

6. Taylor Cole, "The Ministerial System in Tanzania," in *Die moderne Demokratie und ihr Recht: Festschrift fuer Gerhard Leibholz* (Tübingen, 1966), II, 641–668, esp. pp. 657 ff.

7. However, on the uncertain administrative and political relations with the national ministries and regional governmental agencies, see R. Cranford Pratt, "The Administration of Economic Planning in a Newly Independent State: The Tanzanian Experience 1963–1966," *Journal of Commonwealth Political Studies*, V (1967), 38–59.

responses of the students of economics in the United States, reflecting the attitudes of students professionally immersed in graduate study and being interviewed by American social scientists, would have been the same as they would have been in the home countries where they were active participants in the operating *institutions.*

But, fifth, let us assume for the purposes of discussion, that the antipolitical bias of an acceptable sample of clearly defined rational-productivity bureaucrats has been proven. Then, I may ask when and why this antipolitical reaction has developed in a comparatively noteworthy way among this particular subgroup of bureaucrats. My own investigation and inquiries in Nigeria on the nature of the training of public servants in Nigerian universities and institutes, and on the attitudes of public service employers toward these programs, indicate that to the potential employers a major in economics offered certain advantages over a major in other social sciences.[8] Though the reasons offered therefore were not always carefully considered, varied somewhat from respondent to respondent, and were occasionally inconsistent, the economics major was viewed as having a background permitting of special adaptation to different types of positions in the public service (particularly as compared to majors in programs in "public administration"). The employers, usually evidencing the heritage of their British educational experience, felt that the economics major fitted better into a "classical-literary generalist tradition" while the public administration major was too often the victim of the virus of a "mechanistic emphasis and management techniques." Further, it was believed that the economics major possessed certain skills that might find immediate application in the public services, and, perhaps somewhat inconsistently, that the economics major acquired a greater "depth" in a particular discipline than was readily available in other social science disciplines. In short, the public service employer possessed a positive bias toward the initial recruitment of the economist.

8. Unpublished report prepared by Taylor Cole for the Committee on Education and Human Resource Development of Education and World Affairs, "AID and Public Administrative Training Programs in Nigeria" (January, 1966).

At the same time, did the economics major himself acquire during his period of study a distrust for the "politician" (presumably including the public service employers)? Unpublished research on the attitudes of Nigerian students in 1964–65, undertaken at the University of Ibadan by Dr. Charles Rooks indicates that over 78 per cent of those majoring in the social sciences at the University of Ibadan and over 65 per cent of those majoring in the social sciences at the University of Nigeria found government employment preferable to all other types of employment. There are various reasons that may be given for these attitudes, including the limited range of choices open in a country where most employment *is* public employment. But the point is that the economist began his public service career in a setting of acceptance by the public service employer and with a predisposition on his own part toward public employment.

When and why, to repeat, does the alleged bias on the part of the rational-productivity bureaucrat arise? Is it a product of belated recognition by the rational-productivity bureaucrat that the government cannot encourage economic development except within the limits outlined in Spengler's chapter (especially restricted in respect to the "transformation of input into growth-oriented output" and "the economical use of all of the nation's resources")?[9] In particular, is it due to the failure to appreciate and evaluate the politician's concern, commitment, responsibility, and course of action taken for the "survival of the centralized polity and the existing regime, the existence of which is new and uncertain"?[10] Or, is it to be explained on other grounds?

In conclusion, I view this thoughtful study as making a significant contribution to the literature on planning and bureaucratic planners in developing countries. Because of its merits and its pioneering attempts to study the characteristics and ideology of economic planners, I have felt that the author would expect and welcome critical questioning by a "devil's advocate." The ques-

9. Joseph J. Spengler's chapter in this volume.

10. See Warren F. Ilchman and Ravindra C. Bhargava, "Balanced Thought and Economic Growth," *Economic Development and Cultural Change*, XIV (1966), 385–399, esp. 394–395, and p. 396, n. 21, where specific reference is made to Spengler's concept of an autonomous economic system.

tions I have therefore raised are, in summary: (1) Would a more realistic title be appropriate in view of the nature of the contents and main thesis of the chapter? (2) Methodologically, would other ideal types or alternative methods of selection of the group for study, and of sampling it, have been desirable in the light of the author's objectives? (3) Is the evidence presented by the author convincing as to the unique antipolitical attitudes or bias of the economic planners among the rational-productive bureaucrats? (4) Should the examination of the characteristics and attitudes of these economic planners have been made in their institutional and home country setting? (5) On the assumption that the antipolitical attitudes of the rational-productive bureaucrat have been adequately proven, when and why did this antipolitical bias develop?

• 13 •

Administrative Doctrines Diffused in Emerging States: The Filipino Response*

José V. Abueva

"Administrative doctrine" is used here as shorthand for shared goals, norms, beliefs, and technology for administrative modernization. Our concern is limited to the administrative doctrines of those officials, advisers, experts, or consultants of the United Nations and the (United States) Agency for International Development (AID), whose principal mission has been to induce administrative reform and improvement in newly developing countries. Administrative doctrines serve a number of related uses. They are long-range standards, immediate working guidelines, and specialized techniques for those assigned in the field. They also are the bases for program planning, recruitment, research, and evaluation by headquarters in New York or Washington, or in the country missions of the technical assistance agencies.

This usage of doctrine is consistent with its broad conceptualization by the Inter-University Research Program in Institution-Building as "the specification of values, objectives, and operational methods underlying social action."[1] Likewise, our usage is illuminated by the understanding of doctrine "as a series of

* The author wishes to express his appreciation for a grant from the Committee on Research, the Department of Political Science, Brooklyn College of the City University of New York, which covered expenses for research at the Agency for International Development in Washington, D.C. For facilitating the collection of official data, he is indebted to Mr. George Lawson, Jr., and Miss Carol S. Piper of AID and to Dr. Buenaventura S. Villanueva of the Public Administration Division of the United Nations.

1. Milton J. Esman, *The Institution-Building Concepts: An Interim Appraisal*, Inter-University Research Program in Institution-Building (Pittsburgh, 1967), p. 3. See Braibanti's chapter in this volume, esp. n. 128, for further references.

themes which project, both within the organization itself and its external environment, a set of images and expectations of institutional goals and styles of action."[2] Moreover, we accept the view that doctrine may, and often does, spearhead, guide, legitimatize, and rationalize organizational actions. Differing with the program's view, perhaps, we consider technology as a component part of doctrine, for we conceive of technology as the operationalization of, and in practice hardly differentiated from, the doctrine itself.

I. United Nations Administrative Doctrine

In lieu of exhaustive content analysis of agency documents, which could not be done for this study, a few key reports and handbooks were examined. For United Nations administrative doctrine the principal sources were *Standards and Techniques of Public Administration* (1951) and *A Handbook of Public Administration* (1961). *A Handbook of Civil Service Laws and Practices* (1966), *A Handbook of Training in the Public Service* (1966), and *The United Nations Programme in Public Administration* (1967) were also consulted. The first two are codifications of principles, concepts, and practices; the third and fourth are international abstracts presented cafeteria-style for the choice of their users, while the last is a review of the United Nations program since it began in 1950. To a considerable extent the selected materials incorporate beliefs, ideas, and techniques embodied in several other United Nations public administration publications and in indivudal reports by experts.[3]

Standards and Techniques was a "unanimous statement"[4] of the seven committee members who wrote it. They came from the

2. Esman, *Institution-Building Concepts,* pp. 2–3.

3. A thorough analysis of United Nations administrative doctrine would involve at least a content analysis of many more reports and communication, as well as distinguishing between authoritatively stated doctrine and operative doctrine "in the field."

4. United Nations Technical Assistance Administration, *Standards and Techniques of Public Administration with Special Reference to Technical Assistance for Underdeveloped Countries* (New York, 1951). Hereafter cited as *Standards and Techniques.*

Netherlands, the United States, Cuba, Puerto Rico, India, and France. "Such a consensus," the authors averred (p. 2), "constitutes strong evidence that there exists a common body of principle and technique in the field of public administration which has some degree of world-wide and general validity, which may have special applicability to new states and to the less developed areas of the world. . . ." The contribution of several staff members in various United Nations departments and specialized agencies to the committee's work was hailed in the text as confirmation of "the fact that there already exists in the international civil service, supplemented by experts called in for special consultation, a body of common knowledge in the realm of governmental administration and public management which constitutes one of the primary resources available in any evolving international programme of technical assistance looking forward toward social, economic, or administrative development" (p. 3). Having said this, the committee added that any development program or "reform and reconstruction in any of the public services can only succeed if it is supported by machinery and methods established under sound principles of public administration and adapted to the circumstances of the country concerned" (p. 4). In other words, "any attempt to apply the generally applicable principles of public administration must contend with those economic, social and governmental circumstances which seem to be peculiar to underdeveloped areas . . ." (p. 5).

As one form of technical assistance, the international public administration program was traced to a basic goal in the United Nations charter: "to promote higher standards of living, full employment, and conditions of economic and social progress and development."[5] This articulation is based on a cardinal assumption: "A sound system of administration contributes as directly as possible to the economic and social development of the nation and to the raising of the level of economic security and social welfare of the population."[6] Inspired by lofty ideals expressed in the charter and other United Nations declarations, *Standards and Techniques* was unequivocal in affirming a series of Western

5. Art. 55, chap. 9.
6. *Standards and Techniques*, p. 11.

libertarian beliefs as "fundamentals of public administration":[7]

> *Public order, stability,* and *justice* are not only indispensable to, but also fundamental objectives of, an effective system of public administration. (p. 9)
>
> Sound public administration can only flourish under a system for the *administration of justice* based on *equal protection for all, impartial administration* of governmental services, and *adequate provision for social change.* (p. 9)
>
> Governments which abuse their powers, or which habitually act arbitrarily with reference to persons and property or which do not respect fundamental human rights, or which permit dishonesty in the public service, lack an adequate basis for a desirable and stable form of public administration. (p. 9)
>
> An effective system of public administration must be founded on a policy which tends to broaden the range of *personal freedom, economic and social opportunity,* and *political democracy.* (p. 9)
>
> The best system of administration runs the risk of breaking down sooner or later if, in administering the power of the state, it is not *genuinely responsible to the public,* and if it does not subscribe to the elementary precepts of *liberty* and *equality.* (p. 10)
>
> Effective public administration requires a *favourable political leadership and public opinion.* The public must be willing to pay the price in order to achieve the essentials of governmental reorganization, fiscal reform, and civil service improvement. (p. 10)
>
> Sound administration seeks to *share responsibility* and to *enlarge the area of participation* as widely as feasible. A sound system of public administration is solicitous about its relations with the public. (pp. 10, 11)

The authors of *Standards and Techniques* admit that "effective administration adapts its particulars to the life of the nation concerned" (p. 11), that "there is seldom a One-Best-Way in public administration" (p. 12), and that "there may have to be extensive variations in means" toward achieving "generally adopted standards of competent public management" (p. 11). Nevertheless, the document presented a number of "applicable principles . . . common to most developed, and some underdeveloped, systems of administration" (p. 12), under conventional headings in Western administrative systems: governmental or-

7. Italics in the quotations immediately following are the author's.

ganization, public finance, public personnel, administrative management, and planning and development.

If we wish to speculate on the spread and influence of its contents, it is helpful to know that over 7,600 copies of *Standards and Techniques* were printed and that it was "in constant demand as the basic working document for the use of United Nations experts . . . and of Governments to which they were accredited."[8] During the decade of the fifties, it was the United Nations standard general reference in its field.

Its successor, *Handbook of Public Administration*, has been also in great demand. Including its reprint, over 10,000 copies have been circulated, and a second printing has been urged. The *Handbook* was intended as a "clear restatement of the basic elements in a programme of public administration improvement in developing countries" (p. 1) and available United Nations assistance. While the publication it superseded was far less firmly based on field experience in technical assistance, Herbert Emmerich, the American public administration expert who wrote the *Handbook*, acknowledges that "its conclusions are largely based on the reports of United Nations experts and working parties who have now been engaged for almost ten years in public administration work and closely allied fields in most of the developing countries of the world" (p. 1). Although at another part of the *Handbook* the author describes the document as a summary and synthesis of "findings" of United Nations experience, the *Handbook* offers forthright generalized "concepts" and prescriptions. It is therefore noteworthy that, as Emmerich observes, "the experts show remarkable agreement in their suggestions for the improvement of public administration" (p. 1). Nevertheless, the reader is advised to regard them "as guidelines and not as immutable dogmas" (p. 126). Moreover, he is told: "Each country in introducing administrative reforms of the type described will be well advised to adapt them carefully, without impairing their essential purposes, to national needs and national cultures" (p. 126).

In a section entitled "Public Administration and the Citizen,"

8. United Nations, Department of Economic and Social Affairs, *A Handbook of Public Administration: Current Concepts and Practice with Special Reference to Developing Countries* (New York, 1961), pp. 1–2.

the *Handbook* restresses the universal, libertarian, and humane principles proclaimed in the United Nations charter as "the fundamental aims and objectives which an administration should serve . . ." (p. 10). It enjoins the political leaders of the emerging states to uphold those principles. It calls on career officials to implement them loyally in their "role of servants, not masters of the citizen, devoted to the pursuit not of their own interests but of the general well-being" (p. 10). Going farther than *Standards and Techniques,* the *Handbook* spells out five specific rights of the citizen in relation to the public service:

> 1. The right to be treated with due observance of the rule of law, and with justice, impartiality and reasonableness in all his dealings with the administration;
> 2. The right of appeal against administrative decisions as a protection against arbitrary and biased treatment, and to obtain justice;
> 3. The right to know what the laws and regulations are, and his own privileges and duties in regard to them;
> 4. The right to information on the purposes, organization and operations of his government;
> 5. The right to participate in public affairs, as far as possible, at national, regional, and local levels. (p. 11)

Considerable confusion results from the mixture of description and prescription and from the failure to reconcile conflicting ideals of public administration being affirmed. At one point the *Handbook* bewilderingly assumes or piously proclaims that "a country's public administration *is* based on these principles: to serve the general interests, apply the rule of law and carry out decisions made in conformity with the processes of consent" (p. 13). In other parts, similar characteristics are presented as preconditions of administrative modernization. While admitting variations caused by differing evolutionary stages of countries, it flatly states: "But unless the national state is committed to the building of a public administration which will serve these purposes, many of the conclusions that follow [findings and solutions offered] will be inapplicable" (p. 13). And yet, the *Handbook* also upholds the idea that the public service should truly share the society's "culture, its values, its problems and its ambitions" (p. 11). External advice and assistance "must be given an indigenous character" (p. 11). The reader is therefore asked to regard the abundant "findings," "principles," or "elements" concerning public administration in developing countries as merely "the skeletal structure into which every country can breathe life in the best way suited to its society" (pp. 11–12).

If United Nations administrative doctrine is inapplicable in those states that are not committed to building a democratic policy and administrative system—as most emerging states seem not to be—it is pertinent to inquire why United Nations public administration experts are assigned to a number of those states and are introducing there essentially the same tenets and techniques which they are also diffusing in the few emerging democratic states. If democratic commitments are prerequisite to successful administrative modernization, then the prospects for administrative modernization of most emerging states must indeed be poor or nonexistent.[9] If administrative reforms must share the nation's values and elite ambitions, what happens if, at any particular time, these are given the goals and precepts of United Nations administrative doctrine, inimical and counterproductive?

Despite the mélange of imperious command and diffident suggestion, essentiality, universality, and culture-bind characterizing the precepts and methods preferred by the *Handbook,* the net impression is that its author is mightily convinced of their relevance to administrative modernization in the emerging states, irrespective of their condition. The significance of that conviction and its affirmation is revealed in Shor's observation, partially based on United Nations survey reports and mission recommendations: "it is quite evident that these doctrines are faithfully invoked by technical assistance advisers in the developing countries."[10] We might add that not a few of the most sensitive and sophisticated and best-trained among public administration practitioners and scholars in the developing countries also subscribe

9. Only a democratic bias precludes the view that authoritarian and totalitarian systems cannot achieve administrative modernization or political development. These processes can and have been defined without relation to ideological preferences. See, for example, Alfred Diamant, "Political Development: Approaches to Theory and Strategy," in John D. Montgomery and William J. Siffin (eds.), *Approaches to Development: Politics, Administration and Change* (New York, 1966), pp. 25–26.

10. Edgar L. Shor, "Comparative Administration: Static Study Versus Dynamic Reform," *Public Administration Review,* XXII (1962), 158–165.

to those precepts and try to apply those techniques—as they have been diffused not only by the United Nations, but also, even more widely and no less vigorously, by the AID and other governmental and educational institutions of the United States.

For the sake of brevity, the more important values, techniques, and processes discussed in the *Handbook* are enumerated in Table 2 essentially as they appear in the *Handbook*'s detailed table of contents.[11] Not surprisingly, these are consistent with those offered ten years earlier in *Standards and Techniques.* But being twice in length, and having had a decade of field experience as a basis, the *Handbook* has more "concepts and practices" between its covers. Undoubtedly, the most important factor in the consistency between the two key documents is their common source of administrative doctrine and experience. The principal authors were Americans and other Westerners. Table 1 shows the

Table 1. *Country of Origin of United Nations Public Administration Experts, 1950–1966*

Country of origin	Number of experts	Percentage of total (N = 438)
United States	82	18.7
United Kingdom	68	15.5
France	53	12.1
Canada	18	4.1
Netherlands	17	3.9
Belgium	15	3.4
Switzerland	11	2.5
Sweden	10	2.3
India	9	2.0
Egypt	9	2.0
Soviet Union	2	0.5
Subtotal	294	67.0
Other	144	33.0
Total	438	100.0

Source: Compiled from data in United Nations, Department of Economic and Social Affairs, Public Administration Branch, *Public Administration Newsletter,* No. 5 (July, 1966).

11. A wider range of interests and activities of the United Nations in public administration is suggested by varied subjects covered by United Nations meetings and reports; see United Nations, Department of Economic and Social Affairs, Public Administration Branch, *United Nations Programme in Public Administration: Report of the Meeting of Experts* (New York, 1967), pp. 198–205.

Table 2. *Contemporary Concepts and Practice: United Nations Handbook of Public Administration, 1961*

1. *Organization analysis*
   a. Purposes of organization
   b. Political and personal factors
   c. Systematic organization
   d. Types of organization
   e. Organization nomenclature
   f. Organization charts and manuals
2. *Organizational structure*
   a. Limitation of number of agencies
   b. Grouping and definition of related functions in a ministry
   c. Identification of types of functions and duties
   d. Provision for administrative controls
   e. Decentralization of operations
3. *Methods and matériel*
   a. Purposes of good methods
   b. Serving the public
   c. Legality and impartiality
   d. Economy and speed
   e. Simplicity and clarity of forms
   f. Paper work, registry and archives
   g. Office layout and equipment
   h. Matériel purchasing and property control
   i. Suggestion schemes
   j. Organization and methods offices
4. *Career Service*
   a. A career service based on merit and fitness
   b. Political neutrality and the career service
   c. Classification and grading
   d. Just and adequate salary scales
   e. Pensions and social security
   f. Leaves and other benefits
5. *Personnel administration*
   a. Recruitment by objective tests
   b. A planned system of promotion
   c. Discipline, appeals, and consultation
   d. The problem of manpower planning and personnel statistics
   e. A central office of personnel administration
6. *Human relations, supervision, and training*
   a. Human relations as an art and as a science
   b. Special role of the supervisor
   c. Training in public administration
   d. Training new entrants into the career service
   e. Technical and professional training
   f. Training of trainers
   g. Role of national institutes
7. *Decentralization*
   a. Complexities of decentralization
   b. Forms of decentralization
   c. Area administration under central ministries

Table 2 *continued*

- d. Devolution to local and state authorities
- e. Community development

8. *Autonomous institutions and public enterprises*
   - a. The variety of autonomous institutions
   - b. Purposes of public enterprises
   - c. Forms of organization of public enterprises
   - d. Safeguards on corporate autonomy
   - e. Conformity with general government policy
   - f. Conformity with general administrative controls
9. *Budget and financial administration*
   - a. The national budget
   - b. The budget as an instrument of economic policy
   - c. Performance or management approach to budgeting
   - d. Fiscal control
   - e. Auditing
   - f. The revenue side of the budget
   - g. Tax policy as related to national development
   - h. Tax administration
   - i. Tax problems of local authorities and earmarked revenues
10. *Research and planning*
    - a. Elements of the planning process
    - b. Planning with relation to public administration
    - c. United Nations aid in the planning process
    - d. Research and statistics as a basis for planning
    - e. Co-ordination as a basis for planning
    - f. Staffing of central office of planning
    - g. Objectives and priorities of planning
11. *Decision-making*
    - a. Decision-making and operations
    - b. Delegation and clearance
    - c. Decision-making and the career officials
    - d. Decision-making and the minister
    - e. Multiple clearance
    - f. Consultations and hearings
    - g. Policy co-ordination
12. *Public relations and reporting*
    - a. Reporting within the administration
    - b. Reporting to the nation
    - c. Communicating with the individual citizen

predominance of Americans, British, and French experts in the United Nations public administration program during the period 1950–66.[12]

12. Moreover, most of the 1,646 United Nations fellowships awarded to nationals in the developing countries during 1960–65 involved training in Western countries, some 400 in the United States, 300 in the United Kingdom, and 200 in France.

II. AID Administrative Doctrine

In 1960 the Agency for International Development (AID) incorporated ito its manual a series of orders concerning the "philosophy," "nature," "objectives," and "methods" of its overseas public administration program.[13] Since these authoritative documents emerged from a long round of discussions and consultations within the agency, at about the end of the first decade of technical assistance abroad, they may be regarded as a partial "codification" of AID administrative doctrine. Barely ten pages long, and forming part of the agency manual, the AID codification is probably in a more usable format compared to the first two United Nations handbooks described earlier. It should be remembered, too, that AID has disseminated a number of specialized publications, such as the handbooks entitled *Modernizing Government Revenue Administration, Modernizing Government Budget Administration,* and *Improving the Public Service through Training.* Moreover, AID's public administration division maintains an information service which collects technical reports from around the world and circulates them to the agency's public administration advisors "in the field." The bulk of these resources have been produced by AID personnel themselves and by management specialists and professors under contract to the agency.[14]

The AID administrative doctrine mentioned above should be seen in the broader context of the overall foreign aid program which seeks to provide assistance "to help strengthen the forces of freedom by aiding peoples of less developed friendly countries of the world to develop their resources and improve their living

13. For convenience the Agency for International Development is used to refer to all its predecessor agencies. See *International Cooperation Administration Manual,* Order No. 2611.1, "Nature of the ICA Programs in Public Administration"; Order No. 2621.1, "Objectives of Overseas Public Administration Programs"; Order No. 2631.1, "Methods of Providing Technical Assistance in Public Administration Overseas"; Order No. 2651.1, "Philosophy of the ICA Program of Overseas Technical Assistance in Public Administration": all dated June 13, 1960.

14. Department of State, Agency for International Development, Office of Technical Cooperation and Research, Institutional and Social Development Service, "List of Public Administration Publications of AID," December, 1966.

standards, to realize their aspirations for justice, education, dignity and respect as individual human beings, and to establish responsible governments."[15] The United States recognizes that the survival of its free institutions ultimately depends on peace based "on wider recognition of the dignity and interdependence of men" and on "a worldwide atmosphere of freedom." Through foreign aid the United States also deems it "a primary necessity, opportunity, and responsibility" to help "make a historic demonstration that economic growth and political democracy can go hand in hand to the end that an enlarged community of free, stable, and self-reliant countries can reduce world tensions and insecurity."[16]

Accordingly, AID declares that its overseas technical assistance in public administration "is an integral element in U.S. activities abroad."[17] It "is designed to assist co-operating governments in using their resources more effectively in a manner which will both *protect the public interest* and will advance personal freedoms."[18] AID assumes that its perceived deficiencies of the administrative systems of developing countries are "a critical barrier to economic development and a potential threat to political stability."[19] Thus, to begin with, AID seeks to impress upon the leaders of aid-receiving or co-operating countries its assumed causal connection between effective public administration on the one hand and economic development and political stability on the other. AID would like to have those leaders share its faith that the administrative deficiences can be remedied—as, claims AID, the United States and other countries have been able to demonstrate—and that these successful foreign experiences can help the leaders attain their aspirations for their country.

Public administration is broadly conceived by AID. Its manual states: "Public Administration is concerned with not only methods, techniques and principles of management, but also attitudes, social relationships, value judgments, and behavioral pat-

15. Foreign Assistance Act of 1966, Public Law 89–583 (80 Stat. 795), Sec. 102.
16. *Ibid.*
17. *ICA Manual,* Order No. 2631.1, p. 1.
18. *ICA Manual,* Order No. 2611.1, p. 1.
19. *ICA Manual,* Order No. 2651.1, p. 1.

terns."[20] Denying that public administration is an end in itself, its suggested relation to the goals of national development is nevertheless left vague, or, rather, assumed. There seems to be the implication that whatever those goals may be, the basic objective of the agency's overseas program in public administration is "to assist governments in improving the quality of their operations both at the national and local level."[21] It is admitted that assistance has so far been concentrated on the central government agencies, to the relative neglect of local governments. A twofold emphasis has been intended: "*modernization* of administrative practices and procedures of government and . . . the development and application of *sound* management concepts."[22]

In stressing the advisory nature of technical assistance in public administration, AID points up its concern with "the development of people" and its aim to "help governments help themselves."[23] Although diplomatically proper and necessary, certain of its disavowals are sure to evoke a smile from knowing officials in the aided country, if not their disbelief about some inconsistencies with other stated goals and values of United States foreign aid. The manual assures all and sundry that public administration programs "do not . . . encroach upon the sovereignty of the cooperating country." Why? Because those programs "are not concerned with changing the basic form of a government, nor do they attempt to substitute the judgment of U.S. technical assistance for that of responsible country officials." They are "advisory services only" (p. 1). In any event, as already mentioned, they are designed to help the people and their governments to help themselves.

Elsewhere, however, the newly inducted public administration adviser is instructed to orient himself to the political and economic facts of the country of his assignment and contact the corresponding sections of the United States Embassy. He is explicitly reminded thus:

20. *ICA Manual*, Order No. 2631.1, p. 1.
21. *ICA Manual*, Order No. 2621.1, p. 1.
22. *Ibid.*, italics mine.
23. *ICA Manual*, Order No. 2611.1, p. 1.

> In the final analysis the mission of all [AID] programs is political. This can be especially true of work directly with the administrative machinery of cooperating governments where effective government administration can make an important contribution to political stability and internal security. In fact, it is vital that all efforts in this area be kept in step with those being carried on by the political and economic elements of the Embassy staff.[24]

Farther on in the same document the beginning public administration adviser is told that it is his job "to help see to it that [the changes being introduced] are appropriate for the country concerned and realistically related to its future growth and development along lines which tend to broaden the range of *personal freedom,* promote *economic and social opportunity,* and which can be expected to contribute to the growth of *political democracy*" (p. 18). In contrast to the gingerly disclaimers above, the recruit is aroused and exhorted: "In other words, you can take pride in the knowledge that you are playing on the side of history and, in fact, helping to make it" (p. 18).

Nowhere in the manual are "modern" and "sound" administrative concepts, practices, and procedures described or defined. This omission is most likely traceable to an unstated assumption that what are regarded as progressive and workable in American public administration are, *ipso facto,* "modern" and "sound." Implicitly, therefore, the reshaping of existing administrative systems in the underdeveloped countries largely in the image of familiar American models is roughly *the* process of administrative modernization. Given the accent on administrative modernization, and its underlying assumptions, the AID manual specifies the "general objectives" and the related means for achieving them, as follows:

> A. The development and application of sound management concepts by assisting a government:
>
> 1. Appraise its human resources for management and establish plans and arrangements that will generally provide a

24. International Cooperation Administration, Public Administration Division, "Orientation Papers for Public Administration Advisors and Technicians," No. 1, "Improving Public Administration in the Newly Developing Areas of the World," March 1961, p. 13.

sufficient supply of management talent to meet the needs of the government;

2. Develop adequate training and educational institutions devoted to the expansion of managerial skills through in-service training methods and business and public administration educational programs;

3. Establish general appreciation among government officials of the value and need for continuous attention to management improvement;

4. Encourage the growth and recognition of professional standards of conduct among the public service; and

5. Stimulate public support and understanding for sound public administration.

B. The modernization of administrative procedures and practices by providing assistance in the development of:

1. Adequate government organization and staff competence for planning and effectuating country economic and social development plans;

2. An effective focal point for continuous attention to management improvement within the government;

3. A soundly designed and administered system for financial planning and administration, covering taxation, revenue collection, disbursement practices, tariffs customs administration, public debt management, capital accumulation, banking, foreign trade and related matters;

4. A competent, honest, adequately paid, properly motivated and well-managed civil service with high prestige;

5. A sound system of budget formulation and execution, supported by effective systems of fiscal control, accounting, auditing and reporting;

6. Soundly designed and administered central statistical services;

7. Efficiently organized and managed ministries and other government agencies, particularly in the areas to which U.S. assistance is directed;

8. Efficient staff and administrative support for legislative and judicial systems;

9. Effective specialized technical government services in fields such as postal and communication systems, standards bureau, meteorology, land mapping and title recording systems, coinage, patents, and other services of government to business and industry;

10. Proper allocation of functions and effective work relationships between the central government and local government units; and
11. Efficiently organized and operated local government.[25]

Sequentially, AID conceives of its tasks of administrative modernization as consisting of the following steps: (1) determining the extent of understanding and interest among key officials in the co-operating country; (2) identifying major administrative problems and determining priorities in their solutions; (3) providing needed support for administrative improvement; and (4) establishing continuing support for administrative reform.[26]

The initial step is intended to ascertain what further enlightenment and reassurance may be needed by indigenous leaders in and outside the government in regard to administrative modernization and its positive consequences for their country, and, presumably, for themselves as well. The usual devices at this point are observation trips to the United States and one or more third-countries, attendance at consultation meetings and conferences, discussions with outstanding foreign specialists or with leaders and experts in the co-operating country itself, and the dissemination of public administration literature. The diagnostic and priority-setting step usually assumes the form of organization and management surveys which may be government-wide or limited to particular agencies or levels of government. Rather than be confined to the usually narrow scope of administrative surveys, consideration is to be given to "constitutional provisions, policies, legislation, or other traditional and customary practices requiring attention before administrative reform may be developed" (p. 3). The survey may be undertaken by a body of country officials, with or without AID or other outside technical advice. Managerial manpower studies may be also carried out. In any event, the surveys and studies must offer a plan of action to improve public administration.

AID support of the induced, as well as spontaneous, action proposals takes the form of joint projects designed "to increase the

25. *ICA Manual,* Order No. 2621.1, pp. 1–2.
26. *ICA Manual,* Order No. 2631.1, pp. 2–5.

ability of local officials to carry on their own administrative reforms" (p. 3). Actually, reports indicate that the areas of technical assistance are fairly uniform from one country to another: these are economic planning, budgetary administration, tax administration, personnel management, and organization and methods analysis—involving conventional American ideas and methods—as well as university-level education for public and business administration, and statistical services. Technical services are rendered by AID or other United States government staff, individual consultants, management consulting firms, research institutions, or university contract personnel. Training is part of every advisory service project. Like the United Nations AID has established new training institutions for the long-range administrative needs of the co-operating country. In their activities overseas, public administration advisers are urged to co-ordinate with all other aid resources available.

Three methods are prescribed to help insure the viability and progress of administrative reform. The first goes under the awkward heading of "Establishing the Value of the Technical or Educational Developments in Administration" (p. 4). The goal is to achieve active indorsement and support of administrative reform within the officialdom on the basis of their understanding and acceptance of the "new values and benefits" (p. 4). Periodic conferences on administrative improvement and applied academic research are to be encouraged. The second method is to organize professional and public support for administrative reform. Officials and business leaders are to be encouraged "to interpret the purposes and benefits of administrative reforms to the public" (p. 5). Alongside, officials are to be encouraged "to seek professional recognition of their field of interest, to seek support for the growth of professional associations, and to contribute to the issuance of professional literature" (p. 5). The third method is to extend to the international sphere the professional recognition attained in the co-operating country. This may be done through participation in conferences abroad, sponsorship of international meetings at home, supporting United Nation's activities in public administration, and the loan of administrative specialists by the co-operating country to other developing countries or to the United Nations.

In official AID literature the caution is often enough sounded that administrative changes must be tailored to fit differing local situations. As the manual states: "Each situation must be clearly analysed and evaluated, and a program of assistance specifically designed to meet the local situation" (p. 1). In introducing modifications of existing institutions and techniques or outright innovations, "a multiple and balanced approach" is required. This cryptic admonition is left unexplained, except in the succeeding clause, which says that this particular approach has the twin virtue of assuring that "solving one problem does not create others of equal or greater importance, and . . . that assistance in public administration is responsive to and is in turn supported by other U.S. technical assistance and resources" (p. 1). AID has been humble in acknowledging the lessons of success and failure in the admitted "trial and error" way in which it had to undertake its "novel" operation "of trying to adapt United States practices to conditions in the host country."[27] In its orientation paper, entitled "Improving Public Administration in the Newly Developing Areas of the World," AID annotates ten such lessons which the prospective public administration adviser is asked to heed as one who would soon "work in a culture based on a different set of social values than that upon which American civilization is based."[28] Thus far, however, there is much to support Weidner's conclusion concerning United States and United Nations technical assistance alike, namely: "In practice visiting technicians, experts, and professors have provided strikingly similar advice and assistance, country to country. . . . There has been pragmatic application, but only within a small range. It has been a pragmatism of what part of Western public administration to introduce."[29]

Seven years after the 1960 "codification" of AID administrative doctrine, the agency thought it was time to update itself. The

27. ICA, Orientation Paper No. 1.
28. *Ibid.*, pp. 1–22.
29. Edward W. Weidner, *Technical Assistance in Public Administration Overseas: The Case for Development Administration* (Chicago, 1964), pp. 158–159.

whole elaborate procedure of consultations, discussions, and clearances was repeated. The resulting manual order, labeled "Public Administration Guidelines,"[30] is less than half as long as the manual orders discussed above, and it incorporates important parts of the old content in only slightly different wording.

One significant change in the 1967 version of AID administrative doctrine, as embodied in the agency manual, is the emphasis on "development administration," curiously without once using that popular term at all.[31] Another is the open reference to "political development" as an objective. Apparently in response to the justifiable criticism that public administration technical assistance was being divorced from the substance of policy and programs, the new manual order begins by stating: "The objective of the U.S. program of technical assistance in public administration is to assist governments in creating or improving the institutions needed to develop and execute plans for social, economic, and political development."[32] Indeed, it is acknowledged that public administration "takes its direction as much from the substantive program in a given country as from public administration theory" (p. 1). It is recognized that public administration technical assistance performs a "supporting role . . . to sectoral programs, e.g. agriculture, education, health, urbanization (including housing), industrial development, human resources development, the private sector, and labor" (p. 1).

In a manner that would warm the heart of the public administration scholar who regards his field as the vital center of politics, AID's concern in public administration is given its most embracing definition. Thus, public administration is deemed to encompass: (1) "the total structure of government organization objec-

30. *AID Manual,* Order No. 1612.70, "Public Administration Guidelines," March 14, 1967.

31. For definitions of the concept of "development administration" see Weidner, *Technical Assistance in Public Administration Overseas,* pp. 200–208; International Institute of Administrative Sciences, "Programme for Training and Education in 'Development Administration' " (undated, mimeographed); Merle Fainsod, "The Structure of Development Administration," in Irving Swerdlow (ed.), *Development Administration* (Syracuse, N.Y., 1963), p. 2; George F. Gant, "A Note on Applications of Development Administration," in John D. Montgomery and Arthur Smithies (eds.), *Public Policy,* XV (1966), 199–212.

32. *AID Manual,* Order No. 1612.70, p. 1.

tives, functional responsibilities, staffing requirements, and overall effectiveness"; and (2) "the executive, legislative, and judicial branches of the central government, as well as local government units at all levels" (p. 1).

The goals of advancing political democracy and free enterprise or capitalism are evident in the new manual order. Specific reference is made to Title IX of the Foreign Assistance Act of 1966 whose title is "Utilization of Democratic Institutions in Development." The pertinent portion of this provision states: "emphasis shall be placed on assuring maximum participation in the task of economic development on the part of the people of the developing countries, through encouragement of democratic private and local government institutions."[33] Accordingly, three of the six guidelines in selecting priorities among prospective public administration projects are: (1) "motivating government officials for the continuing improvement of operations and services, and stimulation of demand and support among the citizenry of the country for responsive and effective public administration"; (2) "improving local self-government and the degree of social justice available to the people"; and (3) "exploiting opportunities to strengthen management of the private sector and encourage its growth."[34]

As in United Nations technical assistance in public administration, the paramountcy of training is underscored by AID: "The key to successful technical assistance is training." But, presumably reflecting the lessons of experience in many an emerging state, a procedural innovation is suggested: "Indoctrination at the executive level should precede training at the technical level to develop a receptive climate for change" (p. 3). To complement training, a research capability is to be built into local universities and governmental institutes.

A whole new section on evaluation is included in the 1967 manual order. The criteria for evaluation of projects are to be: "U.S. objectives, their support of other U.S. activities, the effec-

33. Foreign Assistance Act of 1966, Title IX, Sec. 281. See Braibanti's chapter in this volume, esp. pp. 11–21.

34. *AID Manual,* Order No. 1612.70, pp. 1–2.

tiveness of the methods and techniques used in their implementation, and the understanding, support, and use of the institution by the host government . . ." (pp. 4–5). Lest these standards prove too difficult to apply, "a clearly defined, comprehensive, realistic and time-phased work plan" (p. 5), jointly developed by AID public administration advisers and their counterparts, should serve as the foundation for project evaluation.

III. Administrative Doctrine as Propositions

Even a cursory interpretation of the normative content, theoretical validity and practical utility of administrative doctrine is aided by recasting some of its content in the form of propositions. When we do this, a number of propositions emerge stating relationships among variables of varying levels of generality and abstraction, and therefore of differing amenability to verification.[35] Once so transformed their underlying assumptions can also be more readily discovered. For convenience and concreteness, we shall engage in this exercise using only AID administrative doctrine, illustrating the relevance of some of its content to public administration technical assistance in the Philippines. It so happens that in the Philippines the United Nations has not supported any public administration project, so officially identified, although it has assigned experts in the country in such related activities as community development, statistics, and planning, and awarded nine public administration fellowships to Filipinos.[36]

At the highest level of objectives and generality would be these propositions:

1. Public administration technical assistance (as part of the total United States assistance program) contributes to international peace, the promotion of human dignity, and a worldwide atmosphere of freedom.

35. For an instructive exploration of the strategy and tactics of proposition-building in the discipline, see Glenn D. Paige, *Proposition-Building in the Study of Comparative Administration* (Chicago, 1964).

36. For cumulative aid received by the Philippines from the United States, the United Nations, and other foreign sources, see National Economic Council, Office of Foreign Aid Coordination, *Annual Report on the Foreign AID Programs in the Philippines, FY 1966* (Manila, 1966).

2. Public administration technical assistance contributes to the national security, the general welfare, and the preservation of the free institutions of the United States.

3. Public administration technical assistance contributes to the American demonstration that economic growth and political democracy can go hand in hand in developing countries.

From official sources relating to the total AID program in the Philippines we can derive this proposition:

4. Public administration technical assistance helps to build a strong Filipino economy which will mean, for the United States, a bastion of strength in the free world.[37]

Obviously, these propositions are almost impossible to test, not only because the independent variable is so small a force in the total configuration of independent variables which impinge in yet unclear ways on the dependent variables, but also because the latter are so vague and complex in themselves. The "validity" of these propositions must be taken on faith. Indeed, they are simply postulated as "true" by policy-makers and technical assistance participants. This fact does not necessarily minimize their doctrinal or ideological value, however.

Two additional propositions are:

5. Public administration technical assistance aids the governments of emerging states in utilizing their resources more effectively, and in a manner that will protect the public interest and advance personal freedom in these states.

6. Public administration technical assistance helps the Philippines to increase its economic capability, achieve political and social stability, and resist communism.[38]

These propositions assume that rationality, democracy, and anti-communism are values that are already regnant among the elite of the emerging states, or, if not, that they could be enhanced or introduced through public administration technical assistance, among other programs of United States foreign aid. A basic thesis

37. From United States International Cooperation Administration/Philippines, *ICA in the Philippines* (Manila, undated, no pagination), which states in part: "In essence the partnership . . . is to build a secure, domestic Philippine economy, which in turn means, for America, a bastion of strength in the free world."

38. *Ibid.*

is that "modern" and "sound" administrative technology developed in the United States is transferable or adaptable to the administrative systems of developing countries and that this diffusion will improve their efficiency and effectiveness. Again, the dimensions of the variables being related to each other, although less grand than those considered above, preclude measurement. Where the democratic values are heavily diluted, if not wholly rejected, practical attempts to make administrative modernization projects promote these values could lead to considerable difficulties with authoritarian and nationalistic elites. On the other hand, of course, the often implicit and indirect advancement of the values through seemingly innocuous administrative projects usually avoids controversy and resistance to change. Much of public administration technical assistance must realistically expect long-range rather than immediate returns in the institutionalization of administrative doctrine.

A further proposition is:

> 7. Public administration technical assistance will improve the capacity of host governments to develop and implement plans for social, economic, and political development.

This proposition carries the efficiency and effectiveness objective one step further by identifying the broad governmental goals to which it is intentionally instrumental. This is a less unmanageable level of correlation. However, perhaps it is only when public administration technical assistance is seen as individual component projects and evaluated in terms of limited project objectives that particular effects may be reasonably attributed to technical assistance inputs. Even here the selection of indicators is no mean task. Understandably, therefore, most evaluation attempts so far have been impressionistic and rhetorical, usually in the form of official reports of accomplishments and testimonial speeches.

A catchall set of propositions might consist of specific projects involving institution-building or new administrative techniques as independent variables and, as dependent variables, the general and specific objectives they are intended to help realize. For the Philippines such a formulation could be schematically stated, as shown in Table 3.

Table 3. ***Aid-Assisted Public Administration Projects in the Philippines****

Independent variables (Technical assistance inputs)	*Dependent variables (Expected technical assistance outputs)*
Project: *Government Management and Procedures Improvement* (FY 1953–56)	
Establish organization and management offices to provide administrative technical assistance to departments and agencies; train 20 participants; commodities. (Total U.S. contribution: $69,000 TC funds.)	Improve organization and management, encourage better planning and more timely decision-making.
Project: *Government Organization and Management* (FY 1954–56)	
Technical assistance in organization, management, and procedures rendered by the AID mission's Public Administration Division (but not chargeable to specific projects); 11 man-years of technical services and train 12 participants. (Total U.S. contribution: $160,000 TC funds.)	Bridge the gaps between public administration projects and between those projects and other phases of the technical assistance program.
Project: *Government Survey and Reorganization Commission* (FY 1955–58)	
Reorganization of structure and procedures of several departments and agencies, reorganization of certain departments; 18 man-years of technical services. (Total U.S. contribution: $265,000 TC funds.)	Improve the economy and efficiency of the executive branch; strengthen the planning, coordinating, and administrative facilities of the president and department heads.
Project: *Wage and Position Classification* (FY 1952–55)	
Wage and position classification survey; 2 man-years of technical services, train 7 participants, and 21 man-years of contractual services with Louis J. Kroeger and Associates. (Total U.S. contribution: $443,000 TC funds.)	Establish a continuing system for standardizing salaries and classifying positions ("Equal Pay for Equal Work," comparability with salaries in private enterprises, and management tool).
Project: *Bureau of Lands Modernization* (FY 1953–55)	
Sixteen man-years of contract services, train 4 participants, and commodities to assist the Bureau of Lands. (Total U.S. contribution: $703,000 TC funds.)	Intensify the survey classification and subdivision of public lands, and issue of titles in conjunction with program to increase agricultural productivity.
Project: *Civil Service Improvement* (FY 1956–59)	
Improve regulations and operations of the Civil Service Commission; 10 man-years of technical services, commodities, and train 5 participants. (Total U.S. contribution: $174,120 TC funds.)	Increase the efficiency of government personnel practices and strengthen the merit system.

Table 3 *continued*

Independent variables (Technical assistance inputs)	*Dependent variables (Expected technical assistance outputs)*
Project: *Revenue Administration Improvement* (*FY 1956–59*)	
Improve organization and procedures for tax collection and enforcement; 31 man-years of technical services, train 76 participants, and commodities for the Department of Finance. (Total U.S. contribution: $629,000 TC funds.)	Improve revenue collections for financing the expanding government operations and activities.
Project: *Modernization of Budgeting and Accounting* (*FY 1952–60*)	
Contract services of Booz, Allen and Hamilton Co. (25 man-years), 7 man-years of technical advisory assistance, train 35 participants, and commodities; organize fiscal policy planning staff, introduce performance budgeting, and improve accounting and auditing policies and systems. (Total U.S. contribution: $1,390,000 TC funds.)	Develop a national fiscal policy and staff and a related cyclical national budget, better allocation, and control of plan by administrators and legislators.
Project: *National Auditing* (*FY 1960–62*)	
Installation of a system of program audits in the national government; installation of internal audit units in 40 agencies of the national government; further development and refinement of fiscal methods and systems in the General Auditing Office; provide 2 man-years of technical services, train 7 participants, and commodities. (Total U.S. contribution: $96,000 TC funds.)	Improve financial controls in the Philippine government.
Project: *Rehabilitation of Bureau Printing* (*FY 1955–56*)	
Rehabilitation by providing 1 man-year of technical services and commodities. (Total U.S. contribution: $145,000 TC funds.)	Enable the Bureau of Printing to undertake the required government printing.
Project: *Government Procurement* (*FY 1954–56*)	
Provide 7 man-years of technical assistance and train 1 participant. (Total U.S. contribution: $91,000 TC funds.)	Overcome delays in government procurement, improve procurement and supply management, co-ordinate purchasing and supply functions for commodities required by AID-assisted projects.
Project: *Institute of Public Administration* (*FY 1952–55*)	
Establish teaching, training, research, and consultation institute in the University of the Philippines; provide 12 man-years of contract services, train 11 participants, and commodities. (Total U.S. contribution: $406,000 TC funds.)	Provide the government with competent administrators, research on governmental and administrative problems, and consultation services to government officials.

Table 3 *continued*

Independent variables (Technical assistance inputs)	*Dependent variables (Expected technical assistance outputs)*
Project: *Statistical Survey* (*FY 1954–59*)	
Provide 14 man-years of technical services and train 12 participants. (Total U.S. contribution: $205,000 TC funds)	Produce statistics on manpower, population, and economic activities; establish reporting systems to keep statistics current; preparation for the 1960 national censuses.
Project: *Economic Policy Development* (*FY 1953–57*)	
Assist the NEC in developing a comprehensive, long-range economic development program, and in the formulation of economic policy, staff organization, and recruitment of professional personnel; provide 11 man-years of technical services and train 14 participants for the National Economic Council. (Total U.S. contribution: $255,000 TC funds.)	Improve the capacity of the National Economic Council to formulate economic plans and policies as the highest economic advisory body to the president.
Project: *National Media Production Center* (*FY 1952–60*)	
Assist the National Media Production Center as the major agency to develop and disseminate audio-visual and printed educational information; provide 31 man-years of technical services, train 1 participant, and commodities. (Total U.S. contributions: $564,000 TC funds.)	Enable the government to carry out programs of mass communication in support of government activities.

Source: Based on Agency for International Development, "106 Completed Projects (FY 1951–1965), AID and Predecessor Agencies" (Washington, 1965).

Alternatively, we might extract two sets of hypotheses from the official documents. One of them would relate public administration technical assistance to political-administrative doctrine, specifically the values of merit and competence, efficiency and economy, rationality and planning, and bureaucratic responsibility and responsiveness. Applying the development administration concept, the other set of hypotheses would relate public administration technical assistance to the accomplishment of particular governmental programs, e.g., rice production and road-building. In the following section we shall use the first approach in evaluating the Filipino response to American administrative (and political) doctrine, many elements of which actually began to be diffused some fifty years before AID.

A noteworthy theoretical and methodological approach to the diffusion of administrative doctrine is being developed by the Inter-University Research Program in Institution-Building which was cited at the beginning of this chapter. Focusing on specific organizations as channels and innovators of administrative and program changes, the program has identified three clusters of institution-building variables for analysis: (1) the *institutional* variables which attempt "to explain the systematic behavior of the institution," which include leadership, doctrine, program, resources, and internal structure; (2) the *linkages* variables or "the interdependencies which exist between an institution and other relevant parts of the society"; and (3) *institutionality* "as the end state . . . an evaluative standard for appraising the success of institution-building efforts."[39] Four pilot studies of institution-building have produced refinements of the original concepts and variables and a number of testable propositions have resulted from their review.[40]

IV. The Filipino Response to Exogenous Administrative Doctrine

The Filipino political system in comparative perspective

The emerging political institutions in the Philippines provide an important framework for any evaluation of the Filipino response to efforts at inducing administrative reform.[41] As conceived by the Filipinos in their Constitution, their government should be one "that shall embody their ideals, conserve and develop the patrimony of the nation, promote the general welfare, and secure to themselves and their posterity the blessings of independence under a regime of justice, liberty and democracy."[42] Also affirmed in the Constitution are the principles of popular sovereignty and

39. Esman, *Institution-Building Concepts*, pp. 3–6. Cf. the seven indices for measuring institutionalization proposed in Braibanti's chapter in this volume, pp. 58–66.

40. Esman, *Institution-Building Concepts*, pp. 62–66.

41. For essays analyzing Filipino political institutions, see José V. Abueva and Raul P. de Guzman (eds.), *Foundations and Dynamics of Filipino Government and Politics* (Manila, 1967).

42. Preamble, Constitution of the Philippines.

republicanism, the unitary system, presidential government, separation of powers, and social justice. "In the interest of the national welfare and defense," the state is empowered to "establish and operate industries and means of transportation and communication" and to assume ownership of private utilities and enterprises.[43] In precept and practice the ideal of bureaucratic responsibility to the chief executive and the Congress is accepted by Filipinos in a way typically their own.

Since independence, in 1946, the legitimacy and stability of the Filipino political system have passed a series of tests.[44] Except for the Communist-Huk rebellion, which was checked in the early fifties, there has been no serious challenge to the authority of the national government. None of the cultural minorities has sought secession. In contrast to four other countries in Southeast Asia, the military in the Philippines has not only respected civilian supremacy but has also been regularly employed to insure free and honest elections. It has been used as well to suppress the Communist-Huk conspiracy and other lawless elements. Political and governmental processes have operated within constitutional bounds, thanks partly to the Supreme Court, which has been vigilant in restraining and reversing unconstitutional acts. Four times the incipient two-party system has seen the alternation of the major parties and the defeat of the incumbent president. Together with the turnover of legislators and local officials, this indicates a highly competitive politics. Accordingly, the people have a sense of democratic control over their leaders. Twice, the vice-president has succeeded to office upon the death of the president, with the full acceptance of political leaders and citizens alike.

Although articulate Filipinos have been severely critical of the malfunctioning of their democracy, available measures record its general approval by the people. During the Magsaysay administration (1954–57), 60 per cent of the respondents in a national survey said "yes" to this query: "In general, do you think that democracy is working out as well as could be expected in a nation

43. *Ibid.*, Art. XII, Sec. 6.
44. José V. Abueva, "Filipino Politics Since Independence," Manila *Times*, September 13–16, 1965.

such as the Philippines?"[45] Another survey, in 1963, reported that 71 per cent believed the government could help them solve their problems and that 58 per cent sensed the government had already begun to do so.[46] A study of "middle civil servants" in 1966 disclosed that "democratic ideals and institutions" were regarded by them as the second most highly prized object of national pride.[47]

Table 4 below shows the consensus among scholars in comparative politics concerning the Filipino political system, in relation to their judgments of other Southeast Asian political systems.

Almond and Coleman chose the Filipino polity as the type-model for "political democracy."[48] Such classification and description, or their equivalents, may be better appreciated against the arrays of developing countries which comprised the universe of some of the cited studies. Thus Almond and Coleman counted only seven Afro-Asian polities, including the Philippines, as "competitive," while classifying twenty-four Afro-Asian polities as "semi-competitive" and fifteen others as "authoritarian" (pp. 542, 564–567). Von der Mehden included the Philippines among the seven "two-party democratic states" within the larger class consisting of twenty-nine "competitive sytems," as against sixteen "semi-competitive systems" and thirty-eight "non-competitive sytems"—a universe of eighty-three states in the underdeveloped world.[49]

What is important for our analysis is that the Filipino polity may be regarded as manifesting many of the political values and institutions which have been assumed by both the United Nations and AID as prerequisite and/or terminal features of the kind of political and administrative systems they have been seeking to help bring about with their technical assistance programs.

45. Carl H. Lande, "Political Attitudes and Behavior in the Philippines," *Philippine Journal of Public Administration,* III (1959), 362.
46. Index, Inc., "A Study of the National Politico-Social Attitudes" (1963, typescript), pp. 25–27.
47. José V. Abueva, "Conditions of Administrative Development: Exploring Administrative Culture and Behavior in the Philippines," Comparative Administration Group Occasional Paper, (Bloomington, Ind., 1966), pp. 20–22.
48. Gabriel A. Almond and James S. Coleman (eds.), *The Politics of the Developing Areas* (Princeton, 1960), pp. 566–568.
49. *Ibid.,* Appendix.

Table 4. *Classifications of Political Systems in Southeast Asia*

	Almond and Coleman (1960)[a]		Von der Mehden (1964)[b]	Janowitz (1964)[c]		Heady (1966)[d]
Country	*Functional profiles*	*Degree of competitiveness*	*National ideology*	*Civil-military relations*	*Political roles of military*	*Political regime and bureaucracy*
Philippines	Political democracy	Competitive	Individualist democracy	Democratic-competitive	Mark of sovereignty	Polyarchal-competitive
Burma	Tutelary democracy	Semicompetitive	Guided democracy	Military oligarchy	Political ruling group	Bureaucratic elite
Cambodia	Conservative oligarchy	Authoritarian	Collective democracy	Authoritarian personal control	Mark of sovereignty	Traditional autocratic
Indonesia	Tutelary democracy	Semicompetitive	Guided democracy	[Military-civil coalition]	[Dominant political bloc]	Bureaucratic elite
Laos	Conservative oligarchy	Authoritarian	Mixed democracy	[Authoritarian personal control]	[Mark of sovereignty]	Traditional autocratic
Malaysia	Poltical democracy	Competitive	Individualist democracy	Democratic-competitive	Mark of sovereignty	Polyarchal competitive
Thailand	Modernizing oligarchy	Semicompetitive	Guided democracy	Military oligarchy	Political ruling group	Bureaucratic elite
Vietnam (North)	[Modernizing oligarchy][e]	[Authoritarian]	Proletarian democracy	[Authoritarian mass party]	[Mark of sovereignty]	Communist totalitarian
Vietnam (South)	Tutelary democracy	Semicompetitive	Guided democracy	[Military oligarchy]	Political ruling group	[Bureaucratic elite]

a. Gabriel A. Almond and James S. Coleman (eds.), *The Politics of the Developing Areas* (Princeton, 1960), pp. 542, 564–567. See pp. 566–576 for description of the typology.

b. Fred R. von der Mehden, *Politics of the Developing Nations* (Englewood Cliffs, N.J., 1964), Appendix. See pp. 122–127 for description of the typology.

c. Morris Janowitz, *The Military in the Political Development of the New States: An Essay in Comparative Analysis* (Chicago, 1964), pp. 10–11, 20–21. See pp. 5–7 for description of the typology.

d. Ferrel Heady, *Public Administration: A Comparative Perspective* (Englewood Cliffs, N.J., 1966). See pp. 74–97 for description of the typology.

e. Classifications in brackets are the author's.

Background of administrative reform

Since the beginning of American colonial rule in 1898, through the period since independence, kindred political and administrative norms have been authoritatively prescribed for all concerned to observe. The first Philippine Commission, in a proclamation on April 9, 1899, specified the following goals and norms among others for American governance of the islands: (1) "a wise, just, stable, effective and economical administration of public affairs,"

(2) "an honest and effective civil service," (3) "a pure, speedy and effective administration of justice . . . whereby the evils of delay, corruption and exploitation will be effectively eradicated," (4) "the collection and application of taxes and revenues . . . upon a sound, honest and economical basis," and (5) "reforms in all departments of the government . . . , conformably to right and justice, . . . that will satisfy the well-founded demands and the highest aspirations of the Philippine people. . . ."[50] As if with the prescience of public administration technical assistance half a century hence, President William McKinley exhorted the members of the second Philippine Commission that they were to establish a government

> designed not for our satisfaction, or for the expression of our theoretical views, but for the happiness, peace, and prosperity of the people of the Philippine Islands, and the measures adopted should be made to conform to their customs, their habits and even their prejudices, to the fullest extent consistent with the accomplishment of the indispensable requisites of just and effective government.[51]

Ensuing organic acts of the United States Congress and legislation passed by the all-Filipino legislatures embodied the American-introduced concepts of administrative "efficiency," "economy," and "responsiveness." The last concept was progressively emphasized by liberal American governors-general and by Filipino nationalists who wished by their proven capacity for democratic rule to hasten the day of the promised independence. Beginning in 1913 the bureaucracy was rapidly Filipinized. Comprehensive government reorganizations were carried out in 1905, 1916, and 1932. The influence of the American civil service reform movement at the turn of the century lingered through the first three decades of American rule in the islands. Bolstered by

50. *Ibid.*, Appendix, pp. 979–980; Dean C. Worcester, *The Philippines Past and Present* (New York, 1921), one volume edition. For a history of administrative reorganization leading to the Government Survey and Reorganization Commission of 1954–56, see Leandro A. Viloria, *U.S. Technical Assistance in Public Administration in the Philippines: Establishing a Management Improvement Program* (unpublished doctoral dissertation, Syracuse University, 1962), chap. 4.

51. "The President's Instructions to the Commission," *Annual Report of the War Department for the Fiscal Year June 30, 1901*, Public Laws and Resolutions Panel by the Philippine Commission (Washington, 1901), pp. 1–10.

the accumulating experience of the Filipinos, the framers of the Constitution in the mid-thirties decided to devote a whole article to the establishment of a civil service system based on merit.[52] The impact of intensive American "technical assistance in political development and public administration"—to use the current terminology—reverberated in the words of Manuel L. Quezon in his inaugural as president of the Commonwealth of the Philippines, on November 15, 1935: "We shall build a government that will be just, honest, efficient, and strong so that the foundations of the coming Republic may be firm and enduring—a government, indeed, that must satisfy not only the passing needs of the hour but also the exacting demands of the future."[53]

Underscoring the need for continuity, but also revealing the essential conservatism of the nation's political elite, Quezon continued to say: "We do not have to tear down the existing institutions in order to give way to statelier structure. There will be no violent changes from the established order of things, except to carry into effect the innovations contemplated by the Constitution."[54] These thoughts gain greater meaning when set against the sporadic uprisings of Filipino radicals and their desperate followers in the provinces around Manila.[55] Nonetheless, somewhat in self-defense and partly inspired by the New Deal in Washington, the Commonwealth government enacted some progressive social, labor, and agrarian legislation.[56]

Following President Franklin D. Roosevelt's Committee on Administrative Management, (the Brownlow Committee), a Philippine Government Survey Board conducted a reorganization study (1936–38) whose implementation clarified and bolstered President Quezon's role as the chief executive: the highest policy-making official and the general manager of the bureaucracy. Now he would be assisted in his policy initiating, directing, co-ordinating, and controlling activities by a new Budget Commission

52. Art. XI.
53. *Messages of the President* (rev. ed.; Manila, 1938), I, 13.
54. *Ibid.*
55. See David R. Sturtevant, "Sakdalism and Philippine Radicalism," *Journal of Asian Studies,* XXI (1962), 199–213; Joseph R. Hayden, *The Philippines: A Study in National Development* (New York, 1945), chap. 15.
56. José V. Abueva, "Bridging the Gap Between the Elite and the People in the Philippines," *Philippine Journal of Public Administration,* VIII (1964), 332.

charged with organization and management on top of its primary fiscal functions. Through this strategic office the President could initiate administrative reforms, classify positions, and standardize salaries.[57] The basis had thus been laid for presidential initiative in effecting administrative reforms when World War II rudely interrupted the transition from Commonwealth to Republic.

Within two months after independence, President Manuel A. Roxas obtained congressional authority to undertake a government-wide reorganization. His announced objectives were to rationalize "the entire bureaucratic structure of the Philippine Government" so as to achieve "maximum efficiency and maximum economy."[58] Barely two years following completion of the Roxas reorganization, however, another major reorganization was in progress, this time at the behest of President Elpidio Quirino who succeeded upon Roxas' death in 1948. Quirino's intentions were variations on a familiar theme. "It is clear that we must reorganize our administrative machinery," he said, "with a view to securing greater efficiency, the improvement of the public service, and economy of means and effort in the discharge of the government's responsibilities, in order to make that machinery more responsive to public need within the limits of our available resources."[59]

What impelled Quirino to embark on another reorganization so soon after the one implemented by his predecessor? Aside from the pride of paternity and the opportunities for patronage which large-scale organizational changes provide a new president, Quirino had urgent and compelling reasons. He had just been elected president in his own right in a national election that was then, and up to now, considered the most notorious Filipino election for its fraudulence and violence. Amidst bitter recrimination and an abortive "revolt" in Batangas province, which symbolized the illegitimacy of Quirino's election in the eyes of some opposition leaders, the Communist-Huk rebellion was rapidly gaining momentum. The triumph of communism in China cast a dark shadow over Aisa.

57. *Executive Order* No. 25, April 25, 1936.

58. Republic of the Philippines, Reorganization Committee, *Report of the Reorganization Committee* (Manila, 1947), p. 2.

59. Inaugural Address, *Official Gazette,* XLV (December, 1949) 5382–5383.

Actually, as in the case of the Roxas reorganization, the outcome of Quirino's endeavor was unimpressive in terms of its avowed ends.[60] Understandably, deeply rooted official graft and corruption remained unchecked. Having no illusions that he could solve the nation's problems with the limited resources at his command, much less by mere organizational reshuffling, Quirino promptly sought American assistance. Opportunely, this was a time when the Communist takeover in China had American leaders worried over the fate of neighboring Asian countries and over America's strategic position in the cold war. Pertinent to the Philippine situation was Secretary of State Dean Acheson's diagnosis of the Nationalist Chinese debacle and its "lesson" for the threatened Communist subversion and penetration of other countries in the region. The spread of communism could not be stopped by military means, Acheson said, but rather by assistance "to develop a soundness of administration of [the] new governments and to develop their resources and their skills so that they are not subject to penetration either through ignorance, or because they believe false promises or because there is real distress in their areas."[61]

To lay the groundwork for economic aid and technical assistance, President Harry S. Truman sent an economic survey mission to the Philippines, which came to be known as the Bell Mission, after its chairman, Daniel W. Bell. At the root of the nation's difficulties, the Bell Mission reported, were inefficient production and very low incomes which led to the government's critical finances and the country's unfavorable international balance of payments.[62] The mission report contrasted official indecision and inaction, as well as private irresponsibility toward the lower income groups, with the evident awareness of Filipino leaders of the many problems plaguing the government and the economy.

The last two of the seven principal recommendations of the

60. See Quirino Austria, "Historical Background and Implementation of the Reorganization Plans of 1955–1956," *International Review of Administrative Sciences*, XXIII (1957), 291–317, esp. 308.

61. Quoted in Charles Wolf, Jr., *Foreign Aid: Theory and Practice in Southern Asia* (Princeton, 1960), p. 44.

62. United States Economic Survey Mission to the Philippines, *Report to the President of the United States* (Washington, October 9, 1950).

Bell Mission were directly concerned with public administration reforms and American technical assistance. Specifically, the following administrative reforms were urged upon the Philippine government: place the civil service on a merit basis; raise salaries; balance the budget; improve efficiency by supervisory training courses, job rotation, and staff assistance in administrative management; modernize fiscal administration to improve fiscal controls; insure efficiency and integrity in tax collection; and clarify functions, duties, and responsibilities of tax agencies. To facilitate these and other actions concerned with economic and social development, an American technical mission would help the Philippine government. To be included in the technical mission would be specialists in public administration, agriculture, industry, finance, and labor and social welfare.[63] The Bell Mission was emphatic on the crucial role of public administration in the total undertaking: "the success of the development program," it said, "may depend more on the efficiency and honesty of the public service than on any other factor."[64]

The recommended loans and grants of $250 million to be made available over a five-year period were "to be strictly conditioned on steps being taken by the Philippine government to carry out the recommendations [of the Bell Mission] . . . including the immediate enactment of tax legislation and other urgent reforms. . . ."[65] Among the other strings attached to the recommended assistance were supervision and control of United States funds by the American technical mission and the co-ordinated use of Philippine funds for development purposes.

In retrospect, the import of these sanctions becomes clear. America's former ward in the Pacific was in dire straits. The sentimental approach of the Philippines to its relations with its acknowledged benefactor—until then not effectively subject to question by a nationalist reappraisal—conditioned it to acquiescence. Only four years earlier, America had extracted equal rights for its citizens to exploit the natural resources and operate public utilities in the Philippines—an extraordinary condition for Ameri-

63. *Ibid.*, p. 100.
64. *Ibid.*, p. 97.
65. *Ibid.*, pp. 4–5.

can individual payments of war damages in excess of five hundred dollars which necessitated amendment of the Philippine Constitution. The concept of conditional assistance was predicated on the belief that the annual channeling of an average of $50 million in loans, grants, and technical advice would determine the realization of the far-reaching reforms sought in public policy, legislative and administrative behavior, and the activities of leaders in private enterprises. In a sense, it might even be said that America was now attempting anew to bring about some basic reforms in the relationships between government and citizens, landlord and tenant, management and labor, and in more basic attitudes toward the nation, government, law, taxes, and work which America was not able to, and could not alone, do in the more than forty years that it had sovereignty over the Filipinos.

Evolving Filipino administrative values, norms, and behavior

In our evaluation of how AID administrative doctrine was applied and how Filipinos responded to it, we shall limit ourselves to four officially professed "administrative values" as organizing criteria. As we stated in Section III, these are (1) merit and competence, (2) efficiency and economy, (3) rationality and planning, and (4) bureaucratic responsibility and responsiveness.[66] Not all the public administration projects enumerated in Table 3 above will be considered. It should be remembered that none of these projects has been evaluated in relation to our chosen criteria. They have all been assessed mainly, if not solely, for their accomplishments in terms of "project completion" and immediate effects. We can do no more here than speculate on some of their intermediate effects in the direction of our selected "administrative values." One way perhaps of appreciating the dimensions of what remains to be done is to intersperse each brief evaluation with some observations based partly upon a recent "panel survey" of fifty-two Filipino administrators conducted by the author.[67]

66. These values pervade the official literature of administrative reform in the United States, the United Nations, and the Philippines, as shown in quotations and references in this chapter.

67. Abueva, *Conditions of Administrative Development.*

Merit and competence. Among the AID-assisted projects aimed at these objectives were: the establishment of the University of the Philippines Institute of Public Administration, the improvement of the organization and operations of the Civil Service Commission, the setting up of the Wage and Position Classification Office, and the training abroad of more than 3,000 government officials (559 or about one-sixth of them in public administration).[68]

The Institute of Public Administration at the state University of the Philippines (now called the College of Public Administration) is widely regarded as one of the most successful centers of its kind in the underdeveloped world. This reputation rests upon its demonstrated viability, capability, and expansion since its formation in 1952. Established under a contract with the University of Michigan, with AID funds, the IPA has received substantial support from the Rockefeller and Ford foundations in addition to continuing government financing. The institute has conferred the master's degree in public administration on some two hundred government officials. It has trained more than two thousand government supervisors. Through the training of over three hundred training officers, the IPA has stimulated scores of government agency training programs. Its steady research output—which excels most other units in the University of the Philippines—has served teaching and training needs in public administration beyond its confines. Institute staff members have been called upon to assist administrators and legislators in their policy-making. The IPA now has a Philippine Executive Academy and a Local Government Center. It has also spearheaded an international body known as the Eastern Regional Organization for Public Administration (EROPA).

Like educational and training institutions around the globe, the IPA's ultimate contribution (to official competence and recognition of merit in the public service) remains a matter of conjecture. The impressive figures for graduates and trainees must be related to the immense problem of transferring values and

68. United States Agency for International Development/Philippines, Training Division, "Participant Training Program, FY 1952–1966" (October 30, 1966, mimeographed).

norms and translating technical skills and knowledge into the kinds of decisions and behavior that realize program objectives. One must also bear in mind the common Filipino predilection for prestigeful education and training as almost an end in itself. Although most IPA staff members are well qualified, their apparent success and reputation endanger their continued effectiveness because of the ever increasing demands for their services to the government. From its inception, the IPA has been hampered internally by confusion over its varied and conflicting values and roles, while being an integral unit of an institution of higher learning.

It is clear that AID-sponsored training abroad and AID-supported local training have given impetus to the professionalization of the public service. Separate organizations have been formed by bureau directors, personnel officers, training officers, budget officers, accountants, auditors, public relations officers, management analysts, legal officers, administrative officers, treasurers, assessors, and supply officers. In addition, there are a few inclusive associations, like the Society for Public Administration of the Philippines which sponsors the yearly celebration of "Public Administration Week" promulgated by the President. As already hinted above, most government agencies have instituted training programs. The example of the Institute of Public Administration has been emulated by a few other universities which have adopted public administration curricula. The trend in civil service examinations is also toward specialization.

However, the training and specialization of many officials, consequent upon AID technical assistance, are not being fully utilized because of the resistance to change of their administrative and political superiors and of citizens with whom they must deal.[69] While they are in a position to set professional standards,

69. A survey of returned Filipino AID participants contains these remarks: Something further can be done to help the participants become more effective change-agents for economic and social improvement. However, the points where action seems to be needed most are in the organizations in the Philippines which are devoted to carrying out these programs of economic and social development. To some extent making these organizations more effective users of foreign training probably means also bringing about necessary changes in the attitudes of those in the highest levels of governments, and in those parts of the public with which these organizations deal.

work for the improvement of public administration through their respective specialization, and give mutual encouragement to colleagues in the face of stubborn odds, these professional organizations may be expected to compete for rewards for their members, which may not be wholly beneficial to the government as a whole or the public. Organized civil servants who use their power for their own benefit could undermine the capacity of the bureaucracy when countervailing citizen groups cannot exert a moderating influence. Presently, the problem is probably more of professional inactivity and ineffectiveness than any self-serving propensity.

The Civil Service Law of 1959 was the culmination of an intensive reform process in which AID technical advisers and Filipino participants in AID technical assistance played major roles. The law was intended to minimize the rampant violations of the merit principle, to remedy deficiencies in personnel practices by modernizing them, and to codify the confusing amendments, executive and administrative orders, and interpretations pertaining to the civil service system. With the Bell Mission findings as point of departure, Filipino and American specialists assisted in personnel administration surveys sponsored by the Budget Commission, President Ramon Magsaysay's Committee on the Civil Service, the Government Survey and Reorganization Commission, and in the drafting of the legislation itself. AID-assisted institutions, such as the Institute of Public Administration, and some professional organizations of civil servants, whose members had received AID training directly or indirectly, were active in the congressional hearings. Revealingly, an analyst of the Civil Service Law discovered a striking parallel between its provisions and four value premises which Frederick Mosher regards as essential for a sound personnel system, namely: (1) the moral, good government, antipatronage premise; (2) the efficiency or profes-

U.S. trained participants are individuals in organizational groups which are operating units of Philippine society. Changes at any level must be related to the readiness to change of other parts of the social structure.

Institute of Social Research, University of Michigan, *Using U.S. Training in the Philippines: A Follow-Up Survey of Participants* (Ann Arbor, 1959), I, 12.

sional premise; (3) the improved and responsible management premise; and (4) the human relations premise.[70]

Enormous difficulties in implementing the Civil Service Law soon arose. To allay fears generated by reported mass layoff of non-eligibles, the President's office enabled the threatened employees to be retained. Temporary employees with less than five years of service were allowed to qualify for permanent tenure upon passing an examination. Little known to the public, President Carlos P. Garcia and the majority congressmen entered into a so-called "50–50 agreement" to share equally in filling some 1,800 new positions in the bureaucracy.[71] To implement this agreement between Malacañang and the House, the speaker appointed a screening committee. Actually, only the formality of the agreement was novel; majority legislators have always enjoyed ample patronage in the public service. Many months would pass before the President acted upon the civil service rules which the Civil Service Commission had promptly submitted to him to govern implementation of the Civil Service Law.

Our 1966 panel survey of "middle civil servants" suggests the tenacity and prevalence of practices that confound the laws and rules intended to promote competency and minimize spoils in the government. With remarkable consistency, most respondents agreed that (1) the two national attributes they were least proud of (objects of national shame) were "graft and corruption in government" and "political partisanship and interference," and that (2) the two principles or standards which, above all, should guide the conduct and administration of the government should be "honesty and integrity" and "merit and political non-interference."[72] In a society that puts a premium on kinship and personal reciprocity, it is not surprising that 40 per cent of the informants admitted their difficulty in refusing undeserving relatives and

70. Florencia S. Medina, "The Civil Service Act of 1949: Reform in the Philippine Civil Service" (unpublished M.P.A. thesis, University of the Philippines, 1960), p. 133.

71. Gregorio A. Francisco and Raul P. de Guzman, "The '50–50 Agreement': A Political-Administrative Case," *Philippine Journal of Public Administration,* IV (1960), 328–347.

72. Abueva, *Conditions of Administrative Development,* p. 30.

friends who seek jobs and other benefits from the government. More telling is the acceptance by about 80 per cent of the panel respondents of these two statements as essentially valid: (1) "In case of conflict between the merit system and the demands of their relatives, most officials would rather please their relatives"; (2) "The truth is that most officials would rather go around the merit system than antagonize a close friend or relative."[73]

Another administrative reform project calculated to enhance merit and competence—through adequate and equitable compensation and well-defined duties and responsibilities—was the establishment of the Wage and Position Classification Office (WAPCO) in the Budget Commission. Its slogan is "Equal pay for equal work." Whatever may be its contribution to rationality in administration, WAPCO has encountered serious impediments. One fundamental obstacle to the payment of adequate salaries (that would in turn partly discourage corruption) and to reclassification to update job descriptions is the fiscal conservatism of Filipino leaders. The Filipinos are one of the least-taxed nations of the world.[74] Their tax structure is regressive, their tax assessments are unrealistically low, and tax collection has been chronically lax. Consequently, progressive policies and laudable programs are handicapped if not nullified by revenue shortages. Pressed to provide employment for a surging labor force, the government is compelled to allocate a large portion of available funds for salaries of inflated agency staffs. This condition partly explains the persistence of personal and partisan patronage, often, although not always, at the expense of the merit system.

Another basic obstacle to systematic salary standardization and position classification is the insistence of various agencies, employee groups, and unions on bargaining for special treatment by legislative or administrative means. Consequently, thousands of government personnel are now legally exempted from WAPCO pay and classification plans. A survey in 1963 also revealed that some 20 per cent of employees covered by WAPCO were not performing the duties and responsibilities in their job descrip-

73. *Ibid.*, p. 28.

74. Amelia B. Abello, *Patterns of Philippine Public Expenditures and Revenue, 1951–1960* (Quezon City, 1964).

tions.[75] Poorly paid and status-conscious personnel will naturally strive to upgrade their titles and salaries, even while mouthing "Equal pay for equal work." Evidently, WAPCO is not seen by many to be distributing far greater benefits than costs compared to customary ways of determining salaries and classifying positions. Incidentally, it may be that 285 occupational groups, 3,416 classes, and 75 pay ranges are too fine distinctions to be made among about 300,000 positions in almost 200 agencies.[76]

Reviewing several innovations designed to modernize public personnel administration from 1950 to 1958, the perceptive AID technical adviser, H. Donald McInnis, concluded:

> But these . . . have hardly more than set the stage. Continuing the theatrical inference, one might say that an adequate structure has been provided, competent performers had been employed, and by usual standards, an effective plot and dialogue had been prepared—but the success of the performance was in doubt. The source of the uncertainty lay in what the audience wanted. The Philippine people have not yet spoken unequivocally in support of the merit principle of government employment.[77]

Efficiency and economy. Efficiency and economy were the expressed objectives of the administrative reorganizations during the postwar administrations of Roxas, Quirino, and Magsaysay. Along with merit and competence, they are undoubtedly also the most readily cited rationale for all kinds of more limited management improvement schemes. Yet efficiency and economy have rarely been demonstrated as the reasonable outcome of planned administrative change. At the only time when actual economies were reported as the consequence of a general reorganization, under Quirino, the spokesman virtually apologized for the meager savings in relation to the 25 per cent target of reduction in government expenditures.

Largely as the result of administrative reforms and the work of

75. Guadalupe R. Mapili, "Development of the Classification and Pay Plans in the Philippine Government: Implementation in Selected Agencies," *Philippine Journal of Public Administration*, VIII (1964), 215–226.
76. *Ibid.*, p. 222.
77. "Terminal Report, August 1958," in United States Operations Mission to the Philippines, *Selected Papers on Public Administration* (Manila, 1959), p. 127.

the Government Reorganization Commission in the mid-fifties—the heyday of AID public administration technical assistance in the Philippines—a number of central staff agencies were created to help insure continuous administrative modernization. The Council of Administrative Management was formed to serve the president as his highest management advisory body. To the Budget Commission was added the Management Service as its organization and methods arm. Performance budgeting was introduced. Improvements in the Civil Service Commission were designed to strengthen it as the president's principal staff arm in personnel administration. The Management Service and the Civil Service Commission were expected to assist and co-ordinate decentralized organization and methods and personnel units, respectively, throughout the bureaucracy. A new Department of General Services, patterned after the United States General Services Administration, was organized to improve procurement, records management, buildings and real property management, government printing, and official media production.

A decade after their creation, no objective appraisal can be sanguine about their individual cumulative performance. The Council of Administrative Management has not been utilized as expected by its innovators, for it has not been a prestigious and forceful advocate. No president has evinced a sustained interest in improving government organization and management. In response to the most urgent kinds of criticism and demands by the citizenry and the press, presidents have paid far greater attention to ombudsman-type agencies directly under presidential surveillance than to either the Council of Administrative Management or the Management Service.[78] The latter's director complained ruefully to the author that organization and methods analysts of the Management Service had been made to serve as auxiliaries to the president's investigators and troubleshooters or have been pirated by agencies which could offer them more meaningful and

78. President Ramon Magsaysay created the PCAC (Presidential Complaints and Action Committee), and this was reorganized by President Carlos P. Garcia into the President's Committee on Administration Performance and Efficiency (PCAPE). President Diosdado Macapagal replaced the PCAPE with the Presidential Anti-Graft Committee. The present agency, under President Ferdinand Marcos, is Presidential Agency for Reform in Government Operations.

profitable work. The Civil Service Commission suffered from a weak and escapist leader until the last five years, when a devotee of administrative reform took over—and took on all comers. Sporadic assessments of the Department of General Services, particularly in respect to procurement, printing, and buildings management, have not been very favorable.

In fairness, it must be said that, given the basic problems and powerful pressures within and without the bureaucracy, it would take at least exceptional leadership, such as that provided by President Magsaysay, Budget Commissioner Dominador Aytona, and Civil Service Commissioner Abelardo Subido, to effect any appreciable administrative improvements. President Magsaysay had no consuming zeal as administrative reformer, and he rejected the reorganization plan to improve his own office. But he had the charisma and overwhelming popular support and the inspired associates that encouraged administrative innovation and unorthodox shortcuts which facilitated program implementation.[79]

Some of the basic conditions obstructing efficiency and economy were not discovered, and therefore could not be consciously counteracted, by the administrative reforms initiated under foreign technical assistance. This is not to say, however, that certain technical assistance projects in public administration and in the substantive program fields may have begun to alter some of those conditions. From the data on our panel survey some hypotheses emerge regarding the commonly observed inefficiency and wastefulness in the government. Most government workers lack the motivation to do their best because of the common concept that personal success is rather undeserved, being a stroke of good fortune, and must therefore be shared by them with their extended family. Few think of personal success in individualistic and professional terms. The modal concept also stresses fatalistic dependence which, although optimistic, minimizes the notion that personal success is achieved and may be manipulated. In their orientations toward time and change most government workers are probably preoccupied with the present and feel little

79. See Abueva, "Bridging the Gap," pp. 345–347.

concern for their future and the future of their agency and country. Time to them is something they have in unlimited abundance, and since today seems no different from yesterday nor tomorrow from today, they do not feel it necessary to be subjected to plans, schedules, and appointments. *Bahala na* is a popular expression which betrays a disinclination to see actions through to their consequences or to think beyond the present. Delayed action is rationalized in terms of the generally slow pace of most people and the tropical climate.[80]

An economizing attitude does not easily develop from the common concept of "public" as something that belongs to no one and therefore is fair game for anybody. This contrasts with the Western view that public property belongs to everyone and should be safeguarded for all. Reports of dishonesty at all levels of the public service feed official cynicism which rationalizes wastefulness in the use of public resources if not their outright misappropriation. When it is often assumed that it is know-who, more than know-how, that leads to advancement in one's career, it takes uncommon commitment and drive to do one's best on the job and to be provident with official resources.

Rationality and planning. Rationality involves choices of appropriate goals and efficient means toward their fruition. Imported administrative doctrines prescribe planning for both kinds of choices. The Philippine government has been *formally* committed to comprehensive planning since the National Economic Council was created during the Commonwealth days. From the birth of the Republic to the intensification of United States economic aid and technical assistance following the Bell Mission report, four economic plans were formulated: the Hibben Memorandum, the Beyster Plan, the Cuaderno Plan, and the Yulo Plan. Thereafter, the National Economic Council produced the Rodriguez Plan (1955–59), the overlapping Social and Economic Development Program for 1957–61, the NEC Three-Year Program of Economic and Social Development (1960–62), the Five-Year Integrated Socio-Economic Development Program (1962–67), and

80. Abueva, *Conditions of Administrative Development*, pp. 15–17.

the current Four-Year Economic Program for the Philippines (1966–69).[81]

United States "technical assistance" in economic planning is evident in the way some of the earlier economic plans were named. From the commencement of United States economic aid and technical assistance in 1950, AID has contributed directly and indirectly to national and agency planning activities. The AID public administration project called Economic Policy Development involved eleven man-years of American technical services to the National Economic Council and the training of fourteen NEC technicians. The AID project that supported the Government Survey and Reorganization Commission, which "revitalized" the NEC, cost about the same amount in American funds, including eighteen man-years of American technical services.

In practice, several NEC functions and a good deal of effective planning have been assumed by the Budget Commission, the Central Bank, and a number of specialized agencies and *ad hoc* bodies. Most of the NEC plans were never adopted by the president. All have been implemented only piecemeal. Although the government has always exercised monetary and fiscal controls, private entrepreneurial groups retain the initiative in planning and launching most economic projects. Expert observers agree that comprehensive planning, as exemplified by the work of the NEC, has failed. NEC Chairman Sixto K. Roxas, an economist and business executive, concluded in his terminal report to President Macapagal that all postwar national plans, presumably including the one he had drafted, "were not really plans but merely statements of general aspirations."[82] More relevant to our purposes, he began with this telling judgment: "The basic premise of this report is that it is meaningless, at this stage, to talk of national planning . . . because neither the Philippine government nor any of its agencies is in a position to draw up a meaningful national plan. The whole public administration system, the

81. James A. Storer and Teresita L. de Guzman, "Philippine Economic Planning and Progress, 1945–1960," in R. S. Milne (ed.), *Planning for Progress: The Administration of Economic Planning* (Manila, 1960), pp. 9–27.

82. *Organizing the Government for Economic Development Administration* (Manila, February 29, 1964, mimeographed), p. 1.

whole government machinery as it stands, is a large, cumbersome, and sticky structure that militates not only against *implementing* a plan, but even against *formulating* a meaningful plan."[83]

An incisive analysis of attempted comprehensive planning in the Philippines is provided by José D. Soberano.[84] He traced the obvious failures in national planning to serious deficiencies in the valuational, technical, and practical requirements of national planning. In his value category are a long-term point of view, an instrumental-rational or pragmatic approach toward goal-values, a secular choice of goal-values and the means for achieving them, and a perception of the public interest for testing the validity of the goal-values. Among the technical requirements are research, prediction, technicalization of means, and growth-sustaining interaction of functions, structures, practices, and values. The practical implications of national planning are sustained political support, administrative support, and effective co-ordination and control.[85]

Shortcomings in these factors are related to the ecology of politics and public administration. The predominant rural sector of Filipino society is relatively undifferentiated, largely self-sufficient, and primary-group oriented. Consequently, rural interests and demands that impinge upon local politicians, urban-based pressure groups, political parties, individual legislators, department heads, and upon the president are characteristically diffuse, particularistic, and short-term in nature. Unavoidably, the more specific, universalistic, and longer-range interests and demands emanating from the developed urban areas tend to be compromised, if not swamped altogether, resulting "in an ambivalent dualism of political and administrative operations—[universalism] of policy and particularism of implementation."[86]

Over the years the president's towering constitutional authority has been steadily challenged and eroded by the Congress. The

83. *Ibid.*, italics mine.
84. *Economic Planning in the Philippines: Ecology, Politics and Administration*, Institute of Public Administration (Manila, undated, mimeographed), 535 pp.
85. *Ibid.*, pp. 477–478.
86. *Ibid.*, p. 487.

president must constantly bargain with individual legislators of his own party for the passage of every piece of legislation and for the confirmation of appointments. As the local political chieftains, who together tenuously form the highest leaders of the majority party, legislators can extract executive patronage and preferment in return for their legislative and electoral support. Lacking the bonds of a distinctive ideological or policy consensus, relative to the minority party, the president and his party colleagues in the Congress have to relate continually to each other on a personal basis. In fact, the president sometimes finds it easier to secure the support of opposition legislators, whose modest demands are more manageable, than that of his own partymen. Two examples will illustrate the assertion of congressional power over the executive. In the reorganization of the National Economic Council in 1955, the inclusion of two senators and two representatives as members was the consequence of the influence of the legislative members of the Government Survey and Reorganization. In 1956 the Congress acceded to the president's adoption of performance budgeting in twelve pilot agencies but retained the line-item budget as the customary basis for the annual appropriations act.

Bureaucratic centralization delays decision and action without always insuring topside direction and control. Behind this paradox is the absence of consensus on administrative values, resulting in personalized value premises, isolationist tendencies among administrative units, and a double standard of behavior.[87] For their own personal and program advancement, career administrators usually form personal alliances with individual legislative patrons, thus further lessening their susceptibility to presidential and departmental co-ordination and control.

Like efficiency and economy, successful planning may be also related to basic orientations toward time, change, work, and success. A preoccupation with the present or the past, the assumption that change and success are not manipulable, the belief that it is futile to plan without full control over needed resources or that good plans are never carried out anyway, the personal experience that leads one to conclude that performance and

87. *Ibid.*, p. 490.

achievement are less important than political connections in getting recognition—these could very well undermine the idea of program planning. When all the obstacles, actual and conjectured, are considered, however, the point must be made that agency planning does take place. In Manila private groups plan and lobby spiritedly for policies and programs which have long-run effects on their interests and concerns. Moreover, political competition drives some ambitious and progressive politicians to the sponsorship of long-range programs and reforms in selected fields. Partly as a consequence of AID technical assistance and specialized training, a growing number of technicians have developed planning and statistical skills which are being employed in agency planning and evaluation. At the least, annual planning in support of requested budgetary outlays must be made. Requests for AID or United Nations assistance, for Japanese reparations allocations, and for international loans must be justified by workable plans.

Bureaucratic responsibility and responsiveness. Few emerging nation-states have had the advantage of the extended and intensive democratic tutelage and experience enjoyed by the Filipinos. They have, consequently, internalized many Western democratic values and adapted these to their circumstances. In fact, many of the national problems facing the Philippines today may be said to stem partly from the relative success of its political system in keeping politicians and bureaucrats responsive to the people's wishes and importunities. This has sometimes been called an "excess of democracy." And yet, the inefficiencies, nepotism, spoils, and corruption, which have been moralistically condemned as unrelieved evils, may have contributed to the viability of the Republic as a young democracy in the emerging "third world."[88]

Certainly, the Filipinos are highly politicized. Conscious of their bargaining influence through their votes and, encouraged by the competitiveness of local and national elections, they rarely

88. José V. Abueva, "The Contribution of Nepotism, Spoils, and Graft to Political Development," *East-West Center Review,* III (1966), 45–54.

hesitate to approach politicians—with particularistic requests. These quickly become pressures on the bureaucrats for employment, services, benefits, or exemptions from the rules. However, most citizens in the provinces constitute still amorphous masses which are poorly integrated with the functioning of the Congress and the bureaucracy. Unorganized as members of associations with common interests, and unable to perceive their individual problems and interests in policy terms, they are ineffectual in influencing legislation. To borrow the concepts of Almond and Verba, most Filipino citizens have developed only the electoral aspect of their "participant role," are still too engrossed in their "parochial role," and yet have to learn their "subject role" as well (as shown by low payment of taxes and high incidence of crimes).[89] In their relatively undifferentiated and loosely integrated state, most citizens can neither assert the necessary policy demands nor contribute the required public scrutiny and support needed by a well-functioning democracy. Unorganized and undisciplined in their participation in administrative decision-making, they tend to lower the capacity of the bureaucracy for achieving program results.

Again, our panel survey data provide us some insights. Although the citizens have a sense of potency in regard to the politician's election and continuance in office, many seem to feel helpless vis-à-vis the unresponsive or overbearing official. Aside from their inability to organize for influencing policy and official conduct, a cultural factor seems to underlie this paradoxical combination of political influence and administrative helplessness. It appears that many officials tend to feel they are providing services or benefits not so much out of a sense of duty but as personal favors that accrue to their official status. In turn many citizens who approach officials for assistance do so feeling more that they are asking personal favors than seeking what is theirs by right.[90] The locally well-known concepts expressed in the democratic saying, "Public office is a public trust," and in the terms "sover-

89. See Gabriel A. Almond and Sidney Verba, *The Civic Culture* (Princeton, 1963), pp. 16–19, and Abueva, *Conditions of Administrative Development*, pp. 51–52.

90. Abueva, *Conditions of Administrative Development*, p. 25.

eign people" and "civil servant," collide with customary expectations in interpersonal relations.

The Filipino emphasis on primary-group values, interests, and techniques often leads to violations of the idealized norms of merit and equal treatment of citizens. Relatives and friends tend to be favored. The more numerous uninfluential persons and strangers are likely to be ignored. Relationships among citizens, politicians, and administrators are often corrupted. Under heavy personal or political pressures, government decision-making tends to be *ad hoc,* face-to-face exchanges in the form of mutual cathexis and individual bargaining—in either of which values loom large and facts recede into the background as decision premises.[91]

However, the foregoing description of decision-making and official-citizen relations should be immediately qualified. There are decisional areas of known and condoned unmitigated cathexis and personal *do ut des,* such as in public works patronage involving semiskilled and unskilled labor. There are decisional areas where universalistic rules are explicit and known, but frequent exceptions are allowed for favored clients—such as in the issuance of business licenses and building permits, in tax collection, and in extending government credit. There are decisional areas where minimal legal requirements are invariably observed but where favoritism is occasionally practiced among those who are eligible—as in appointments to the classified civil service. Then there are decisional areas where rules are observed with rare deviations because officials customarily discharge their defined duties and responsibilities—all legally eligible persons receive the service or benefit due them, although certain persons get attention earlier or get more than the usual amounts permissible—for example, in extending loans from government insurance or social security funds. Finally, there are areas of decision where, generally, rules are applied and services rendered in an objective and universalistic manner, where official duties and obligations

91. See Herbert A. Simon, *Administrative Behavior: A Study of Decision-Making Processes in Administrative Organization* (2nd ed.; New York, 1957), pp. 4–8, 45–60. The author's analysis draws heavily from *Conditions of Administrative Development,* pp. 52, 54.

clearly transcend cathexis and bargaining as the mode of exchange between the parties to the official transaction. Examples are public education, public health services, postal and telegraphic services, and the obvious free citizen access to public roads and parks.[92]

92. *Ibid.*, pp. 54–55.

• 14 •

Allocation and Development, Economic and Political

Joseph J. Spengler

> They were both by nature sharp-eyed foxes, inescapably aware of sheer, *de facto* differences which divide and forces which disrupt the human world, observers utterly incapable of being deceived by the many subtle devices, the unifying systems and faiths and sciences, by which the superficial or the desperate sought to conceal the chaos from one another.
>
> ISAIAH BERLIN,
> *The Hedgehog and the Fox*

This essay does not deal with administrative reform as such. It has to do rather with an aspect of the interrelation between the state and process of political development and the state and process of economic development. This aspect is allocation and its administration. In the absence of simple indicators of economic and political development and of their interrelations I shall make use of somewhat arbitrary measures. Moreover, I shall confine my discussion to societies with economies comprising a public and a private sector, though the mode of analysis employed is readily extendable to a society in which the state has come to dominate the national community instead of merely serving as its agent.

I shall assume that the movement of per capita income roughly reflects the course of economic development, though not necessarily that of well-being. After all, as Durkheim observed, "our capacity for happiness is very limited," much more so than our capacity to produce goods and services.[1] No correspondingly simple and generalizable index of political development is available; after all, political phenomena are less universal than economic and more conditioned by the political systems in which they are embedded. I shall therefore assume, for purposes of discourse, that in the long run, albeit not always in the short run, increase in the range of political choice probably reflects progress in political development as well as does any alternative indicator.[2] For, as output per head rises in an economy, more means per head become available to the polity or public sector and thus increase the capability of those controlling this sector to accomplish any or many objectives. I shall also assume that if one had at hand a satisfactory community welfare index, its level would tend to be correlated with the width of the range of political choice open to individuals as well as with the level of average income. This assumption does not preclude the possibility that in

1. Emile Durkheim, *The Division of Labor in Society,* trans. George Simpson, (Glenco, Ill., 1933), p. 235, also Book II, chap. 1. Economists agree. "We must be highly skeptical of the view that long-term changes in the rate of growth of welfare can be gauged even roughly from changes in the rate of growth of output." Changes in output may "involve profound changes in social and economic organization" and in our manner of earning and using income. We "cannot assume that a social utility function remains stable," nor, should it remain so, have we adequate information "about the relation between increments to output and increments to utility." As monetization and the growth of output proceed, the ratio of both free goods and non-marketed goods to all goods diminishes and so do the ratios of final product and of consumables to total product. See Moses Abramovitz, "The Welfare Interpretation of Secular Trends in National Income and Product," in Abramovitz (ed.), *The Allocation of Economic Resources* (Stanford, 1959), pp. 1–22, esp. 4–6, 20–21. E. J. Mishan writes in a similar vein. Having noted that one cannot bring the things on which happiness ultimately depends into a practical relation with the measuring rod of money, he remarks: "The triumphant achievements of modern technology, ever-swifter travel, round-the-clock synthetic entertainment, the annual cornucopia of sleek and glossy gadgets, which rest perforce on the cult of efficiency, the single-minded pursuit of advancement, the craving for material success, may be exacting a fearful toll in terms of human happiness. But the formal elegance of welfare economies will never reveal it." See his "A Survey of Welfare Economics, 1939–59," in American Economic Association and Royal Economic Society, *Survey of Economic Theory* (New York, 1965), I, 154–222, at 213. Investment, the source of growth, can, of course, be made the final output to be maximized, subject to given conditions, among them social purposes which reduce the rate of growth. T. Lefeber and S. Chakravarty, "Wages, Employment and Growth," *Kyklos,* XIX (1966), 602–619; also Harvey Leibenstein, "Long-Run Welfare Criteria," in J. Margolis (ed.), *The Public Economy of Urban Communities* (Baltimore, 1965), pp. 39–51.

2. Mishan accepts " 'an expansion of the area of choice' as synonymous with an increase of welfare, and as an unexceptionable norm of policy," but he objects to treating "a rising standard of living" as the "certain instrument of an expanding horizon of opportunities" ("Survey of Welfare Economics," p. 212).

the short run acceleration of the rate of economic (political) change may have a destabilizing impact upon the existing political (economic) structure.[3] Ease of discussion presupposing the use of an index of political progress, the one proposed above will at least serve this purpose.

My inquiry is focused primarily upon allocative processes and their determinants, together with contrasts between the allocative systems employed in the public sector and those found in the private sector. It also touches upon the role of the entrepreneur as contrasted with that of the bureaucrat.[4] It takes for granted that allocation is the main regulator of economic development and hence indirectly of the limits imposed upon the course and content of political development within the structure of any concrete political system.

An inquiry of the present sort is handicapped by the fact that public agencies are only beginning to be conceptualized in terms parallel to our conceptualization of private firms. This is being done through study of the budgetary mechanisms of public firms and comparison of them with those of private firms. As yet, however, the agencies comprising the apparatus of state have not been translated into terms of a system resembling the system of firms comprising the private sector, but equilibrating mechanisms are being uncovered. Moreover, even should the agencies operating within the public sector be dealt with as a system of interrelated units, it would not yet become clear why only so many and no more "means" or "facilities" are at the disposal of the public sector. Eventually, of course, the process of equilibration operative within the public sector or system may become sufficiently delineated to permit comparison with that found in the private sector.[5] Then we shall have a better understanding of the nature

3. See Charles Wolf, Jr., *United States Policy and the Third World* (Boston, 1967), chaps. 2, 6.

4. It is the contemporary bureaucrat with whom I am concerned, not the generalist who maintained law and order in traditional societies in the age of European suzerainty, but his ever more numerous specialist successors. See Ralph Braibanti and Associates, *Asian Bureaucratic Systems Emergent from the British Imperial Tradition* (Durham, N.C., 1966).

5. J. Tinbergen discusses how co-ordination of policies is obtained in a more or less planned economy. *Economic Policy: Principles and Design* (Amsterdam, 1956), chap. 8. See also W. A. Lewis, *Development Planning* (New York, 1966), and R. A. Solo, *Economic Organization and Social Systems* (Indianapolis, 1967).

and source of such balance as develops between the economic system and the political system, between the public and the private sectors, and between "political" allocation and "market" allocation, as well as of such changes as take place in this balance (e.g., as when the importance attached to "public goods" changes).[6] In Section VII I touch upon the role played by exchange in the public and the private sector, respectively, and in their interrelations. Under present circumstances, of course, comparison of entrepreneur with administrative bureaucrat, or of firm or industry with government agency, or of political system with economic system, must fall quite short of what is essential to effective comparative analysis.

This essay is divided into seven distinct though somewhat interrelated sections: (1) stationary vs. non-stationary society and economy; (2) costs of growth and development; (3) political and economic development (4) allocation; (5) allocative mechanisms compared; (6) optimizing the state's role in allocation and development; and (7) the universality of the role played by exchange in allocating goods, services, and power.

I. Stationary vs. Non-Stationary Society

My discussion relates to essentially autonomous societal systems (one might say sovereign nation-states) which normally

---

This work, which came to my attention after this chapter was completed, deals with the allocation problem in different social contexts.

6. See O. A. Davis, M. A. H. Dempster, and A. Wildavsky, "A Theory of the Budgetary Process," *American Political Science Review,* LX (1966), 529–547; M. Holden, Jr., "'Imperialism' in Bureaucracy," *ibid.,* pp. 943–952; A. Wildavsky, *The Politics of the Budgetary Process* (Boston, 1964). See also Gordon Tullock (ed.), *Papers on Non-Market Decision-Making,* Vols. I–II (Charlottesville, Va., 1966–67); R. A. Dahl and C. E. Lindblom, *Politics, Economics and Welfare* (New York, 1953), chap. 12; C. E. Lindblom, "Policy Analysis," *American Economic Review,* XLVIII (1958), 298–312, and *Bargaining: The Hidden Hand in Government,* RAND Corporation Research Memorandum RM-1434-RC (Santa Monica, 1955); Albert Breton, "The Demand for Public Goods," *Canadian Journal of Economics and Political Science,* XXXII (1936), 453–467; A. O. Hirschman, *Journeys Toward Progress* (New York, 1963), pp. 276–297, on models of "reform mongering"; J. S. Saloma, *The Responsible Use of Power,* American Enterprise Institute (Washington, 1964); and R. N. McKean, "The Unseen Hand in Government," *American Economic Review,* LV (1965), 496–506. On the political forces governing development within the American city, see A. A. Altshuler, *The City Planning Process* (Ithaca, N.Y., 1965).

consist of an economy which produces goods and services, a polity which mobilizes the productive capacity of a society to realize collective or systemic goals, and subsystems that maintain various social patterns (e.g., the family) or commit a member of a society to values agreed upon.[7] An economy (and perhaps a polity) may undergo either development, or growth unaccompanied by development, or mere replacement answering closely to Levy's description of renovative social change (e.g., that characteristic of traditionl China).[8] It is to economic and political development that I shall devote major attention.[9]

A societal system is *inter alia* a collection of interacting individuals of various ages, each of whom is born, grows and develops, and eventually dies. It differs from its individual components in that it persists, whereas each component dies. It may be stationary, or it may increase or decrease at a rate that is constant or subject to variation. If the number of births just balances the number of deaths, the collectivity will be stationary. It will grow if births exceed deaths; it will decline if deaths exceed births. It tends to disappear when the number of individuals descends below some critical point. Of importance in this connection is the fact that some behavior of a society is a function of its size. Of importance also is the fact that politico-economic viability presupposes the existence of a set of minimal conditions.[10]

The culture of a society tends to change independently of its size or of changes in this size. The experience of each new member of a society will differ from that of older members and

7. Talcott Parsons and N. J. Smelser, *Economy and Society* (Glencoe, Ill., 1956), chap. 2; also, N. J. Smelser, *The Sociology of Economic Life* (Englewood Cliffs, N.J., 1963), chap. 3; Marion J. Levy, Jr., *Modernization and the Structure of Societies* (Princeton, 1966), *passim.*

8. *Modernization and the Structure of Societies,* pp. 487–488. For a quite different notion, see Hellmut Wilhelm, *Change: Eight Lectures on the I Ching* (New York, 1960).

9. Dynamical theory is dealt with by Paul A. Samuelson in his *Foundations of Economic Analysis* (Cambridge, Mass., 1947), chap. 11. R. A. Solo's approach is dynamical in that he treats the process of development as "a continuous transformation of the system of cognition" (*Economic Organization,* pp. vi, 417–419, 454–455, 480–485).

10. On theoretical but not empirical aspects of viability, see K. E. Boulding, *A Reconstruction of Economics* (New York, 1950), chap. 1, and *Conflict and Defense: A General Theory* (New York, 1962), chaps. 4, 10, 12.

bring about some change even as does the replacement of depreciated artifacts by new artifacts. Therefore, change tends to be at a minimum in a society that is declining in size. Change does not, however, tend to be at a maximum in a society that is growing rapidly, even though the ratio of additions (births) to departures (deaths) then is relatively high. This seeming advantage tends to be offset by a shortage of new capital per capita. In a slowly growing collectivity, on the contrary, provision can readily be made for capital formation essential to economic development and change.

A distinction needs to be made between growth as such and economic development. Growth as such, or simple growth, here denotes addition to an aggregate of elements but without change in the composition of that aggregate. Development, or complex growth, also denotes the addition of elements to an aggregate, but with the qualification that some of these elements are new and novel and *different* from any already present. Simple growth gives rise to a larger aggregate but not to one made up of different ingredients. Complex growth gives rise to distinctly new types of aggregates. It is truly evolutionary in character.[11]

It is inferable that if a society is non-stationary it is generating a social surplus. Indeed, the developmental potential of a society is conditioned by its social surplus, that is, by the excess of goods and services it produces per annum above what is required to meet the elementary consumption requirements of the population and keep its productive apparatus intact. This is not quite the same as Marx's "surplus value," a term he used to denote the difference between the number of hours a society's labor force worked and the number of hours required to supply that labor force with subsistence. A society's social surplus does, of course, include a great deal of that portion of its income—property income—consisting of profits, rent, and interest, together with a fraction of its wage and salary income. The latter fraction is very small in societies in which average and wage incomes are very

11. See my "Social Evolution and the Theory of Economic Development," in H. R. Barringer *et al.* (eds.), *Social Change in Developing Areas* (Cambridge, Mass., 1965), pp. 244–252.

low; there property income is virtually the only source of a surplus. Inequality thus is a necessary though not a sufficient condition for the emergence of a social surplus.

The size of a social surplus may be affected by the organization of a society and its economy. For even though this organization should not affect output per capita, it might make per capita capital formation greater or smaller than it otherwise would be. For example, consumption may be reduced through taxation, or it may be augmented by governmental or other arrangements which transfer purchasing power from higher- to lower-income groups.

In reality, the size of a society's social surplus depends largely upon the rate of growth of per capita income—that is, upon the extent to which the rate of growth of aggregate output exceeds that of population. Consumption tends to press upon income in all but highly puritanical societies. Income that has been looked upon as non-permanent comes to be viewed as permanent and hence spendable.[12] The forces that bring about income growth also bring new products into existence and thereby sustain or elevate the marginal propensity to consume.[13] Resources may also be used to intensify old and generate new wants and thereby augment a population's want-generating power. Demonstration effects may be experienced as well.[14] In short, should average income not continue to rise, it would presently be approximated by average consumption in all classes of society except perhaps those made up of very wealthy persons. Increments to average income, however, tend to contribute to a society's social surplus, until they become committed to some form of consumption.

It is the magnitude of social surplus per capita with which the potential if not also the actual rate of economic growth and development per capita is highly correlated. This magnitude depends largely upon a country's rate of population growth, since 4

12. See Milton Friedman, *A Theory of the Consumption Function* (Princeton, 1956), pp. 220–221, 233–239.
13. See my "Product-Adding versus Product-Replacing Innovations," *Kyklos*, X (1957), 249–277.
14. See Peter Bauer and B. S. Yamey, *The Economics of Underdeveloped Countries* (London, 1957), pp. 137–142.

to 6 per cent of a country's national income is absorbed by a 1 per cent per year rate of population growth.[15] Since, as a rule, the gross reproduction rate in underdeveloped countries generally exceeds 2 per cent and their populations are growing 2 or more per cent a year, population growth is absorbing 8–12 or more per cent of the national income and thus reducing by 1–2 percentage points the annual rate of growth of per capita income.[16] Excessive population growth thus constitutes perhaps the greatest persisting threat to economic development in the underdeveloped world, one on a par with the threat of military belligerence and/or utopianism to the emergence of opulence in the developed world. Given the high rates of population growth currently prevailing in much of the world, political as well as economic development will be greatly retarded.

The existence of a social surplus is a necessary though not a sufficient condition of economic and political development. Indeed, throughout much of man's history, he must have had a social surplus, but he so used it that average output and income grew only very slowly and intermittently. Much of this social surplus was used unproductively by the priestcraft, the military, landowners, and the political ruling class and their bureaucratic retainers (i.e., mandarins, etc.) As a rule, only the "middle class" or bourgeoisie were important capital formers; they alone were animated by values which made for the accumulation of wealth in productive form as well as for the use of improved methods. It is not surprising, therefore, that average incomes remained low in much of the world; as late as the 1950's they were often at levels much below those encountered in Western Europe about the time of the French Revolution.[17] Indeed, it is because the social surplus was put to such unfruitful uses in most non-primitive societies that many retained their traditional character and re-

15. Here I conceive of capital as described in the next section and allow for the unfavorable effect of high fertility upon the age structure of a population.

16. On fertility see United Nations, *Population Bulletin of the United Nations*, No. 7 (New York, 1963), pp. 1, 16–20, chap. 9.

17. See, for example, Simon Kuznets, *Economic Growth and Structure* (New York, 1965), pp. 176–212; also, H. J. Habbakuk's essay in L. H. Dupriez (ed.), *Economic Progress* (Louvain, 1955), pp. 149 ff.

mained essentially stationary, trapped in preindustrial equilibria until freed by social revolution or its equivalent.[18] Conflict over the use of the social surplus remains alive today. There is conflict between those favoring rapid development and those who attach more weight to welfare objectives than to growth objectives.[19] There is conflict between those who favor more rather than less rapid "modernization," not only within undeveloped countries but also within European countries which lag markedly behind the United States in growth-oriented methods, values, and purposes.

II. Costs of Growth

Growth and development, as Sismondi realized during the industrial revolution, entail costs for many members of a society, some of which are unrequited.[20] I shall touch upon three types of costs, namely, the economic cost of capital, that of changes in a society's input structure, and the socio-psychological costs involved in modernization and development.

1. The most important economic cost of growth consists in capital, formed mainly through setting idle resources to work[21] and transforming all or most of the marginal increment in output per capita into capital. One may, in fact, say that economic development consists essentially in increase in capital per head.

18. On the issue here posed see Barrington Moore, Jr., *Social Origins of Dictatorship and Democracy* (Boston, 1966). See also T. W. Schultz's analysis of traditional agricultural equilibrium in *Transforming Traditional Agriculture* (New Haven, 1964).

19. The issue is touched upon by R. M. Titmuss in his *Essays on the Welfare State* (London, 1966). See chap. 11 on "The Irresponsible Society," esp. pp. 216–219.

20. See, for example, M. Bronfenbrenner, "The High Cost of Economic Development," *Land Economics,* XXIX (1953), 93–104, 209–218; Klaus Knorr and W. J. Baumol (eds.), *What Price Economic Growth* (New York, 1961); Thomas Wilson, *Planning and Growth* (London, 1965), pp. 62–81; P. J. D. Wiles, "Growth Versus Choice," *Economic Journal,* LXVI (1956), 244–255, and *The Political Economy of Communism* (Cambridge, Mass., 1962), Part III, esp. chap. 11; Jacques Austruy, "Le prix de la croissance," *Revue d'économie politique,* LXXII (1962), 830–858. On Sismondi's reaction in and before the 1830's see Charles Gide and Charles Rist, *A History of Economic Doctrines* (Boston, 1948), pp. 205–211.

21. John C. H. Fei and Gustav Ranis, *Development of the Labor Surplus Economy: Theory and Policy* (New Haven, 1964).

It is for this reason that, in the previous section, development was said to be conditioned if not dominated by a society's social surplus. For capital, the source of development, comes out of a society's social surplus. Here, of course, we define capital more broadly than is customary. The classical economists stressed working capital, wage goods. Their successors allowed greater weight to fixed equipment. Even modern writers tend to conceive of capital in terms of "hardware." This conception answers some analytical needs. It does not, however, answer all of the needs of the student of economic development, nor does it meet adequately those of the social-cost accountant in an age when "brains" have superseded muscle and electronic developments are swamping mechanical power. Today, therefore, a great deal of investment results in the augmentation of science and skill rather than in the increase of productive physical wealth.

Much more useful is Harry G. Johnson's approach, designed to meet the analytical needs of an age of opulence.[22] Johnson regards

> "capital" as including anything that yields a stream of income over time, and income as the product of capital. . . . The growth of income that defines economic development is necessarily the result of the accumulation of capital, or of "investment"; but "investment" . . . must be defined to include such diverse activities as adding to material capital, increasing the health, discipline, skill and education of the human population, moving labour into more productive occupations and locations, and applying existing knowledge or discovering and applying new knowledge to increase the efficiency of productive processes. All such activities involve recurring costs, in the form of use of current resources; and investment in them is socially worthwhile if the rate of return over costs exceeds the general rate of interest, or if the capital value of the additional income they yield exceeds the cost of obtaining it. . . . Efficient development involves allocation of investment resources according to priori-

22. "Towards a Generalized Capital Accumulation Approach to Economic Development," in his *The Canadian Quandary* (Toronto, 1963), chap. 14. See also Harvey Leibenstein, "Allocative Efficiency vs. 'X-Efficiency,'" *American Economic Review*, LVI (1966), 392–415; Mason Haire, "The Social Sciences and Management Practices," *California Management Review*, VI (1964), 3–10; J. R. Platt, *The Road to Man* (New York, 1966).

> ties set by the relative rates of return on alternative investments.[23]

In other words, capital consists of expenditure, of the use of inputs or resources, in such ways as will make tomorrow's income stream greater than it otherwise would have been, and in particular, tomorrow's income stream per capita. It follows that any expenditure made today and having that effect tomorrow is "capital." Capital, therefore, includes the devotion of inputs to such outputs as productive education and training and retraining, the accumulation of scientific knowledge, the conversion of that knowledge into applied science, invention, and innovation, buildings and equipment, so-called public capital as well as household capital, improvement and preservation of health.

2. Economic development entails a second type of cost in that it is accompanied by change in the relative importance of actual and potential inputs and hence in their relative scarcity and the scarcity rents (if any) which they command. Let us call the inputs in use before an important developmental change I_o and the *new* ones in use after such change I_n. Some types of inputs included in I_o will become obsolete as a result of the change and command a price much below what they formerly commanded, whereas others will continue to command roughly the same prices as they did formerly. Those which become relatively or completely obsolete no longer command the rents (if any) they commanded before derived demand for their services declined. Meanwhile, some of the inputs included under I_n begin to command prices, often inclusive of rents, for the first time. Striking instances of the emergence of such rents are those which various formerly worthless wave channels would now command explicitly were governments (in which their ownership usually is vested) to charge for their use. In sum, every major economic change alters the composition of derived demands and with it the structure of rents and quasi-rents, some of which rise while others fall.

Threat of loss of rents sometimes gives rise to opposition to

23. Johnson, "Towards a Generalized Capital Accumulation Approach," p. 230.

economic development and thus reinforces opposition on the part of those whose position in the power structure, together with perquisites attached thereto, is reduced.[24] These losses, the products of substitution effects, may be somewhat counterbalanced, however, by income effects which accompany economic development when it decidedly augments aggregate output and income. Indeed, it is generally true that just as the rate of growth of average output constitutes a good measure of the progress of economic development, so does the rate of growth of average income constitute a good index of a society's capacity to tolerate losses and disadvantages associated with economic progress. Otherwise these would produce revolt or demands for reduction of income inequalities.

The aspect of emerging demand for new inputs I_n of greatest importance here is the fact that some of these are not only very significant but also in quite limited and inelastic supply. They thus constitute limitational factors and set the pace at which an economy can progress. Illustrative are various types of educated personnel,[25] above all, personnel with decision-making capacity[26] and personnel with specialized technical capacities of a sort seldom possessed by old-line civil service generalists.[27] We shall return later to means of coping with this form of scarcity, sensed already by Henri Saint-Simon in the early nineteenth century.[28]

3. Transformation, whether complete or incomplete, of the so-

24. Zbigniew Brzezinski discusses these and other costs of development in "The Politics of Underdevelopment," *World Politics*, IX (1956), 61. See also George Rosen, *Democracy and Economic Change in India* (Berkeley, 1966), pp. 4–5, 220–221, also chaps. 8–10.

25. See, for example, F. Harbison and C. A. Myers, *Education, Manpower and Economic Growth* (New York, 1964), esp. chaps. 2–3, 8; C. A. Anderson and M. J. Bowman (eds.), *Education and Economic Development* (Chicago, 1963), chaps. 3–4; Lewis, *Development Planning*, pp. 104–110, 222–234.

26. S. M. Lipset and Aldo Solari (eds.), *Elites in Latin America* (New York, 1967), pp. 152–153; A. O. Hirschman, *The Strategy of Economic Development* (New York, 1959), pp. 23–26. Cranley Onslow (ed.), *Asian Economic Development* (New York, 1965), pp. 181–185; A. H. Hanson, *A Study of India's Five-Year Plans* (London, 1966), pp. 20–22, also chap. 8.

27. Rosen, *Democracy and Economic Change in India*, pp. 108–109. See also Inayatullah, "Changing Character of District Administration in Pakistan," in W. T. Ross (ed.), *Five Articles on Development Administration in Pakistan*, Asian Studies Papers, No. 1, Michigan State University 1966–67 (East Lansing, Mich., 1967), pp. 35–48.

28. See, for example, F. E. Manuel, *The New World of Henri Saint-Simon* (Notre Dame, Ind., 1963), chap. 21, also pp. 189, 301.

cial structure of a premodern society into that of a modern society entails costs in addition to those included under 1 and 2. These costs are in considerable part social and political in nature and must be allowed for whether one adopts the holistic conception of society put forward by Marion J. Levy, Jr.,[29] or a less holistic coneption of society and political change such as that which Whitaker calls "dysrhythmic."[30] According to Levy, the premodern whole is replaced by a modern whole, with the replacement process set in persisting motion by an initial penetration of modernization patterns into the premodern whole. According to Whitaker, on the contrary, an initial penetration of modernization patterns may produce only limited results, some of which may partly countervail the stimulus of the initial penetration. Under either theory economic development cannot progress far in a backward country in the absence of a profound transformation of its society. This transformation requires time and entails costs, among them the subversion and destabilization of much of the traditional social structure. Whence accomplishment of modernization may call for aggressive and determined leadership which, while bent upon modernization,[31] may long have to acquiesce in the persistence of unavoidable economic dualism.[32] This leadership may not be forthcoming, or it may prove inadequate as in Egypt[33] and India.

Leadership may prove unequal to the task of economically transforming a society for one or both or a combination of two

29. See his *Modernization and the Structure of Societies.* On interrelated indicators of socio-economic development and the identification of stages of development see Bruce M. Russett, *World Handbook of Political and Social Indicators* (New Haven, 1964); Irma Adelman and Cynthia T. Morris, *Society, Politics, and Economic Development* (Baltimore, 1967); and Arthur S. Banks and Robert Textor, *A Cross-Polity Survey* (Cambridge, Mass., 1963). See also Wolf, *United States Policy and the Third World;* Hadley Cantril, *The Pattern of Human Concerns* (New Brunswick, N.J., 1966).

30. C. S. Whitaker, Jr., "A Dysrhythmic Process of Political Change," *World Politics,* XIX (1967), 190–217.

31. On aspects of the genesis and impact of authoritarianism and the use of force in developing societies, see Wolf, *United States Policy and the Third World,* chap. 2; Lipset and Solari (eds.), *Elites in Latin America,* chap. 5. See also Braibanti's chapter in this volume, pp. 3–106.

32. Industrial dualism, the coexistence of many inefficient small undertakings with modern large-scale enterprises, succumbs only very gradually to the progress of an economy and its large-scale units. Seymour Broadbridge, *Industrial Dualism in Japan* (Chicago, 1966), esp. chap. 1 and pp. 87–96.

33. See Phillip Dorn, "Egypt's Paralyzed Revolution," *New Leader,* January 30, 1967, pp. 11–14.

reasons, resistance issuing from a people's socio-cultural milieu, and weakness in leadership circles as such. India may serve as a case in point. Much has been written regarding the adverse effects of India's otherworldly tradition, caste system, joint-family system, inheritance system, etc., though note has often been taken of the fact that practical values such as wealth have also been stressed.[34] One concomitant of India's culture, manifest also in other of Asia's village-based societies, is parochialism and apathy; for example, it is reported that barely one Indian villager in three knows about his country's five-year plans and that three out of four do not care whether the plans fail or succeed.[35] Parochialism (or its sources) constitutes a major barrier to economic development in predominantly agricultural societies in which current agricultural output is about as large as it can be under traditional methods of cultivation.[36] Not even a better use of the price system can help much so long as agricultural methods remain essentially traditional.[37] It is for this parochialism, therefore, that India leaders as well as other countries' developers must find a solvent.[38]

34. See, for example, Vikas Mishra, *Hinduism and Economic Growth* (Bombay, 1962), esp. pp. 195–206; John Goheen *et al.*, "India's Cultural Values and Economic Development: A Discussion," *Economic Development and Cultural Change*, VII (1958), 1–12; Ajit Dasgupta, "India's Cultural Values and Economic Development," *ibid.*, XIII (1964), 100–103. See also M. N. Srinivas, *Social Change in Modern India* (Berkeley, 1966); Norman Jacobs, *The Origin of Modern Capitalism and Eastern Asia* (Hong Kong, 1958), pp. 217–219. We are here dealing with what some have called "national character" and its sources, discussions of which, especially of effects of despotism, appear already, as Potter notes, in Herodotus, *Histories*, V, 78, and Hippocrates, *Airs, Waters, Places*. See D. M. Potter, *People of Plenty* (Chicago, 1954), Part I.

35. See J. Anthony Lukas' report in the New York *Times*, December 11, 1966, Sec. I, p. 11, a report based upon a survey published in *Yojana*, the Planning Commission's official journal. Whether this survey is truly representative of Indian villagers' attitudes is not clear. See also Susan Shechan, *Ten Vietnamese* (New York, 1967).

36. See, for example, T. W. Schultz, *Transforming Traditional Agriculture;* also Rosen, *Democracy and Economic Change in India*, pp. 214, 217–218.

37. Rosen, *Democracy and Economic Change in India*, pp. 214–219. I. M. D. Little concluded that "there are prima facie reasons for believing that all important prices in India may diverge seriously from the prices which would ensure overall 'economic efficiency.'" See "The Real Cost of Labor and the Choice Between Consumption and Investments," *Quarterly Journal of Economics*, LXXV (1961), 15; also, A. M. Khusro, "The Pricing of Food in India," *ibid.*, LXXXI (1967), 271–285.

38. William Letwin concludes: "If India wants to achieve economic development, it will have to try, by the process of education, to persuade the peasants and unskilled laborers to want and strive for a much higher standard of living" ("What's Wrong with Planning: The Case of India," *Fortune*, June, 1963, p. 151). Gross domestic product in India grew about 4 per cent per year between 1953 and 1963.

The tasks faced by India's leadership are very great, even given the best of leadership.

Leadership may, of course, prove inadequate. Concerning India, V. D. Kennedy suggests (and I. R. Sinai seems to agree, though various commentators do not) that too many of its leaders are animated by "tendermindedness," a syndrome of symptoms reflecting attitudes unfavorable to economic development, a "highmindedness insufficiently disciplined by intellect" and indisposed to bring common knowledge to bear upon pressing problems.[39] "Mystical confidence that in Hinduism and Indian traditions and culture there is a special essence . . . which will carry India through many troubles" is joined with both "idealization of the peasant as the central figure in an agrarian mystique" and "veneration of the rural way of life." Indian leadership has a "strong emotional identification" with an ethic embracing such values as "equality, freedom for the individual, nonviolence, trusteeship, responsibility of the rich to the poor and of the strong to the weak, morality in all human conduct, and cooperation between individuals and between organizations." Indian "socialism" signifies "the morality of a social order which embodies the above values and in which these values are assured by giving government primacy over private enterprise." There is "an almost eighteenth century faith in the rationality and goodness of man; a belief in his ability to remake society through universal education, laws, science, codes of correct behavior, reform movements, and appeals to moral conscience." Form is put above substance in both education and family life, and ceremony above substance in public and administrative life. Finally, there is "reluctance to face up to the realities of power," to use it to achieve certain social ends. This attitude is based on the belief that use of power is not consistent with belief in man's goodness and reasonableness, or with the democratic rights and harmonious relations "deemed to have been characteristic of traditional India and to be essential to

39. Van D. Kennedy, "India: Tendermindedness vs. Tough Problems," reprinted from *Industrial Relations,* V (1965), 1. See also I. R. Sinai, *The Challenge of Modernisation* (New York, 1964), pp. 190–200. For a more favorable interpretation of India's leadership see Rosen, *Democracy and Economic Change in India,* and Hanson, *India's Five-Year Plans;* also William Clifford, "Hope for India's Hungry," *Think,* July–August, 1967, pp. 31–36.

a socialistic society."[40] India's leaders object to "power politics" but not to "good politics."[41] They appear to be oblivious to the fact that the role of politics is to restrain conflict, not abolish it, to circumscribe interests and interaction among interests, not deny them.[42] They forget that effective sanctions are essential to the securing of good performance. They remain disinclined to make "decisions, particularly those that may be unpopular or involve an exercise of government power in a context of conflicting group interests."[43] Kennedy finds support for his analysis in the failure of Indian authorities to deal more effectively with agricultural, population, and higher-educational problems.[44]

Kennedy identifies four main sources of "tendermindedness": (1) India's British heritage with its emphasis upon generalists and its failure to provide practical experience and non-evadable responsibility; (2) India's own history and culture, with its non-secular philosophy and lack of emphasis upon history and objective reality; (3) the influence of Gandhi and his themes; and (4) the coincidence in time of the emergence of the modern welfare state and the emergence of an autonomous Indian state confronted by many burdensome problems, solution of which will long preclude adoption of the costly and unproductive standards of a welfare state.[45] To these sources one may perhaps add a fifth, the deposit in Indian socio-economic thought of the more or less syncretistic views of India's late nineteenth-century and early twentieth-century reform-oriented jurists and economists. M. G. Ranade (1842–1901), father of Indian economics, is a case in point.[46]

Only a detailed study would reveal the degree to which Ken-

40. These traits are described in Kennedy, "Tendermindedness vs. Tough Problems," pp. 3–7.

41. *Ibid.*, p. 7. Even in England the subject of power has recently ceased to be popular. See Titmuss, *Essays on the Welfare State,* pp. 218, 238 ff.

42. On the role of politics see K. R. Minogue, *The Liberal Mind* (New York, 1964).

43. Kennedy, "Tendermindedness vs. Tough Problems," p. 8.

44. *Ibid.*, p. 13.

45. *Ibid.*, pp. 9–13. See also Gunnar Myrdal, *Asian Drama* (New York, 1968), Part 4.

46. See, for example, Ralph Price, "M. G. Ranade's Theory of Development and Growth," *Explorations in Entrepreneurial History,* IV (1966), 40–52, and H. K. Majumdar's comment, *ibid.*, pp. 53–56.

nedy's assertions are valid. Even then, should support for them be found, it would not follow that the system of selecting leaders in India would always push forward individuals with the attributes described by Kennedy. These surely do not describe the leaders found in the private sector. Moreover, Kennedy's account of the origins of "tendermindedness" suggests that its influence will steadily diminish. The British heritage, especially its emphasis upon generalists, is weakening. The materialistic elements in Indian cultures are becoming stronger. It is becoming increasingly evident that, if income acceleration is the major objective, values antithetical thereto must decline in importance as must diversion of resources to welfare purposes that do not further economic development. It is in the making of this choice and its implementation that the costs of transformation lie.

Sinai[47] implicitly agrees with Kennedy that lack of a determined, self-disciplined leadership is a major cause of the slowness with which modernization and development are proceeding in Asia, both in and outside India. He describes competent leadership as more important than capital, as the key agent of developmental change and means to the effective use of applied science, advanced technology, and competent personnel. He finds in Asia's history an explanation of the comparative absence of those individual character traits (e.g., assertive individualism, secure and well-defined ego, drive to learn and master) which made for development in Europe in the eighteenth and nineteenth centuries. Asia, he argues, has always been traditionalist in character, subject to despotic rule, and without the experience of a Renaissance, Reformation, and Enlightenment, without "those political and social revolutions which have inaugurated a new epoch of civilization, which have changed the lives, the habits, and the values of whole peoples." There has been "hardly a sign of any mass aspiration to freedom." "Asia never found what Europe

47. *The Challenge of Modernisation.* On why the role played by the industrial elite and the urban middle class is no more powerful in Latin America, see Lipset and Solari (eds.), *Elites in Latin America,* chaps. 2–3. According to F. H. Cardoso, however, the industrial elite is quite powerful and in favor of a predominance of the private sector. See "The Entrepreneurial Elites of Latin America," *Studies in Comparative International Development,* II, No. 10 (1966), 147–159.

discovered—man—individual, self-conscious, expansive, seeking, acquiring and tormented."[48] Western imperialism, with its dependence upon direct rule and its small complement of European personnel, did not materially change the traditional character of Asia or Africa; their "ponderous subterranean foundations" were not affected. Whence a new civilization could not come forth in Asia, or dissolve an omnipresent and stagnating tribalism in Africa.[49] Even though some of the elite acquired a taste for Western life styles and trappings, they seldom developed the ideas and skills essential to the support of these styles.[50]

What is needed, Sinai believes, is "a new elite of reformers and innovators, ready and willing to assume the hardships and risks of modernisation," a "new ideology with the power to bring about a cultural revolution," a state capable of imposing very heavy collective costs upon the population, and a new elite committed to force-marching their people into the modern world.[51] What is needed, Sinai seems to believe, are leaders of the Kemal Ataturk type who subordinate democratic and diplomatic niceties to the tasks of modernization. Whether such action would greatly increase human happiness is not considered, probably because economic development is the central objective. Whether such action will succeed depends in part, as did the set of policies pursued in Stalin's command economy, on whether the constellation of conditions present in a country at a given time makes for toleration of life under a forced-draft economy.[52]

It may be noted, as earlier suggested, that while economic and political development are correlated in the long run, economic development can give rise to short-run political costs. (1) Economic development weakens traditional controls, facilitating revolution in the short run, though with the possibility of "stable

48. Sinai, *The Challenge of Modernisation*, pp. 45, 46, chap. 1. Sinai's analysis may be contrasted with that of David C. McClelland in *The Achieving Society* (New York, 1961), and Everett E. Hagen in *On the Theory of Social Change* (Homewood, Ill., 1962).

49. Sinai, *The Challenge of Modernisation*, chap. 2.

50. *Ibid.*, chap. 5.

51. *Ibid.*, pp. 216–218. See also Moore, *Social Origins of Dictatorship and Democracy*.

52. See, for example, P. J. D. Wiles, "The Political and Social Prerequisites for a Soviet-Type Economy," *Economica*, XXXIV (1967), 1–19.

pluralism and decentralization" in the longer run. (2) Economic development "can create new links and points of contact in society" and thereby increase its capacity for non-authoritarian conflict-resolution, though not in such wise as always to prevent "coercive centralization of power." (3) Economic development tends to be accompanied by redistribution of economic and political power, though not necessarily with anti-authoritarian results. (4) Economic development may generate non-satisfiable aspirations and thus contribute to political instability. The capacity of economic development to produce these effects lends support to the view that development within the economic sector is a more powerful "cause" of change in general than development within the political sector.[53]

III. Political vs. Economic Development: Interdependent?

Opinion respecting the contribution of political development to economic development has varied greatly over time in the West. It has varied for theoretical as well as for other reasons.[54] Emphasis upon the economic role of the state declined between the early eighteenth century and World War I but has since increased. It declined for ideological reasons, because of improvements in the apparatus of economic thought and in the self-sufficiency of the business community, and because average income began to rise faster in more democratic than in less democratic nations after 1700 and especially after 1800. It has risen since the 1940's, in large part because many believe that only through almost exclusive emphasis by the state upon the fomentation of economic growth can low-income nations reduce the spread between their income levels and those found in ad-

53. On these effects see Wolf, *United States Policy and the Third World,* pp. 113–114. Dye finds that within the United States economic "causation" outweighs political. Thomas R. Dye, *Politics, Economics and the Public Policy Outcomes in the American States* (Chicago, 1967), chap. 11 and *passim.*

54. For an attempt to determine the relation of political action to economic action, see J. M. Buchanan and Gordon Tullock, *The Calculus of Consent* (Ann Arbor, 1962), pp. 17–30.

vanced lands.[55] Had the ideology of the French Revolution and industrialization spread throughout Europe and into Asia, the middle class would have increased more rapidly and international inequality would be less pronounced today than it is; then presumably the current demand for state intervention would be less pronounced.

As it is, international income disparity is so marked that it will prove very difficult to reduce it notably. Average incomes in advanced countries are something like ten to twenty times those recorded in backward countries.[56] Even if average income should rise 50 to 100 per cent faster in underdeveloped than in developed countries, it would take two or more centuries for averages in many of the former to overtake those in the latter.[57] Moreover, the absolute spread between advanced and underdeveloped countries would increase over much of this period, even should backward countries manifest a capacity to catch up in the long run. Only if the demand for leisure should grow fast enough to countervail income-increasing forces in the advanced countries might one be sanguine about the capacity of underdeveloped countries to catch up.

55. In Isaiah Berlin's terminology, the fox type, with emphasis upon "many ends, often unrelated and even contradictory," became ascendant in the eighteenth and nineteenth centuries, only to give way, in some backward lands in the present century, to the hedgehog type. The hedgehog knows only "one big thing." He relates "everything to a single central vision . . . a single, universal, organizing principle" (see *The Hedgehog and the Fox* [New York, 1957], pp. 7–8). Hegel answered to the description of a hedgehog and, in single-minded devotion to economic growth, so did Stalin. See Wiles' account of Stalin's economy in "Prerequisites for a Soviet-Type Economy." On the spread of the modern industrial system see G. M. Meier and R. E. Baldwin, *Economic Development: Theory, History, Policy* (New York, 1957), Part 2, and William Woodruff, *The Impact of Western Man* (New York, 1967). On the resulting increase in international inequality, see L. J. Zimmerman, *Poor Lands, Rich Lands: The Widening Gap* (New York, 1965), chap. 2. In 1860, 50 per cent of the world's population got about 73 per cent of the world's income; in 1960, about 90 per cent (*ibid.*, p. 38). On the spread of science, see W. H. G. Armytage, *The Rise of the Technocrats: A Social History* (Toronto, 1965).

56. See, for example, W. Beckerman, *International Comparisons of Real Incomes*, OECD Development Centre studies (Paris, 1966), pp. 19, 36–37.

57. Suppose average income in A is fifteen times that in B. Suppose also that average income increases 1.5 per cent per year in A and 2.5 per cent in B. Then it will take about 275 years for the average in B to overtake that in A. Between 1953–54 and 1962–63 gross domestic product in underdeveloped countries grew annually 1–7 per cent, but from this must be deducted a 2–3 per cent rate of population growth (United Nations, *World Economic Survey, 1965* [New York, 1966], Part I, p. 15).

It is therefore not surprising, in view of the apparent lack of capability on the part of many of the underdeveloped countries to do easily what is required to catch up, that the apparatus of state (whether suited to the task or not) is looked upon as the developmental instrument of last resort. This view is strengthened, moreover, by current anticapitalist and anti-free-enterprise ideology as well as by misinterpretation of the emergence of Western welfare and uplift states. As a result the idol of the State becomes ascendant over other idols and *étatistic* theory and ideology displace classic liberal theory and ideology.

Men agree, of course, that there is interaction between economic and political development, though they may disagree about whether politics or economics is primary. Yet the relation of the one to the other is not hard, fast, and continuous, and man's interpretation of the relation is subject to great variability.[58] How one describes the nature of the relation between these two processes turns upon one's definition of each process and upon how holistic is one's conception of the interrelation of the subsystems constituting a total social system. It turns also upon the nature of the quaesitum of one's inquiry, since one may distinguish more or less sharply that upon which one wishes to focus his analytical instruments. Since my central concern is resource allocation, I shall limit my implicit definition of the process of political development to that which appears to bear significantly upon resource allocation; this simplifies theoretical analysis. After all, as Milton Friedman points out: "Viewed as a language, theory has no substantive content; it is a set of tautologies. Its function is to serve as a filing system for organizing empirical material and facilitating our understanding of it; and the criteria by which it is

58. Industrialization (as noted in the section on costs of growth) imposes many costs which tend to generate strong political response and make for authoritarian and/or one-party rule, but this response lies somewhat outside the purview of this essay except insofar as it notably affects economic development. See, for example, Gideon Sjoberg, "Political Structure, Ideology, and Economic Development," in *Studies in Comparative International Development* (Washington University), II, No. 7 (1966), 109–115; Mancur Olson, Jr., "Rapid Growth as a Destabilizing Force," *Journal of Economic History*, XXXIII (1963), 529–552; Karl de Schweinitz, *Industrialization and Democracy: Economic Necessities and Political Possibilities* (Glencoe, Ill., 1964); Jason Finkle and Richard Gable (eds.), *Political Development and Social Change* (New York, 1966), Part III; Wolf, *United States Policy and the Third World*, chaps. 2, 6.

to be judged are those appropriate to a filing system."[59] Acceptance of this approach need not, of course, always entail acceptance of Friedman's emphasis upon capacity for prediction as the main test of the validity of a hypothesis. The universe of conditions may not always be adequately specifiable.[60] Whatever the conditions, however, the economist is interested in "explaining" much by little, not little by much.[61]

Attainment and maintenance of a given state of political development presuppose the presence of a set of minimal economic preconditions. Similarly, the attainment and maintenance of a given state of economic development presuppose the presence of set of minimal political preconditions. A government must be able to perform a set of prerequisite tasks, though there is disagreement over what tasks must normally be included in this set. Indeed, social scientists can agree on the contents of this set only if the societal universe envisaged is specified in sufficient detail. For example, Diamant, following Almond, believes a government must have the capacity to perform a number of functions associated with the facilitation of modernization: creation of national unity and a centralized bureaucracy, international accomodative capability, "widespread dissemination of welfare standards and accomodation between political and social structures," and so on.[62] Performance of these functions, whether or not all are essential to economic development, entails that the polity draw upon the economy for a sufficiency of facilitating resources. The economy may, however, be unequal to this burden; it may be overloaded as were many economies during World War II. When this proves to be the case, the state tends to become more authoritar-

59. *Essays in Positive Economics* (Chicago, 1953), p. 7.
60. On this problem, see Harvey Leibenstein, "What Can We Expect From A Theory of Development?" *Kyklos* (1966), 1–21.
61. Friedman, *Positive Economics*, p. 14.
62. See Alfred Diamant's "The Nature of Political Development" and Gabriel A. Almond's "A Developmental Approach to Political Systems," reprinted in Finkle and Gable (eds.), *Political Development and Social Change*, pp. 91–118, esp. pp. 94–95, where Diamant describes as too restricted the set of minimal conditions listed in my "Economic Development: Political Preconditions and Political Consequences," also reprinted in *ibid.*, pp. 253–268, at 263–264. See also J. D. Montgomery and W. J. Siffin, *Approaches to Development: Politics, Administration and Change* (New York, 1966), and Almond's Introduction in Gabriel A. Almond and James S. Coleman (eds.), *The Politics of the Developing Areas* (Princeton, 1960), pp. 3–64.

ian in character and to subordinate the economy to the polity (as in the Soviet Union).[63]

The situation just described poses on a national scale the problem faced by each individual—how to allocate resources among alternative uses in order to realize the most desirable collection of goods and services. A society, together with its members, is confronted by conflicting goals and claims which must somehow be conciliated if political stability and politico-economic development are to prevail. How is this conciliation to be accomplished, and at what cost? We attempt to answer this question later. Here, however, it is to be noted that every society has had to make provision for allocation, in part because, as Thomas Hobbes stressed, the totality of a society's demands flowing mainly from its polity and its underlying population generally exceeds the capacity of its economy to supply. This shortfall may be accentuated by misinvestment (e.g., by underinvestment in agriculture, neglect of small-scale enterprise, etc).[64]

Arrangements for political and economic allocation constitute only some of the many elements common to all societies, modern and non-modern. The nature of these elements, together with the degree of their interdependence, changes as modernization progresses and the area occupied by a societal system grows. Many of the primary units composing a folk or feudal society are virtually self-sufficient; yet the autonomy of each unit is limited by the nature of that society's culture, together with the smallness of the space which it occupies. It is probably valid to say, therefore, that the subsystems of a traditional folk and feudal society, among them its polity and its economy, are less autonomous and more integrated into the societal totality than are the subsystems constituting a modern societal system, especially one occupying considerable space. Even so, modern societal systems resemble one another much more closely than do premodern societies. Levy concludes, contrary to some opinion, that "relatively modernized

63. See, for example, Wolf, *United States Policy and the Third World,* pp. 33–35, and Edward Shils, *Political Development in New States* (The Hague, 1962), pp. 27–28.

64. See discussion in Dahl and Lindblom, *Politics, Economics and Welfare,* Part 5, and Lewis, *Development Planning,* pp. 38–39, 45, 54, 60–61, 154–155.

societies tend to become more similar to one another as modernization progresses" and that modernization, while subject to upper limits, tends to increase.[65] This trend is comparable, however, with one giving rise to greater autonomy in subsystems, especially in the economic subsystem.

Modernization tends eventually to favor increasing economic autonomy. First, the increasingly technical and dynamic character of the economic subsystem makes increasingly costly interference by the polity or any other subsystem with the economy's performance of its task of transforming inputs into output. In the United States, for example, the federal government has been quite successful in its efforts to prevent restraint of trade,[66] but it remains incompetent to regulate trade practices and enforce so-called fair competition.[67] Second, when a society has attained its main systemic goals and routinized their support, it tends to concern itself with essentially private, individualistic problems

65. *Modernization and the Structure of Societies,* p. 711. Reduction in economic differences between two countries does not necessarily entail reduction in differences between their political systems. So conclude Z. Brzezinski and Samuel Huntington, in *Political Power: USA/USSR* (New York, 1964).

66. It is taken for granted that "individuals and economic entities will be motivated by and act in accordance with their own self-interest" and that a "competitive economy neither assumes nor requires individual unselfishness or nobility beyond compliance with the laws establishing general legal standards." So writes Lee Loevinger, member of the Federal Communications Commission, in "Regulation and Competition as Alternatives," *Antitrust Bulletin,* XI (1966), 101–140, at 108. The United States Supreme Court has declared that

> the Sherman [antitrust] Act was designed to be a comprehensive charter of economic liberty aimed at preserving free and unfettered competition as the rule of trade. It rests on the premise that the unrestrained interaction of competitive forces will yield the best allocation of our economic resources, the lowest prices, the highest quality and the greatest material progress, while at the same time providing an environment conducive to the preservation of our democratic political and social institutions.

Northern Pacific Ry. v. *United States,* 356 U.S. 1, 4 (1958). The intent of this declaration is plain although, as M. Bronfenbrenner shows, the concept of economic freedom has a number of connotations in the universe of discourse ("Two Concepts of Freedom," *Ethics,* LXV [1955], 157–170).

67. "An understandable lack of detailed knowledge of the workings of our industrial economy constitutes a substantial barrier to effective regulation of trade practices by government." This lack of knowledge is due to personnel turnover on regulatory agencies and to "the second American revolution," a proliferation of products and industries, together with continual change in the marketing structure. See J. G. Van Cise, "Regulation—By Business or Government," *Harvard Business Review,* XLIV (1966), 53–56. Durkheim argues that the regulatory power of government decreases as division of labor increases and detail multiplies (*Division of Labor in Society,* pp. 359–362).

and tasks associated with making adjustments to its physical and international environment.[68] Third, as a society develops and average income rises, more of the representative individual's time and income become discretionary, and relatively less of a nation's resources assumes the form of capital, especially of productive physical equipment. As a result, the economy must be adjusted much more closely to consumer preferences, the effective satisfaction of many of which depends upon an economy's sensitivity to the changing requirements of consuming populations. Industries suited to the centralization of entrepreneurial decision-making therefore tend to decline in relative importance when average income ascends above a critical level.[69] For, even though an affluent society generates a relatively large demand for goods that are public in character, or are treated as if they are public or indiscriminate in character, these goods and services may be produced in the private sector.

While agencies of the state may be mobilized to accelerate the rate of economic growth, the progress of political development is conditioned by the progress of economic development. Not only is the role of the state relatively small in non-Communist underdeveloped countries,[70] the size of a state's political role depends also upon the magnitude of the amount of social surplus generated in the private sector and appropriatable for use in the public sector. This magnitude sets outer limits to the state's role, but it does not determine the actual limits. These are determined in considerable measure by a variety of ideological and real circum-

68. See B. F. Hoselitz, "Economic Policy and Economic Development," in H. G. J. Aitken (ed.), *The State and Economic Growth* (New York, 1959), pp. 325–352, also my comments, *ibid.*, pp. 370–372.

69. J. K. Galbraith identifies some of these industries in *American Capitalism* (Cambridge, 1952), chap. 12.

70. The ratio of government receipts or expenditures to gross national product is two to four times as high in developed as in less developed countries. See, for example, Harry T. Oshima, "Share of Government in Gross National Product for Various Countries," *American Economic Review*, XLVII (1957), 381–390; see also "The Increasing Role of the Public Sector," in United Nations (ECAFE), *Economic Survey of Asia and the Far East 1960* (Bangkok, 1961), pp. 53–56, and United Nations, *World Economic Survey, 1965*, Part I, pp. 22, 27. W. A. Lewis estimates that in underdeveloped countries current governmental expenditures will run at least 13 per cent of national income, with capital and other expenditures 4 to 7 per cent. He adds that most underdeveloped countries can raise revenue in an amount approximating at least 17 per cent of gross domestic product (*Development Planning*, pp. 115–117, 127–129).

stances which seem to behave stochastically and cumulatively for long periods until interrupted by other unpredictable sets of circumstances.[71]

V. Allocation

Every society is equipped with structures and mechanisms for the allocation of goods and services as well as for the allocation of power and responsibility.[72] The outcomes of these two types of allocation are only partly independent of one another. He whose economic share is relatively large tends to enjoy a relatively large political share, and he whose political share is relatively large tends to enjoy a relatively large economic share. The degree of correlation between these two relative shares tends to be lower, of course, in societies in which democratic institutions and practices prevail and the economy is one in which free enterprise and the market play major roles.[73] In modern societies, however, as well as in less modern societies emulative of modern societies, allocation may be significantly modified through use of the apparatus of state by those currently in possession of it. This happens almost automatically when the underlying population has acquiesced in a progressive tax system as it tends to do in the wake of war and crisis. For the propensity of a government to spend revenue yielded by its set of taxes tends to approximate unity; it may even exceed unity when the generation of wants deemed satisfiable by the state progresses more rapidly than its inflow of revenue.[74] Since my chief concern is with the impact of allocation

71. On the role of cumulative causation which resembles a stochastic drift see K. W. Kapp, "Social Economics and Social Welfare," reprinted from T. K. N. Unnithan *et al.* (eds.), *Towards a Sociology of Culture in India* (Delhi, 1965), pp. 6–12; also Paul Streeten (ed.), *Value in Social Theory* (London, 1958).

72. See, for example, Levy, *Modernization and the Structure of Societies*, II, pp. 667–673; Dahl and Lindblom, *Politics, Economics and Welfare*, Part 5.

73. While the market determines the return per unit of resources, it does not tend to aggravate the degree of inequality in the ownership of resources. "Any given degree of inequality is a much more serious one in an economy which is governed by status or tradition than in a market economy where there is much chance for shifts in the ownership of resources" (see Milton Friedman, *Price Theory: A Provisional Text* [Chicago, 1962], p. 11).

74. See, for example, E. S. Phelps (ed.), *Private Wants and Public Needs* (New York, 1962). On the behavior of public expenditures, see A. T. Peacock and

upon economic and political development, the interrelation of economic and political allocation is of significance only insofar as it affects the amount and the efficiency of use of inputs directed into political and economic development and as it increases or decreases the supply of human effort and thereby affects the size of the gross national product. Some decrease in economic inequality seems to accompany economic progress, however.[75]

While the ownership and the allocation of inputs dominate the allocation of pretax income, the income side of the distributive coin may be neglected even though the manner in which income is distributed does affect both the overall rate of "saving" and the supply of effort. We may then view input allocation from two vantage points. If our society is comparatively static, we may simply ask if the distribution of inputs among uses meets the requirements of optimality at the relevant margins.[76] This aspect of distribution is not so important, however. Total output is lower, as a rule, than it might be. Yet, even if it were 10–20 percent lower, this amount would represent the maximum gain obtainable through optimization of allocation, and much of this would probably be consumed or taken out in the form of leisure and hence not be available for economic and political development.[77] The form of allocation of predominant importance for

---

Jack Wiseman, *The Growth of Public Expenditures in United Kingdom* (Princeton, 1961). See also R. A. Musgrave, *The Theory of Public Finance* (New York, 1959), chap. 3, and E. Halévy, *The Era of Tyrannies* (Garden City, N.Y., 1965), pp. 265–285. Halévy's essay dealing with war and *étatisme* was written in 1936.

75. See, for example, Simon Kuznets, "Distribution of Income by Size," No. 8 in his series, "Quantitative Aspects of the Economic Growth of Nations," *Economic Development and Cultural Change,* XI (1963), 68–69; Colin Clark, *Conditions of Economic Progress* (3rd ed.; London, 1957), chap. 12; also (2nd ed.; 1951), chap. 12.

76. See, for example, I. M. D. Little, *A Critique of Welfare Economics* (2nd ed.; London, 1960), chaps. 8–9. Optimum conditions of production and exchange do not, of course, insure maximization of welfare (*ibid.,* chaps. 6–7). Mishan suggests that it may not be too difficult, given commercial rivalry, to keep output fairly close to ideal output, and that an income tax reduces somewhat the income inequality associated therewith ("Survey of Welfare Economics," pp. 209–211). Gordon Tullock finds that even this "majority voting process leads to a determinate outcome . . . reasonably satisfactory" ("The General Irrelevance of the General Impossibility Theories," *Quarterly Journal of Economics,* LXXXI [1967], 256–270).

77. See Harvey Leibenstein, "Allocative Efficiency vs. 'X-Efficiency,'" pp. 392–415. It is very important, of course, that the price system remain flexible and free of restraints, especially in a dynamic economy. Otherwise inputs will not be continually redistributed in sufficient measure to preserve an optimum set of relationships as conditions of supply and demand change.

economic and political development is the division of inputs between activities supplying current consumption and activities designed to augment future productive capacity. This was discussed in Section I, where the growth of output and hence of opportunity for development was said to rest upon the rate of growth of generalized capital per capita. It is upon the magnitude of this rate and upon the efficiency with which this capital is used that the rate of economic and political development depends. It implies in particular that the efficiency with which human skills are used, together with the degree to which these skills are developed, may be of predominating importance.

Co-ordination and allocation take place within two subsets of the inclusive set, or economy, which has been described as "islands of conscious power" in an "ocean of unconscious co-ordination."[78] This description, of course, fits a command economy (that of the Soviet Union) much less closely than an essentially free-enterprise economy (the American) or a mixed economy (the British).[79] An island of "conscious power" denotes a business firm, co-ordination and allocation within which are ultimately determined by the individual or collective entrepreneur controlling this firm; he acts in light of his profit-oriented plans of production, of available or expected prices, and of accessible production functions, all of which condition his profit potential. Within the firm, therefore, be it integrated or not, the price mechanism is superseded by the entrepreneur–co-ordinator and his allocating instruments. Outside the bounds of firms and in the "ocean of unconscious co-ordination," however, allocation and co-operation are governed by the price system; "price movements direct production, which is co-ordinated through a series of exchange transactions on the market." A society may thus choose between these two modes of allocation and co-ordination, subject perhaps to constraints imposed by the state. Why is one mode rather than the other chosen in particular instances?

The answer to this question lies in the net advantage of one

78. D. H. Robertson, *Control of Industry* (London, 1946), p. 85.
79. On the command economy see Wiles, *Political Economy of Communism,* chaps. 4–6; also A. Balinky *et al., Planning and the Market in the U.S.S.R.* (New Brunswick, N.J., 1967).

mode as compared to the other. Each mode entails costs; each yields certain gross advantages. It costs a firm to make use of the price mechanism—to acquire market information, to negotiate many small transactions,[80] to enter into contracts of suitable length, etc. At the same time, it costs a firm in various ways to perform allocative and co-ordinating functions within the firm. These costs vary with the size of the firm as well as with other technological and economic circumstances and may change as these various determinants change just as may costs associated with a firm's making use of the market and the price mechanism. In general, therefore, it will pay an entrepreneur to substitute intrafirm co-ordination for extrafirm co-ordination, up to the point where the "costs of organising an extra transaction within the firm become equal to the costs of carrying out the same transaction by means of an exchange on the open market or the costs of organising in another firm." There is not, therefore, a fixed line demarcating the area of intrafirm from that of extrafirm allocation and co-ordination. The actual boundary may shift in either direction, though only within limits, for reasons indicated below.[81] This boundary probably shifts toward the firm as it increases in size and augments its capability for intrafirm allocation and co-ordination.

The price or market system can play several types of roles in a society, each of which is conducive to economic growth. Through decentralization of decision-making it mobilizes incentives present in society. It assembles and transmits accurately information regarding the alternative use values of all resources or inputs and thereby facilitates allocation and co-ordination in a specialized world. It supplies each producer with the buying and selling

80. Consumers too may be disadvantaged by small transactions when these understate the magnitude of actual and potential demand. "It is an inherent characteristic of a consumer-sovereign, market economy that big changes occur as an accretion of moderate-sized steps, each of them the consequence of 'small' purchase decisions, small in their individual size, time perspective, and in relation to their total, combined, ultimate effect." The results may "conflict with the very values the market economy is supposed to serve" (see A. E. Kahn, "The Tyranny of Small Decisions: Market Failures, Imperfections and the Limits of Economics," *Kyklos*, XIX [1966], 23–45, esp. 44–45).

81. The discussion in this and the preceding paragraph is based upon R. H. Coase, "The Nature of the Firm," *Economica*, IV (1937), 386–405; citations are from this source unless otherwise indicated.

prices he needs to carry out his production plans, thereby avoiding the collection and processing of data required in a centralized economy.[82] It provides resource-suppliers with comparable information. It makes it possible for workers and others to remain mobile, to move from employments that pay less well to those that pay better, and thereby to reduce inequality; these opportunities are much less prevalent in a command economy.[83]

The price system, in short, enables a society to meet each of the five interrelated types of economic problems facing it. (1) It rates competing ends in comparable monetary terms and thus permits their efficient choice and reconciliation. (2) It facilitates the allocation and co-ordination of available productive forces among industries and firms by putting scarcity-reflecting prices on inputs and outputs and thereby avoiding waste in the use of scarce inputs.[84] (3) It helps to distribute the product by putting efficient prices on the inputs supplied by factor-owners. (4) It facilitates the maintenance and accumulation of capital by putting an economic price on that which is used today for the benefit of tomorrow. (5) It rations particular products and thus adjusts consumption to production.[85] It also generates supplies by espe-

82. T. C. Koopmans, *Three Essays on the State of Economic Science* (New York, 1957), pp. 22–23; F. A. Hayek, *Individualism and the Economic Order* (London, 1949), pp. 86–91; J. E. Meade, *Planning and the Price Mechanism* (New York, 1949).

83. See N. J. Smelser and S. M. Lipset (eds.), *Social Structure and Mobility in Economic Development* (Chicago, 1966).

84. Economically incorrect prices have occasioned much loss in the Soviet economy. M. S. Prybla writes: "In spite of impressive quantitative performance over the years, the Soviet economy continues to suffer inefficiency in all but a few priority sectors." Poor-quality goods and poor planning and management are responsible. Moreover, pricing itself runs in average instead of in marginal terms ("The Soviet Economy: From Libermanism to Liberalism," *Bulletin of the Institute for the Study of the USSR*, XIII [1966], 19, 26). Given the present planning machinery, the Soviets will need (according to a Soviet estimate) "something like one million computers working day and night at the rate of 30,000 operations per second" (*ibid.*, p. 21, also p. 22 where the world stock of computers is put at 30,000). Wiles points out that Lenin, following Marx, had no clear notion of resource scarcity and allocation and hence of the role of the market. Whence they were predisposed to a command economy (see "Prerequisites for a Soviet-Type Economy," pp. 10–15).

85. See F. H. Knight, *The Economic Organization* (New York, 1951), pp. 7–22, and *Freedom and Reform* (New York, 1947), pp. 335–369. As J. M. Buchanan points out, however, it is misleading to reify a "society" or an "economic system" and represent it as seeking "social welfare" when what is at issue is individuals and their behavior ("What Should Economists Do?" *Southern Economic Journal*, XXX [1964], 214–216).

cially rewarding the providers of that which is scarce, whether particular inputs or enterprise.

The advantages of the price system or free market are of two sorts. First, by making spontaneous instead of imposed order possible, it permits individuals and groups to work toward divergent goals, each making use of his own knowledge, without generating conflict or disorder.[86] Second, the price or market system works automatically, at little cost even to those using it, making new information continuously available and thus providing a flow of feedbacks. "It requires no big administrative apparatus, no central decision-making, and very little policing other than the provision of a legal system for the enforcement of contracts."[87] Wiles, contrasting the market system with the alternative systems found in command economies, indicates that while "a market does not require much less *knowledge* in its participants than a central planning system," it has several advantages. It requires no apparatus "to give orders," the profit motive serving and enforcing this purpose, whereas a central planning system requires an "immense apparatus" to communicate and enforce orders, together with relatively scarce technical personnel at both the order-giving and the order-receiving ends.[88] Even in an essentially free-enterprise economy such as the United States in which information, though not free, is economically supplied,[89] a vast amount of paper work is required, much of it to satisfy innumerable requests on the part of the governmental bureaucracy.[90] On

86. See, for example, Michael Polanyi, *The Logic of Liberty* (London, 1951), chap. 10, and F. A. Hayek, *The Constitution of Liberty* (Chicago, 1960), pp. 159–161.

87. Harry G. Johnson, *Money, Trade and Economic Growth* (Cambridge, Mass., 1962), pp. 156–157.

88. *Political Economy of Communism*, pp. 138–139. To this heavy and inefficient use of technical personnel in communications Wiles traces the excessive use of engineers in the Soviet Union. The objectives of a planned economy "can be achieved in an efficient and free society only if an extensive use is made of the mechanisms of competition, free enterprise, and the free market determination of prices and output" (Meade, *Planning and the Price Mechanism*, pp. v–vi).

89. See, for example, George Stigler, "The Economics of Information," *Journal of Political Economy*, LXIX (1961), 213–225.

90. In a single year one farm-products company filed 37,683 reports to federal agencies. About 12 billion pieces of paper are annually added to federal files; paper-handling occupies much of the time of three government workers out of ten (see J. F. Ter Horst, "Paper Proliferation," Durham *Morning Herald*, May 1, 1966, p. 4; also *Time*, April 24, 1964, p. 94).

the whole, the market system is relatively less well adapted to the needs of fragmented underdeveloped economies than to those of developed countries.[91] This weakness does not, however, constitute an argument for an alternative system; for the inferiority of underdeveloped to developed economies is even more pronounced in respect of alternatives to a price or free-market system. Improvement is most readily found in provision of information, knowledge, and market education to residents of underdeveloped lands so that they can make more effective use of the price system and thereby improve its functioning.

In theory, the price system could function as well in a socialist or collectivized economy as in a free-enterprise economy. This conclusion was an outcome of considerable discussion of pricing in the "socialist state,"[92] stimulated in part by Pareto's work. A. P. Lerner has described with care a set of marginal and related rules for the guidance of the state and the economy's managers. Compliance with these rules would result in the maximization of economic welfare, as defined, just as would result under ideally perfect competition.[93] At issue, however, is whether, under the institutional matrix Lerner implies, the price system would work homeostatically. Would managers and consumers be sensitive to feedbacks as the rules require? Would there exist enforceable sanctions to secure compliance? Or would managers behave as Thomas Hobbes feared men would behave under "Covenants,

91. See, for example, Johnson, *Money, Trade and Economic Growth,* p. 157; K. B. Griffin, "Reflections on Latin American Development," *Oxford Economic Papers,* XVIII (1966), 1–2, 11–12, 17–18; T. Balogh, "Economic Policy and the Price System," United Nations (ECLA), *Economic Bulletin for Latin America,* VII (1961), 41–54; and Lewis, *Development Planning,* pp. 28–31, 58–65.

92. See, for example, B. E. Lippincott (ed.), *On the Economic Theory of Socialism* (Minneapolis, 1938). This consists mainly of papers by Oskar Lange and F. M. Taylor. See also Oskar Lange, *The Working Principles of the Soviet Economy,* Russian Economic Institute, Pamphlet No. 1 (New York, 1944); F. A. Hayek (ed.), *Collectivist Economic Planning* (London, 1935); and Bela A. Belassa, "Success Criteria for Economic Systems," *Yale Economic Essays,* I (1961), 32–7. V. Pareto's analysis, in his *Manual d'economia politica* (Milan, 1906), foreshadowed some of the later discussion. See also Abram Bergson, "Market Socialism Revisited," *Journal of Political Economy,* LXXV (1967), 655–673.

93. *The Economics of Control* (New York, 1944). See also Koopmans, *Three Essays on the State of Economic Science,* pp. 41–66. While Lerner also treats improvement in the division of income, his formal analysis does not stand up as well as that dealing with input allocation. See, for example, Friedman, *Positive Economics,* pp. 307–316.

without the Sword" which "are but words, and of no strength to secure a man at all."[94] Wiles believes that enforcement of Lerneresque socialism would "undoubtedly mean a degree" of "centralized market" economy under which "all decisions as to *intermediate* resource allocations are centralized in a planning office" whereas other decisions are left to the market to which the planners respond.[95] Friedman points out that arrangements such as those proposed by Lerner must

> be judged in part by (1) the practical administrative problems entailed in so operating them as to approximate the economic optimum, and (2) as a corollary, the extent to which they lend themselves to abuse, i.e., the ease with which they can be used for objectives other than the general welfare. Economic institutions do not operate in a vacuum. They form part, and an extremely important part, of the social structure within which individuals live. They must also be judged by (3) their non-economic implications, of which the political implications—the implications for individual liberty—are probably of the most interest and the ethical implications the most fundamental.[96]

Unfortunately not enough empirical work has been done on issues raised in this or the next section to permit answers in which we may always place unqualified confidence. Reiterated condemnation of governmental economic intervention produces only superficiality. Much of the discussion of the formulation and administration of economic policies remains as if we were still in the seventeenth century.[97] Yet, as Stigler shows, the measurement of

94. *Leviathan* (1651), Everyman's Library (London, 1943), chap. 17, p. 87. See Dahl and Lindblom, *Politics, Economics and Welfare*, pp. 210–218.

95. Wiles, *Political Economy of Communism*, pp. 68, 78. Wiles describes (p. 80) Lange's model (see Lippincott [ed.], *Economic Theory of Socialism*) as approximating that of a "centralized market" economy.

96. *Positive Economics*, pp. 317–318. Loevinger reasons in a manner parallel to Friedman's when he observes that "the regulatory function will be effective only as it recognizes and accomodates the realities of social and individual human conduct. . . . The only [regulatory] system which has any chance of success is one that takes men as they are and is capable of functioning with normal, imperfect and somewhat selfish human beings" ("Regulation and Competition as Alternatives," p. 137). As C. A. Reich points out, the increasing importance of governmental largesse poses economic as well as ethical questions, among them some affecting motivation ("The New Property," *Yale Law Journal*, LXXIII [1964], 733–787).

97. See George Stigler, "The Economist and the State," *American Economic Review*, LX (1965), 1–18, and "Private Enterprise and Public Intelligence," in American Bankers Association, *Proceedings on Business-Government Relations* (New York, 1966), pp. 36–46.

economic relationships has greatly improved, and economists will soon be testing economic policy-legislation and related legal matter to determine whether particular laws should be retained or discarded. Our current capacity to anticipate the effects of legislation, already considerable, should therefore be appreciably augmented.[98]

VI. Allocative Systems Compared

In the preceding section some comparisons were made of market and non-market or partial-market systems.[99] Detailed comparison is possible only in the light of selected criteria such as income distribution, consumer satisfaction, efficiency in resource allocation, dynamic efficiency, rate of growth of national income, etc. One mode of organization is likely to be rated unambiguously superior to another only when no more than one or two criteria are employed; when this number is increased, one mode is likely to rate high in terms of one or more indicators (e.g., rate of growth) but low in terms of others (e.g., consumer satisfaction). Since our concern is development we may emphasize indicators positively correlated with development, but we must remain sensible of the costs of this development, especially if they prove to be high.

Before contrasting market and non-market systems as such, two questions need to be posed with respect to underdeveloped countries. (1) Which system incorporates the set of incentives, disincentives, and feedbacks best suited to impel decision-makers and the relatively passive underlying population to achieve economic and political development? This question is dealt with below. It is not answered in entirety, since detailed study has not been made of all the various settings or structures in which decision-makers and the labor force may carry on. On a priori grounds, however, the free market seems the preferable structure, given occasional corrective intervention.[100]

98. Spengler "The Economist and the State," pp. 16–17.

99. On the shortcomings and advantages of price-system and centrally controlled allocation, respectively, see Dahl and Lindblom, *Politics, Economics and Welfare*, chaps. 9, 14–16.

100. See, for example, Meade, *Planning and the Price Mechanism.*

(2) Which system tends to select and elevate active decision-makers interested in performance rather than in tranquility? On this score the free-market system is superior to any other. The bureaucrat, as Johnson points out, has a "natural propensity to regulate," be he mandarin, district officer, or what. "A good civil service, or a bad one, is rarely prepared to decide that non-intervention is the best policy; and to the bureaucratic mind the functioning of the price system as a regulator appears mere disorder and chaos." The bureaucrat tends to be hostile to entrepreneurship; after all "the entrepreneur is an agent of change and as such disturbs the orderliness of the economy and makes it more difficult to regulate." To this statement there are exceptions, of course, in that "civil services have, at times, played important entrepreneurial roles themselves, though usually under the pressure of political events." As a rule, literate and "responsible" civil servants are antipathetic to the semiliterate, socially unacceptable types who manifest a knack for trading and perhaps a capacity for helping to get development underway. Even when intervention for the sake of development is indicated in an underdeveloped country, few honest civil servants are likely to prove capable of such intervention.[101] When civil servants are dishonest, bribes may prove instruments of progress should they displace man-made barriers to economic development or correct allocational externalities.[102]

101. My discussion under (2) draws on Johnson, *Money, Trade and Economic Growth,* pp. 154–155. See also Anthony Downs, *Bureaucratic Structure and Decision-Making,* RAND Corporation Memorandum RM–4646–PR (Santa Monica, 1966); Dahl and Lindblom, *Politics, Economics and Welfare,* pp. 220–226, 243–261; Gordon Tullock, *The Politics of Bureaucracy* (Washington, 1965). W. A. Lewis stresses the crucial importance of a good civil service in underdeveloped countries seeking economic growth, together with the usual shortage of such civil servants (*Development Planning,* pp. 100, 156, 272–273).

102. Bribes do not, of course, always function effectively. See M. I. Kamien, N. L. Schwartz, and F. T. Doebear, "Asymmetry between Bribes and Charges," *Water Resources Research,* II (1966), 147–157; also Buchanan and Tullock, *Calculus of Consent,* pp. 186–187, 197–199. Theodore Morgan finds that "corruption can, in extreme cases, be not only desirable but essential to keep the economy going" ("The Theory of Order in Centrally-Directed Economic Systems," *Quarterly Journal of Economics,* LXXVIII [1964], 414–415). On the extent of bribery see Hirschman, *Journeys Toward Progress* (see index), and Braibanti and Associates, *Asian Bureaucratic Systems* (see index). On causes of corruption, together with its correction, see Ralph Braibanti, "Reflections of Bureaucratic Corruption," *Public Administration* (London), XL (1962), 357–372, and Nathaniel Leff, "Economic Development Through Bureaucratic Corruption," *American Behavioral Scientist,* VIII (1964), 8–14.

It is notable in passing that bureaucratic organization may accentuate traits likely to be present in those who elect to become civil servants.[103] Where one works may condition one's solutions to political as well as to other problems.[104] Even within the private sector bureaucratic organization can sometimes virtually petrify executives and orient them to routinized community and public service.[105]

Within both the private sector and the public sector in advanced societies a number of forces are operating to weaken the grip of pyramidal bureaucratic organization. Among these, at least in the private sector, are rapid and unexpected change, complexity of operations which increases with a firm's size, increasing complexity of modern technology and the concomitant need for highly specialized competence, and changes in the philosophy of management resulting in greater emphasis upon personal development.[106] In the public sector satisfaction with "wisdom" and "folk knowledge" (so characteristic of departments of foreign affairs) is giving way to recognition of the central role played in modern social systems by science and information, especially social science and information and the policy-shaping images which they generate.[107] In both the public sector and the

103. In the United States the greatest appeal of civil service is "to the insecure, the less well educated, the less ambitious, the less adventursome"; the least is "to those the civil service needs most: well-trained people with good minds who are willing to try new ideas that could change the fate of men." Unfortunately, high school teachers are the most faithful exponents of civil service. See John Lear, "To Restore Adventure to American Democracy," *Saturday Review of Literature,* September 7, 1963, pp. 39–42, at p. 41. This is based upon F. P. Kilpatrick, M. C. Cummings, and M. K. Jennings, *The Image of the Federal Service* (Washington, 1964). See also Gordon Tullock, *The Politics of Bureaucracy* (Washington, 1965); J. H. Crider, *The Bureaucrat* (New York, 1944); and Harry Cohen, *The Demonics of Bureaucracy* (Ames, Iowa, 1967).

104. S. M. Lipset and M. A. Schwartz, "The Politics of Professionals," in H. Vollmer and D. L. Mills (eds.), *Professionalization* (New York, 1966), p. 304; Dahl and Lindblom, *Politics, Economics and Welfare,* pp. 218–226.

105. See E. E. Jennings, *The Executive: Autocrat, Bureaucrat, Democrat* (New York, 1962). See also discussion of entrepreneurship and management in United Nations (ECAFE), *Economic Bulletin for Asia and the Far East,* IX (1958), 30–33.

106. W. G. Bennis, "The Coming Death of Bureaucracy," *Think,* November–December, 1966, pp. 30–35. Although underdeveloped countries usually are short of large-scale entrepreneurship, the local civil service cannot make up that lack, which is best solved through use of foreign entrepreneurship (Lewis, *Development Planning,* pp. 156, 271–272).

107. See K. E. Boulding's critical review of D. K. Price's *The Scientific Estate* (Cambridge, Mass., 1965), in *Scientific American,* CCXIV (1966), 131–134; also K. E. Boulding, *The Impact of the Social Sciences* (New Brunswick, N.J., 1966).

private sector a growing interest in long-range forecasting and planning is proving inimical to stereotyped bureaucratic organization. Meanwhile, the so-called contract state is accentuating the flow of information between the public and the private sector and affecting the views of decision-makers. In general, built-in change is continually countervailing bureaucratic efforts to contain it.

Returning now to our comparison of systems of organization and their impacts upon consumption and through it upon development. Whatever favors consumption beyond the point where increments in consumption beget offsetting increments in output tends to check production and growth. Emphasis upon consumer satisfaction has this effect and so does undue reduction in the inequality with which income is distributed. Consumer freedom and sovereignty therefore tend to slow down economic development as well as (in the opinion of some economists) to make for less satisfaction than arrangements imposing some constraint on what consumers do.[108] Holzman argues, therefore, that the concept of consumer sovereignty needs to be revised, not in keeping with highly authoritarian dictates, but in such wise as to narrow "the gap between planner and consumer sovereignty concerning the appropriate rate of investment."[109] Such narrowing does not violate consumer sovereignty "by as much as is generally assumed" since it increases welfare in the near future and since, had consumers hindsight, they would invest more than they actually do.[110] The market is not, after all, adapted to anticipating the future in such wise as to determine what constitutes optimal investment.[111] In reality, therefore, actual investment may be ex-

108. See, for example, Balassa, "Success Criteria for Economic Systems," pp. 22–26.

109. F. D. Holzman, "Consumer Sovereignty and the Rate of Economic Development," reprinted from *Economia Internazionale*, XI (1958), 5.

110. *Ibid.*, pp. 16–17. See also Dahl and Lindblom, *Politics, Economics and Welfare*, pp. 375, 377, 385–393, 413–434; H. A. Simon, "The Planning Approach in Public Economy: A Reply," *Quarterly Journal of Economics*, LV (1941), 325–330; and J. G. March and H. A. Simon, *Organizations* (New York, 1958).

111. As K. J. Arrow remarks, "there is an inadequate number of future markets to achieve the allocation of resources over time that is required by the theory of resource allocation" (see "Tinbergen on Economic Policy," *Journal of American Statistical Association*, LIII [1958], 95).

cessive or too little; it may be correctly or incorrectly allocated;[112] it may or may not yield visible results that induce a people to put up with the austerities involved.[113]

The market system may not necessarily give rise to either static or dynamic efficiency and thus maximize the gross output out of which gross savings flow. Given external effects,[114] increasing returns to scale, product indivisibility, and other traits of "publicness," the market will not give rise to an optimum solution even if information is complete. There exists a category of public and quasi-public goods to whose production and distribution the market is imperfectly adapted. Then, if deviations from the optimum emerge, private and social costs diverge, and essentially collective or public goods are forthcoming in deficient quantity, econoists believe, even as did Adam Smith, the state must intervene with taxes and subsidies to equalize costs and correct the deviations or with alternative arrangements. Economists may differ, however, regarding the mode of action, or the degree to which it is pursued. They may believe that externalities are not very important, or that they are capable of being negotiated, or that the costs of correction often approximate or exceed the gains.[115]

112. See Gerald M. Meier (ed.), *Leading Issues in Development Economics* (New York, 1964), pp. 416–418, 431–439. "Economic growth is not merely a matter of investment as such," writes J. R. Hicks, "but of investment in ways that are sufficiently productive" (*Essays in World Economics* [Oxford, 1959], p. 177). See also Lewis, *Development Planning*, pp. 265–273. Subjection of planning to input-output analysis and linear programming makes for balance and avoidance of imbalance within the framework of a national plan (*ibid.*, chap. 3, also pp. 36–38).

113. Wolfgang Stolper, "Politics and Economics in Economic Development," reprinted from *Rivista di Politica Economica*, Vol. LIII (1963); Wiles, "Prerequisites for a Soviet-Type Economy," pp. 8–9, 18.

114. B. P. Herber, "The Social Balance Controversy in Perspective," *Quarterly Review of Economics and Business*, VII (1967), 29–36; Breton, "The Demand for Public Goods." The role of external economies in underdeveloped countries tends to be exaggerated. What these economies are expected to do in a closed economy is done by international trade and the integration of underdeveloped economies (which are always open economies) into the world economy (W. F. Stolper, "External Economies from a Planning Standpoint," *Zeitschrift für die Gesamte Staatswissenschaft*, CXIX [1963], 195–217, esp. 197–199). W. A. Lewis puts more stress upon external economies in underdeveloped countries (*Development Planning*, pp. 31–36, 258).

115. See Stanislaw Wellisz, "On External Diseconomies and the Government-Assisted Invisible Hand," *Economica*, XXXI (1964), 345–362, and reply by O. A. Davis and A. B. Whinston, "On Externalities, Information and the Government-

That a planned system may be more dynamically efficient than a market system is sometimes asserted on the ground that the former can both foster a higher rate of capital formation and co-ordinate investment and research decisions *ex ante*. In reality, of course, the final outcome may be more favorable now under the one, and now under the other system.[116] That a planned system will almost automatically produce more capital than will a free-market system is admissible,[117] since the state may intervene to elevate the rate of capital formation as well as seek to allocate it more appropriately among competing investment projects. Yet should uneconomic pricing or other adverse effects be permitted, these effects may offset the efforts of the state to step up the effective rate of investment.[118]

Certain weaknesses inhere in centrally directed systems, be they public or private. Mention may be made of recurring "discrepancies between targets and results at the plant level and uncoordinated decisions taken by officials at various echelons in the hierarchy";[119] of the "administrative limitations of a system of

Assisted Invisible Hand," *Economica*, XXXIII (1966), 303–318; Alan Williams, "The Optimal Provision of Public Goods in a System of Local Government," *Journal of Political Economy*, LXXIV (1966), 18–33. See also Herber, "The Social Balance Controversy"; Balassa, "Success Criteria for Economic Systems," pp. 8–13; William Baumol, *Welfare Economics and the Theory of the State* (Cambridge, Mass., 1952), chap. 14; R. H. Coase, "The Problem of Social Cost," *Journal of Law and Economics*, III (1960), 1–44; and Johnson, *Money, Trade and Economic Growth*, p. 158. But see K. W. Kapp, *The Social Costs of Private Enterprise* (Cambridge, Mass., 1950).

116. Balassa, "Success Criteria for Economic Systems," p. 13.

117. Wiles, *Political Economy of Communism*, chap. 13, also chap. 19; also, Anthony Downs, "The Public Interest: Its Meaning in a Democracy," *Social Research*, XXIX (1962), 34–36. A rule of thumb might be, Lewis suggests, that 50 or more per cent of the per capita "increase in (gross) output must go into private consumption," and the balance to savings (*Development Planning*, pp. 160–164).

118. Balassa, "Success Criteria for Economic Systems," pp. 17–20. See also Vera Lutz, *French Economic Planning*, American Enterprise Institute (Washington, 1965). She was unable to determine if the French system of planning investment had actually increased France's rate of growth (*ibid.*, p. 95). On uneconomic pricing in planned economies, see Wiles, *Political Economy of Communism*, chap. 6, esp. pp. 108–109, 116–119, 121–125, 128, also pp. 135, 137, 143–146, and chap. 10; also, Meade, *Planning and the Price Mechanism*, chap. 1; also Z. M. Fallenbuchl, "Investment Policy for Economic Development: Some Lessons of the Communist Experience," *Canadian Journal of Economics and Political Science*, XXIX (1963), 26–39.

119. J. M. Montias, "On the Consistency and Efficiency of Central Plans," *Review of Economic Studies*, XXIX (1962), 289.

central direction";[120] and of a tendency for restraints to proliferate, at least at times.[121] There is present also, Morgan believes, an incapacity to avoid faults and cumulative errors associated with size:

> First, such organizations drift toward fewer but bigger general errors than does the decentralized system. Second, central direction tends toward delay, excessive optimism, and extensions of controls. As to incentives: the centrally-directed system offers the contrast of compulsive and completely adequate incentives to the executive and his group, offset by modest incentives or the treadmill for the many. The desire of the central director for public approval means that he will systematically tend to choose conspicuous actions in accord with the community's conventional wisdom—and that usually deviates more or less from what is actually best. Notably, central authorities often rely on what are considered the highest motives; but the work of the world gets done best when reliance is on the strongest motives. Fourth and finally, the divergence between the highest and the strongest motives, and between public and private interests, leads to hypocrisy. Hypocrisy is plainly a social loss, but the latter resorts can on occasion be socially useful, offering the only way that wooden-headed or unlucky policies can be made reasonably consistent with economic survival or progress.[122]

There is finally weakness in the error-correcting capacity of feedback mechanisms present in large-scale centrally directed systems, above all those established on a country-wide basis. Not only are the indicators fewer and weaker than in a free-market system; bureaucratic officials are also interested in covering up failures or difficulties,[123] instead of being motivated to recognize them, as do private entrepreneurs or their agents, and taking corrective action.

120. Polanyi, *The Logic of Liberty*, chap. 8. See also Janos Kornai, *Overcentralization in Economic Administration* (Oxford 1959), chaps. 5–6.

121. L. Athanasion, "Some Notes on the Theory of the Second Best," *Oxford Economic Papers*, XVIII (1966), 81–87, at 86.

122. "Theory of Order," p. 419. See also Holland Hunter, "Optimum Tautness in Developmental Planning," *Economic Development and Cultural Change*, IX (1961), 561–572.

123. The role of criticism, especially that flowing from a critical opposition, may not be appreciated. See Stolper, "Politics and Economics," pp. 8–10.

VII. Optimizing the Role of the State in Economic Development

In this section we touch upon the role that the state, the people's political instrument, may optimally play in the fomenting of economic development and (hence) such political development as is complementary to economic development. The developmental role of the state is limited in two respects: (1) by characteristics of the penalty-reward system operative in the public sector; and (2) by the fact that the apparatus of state in underdeveloped countries operates under limitations imposed by dearth of critical inputs. These limits, together with their implications, may be examined in order.

1. The system of incentives and disincentives operative in the public sector, together with the generation, flow, and use of information in that sector, is less conducive to creative entrepreneurship, factor mobility, and economy in resource use, than its correspondents in the private sector. In the bureaucracy, especially in its upper reaches, "the superior-subordinate relationship is most characteristic";[124] one gets promoted by finding out what one's immediate superiors want done and doing it. The criterion of remuneration then is not always productivity of predetermined objects preferred by society but compliance with the desires of immediate superiors. The harm resulting would be less if orders stipulating objectives flowed speedily downward from the apex of a bureaucratic pyramid to those in its lower reaches where the prescribed actions were carried out. This seldom happens. Moreover, the process is inferior to one involving optimum decentralization of the making and execution of decisions.[125]

When both decision-formation and decision-execution are decentralized among departments, the probability increases that the bureaucrats controlling a given department will endeavor to

124. Tullock, *The Politics of Bureaucracy*, pp. 11–14.

125. *Ibid.*, pp. 141, 157, 168, 221, 224. See also pp. 161–164 for Tullock's comparison of the army's comparative inefficiency in supplying its vehicles with spare parts when needed with the market system's comparative efficiency in supplying owners of private vehicles.

augment its size and undertakings. This tendency is somewhat held in check, however, by the hidden hand present in the government sector. Interagency and related bargaining representing a multiplicity of interests gives rise to decisions "closer to satisfying the welfare equation than they would if no such mechanism existed."[126] Even so, policy may be influenced by the desire of upper-level officials to win or retain position, unless they are unusually committed to the "public interest."[127] It is essential, therefore, to "design social mechanisms that utilize men's actual motives to produce social conditions as close as possible to our ideal of 'the good society.' "[128]

2. Economic development entails four types of action: (*a*) transformation of inputs into growth-oriented output; (*b*) diversion of resources from current to future-oriented use; (*c*) economical use of all of a nation's resources; (*d*) specification of output required in economic development. The role of the state is likely to be much smaller in accomplishing *a* and *c* than *b* and *d*.

a) The state is poorly qualified to transform inputs into some types of output. Its bureaucratic personnel usually lack competence, indicators of performance, a relatively simple communication system, and freedom to modify the character of the product when such modification will better or cheapen it. The bureaucrat is much more bound by the blueprint which can be a progress-retarding constraint when the product defined is a new one.[129] It is in keeping with the principle of specialization, therefore, that responsibility for transformation of inputs be vested largely in the private sector. Some services, of course, can be best supplied by agencies of the state. When the state becomes involved in the

126. McKean, "The Unseen Hand in Government," pp. 409–505.

127. Downs, "The Public Interest," pp. 31–33; R. E. Flathman, *The Public Interest* (New York, 1966).

128. Downs, "The Public Interest," pp. 32.33. See also Peter Bernholz's comments upon the impact of a country's economic structure upon the political behavior of voters and the response thereto of politicians, in "Economic Policies in a Democracy," *Kyklos*, XIX (1966), 48–79.

129. See, for example, J. S. Livingston, "Decision Making in Weapons Development," *Harvard Business Review*, XXXVI (1958), 127–136; also unsigned "Defense Procurement," *Time*, September 8, 1958, p. 86. The behavior of contractors in respect of risk aversion is treated by F. M. Scherer, in "The Theory of Contractual Incentives for Cost Reduction," *Quarterly Journal of Economics*, LXXVIII (1964), 257–280. See also Lewis, *Development Planning*, pp. 265–274.

supply of particular goods and services, however, it may have to choose among alternative modes of organization, of which the public corporation is often the preferable form.[130]

b) The state can divert resources from non-development to development-oriented use. It can do this through subsidies, tax concessions, and cheap credit to private enterprise, through appropriate taxation and diversion of the funds collected to enterprise,[131] and through stimulating savings by offers of higher interest rates to private savers. Of great importance also is reduction of military, paramilitary, police, showpiece-capital (e.g., airlines, steel mills), and public-luxury expenditures.[132] Of even greater importance is diminution of natality, now a major absorber of potential capital resources in most underdeveloped countries.

c) While agencies of the state may not be highly adapted to utilizing given resources economically, they can contribute importantly to making known the range of resources and productive potentials available for economic exploitation. The real lack in underdeveloped countries, Watson and Dirlam conclude, is not capital or foreign exchange or natural resources. It is lack of information,[133] lack of suitable projects ready for implementation, and lack of qualified personnel. There is little statistical and related information essential to planning.[134] This lack of information in turn results in the turning up of very few implementable projects, even when funds for such projects are available. "The lack of skilled human resources is generally more serious than any other resource lack, and is at the root of all the other main shortages characteristic of underdevelopment." This shortage

130. See, for example, A. H. Hanson, *Public Enterprise and Economic Development* (London, 1959), chap. 11.

131. M. Bronfenbrenner points to the importance of sales, land, capital-gains, and income taxes confined to higher brackets ("Some Development Pitfalls and Their Avoidance," *Philippine Economic Journal,* IV [1965], 98–99). See also Ursula Hicks, *Development Finance Planning and Control* (New York, 1965); A. Basch, *Financing Economic Development* (New York, 1964); and Johnson, *Money, Credit, and Economic Growth*, pp. 160–164.

132. Bronfenbrenner, "Some Development Pitfalls," pp. 102–104.

133. See W. F. Stolper, *Planning Without Facts* (Cambridge, Mass., 1966). This work is based upon Stolper's experience as a planner in Nigeria.

134. Even in advanced countries economic policy has been misguided by inadequate statistics. See, for example, W. Allen Wallis, "Economic Statistics and Economic Policy," *Journal of the American Statistical Association,* LXI (1966), 1–10; K. J. Arrow, "Statistics and Economic Policy," *Econometrica,* XXV (1957), 523–531; and Fernand Martin, "The Information Effect of Economic Planning," *Canadian Journal of Economics and Political Science,* XXX (1964), 328–342.

may be accentuated by collectivized planning.[135] Watson and Dirlam conclude, therefore, that the main initial undertakings in a country seeking to develop should be directed to gathering essential statistical information, to inventorying natural resources, to programming in as much detail as possible the range of possible projects (*inter alia*, legal, fiscal, and administrative reforms), and, above all, to developing "a more enlightened and capable labor force at all levels, for both the government and the private sectors."[136]

> More can be achieved if the government creates conditions which will encourage maximum activity in the private sector—that is, if the greatest possible amount of talent and capital, which for one reason or another lie beyond the government's control, is mobilized. To obtain such increments, however, the government may have to be content to lose much control over the economy. It may even have to reconcile itself to a considerable measure of foreign domination of economic life.[137]

It should be noted also that import substitution beyond a point may draw on relatively scarce domestic resources and thus check investment in export industry even when the latter is yielding a higher return than import substitution.[138] Foreign protectionism serves, of course, to stimulate attempts at import substitution even when the domestic market is small.

d) The state can play a principal role in determining the composition of output and orienting it to economic development. It will do this, not by engaging in the transformation of input into output, but by modifying the composition of aggregate demand. This entails interfering with consumer sovereignty and freedom

135. See, for example, Z. M. Fallenbuchl, "Collectivization and Economic Development," *Canadian Journal of Economics and Political Science*, XXXIII (1967), 12. If a manpower budget is carefully prepared and governmental undertakings are neither excessive nor overmanned a central plan should not prove wasterful of human resources.

136. A. M. Watson and J. B. Dirlam, "The Impact of Underdevelopment on Economic Planning," *Quarterly Journal of Economics*, LXXIX (1965), 167–194, at 192.

137. *Ibid.*, pp. 193–194. See my "Bureaucracy and Economic Development," in Joseph La Palombara (ed.), *Bureaucracy and Political Development* (Princeton, 1963), pp. 215–223. Whether nationalism greatly stimulates the growth of per capita income remains subject to dispute. See Morris Silver, "The Relationship Between Nationalism and Per Capita Gross National Product: Comment," *Quarterly Journal of Economics*, LXXXI (1967), 155–157.

138. Harry G. Johnson, *Economic Policies Toward Less Developed Countries* (Washington, 1966), pp. 57–59, 71–74.

of choice and diverting inputs to the production of output prerequisite to economic development but not forthcoming within the private sector or the public sector as currently financed. Most of the output required answers to the description of infrastructure and overhead capital inclusive of provision for education. The major problem aside from making adequate total provision is that of avoiding excessive or inadequate provision for particular components of that for which the state is responsible. It may also be necessary for the state to prevent underinvestment in regions with potential; this is most likely to occur in former colonies dominated by primate cities.

A very important advantage flows from limiting the role of the state to the supply of so-called orthodox types of government service and the developmental role of the bureaucracy to the gathering of essential information and the discovery of lines of productive activity strongly contributive to economic development. This advantage consists in economy in the use of skilled personnel, the most strategic as well as the scarcest of the growth-favoring agents of production to be found in underdeveloped countries. For then it is possible to devote a large fraction of a nation's skilled personnel, together with personnel possessed of entrepreneurial skill, to the business of transforming input into output, much of it growth-oriented. It also becomes easier to overcome the politically destabilizing presence of large numbers of unemployed and underemployed in cities, attracted there by illusory prospects of a better life than is to be had in the rural areas. For the generation of employment depends more upon the availability of entrepreneurs than upon that of "capital."[139]

VIII. The Universality of Exchange

In the preceding sections attention has been focused upon allocation. Allocation implies scarcity of that which is allocated, and hence conflict respecting its use; where there is enough of something to satisfy all requirements at zero price, the need to allocate it does not arise. Allocation therefore presupposes the

139. It depends also upon the avoidance of supra-equilibrium wage levels. See B. I. Cohen and N. H. Leff, "Employment and Industrialization: Comment," *Quarterly Journal of Economics*, LXXXI (1967), 162–164.

presence of allocative mechanisms, which involve varying degrees of exchange except when distribution is arbitrarily and dictatorially administered by an absolute ruler. Exchange does not, of course, increase the amount of that which is allocated, at least in the short run. But it does increase the amount of service or utility derivable by exchanging individuals from a given amount of scarce resources; it is thus a positive-sum game. Exchange thus not only organizes the economic world but also, in so doing, allocates resources. One may therefore approach the study of allocation through the study of exchange. Indeed, if we do this, we deal with a process that operates within the public sector, within the private sector, and within the realm of relationships knitting the two sectors into an all inclusive resource-using totality. We then have in hand a universal mechanism—bargaining and exchange in the face of scarcity—use of which permits us to reduce what happens in the public and the private sector, respectively, to comparable if not quite identical terms.

It seems to have been early recognized that free exchange is a positive-sum game, at least in the economic world. Exchange served to hold a community together so long as the terms of exchange were just, Aristotle believed.[140] It remained for eighteenth-century economists (especially Adam Smith) to note the important economic role of exchange and for Archbishop Whately to express a view that some economists continued to stress: "Man," observed Whately, "might be defined, 'An animal that makes Exchanges'"; but, being concerned only with "economics," he went on to describe this science as "Catallactics, or the 'Science of Exchanges.'"[141] The usefulness of this approach has recently been stressed by students of decision-making in market and non-market situations,[142] as well as by those concerned with the resolution of conflict situations.[143]

140. *Nichomachean Ethics,* 1132b, 1133a. Compare Durkheim, *Division of Labor in Society,* Book II, chap. 2, also pp. 706–709; also Plato, *Republic,* 462–464.

141. Richard Whately, *Introductory Lectures on Political Economy* (London, 1831), p. 6, also p. 7.

142. Buchanan, "What Should Economists Do?" pp. 213–222. He prefers "symbiotics," or "study of the association between dissimilar organisms," to both "economics" and "catallactics" (*ibid.*, p. 217).

143. See, for example, Boulding, *Conflict and Defense, passim,* and "Towards a Pure Theory of Threat Systems," *American Economic Review, Papers and Pro-*

The universality of exchange phenomena, though implied in premodern documents,[144] was slow to be recognized. Recently, however, Blau has defined exchange as "a social process of central significance in social life," one that guides a great deal of human behavior. It must, however, "be oriented towards ends that can only be achieved through interaction with other persons, and it must seek to adapt means to the further achievement of these ends."[145]

Of especial pertinence for the present discussion is Buchanan's conclusion respecting the interrelation of economics and politics.

> The distinction to be drawn between economics and politics, as disciplines, lies in the nature of the social relationships among individuals that is examined in each. In so far as individuals exchange, trade, as freely-contracting units, the predominant characteristic of this behavior is "economic." And this, of course, extends our range far beyond the ordinary price-money nexus. In so far as individuals meet one another in a relationship of superior-inferior, leader to follower, principal to agent, the predominant characteristic in their behavior is "political," stemming, of course, from everyday usage of the word "politician." Economics is the study of the whole system of exchange relationships. Politics is the study of the whole system of coercive or potentially coercive relationships. In almost any particular social institution, there are elements of both types of behavior, and it is appropriate that both the economist and the political scientist study such institutions. What I should stress is the potentiality of exchange in those socio-political institutions that we normally consider to embody primarily coercive or quasi-coercive elements. To the extent that man has available to him alternatives of action, he meets his associates as, in some sense, an "equal," in other words, as in a trading relationship. Only in those situations where pure rent is the sole element in return is the economic relationship wholly replaced by the political.[146]

---

ceedings, LIII (1963), 424–434; T. C. Schelling, *The Strategy of Conflict* (Cambridge, Mass., 1960).

144. See, for example, Marcel Mauss, *The Gift* (Glencoe, Ill., 1954), pp. 1–5 and *passim.* See p. xiv for lines from the *Edda,* cited also by Gustav Cassel in his *Theory of Social Economy,* trans. S. L. Barron (New York, 1932), p. 371. See also David Easton, *A Framework for Political Analysis* (Englewood Cliffs, N.J., 1965), pp. 47–48, 107–111.

145. Peter M. Blau, *Exchange and Power in Social Life* (New York, 1964), pp. 4, 5.

146. "What Should Economists Do?" pp. 220–221.

Four sectors, or sets, of situations, *within* which some degree of freedom to bargain exists may be identified. (1) The bargaining units within the private sector are relatively free of constraints other than those imposed by market imperfections or by the state. (2) *Within* the public sector some bargaining is possible, among the policy-makers of any one public entity, and between spokesmen for a given public entity and some other entity. The amount of bargaining possible, however, is quite small, and its scope is bounded also by the resources available to the public sector and to particular entities. (3) The relationship *between* the public sector and the private sector is essentially a bargaining one. Of less importance are the contracts under which private entities perform services for entities in the public sector. Of major importance is the bargaining of spokesmen for the public sector with spokesmen for all non-public interests respecting how much of the nation's resources are to be made available to particular public entities and to the public sector as a whole. Here a middleman role may be played by the legislature intermediating between the demands flowing from the public sector and from reluctant taxpayers, respectively. The contribution of parties to this bargaining process may be accommodated here. (4) This is a residual sector or category in which may be placed bargainers who do not fit nicely into sectors or categories 1–3. We end up with a universe of bargaining entities, between each of which and one or more other entities a bargaining and exchange nexus exists. We thus have a universe of interdependent components, though not one as sensitive in all its sectors as is a system of interdependent prices. This universe tends to equilibrium, though it seldom if ever attains it, given continuous redistribution of power as well as other sources of change.

Exchange is most free in sector 1 where coercion is at a minimum. It is least free in sector 2 and only partially free in sector 3. In 2 and 3 varying amounts of coercion constrain the bargaining process; participants in the process possess varying degrees of power over others, with the result that the outcome is different from what it would be if it reflected economic rationality alone.[147]

147. See Vincent Lemieux, "La dimension politique de l'action rationelle," *Canadian Journal of Economics and Political Science,* XXX (1967), 190–204. See also his references to the work of R. A. Dahl, J. Harsanyi, and J. G. March.

The degree of coercion present in sector 3 is reduced, of course, as weight is given to the benefit approach to taxation;[148] it tends to rise as "public goods" increase in relative importance and ethical and related values become more subordinate to a society's "power structure."[149]

The probability that exchange, even when free and between two individuals, will produce a stable, mutually satisfactory outcome depends mainly upon the specificity of the medium of exchange guiding the transactors and upon the quality of the information that enlightens the "reason" of each transactor. Comparison of a barter transaction, involving as it does a fourfold coincidence, with one accomplished through use of stable money suggests the fundamental significance of money—a significance formerly stressed in the economists' natural history of division of labor, co-operation, and money.[150] Monetary media of exchange play a more important role in sector 1 than in sectors 2 and 3, even though the prices and scales ruling in 1 are drawn upon to supply comparison and guidance in 2 and 3. Furthermore, in sector 1 the market, together with its facilitating agencies,[151] supplies more information and contributes more powerfully to the organization of life than in sectors 2 and 3. In sum, as was argued in earlier sections, the market is generally, though not always, an instrument of "economical administration" superior to alternatives. It had best be used as far as possible in the solution of a society's allocation problems. Of course, should greater progress be made in the realm of non-market than in that of market allocation, the margin of superiority of the latter would decline, though hardly enough to permit the market to be surpassed by non-market alternatives. Even so, it is advisable to transfer into

148. See discussion in Musgrave, *Theory of Public Finance,* chap. 4.

149. Breton, "The Demand for Public Goods," p. 467.

150. "General media of exchange seem to have come gradually into use in connection with the development of calculation in prices." Cassel, *Theory of Social Economy,* p. 376. Division of labor and specialization generate a "net-work of co-operation" impossible of achievement in the absence of a money nexus (P. H. Wicksteed, *The Common Sense of Political Economy* [London, 1933], I, chap. 4).

151. The market "is the machinery by which objective equilibrium in the marginal significance of exchangeable things is secured and maintained in a catallactic society" (Wicksteed, *Common Sense of Political Economy,* I, 212).

non-market situations as much as possible of the mechanisms that give rise to efficiency in sectors dominated by the market.

IX. Conclusion

Allocation produces optimum results when the allocative mechanisms are suited to the task of maximizing that which is to be maximized. A change in quaesitum may, therefore, call for a change in allocative mechanism, and a change in allocative mechanism is likely to produce a change in the results achieved. Underlying changes in mechanism, or in quaesitum, may be a change in the power structure, or in the structure of values, or in the state of the arts. Presumably the nature of the exchange system itself sets outside limits to the modifiability of the mechanisms of exchange employed in a society.

• 15 •

Conspectus

Ralph Braibanti

Some effort to relate the various themes of this book and to arrange them in a preliminary sort of paradigmatic sketch was made in Chapter 1. In the present chapter we shall summarize the principal observations and findings of the preceding chapters. In so doing we shall recast the line of thought of each chapter using largely the language of each author. Only occasionally in these summaries will the argument be extended or questions raised concerning the relationship of one chapter to another. We make no pretense at co-ordination of thematic perceptions except in a rudimentary way. Nor do we present agreement on a line of thought; indeed, agreement was never our objective. From one point of view, it is a deficiency of this volume that we have not built a model of dazzling complexity and architectural splendor which can be conveniently corroborated or demolished by subsequent research. There may be compensating advantages in the many different fronts and interstices which these chapters reveal and where subsequent research and speculation can be directed. Perhaps we may take comfort in Pareto's defense of disregard for particulars now and then in the evolution of a discipline. "One must first obtain a general concept of the thing one is studying, disregarding details, which for the moment are taken as perturbations; and then come to the particulars afterwards, beginning with the more important and proceeding successively toward the less important."[1] We can only hope that, since many more facets have been exposed than the four sides of a general model would

1. Vilfredo Pareto, *The Mind and Society* (New York, 1935), I, 540.

reveal, varying combinations of the theoretical insights, historical perspectives, and practical experiences may be provocative of further exploration.

Despite the foregoing remarks, there appear to have emerged the glimmerings of a common perspective with respect to the purposes of development, the configurative or ecological tissue in which administration is embedded, the indigenization of political institutions, and the insistence on typological schema, however obscure and complex they may be, by which subsequent comparative evaluation may be made. Apart from what appears to be a group of not greatly divergent points of view toward these problems, there are on some issues conflicting emphases, uneconomic variations in terminology and constructs, and varying perceptions of the same problems of political and administrative development.

It may be of some prospective utility to identify some of the themes which recur, though in various keys, throughout the volume. This is done in the final section of the present chapter. We have refrained throughout this chapter from summarizing or even commenting on the critiques by Sartori, Landau, and Cole on the assumption that those commentaries are brief enough to be easily retrieved and are already carefully and purposefully integrated with the main chapters which they follow. Additional analysis of them would appear to be redundant.

I

The central theme of Chapter 1 is the cruciality of institutions in a political system. Excessive attention has been given in development literature to the (input, mobilization) issues accelerating political participation. This chapter seeks to rectify this imbalance by focusing attention on the institutional means for maintaining political order and for accommodating to demands created by extended participation. Title IX of the Foreign Assistance Act, while providing no answer to the problem of political development, does serve to direct attention to some formulation for the engineering of political systems. If such a formulary is to transcend idiosyncratic and ethnocentric limitations we must leaven our insights with the colonial experience of major imperial powers such as France and Britain and with the half-century of experience of those states which formally embraced Marxism. Only such linkages of knowledge can provide us with a formulation unconstrained by geographical or ideological bias. Four characteristics of political development—architectonics, power diffusion, institutions, and innovative capacity—are used to indicate that a strong institutional base is necessary not only for the creation and maintenance of order but for the suffusion of values in the whole fabric of society.

A distinction is drawn between institution, structure, and sector. This chapter is silent on the construct of structural functionalism, preferring instead the construct of process or flow of events through institutions. Much attention is given to the capacity of institutions to receive, reformulate, and project values in the whole social order. Seven indices for assessing institutionalization are then advanced. These indices can be conveniently grouped under the acronym RABCIRR. A basic scheme is advanced for measuring capacity of institutions, structures, and sectors in terms of these seven indices. This measurement might eventually reveal structural and substantive differentials in institutions. This comparative analysis might then be used as a base for determining which institutions need strengthening and, indeed, for determining the contrived assignment and transmutation of functions from one institution to another. It is held in this chapter that without such a rational and systematic evaluation of institutions no formulation with respect to administrative and political development is possible.

Any strategy proposed to assist in inducing political development must be very tentative; moreover, there must be provision for an extensive degree of ecological adjustment as a political system seeks to find its own roots and to develop a political form suited to its peculiar needs. Such a strategy, therefore, must have an indigenizing dimension as well as a dimension allowing for the transnational induction of norms. Central to this is the question of the demand-conversion dilemma. It would seem that the demand side of this dilemma, namely the nature and the rate of increased participation in the political system, might best be left to the indigenizing component of such a strategy. The quantum, nature, and incidence of demands are phenomena which should be determined by the indigenous needs of the system itself. This is particularly true of that participation characterizing the electoral process. This chapter has distinguished four kinds of participation: electoral, occupational, community development, and interstitial. The last of these is comparable to the lateral relationships described by Montgomery. The first three might better be left to indigenous impetus since they are closely connected with internal political issues and polycommunality. Interstitial participation can probably be assisted by external assistance. The nature of such assistance and the loci of effective participation can be determined only after institutional analysis of the kind suggested by the RABCIRR formulary, combined with the PEWBSARD construct of Lasswell and Holmberg. Increasing the efficiency of the legislative process and reducing its ambiguity can enhance the quality of participation. Rectification of the administrative process can not only increase the psychic satisfaction of those whose lives are spent within its embrace, but can also serve as a diffuser of architectonics in the whole social order. In short, an emphasis on institutional rectification, together with an acute sensitivity to human values while leaving the problems of participation of the first three types to the natural indigenous forces at work in the system is the only formulation we now suggest.

II

The inattention in influential political development literature to the ultimate purposes of development—the questions about which men fight—is noted by Friedrich. Empirical evidence forces us, he asserts, to the conclusion that no rank or hierarchy of values exists and that man adjusts to value preferences as the situation requires. Nevertheless, there must be some means of determining what the objectives of various political orders in the past have been. Two such means seem to be useful. The first is to compare various systems and identify the objectives which seem to recur in all or most of them. The second is to look for specific objectives which appear to have unique values springing from highly particularistic beliefs. Four recurring objectives which can be explicated by these means are: (1) security and territorial expansion, (2) reduction of external friction, (3) prosperity, and (4) reduction of internal friction. These four paramount objectives subsume three correlative objectives—equality, order, and freedom. Order is subsumed under the reduction of internal friction and the related value of justice, for if all men are treated justly then perfect order would prevail and there would be a minimum of internal friction. Similarly, equality is a corollary of justice. It is true that egalitarian trends, for example in Negro problems in the United States, are much more significantly at work now than they have been at other times in the past. Even so, equality as a corollary of justice comes within the objective of reducing internal friction. The correlative objective of freedom has three dimensions—freedom of independence, of participation, and the creative freedom of political innovation. The last dimension, commonly overlooked, is in reality closely related to the development of human dignity simply because the universe of choice is much larger when unknown alternatives newly discovered are added to alternatives known to exist. Freedom of independence was conceived in most of the developing countries in communal rather than personal terms, and as it was achieved it merged with the first objective, that of security. As to freedom of participation, Friedrich seriously questions the widespread assumption that *the* major objective of modern government has been to maximize freedom, including freedom of participation. There are limits which are imposed by the dialectics of freedom itself. When freedom of participation is increased, the sphere of freedom of independence is thereby reduced. Experience has taught us that human beings desire a minimum rather than a maximum of freedom.

With respect to security as a primary objective, it should be noted that the high cost of security of modern nations has slowed the whole process of development. Further, the existence of a strong independent military establishment in a political community which has not yet been unified may represent a considerable danger to the attainment of viable constitutional government. Both of these may be thought of as high costs of security under developmental conditions. These costs would lead one to suggest that some sort of external arrangements for security might be evolved. Puerto Rico is an example of a nation which uses the power of a larger nation for its own security. An international police force can also be seen in this perspective. A second primary objective, the reduction of external frictions, arises from the increasing awareness that a political community under modern conditions has more to gain than to lose from the maintenance of peace. A slowly evolving legal framework of an international community seems to corroborate the emergence of this major objective of modern government. The reduction of external friction is closely related to the achievement of prosperity, which is the third primary objective. We must beware of the notion of "take-off" in development being facilitated by a government ill-equipped to play a major role in development. The evidence often adduced from France, China, England, and Japan is misleading in this respect. None of the developing systems with which we now deal is as autonomous as those systems once were. Moreover, the very concept of "take-off" is itself a dubious one. Economic development in England and France was greatly stimulated by power struggles generated by the discovery of gold and silver by the Spaniards in America. Mercantilism and cameralism, having as their goals an increase in wealth, were indications of international factors helping in the development of those states; foreign aid may very well play a comparable role as a factor in contemporary development.

There are no absolute priorities among the four objectives reviewed above, and yet concrete policy must balance the rival claims and thrusts. Emergent political systems have three tasks to perform in order to achieve an effective political order. These are (1) the transformation of a political community by continuing internal renewal, (2) the planning of actions to meet the needs of a community, and (3) the implementation of such plans and policies. A comparison of effective political systems of the past would reveal that a satisfactory system would exhibit six features: (1) the capacity to cope with the technological requirements of survival (including planning), (2) enforcible restraints upon government to protect citizens and enable them to act as political persons, (3) some operative participation of adult and sane members of the community, (4) general rules expressing shared values, (5) a judiciary to settle disputes, and (6) voluntary associations which can put forth candidates for public office and compete with each other in determining public business. Existing political orders exhibit one or more of these features but not all of them. While these six features may constitute a tentatively advanced model for political development they should not be mistaken for the four basic objectives themselves. We cannot be as certain as either Plato or Aristotle were in designing political systems. As the community evolves, its government must reinterpret basic objectives; the six characteristics and their sequential timing in terms of priorities must change accordingly. But the four paramount objectives are much less susceptible to change, and the three correlative objectives, while somewhat more yielding in their application, would seem to be more requisite than the six characteristics.

III

The immense difficulty in identifying the ends of political development is also alluded to by Kariel. One means of determining them would be to consider the suggestions of H. L. A. Hart, derived from what he regarded as the minimum content for natural law without which there can be no survival. The substance of this formulation is human vulnerability, approximate equality, limited altruism, limited resources, and limited understanding and strength of will. This emphasis on the maintenance of life leads us into the question of the quality of living, which we assume would incorporate the greatest range in a variety of manageable experiences. This in turn leads us into a psychological, therapeutic perspective, which should further lead us to study, as Christian Bay has indicated, the effect of social institutions on human well-being. The impact of the social order on human personality thus is central to Kariel's analysis. An acceptance of this paramount objective of a political system, he maintains, would free us from a restrictive ideological interest in what has worked in the past. We would thus be intellectually emancipated to specify the general requisites for optimal human development. This would allow us to concentrate on the psychological effects of human development and on how we might institutionally accommodate and promote the healthy personality. Drawing strength from Kant's categorical imperative, Kariel maintains that we need not take our bearings from modes of human behavior as we observe them; rather we can posit a certain kind of personality as normatively healthy even though it may not be the model we find around us. We must therefore conceptualize man in terms of an open-ended system. But it is extremely difficult to define free man. We can draw on various figures from the novelists: Huck Finn, Ishmael in *Moby-Dick,* and similar literary figures give us insight into the requirements of man's spirit. Yet we often reject them because they are men who have chosen to fail. We find it difficult to conceive of rewards inherent in the mere act of communicating and in the process of learning rather than in a final product or in a lesson learned. We must, Kariel is saying, be prepared to accept and respect psychic, spiritual, non-temporal values projected by the human personality and to acknowledge that society may depress and distort such values to the detriment of man. In addition to literary wisdom we can also be helped by various characterizations of the healthy personality in modern personal and social psychology. But all of these indicators raise ambiguities and queries.

Our fundamental problem here, Kariel continues, is to make

the administrative arena approximate our ideals of the healthy personality. In developing states where bureaucracy has a dominant role in determining the ethos, the quality, and the structure of life and where it is the largest and often the sole employer, this is especially crucial. We shall then have to raise such questions as the kind of structures which give greater personal opportunity for development. This may lead to a new, more sympathetic assessment of participatory entities such as neighborhood-controlled schools, civilian review boards, community corporations, and the like. This participatory need can be answered in part by the emergence of interstitial participation developed elsewhere in this volume. The overriding imperative is that we emphasize our independence as personalities. It is extremely difficult to implement this, and all we can venture here is to set forth the problem with the hope that its recognition will make us increasingly sensitive to institutions and to procedures which tend to frustrate human development. Yet it is acknowledged that in underdeveloped countries where men must be disciplined merely to survive, creation of institutions which would provide for this kind of independence is even more difficult. Perhaps ideal administrative structures should be based essentially on the concept of role-playing rather than on one of total psychic dedication to a particular function. This perspective may lead us to pay greater attention to heterogeneous organizations, to multi-interest groups, and to persons who succeed in integrating a variety of roles. This might make for more ambiguity in the system; certainly it would test our capacity for tolerating ambiguity. But this appears to be necessary if we are to raise the concept of the individual personality to the highest level. Such a system as that proposed by Kariel raises the question of the role of order; indeed, the veritable utopian freedom which he poses for the individual may be nothing more than anarchy. On the other hand, it is a logical extension of the maturation of thinking concerning individuality and the uniqueness of human personality, and it raises the fundamental issue of seeking to adjust institutions to agreed upon personality needs rather than conceiving of the personality as being required to adjust to the institutions with which he finds himself associated.

IV

LaPalombara explores the theoretical relationships between generalizations growing out of administrative thought and the value commitments and ideological orientation underlying that thought in the political systems of the West. The technical assistance activities engaged in by AID and the United Nations and other organizations assume that there is an administrative technology universally applicable. This assumption is corroborated by Abueva's case study of the Philippines in Chapter 13. LaPalombara's exploration of these problems is designed to shed light on whether some particular system of values or ideologies may be incompatible with certain types of structures and behaviors in administration. Accepting the view of Rosenberg and others that the modern administrative state as we know it is an invention of the West, he discusses what he calls "a consciously idealized decalogue" of the characteristics of a bureaucratic system as developed by Max Weber. This Weberian description of administration has greatly influenced Western administrative thought, and the decalogue is reflected in patterns of reform and operational codes put into effect in various developing states. Again Abueva's analysis of the doctrinal content of AID and United Nations administrative reform documents substantiates this assertion. The Weberian model was closely associated with the concept of power as an overriding value. The question here is whether or not the same kind of authoritarian power structure which theoretically undergirded the Weberian model is essential as a prerequisite for administrative systems developed in the new nations in which the demands for participation and diffusion of power make such an authoritarian model difficult to attain. La Palombara seeks to analyze this point by reviewing the administrative development of Brandenburg-Prussia, England and France. Although it is clear that the Prussian rulers utilized the new public administration system as a mechanism of power to achieve national unity, there were interesting by-products which subsequently helped precipitate the liberalism of the nineteenth century. The first of these was absolutism, which in destroying local decentralizing tendencies of feudalism also served to separate public and private functions. Indeed, this separation emerged as a cardinal principle of government. Second, the concept of sovereignty as belonging to the nation-state carried with it the notion of contractual delegation of authority from the people to the nation, thus demolishing the concept of personal power wielded under divine mandate. Third, centralized power necessarily accelerated the growth of the bureaucratic apparatus. These three by-products in turn led to increased functional differentiation in bureaucratic activity. They also led to the opening of some public service positions to the middle class, the emergence of a class of public servants compensated by salary, the establishment of a hierarchical organization in the bureaucracy, and last, the notion that the rule of law would apply evenly in bureaucratic administration. A second major value, probably of an importance equal to that of absolutism and power, is the desire for economic gain or wealth reflected in a public policy dominated by mercantilism. Such values as accountability, honesty, and efficiency therefore easily transferred from commercial and industrial enterprise into bureaucratic activity. A third important value is the concept of popular sovereignty which dramatically emerged in France, thus giving rise to the matrix of pluralism and participation and to the concept of a bureaucracy as servants of the people. These issues have engaged thoughtful scholars ever since. This third value can be called the service aspect of administration. When such a value is dominant other values such as efficiency, professionalization, and rationality can, and often do, take second place. This service aspect became in a sense the structural means for viewing the political system in humanistic terms which seek to elevate the human personality and hence considerations of equity to a high plane.

The developments on the Continent described above, however, did not necessarily occur in the same sequence in Britain and the United States, which we can characterize as antibureaucratic states. While it is true that England developed a highly centralized system even before it emerged on the Continent, a different attitude toward mercantilism and the concept of the "gentlemanly administrator," as well as a doctrine which deferred to continuity of tradition, slowed English administrative change. The establishment of a civil service as a consequence of the Northcote and Trevelyan report of 1853 was the first major move toward the development of a bureaucratic state in England. The introduction of the administrative class maintained a highly elitist system, and a separation of generalists from technical functions even now has not significantly changed in the British system. The development of public administration in the United States was equally affected by historical and ecological circumstances.

LaPalombara agrees with Friedrich that human dignity and freedom of the individual cannot best be obtained by limitations on bureaucratic behavior which are self-imposed by benevolent guardians. He concurs also with Alvin Gouldner that we need not focus all of our attention on the bureaucratic foundations of Weber, which were essentially those of quiescence and neutralism. The important question now is to examine organizations in terms of their projection of humanitarian and democratic values. This sort of examination or evaluation is difficult to implement. While LaPalombara does not allude to it, the Lasswell-Holmberg PEWBSARD construct is a beginning effort to systematize such evaluation. LaPalombara concludes by saying that the context in which administrative reform must occur in the developing countries is one in which all of the demands or crises which were spread out in the West over a period of several centuries are now simultaneously present. Somehow we should be able to free our concepts of administrative and political development from Western bias. This might mean that some of the prescriptions drawn from Western experience would prove to be unworkable.

V

Riggs seeks to analyze the impact other structures of a political system have on bureaucracy. Using the terms "structures" and "institutions" interchangeably (and therefore using them in not necessarily the same sense in which they are used in Chapter 1), he asserts that the functions performed by particular structures have been transformed in various ecological settings. Rather than examine the causes of these transformations, Riggs seeks to assess their consequences, and especially how new structures of government and the transformed functions of those structures affect the behavior of public bureaucracy. He views ecological change as embracing three types: development, democratization, and modernization. He regards development as an extensive transformation in society embracing such characteristics as the differentiation of roles and an increase in the functional specificity of social structures. The transformations which occur, particularly as they involve more differentiated structures, need a greater degree of integration. At the popular level increased politicization is also generated. Certain governmental institutions (structures) must be strengthened or the developmental revolution will be impeded. The second dimension of transformation is democratization, by which Riggs means the extent to which access to the values prized in a society are equally shared. He believes that democracy can be a constraint on development and that there are some structures which are compatible with both the developmental revolution and with democracy and others which may be favorable for development but not for democracy. The third kind of transformation is modernization, which he regards as emulative acculturation in which certain practices, forms, and technologies are deliberately transferred from one society to another. The mere emulation of structures does not mean that functional transformations will automatically occur; indeed, the whole problem of modernization focuses on the irrational, uncontrolled, and chaotic manner in which new structures are introduced without regard to ecological consequences. What has occurred for the most part in the past few decades is the remarkable spread of emulated structures of government; that is, modernization has spread throughout the world without regard to the relationship between these structures and ecological circumstances. Such modernization has been more widespread than either development or democratization. With respect to administrative reform, we must not overlook the importance of the constitutive system in a political order. As bureaucratic functions have become transformed from a mixture of the political and administrative into primarily administrative it is necessary to establish a constitutive system capable of exercising power and imposing effective controls over the bureaucracy. Describing an elaborate classification of polities using adjectives derived from the root word "tonic," Riggs seeks to associate types of polities with different bureaucratic systems. This classification is preliminary, but he contends that no meaningful analysis of the effect of the political system on bureaucratic subsystems is possible until such a classificatory scheme is produced. This classification scheme and the problems of terminology implicit in it have been commented on extensively in Landau's chapter and need not be repeated here. Riggs rejects the classification of political systems based on functional criteria. The typology of polities he presents is not designed as an explanation for developmental change. It is a typological requisite and must be antecedent to such explanation. But the ultimate explanation, he asserts, is to be found not in the typology itself but in what he calls ecological theory and the political process.

VI

The provisional outline developed by Lasswell and Holmberg focuses on the capability of institutions to project certain values in the political system. In this respect, it is closely related to the question of the impact of institutions on personality as developed by Kariel and Pye, and mentioned by LaPalombara. It is also related to the indices (RABCIRR) for measuring institutionalization as developed by the present writer in Chapter 1. Lasswell and Holmberg propose eight categories of values which might be grouped for expository convenience under the acronym PEWBSARD. These values are power (P), enlightenment (E), wealth (W), well-being (B), skill (S), affection (A), respect (R), and rectitude (D). The projection of these value categories as a scheme differs in perspective though not in fundamental objective both from the use of functional categories employed by Almond and Coleman and from the use of institutional categories employed by this writer in Chapter 1. The central focus is on values and it assumes that the fitting of institutions and functions in various societies with these values will make possible a greater degree of flexibility in tracing institutional-functional relationships. This system for comparative analysis is exceedingly difficult (indeed, it may be impossible) to apply, and it should be noted that the model here is merely a tentative one which has not yet been put into extensive operation. The scheme proposed by Lasswell and Holmberg is highly dynamic, being based essentially on the process of the flow of events. It reflects the same emphasis on the relationship between process and institution which Lasswell has developed in earlier studies. The model reflects also the significance of institutions as the accumulators, repositories, and diffusers of values. While it may be extremely difficult, if not impossible, to implement the Lasswell-Holmberg model, it nevertheless calls attention in a very dramatic way to the importance of the value content and diffusional power of institutions.

The processing of events through institutions includes preparatory events known as value-shaping and outcome events which are value-sharing. If measurement of institutions in terms of their value content is to be achieved, a unit of measurement must be devised. Lasswell and Holmberg formulate such units in terms of interactions which are defined as sequences of communication and collaboration. Interactions consist of symbols, signs, and resources. The frequency of these three references thus constitutes the units by which values can be measured. The units must be measured at various points in the process or flow of events through institutions. These points are the pre-outcome, outcome, and post-outcome phases of process. When this inspection of process is made, the value or adequacy of process as it relates to institutional flow will be perceived. These three categories of outcomes are performed by at least seven types of action: prescription, intelligence, promotion, invocation, application, appraisal, termination. When an association has been established between value units and types of action in the process of events in institutions, strategies may be devised for innovation of institutions along desired lines.

Lasswell and Holmberg conclude by suggesting six implications of this value-measurement model for developing states: (1) a self-sustaining level of power accumulation, (2) participation in power, (3) power to maintain independence, (4) responsibility in world politics, (5) increased participation in all values, and (6) sequence in timing of factors in development.

While the Lasswell-Holmberg construction may be too abstract, it is nevertheless a pioneering contribution to the study of development. By riveting attention on values and correlatively by almost ignoring institutions and functions as separately analyzable phenomena, it forces the analyst to locate institutions only in terms of their values. By analyzing institutions in the context of the processual flow of events, it makes possible the evaluation of components of institutions in terms of the events in the flow outcomes. This lays the base for a remarkably flexible, comprehensive, and sophisticated measuring construct. But it should be pointed out that it provides *only* the most basic and most primitive schematic outline, which must be tested and refined. It places values in a paramount position, institutions in an ancillary position, and ignores (as Lasswell has consistently) function as a determinate phenomenon. Function is subsumed in process—which is the flow of events through institutions. By forcing a continuing evaluation of institutions and process in terms of value units, this scheme reflects the greater importance of the personality and its development over institutions. In this respect it is conceptually though not methodologically related to the theme of the chapters in this volume by Kariel and Pye.

VII

The relationship between bureaucracy as an institution and human behavior is explored in a different way by Pye. He deplores the lack of constructive attention formerly given to the problem of institution-building. For a time, he maintains, an institutional approach was held to be a significant advance in the history of knowledge, but it gradually became excessively legalistic and static. Dissatisfaction with the institutional approach encouraged the advent of behavioralism, which reasserted the simple fact that an institution was, after all, composed of the acts of individuals and that both the act and the individual should be the objects of attention. This return to the centrality of the individual was accompanied, however, by increasing scientific rigor and a concern for precision and measurement in methodology which in turn neglected more humane aspects of analysis of the individual. Thus the static character of the old institutionalism was replaced by the equally static emphasis of much of the new behavioral school. What is now needed is the establishment of a relationship between individual acts which create and mold institutions and the effect which institutions have on human behavior and personality. If institutionalization is essentially "the internalizing of norms," then it must be essentially a psychological phenomenon.

It is illuminating to examine two different patterns of institutionalization in the building of bureaucracies during two historical periods. The first of these occurs with the establishment of the administrative systems in the old empires and colonies. Viewed from the perspective of a whole society, it is remarkable how quickly colonial authority was institutionalized in most of these areas. The effect of this colonial institutionalization, however, on human personality has not received much attention. Here the concept of the "spirit of the clerk" is especially instructive. The indigenous administrator who entered the civil service developed a set of attitudes and a mode of behavior induced by his subordination to his colonial superiors. In their relations with their superiors these functionaries had to exercise the most complete self-control of behavior. The deference which they were accorded and which they extracted from the citizenry at large may very well have been an escape from the constrained behavior in relation to their superiors. They tended to ascribe almost magical powers to words in the texts with which they dealt, texts which became virtually sacred. When colonial rule ended, however, the kind of personality required for development was quite antithetical to the imperial type. Now the old discipline and hierarchical order were replaced by one of highly dynamic and reciprocal power relationships. The required behavior is no longer that of repressing emotions, following ritualistic behavior, and behaving arrogantly toward subordinates. Rather, the requirement now is an ability to be effective in the context of the give-and-take of politics. Pye adverts to this as the adversary relationship. The urgent contemporary need in administrative development is in the building of new institutons of administration around conflict or adversary situations. This has been made more difficult by communal sensitivities which in many ways have been aggravated by the end of colonialism. In consequence the need for each communal group to adjust its competitive position with other groups has been accelerated and has brought about an increase in suspicion and political competition. The paramount need, therefore, is to change bureaucratic behavior from ritual to that kind of inventiveness "inherent in game situations." The efforts in public administration training have been on technical skills rather than on teaching the art of adversary relationships. Ideal adversary relationships include the ability to live with and abide by the rules of the game, the ability to cope with debate, argument, and confrontation while still carrying on with the task without being scarred by deep emotional resentments impairing creativity and objectivity. Above all, the depersonalization of defeats in argument and capacity to deal constructively with conflicting points of view is needed. Pye concedes that a high degree of personal security is required if officials are to be successful in coping with aggression from others and in operating within the adversary context he prescribes. He concludes by saying that bureaucratic institutions must be constructed so as to create a context in which a high degree of psychic satisfaction will be found in a combination of technical and personal skills. These skills should find outlets in a broad-based decision-making process characterized by constructive adversary relationships.

VIII

Administrative reform, suggests Montgomery, is generated by such power sources in government as rulers and policy-makers, by other elements in the social order which are not a part of government, or by the administrative system itself. From the point of view of the bureaucracy these three sources of reform can be thought of as representing its upward, lateral, and internal relationships. Bureaucratic change cannot be viewed narrowly or merely as a legal or procedural problem; rather, it is part of a larger social phenomenon. Montgomery rejects the analysis of Eisenstadt and others which asserts that reform is generated primarily by a class struggle and which regards this as an explanation applying with equal force to all societies. Instead, he favors what he calls the "annoyance principle," the use of which enables him to examine the sources of reform in different systems and in several interacting layers. He examines three types of government (autocracy, Western democracy, developing states) with respect to three sources of reform (upward, lateral, and internal). In traditional autocracies reform was often induced by weeding out sources of disloyalty and by linking through effective sanctions the interests and loyalties of subordinates with those of superiors. Lateral relationships could produce reform because of the need for the administrative system to collect revenue. Internal relationships focused largely on indoctrination in an ethos, pride of service, or a mystique. Reform tends to focus more on outward manifestations of behavior than on commitment to an inner creed, however, even in autocratic states.

Montgomery then examines these three relationships which have influenced reform in the Western democracies. The mechanism of loyalty, in the personal sense, which was so important in upward relationships in authoritarian regimes, loses its importance in the constitutional democracies because it becomes pluralized. In lateral as in upward relationships, reforms in the democracies seem to have broadened the purpose and the outlook of the bureaucracy. Moreover, the impact of norms of efficiency and economy from the old social order appear to have been substantial in generating reforms within the administrative system itself. Codes of honor or mystique seem seldom to have been the source of reform in internal relationships in the democracies. Procedural changes such as in budgeting and in PPBS have, however, in recent years been more important generants of change than have modifications in structure.

Montgomery goes on to analyze these means of change in the modernizing polities (developing states). In the new states loyalty is not to a personal ruler, institution of government, or even a class, but rather, to the sources of power which will have to be integrated to establish a nation-state. Montgomery refers to this dimension as "polycommunality." The drive to achieve representation of various communal groups has resulted in not only the indigenization of the bureaucracy but also the selection of nationals from the various ethnic, religious, and other groups in politically acceptable proportions. Reforms induced by lateral relationships appear to be for the purpose of achieving effective performance rather than efficiency or even responsibility. This pattern seems to be encouraged by the introduction of Western advice which is technical rather than managerial. As a consequence, the impetus is for technical effectiveness rather than bureaucratic efficiency. Reform may be induced within the context of internal relationships by the politicization of the bureaucracy. This appears to be essential because it becomes itself an instrument for the political socialization of the masses. This variation in bureaucratic function requires a change in outlook and, in some instances, even in organization and thus becomes a source of reform.

Montgomery cautions us that the rather unconventional mode of analysis he has provided must be supplemented by careful studies of the nature and effects of past reform measures. It does appear clear, however, that so far as developing states are concerned, the experimental alternatives available now are far more numerous than those available to the older systems at any time in history. This also means, he concludes, that Western administrative doctrine may be of less immediate relevance to their problems than Western understanding of political society and the methods used for examining them.

IX

The roots of what Ilchman calls a rational-productivity bureaucracy can be found in the earlier concept of technocracy, although that concept was developed in a provisional and imprecise way. Some significant developments in Europe and the United States, particularly in the twentieth century and mostly within the ambit of planning, are indicators for him of the emergence of rational-productivity as a new orientation toward action. These characteristics, namely, technical knowledge, loyalty to substantive programs, and commitment to productivity, seem to unite rational-productivity bureaucrats in a common bond of intellectual outlook, training, and view of the universe. This unity seems sufficient to make them an ideal type for analysis. Such bureaucrats, Ilchman feels, regard politics as inherently unproductive and claim their own knowledge to be superior to that of the politician or the statesman.

The number and importance of the rational-productivity bureaucrats is increasing throughout the world. One of the most important members of this group is the economic planner. Ilchman interviewed over a period of two years thirty-three mid-career planners from eighteen countries who were students in the United States at the time of interview. After analysis of the background of the planners thus interviewed, Ilchman designs a profile of their ideology of economic development. They agreed that modernization and especially industrialization are essential for their countries. Both modernization and industrialization assume a high degree of rational planning and rational-productivity. The planners also seemed to agree that it is essential to push beyond the economic sphere and to manipulate the underlying cultural values of the society which are regarded as an impediment to economic development. For the most part the planners felt that the private business sector was a major contributor to economic development. They also felt that trade unions were, with some limitations, useful. The antipolitical bias of the planners is suggested by the fact that they appeared to regard any planning which involved such questions as distribution, regional equality, and prestige expenditures as wasteful and irrational. This was indicated further by their attitudes toward foreign economic and technical assistance.

Ilchman then analyzes five variables which may be relevant to the attitudes developed by the planners he interviewed. The first is the regime in which the planner works. Most seemed to feel that the monopoly party regime is most conducive to their values and methods. Other categories of regimes are difficult to rank in terms of their preference. The second variable is the relationship between the income level of the country of the planner and his attitudes. In general, planners in countries of higher per capita income find the public and the bureaucracy somewhat more congenial to their development efforts. A third variable is the kind of bureaucratic function being performed by the planner. While generalizations here are complex, it can be tentatively said that the less contact the bureaucrat has with the public the more he regards traditional factors as being impediments to development and the more he tends to think of government as the main support of his own efforts. The fourth variable is the source of the planner's education; here it appears that those educated abroad reveal a more unqualified support of modernization. The fifth and final variable has to do with social status of the planners. The new elites seem to have a more unqualified indorsement of modernization, and the traditional social elites seem to be somewhat more sympathetic toward the past, probably because they have links with those who formerly ruled the country.

Ilchman concludes his analysis with three possible implications for administrative reform. The first is that an imported intellectual technology will not necessarily be subordinated to the power needs of the political leaders of a developing state. So far as the planners are concerned, they downgrade politics, have identifiable propensities of their own, and may become a powerful political force. Second, administrative reform should distinguish between the idioms of the orthodox bureaucracy and the rational-productivity bureaucracy, each of which can carry out certain kinds of programs more effectively than the other. Third, there is a relationship between structure of authority and ultimate program effectiveness. A rational productive activity can be carried out in less authoritarian structures with more informal channels of communication. Last, Ilchman asserts the necessity for analyzing emerging political, economic, and social forces in all their political variety without the constraints of models which predicate direction or congruence.

X

Abueva analyzes the content of United Nations handbooks, AID doctrine, and AID program reports relating to administrative reform. From these sources he describes the administrative doctrine these agencies have sought to diffuse transnationally. Here the influence of the United States has been great; even in the United Nations nearly 19 per cent of the experts between 1950 and 1966 came from the United States and 28 per cent came from the United Kingdom and France. Abueva then recasts the doctrine embedded in United Nations and AID administrative reform manuals into a series of propositions each of which he discusses. He evaluates the Filipino response to administrative doctrine which has been introduced externally. In so doing he first indicates that the Philippine Republic is a fairly viable political system, having passed most of the tests of legitimacy and stability since independence in 1946. This judgment is confirmed by a table showing that most of the comparative analysts who have typed governmental systems have classified the Philippines as being a relatively mature and viable system. This seems to indicate that the Philippines may be regarded as having many of the political values and institutions which were assumed by administrative reformers as being prerequisite to further administrative development. Following independence the Philippines undertook a series of relatively sophisticated administrative reform efforts, many of them molded after comparable reforms in the United States. One was the Bell Mission which, although it laid the groundwork for economic aid and technical assistance, also made recommendations with respect to administrative reform.

Having suggested a relatively felicitous context for the reception of new norms and ideas, Abueva then evaluates the Filipino response to four officially proclaimed administrative values. This evaluation is derived from a panel survey of fifty-two Filipino administrators interviewed in 1966. The first administrative value thus surveyed is merit and competence. Abueva indicates that kinship and family ties continue to take precedence over an objective interpretation of a merit system. It is also clear that economic conditions, and especially tax policy, in the Philippines require the bureaucracy to provide employment for a rapidly growing labor supply. This in turn distorts the otherwise rational position and classification plans that have been specified in the context of a second professed aim, namely, efficiency and economy. Cultural forces similarly impede the implementation of these aims. Inefficiency and wastefulness in government seem to be engendered in part by the fact that personal success is still regarded as being a stroke of good fortune which must be shared with the extended family. Orientations toward time and change and a disinclination to see actions through to their consequences are further cultural factors which impede efficiency as it is known in other systems. Corruption is facilitated by the fact that the concept of stewardship is not deeply ingrained in the culture; on the contrary, the concept of "public" as something that belongs to no one and is therefore fair game for everyone is deeply embedded in the system. The fourth attribute is that of rationality and planning. Here again the impedances are largely cultural and include basic orientations toward time, change, work, and success as well as such structural factors as intense centralization. The Filipino system is highly politicized, and for this reason the political system is remarkably responsive to the wishes of the public. This has sometimes been called an excess of democracy. In terms of the concept of civic culture advanced by Almond and Verba, however, the Filipinos have developed only the electoral aspects of their participant role and not their subject aspect of participation.

XI

Spengler seeks to contrast the allocative systems employed in the private sector with those found in the public sector. He concedes that his inquiry is handicapped by the fact that rigorous comparisons of the private and public sectors have not yet been worked out although a beginning is being made through the comparison of the budgetary mechanisms of the two sectors. The concept of social surplus is central to the thesis developed by Spengler, which is not to be confused with Marx's theory of surplus value even though social surplus does include some elements of Marxian surplus value. The existence of a social surplus is a necessary condition of economic and political development. Indeed, conflict respecting its use remains alive in developing economies and in those which are deemed to be developed. He analyzes three types of the costs of growth: the economic costs of capital, changes in the society's input structure, and the socio-psychological costs involved in modernization and development. In developing the last he alludes to India as an example. Leadership may often prove inadequate to the task of transforming a society. In this respect he refers to the tendermindedness of Indian leaders, which has been described as "a highmindedness insufficiently disciplined by intellect." Spengler agrees with Sinai, to whose work he alludes, that what is needed is not only a new ideology capable of bringing about a cultural revolution but a new elite of reformers and innovators highly disciplined, ready and willing to assume the hardships and risks of modernization. The role he thus assigns to leadership in the development process is similar to that of Friedrich in Chapter 2 and of the present writer in Chapter 1. While there is agreement that there is interaction between economic and political development, there is disagreement about whether politics or economics is primary.

The relationship between the arrangements for political and economic allocation undergoes constant change. Spengler agrees with Levy that relatively modernized societies tend to resemble each other as modernization progresses, and he adds that this probably gives rise to greater autonomy in subsystems. The more technical and dynamic the subsystem becomes, the more costly becomes interference by the polity or other subsystems. Not enough empirical work has been done to make possible unqualified judgments on the role of government intervention in the allocation of resources. The state, however, is limited in the role it can play in economic development and hence in political development insofar as it is complementary to economic development. These limitations are derived first from the characteristics of a system of incentives which operate in the public sector. These incentives are opposed to an entrepreneurial propensity and are too highly centralized. It is also difficult for the state to transform inputs into outputs sufficiently. A concept of exchange phenomena applicable to the relationship of government to economic development is important. The fundamental relationship between the public and private sectors is essentially a bargaining one. The degree of coercion in the exchange process should be watched carefully, for it is likely that the greater the coercion the farther the exchange relationship will depart from economic rationality.

XII

Tentative observations on recurrent themes are now ventured.

1. Viewed retrospectively the chapters taken as a whole reassert the importance of considering the ends of the state and the eminence of human spirit as ultimate aims of political and administrative development. While this is nothing new, its explicit assertion has been uncommon in the past twenty years. To this extent the volume as a whole may be viewed as a departure from trends in the literature on political development of the past two decades. At the same time it is a reflection of a growing concern,

particularly on the part of theoretically oriented students of political development, for the need to reconsider these values. The perennial problem of balancing values has not been resolved here, but the attention given to it may serve to place means in a proper perspective and hence encourage a propensity to regard all means as relative and contingent on factors of time, space, and belief. The consideration of values is approached quite differently by writers in this volume. Friedrich, for example, would have us approach them from the point of view of four objectives of the state, thus allowing for a versatile combination of institutional and structural arrangements in varying sequences and combinations suiting the particular need of a political system and its stage of development. Pye and Kariel especially would have us consider values in terms of the psychological impact of institutions on the development of human personality. Lasswell and Holmberg consider a tentative scheme (PEWBSARD) for the measurement of eight values as they are diffused by institutions in the whole order.

2. Another theme relates to the many ways of viewing institutions in development. Even contributors such as Pye and Kariel, whose emphasis is on psychology, base their concern for human development on the impact of institutions. The dilemma thus raised is one which has vexed theorists for centuries. There is a reciprocal relationship between institutions and personality and the extension of personality, namely, behavior. It is doubtful that institutions can be molded perfectly to fit transitory personality demands. The state and, indeed, all institutions in a social order always exert pressure upon the individuals who constitute it. Ortega describes the relationship:

> The state is but one of the strongest among such social pressures. The limitation of our free will which the state unquestionably implies is of the same order as that imposed upon our muscles by the hardness of bodies, and therefore must be recognized as inalienable part of the make-up of man. A society is not a man-made institution, as eighteenth-century philosophers thought, but a condition in which man finds himself irremediably and without any hope of true escape. . . . Political freedom cannot be defined as absence of pressure; for that situation does

> not exist. The decisive point lies in the fashion in which pressure is brought to bear. Are we not at any moment subject to the pressure of the atmosphere? Yet when this pressure affects us in a certain way it imparts a glorious sense of "free movement" and the leather strap that, girding our loins, fosters a carriage of springy ease will, tied around our wrists make us cry out to heaven that we are manacled. The pressure of state becomes manifest in the form of "institutions." With this remark we have definitely cornered our problem. Man is not free to elude the permanent pressure of the collective body upon his person. But certain nations in certain epochs succeeded in giving that coercion institutional forms of which they fully approved; *they shaped the state after their vital preferences.* This is what we call "life in freedom."[2]

Here then is the problem—the reciprocally affective relationship between the individual and political institutions. Innovation of institutions always occurs, but at times certain major or episodic transformation or adjustment seems called for. It may be that in certain developed nations the great emphasis placed on individuality and the human personality now calls for major renovation and adjustment of institutions. But we face the question of timing. Is the same kind of epochal renovation called for in the developing states which struggle to achieve and maintain a modicum of order in the system?

3. The assumption that there is a reciprocal relationship of values and institutions requires some means by which that relationship can be ascertained more precisely. The formulation RABCIRR given in Chapter 1, combined with the construct PEWBSARD given in Chapter 8, may be the primitive beginning of such a measure. The RABCIRR measure may be useful in determining institutional adequacy with respect to performance in a political system and in plotting transmutations of function. PEWBSARD can help determine a relationship of specified values to particular institutions and can help associate the effect of values as transmutation occurs. If we are to consider further the institutional impact on human personality, then some formulation like RABCIRR is essential. Since political order must be main-

2. José Ortega y Gasset, *Concord and Liberty,* Norton Library edition (New York, 1946), pp. 34–35.

tained while at the same time it adjusts to personality demands, a formulation like PEWBSARD is also required. In this respect, then, the dual formulations of RABCIRR and PEWBSARD are provisional means of ascertaining institutional capacities to maintain order in the system and at the same time to adjust to changing demands by diffusing values.

4. Several of the chapters direct our attention to the perennial problem of the relationship of ecology or indigenous factors to externally induced ideas and institutions. This is forcefully brought to our attention by LaPalombara, Riggs, and Abueva, among others. The ideological component is brought out with particular cogency by LaPalombara. Certainly we are much more keenly aware of the need to adapt to indigenous circumstances than we were twenty years ago when we first engaged in this activity in the occupation of Japan. In the interim, however, there has been so massive an infusion of norms and ideas and these have become so mixed with those already found in the system that it is extremely difficult to separate them. Moreover, in the case of India and other nations which experienced long periods of imperial rule, administrative and political institutions then introduced may be no more or less indigenous than those introduced under Mogul rule. It is extremely difficult, if not impossible, to determine the difference (except on a temporal basis) between exogenous and endogenous institutions. In research on political development our faith in the transferability of lessons of development from the West should be seriously shaken and our minds should be free to look with new respect upon indigenous needs and the evolution of indigenous institutions. These may occur in different combinations which seek to carry out such fundamental goals and aims of the political order as those advanced by Friedrich.

5. The rudiments of a typology establishing an association between the total political system and the administrative subsystem are found especially in the chapters by Montgomery and Riggs. Riggs's detailed analysis of constitutive systems may ultimately be used as a basis for determining the kind of bureaucratic system best suited for a particular type of political system.

This relationship is crucial if a powerful bureaucratic system capable of carrying on the activity of government is also to be controlled, responsible, and imbedded in its proper place in the government. Riggs's typology further refined by empirical research would lead us to a formulation of immense utility. The consideration by Montgomery of upward, lateral, and internal relationships presents us with the rudiments of another formulation of considerable utility.

Insufficient attention has been given to the relationship between politics and economics. It is unfortunate that the disciplines of economics and political science have lost some of their close association and that each has been attracted to sociology rather than to each other. Spengler's analysis indicates a very delicate role for the state which must be powerful enough to maintain its legitimacy and a system of order and at the same time should not, in Spengler's view, dominate or crush the entrepreneurial spirit. How to achieve a strong bureaucratic system which operates with that effectiveness and delicacy necessary to stimulate the private sector is another dilemma. This kind of relationship of political power to the economic system might also be combined with the typology advanced by Montgomery and Riggs.

Index

Abbassid Empire, 435
Abello, Amelia, 576n.
Abramovitz, M., 589n.
Absolutism, 189, 648; and administrative organization, 179–180; in England, 197–198, 200; in France, 192; in Prussia, 192
Abueva, José V., 8n., 344, 562n., 563n., 564n., 567n., 575n., 579n., 580n., 584n., 585n., 647, 660, 661, 666
Academic research: and foreign assistance operations, 21–32, 545; links to AID and SEADAG, 26–30; and need for field work, 29; relating to political development, 21–26; in United Kingdom, 30–31
Accountable executive, 322
Accumulation of values, 364–367, 385, 397
Acheson, Dean, 569
Act of Settlement of 1701, 129, 196, 201
Adelman, Irma, 600n.
Adjudication, administrative, 193
Adler, M. J., 120n.
Administrative doctrines: of AID, 546–556, 571, 660; definition of, 536; Filipino response to, 563–587, 660–662; as propositions, 556–562; relevance in emerging states, 542; of United Nations, 537–545
Administrative organization: in anti-bureaucratic state, 195–212; in bureaucratic state, 170–195; capacity for, 33, 261–263, 322; "monocratic" form, 172; values and ideologies in, 166–219
Administrative reform: and adjudication, 193; American concepts of, 549, 566; and class struggle, 430; and constitutive system, 651; factors in, 538, 649, 659–660; goals of, 144; need for, 464–465; in Philippines, 565–571; and political order, 427–431; as social phenomenon, 429; sources of, 428, 656; universally applicable technology in, 169, 647
Adversary power, 414, 420–422, 655
Advisory services of AID, 548
Affection, as value-institution category, 356–357, 363, 371
Afghanistan, 70
Africa, 169; bureaucratic behavior in, 220, 251, 271, 309, 313, 527; East Africa, 502; expansionism in, 126; independent countries of, 280, 307, 388; institution-building in, 402, 410; liberation from colonial rule, 118; South Africa, 271; tribalism in, 605; West Africa, 421n., 485, 491, 495, 497, 520, 531
Afro-Asian states, bureaucratic development in, 421, 564
Agency for International Development (AID), 6n., 88n.; administrative doctrine of, 536, 546–556, 561, 571, 660; advisory services of, 548; attitudes of, 5–10, 13; and implementation of Title IX, 15–17; link with academic research, 26–30, 103; programs in India and Pakistan, 96; propositions from administrative doctrine of, 556–558; publications of, 546, 554n.; recommendations of, 520, 521, 543; role of, 17, 20–21; strategy of, 16, 104; study tours sponsored by, 94; technical assistance programs of, 548, 557, 564, 572–574, 577–578, 581, 584, 647
Agency for Reform in Government Operations, 578n.
Aggression, controlled, 414–425
Agriculture, areas for improvement in, 500–501
Akali Dal, 81
Akzin, B., 53n.
Albania, 307
Albonetti, A., 475n.
Alker, H. R., 125n.
Alliance for Progress, 11, 15
Allocation, 613–621, 632–633, 662–663;

comparison of systems, 621–627; in private sector, 590, 662; in public sector, 501–503, 590, 662
Allport, G. W., 154n, 155, 404n.
Almond, Gabriel A., 48, 56, 57, 107n., 109n., 112n., 124n., 136n., 142, 145n., 341, 406n., 416n., 564, 565, 585, 609, 652, 661
Altshuler, A. A., 591n.
Ambiguity in political structure, 82–86
American Political Science Association, 16, 65
American Revolution, 199
American Society for Public Administration, 65
Anatonic polity, 322
Anderson, C. A., 599n.
Angevins, 196, 198
Ankrah, General, 292
Annoyance principle, 428, 431, 656
Antetonic polity, 322
Antibureaucratic systems, 200, 648
Anti-Graft Committee, 578n.
Antitonic polity, 322
Appleby, Paul H., 101, 102
Applications of power, 378
Appraisal of power, 378
Apter, David E., 101n., 167, 281, 303, 304n., 313, 314, 315, 480, 481n., 483, 506, 518, 519n., 531n.
Aquinas, Thomas, 110
Arab socialism, 494
Arakanese, 419
Architectonics, 37–47, 640
Arendt, Hannah, 151n., 160n., 161
Arens, R., 36n.
Argentina, 317n.
Aristotle, 34, 63, 110, 114, 115, 135, 168, 233, 633, 644
Armytage, W. H. G., 607n.
Aron, Raymond, 126n.
Arrow, K. J., 624n., 630n.
Ashford, Douglas, 95
Asia: bureaucratic behavior in, 220, 251, 271, 309; civil service in, 410; and communism, 568; as developing country, 169; government institutions in, 313, 402; independent countries in, 307; middle class in, 607; traditionalist character of, 604, 605; village-based societies in, 601. *See also* Southeast Asia
Asia Society, 17, 28
Asian Development Bank, 25, 88n.
Asian and Pacific Affairs, subcommittee on, 17
Assemblies, elected, 245, 323, 329, 330
Ataturk, Kemal, 69, 70, 295, 605
Athanasion, L., 627n.
Athens, constitution of, 135
Atonic polity, 322
Attitudes toward development programs, 497–498
Attlee, Clement, 445
Augustine, Saint, 116
Australia, 317n.
Austria, 317n.
Austria, Quirino, 569n.
Austruy, J., 596n.
Authoritarian power structures, 647
Authority: in bureaucracy, 171; concepts of, 422–425; of judiciary, 194; symbols of, 409
Autocracies, traditional, 431–442, 656
Autonomous institutions, 545, 591–592
Autotonic polity, 322
Avineri, S., 166n.
Aytona, D., 579
Ayub Khan, 24, 70, 97, 462

Bachrach, P., 162n.
Baerwald, H. H., 87n.
Bailey, F. G., 418n., 519n.
Bailey, Stephen K., 475n.
Bakufu government, Japan, 432
Balance, definition of, 322
Baldwin, R. E., 607n.
Balfour, D., 133
Balinky, A., 615n.
Balogh, T., 619n.
Balwantray Mehta, 96n.
Banks, Arthur S., 600n.
Barber, E. G., 437n.
Bargaining between public and private sector, 635
Barker, Ernest, 177n., 188, 189, 190, 191, 193, 198, 432n., 439n., 440n., 475n.
Barnard, Chester I., 62n., 401n., 455n.
Barnett, D., 272, 282
Barron, F., 155, 404n.
Basch, A., 630n.
Basic Democracies, 97, 98, 99
Batangas province, 568
Bates, F., 62n.
Bateson, G., 422n.
Bauer, Peter, 594n.
Baumol, W. J., 596n., 625n.
Bay, Christian, 145n., 147, 148, 645
Bay of Pigs, 24
Bayley, David, 16
Becker, S. W., 85n.
Beckerman, W., 607n.
Beer, Samuel H., 443n.
Behavioralism, 401, 654
Belassa, B. A., 619n., 624n., 625n.
Belgium, 239, 317n., 543
Bell, David E., 26, 27n.
Bell, Daniel W., 569
Bell Mission, 569, 570, 580, 661

Bellagio conference, 100n., 166n., 213, 220n., 522n.
Beloff, Max, 433n.
Bendix, Reinhard, 175, 195, 476n., 477n.
Bengal, 410
Bennis, W. G., 480n., 525n., 623n.
Bentham, J., 204, 208n.
Benthamism, 204, 206, 207
Benveniste, G., 472n., 482n.
Berelson, B., 164n.
Berger, Morroe, 484n.
Bergson, A., 475n., 619n.
Berlin, Isaiah, 121n., 176, 588, 607n.
Berman, H. J., 130n.
Bernholz, P., 629n.
Berreman, G. D., 41n.
Berry, W., 50n., 90n., 95n.
Beveridge Reports, 475
Beyer, W. C., 441
Beyster Plan, 580
Bhargava, R. C., 516n., 534n.
Bigelow, K. W., 29n.
Biller, R. P., 472n.
Binder, Leonard, 44n., 183n., 483n.
Bismarck, 69
Black, C. E., 23n., 170n., 219
Black, J. B., 434n.
Black Horse Cavalry, 348
Black Power movement, 41
Blaise, H. C., 52n.
Blau, Peter M., 633n., 634
Bloch-Laine, François, 480n.
Boak, A. E. R., 433n.
Boguslaw, R., 476n.
Bond, J., 153
Boniface, Pope, 183
Bottomore, T. B., 162n., 519n.
Boulding, Elise, 425n.
Boulding, K. E., 592n., 623n., 633n.
Bowman, M. J., 599n.
Braibanti, Ralph, 12n., 29n., 39n., 43n., 45n., 49n., 59n., 78n., 121n., 162n., 164n., 191n., 220n., 225n., 325, 333, 338n., 340n., 342, 416n., 444n., 462n., 475n., 514n., 532, 536n., 562n., 590n., 600n., 622n.
Brandenburg-Prussia. *See* Prussia
Brayne, F. L., 96
Brazil, 10, 127n.
Brecht, A., 110, 171n.
Bréhier, L., 433n., 434n.
Brenner, M., 472n.
Breton, A., 591n., 625n., 636n.
British East India Company, 409, 410. *See also* United Kingdom
Brittain, S., 475n.
Broadbridge, S., 600n.
Brodie, B., 476n.
Bronfenbrenner, M., 596n., 611n., 630n.
Brookings Institution conference, 78n.
Brookings Study Group, 8
Brown, N. O., 153n.
Brownlow (Louis) Committee, 567
Brownson, F. O., 85n.
Bruhns, F. C., 53n.
Brzezinski, Z. K., 114n., 130n., 599n., 611n.
Buchanan, J. M., 606n., 617n., 622n., 633n., 634
Buddhism, 115, 418
Budget and Accounting Act, 93
Budget Commission, 567, 574, 576, 578, 581
Budget and financial administration, 545
Bulgaria, 87n., 234, 239
Bunche, Ralph J., 117n.
Burchard, W. W., 159n.
Bureaucracy: and administrative reforms in democracies, 447; in America, 190, 447; in ancient societies, 167; and antipolitical bias, 472–535; in Brandenburg-Prussia, 175–177, 179–180, 183, 184, 188–189; British, 184n., 215–216; Byzantine, 314; careers in, 100–101; characteristics of, 170–171, 649; in China, 272, 314; in colonial administrations, 408–414; and communal multiplicity, 459; and communism, 222–223, 254, 271, 298; compensated, 263, 322; complex types, 238–243, 253–262, 322, 329; compound, 241–243, 322; definition of, 322, 330; and democracy, 190–191, 217; development of, 400–426; diffusion rates in, 250–253; efficiency of, 261–263, 322, 464–465; evils of, 452–453; forces weakening organization of, 623–624; in France, 185–186, 190; and free market system, 622; function of, 161; goals in underdeveloped countries, 462–463; growth of, 648–649; "guardian" type, 184n.; and human behavior, 653; and ideology of development, 506, 510–511; in Japan, 87; legal-rational, 476–479; in modern states, 170–171, 238–243, 456; Napoleon influencing, 190; in new states, 424–425; in Ottoman Empire, 314; in Pakistan, 88; partisanship in, 259–262; patronage in, 206–207; in Philippines, 563, 566; politics and administration of, 221–225; political orientation in, 259–262; and political socialization, 467; postcolonial, 414–422; in private sector, 623, 624; rational-productivity, 474, 476–483, 523, 527, 529, 530, 658; reforms in, 427–471, 656–657;

responsibilities in new countries, 457, 584–587; Roman, 314; simple, 238–243, 324; six types of, 324, 651; in tonic polities, 250–268; traditional, 238–243; Type I, 257, 262, 263, 264, 265, 267, 268, 272, 324; Type II, 257, 263, 267, 268, 324; Type III, 257, 263, 267, 268, 272, 324; Type IV, 257, 262, 263, 266, 267, 268, 272, 324; Type V, 257, 258, 266, 268, 324; Type VI, 324; types of bureaucrats, 529; underlying values in, 170–195; views on, 216–219. *See also* Administrative reform; Civil service; Government
Burgess, J. W., 32
Burin, F. S., 190n.
Burke, E., 144, 202, 203, 208n., 448
Burks, Ardath, 87n.
Burma, 286, 300, 388, 389, 409, 412n., 461, 462, 519n.; Buddhism in, 418; minority groups in, 419; political system in, 565
Burns, T., 525n.
Burtt, H. E., 455n.
Busia, K., 292
Butwell, R., 419n.
Byzantium, 430n., 433, 434n., 438

California, University of, 472n.
Cambodia, 565
Camelot Project, 24, 60
Cameralism, 643
Camus, A., 151
Canada, 239, 317n., 543
Cantril, H., 600n.
Capital, broad conception of, 597–598
Cardoso, F. H., 604n.
Career service, 100–101, 544
Carlyle, T., 345
Carmel, SEADAG development administration, seminar in, 28, 31, 78n., 90n.
Carstairs, G. M., 421n.
Cary, Joyce, 410n.
Caserta, public administration in, 173
Cassel, G., 633n., 636n.
Catallactics, 633
Catholic Church, influence of, 213
Cecil family, 119, 134
Central Bank, in Philippines, 581
Centralized power, in bureaucracy, 170, 171; weakness of, 626–627
Ceylon, 418n., 462; constitution of, 43n.
Chadwick, E., 446n.
Chakravarty, S., 589n.
Change: conditions needed for, 68–76; as cost of growth, 596, 598–599
Chapman, B., 178, 179n., 180, 189n., 192, 209, 210n.
Chardin, P. T. de, 109n.
Charisma and leadership, 69
Charles I, 201
Charles II, 197n.
Charlick, R. B., 32n.
Chawla, V. N., 97
Cherry, C., 327n.
Chester, D. N., 278n.
Chiang Kai-shek, 295, 298
Chile, 169, 271
China: administrative reform in, 234, 238, 282, 284, 285, 592, 643; ancient civilization in, 166, 223, 227, 307, 430; censorial system in, 102, 241, 435n., civil service in, 170, 171, 440; communism in, 126, 272, 568, 569; constitution of, 43n., despotism in, 438; dynasties in, 184n., economic development of, 127–128; emergence of, 25; eunuchs used in, 433; influence in Malaya, 461, 462; population and resources in, 319; reforms in, 69; size of, 239
Chins, 419
Chrimes, S. B., 197n.
Christensen, A., 434n., 440n.
Cicero, 517
Citizen's rights in public service, 541
Civil service: in America, 450; attitudes toward development plans, 496; British, 443–447, 449, 450, 649; in China, 170, 171, 440; class changes in, 447, 648; in colonial environment, 413; in France, 451, 454; in Germany, 451; in Ghana, 292; international, 538; in Pakistan, 70; in Philippines, 566–567, 572–579; politicization of, 466; postcolonial problems, 414–415, 420–421; professionalism in, 452; in Prussia, 432; recruitment of workers for, 448–449; role of, 78; status of workers in, 412; training of employees, 410–411. *See also* Bureaucracy
Clark, Carolyn, 482n.
Clark, Colin, 613n.
Clark, G., 434n.
Clark, P., 519n.
Class changes in bureaucracy, 447, 648
Class interactions, 388–389, 446
Classification of political systems, 565, 651
Clerks: role in colonial administration, 413; spirit of, 410, 654. *See also* Civil service
Cleveland, H., 8n.
Clifford, W., 602n.
Coase, R. H., 616n., 625n.
Cobban, A., 186n., 187n.
Cobbett, W., 446

Codding, G. A., 119n.
Coercion in exchange process, 663
Cohen, B. I., 632n.
Cohen, Harry, 623n.
Cohen, R., 49n.
Colbert, J. B., 119, 185, 186, 192
Cole, G. D. H., 162n.
Cole, R. Taylor, 216n., 218n., 460, 461, 522n., 532n., 533n., 639
Colegrove, Kenneth W., 43n.
Coleman, J. S., 56, 57, 520n., 564, 565, 652
Collaboration of scholars, basis of, 28
Collis, M., 410n.
Colombia, 492
Colonial institutions, development of, 409–413
Combined Opposition party (COP), 97
Comilla, Pakistan, 99n.
Common good as political goal, 144
Common law, 194
Commonwealth countries, polities of, 319
Commonwealth of the Philippines. *See* Philippines
Communism: and bureaucracy, 222–223, 254, 271, 298; in China, 126, 272, 568, 569; economic planners interviewed, 484, 504; in India, 80; in Indonesia, 298; objectives of, 113–114; as orthotonic polity, 271, 273–275; as political order, 379; and totalitarian oligarchy, 307–308
Communist-Huk rebellion, 563, 568
Community development, role of, 95–100, 641
Community welfare and range of political choice, 589
Comparative Administration Group (CAG) of American Society for Public Administration, 28–29, 88n.
Compensated bureaucracy, 263, 322
Competence as administrative value, 572–577
Competition and economic development, 128
Competitive politics: in constitutive system, 322; and development programs, 507, 531; in Philippines, 563
Complex bureaucracy, 238–243, 253–262, 322, 329
Compound bureaucracy, 241–243, 322
Comprehensive planning, aspects of, 499, 581–582
Comte, A., 474
Concepts: of man, 150–156, 646; and naming, 326
Conditional assistance, concept of, 571
Conflict between planners and politicians, 518–519, 520–521
Confucius, 115
Congo, 300, 418n., 461
Congress: of Philippines, 563, 582, 583, 585; of United States, 5, 6, 9n., 14, 29, 252, 285, 443, 454
Congress party, India, 274, 300
Conseil d'Etat, 185, 194, 209, 210, 211
Conseil des Finances, 185
Constitution: of Ceylon, 43n.; of China, 43n.; of Germany, during occupation, 43n.; of India, 39, 43n.; of Japan, 43n.; of Malaysia, 43n.; of Pakistan, 39, 43n., 98; of Philippines, 562
Constitutionalism, 32, 44n., 132, 133, 216
Constitutive systems, 243–246, 262, 651, 666; definition of, 322, 329; in tonic politics, 268–273
Consultation and political participation, 101
Consumer sovereignty, and development, 624
Contextuality and directed change, 354
Continuity in government, 567
Contratonic polity, 323
Convention People's party, Ghana, 292
Coombs, P. H., 29n.
Cooper, J. S., 9
Cooperative League of the U.S.A., 17
Cooperatives, value of, 9, 15, 17, 18, 161
Copi, I. M., 334n.
Cornelius, A. R., 98n., 100
Corruption, 435, 438, 661
Cost: of growth, 596–606, 662; of security, 643
Costa Rica, 271
Council of Administrative Management, 578
Council of Economic Advisers, 475
Creativity, 422–425
Crider, J. H., 623n.
Crimean War, 204
Cromwell, O., 198
Crozier, Michel, 73, 75, 76, 174n., 213n., 453, 454, 480n., 482n.
Cuaderno Plan, 580
Cuba, 22, 307, 317n., 538
Cultural factors, effects of, 592–593, 661
Culver, J., 20
Cummings, M. C., 623n.
Cunningham, W., 113n., 128n., 129n.
Cyprus, 25, 317n.
Czechoslovakia, 317n.

Dacca Centre of Pakistan Council for National Integration, 98n.

Dahl, Robert A., 591n., 610n., 613n., 620n., 621n., 623n., 624n., 635n.
Dandekar, N., 90n.
Dasgupta, A., 601n.
David, Paul T., 53n.
Davies, J. C., 147n.
Davies, R. W., 434n.
Davis, O. A., 591n., 625n.
Davis, R. H., 13n.
Dawes, C. G., 93, 94n.
Decentralization, 544–545
Decision-making, 395–396, 545
Deductive method, inverse, for political study, 141–142
Defense Department, U.S., 94
Delany, W., 525n.
Demand-conversion crisis, 16, 105
Democracy and bureaucracy, 190–191, 217
Democratic party, 82
Democratization, 233–234, 323, 650
Dempster, M. A. H., 591n.
Denmark, 239, 317n.
Desai, C. C., 90n.
DesRoutours, R., 430n., 433n., 435n.
Deutsch, Karl W., 47, 107n., 115n., 155n., 397–399
Developing states: means of change in, 656–657; political systems in, 643–644; resource lacks in, 630
Development: and administration, 554; definition of, 323; as ecological change, 230–233; grants for, 11; objectives of, 641–642, 650; supporters of programs for, 494–498. *See also* Economic development
Development Loan Fund, 11, 15
Dewey, J., 351, 352, 353n.
Diamant, A., 157n., 171, 218n., 542n., 609
Dicey, A. V., 181n., 197n.
Diehl, C., 433n., 434n.
Diem regime, 462
Diet (Parliament) of Japan, 87, 89, 94
Diffusion of power and political development, 45, 47–52, 383–385, 640, 647, 652
Dimock, M. E., 480n.
Diogenes, 161
Directional dimensions in value changes, 391–393
Dirlam, J. B., 630, 631
Dissatisfaction with government, causes of, 131
Djakarta, 409
Doctrine related to myth, 380
Doebear, F. T., 622n.
Dorn, P., 600n.
Dorn, W., 435n.
Dorsey, John T., 462n.
Dorwart, R. A., 176, 177, 179n., 182, 184, 187, 432n., 435n., 436n., 437n., 438n., 439n., 440n.
Dostoevski, 148
Downs, Anthony, 622n., 629n.
Drucker, P., 162n.
Druesne, M., 474n.
DuBois, Cora, 417n.
Dunlap, J., 433n.
Dupree, A. H., 475n.
Durkheim, E., 157, 588, 611n., 633n.
Dutch in Indonesia, 408
Dutch East Indies Company, 410
Duverger, theories of, 315
Dye, T. R., 606n.

Easton, D., 83n., 142, 633n.
Eberhard, W., 430n.
Ebtehaj, 520
Eckstein, H., 125n.
Ecological change: democratization as, 233–234; development as, 230–233; modernization as, 234–236; types of, 230–236, 650
Ecology: and indigenous institutions, 106; and political development, 25, 198, 317
Economic aid. *See* Foreign aid
Economic development: autonomy and modernization in, 611–612; and cost of growth, 596–598, 662; and efficiency, 577–580, 661; four types of action in, 629–632; and ideology, 505, 508–510; impediments in, 491–493, 499; optimizing role of state in, 628–632; and political costs, 605–606; and political development, 33, 595, 597, 634, 667; reflected in per capita income, 588; "take-off" in, 127, 643
Economic planners. *See* Planners
Economic Policy Development, 581
Economist as trained public servant, 533–534
Edel, A., 148n.
Education: of economic planners, 485–486; and ideology of development, 506, 511–513; role of, 101, 112
Edward IV, 198
Effective political systems, features of, 644
Effective public administration and political stability, 547
Efficiency: in bureaucracy, 261–263, 322, 464–465; and economy, 577–580, 661; market systems affecting, 625–626
Egalitarian trends, 119, 642
Egypt: ancient empire of, 167, 223; bureaucracy in, 239, 438; expansion-

ism in, 126; incentives for planners in, 521; and Israel, 39; leadership in, 600; modernization in, 489; prestige of, 504; U.N. experts from, 543
Eire, 239
Eiseley, L. C., 109n.
Eisenstadt, S. N., 53n., 157n., 167, 171n., 223, 341, 429n., 430, 433n., 434n., 437n., 452n., 466n., 523n., 525n., 656
Elder, Robert E., 475n.
Elected assemblies, 245, 323, 329, 330
Elections: definition of, 323, 329, 330; legitimizing, 323; in Philippines, 563
Electoral participation, 100, 641
Elizabeth I, 434n.
Elliott, W. Y., 8n.
Ellsburg, D., 85n.
Ellul, J., 480n.
Emerson, Rupert, 107n., 408n.
Emery, F. E., 525n.
Emmerich, Herbert, 540
Empathy and political development, 74–75
Empiricism, 146–148, 159
Employment Act of 1946, 475
England: absolutism in, 197, 198, 214, 648; administrative history of, 204–209, 647, 648; bureaucracy in, 184n., 195–196, 203, 206, 209, 251, 264, 443, 447, 649; civil service in, 443–447, 449, 450, 649; colonial experience of, 640; concept of rule of law, 180, 193, 194; crisis management in, 183, 184; economic development in, 127–128, 200, 474, 475, 643; elected assemblies in, 245; experts from, 543, 545n., 660; foreign aid policies of, 30, 31, 94; Glorious Revolution in, 199, 201, 448; government powers in, 199–201, 211, 284; historical tradition in, 191; influence in India, 408, 603; mercantilism in, 202; modernization in, 170n., 186, 234, 239; monarchy in, 182, 188, 196–199, 210, 247; per capita income, 318n.; public services of, 187; staffing patterns in, 278n., 280; training of personnel in, 92; wages of civil servants in, 89; and world affairs, 395
Enlightenment as a value, 356–357, 358, 361, 370
Entrepreneurs and bureaucrats, 622
Epictetus, 143
Epstein, T. S., 418n.
Equality as objective of government, 117–119, 642
Erikson, E. H., 411n.
Esman, Milton J., 29n., 52n., 53n., 78n., 218n., 456n., 536n., 537n., 562n.
Etat de Droit, 211, 214
Ethiopia, 223, 239, 294, 307, 313, 459
Ethnic factors in developing countries, 459–462
Etzioni, Amitai, 401n., 525n.
Europe: absolutism in, 178, 181, 182; administrative development in, 171, 173, 181, 190, 211; bureaucracy in, 170, 242, 250, 251, 252, 448; Catholic Church in, 213; Common Market in, 475; course of development in, 110, 604, 607, 648, 658; Eastern states, 251, 271, 307, 319, 481, 512; economic development in, 491, 595; economic planners in, 481; expansion of, 394; feudal system in, 224, 227; influence on planners, 486, 504, 512; issue of equality in, 118, 607; lack of political parties in, 223; liberalism in, 189; mercantilism in, 185; military planning staff in, 474; monarchs in, 167, 183, 247; nation-states in, 121, 176, 178; political development in, 134; polities in, 251, 319; public services in, 191n.; Recovery Program, 475; as threat to England, 204
Evaluation of projects, criteria for, 555–556
Evans-Pritchard, E. E., 167n.
Exchange, universality of, 632–637
Executive, role of, 246–249, 323, 329, 330
Expansionism as objective of government, 116–126
External inducement of institutional change, 3, 4, 77–103. *See also* Foreign aid

Fagan, R. R., 39n.
Fainsod, Merle, 461, 463n., 554n.
Fallenbuchl, Z. M., 625n., 631n.
Fascist party, 379
Federalists, 45, 211, 450
Fei, J. C. H., 596n.
Feith, H., 419n.
Fesler, James W., 254
Festinger, L., 424n.
Field, G. L., 197n.
Field, M. J., 421n.
Finer, H., 187, 197, 452
Finer, S. E., 125n., 126n., 166n., 179n., 203n., 205, 220n., 257n., 288n., 317, 446, 447n.
Finkle, J., 608n., 609n.
Finland, 317n.
Finlay, D. J., 39n.
Finn, Huck, 151, 153, 645

Fisher, L. E., 430n., 435n.
Fisher, W., 207n.
Five-Year Integrated Socio-Economic Development Program, 580
Flacelere, R., 517n.
Flash, E. S., 475n., 476n.
Fleishman, E. A., 455n.
Follett, Mary, 162n.
Foltz, W. J., 107n.
Ford Foundation, 572
Ford, Franklin L., 429n., 430n., 434n., 437n., 439n.
Ford, Henry Jones, 336
Foreign Affairs, House Committee on, 5–6, 14, 15, 17n., 18, 23n.
Foreign aid: academic and government theories of, 26–30; agricultural assistance, 96n.; aims of, 546–547; developments in U.S., 3–32; duration of need for, 503; as factor in developing states, 128, 643; in Philippines, 556–587; strategy in, 77–103. *See also* Agency for International Development
Foreign Assistance Acts: of 1961, 5, 9n.; of 1962, 10n.; of 1966, 5, 11n., 13, 15n., 16, 17, 18, 51, 82, 555; of 1967, 4–32, 51, 78, 103; and Title IX, 4–21, 25, 32, 66, 79, 82, 103–106, 555, 639
Foreign Relations Committee of U.S. Senate, 5n., 6, 13n.
Formula as component of myth, 380
Fortes, M., 167n.
Four-Year Economic Program for Philippines, 581
Fox, C. J., 203
France: absolutism in, 192; administrative changes in, 177, 179, 184, 197, 647; bureaucracy in, 187, 188, 191, 203, 209, 442, 648; colonial experience of, 640; economic development of, 127–128, 185–186, 643; economic planning in, 626n.; emergence of, 25; experts from, 538, 543, 545, 660; government of provinces, 173; judicial power in, 129, 186, 194n., 201; lack of political parties in, 223; legislature on civil service, 454; medieval government of, 239, 437; mercantilism in, 202; national identity of, 183; per capita income in, 318n.; reforms in, 429; Revolution in, 188–193, 595, 607; sale of offices in, 438, 447; Third Republic of, 451; world position of, 504
France, Anatole, 123
Franchise, and electoral mechanisms, 100
Francisco, G. A., 575n.
Franda, Marcus, 16
Fraser, Donald M., 13, 14, 16, 20
Frederick II of Prussia, 127n., 438, 440
Frederick II of Sicily, 171n.
Frederick William I of Prussia, 171, 176–177, 179, 180n., 182n., 184, 187, 192, 212, 432, 435, 436n., 438, 439, 440
Free market: attitudes toward, 622; and economic development, 621
Freedom: in bargaining, 635; dimensions of, 120, 163, 642; as government objective, 122–123, 140
Freud, S., 124, 158n.
Friction, reduction of, 642, 643
Friedman, M., 594n., 608, 609, 613n., 619n., 620
Friedrich, C. J., 7, 22n., 33n., 37, 41n., 43n., 49n., 53n., 54–57, 67, 68n., 69n., 75, 87n., 108n., 112n., 114n., 115n., 116n., 117n., 118n., 119n., 120n., 122n., 126n., 127n., 128n., 130n., 134n., 136–142, 145, 174, 175, 185, 188n., 199, 200, 216, 218, 325, 335, 342, 347, 352, 451n., 452, 476n., 641, 642, 649, 662, 664, 666
Frohock, F. M., 147n.
Fueter, E., 400n.
Fukuda, Masaru, 88n.
Function: distinguished from structure, 225–230; technical definition of, 323
Fustel de Coulanges, N. D., 166n.

Gable, Richard, 608n., 609n.
Galbraith, J. K., 612n.
Gandhi, M., 69, 96, 603
Gant, George F., 554n.
Garcia, C. P., 578n.
Gardner, J. W., 27
Gaud, W. S., 13, 28, 29
Geertz, C., 419n., 421n.
General Directory, Prussian, 189
General Services Department, Philippine, 578, 579
George III of England, 203n.
Germany: bureaucracy in, 190, 345; East Germany, 317n.; Federal Republic of, 125; judiciary concepts in, 181, 182n., 194, 210; leadership in, 69; modernization in, 170n., 234; monarchical tradition in, 209; occupation of, 8, 22, 43n., 87n.; organization patterns in, 240; reforms in, 429; sale of offices in, 447; specialization in, 215; after Thirty Years War, 176; West Germany, 210n., 317n.
Gerth, H. H., 172n., 476n.
Ghana, 260, 286, 291, 293, 300, 459, 460, 464, 519n.
Gide, C., 596n.

Ginsburg, N., 417n.
Goal models for political development, 393–399
Goering, H., 215
Goethe, 121
Goheen, J., 601n.
Gold Coast, Africa, 410
Gooch, G. P., 400n.
"Good life" concept, 114–115
Goodman, P., 162n.
Goodnow, Frank, 336, 337, 349
Goshal, A. K., 171n.
Gouldner, A., 162, 217, 346, 649
Goulet, D. A., 35n.
Government: functional relationships in, 261; modern patterns of, 113, 237–250; objectives of, 113; as opposed to state or political order, 139–140; and private sector, 623, 635, 662, 663; related to academic research, 26–30; separation of public and private functions, 177, 648; traditional patterns of, 237–250
Government Survey and Reorganization Commission, Philippine, 566n., 574, 581, 583
Great Britain. *See* England
Great Elector in Prussia, 171, 175–177, 183, 199, 212
Greaves, H. R. G., 114n., 208n.
Greece, 25, 166, 234, 245, 294, 297, 313
Greene, G., 151, 152
Greenstein, F. I., 52n., 154n.
Greenwood, E., 515n.
Gretton, R. H., 197n.
Griffin, K. B., 619n.
Griffiths, P. J., 408n.
Gross, Bertram M., 167, 168, 482n.
Gross, N., 62n.
Gross National Product, 317–319
Gross and net outcomes, 359–364
Growth: costs of, 596–606, 662; versus development, 593
Guatamala, 459
Guided Democracy period, in Indonesia, 297
Guild system in Europe, 185–186
Guilland, R., 433n., 434n.
Gumplowicz, L., 126n.
Gurgaon district of Punjab, 96
Guyot, James F., 462n.
Guzman, R. P. de, 562n., 575n.
Guzman, Teresita L., de, 581n.

Habbakuk, H. J., 595n.
Hackett, Anne-Marie, 475n.
Hackett, J., 475n.
Hagen, E. E., 389, 407n., 423n., 516, 605n.
Haider, S. M., 47n.
Haire, M., 597n.
Haldane Report on Machinery of Government, 208
Halévy, E., 613n.
Hallowell, J. H., 35n.
Han Dynasty, 430n.
Handbook of Public Administration, 540–545
Hanson, A. H., 475n., 599n., 602n., 630n.
Hapgood, D., 13n.
Happiness as government objective, 114–115
Hapsburg, 128
Harbison, F., 599n.
Haring, C. H., 430n., 433n., 435n.
Harris, E. F., 455n.
Harsanyi, J., 635n.
Hart, H. L. A., 147, 644
Hastings, P. K., 409, 472n.
Hatch Act, 434
Hayden, J. R., 567n.
Hayek, F. A., 617n., 618n., 619n.
Hayter, Teresa, 32n.
Heady, F., 78n., 171n., 565
Healthy personality, concept of, 645–646
Hecksher, E., 128, 129n.
Hegel, G., 607n.
Held, Virginia, 94n.
Heller, W. W., 476n., 480n.
Hemingway, E., 151
Hempel, C. G., 338n., 343
Henderson, A. M., 172n., 403n.
Herber, B. P., 625n.
Hermes, spirit of, 74
Herodotus, 601n.
Heterotonic polity, 263, 323
Hewart, Lord (of Bury), 46
Hibben Memorandum, 580
Hicks, J. R., 625n.
Hicks, Ursula, 630n.
Hierarchy: in bureaucracy, 648; of government goals, 141
Hinduism, 409, 462, 468, 601n., 602
Hintze, O., 435n.
Hippocrates, 601n.
Hirschman, A. O., 4n., 591n., 599n., 622n.
Hitch, C. J., 476n.
Hitler, A., 118n., 295
Hobbes, T., 110, 116, 124, 200, 610, 619, 620n.
Hohenzollerns, 173, 182, 187, 188, 191, 440
Holborn, Hajo, 166n.
Holden, M., 591n.
Holmberg, A. R., 641, 649, 651, 652, 653, 664

Holmes, Oliver Wendell, 444
Holsti, O. R., 39n.
Holt, Robert T., 113n., 127n., 179n., 184n., 186n., 200
Holzman, F. D., 624
Homotonic polity, 251, 263, 264, 286–293, 323
Hoover, H. H., 454
Horowitz, I. L., 23n.
Hoselitz, B. F., 128n., 438n., 612n.
Hovde, B. J., 440n.
Hoyle, F., 472
Hucker, C. O., 435n.
Hughes, E., 515n.
Hughes, J. W., 62n.
Hughes, R. B., 13n.
Human development: institutions affecting, 164, 649, 664–665; optimal, 645
Human relations, supervision and training, 544
Humphrey, H. H., 9, 10, 17
Hungary, 87n., 317n.
Hunter, H., 627n.
Huntington, Samuel P., 17, 23n., 33, 53n., 59, 60, 79, 80, 81, 119n., 124n., 157n., 170n., 402n., 475n., 611n.
Hyneman, C., 190, 443, 452, 454n.
Hypertonic polity, 323
Hypotonic polity, 323

Ibadan, University of, 530, 534
Iceland, 317n.
Ideologies: and administrative organization, 166–219; and economic level, 505, 508–510; and education, 506, 511–513; variables affecting, 505–506
Ilchman, Alice Stone, 472n.
Ilchman, Warren F., 29n., 63n., 161, 345, 348, 472n., 476n., 516n., 522n., 527, 534n., 658, 659
Impediments to economic development, 491–493, 499
Inayatullah, 599n.
Inca Empire, 438
Income: international disparity in, 607; per capita, 588
Independence: as dimension of freedom, 120–121, 642; as political goal, 394
India: adjustment to imbalance in, 83; administration changes in, 4, 40; ancient civilization of, 166; civil service changes in, 206, 459, 462, 519n.; colonial administration of, 295, 296, 312, 388, 408–410, 413n., 418n., 666; communism in, 80; community development in, 41, 50, 95–99; Congress party of, 274, 300; constitution of, 39, 43n.; experts from, 538, 543; Five-Year Plans in, 102, 475, 599n., 601; foreign aid in, 11, 79n.; leadership in, 69, 467, 600, 602–605; legislative system in, 88–92, 95, 286, 300; military aid to, 25; modernization in, 489; orthotonic polities in, 271, 307, 388; per capita income in, 318; "skimming" practices in, 438; sociology of culture in, 613n.; tradition-oriented groups in, 81; as transitional culture, 420n., 421n., 461, 468
Indigenous institutions, 20, 96–100, 106, 286, 639, 641, 666
Individual development, institutions affecting, 164, 649, 664–665
Indonesia: colonial administration of, 408; communal groups in, 419; economic development in, 492; expansionism in, 126; industrialization in, 491; leadership in, 69, 297–298; military officers in, 286, 506; political system in, 565; seminars concerning, 28; as transitional culture, 421n., 461
Inductive method for political study, 138
Industrialization: and administrative organization, 213; valued by economic planners, 488. *See also* Modernization
Inequity before law, 118, 119
Inkeles, A., 74n.
Innovation: as dimension of freedom, 120–121; as institutional pattern, 383–385; and political development, 66–77, 640
Inoke, Masamichi, 86n., 89n.
Inonu government, 521
Institute of Constitutional and Parliamentary Studies in Delhi, 90
Institute of Development Studies, Sussex, 30, 31
Institute of Public Administration, in Philippines, 572, 573, 582n.
Institutions, 402–406; in development programs, 19, 397–399; evaluation of, 59–63, 640; and human development, 4, 164, 649, 651, 664–665; indigenization of, 96–100, 106, 286, 639, 641, 666; interaction situations, 378–380; and political development, 639–640; in precolonial and postcolonial periods, 406–422, 654; related to academic research, 26–30; strategies of, 381–383; strengthening of, 5, 25, 105–106, 650; sub-outcomes of, 373–378; validity of, 106; and values, 385, 665; variables in building of, 558, 562
Intellectuals and development programs, 496–497
Intelligence and power, 377

Interaction by collaboration and communication, 368–369
Interdependence, mutual, 350–352
Internal relationships: in bureaucracy, 428, 657; in democracies, 450–455, 656; in developing countries, 465–468, 656; in traditional autocracies, 439–442, 656
International Bank for Reconstruction and Development (IBRD), 520, 521, 530
International Cooperation Administration (ICA), 96n., 546n., 549n., 553, 557n.
Interstitial participation, 100–103, 641, 646
Inter-University Research Program in Institution-Building, 536, 562
Intervention, sensitivity to, 24
Inventive method for political study, 138
Invocations, power, 378
Iqbal, 42
Iran: bureaucracy in, 297; economic planners in, 520, 521; leadership in, 70; modern institutions in, 239; monarchy in, 294; political system in, 307, 310, 313
Ireland, 317n.
Ishmael, 151, 645
Isotonic polity, 323
Israel, 25, 39, 260, 271, 317n., 504
Italy, 69, 215, 279, 317n.

Jackson, A., 145, 205, 210, 447
Jacobins, 191
Jacobs, N., 601n.
Jafri, S. R. A., 97n.
Jagota, S. P., 459n.
Jaguaribe, Helio, 89n.
Jaipur district, 97
Jamaat-e-Islami, 81, 84
Jamaica, 271, 286
Jana Sangh, 81, 90n.
Janowitz, Morris, 125n., 519, 565
Japan: administration changes in, 4; Children's Welfare Law in, 102; constitutive system in, 252; economic development in, 127–128, 643; evolution of, 388; feudal system in, 227; industrial dualism in, 600n.; leadership in, 69, 70; legislative system in, 88, 89, 91; as model for development, 504, 508; modernization in, 234; occupation of, 8, 22, 86–87, 94, 101, 666; per capita income in, 319; political system in, 271, 307
Java, 410, 421n.
Jefferson, T., 145
Jena, 173, 188
Jennings, E. E., 623n.
Jennings, I., 43n.
Jennings, M. K., 623n.
Jinnah, 69
Johnson, A., 186n.
Johnson, H. G., 597, 598n., 618n., 619n., 622, 625n., 630n., 631n.
Johnson, J. J., 125n.
Johnson, L. B., 6
Joint Commission of Rural Development (JCRD), 12–13, 21
Joint Commission of Rural Reconstruction in China (JCRR), 12
Jordan, 294, 313
Jouvenel, Bertrand de, 53, 111
Judd, W. H., 13n.
Judiciary. *See* Legal development
Justice as objective of government, 116, 129–130, 134, 642

Kachins, 419
Kahin, George McT. 164n.
Kahn, A. E., 616n.
Kahn, R. L., 162n., 425n.
Kamien, M. I., 622n.
Kant, I., 110, 119, 123n., 149–150, 182n., 645
Kaplan, A., 38n., 54, 55, 56, 57, 137
Kapp, K. W., 613n., 625n.
Karens, 419
Kariel, Henry S., 4, 52n., 325, 335, 340n., 342, 345, 346, 347, 514n., 644, 645, 646, 651, 653, 664
Katz, D., 162n., 425n.
Kearney, Robert N., 462n.
Keith, A. B., 408
Kennedy School of Government, 44n.
Kennedy, V. D., 602, 603, 604
Kerala, 80
Khanna, R. L., 97
Khrushchev, N., 284
Khusro, A. M., 601n.
Kilpatrick, F. P., 623n.
King, J. E., 185n.
Kingsley, J. Donald, 101, 444, 445, 446, 448n., 450n., 451, 459, 464, 466n.
Kinross, Lord, 70n.
Kirchheimer, O., 181n.
Kitt, Alice, 63n.
Kluckhohn, C., 112
Knight, F. H., 617n.
Knorr, K., 596n.
Kochanek, S. A., 95n.
Koopmans, T. C., 617n., 619n.
Korea, 70, 79n., 86n., 307
Kornai, J., 627n.
Kornhauser, W., 476n.
Krieger, L., 87n.
Kris, E., 424n.

Kuhn, Thomas S., 333
Kurtz, P., 147n.
Kuwait, 313, 317n., 318
Kuznets, S., 595n., 613n.

Labour party, 444, 445, 475
Ladd, J., 119n.
Laevinger, 620n.
Laissez faire, 186
Landau, Martin, 164n., 336n., 337n., 341n., 350n., 639, 651
Lande, C. H., 564n.
Lange, O., 619n., 620n.
Laos, 10, 565
LaPalombara, Joseph, 38, 44n., 48, 53n., 77n., 78n., 144, 157n., 183n., 210n., 218n., 274n., 325, 332, 334, 340, 341, 342, 345n., 346, 347, 350, 403n., 416n., 438n., 464n., 647, 649, 651, 666
LaPorte, T. R., 525n.
Laski, 345
Lasswell, Harold D., 33, 35, 36n., 38, 47, 48, 51n., 54, 55, 56, 57, 58, 67, 68, 70, 75, 79n., 154, 162n., 401, 407n., 641, 649, 651, 652, 653, 664
Lateral dimensions in development, 391–393
Lateral relationships: in autocracies, 437–439; in bureaucracy, 428, 657; in democracies, 447–449; in underdeveloped countries, 462–465
Latin America: bureaucracy in, 220; developing countries of, 169, 619n.; economic planners in, 483, 484, 485, 489, 493, 494, 496, 497, 502, 520, 531; elites in, 600n., 604n.; orthotonic polities in, 271, 319; political system in, 307
Lautman, J., 482n.
Law. *See* Legal development
Lawrence, D. H., 151
Lawson, G., 536n.
Lawson, Kay, 472n.
Leadership necessary for change, 68–70
Lear, J., 623n.
Lebanon, 271
Lefas, A., 451n.
Lefeber, T., 589n.
Leff, N., 622n., 632n.
Legal development: factors in, 105, 193–194, 453; international framework of, 643; and rule of law, 11, 12, 21, 195, 201n., 648
Legal-rational bureaucracy, 476–479
Legislative process in new states, 105, 641
Legislative Reference Service, 91, 94
Legislatures, 86–94
Leibenstein, H., 589n., 597n., 609n., 613n.
Leighton, A. H., 57, 76
Leites, N., 407n.
Lemieux, V., 635n.
Lenin, N., 216, 617n.
Lerner, A. P., 619, 620
Lerner, Daniel, 47, 74n., 124n., 163n., 389
Letwin, W., 601n.
Levellers, 200
Levi, W., 158n.
Levy, M. J., 592, 600, 610, 611n., 613n., 663
Lewis, W. A., 78, 117n., 590n., 599n., 610n., 612n., 619n., 622n., 623n., 625n., 629n.
Li, H., 435n.
Liberalism, 182n.
Likert, R., 455n.
Lindblom, C. E., 591n., 610n., 613n., 620n., 621n., 623n., 624n.
Linkages variables, 562
Lipset, S. M., 23n., 515, 516n., 599n., 600n., 617n., 623n.
Lipson, L., 166n.
Lissak, M., 519n.
Little, I. M. D., 601n., 613n.
Livingston, J. S., 629n.
Lobo Prakhu, J. M., 90n.
Local Government Center, Philippine, 572
Locke, J., 110, 119, 129
Loevinger, L., 611n.
Lok Sabhah, 90
Lord, H. M., 94
Louis XIV, 127n., 177, 183, 185n., 186, 187n., 188n., 193, 194n., 198, 199, 212, 429
Lovejoy, A. O., 346
Low-income countries, economic planners in, 481–493
Lowell, A. L., 336, 337
Loyalty in democratic bureaucracy, 443, 445
Lukas, J. A., 601n.
Lutz, Vera, 625n.
Luxembourg, 317n.
Lybyer, A. H., 171n.
Lystad, R. R., 519n.

MacArthur, D., 87
MacDonnell Commission, 449
McCamy, J. L., 476n.
McCarthy era, 434, 444
McClelland, D. C., 74n., 153n., 389, 605n.
McDougal, M. S., 36n.
McEachern, 62n.
McInnis, H. D., 577

McKean, R. N., 476n., 591n., 629n.
McKeon, R., 118n.
McKinley, W., 566
Macapagal, D., 578n., 581
Machiavelli, 110, 144, 168
Mackenzie, W. J. M., 41n., 166n., 207n.
Macy, R. M., 8n.
Magna Carta, 201n.
Magsaysay, R., 563, 574, 577, 578n., 579
Mahendra, King of Nepal, 70
Maine, H., 171n.
Maistre, J. de, 157
Majlis, 297, 521
Majumdar, H. K., 603n.
Malacañang, 575
Malamud, B. 151
Malaysia: constitution of, 43n.; guerrilla emergency in, 467; modernization in, 490, 492; orthotonic polities in, 271; political system in, 565; postcolonial government in, 286, 463; public services in, 459, 460, 461, 462
Malenbaum, W., 467n.
Man: concepts of, 150–156, 646; as self-governed agent, 163
Management Service, Philippine, 578
Manchu bureaucracy, 438
Mangone, G. J., 8n.
Mann, T., 151, 152
Mansur, F., 519n.
Manuel, F. E., 599n.
Mapili, G. R., 577n.
March, J. G., 624n., 635n.
Marcos, F., 578n.
Marcuse, Herbert, 345
Market system: and efficiency, 625–626; free market, 621, 622
Markewitz, I. G., 292n.
Martin, F., 630n.
Marvick, D., 520, 531n.
Marx, F. M., 176, 180n., 184n., 187, 188, 210n., 215, 442, 444n., 446n., 451, 452n.
Marx, K., 144, 145, 161, 593, 617n., 640, 662
Masihuzzaman, 191n.
Maslow, A. H., 147n., 154n.
Mason, W. S., 62n.
Massachusetts Institute of Technology, 16
Massé, P., 480n.
Masselman, G., 408n.
Masson, F., 443n.
Masters, J., 410n.
Mathur, M. V., 97n., 99n.
Maulana Maudoudi, 84
Mauss, M., 633n.
Mayo, Elton, 470n.
Meade, J. E., 617n., 618n., 621n., 625n.
Means-end relationship, 350–353
Medina, Florencia, 575n.
Mehta, A., 40
Meier, G. M., 607n., 625n.
Meiji Reform, Japan, 69, 70
Mekong development, 28
Mercantilism, 128, 129, 185, 202, 643
Merit and competence, as administrative values, 572–577, 661
Merkl, P. H., 87n.
Merritt, R. L., 87n.
Merton, R. K., 63n., 345, 347n.
Methods and matériel, 544
Mexico, 127n., 239, 271, 488, 489
Meynaud, Jean, 88n., 474n.
Mezirow, J. D., 96n.
Michigan, University of, 572, 573n.
Middle Ages, 179n., 181, 193
Middle civil servants, 575
Middle East, 171, 472n., 484, 485, 491, 495, 496, 501, 502, 520, 521, 528
Miles, M., 161
Military regime, and development programs, 58, 94, 286, 506, 508, 531
Mill, J. S., 122n., 141, 145, 149
Miller, J. G., 57, 58
Millikan, Max F., 13n., 16
Mills, C. W., 172n., 476n.
Ming Dynasty, 435n.
Minogue, K. R., 603n.
Miranda as component of myth, 380
Mishan, E. J., 589n., 613n.
Mishra, Vikas, 601n.
Mitchell, W. C., 53n.
Mobilization and power diffusion, 49
Model political order, 131–135
Modernization: aspects of, 488–489, 536, 662, 663, 650; as ecological change, 234–236; and economic autonomy, 611–612; and economic development, 489; and industrialization, 490–491; leadership for, 600; and monopoly-party regime, 507–508; and productivity, 489; technical definition of, 323; valued by economic planners, 488; versus Westernization, 489–490
Modernizing polities, 455–468
Mogul rule, 666
Mohsen, A. K. M., 99n.
Monnet Plan, 475
Monopoly-party regime, 507–508, 531
Monotonic polity, 323
Mons, 419
Montesquieu, 129, 198, 438
Montgomery, J. D., 4n., 8, 13n., 16, 22n., 29n., 32n., 79n., 101n., 348, 349, 457n., 460n., 609n., 641, 656, 666, 667

Montias, J. M., 625n.
Moore, B., 181n., 586n., 605n.
Morgan, T., 622n., 627
Morocco, 313
Morris, Cynthia, 600n.
Morris-Jones, W. H., 4n., 95n.
Morse, F. B., 14, 82
Morse, Nancy, 455n.
Mosher, F., 574
Mossadegh, 297
Motivation of government workers, 579–580
Munns, Joyce, 472n.
Murphy, G., 423n.
Musgrave, R. A., 613n., 636n.
Muslims, 84, 409, 438, 462
Mussolini, 295
Mutiny in India, 409
Myers, C. A., 599n.
Myrdal, G., 53n., 603n.
Myth, description of, 380, 381

Nahar Mahmood, Shamsun, 84
Nair, K. K., 90n.
Names and concepts, 326–334
Napoleon I, 173, 188, 189, 190, 192, 193, 209, 213n.
National Assembly, Pakistan, 84, 89n., 90
National Council of Civil Liberties, 444n.
National Economic Council (NEC) in Philippines, 580, 581, 583
National Economic Development Council, England, 475
National Farmers Union, 17
National Institute of Planning, Egypt, 519
National Liberation Council, Ghana, 291
Nazi party, 379, 441, 444
Negroes, in U.S., 114, 118, 642
Nehru, 69
Neotonic polity, 249–250, 301, 323
Nepal, 70, 294, 313
Net outcomes, 359–364
Netherlands, 317n., 538, 543
Nettle, J. P., 47n.
New Deal, 66, 567
New Delhi, 90n., 95n.
New Zealand, 317n., 452
Newman, Lionel J., 62n.
Nietzsche, 154n.
Nigeria: bureaucracy in, 239; civil war in, 457; constitutive system in, 295; economic planning in, 519n., 527, 630n.; foreign aid in, 10; military officers in, 286, 506; modernization in, 490; political parties in, 418n., public service in, 459, 460, 461, 530; training of civil servants in, 410, 533, 534; University of, 530, 534
Nigro, Felix A., 452n.
Nisbet, R. A., 23n.
Nivison, L. B., 435n.
Nkrumah, Kwame, 260, 292
Non-orthotonic polities, 323
Non-stationary society and social surplus, 593
Non-tonic polity, 251, 323
Nordlinger, Eric A., 51
Norman Conquest, 196, 205, 212
North American countries, 251, 319
North Indian state, 485
Northcote-Trevelyan Report, 206, 208, 448, 649
Northern Pacific Railway, 611n.
Norway, 317n.
Nyerere, Julius, 532

Objectives of government, 116, 123, 134, 136, 137, 148; values in, 112
Occupational participation, 102, 641
Ogg, D., 197n.
Okada, T., 87n.
Okinawa, 22, 86n.
Olson, M., 608n.
Onslow, C., 599n.
Oommen, T. K., 69n.
Oppenheim, F., 120n., 122n., 151n.
Optimal human development, 645
Order as objective of government, 117, 642
Organization analysis and structure, 544
Orientation: in bureaucracy, 478–479; and successful planning, 583–584
Ortega y Gasset, José, 38, 664, 665
Orthotonic polity, 251, 263, 264, 324; and GNP, 317–319; types of, 273–280
Orwell, G., 118, 410n.
Oshima, H. T., 612n.
Ostrogorsky, 437n.
Ottoman Empire, 173, 239
Outcomes: gross and net, 359–364; in value-institution model, 385
Overman Act of 1918, 454
Overseas Development, Ministry of, 30

Packenham, R. A., 8, 32, 33n., 143n., 150n.
Pagès, G., 435n., 437n.
Pages, M., 525n.
Pahlevi, Reza, 70
Paige, Glenn D., 556
Paine, J., 145
Pakistan: administration changes in, 4, 46, 169, 599n.; advisory councils in, 102; bureaucracy in, 190, 191n.;

community development in, 50; constitution of, 43n.; divisive factors in, 40, 42; ethnic groups in, 461, 462; evolution of, 388; foreign aid in, 10, 79n.; ideology of, 95, 96; leadership in, 69, 70; legislative system in, 88, 89, 92; military officers in, 286; modernization in, 488; oligarchy in, 310; "Pan" case in, 47, 91; political system in, 39, 83, 84, 85, 97–98; resentment of U.S. intervention, 24–25; rural works program in, 99; stress and crisis in, 77; traditional groups in, 81
Palmer, R. R., 194n.
Panchayati Raj, 96, 97n.
Paraguay, 126
Paratonic polity, 324
Parenti, M., 41n.
Pares, R., 203
Pareto, V., 109, 136, 619, 638
Park, R. L., 420n.
Parliament: British, 201, 202, 447; Indian, 300
Parochialism and economic growth, 601
Parris, H., 166n., 194n., 201n., 203n., 204, 205, 209n.
Parry, J. H., 435n.
Parsonian pattern-variables, 238
Parsons, M. B., 464n.
Parsons, Talcott, 54, 55, 142, 172n., 403n., 472, 514n., 592n.
Participation: and community development, 95–100, 641; as dimension of freedom, 120–123, 642; electoral, 100, 641; interstitial, 100–103, 641, 646; as long-run goal, 393; occupational, 102, 641; role of, 9, 12, 15, 18, 20–21, 49, 145, 555, 648
Participants in value-institution model, 385, 386
Partisans in bureaucracy, 259–261, 264–265, 324
Party, technical definition of, 324, 329, 330
Pasteur, L., 99
Patronage, effects of, 206–207, 447, 575–576
Pauker, G. J., 125n., 164n.
Paul VI, 34
Paulet, 438
Peace as objective of government, 116, 126–127, 134
Peacock, A. T., 613n.
Penalty-reward system, 628–629
Pennock, J. R., 7n., 35, 53n., 54n., 157
Per capita income as index of economic development, 588
Peron, J., 295, 298
Persia, 223, 433. *See also* Iran
Personality: healthy, concept of, 645–646; institutions affecting, 664–665
Personnel administration, 544
Peru, 127n.
PEWBSARD, 35–36, 366–367, 641, 649, 651, 664, 665, 666
Phelps, E. S., 613n.
Philip the Fair, 183
Philippines: American experience in, 22, 252; budgeting in, 464; colonial administration in, 409; constitutive system in, 295; leadership in, 70; orthotonic polities in, 271, 285, 286, 299; public administration technical assistance in, 173, 556–587, 647, 660, 661; as tutelary democracy, 312
Pierson, W. W., 435n.
Piper, Carol S., 536n.
Pitkin, Hanna F., 101n.
Plan Organization, Iran, 520
Plank, J., 16
Planners: attitudes of, 658–659; characteristics of, 515–518; policy control of, 524; politics affecting, 505, 506–508, 518–525; as rational productivity bureaucrats, 481–482, 658; status of, 506, 513–514; value to low-income countries, 482–483; variables affecting movements of, 523–524; views on modernization, 488–493
Plato, 110, 116, 121, 135, 150n., 161, 168, 433, 633n., 644
Platt, J. R., 597n.
Play, need for, 157–158
Plumb, J. H., 23n.
Plunkett, G. W., 338
Pluralism and participation, 648
Plutarch, 520
Poland, 239, 317n.
Polanyi, Michael, 120n., 618n., 627n.
Polenberg, R., 443n.
Police force, international, 643
Political development: and administrative development, 32–77, 427–431, 640; analysis of politics, 137–142; and architectonics, 37–47; characteristics of, 32–77, 640; and diffusion of power, 47–52; and ecological adjustment, 640; and economic aid, 8–9, 554; and economic development, 494–496, 606–613, 667; goals of, 393, 561, 663; and innovation, 66–77, 642; and institutions, 52–66, 104–105, 108; manipulation of forces in, 23–25; norms of orthodox theorists, 145; and range of political choice, 589; responsiveness in, 261–263, 324; systems of Southeast Asia, 565

Political parties, role of, 133, 245–246, 259, 507
Politicians relating to planners, 505, 506–508, 518–525
Politicization of civil service, 324, 466
Polities, 324, 329: anatonic, 322; homotonic, 286–293; orthotonic, 273–280; protonic, 249–250, 293–302, 324; syntonic, 280–286; tonic, 304–315
Pollard, S., 474n., 475n.
Polycommunality, 40–41, 457, 458, 461, 462, 641
Poor Law of 1834, 206
Population growth and economic development, 595
Populorum Progressio, 7, 343
Port, F. J., 195n., 201n., 209n.
Potter, D. M., 601n.
Powell, G. B., 56, 57, 107n., 109n., 136n., 341n., 416n.
Power: adversary, 414, 420–422; arenas of, 378–380; authoritarian structures, 647; in bureaucracy, 173; diffusion of, 45, 47–52, 383–385, 640, 647, 652; and economic competition, 128; gross and net outcomes, 360; unit of, 369–370; as a value, 356–357
Pratt, R. C., 532n.
Preference models in social change, 355, 359–364
Prescriptions, role of, 373–377
President's Committee on Administration Performance and Efficiency, 578n.
Presidential initiative, basis for, 568
Presidential Complaints and Action Committee (PCAC), 578n.
Presthus, R., 480n.
Price, D. K., 475n., 476n., 480n., 623n.
Price, R., 603n.
Price system and economic problems, 616–621
Primary-group values and idealized norms, 586
Priorities in government objectives, 130
Pritchett, C. H., 475n.
Private sector, influence of, 64, 93–94, 145, 623, 635, 662, 663
Privy Council, 196, 200, 202, 241
Procedural precedence for attainment of government goals, 141
Processing of events through institutions, 652
Productivity, and policy control by planners, 524
Professionalization of public service, 573
Program Planning Budgeting System in America (PPBS), 475, 657
Programmatic action and economic development, 499
Prohibition party, 379
Prokovsky, M. N., 435n.
Promotion as institutional system, 377–378
Property rights, 145
Prosperity, as objective of government, 116, 127–129, 134, 642, 643
Protonic polity, 249–250, 293–302, 324
Prussia, 170–184, 187–192, 201, 203, 208, 209, 345, 429, 432, 434–436, 440
Prybla, M. S., 617n.
Public administration. *See* Administrative doctrines
Public order and political development, 395
Public relations and reporting, 545
Public sector. *See* Civil service; Government; Political development
Puerto Rico, 22, 125, 317n., 528, 643
Pulleyblank, E. G., 430n.
Punjab, 96, 97
Putney, England, 199, 201
Pye Lucian W., 4, 16, 33, 77n., 107n., 125n., 149n., 162n., 164n., 183n., 339, 340, 389, 411n., 420n., 466, 467n., 519n., 531, 651, 653, 655, 664

Qadir, Manzur, 70
Quezon, M. L., 567
Quirino, E., 568, 569, 577

RABCIRR, 60, 640, 641, 651, 665, 666
Rahman, A. T. R., 50n., 99n., 191n.
Rajasthan, 97, 99
Ranade, M. G., 603
RAND Corporation, 94
Ranis, G., 596n.
Ranke, L., 400n.
Rational-productivity bureaucracy, 474, 476–483, 523, 527, 529, 530, 658
Rationality and planning, 580–584
Ratzenhofer, G., 126n.
Rawls, J., 118n.
Rectitude, 356–357, 364, 371–372
Redfield, R., 423n.
Reforms. *See* Administrative reform
Regional Cooperative Development, 25
Reich, C. A., 620n.
Reiner, E., 455n.
Reisman, W. M., 36n.
Reorganization Committee, Philippine, 568n.
Representation and power diffusion, 49
Republican party, 82, 211
Research. *See* Academic research
Respect as a value, 356–357, 364, 371

Responsibility: and bureaucratic evolution, 174; and political development, 394–395
Restriction of patterns, 383–385
Reward-penalty system, 628–629
Rhee, Syngman, 298
Rhodesia, 271
Richelieu, 134
Riesman, D., 123n., 158n.
Riggs, F. W., 4, 29n., 53n., 56, 57, 77n., 157n., 162n., 164n., 224n., 229n., 237n., 242n., 244n., 248n., 251n., 261n., 278n., 287n., 295n., 305n., 314, 321n., 325–334, 339, 341n., 457n., 463n., 464n., 466, 649, 650, 666, 667; glossary of terms used by, 322–324
Rist, C., 596n.
Ritual in colonial administration, 411–412
Robertson, D. H., 615n.
Robinson, Mary E., 8n.
Robinson, R. D., 70n.
Robson, W. A., 452n.
Rockefeller Foundation, 472n., 572
Rodriguez Plan, 580
Rogers, C. R., 154n.
Rokeach, M., 154n.
Role theory, 514, 646
Roman civilization, 166, 171, 227, 245, 433
Rooks, C., 534
Roosevelt, F. D., 449, 454, 567
Roper Center for Public Opinion Research, 472n.
Rosen, G., 418n., 599n., 601n., 602n.
Rosenberg, H., 170, 173, 180n., 187n., 188n., 189, 429n., 432n., 435n., 436n., 437n., 438n., 440n., 647
Ross, W. T., 599n.
Rossiter, C. L., 122n.
Rostow, W. W., 128n.
Roth, G., 69n.
Roumania, 87n.
Rousseau, 145, 150n., 157, 193n.
Roxas, M. A., 568, 569, 577
Roxas, S. K., 581
Rubenstein, R., 162n.
Rudy, Helen, 472n.
Runciman, W. G., 147n., 430n.
Runneymede, meeting at, 199
Russett, B. M., 125n., 317n., 600n.
Russia. *See* Soviet Union
Rustow, D. A., 183n., 401n.

Safran, Nadav, 126n.
Sagnad, P., 185n., 430n., 433n.
Saint-Simon, H., 474, 599
Saloma, J. S., 591n.
Samson, A., 472n.
Samuelson, P. A., 592n.
Sanford, N., 155n.
Santiniketan, 96
Sarbin, T., 62n.
Sarfatti, Margali, 472n.
Sartori, Giovanni, 4, 43, 44, 45, 48, 50n., 53n., 100, 101n., 166n., 181n., 182n., 189n., 192, 193n., 220n., 278, 315, 639
Saxon institutions, adaptations of, 199
Schaffer, B. B., 31
Scharpf, F., 166n., 193n., 210n.
Schelling, T. C., 633n.
Scherer, F. M., 629n.
Schmoller, 129n.
Schott, John R., 16
Schultz, T. W., 596n., 601n.
Schwartz, B., 475n.
Schwartz, Mildred, 515, 516n., 623n.
Schwartz, N. L., 622n.
Schweinitz, K. de, 608n.
Schweitzer, A., 148
Scott, W. G., 425n.
Sears, Roebuck, 93
Sectors, 58, 640
Security as objective of government, 116–126, 134, 642, 643
Security Council, 335
Self-discipline and individual growth, 165
Self-help, 6, 11, 19
Selznick, P., 54n.
Sensitivity to human values, 641
Separation of public and private functions, 177, 648
Service value of public administration, 194
Seton-Watson, H., 87n.
Sharp, Walter R., 443n., 454n.
Shearer, J. C., 480n.
Shechan, S., 601n.
Sherif, M., 63n.
Sherman Antitrust Act, 611n.
Shils, E. A., 107n., 125n., 304–315, 482, 610n.
Shonfield, A., 475n.
Shor, E. L., 542
Siam, 223
Sibley, Mulford Q., 35n.
Siffin, William J., 131n., 136, 609n.
Sigmund, P. J., 457n.
Silcock, T. H., 418n.
Silone, 151, 152
Silver, M., 631n.
Silvert, K. H., 520, 531n.
Simon, H., 351n., 454, 586n., 624n.
Simple bureaucracy, 238–243, 324
Sinai, I. R., 602, 604, 605, 662
Singapore, 271, 286, 317n., 409
Singhvi, L. M., 90n.

Sinn Fein strike, 444
Sismondi, 596
Sisson, C. H., 209, 215n., 216
Sjoberg, G., 608n.
Skill, 356–357, 371
Sklar, R. L., 418n.
Smellie, K. B., 203, 204, 205, 207, 208
Smelser, N. J., 592n., 617n.
Smith, Adam, 129, 204, 625, 633
Smith, B. L. R., 476n.
Smith, D. H., 74n.
Smith, T. M., 472n.
Smithies, A., 32n.
Soberano, J. D., 582
Social change, characteristics of, 355–356
Social and Economic Development Program, 580
Social order: administrative patterns in, 166; effects of, 645; primitive, 167; and political development, 33
Social Science Research Council, 33, 44n., 86n.
Social Science Research Institute, 220n.
Social sciences, 400, 401
Social status of planners, 506, 513–514
Social surplus, 593–596, 662
Social values, 34–36
Socialization and interaction, 391–392
Societal system, description of, 592
Society for Public Administration of Philippines, 573
Socio-psychological costs in modernization, 596, 599–606
Socrates, 34, 135
Sofer, C., 525n.
Sola Pool, Ithiel de, 162n.
Solari, A., 599n., 600n.
Solo, R. A., 590n., 592n.
Sombart, W., 127n., 128n.
Somit, A., 401n.
South Africa, 271
South America. *See* Latin America
Southeast Asia: allocation of resources in, 501, 502; commonwealth economy in, 418n.; planners in, 484, 485, 489, 490, 492, 494, 495, 496, 520, 528; political system in, 563, 564, 565; programs in, 15, 569n.; unions in, 497
Southeast Asia Development Advisory Group (SEADAG), 17, 26–31, 78n., 90n., 103
Sovani, N. V., 468
Sovereignty, 178, 192, 648: in absolutist systems, 178; consumer, 624; popular, 648
Soviet Union: anatonic polities in, 319; bureaucracy in, 222; developmental revolution in, 233; economy in, 610, 615, 617n., 618n.; expansionist tendencies of, 126; experts from, 543; five-year plan of, 475; modernization in, 234; objectives of, 113–114; orthotonic polities of, 271; per capita income in, 318n.; political system in, 307, 611n.; in prewar Stalinist years, 284; relations with Britain, 444; ruling party in, 274; size of, 239; states depending on, 395; units detached from, 25. *See also* Communism
Spain, 169, 171n., 184
Spanish-American colonies, 435n.
Spanish Indies, 435n.
Specialists, status of, 71
Spengler, J. J., 186, 325, 342, 416n., 457n., 534n., 593n., 594n., 609n., 621n., 631n., 662, 663, 667
Spengler, Oswald, 74n., 128n.
Spinoza, 115
Spiro, H., 43n.
Srinivas, M. N., 601n.
Stalher, G. M., 525n.
Stalin, 295, 298, 605, 607n.
Standards and Techniques, 539–540, 541, 543
Stange, H. O. H., 437n.
State, as opposed to government or political order, 139
State Department, 16, 94, 241, 475, 546n.
Stationary vs. non-stationary society, 591–596
Status of planners, 71, 506, 513–514
Statutory law, 194
Steere, D. V., 35n.
Stein, E., 437n.
Stein, Gertrude, 212
Stein, M. B., 46n.
Stein reforms, 440
Stevenson, C. L., 334n.
Stigler, G., 618n., 620
Stokes, Sybil, 171n.
Stolper, W. F., 625n., 627n., 630n.
Stone, D. C., 161
Storer, J. A., 581n.
Strategies as social institutions, 381–383, 385
Streeten, Paul, 613n.
Structure, 55–58, 82–86, 105, 142, 478–479, 640, 650; technical definition, 225–230, 324, 330
Stuarts, 201n., 434n.
Stubbs, T., 400n.
Sturtevant, D. R., 567n.
Subido, A., 579
Subramaniam, V., 101n.
Sudan, 169, 310, 460, 489, 506
Sufi, M. H., 96n.

Sukarno, 69, 295, 297, 298
Sullivan, H. S., 154n.
Sun Yat-sen, 69
Sung period in China, 184n.
Superannuation Act, 449
Supreme Court in Philippines, 563
Suri, S. S., 90
Surplus value, 593
Survey of economic planners, 483-493
Sussex, University of, 30, 31
Swart, K. W., 187n., 437n., 439n.
Swatantra party, 90n.
Sweden, 317n., 452, 543
Switzerland, 119, 170n., 184, 209, 218, 317n., 543
Symbols of authority, 409
Syntonic polity, 263, 264, 280–286, 324

Tagore, R., 42, 96
Taiwan, 70
Take-off in development, 127, 643
Tanenbaum, J., 401n.
Tanganyika, 532
Tanzania, 527, 532
Tarrow, S., 166n.
Taub, R. T., 519n.
Taylor, C. W., 404n.
Taylor, F. M., 619n.
Tead, O., 162n.
Technical assistance: attitudes toward, 25; objectives of, 538, 554
Technology: and bureaucracy, 70–71, 103; as component of administrative doctrine, 537
Ter Horst, J. F., 618n.
Termination function, 378
Textor, R., 600n.
Thailand: bureaucracy in, 239, 251n., 260, 287, 459; constitutive system in, 289; evolution of, 388; foreign aid in, 10; planners in, 490; political system in, 307, 565
Thirty Years War, 176
Thoenig, Jean-Claude, 482n.
Thompson, V. A., 480n., 525n.
Tilman, R. O., 461n., 467n.
Tinbergen, J., 590n.
Tinker, Irene, 420n.
Tiryakian, E., 41n.
Title IX. *See* Foreign Assistance Acts
Titmuss, R. M., 596n., 603n.
Tokugawa Japan, 239, 432
Tonic polities: and bureaucracy, 263–268; and constitutive systems, 268–273; definition of, 248, 324, 328–330; and regime types, 304–315; types of, 301
Totalitarianism, 132
Tout, T. F., 171n., 196n.
Toynbee, A., 9
Trade unions and development programs, 497
Trades Union Congress, 444
Traditional autocracies, 431–442, 656
Traditional bureaucracy, 238–243
Traditional societies, 245
Traditional values, influence of, 492, 493
Training, importance of, 555
Trinidad-Tobago, 271, 286, 317n.
Trist, E. L., 525n.
Truman, H. S., 569
Tudor Age, 434n.
Tullock, G., 22n., 591n., 606n., 613n., 622n., 623n., 628n.
Tunisia, 10, 275
Turkey: administration changes in, 4; conflict with Greece, 25; councils in, 102; evolution of, 388; foreign assistance in, 11; leadership in, 69, 70; legislature in, 91; planners in, 488, 490, 521; public administration in, 173
Turner, E. R., 197n., 200
Turner, J. E., 113n., 127n., 179n., 184n., 186n.
Turner, R. H., 63n.

U Ba U, 412n.
U Nu, 418, 419n.
Uganda, 167n., 169
Ukita, G., 70n.
Union of Post Office Workers, 444
Unions and development programs, 497
United Arab Republic, 310
United Kingdom. *See* England
United Nations: activities in public administration, 552, 555, 556; administrative doctrine of, 8, 537–545, 647, 660; administrative values of, 571n.; advisers from, 520, 536; economic survey of, 607n., 612n., 619n., 623n.; economists in bureaucracies of, 481; institutes of economic commissions of, 485; political values of, 564; population bulletin of, 595n.; publications on community development, 95n., 98n.; requests for assistance from, 584; as security for developing countries, 125; Technical Assistance Administration, 537n.; technical assistance doctrine, 7, 95, 169, 173, 553
United States: administrative concepts in, 566; administrative development in, 161, 169, 170n., 179n., 187, 190, 191, 203n., 210, 211, 447, 449, 453, 648–649, 658; aid in India, 96, 97; atonic polity in, 284; Camelot project in, 24, 60; civil service appeal in, 623n.; class orientation in, 450; as

developing country, 128, 448, 643; developments in foreign assistance, 3–30, 95, 548; economic planners in, 481, 484; economics and public policy in, 600n., 606n.; economy in, 611, 618; ethnic pride in, 42; experts from, 538, 543, 545n.; government-academic relations in, 103; individual development in, 164n.; influence on planners, 486, 504, 512, 528; isotonic polity in, 277; leadership exchange program of, 94; legislative renumeration in, 88, 89; loyalty in bureaucracy of, 434, 443, 444; one-dimensional bureaucrat in, 353; party organizations in, 80, 82, 379; patronage in, 205; per capita income in, 317n.; political equality of women in, 119; presidential form of government in, 228; private commerce in, 93; racial issue in, 118; relation to Puerto Rico, 125; role in Philippines, 562–587, 660–661; staffing patterns in, 278n.; syntonic polity in, 264, 280; technical assistance programs, 173, 546–562; as threat to England, 204; training of personnel in, 92. *See also* Agency for International Development; Foreign assistance
Uphoff, N. T., 472n., 522n.
Upward relationships, effects of, 428, 432–437, 442–447, 458–462, 656–657
Uruguay, 271, 317n.
Utilitarians, 214

Valkenier, Elizabeth, 32n.
Value-institution model, 385–391
Values: accumulation and enjoyment of, 364–367, 385, 397; and administrative organization, 166–219; and agnosticism, 109, 136; and community culture, 112; eight groups in PEWBSARD, 356–357, 664, 665; exchange among institutions, 103, 105; flow of gross and net outcomes, 359–364; functional and conventional meaning of, 358–359; and myth, 380–381; and political analysis, 109; priorities in, 110–111, 124, 641; shaping and sharing of, 357–358, 372–373, 652–653; units of, 368–373
Van Cise, J. G., 611n.
Veblen, O., 474
Venezuela, 317n., 435n.
Verba, S., 48, 112n., 124n., 145n., 585, 661
Vietnam, 10, 23, 28, 79n., 82, 300, 307, 353, 462; political systems in, 565
Villanueva, B. S., 536n.
Viloria, L. A., 566n.
Viner, J., 128n.
Visva-Bharati, 96
Von der Mehden, F. R., 418n., 564, 565
Von Mises, L., 171n., 190
Von Schön, 429
Vom Stein, Baron, 188, 189

Wage and Position Classification Office (WAPCO), 572, 576, 577
Wages in legislative profession, 89
Waldo, D., 161n., 174n., 333n., 476n.
Waldschmidt, E., 437n.
Wallis, W. A., 630n.
Wang, Y. C., 430n.
Ward, R. E., 44n., 86n., 87n., 183n.
Warshay, L. H., 75n.
Washington, George, 450
Watkins, F. M., 147n., 148n.
Watson, A. M., 630, 631
Wealth as a value, 356–357, 358, 361–362, 370–371, 648
Weber, A., 440n.
Weber, M., 32, 109, 111, 113n., 124, 126, 168, 170n., 171, 173, 174, 175, 180, 188, 190n., 203, 205, 209, 211, 213n., 215–216, 217, 238, 332, 342, 343, 344, 346, 347, 348n., 349, 403, 472, 476, 647
Weidner, E. W., 134n., 553, 554n.
Weil, Simone, 124n.
Weiner, M., 16, 44n., 183n., 274n., 418n.
Well-being as a value, 356–357, 358, 362, 371
Wellisz, S., 625n.
Western civilization: administrative development in, 212, 214, 218–219, 647, 666; advisers from, 238; democratic regimes in, 233, 271, 442–455, 656–657; government structures in, 228, 231, 237; liberal tradition in, 149; and modernization, 234–235, 489–490; socialist ideology in, 216; traditional societies in, 245
Westphalia, Peace of, 173
Whately, R., 633
Whinston, A. B., 625n.
Whitaker, C. S., 237n., 600
White, L. D., 447, 450, 451n.
White, R., 154n.
Wicksteed, P. H., 636n.
Wildavsky, A., 591n.
Wilensky, H. L., 515n.
Wiles, P. J. D., 482n., 596n., 605n., 607n., 615n., 617n., 618, 620, 625n.
Wilhelm, H., 592n.
Williams, A., 625n.
Williams, J., 44n.
Williamson, J. A., 434n.

Willner, Ann Ruth, 69n.
Willner, Dorothy, 69n.
Wilson, R. R., 12n.
Wilson, T., 596n.
Wilson, Woodrow, 32, 190, 336, 337n.
Wiseman, J., 613n.
Witherspoon, J. W., 101n.
Wittfogel, K. A., 166n., 224, 429n., 433n., 434, 436n., 438n., 440n.
Wolf, C., 569n., 590n., 600n., 606n., 608n., 610n.
Wolff, K., 181n.
Woodruff, P., 410n., 413n.
Woodruff, W., 607n.
Worcester, D. C., 566n.
World War I, 606
World War II, 22, 69, 118, 460, 481, 568, 609
Wriggins, W. Howard, 418n.
Wright, A. F., 435n.
Wright, T. P., 23n.

Yale University, 317
Yamey, B. S., 594n.
Yanaga, Chitoshi, 88n.
Young, C., 418n.
Young, K. T., 17, 28
Young, M., 480n.
Younger, K., 459, 460, 461
Yugoslavia, 494, 504
Yulo Plan, 580

Zablocki, C. J., 9, 10, 13
Zahir, King of Afghanistan, 70
Zeller, G., 435n.
Zimmerman, L. J., 607n.
Znaniecki, F., 517n., 518n.
Zwerling, S., 472n.